From Sight to Insight

The Writing Process

Seventh Edition

Jeff Rackham

The University of North Carolina—Asheville

Olivia Bertagnolli

The Sage Colleges—New York

Australia • Canada • Mexico • Singapore • Spain • United Kingdom • United States

From Sight to Insight / Seventh Edition

Jeff Rackham, Olivia Bertagnolli

Publisher: *Michael Rosenberg*
Acquisitions Editor: *Dickson Musslewhite*
Development Editor: *Christine Caperton*
Production Editor: *Diana Baczynskyj*
Marketing Managers: *Ken Kasee, Katrina Byrd*
Director, HED Marketing: *Lisa Kimball*
Manufacturing Supervisor: *Marcia Locke*
Compositor: *Carlisle Communications, LTD.*
Project Manager: *Emily Bush*
Photo Researcher: *Sheri Blaney*
Cover Designer: *Diane Levy*
Printer: *Phoenix Color Corporation*

Printed in the United States of America
1 2 3 4 5 6 7 8 9 10 06 05 04 03 02

For more information contact Heinle, 25 Thomson Place, Boston, Massachusetts 02210 USA, or you can visit our Internet site at http://www.heinle.com

0-15-505916-5 (Student Edition)
0-8384-0700-5 (Student Edition with Info Trac®)

Library of Congress Cataloging-in-Publication Data

Rackham, Jeff.
From sight to insight : the writing process / Jeff Rackham, Olivia Bertagnolli.—7th ed.
p. cm.
Includes index.
ISBN 0-15-505916-5
1. English language—Rhetoric. 2. Report writing. I. Bertagnolli, Olivia. II. Title.

PE1408.R13 2002
808'.042—dc21

2002027496

. . . both sight and insight derive from fierce consciousness, whether it begins in looking at a small object or in paying attention to all of the implications and resonances of an idea or image.

MARVIN BELL

Preface

This new edition of *From Sight to Insight* continues the goal of first edition: to assist first-year students in discovering the relationship between thinking and writing, language and voice, and ideas and values.

In its original inception more than twenty years ago, *From Sight to Insight* was a radical book designed around a basic conviction that thinking and writing are both aspects of a complex process, that ideas occur and are shaped during the preparatory act of exploring a subject—long before one ever puts a word to the page—as well as in the act of writing and revising itself. Today, after serving thousands of students, that original model, while no longer radical, remains remarkably successful in helping students develop sound critical thinking and writing skills.

What's New in This Edition

We have updated this edition of *From Sight to Insight* by adding new examples and illustrations and by making changes that update the research and documentation information as well as refining organization.

- We have replaced nine of the professional essays and three of the poems. The new readings include the following:

  "Dumpster Diving" by Lars Eighner (essay)
  "It's a Jungle Out There" by Camille Paglia (essay)
  "The Insufficiency of Honesty" by Stephen L. Carter (essay)
  "America's Emerging Gay Culture" by Randall E. Majors (essay)
  "American Dreamer" by Bharati Mukherjee (essay)
  "Coming Home Again" by Chang-rae Lee (essay)
  "Earth's Eye" by Edward Hoagland (essay)
  "Academia Goes to War" by William Forstchen (essay)
  "Join Hands Across the Divide of Faith" by Cardinal Francis Arinze (essay)
  "Love Poem" by Denise Levertov (poem)
  "I Wash the Shirt" by Anna Swir (poem)
  "The Peace of Wild Things" by Wendell Berry (poem)

- We have fine tuned Part 3, Factual Reporting, by covering Finding and Selecting Facts, and Basic Forms in Factual Reporting before students cover Context, Purpose, and Voice.
- Chapter 11, The Objective Eye, now contains a stunning visual writing prompt: one of Dorothea Lange's thought-provoking photos from *Migrants*.

- Chapter 28, Awareness of the Arts, offers two new photos of art for criticism, William Hogarth's *The Marriage Transaction* and Jean-Baptiste Greuze's *Village Betrothal,* in addition to two comparison works of the *David,* one by Donatello and another by Michelangelo.
- Part 8, Scholarly Research, is updated to provide more information on electronic research, and a revised and clarified style sheet offers the newest APA and MLA guidelines, including the most up-to-date suggestions for documenting electronic sources.
- A new design better highlights hundreds of writing samples that illustrate how style and voice can be used effectively.

Features of *From Sight to Insight*

We have attempted to retain those features that have made *From Sight to Insight* a best-selling reader-rhetoric for over two decades.

- The text remains centered around six different writing experiences: exploring the subject, identifying an audience, discovering form, drafting, revising, and editing.
- As a student moves through the text, each of these activities is expanded upon and presented at an increasingly higher level of challenge.
- Simultaneously, students move from writing that is personal, imaginative, and concrete, to writing that quickly becomes more critical, abstract, and objective. Students progress from focusing on the senses and emotions to exploring ideas and values.
- Throughout the text we continue to offer numerous student and professional models. In this edition, first-year students will encounter almost fifty examples from their peers, plus ten complete student essays and twenty-one professional essays.
- Although most writing texts provide little or nothing on the arts, we continue to offer a complete unit on how to develop an awareness of the arts, how to evaluate literary significance, and how to write a formal critique.
- Finally, in Part 8, we offer up-to-date information and techniques for conducting both traditional and computerized research, providing students with detailed models and extensive advice for writing college level research papers.

We want to stress that although the text is organized to allow instructors to move through each unit successively, each unit and chapter is also designed to stand on its own merits. Instructors can rearrange the sequence of projects or mix and match individual chapters for classroom needs. Because the writing process is never identical for any two of us (and seldom identical even for the same individual on any two writing projects), it has always been important to offer students as many options as possible for discovering their own potential. We have therefore continued to illustrate how varying types of writing skills—those of the creative writer, journalist, professional essayist, as well as those skills developed through academic and rhetorical models—should be understood as different aspects of a writing process available to us all.

Introduction: The Writing Process

From Sight to Insight is designed, chapter by chapter and unit by unit, to follow the general sequencing that most professional writers move through in almost any given act of composing: exploring a subject, identifying an audience, discovering form, drafting, revising, and editing. We make clear that the process is not something a writer progresses through step-by-step, so much as it is a recursive act. Yet we have also found from experience that some degree of oversimplification at the beginning is most effective with new students. The introduction to *From Sight to Insight* therefore provides a simplified overview of both the organization of the text and of the writing process itself. Instructors may want to begin their course at almost any part of the book, depending upon student backgrounds and class goals, but we strongly recommend all students begin, if at all possible, with the Introduction: The Writing Process.

Part 1: Writing from Experience

The introductory unit begins with the senses, as all human experience must, emphasizing for first-year students that honesty to one's own experience, as well as the discovery of one's own voice, is critical to ultimately finding a style as well as original insights. Although many writing programs begin immediately with academic writing, we have found through the years that at least some degree of writing about or from personal experience can ease almost all students into a writing program with more immediate positive results. The unit ends by tracing a first-year writer's efforts from the earliest rough draft to a final polished piece of prose. Most of our own students find this draft enlightening, and many find it a great relief to discover that such a rough start can end in a rather effective piece of work. In addition to two student essays, this part contains "Shame" by Dick Gregory and "Living South of L.A." by Mike Rose.

Part 2: Writing About People and Places

Part 2 builds on the first unit, re-emphasizing the need to begin any act of writing with an act of perception, this time focusing on perception of character or place. Students are introduced to basic elements of scene, and shown how those elements can be used effectively (in varying degrees) in almost any kind of writing, including descriptive and narrative works. Over the years, there have always been students who complain: "But I don't want to be a creative writer." And it is for them we have included a special section toward the end of the unit that specifically illustrates how the strategy of learning to seek out concrete details relates directly to enriching any kind of essay, including the most formal academic analysis. "Coming Home Again" by Chang-rae Lee has been added to the selections in this part, which include "Sister Flowers" by Maya Angelou and "Beneath My House" by Louise Erdrich.

Part 3: Factual Reporting

In Part 3 we focus on several conventional techniques used by professional journalists to seek out and gather information. It should be made clear that our interest in reporting lies not in the promotion of journalism per se, but only in how journalists identify certain patterns of action such as *change, conflict,* and *consequences* as a methodology for selecting the most important data and information in any given investigation. This unit also introduces students to the earliest stages of objective reasoning, with a strong emphasis on how to evaluate evidence and opinions. Finally, we show how these journalistic techniques actually contribute to any kind of academic investigation. In addition to a student essay, this part contains "Trouble for America's 'Model' Minority" by David Whitman and "Soup" by an anonymous author.

Part 4: Investigating Concepts

By the time most students reach Part 4, Investigating Concepts, they should be ready for the transition from reporting and explaining facts, to investigating and defining concepts. Consulting an expert or seeking information, ideas, and interpretations is described as an outgrowth of earlier interviewing techniques. Students are directed toward those crucial first steps in both library and online research. Evaluation of sources and evidence is especially stressed for computer searches. Finally, organizational strategies focus on introducing and integrating more complex materials. This section contains three new essays: "Dumpster Diving" by Lars Eighner, "American Dreamer" by Bharati Mukherjee, and "Earth's Eye" by Edward Hoagland.

Part 5: Strategies for Academic Writing

Part 5 introduces students to traditional rhetorical patterns: comparison and contrast, classification, definition, and various kinds of analysis, all as critical strategies for exploring and writing about complex ideas. The unit includes techniques for developing a focus or working thesis, as well as a complex student essay with marginal notations pointing out every key development. A revised collection of professional readings provides models for students to study, discuss, and imitate. New essays have been selected for their diversity of thought—"The Insufficiency of Honesty" by Stephen L. Carter and "America's Emerging Gay Culture" by Randall E. Majors—and complement engaging essays that remain in this edition, "The American Dream" by Betty Anne Younglove, "The Arab World" by Edward T. Hall and "Debating Moral Questions" by Vincent Ray Ruggiero.

Part 6: Analysis and Argument

As a natural follow-up, Part 6, Analysis and Argument, offers additional materials to stimulate critical analysis and argumentation. An updated collection of professional arguments provides sources for students to analyze the practice of analysis itself, and—if the instructor desires—for stimulating students to write argumentative essays of their own on related topics. This new material now pairs controversial works "It's a Jungle Out There" by Camille Paglia and an excerpt on *Sexual Harassment and Sexual Politics* by Catharine MacKinnon, as well as offering William Forstchen's provocative conservative argument that college faculties are blinded by political correctness. Finally, we have included a passionate commencement address "Join Hands Across the Divide of Faith" by Cardinal Francis Arinze.

Part 7: Critiquing the Arts

Part 7 includes a wealth of literary works—poetry and fiction—and art as visual writing prompts. We have always offered Part 7, Critiquing the Arts, as an option, and one which we believe is highly valuable. It helps train students to read and think critically, even if their intended fields of study include agriculture or accounting. In learning how to study the subtleties of art, we bring our critical skills to the total life experience. We learn how to read with intense scrutiny. We learn how to evaluate our own emotional responses and how to make meaning out of those emotions or feelings that often make our lives turbulent. Chapter 28, Awareness of the Arts, includes "Traveling Through the Dark" by William Stafford, "The River Merchant's Wife" by Ezra Pound, and "Snow" by Ann Beattie. Chapter 29, Literary Significance, includes "The Book of the Grotesque" by Sherwood Anderson, "Those Winter Sundays" by Robert Hayden, "This Is Just to Say" by William Carlos Williams, "Remember" by Joy Harjo, and "The Parable of the Good Samaritan" from the New Testament, Luke 10:30–37. Part 7 concludes with "Trinity" by Pattiann Rogers, "Three Thousand Dollar Death Song" by Wendy Rose, "The Ones Who Walk Away from Omelas" by Ursula K. Le Guin, and new selections "The Peace of Wild Things" by Wendell Berry, "I Wash the Shirt" by Anna Swir, and "Love Poem" by Denise Levertov.

Part 8: Scholarly Research

Finally, Part 8 offers a thorough and extended discussion of scholarly research. This unit has been significantly updated to include more comprehensive materials on electronic research. Both professional and student models are provided, some with marginal notations and comments, followed by two complete student essays that can serve instructors who wish to point out differing approaches to research, as well as differing strengths and weaknesses. The MLA and APA guidelines have been updated to reflect current standards.

Exercises and Explorations

Each unit in *From Sight to Insight* begins with a brief overview and suggested writing projects for the unit. Each unit also offers a Group Inquiry assignment that can assist students in becoming engaged in and often excited about the approach or the writing project coming up.

Throughout the text, both within chapters and at the end of most chapters and all units, we continue to offer a variety of student activities, exercises, or group inquiries. Numerous journal-like activities also encourage students to explore further writing on their computers or in their journals.

Finally, we offer numerous copying exercises, something that may sound odd or foreign. But copying is one of the oldest methods of learning how to compose, and it has proven dramatically successful throughout the years and across cultures. From ancient China to Shakespeare, to Ben Franklin, to the most contemporary poets, finding model passages and imitating them, sometimes copying word for word, has proven effective training. We recommend passages to copy and imitate from such writers as John F. Kennedy, Louise Erdrich, and Richard Rodriguez. The results are often startling, and always fun.

Instructor's Manual

Special mention should be made of the excellent *Instructor's Manual* that accompanies this edition of *From Sight to Insight.* Prepared by master teacher Eileen Crowe at the University of North Carolina at Asheville, the manual illustrates how material in the text applies to current reading-writing theory, offers suggestions toward the use of portfolio evaluation and other alternative grading possibilities, describes how the dialectical journal can be used as a learning-writing tool, reviews classroom dynamics for first-time instructors, and much more.

Acknowledgments

We want to express our appreciation to Janet Ferguson of the University of North Carolina–Asheville for her extensive assistance in preparing up-to-date electronic research information. And last, but certainly not least, we want to thank our editors, Christine Caperton, for her untiring patience and guidance, and Sarah Greer Bush for her superior copyediting.

We are especially indebted to numerous instructors who use and are enthusiastic about *From Sight to Insight.* The following provided valuable feedback for this revision:

Cathryn Amdahl, *Harrisburg Area Community College*
Adam Frisch, *Briar Cliff University*
Robert Furstoss, *Ocean County College*
Fran Haiden Goldman, *California State University, Northridge*
Linda S. Houston, *The Ohio State Agricultural Technical Institute*
Jeff Kosse, *Iowa Western Community College*
Hallie S. Lemon, *Western Illinois University*
Margaret Studenc, *Haywood Community College*

Early editions of *From Sight to Insight* were written by Jeff Rackham who used a first-person, informal voice, attempting to speak as directly as possible to students. Both students and instructors found it one of the strengths of the text. When Olivia Bertagnolli became co-author, it was decided to retain the first-person voice even though the content of the book now reflects a shared philosophy.

Jeff Rackham
Olivia Bertagnolli

Contents in Brief

Contents

PART 4 Investigating Concepts 176

INTRODUCTION

The Writing Process

Sometime during the nineteenth century, Japanese potters became frustrated with their own efforts. They knew that Korean masters produced the most beautiful pottery in the world. No one knew how.

The Japanese elected a committee of distinguished artisans to study and analyze Korean pots. After years of labor the committee announced it had discovered ten irreducible elements of beauty. Japanese potters were told they must reproduce those ten elements if they wished to achieve superior works of art. Try as they might, the Japanese turned out stiff and awkward pots—mere copies—lacking all grace and virtue. Korean pots remained mysteriously more beautiful. Only later did the answer become clear: The committee of experts had studied form, symmetry, color, even quality and density of clay. The Japanese potters bravely attempted to imitate each of the findings, but the findings were based on conscious analysis of finished products. The committee had not investigated the largely unconscious process used by the Korean masters in their daily work, in the actual making of the pots. It was the process, not the product, that held the secret.

Effective writing also seems to many students like a mysterious accomplishment. You may be one of those for whom writing has always seemed impossible. You may even hate to write. A lot of people do. One reason may be that so much emphasis has focused on the study of finished products, on essays and poems by famous authors. We've analyzed well-written arguments by George Orwell and profound moral essays by Bertrand Russell. We've categorized how great authors organized, shaped, selected, and envisioned their materials; and we've given names to the most successful and traditional models: narration, exemplification, exposition, and so on. Yet when we try to imitate such models for our own work, most of us feel frustrated and helpless. I always have. What I have to say never seems to fit into those honored rhetorical patterns. Over the years, I've found many of my students feeling the same frustration. By comparison with the masterpieces of English prose, our awkward essays read like failures, lacking all grace and virtue.

Perhaps, like Japanese potters, we've been looking too long at the product instead of the process. The best analysis of a well-written novel, essay, or research paper cannot reveal the false starts, the thrown-away words and paragraphs, or the agony the author feels each morning staring at the blank page or the blank computer screen. Nor does it reveal how an author finally discovered what it was he or she wanted to say.

This book, then, is about a process rather than about rules and models. I confess sometimes I'll analyze or explain a rhetorical pattern—and there will be many discussions of craft—but I hope these will be seen only in a context of helping you find a method for getting ideas onto the page—your method.

Because we are individuals, the writing process itself cannot be identical for each of us. We cannot establish "ten steps" or "twenty-two stages" for writing. Repeated studies have shown that writers move through a "recursive" series of mental activities. The drafting of an idea may begin with a clear focus on the subject, only to be interrupted by consideration of a particular sentence structure, then back to the idea, only to be stumped by the question of whether the audience for the paper will understand a certain point. Goals are set, reconsidered, shifted, and reset. Some writers (and I'm one of them) struggle with each phrase. The mind creeps like a mud turtle in rainy season: Is this what I really think? Does this make sense? Should there be a comma here? Do I need another example? Other writers, by contrast, work at incredible speed. Ideas tumble out like socks from a dryer, page after page. Yet their mental process is also moving (perhaps even more rapidly) through an endless shifting of similar goals and questions.

For all the variety and complexity, certain phases seem to recur, enough so that we can identify six general activities the mind seems to move through. These activities are seldom sequential, as I present them here. For purposes of studying them, learning them, and practicing them, however, it can be helpful to divide them arbitrarily into separate and distinct stages, keeping in mind that as you write your own essays, each seemingly separate activity is actually part of an interwoven whole.

Exploring the Subject

All writers need to know about their subject; they also need to learn how to know about it: how to look, how to investigate, how to see relationships. In many ways, this first stage in the writing process is the single most important element in achieving meaningful, intelligent prose. Exploration begins with perception, a sensory act. You must see your subject (and sometimes hear it, taste it, touch it, smell it). Ideas do not float in midair. You discover them in the process of looking at specific details, searching out patterns, bringing together seemingly unrelated parts. A business executive makes a special trip to Texas, where she personally observes the market for her product; she listens to opinions from local officials; she surveys the community's needs; she takes notes on facts found in a government report; she studies statistics provided by a university analysis. Only then does she write her report to the company president. A social worker needs funds to develop housing projects for the aged. He searches for supporting evidence in local welfare records;

he interviews supporters of the project; he selects two good examples from more than fifty case studies; he makes a visual survey of the neighborhood to gather concrete impressions. Only then does he begin to write his grant proposal. No matter what your goal in writing, the first step is to see the subject clearly.

Yet the mind can be overwhelmed by too many details. Part of the perception process involves learning how to focus intensely on a manageable part of the whole subject and then how to select only the most significant details from the smaller part. Learning how to focus and select requires practice. Most writing assignments, whether in school or in a job, will already have some degree of focus: Write a ten-page analysis of economic relations between Cuba and Haiti; write an essay on character growth in *The Adventures of Huckleberry Finn.* But even these subjects will usually prove too broad. The writer always has the responsibility for narrowing a subject. Otherwise, a jumble of impressions leads to a confused and unfocused paper, like a home video that jumps from "Our Vacation in the Rockies" to "Esther's Third Birthday." Focusing and selecting must become automatic steps for every writer.

Perception is ultimately the source of your ideas. In working through facts, details, and statistics; in listening to others' opinions; in personal observation, you begin to combine and compare, to differentiate, to see relationships and patterns. For many, the understanding of a subject, the ideas and insights, will occur even before a word has been written; for others, like me, the act of writing may be the only way to force the mind to shape and order the material. Obviously, I am using the term *perception* in a general sense to include a great many acts that go on in the mind. But the original meaning of the term includes the notion of "seeing all the way through a subject," of reaching "understanding." I think, then, that if we accept the concept in its broadest sense, we can fairly say that a well-written paper is the result of an intense perceptual process.

Identifying the Audience

Writing is an act of communication with a reader (an audience). Few beginning writers realize how significant the audience is, both in the way they perceive the subject and in the way they write about it.

The audience may well influence the way a writer looks at a subject. If a lawyer writes a brief for a judge, it must be logical and concise; it must be documented with facts and precedents. But that, in turn, means the lawyer must see the subject in the same way. The client may have wrecked a car one warm summer night when waves pounded against the beach and the scent of orange blossoms hung in the air. Those are all good sensory details derived from perception. But they won't influence the judge. A different selection of details is called for. The lawyer needs facts on road conditions: a broken safety barrier and the number of other accidents that have recently occurred on that same curve. The details a writer searches for depend not only on the subject but also on the audience—and on the way the writer hopes to affect that audience.

Writing is often a private act. But the product (the essay, report, critical analysis) is a public performance. As in all social actions, convention and custom influence the parties involved. The shaping of your ideas, the voice you speak in, the level of your vocabulary, the formality of your sentences, even your grammar and punctuation may be influenced by the type of audience you're trying to reach. You would probably agree that safety instructions to plant employees should be written in short declarative statements that allow for no ambiguity. Regardless of the shop supervisor's poetic spirit or need to express his inner self, that supervisor cannot be allowed to write safety instructions in free verse. Yet an essay written for a Shakespearean scholar assumes a different audience with a different set of expectations. We can speculate that the Shakespearean scholar might quickly become bored with a paper written in short declarative sentences. Why, she asks the student, can't you let a little more of yourself come through? Where is your voice, the flow and rhythm of some kind of personal style? Successful writers anticipate the reader's needs. They recognize that conventions exist not as unbreakable rules but as traditional patterns that have proved successful in easing communication.

Identifying the audience and its needs probably occurs simultaneously with the first phase of the writing process: exploring the subject. And just as your understanding of your subject continues to evolve and grow as you write, the recognition of your audience's needs will probably continue to influence every stage of the writing process. Honest writers will not change their ideas to please a particular audience, but they must often be willing to change many other elements—selection of evidence, organization of details, tone, and level of vocabulary—all for one reason: to communicate their ideas as effectively as possible.

Discovering Form

In spite of Wordsworth's famous assertion that poetry is a "spontaneous overflow of emotion," no writing, not even poetry, is ever totally spontaneous. No doubt the best writing often sounds spontaneous, but some sort of organization or form, always disciplines content. In prose, most forms, such as the essay or narrative, are open-structured, allowing enormous freedom for exploring and developing a subject. Other than a few obvious requirements like beginnings, middles, and ends, no inflexible patterns exist. You may be suspicious of the whole notion. Organizing, shaping, and forming have always been the great stumbling blocks to professional writers as well as to students. The reason is easy to identify: Finding form in a subject is a process of ordering chaos. In other words, it's hard work. You may have focused on your subject, selected your details, and clearly identified your audience; but if you're like me, you'll still have a head jumbled with subpoints, half-formed ideas, images, and hunches. No outburst of spontaneous writing will magically shape that material into a coherent message. From time to time, exhilarating moments of inspiration do occur, but most attempts to organize require sustained effort.

Placing *discovering form* as the third activity in the process, however, is merely arbitrary. The organization of a paper may be determined by the writer's special perception of the subject or by the limitations and biases of a particular audience. Form may be consciously organized with a Roman-numeral outline, or it may evolve gradually from the writing itself. Knowledge and practice of techniques developed by professional writers can often ease your way. For example, professional writers have developed something called the "lead." A lead quickly defines and limits your subject, establishes tone, and suggests a pattern of organization, all in a sentence or two. Other successful writers make line drawings to "design" their work or jot down informal lists of words and phrases. Still others depend on traditional forms, arguing that they can give more attention to internal subject matter if they allow convention to establish external outlines. Each of these different methods will be reviewed later to provide you with a number of options for any writing situation.

Drafting

Ray Bradbury once said that "writing must be as immediate as life, or there are no juices, no chance to involve yourself or others in your vitality." I've known many students who approached the act of writing with such dread that the product they produced expressed little of their lives and nothing of their vitality. Many student papers read as if they were written by a faulty computer: awkward sentences, distorted vocabulary, too many words and not enough substance, a stumbling lack of logic. Where are the juices? Where are the human beings who never seem to emerge from these shapings of their native language? Other students write with remarkable fluency, with a zest that reveals their own voice and spirit. Some even feel free to let ideas grow out of accidents, to play with words. Surprisingly, the difference does not seem to lie in natural ability as much as in the initial attitude a writer brings to the blank page. Perhaps one of the most serious misunderstandings about the writing process is a failure to envision the first draft and the many drafts that may follow as essential stages requiring separate mental attitudes.

In discussing creativity, psychologist Abraham H. Maslow suggests distinguishing between a primary phase and a secondary phase. During the primary phase, you as a writer must lose your past and future. You must live only in the moment, "immersed, fascinated and absorbed in the present, in the current situation, in the here-now, with the matter-in-hand." While drafting, you may want to suspend—at least temporarily—a critical attitude. If possible, teach yourself to let it flow, to write fast, talking to the page to discover what you know; you must allow digressions to occur. Drafting is the primary phase of creativity, the point where you get down your perceptions, follow your hunches, see the subject intensely in your mind as you write, often ignoring your notes or your outline. Drafting is the stage where you allow yourself to make mistakes, where, if possible, you should not worry about the rules, the right word, or the conclusion. You just write.

You might think of all this as a process of creating a rough sketch of your ideas, a process of writing an extended note to yourself. You'll have time later to judge what you've written, to revise, and to correct. But unless you've explored the subject freely with your own voice, you'll have nothing to improve upon. Vitality in writing usually has its origin in the first draft.

Revising

New writers sometimes believe that novels like *Anna Karenina* simply burst forth from the mind of an author, each perfect sentence following another. In reality, Tolstoy repeatedly revised *Anna Karenina.* After submitting the 1000 page pen-and-ink manuscript to the publisher, the printed galleys were returned to Tolstoy for proofreading. But Tolstoy was disappointed by what he saw in print. Instead of merely correcting errors, he revised the entire novel on the back of the galleys. The publisher reset the novel, and again sent Tolstoy the galleys, which Tolstoy immediately used for revising the novel once more, each time reorganizing, re-envisioning, and polishing. When the third set of galleys arrived from the publisher, Tolstoy's wife mailed them back without showing them to her husband, knowing that he would likely continue the process of revision as long as he could.

Painters, architects, sculptors—and writers—all work from rough sketches that only gradually take on shape and substance. The experienced writer knows that quality writing often does not begin until the revision stage.

Fortunately, the computer has made the entire process remarkably easier than anything Tolstoy could have dreamed of. The speed and ease of the keyboard, the exciting new developments in contemporary software, all allow the act of composing to proceed almost as fast as the mind can work. The early working draft may take shape as swiftly as the fingers can move. And for many, revision has now become a pleasure rather than a labored chore of cut and paste—or rewriting by hand on the backs of galleys. Words, sentences, and whole paragraphs can be deleted with a keystroke; ending paragraphs can be moved to the beginning, and new material can be added easily.

More than ever, revising may overlap drafting. Revising should be seen as an equally creative act of the mind where you attempt to "re-see" the subject and, in light of the needs of your audience and your own desires, reshape, reform, and when necessary, re-investigate. Many professional writers even say that writing *is* revising.

Editing

After drafting and revising, much remains to be done. Editing requires a cool, slow, line-by-line examination. For some writers, this phase may partially overlap the revising phase. For others, it seems most successful as a final and separate act. Often the work is laid aside, the intense involvement in the subject allowed to cool. Later, the writer returns to the paper with a critical eye, acting as his or her own editor.

As an editor you bring to your manuscript the attitude of an old craftsman. You want every word to be precise; you feel every unnecessary word should be eliminated and every verb should be strong. Sentence structures must be grammatically acceptable. You want each sentence to move the idea, the feeling, the rhythm of your voice easily toward the next sentence. Paragraphs must be coherent, focused, and unified. Each paragraph must relate to the preceding and following paragraphs. As an editor, you won't hesitate to relocate a paragraph or strike it entirely if it does not contribute. Finally, the order and logic of the whole must seem apparent. The title must be considered as carefully as the conclusion. No detail is forgotten, not even (alas) punctuation and spelling.

Learning how to edit means learning when to edit. If you begin too soon in the writing process, you may edit out your own personality in favor of safe, anonymous-sounding prose; you may even prevent your ideas from reaching their most developed form. That's why an understanding of writing as a process can be so valuable to your writing. Editing and polishing should probably constitute the final phase (or at least occur no sooner than the revising phase). Editing must come at the point when what you have to say is important enough that every detail about how you say it seems worth perfecting.

Final editing of your manuscript is your responsibility. Someday you'll need to write a lab report for your team manager or a regional analysis for your county supervisor or a critical evaluation of court procedures for your law firm. No English instructor will be standing by to correct your paper in red ink. And your secretary may not be a good editor. Better to set high standards now and teach yourself how to reach them. Editing will not in itself make for good writing, but good writing is simply not possible without careful editing.

The Final Synthesis

The writing process is not a mechanical formula. At best it should suggest a pattern, not a rigid prescription. As you work on assignments, you'll find that the separate activities described here merge and overlap. Instructors often use the term "recursive" to describe this flux of mental activities. To divide exploring, organizing, drafting, and revising into individual phases is an act of analysis. To draw them all together—as eventually you must—requires an act of synthesis. Just as you learn tennis by studying the forehand, backhand, and serve separately and consciously, you must eventually begin to play the game intuitively. We do not know how intuition works. We cannot teach it in the classroom. Yet this inner thing, this inner sensing for which we have no satisfactory explanation, is as much a part of successful writing as the process outlined here.

Gradually, with hard work and self-discipline, practice in the writing process sets in motion an inner growth. Those Korean pots were not beautiful merely because of correctly learned skills and techniques; they were beautiful because in the process of creation the artisan discovered something about himself and the clay. The pottery became an expression of some part of him. By working through the writing process, you work through the very process necessary to begin an understanding of yourself; you work with the way the mind perceives, selects, shapes, and envisions the world. Good writing is always an exploration and articulation of intelligence, of the uniqueness of individual human natures. That is why writing is, or should be, a humanistic act. It extends our imaginations and makes us receptive to our intuitions. Writing increases our sensitivity to emotion, clarifies thought, and makes judgment more rigorous. The writing process is the beginning of movement from sight to insight.

PART 1

Writing from Experience

Suggested Writing Projects

Personal experience is where you start from. Your family, your friends, your culture, your ethnic background, the events of your childhood, even the books you've read and the movies you've seen. All this and so very much more contributes to who you are as a person. To explore and share some small element of this experience begins a process of self-discovery: a process of clarifying your values, your goals, your place in a social world.

To write about yourself, then, is to initiate the first stage of critical thinking. Even though your essay may focus on human interaction, the conflict of emotions, or the sensory details that constitute an event, you are engaging in the act of critical judgment: Which details will you select? How should you organize the experience? How will you present characters and actions? How will you want your audience to respond? And most importantly, what is the meaning or value of this experience within the context of your total life?

Here are some suggestions for where you might begin.

- Consider writing an essay on an object owned and valued by you or by some member of your family. Your mother may own a wicker basket brought from Hungary by her grandmother in 1822. Your brother might think his arrowhead collection is the most magical thing in his life. Your father may have saved a battered trumpet he played in a high school marching band. Your job is to look at the object, perceive it physically (sight, smell, touch, taste, sound), and to write about its special history or meaning. Lead the reader toward an insight or understanding of its emotional or personal significance.

- Recall a particularly good or bad experience in your life caused by a single event (perhaps the night you went camping in Oregon or the summer afternoon you spent shopping with your Italian aunt). Look in detail at all the sensory elements that return to your memory. Re-create the experience in such a way that the reader can see, hear, and feel the whole of it. At the end, reflect on the significance of the experience today (which might be different than how you felt about it at the time).

- Write about a direct confrontation with someone who had an influence on shaping your life. Help the reader see and experience it: the way your math teacher's belly hung over his belt when he suggested you become a scientist, or the tone of voice of the parish priest as he told you he did not think the priesthood was right for you. Focus your essay on the primary moment; share all the details with your reader. At the end, briefly consider in broader terms the effect such an experience had on your life. Most families share favorite stories that create an informal history of family experiences—stories about moving from place to place, legendary characters, unusual relatives, or strange events. Retell one of those family stories and explain its significance to you.

Group Inquiry

After you've had time to consider several possible events or experiences to write about, test your ideas on two or three other students from your class. List the main ideas or outline the "story" that you think might hold the most potential. Ask the group of students to respond: What seems to be the most important element of your story (as they've heard it)? What seems the least important? What did they "learn" or "feel" from it? Why did they think it might have been an important or meaningful event in your life? Listen carefully to your fellow students' responses. Ask them to be honest with you and, in turn, listen carefully to their stories. Respond with sincerity and honesty. Afterward, reflect on how you might reshape or focus the incident you plan to write about to best affect a reading audience. The chapters in this unit will give you ideas about where to begin the writing process itself.

CHAPTER 1

The Senses

Accuracy of observation is the equivalent of accuracy of thinking.

WALLACE STEVENS

All human experience begins with sensory perception. We may know some things intuitively, and like most other animals we possess innate drives—to defend a plot of land or to reproduce sexually. But even our awareness of such primal elements in human nature comes from our ability to see and hear. Anthropologists know something about human social development because they have *observed* it in varying cultures. Psychologists know something about the workings of the mind because they have *listened* to thousands of patients. As a child, you learned about the world only through your sensory perceptions of it. You learned that rocks taste slick and cold when you suck on them, that dandelions smell pungent, that the touch of your mother's hand feels warm. Our emotions are especially affected by sensory experience. You do not fall in love with an abstraction. You love a specific young man or woman with red or blond hair, with blue or black eyes, with a soft voice and a dimple in the chin—and a name: Lynn, Bob, Garvin, Maria. Most of us even feel differently when we see a sunny sky than when we wake up and see dark rain streaking our window. All intellectual and emotional experience begins with the senses: seeing, hearing, smelling, touching, and tasting.

Your perception of the subject through your senses is also the beginning of almost every writing project. Good writing is essentially good thinking. And good thinking derives from the ability to perceive critically, to discriminate between important details and unimportant details, to be sensitive to subtleties, to recognize relationships. Each of these concepts involves an act of perception. Beginning now to exercise and extend your perceptive ability through the senses—as well as imaginatively and critically—leads to the process of self-education that is the ultimate goal of a university experience.

Professional writers have always known the value of the senses. They know that because we learn about the world through sight and sound, they must use language that communicates as directly as possible to the eye and ear. The more sensory details, the more likely a reader is to become involved—not just intellectually but emotionally and even physically. Advertisers know they can sell dishwashing detergent if they say it smells like lemons; they can sell mouthwash by asserting that because it tastes like medicine, it must be good for us; they can sell automobiles by calling attention to the heavy "thunk" when the door slams. The appeal to sensory experience actually makes us willing to spend hard-earned money even when we may not need the product.

In 1932 James Agee visited the home of a tenant farmer in Georgia. Agee felt deeply moved by the experience, by the poverty and the shattered lives. He wrote about his first overnight stay with the family. Had he not known the value of sensory perception, this is what he might have told us.

> The bedroom was as shabby as the rest of the cabin and very uncomfortable. I lay down on the bed but found it difficult to sleep. It was miserable and the mattress made noises. After a while I discovered bugs. Just lying there was more than I could stand, so I tried to kill as many as I could find.

But Agee knew that if he wanted us to share his experience, he had to provide sensory details. He had to stimulate our sight and touch the way his had been stimulated. Here is what he actually wrote in *Let Us Now Praise Famous Men.*

> [I saw] how the shutters filled their squares of window and were held shut with strings and nails: crevices in the walls, stuffed with hemp, rags, newsprint, and raw cotton: large damp spots and rivulets on the floor, and on the walls, streams and crooked wetness; and a shivering, how chilly and wet the air is in this room. . . .
>
> I sat on the edge of the bed, turned out the lamp, and lay back along the outside of the covers. After a couple of minutes I got up, stripped, and slid in between the sheets. The bedding was saturated and full of chill as the air was, its lightness upon me nervous like a belt too loosely buckled. The sheets were at the same time coarse and almost slimily or stickily soft: much the same material floursacks are made of. There was a ridgy seam down the middle. I could feel the thinness and lumpiness of the mattress and the weakness of the springs. The mattress was rustling noisy if I turned or contracted my body. The pillow was hard, thin, and noisy, and smelled as of acid and new blood; the pillowcase seemed to crawl at my cheek. I touched it with my lips: it felt a little as if it would thaw like spun candy. There was an

> odor something like that of old moist stacks of newspaper. . . . I began to feel sharp little piercings and crawlings all along the surface of my body. I was not surprised; I had heard that pine is full of them anyhow . . . it was bugs all right. I felt places growing on me and scratched at them, and they became unmistakable bedbug bites. . . . To lie there naked feeling whole regiments of them tooling at me, knowing I must be imagining two out of three, became more unpleasant than I could stand. I struck a match and a half-dozen broke along my pillow: I caught two, killed them, and smelled their queer rankness. They were full of my blood. I struck another match and spread back the cover; they rambled off by the dozens. I got out of bed, lighted the lamp. . . . I killed maybe a dozen in all; I couldn't find the rest; but I did find fleas, and, along the seams of the pillow and mattress, small gray translucent brittle insects which I suppose were lice. . . .

More than half a century has passed, yet Agee still involves us directly in his experience.

Sight	shutters held together with string crevices in the wall stuffed with rags bedbugs bloated with blood running in the matchlight
Touch	chill in the air wetness on the walls slimy sheets a ridgy seam bedbugs crawling on his body
Sound	the rustling mattress the striking match
Smell	the odor of old moist newspapers a pillow that smells like acid and new blood the queer rankness of the bedbugs

To use sensory experience as part of your writing, you must first train yourself to perceive more clearly and fully. I know that by the time I reached college, I had become dulled to my senses. I was no longer excited as I had been as a child by the touch of a shiny doorknob or the brand-new taste of chocolate chips melting on my tongue. Nor did I even trust my experience to be important or meaningful to others. Yet writing that omits sensory details leaves out the human element of our world, and, more often than not, the human element makes writing interesting, even vital, to a reader. Using the writer's journal is one way to train and develop your perceptive abilities. With effort and practice, all of us can reinvigorate our senses and make ourselves once more conscious of our aliveness. Only when we begin to see clearly will we begin to write clearly.

Practice

Keeping a private journal has proven over the centuries to be an important personal and intellectual exercise. Historians, scientists, naturalists, explorers, painters, writers, and others have all kept journals. A very short list would include Leonardo da Vinci, Thomas Jefferson, Lewis and Clark, Nathaniel Hawthorne, Charles Lindbergh, Winston Churchill, Paul Gauguin, Woody Guthrie, Loren Eiseley, Sylvia Plath, and Kathie Kollwitz.

Write on paper in a special bound journal, or write on a computer disk, but write. Every writer needs a place to let the mind flow freely, to experiment, doodle, explore, digress, and reflect. We still know little about creativity, but what we do know reveals that journal keeping has often been one of the central stages of the creative process, and this is never more true than in writing.

Practicing writing encourages you to explore your experiences, observations, memories, and reflections. It allows you to take risks, to discover your own voice. It serves as a storehouse for ideas and feelings which may later be developed in more formal writing. The important thing is to write every day in a notebook or special file on your computer. Write what is important to you, accept what comes, trust yourself. Focus on sensory details: smell, taste, sight, touch, sound. This might seem elementary, but it will prove to be surprisingly difficult if you avoid generalizations and attempt to use precise sensory details.

Here's how David Knox, a first-year student, wrote about his observation of a candle:

> The candle has burned once before tonight. Yellow, cylindrical, and four-inches wide, streams of molten wax run down the sides of it. One side has folded over in the shape of an ear. The flame grows taller as the wax center builds up. A little pool gets deeper before the wax melts on the sides. The wick burns slowly, and the blackness creeps down lower and lower. The inside of the candle edge is shaped like the underside of a mushroom, thin ridges between deep valleys. Smooth pollen-like grains make a flat surface from the mushroom edge to the pool of liquid wax. One edge looks like an apricot all shriveled and curled.

1. Write freely about an event from your past: the divorce of your parents, the award you won in football, the discovery of a special talent, the time your best friend moved away. Use all your sensory memory to describe the scene: the light, the sounds, the place, your friend's face, and voice.
2. Write about the time you first discovered something important about yourself: the day you refused to smoke pot with your friends (or the day

you gave in and smoked pot because you were afraid your friends would mock you); or that moment in biology class when you looked through a microscope and knew for the first time what you wanted to do with your life; or the year your family's business failed and you realized that you would be expected to go to work instead of college. Try to recall all the small details of the experience: sights, smells, touch, taste, and sound, as well as the emotions.

3. Write about disappointing one of your parents: the day your mother cried when she discovered you had pierced your tongue; the evening you came home from soccer practice and told your father you hated sports. Include as many sensory details as possible to make the memory come alive on the page.

Exercise

1. Consider the types of words each writer uses in the following passages. Look closely. Circle the general, abstract terms; underline the concrete or specific terms. Compare your answers with those of other students.

The rain fell periodically on my window. Soundless. Each blurred streak looked gray and warped. I could hear my dog Harper sleeping in the kitchen. He snores when he sleeps and bubbles ooze between his lips. The rain had begun to melt the old rusted snow in the gutters.

Student Journal

The influence of custom is indeed such that to conquer it will require the utmost efforts of fortitude and virtue, nor can I think any man more worthy of veneration and renown, than those who have burst the shackles of habitual vice.

Samuel Johnson

Standing perfectly still like that, I discover my shadow. At first it was just a dark spot on the bamboo mats that covered the court yard bricks. It had short legs and long arms, dark coiled braids just like mine. When I shook my head, it shook its head. We flapped our arms. We raised one leg. I turned to walk away and it followed me. I turned back around quickly and it faced me. I lifted the bamboo mat to see if I could peel off my shadow, but it was under the mat, on the brick. I shrieked with delight at my shadow's own cleverness. I ran to the shade under the tree, watching my shadow chase me. It disappeared. I loved my shadow, this dark side of me that had my same restless nature.

Amy Tan

Cans. Beer cans. Glinting on the verges of a million miles of roadways, lying in scrub, grass, dirt, leaves, sand, mud, but never hidden. Piels, Rheingold, Ballantine, Schaefer, Schlitz, shining in the sun or picked by the moon or the beams of headlights at night; washed by rain or flattened by wheels, but never dulled, never buried, never destroyed.

Marya Mannes

At sunset I sometimes make bread or roast a chicken in a camp oven on the little islet with twenty eager helpers shrieking, exclaiming, running to throw rotten eggs in the sea or to fetch firewood for a dying fire.

Margaret Mead

My father is a great guy. The whole family looks up to him and admires him. Ever since I was old enough to walk, I think I wanted to be just like him and I still find myself imitating him all the time.

Student Journal

About three to six gallons of a dyed and perfumed solution of formaldehyde, glycerin, borax, phenol. Alcohol and water is soon circulating through Mr. Jones, whose mouth has been sewn together with a needle directed upward between the upper lip and gum and brought out through the left nostril, with the corners raised slightly "for a more pleasant expression." If he should be bucktoothed, his teeth are cleaned with Bon Ami and coated with colorless nail polish. His eyes, meanwhile, are closed with flesh-tinted eye caps and eye cement.

Jessica Mitford

CHAPTER 2

Perception, Language, and Honesty

Along with Shakespeare, Tolstoy, Mark Twain, and other writers who have endured, James Agee knew a simple truth about words: Concrete, specific, and particular words stimulate sensory pictures in the mind. They help a reader share your experiences more fully. Concrete words suggest or name something we can see, hear, touch, smell, and taste, such as *trout, French bread, daffodils,* and *silk.* By contrast, general, abstract terms identify classes, qualities, or ideas—for example, *fish, nutrition, vegetation,* and *clothing.* The ability to abstract is one of the distinctions that separates our brains from the brains of other animals. Truly to think, we must abstract from sensory experience and reach an understanding of it. Indeed, without higher abstractions like *justice, democracy, hope,* and *human nature,* our thoughts would be severely limited. But such terms tend to be vague and, when overused, meaningless. More to the point, in writing about personal experience, if you allow yourself the comfort of the easy generalization, you'll find yourself failing to stretch your senses, failing to *look* for the real and immediate level of experience, and, of course, failing to share anything significant with your reader.

Here, for example, is a student's description of his three-year-old cousin.

> Willa has beautiful hair. It smells nice and feels wonderful.

The writer obviously wants us to know how lovely his cousin is. He tries to bring in sight, smell, and touch. But in each case, the choice of words fails to help the reader experience anything. The description is so vague that no one could ever select Willa out of a crowd. *Beautiful, nice,* and *wonderful* are words that express the author's opinion of his subject. They tell us what he thought about his perception, but they don't *share* his perception in a sensory or specific way. The same is true of this effort by student Carol Eisley:

> There was no chance of working well at home. First I dropped my pencil and it made an interesting sound as it struck the floor. I was trying to decide how to describe it when my little brother came in making lots of ugly noises.

The reader has little idea what *interesting sound* the pencil made and cannot even guess at which of the thousands of *ugly noises* the writer's little brother happened to be making. Both *sound* and *noise* are too general; we can think such words, but we can't hear anything specific in them.

Here is the same scene after Carol went back in her memory and attempted to share the actual experience:

> There was no chance of working well at home. First I dropped my pencil. It skittered across the tile floor. I was down on my knees looking for it under the refrigerator when my six-year-old brother skipped in whistling a two-note song he had invented. He watched me, first on one foot, then on the other. He began sucking through the gap in his front teeth. It sounded like garbage water sucked down an open drain. I had my arm under the refrigerator as far as I could reach. All I could find was a broken potato chip sticky with green mold, so old and mossy it seemed to have eyes. The mold smelled like curdled yogurt. My little brother began making a wet plopping sound by sticking his thumb inside one cheek and popping it out.

Concrete, specific words name things or describe sensory details, objects, emotions, and facts in such a way that the reader can actually experience in the imagination the named quality. When a pencil *skitters* across a tile floor or when a little brother *sucks* through his front teeth or makes a *wet pop* by pulling his thumb out of his cheek, readers can hear it in their imagination, just as they can see and smell a *green, moldy potato chip.* Specific names or details call up whole pictures that affect both mind and emotion. By knowing in advance that you must describe details in your experience, you discipline your senses to work more actively. To be specific, you must first look and listen for the specific. Knowing a vocabulary of the senses thus works in two ways: It stimulates you as a writer to search deeply into your experience; and it stimulates the imagination of the reader, helping him or her to share your experience.

Concrete, specific words are not limited to personal writing. Even philosophers have known that the more abstract an idea is, the more difficult it is to communicate. Plato, for example, in writing his famous "Allegory of the Cave," attempts to show that most of us live in darkness and that we are reluctant to face higher truths. Plato describes—in sensory images, not in abstractions—the problem of several prisoners who live their lives in a cave with their backs to the entrance. On the back wall of the cave, the men watch shadows pass back and forth. They insist that shadows are real life. But one prisoner is forced to walk to the cave entrance where he is dazzled by the light. He would almost prefer the shadowy illusions on the wall to the pain of exposure. Yet, Plato argues, after finally accustoming himself to the sun and lake and trees, the prisoner would rather die than return to the misery of the cave. Plato's dialogue deals with the nature of truth and the manner in which people both find and resist it. He constructs his argument on a simple, sensory-based story. The senses provide us with a tangible point from which Plato hopes we can reason to higher levels.

In your writing, you'll need both kinds of words—general and abstract terms as well as concrete, specific terms. You should make yourself aware of the differences and attempt to become rich in both vocabularies. Knowing a language of the senses can increase your powers of perception, just as knowing the words that express ideas helps you to think about ideas.

Showing Versus Telling

The use of concrete, specific words, especially sensory words, creates *images.* An image is a sensory picture in the mind. If I write that *several people came into my shop,* you receive the communication in the abstract. You understand what I mean. I have used proper grammar and good syntax. But you have no particular image in your mind; you don't know whether six Chinese diplomats came into my shop or twenty-two Nebraska farmers. But if I write *the Hell's Angels gang stomped into my shop,* you'll probably have a fairly instant recognition. *Hell's Angels* suggests motorcycle jackets, chains, greased-back hair, black boots, and perhaps an undercurrent of tension or fear.

The word *imagination* is built from the word *image.* Our imaginations are created by sensory experience. A person without an imagination is a person who neither sees nor helps the reader to see. We might say, then, that one of the first principles of good writing is to *show* instead of *tell,* for showing affects the imagination. Show the reader through some kind of concrete, sensory-related words, if possible, instead of merely telling the reader in abstract concepts. General, abstract words inform the rational side of our minds; specific, concrete words stimulate the imagination.

Telling is vague.

I hurt my finger.

Showing is specific.

I poked a needle through my finger.

Telling communicates an idea or concept.

Downtown traffic was heavy.

Showing demonstrates an idea or concept.

City buses coughed black smoke; taxis honked at a stalled delivery truck. Even a policeman on a motorcycle couldn't squeeze through the rumble of cars.

In her novel *Girl with a Pearl Earring,* Tracey Chevalier shows a young seventeenth-century Dutch woman piercing her ear:

> I took the needle out of the flame and let the glowing red tip change to dull orange and then black. When I leaned towards the mirror I gazed at myself for a moment. My eyes were full of liquid in the candlelight glittering with fear. . . . I pulled the earlobe taut and in one movement pushed the needle through my flesh.

It is almost impossible to read this passage without flinching. We have a reaction that involves both mind and body.

Many inexperienced writers believe that abstract language sounds more intellectual. Some writers use abstract generalities in the hope of impressing the reader with their intelligence. The impression quickly wears thin. Most of us are soon bored with a continuous dose of abstraction, and often it sounds pretentious. George Orwell once demonstrated this principle by calling attention to how simply and specifically the following passage from Ecclesiastes is written.

> I returned, and saw under the sun, that the race is not to the swift, nor the battle to the strong, neither yet bread to the wise, nor yet riches to men of understanding, nor yet favor to men of skin; but time and chance happeneth to them all.

Orwell then rewrote the passage entirely in abstractions.

> Objective consideration of contemporary phenomena compels the conclusion that success or failure in competitive activities exhibits no tendency to be commensurate with innate capacity, but that a considerable element of the unpredictable must inevitably be taken into account.

The passages say approximately the same thing, but the second version speaks only to the mind, whereas the first speaks to our mind, our imagination, and our emotions.

Being Honest to Your Experience

Nothing should be easier than writing down in simple, concrete terms what you see and hear. Yet not only do your emotions, hopes, and fantasies get in the way, so also do the biases of the world you grew up in—especially when you are writing about personal experience. Ernest Hemingway spoke for most of us when he said that one of the great difficulties for a writer was to discover what "you really felt rather than what you were supposed to feel." Yet honesty of perception seems to be an ideal we constantly slip away from, tempted as we are to produce the familiar response or the trite phrase. We have a seemingly instinctive desire to please by writing down what we think others want to hear instead of what we truly see or think for ourselves.

Here, for example, is what Greg Eaton wrote in his notebook when asked to write about the sunrise.

> In that hushed moment before dawn broke and the sky was like black velvet, there was a hovering solitude as all creatures waited for Midnight to disrobe her garments. Suddenly, golden light radiated forth from the trembling clouds. The branches of the trees began to do deep knee bends to get the circulation going again, and all the awaiting animals began a symphony of noise: birdlings warbled in chorus, puppies yapped in counterpoint, insects buzzed in harmony—while the concert master, the breeze himself, tickled the undersides of the leaves in the trees.

Greg wrote down what he thought an English instructor would approve of. He tried to imitate the gleanings of some vaguely remembered poetry, but he did not look or smell or listen for himself, probably because he did not yet have the courage to trust his own perceptions. If, as he thought, writers from earlier centuries had written about the "hovering solitude" before the dawn, then why shouldn't he? Who was he to say that branches don't do deep knee bends or that the breeze is not a concert master running around tickling leaves on their bottoms? The notebook entry does not express his perceptions because it seemed both safer and easier to describe the dawn in acceptable "literary" terms. This kind of faking does not necessarily imply a conscious attempt to deceive. Usually, such dishonesty is unintentional. We simply don't know we are not yet seeing for ourselves. We assume that the way we think something has always been done is the way it should be done. We may actually know of no other words to express something because it has always been expressed in the same words. We tend to grow familiar and comfortable with conventional ways of looking at the world. Trying to challenge the norm either leaves us with a dark hole into which our imagination refuses to leap or gives us a headache thinking about it.

But here is what Greg wrote when urged to report the scene again as he honestly perceived it with his own senses.

> I shivered in the dark. My nose started to run. On the other side of Hennly's pasture, about a quarter of a mile away, diesel trucks rumbled along the highway with their lights on. I sat on a mean rock in the dark listening to the trucks.
>
> The last truck by thundered away down the highway. The sound faded away to a mute grumble. For several minutes there was a silent red glow in the distance, and I couldn't hear anything at all because my ears were still filled with the engines and whirring tires. Then the glow faded and my ears went

> empty. I heard the weeds brushing against my feet. I felt a soft wind come up. Sometimes I could hear water lapping in the creek that wound through the pasture. After a few moments I heard another truck coming, just a whisper at first, mumbling real low like it was pushing the sound ahead of it kind of angry, then louder and louder until it was booming right in front of me, the tires zinging over the pavement, then past me with the engine growing dull and retarded and passing another truck coming from the other direction in a flash of mixed up lights, with the new sound grumbling back toward me.
>
> And somehow it was light. I don't know when or how. I just realized I could see mist hovering over the creek like faint smoke. A few cars appeared on the highway, some without lights, zizzing along like dark beetles.
>
> Just light. Gray at first. On the other side of the highway the woods took shape, black and smoky and wet. While the mist in the pasture faded gradually and the rim of the mountain in the east looked silver.

Little of Greg's second entry deals with the sun coming up at all. In the process of trusting his experience to tell him what was genuine and real, he discovered a sensory world he had previously ignored. Instead of birdlings singing in chorus, Greg heard diesel trucks thundering, grumbling, mumbling, whirring, their tires zinging on the pavement. Instead of branches doing deep knee bends, he saw a black and smoky woods. The light itself appeared so gradually it was almost unnoticed—all this while he was sitting on a "mean rock" with his nose running. This second attempt convinces the reader. Greg is no longer faking. As an almost inevitable consequence, the writing is more powerful, more memorable. Greg has begun to see honestly, and the reader shares the uniqueness of his experience.

The Villainous Cliché

Part of Greg's problem in his first journal entry was his dependence on clichés to do his thinking for him. A cliché is a phrase that has been repeated so often that it no longer communicates anything fresh. A cliché may be false or true, but it is so familiar to our ear that we simply don't think about it. Clichés fool us into thinking that we are saying something meaningful. How familiar to your ear are the clichéd phrases "white as a sheet," "playing with fire," and "dead as a doornail?" More than one student writer has found that he or she could pad a whole essay with clichés, although seldom with the wit Peter Carlson uses in this excerpt from *Newsweek.*

> As every school child knows, the cliché has a long and glorious history here in the land of the free. Clichés were here long before I was born and they'll be here long after I'm dead and buried. Clichés traveled from the Old World to

> the New to follow their manifest destiny. They crossed the Great Plains, forded the rushing rivers and traversed the burning sands of the steaming deserts of this teeming continent until they stretched from sea to shining sea. . . .
>
> And these clichés did not crawl out of the woodwork. Many of our Founding Fathers added their 2 cents to the nation's great storehouse of clichés. Jefferson, Lincoln, and Roosevelt created enough clichés to choke a horse, and Franklin coined more phrases than Carter has pills. Since then, these immortal words of wisdom have become landmarks on the American scene. . . .
>
> Let's face facts: You can fool some of the people some of the time, but you can't change human nature. This is a free country and a man has a right to say what he pleases—even if it's a hackneyed cliché. In this increasingly complex society, where the only constant is change, clichés still occupy a warm spot in our hearts. They are quicker, easier, and more economical than other forms of talk. They also require less energy than thoughtful, carefully constructed sentences. And in this day and age, that's nothing to sneeze at.

Carlson makes appropriate fun of the cliché, but unfortunately there is a serious side to all of this. Because clichés are used so often, they deaden our perceptive powers; they stifle our ability to think for ourselves. Clichés substitute for a genuine attempt to express the uniqueness of our experience.

Here's what one student wrote when asked to describe someone she cared about deeply.

> The first time I met Hodges he came up to the desk in the library with determination written all over his face. I could tell he was buried deep in thought, perhaps about an assignment that had been given in class that morning. I'm sure he didn't know I was in the same class with him so I just asked him how I could help, but inside I had butterflies in my stomach.

Although the reader gets a certain feel for the situation here, the author makes it difficult for us to trust her perceptions. Did Hodges really have "determination written all over his face"? There must have been some actual physical quality, but neither the author nor the reader has seen it. And what about being "buried deep in thought"? What exactly did Hodges do or say that made the author think so? Is it even possible to be buried in thought and show a face with determination written on it at the same time? The clichés begin to sound like easy substitutions for what really happened in the author's experience. The final statement about "butterflies in my stomach" confirms such a judgment. This is lazy writing in which the author has made no honest effort.

Yet it is not enough to say that a writer must avoid clichés. We must also say how to avoid them. The answer does not lie in turning to a thesaurus for an alternative word or phrase. The fault lies not in language, but in the substitution of old language for new perception. *Only by seeing what is actually there in-*

stead of what you think you are supposed to see will your writing become meaningful. The honesty of the writer demands an honesty to his or her experience—and perhaps the only way to begin is with a series of questions: Is my experience here real, or am I feeling this way because my parents or teacher expect me to? Am I hearing or seeing something in a certain way because the cliché tells me I am supposed to hear and see in that way? Just because something has always been said this way before, are the words true to my experience?

Here is a revision of the Hodges paper.

> I was working from nine to midnight behind the checkout desk when Hodges came in. He marched straight up to the desk and let a book drop on it. I remember how I watched his jaw thrust out and pull back. At the time I was so fascinated by him I thought the thrusting jaw meant that he was a determined young man who demanded his own way, but later I came to realize that he did it whenever he was nervous. He kept his eyes on the lighted computer board behind the desk while his slender fingers twisted the corner of the book. The other girls only giggled and pretended to be busy. I had to cross ten feet of open space to get to the counter. It felt like I had forgotten how to walk. I felt my arms and legs were sponging about in all kinds of directions. When I reached the counter I took hold, hung on, and asked if I could help, all without ever looking at his eyes.

This time, in using her five senses and then in attempting to be exact in describing her sensory experience, the writer has eliminated clichés. Her experience now seems genuine to us. It may be impossible to eliminate all clichés from your writing. Yet only when you begin to challenge yourself to see and feel what is really there in front of you can you be sure you are at least making an honest effort. Honesty may sometimes be painful, yet it is essential if you are to begin the process of finding truth in your experience of the world about you.

Exercises

1. Revise each abstract "telling" that follows. Make it concrete. **Group Inquiry:** Work in pairs or trios. Rely on the actual experiences of members in the group.

a. She fed us well.

b. The party was awful.

c. She dresses funny.

d. I just love nature and the woods and all that.

e. Roberto looked terrible after the fight.

Here are three examples.

Original	**Revision**
The door sounded awful.	The door squeaked as I closed it.
The mirror didn't work.	The mirror looked like a car windshield early in the morning after a heavy dew.
We had a pleasant time riding horses.	We took the old gray stallion and a dingy white mare and went exploring gentle hills. We followed the lazy creek to its source near a jagged clump of rocks where the water was the coldest and clearest I've ever seen. So cold it made your teeth ache. Later we followed the narrow creek for a mile or so until it widened and warmed.

2. Clichéd writing may be caused by laziness, or it may occur because the beginning writer is not yet widely read and not yet aware of phrases and terms others consider hackneyed and worn out.

   In which of the following sentences do you detect a cliché? **Group Inquiry:** Compare your responses with those of classmates. Did they recognize the clichés that you did?

   a. Snow blanketed the park.
   b. For better or worse, the general died on the battlefield.
   c. Movie actors come from all walks of life.
   d. In this modern-day society we seldom see students burning the midnight oil.
   e. Investing in the stock market when it's down is a tried and true plan.
   f. I had a sneaking suspicion that she was guilty.
   g. Last but not least, you have to face the fact that writing always requires effort.

Practice

1. Write about an experience you had with someone important to you. Look deeply into your memory for the actual details. Write with feeling for yourself (you are your own audience), but this time write in third person, as if you were watching the experience happen at an earlier time in your life. Use the five senses to help you recall images.

   George Powers, a physics major, chose to write about his memory of his grandmother in the hospital just before she died.

   The family stood back from the bed as the nurses spread and tucked a blanket over Gran. Skin hung in folds from her thin body. She made a small package wrapped in a yellow hospital blanket. Her eyes stared out of small caves, moving slowly from the face of one person to another. Little brown splotches covered her wrinkled face. One under her left eye, one under her forehead. Many speckled her cheeks.

Her feet poked out from under the covers. Ten toenails grew in different angles, curved and long, like small birds' beaks on small birds' heads. Her feet were almost white and they smelled of old stockings and hospital alcohol. The feet never moved. He thought of her walking through the garden, the feet busy nudging stones away from young corn.

Her arms lay across her stomach. The loose splotched skin on her arms outlined the bones underneath. The IV site on her wrist was black in the center changing to a two inch blue circle. Raw skin surrounded the circle. The arms had shrunk to half their previous size.

Her hands looked worst of all. Thin crooked fingers lay entwined together. Strips of skin peeled away from the ends of her fingers and curled back to expose pink flesh. The tendons on the backs of her hands ran like small tubes under the splotched skin.

"George, is that you?" She could barely whisper now.

"Yeah, it's me." He leaned over and kissed her cheek. A little wisp of white hair tickled his cheek.

2. Reread one of your practice writings. Find a passage that could be more concrete, more sensuous, more honest and moving if you had shared more details. Rewrite it, telling the story through images. Avoid clichés. Find the actual details that make the experience come alive.

CHAPTER 3

The Appropriate Voice

As you've looked at the world about you and sharpened your senses, you've also been redefining yourself. Consciously or unconsciously, you've been exploring concrete relationships between yourself and your immediate environment. In that sense, writing from personal experience may sometimes seem to be a private act. But almost all writing, even a journal, may reach an audience if you choose to share it. Although writing often serves to help us formulate a better understanding of ourselves, it never ceases to function as an act of communication. One of the earliest phases in the writing process, then, perhaps one that occurs as an almost simultaneous act with exploring the subject, is identification of audience. Who are your readers? Why are they reading? What do they expect from you?

The Ever-Changing Audience

If you were writing an objective research paper for a history professor, you might begin like this:

> Our knowledge of Queen Elizabeth's era is limited by the scarcity of unbiased historical data. According to C. P. Sharksey, professor of history at Oxbridge, historical information from the sixteenth century is drawn almost entirely from the men directly involved in making the history and, therefore, must be seen as containing an inherent favoritism toward one party or the other.

But you would not write a letter home in the same manner. Instead, you would probably relax and compose the sentences exactly as they came to you.

> Hi Mom,
> Working on a history paper for old Donaldson this week. Wants footnotes. The whole works. I've been up until 3 A.M. every night. Got kicked out of the library Thursday night for eating chocolate cake in the computer room.

Professor Donaldson would never accept the informality of your letter; your mother would never accept the rather stiff voice you used for Donaldson. You make such adjustments because you know each reader expects something different from you. All successful writers know they must make repeated shifts in word choice, sentence length, voice, and tone if they are to convince whatever reader they are addressing at the moment. When, for example, advertising copywriters turn out TV scripts for Crispy Pop cereal, they write with a vocabulary and voice that they hope will sway an audience of children; when bank presidents write their annual reports, they write to inform the banks' stockholders; and when students write papers about Freud's Oedipal theory, they usually write to convince a single professor that they understand the subject. Yet writing *for* an audience does not mean that you abandon your ideas or standards; it does not mean "selling out." Rather, it means using common sense. It means learning to be flexible enough to meet your readers where they are, even when the goal may be to lead those readers somewhere else. That requires you to know something about the audience *before* you begin to write.

What, then, should you know about the audience for personal or expressive writing? By its very nature, the writing found in personal letters, journals, and essays is usually addressed to a more intimate group of friends or at least to a sympathetic reader. Such an audience is presumed to be interested in sharing insights drawn from your observations and experiences. Your aim may be nothing more than to entertain, or it may be to inform and persuade your reader about values and personally held truths. Either way, one common element holds all personal writing together: the natural voice. The reader will expect it and may even be offended by overformality.

The Natural Voice

Listen for a moment with your inner ear to the voice of Virginia Woolf. The year is 1929; the location, a women's college in England.

> Here was my soup. Dinner was being served in the great dining-hall. Far from being spring it was in fact an evening in October. Everybody was assembled in the big dining-room. Dinner was ready. Here was the soup. It was a plain gravy soup. There was nothing to stir the fancy in that. One could have seen through the transparent liquid any pattern that there might have been on the

> plate itself. But there was no pattern. . . . Next came beef with its attendant greens and potatoes. . . . Prunes and custard followed. . . . Biscuits and cheese came next, and here the water-jug was liberally passed round, for it is the nature of biscuits to be dry, and these were biscuits to the core. That was all. The meal was over. Everybody scraped their chairs back; the swinging doors swung violently to and fro; soon the hall was emptied. . . . Conversation for a moment flagged. . . . A good dinner is of great importance to good talk. One cannot think well, love well, sleep well, if one has not dined well. [But] the lamp in the spine does not light on beef and prunes.

Virginia Woolf sees clearly. She senses, names, shares the experience in concrete images. But she also talks to us in a human voice, a warm and familiar voice—almost conversational but a little more rhythmical and controlled, as prose must always be. Look closely and you find simple sentences (*Here was my soup*), simple words (*biscuits, beef,* and *prunes*), mixed only occasionally with a longer, more complex thought. Among other qualities, it is this intimate voice of a real person speaking to our inner ear that makes "A Room of One's Own" such a forceful essay. Yet one misfortune of our educational system is the tendency for all of us to write in the same voice: an objective, impersonal monotone.

Listen to Irwin Parker, in his first term at college, trying to write about a personal experience in high school.

> The most interesting course that was taken by me in high school was taught by Mr. Frank. It was a course in chemistry. Mr. Frank developed student minds by involving them in experiments which were a daily part of the content of the experience that Mr. Frank wanted them to have. One liked the course because of the excitement. One never knew what exciting type of experiment Mr. Frank would come up with next.

After Irwin Parker read this paper to the class (this is only the first paragraph), he admitted he did not talk that stiffly in real life. It sounded nothing like his voice. In fact, the class decided the essay was rather boring.

One problem was tone. *Tone* is the attitude or feeling the writer takes toward both subject and audience. Parker's tone is distant and rather cold.

> *The most interesting course that was taken by me . . . One liked the course . . . One never knew what exciting . . .*

Any reader would find it difficult to feel "excitement" when the prose is so stiff. The use of the third-person *one* instead of the first-person *I* removes the human element. Other forms of writing—a critical analysis, a laboratory report—

demand that the writer take an objective tone toward his or her subject. But the personal essay ought to sound personal.

Irwin tried to rewrite it using a more natural voice. "Begin again," the class told him, "Keep it simple, and try talking to the page."

> I liked Mr. Frank because he was a good chemistry teacher in my high school. He made us think. We were always doing experiments in class, and sometimes we would get so involved that no one would hear the bell. Once, Mrs. Shaw, the principal, had to come in and drive us out because we were all late for our next class.

"Better," the class told Parker after he read the second version. "Much more human and more readable." This would probably be an acceptable voice for a personal essay. But it was still not the voice Irwin Parker used outside the classroom walls. Could he tell it to the page as if the page were his friend? Could he tell the page concretely what he saw in his memory and pretend his audience was not an English teacher but a group of his own peers?

> Mr. Frank was a super dude. He wore bow ties so big they held up his chin. A little guy, all squeezed up in an old suit spotted with chemicals and this giant butterfly of a bow tie. We would start experimenting with iron sulfide and hydrochloric acid, and pretty soon the whole room would smell like a rotten egg, and then everybody would be wiping their eyes and gasping and laughing, and old Mr. Frank would be dancing around the room saying, "Wow, it worked. You see what happened? You see what happens when you make hydrogen sulfide?" And that's when old Mrs. Shaw would stumble in gasping and holding a pink handkerchief over her nose. "You've all god to ho to quass." She would turn red and Mr. Frank would act shocked, like how did he know what time it was, and we would all just be laughing so hard you couldn't breathe.

"Good!" said the class. "Now we can hear the genuine voice of Irwin Parker."

And notice what has happened in the process of working toward that voice. The first essay is almost totally abstract.

> *One liked the course because of the excitement.*

But in the final paper Parker involves the reader by using concrete, sensory details.

> *. . . pretty soon the whole room would smell like a rotten egg, and then everybody would be wiping their eyes and gasping. . . .*

By finding his natural voice, Parker has been able to let his imagination flow more freely. The tone has become informal, even conversational; and the reader feels the emotion and excitement of the class.

> *. . . like how did he know what time it was, and we would all just be laughing so hard you couldn't breathe.*

In listening once again to all three versions, the class decided that the first voice probably revealed Parker's nervousness about writing anything. He wrote stiffly, perhaps on the assumption that his audience would expect "dignified," formal writing at college. In the second version, he wrote more directly to a particular English instructor who told him that he could relax and be natural. But in the third version, he wrote for his fellow students, using the same voice he would actually talk in.

The point is clearly that beginning writers should become aware that they have a choice of voices, just as they have a choice of vocabulary, and that the audience as well as the subject helps determine which voice is appropriate for the purpose. Writers who find themselves locked into the same voice in every paper, no matter what the audience or intention, find themselves locked into repetitive dullness. Even the most formal research paper can be made more lively and interesting by the carryover of a genuine voice. What we are talking about here is a matter of degree. The beginning writer must recognize that dull writing lacks any voice at all. It sounds anonymous, as if written by committee. Effective writing, even formal and scientific prose, can still have a voice, a liveliness or felicity or uniqueness that makes the reader say, "This could only come from Irwin Parker or Salinda Rodriquez or Corrine Golden."

Exploring Your Voice

Finding a natural voice may open doors to your imagination that a wrong voice will permanently block. The right voice relaxes you and frees you to speak your mind. The wrong voice makes you uncomfortable and distracts your attention from the subject to the writing itself.

Listen to Jim Brown, a star football player of the late 1950s and early 1960s:

> I get a little weary of hearing broken homes blamed for 96.3 percent of American youth's difficulties. . . . My guess is that thanks to all the yakking about broken homes, a lot of kids have found a good excuse to get into trouble. The broken home is their crutch in Juvenile Court. I am not dogmatic about this. Looking back on my own boyhood, there were many times when I came perilously close to becoming a no-account.

Compare Brown's voice with that of E. B. White, a novelist and an essayist:

> One summer, along about 1904, my father rented a camp on a lake in Maine and took us all there for the month of August. We all got ringworm from some kittens and had to rub Pond's Extract on our arms and legs night and morning, and my father rolled over in a canoe with all his clothes on; but outside of that the vacation was a success and from then on none of us ever thought there was any place in the world like that lake in Maine.

Both voices sound natural, informal, and relaxed. Both put the reader at ease, yet they are not the same voice. Brown uses more conversational words. Conversational words reflect the vocabulary we use in our most casual speech, for example, *I get a little weary . . . My guess is . . . all the yakking about . . . a lot of kids . . . becoming a no-account.* Of course, no written language is identical with the spoken voice. But good writing almost invariably has the sound of the spoken voice. Brown achieves that sound, the impression that he is speaking to us from the page.

E. B. White achieves the same effect, but his word choice is *informal,* not conversational. Excluding the more casual or slang vocabulary found in conversational writing, the informal voice simply uses everyday words and phrases: *We all got ringworm . . . but outside of that . . . and from then on . . . there was any place in the world like. . . .*

The following list contrasts informal and conversational language with a more formal vocabulary.

Conversational	**Informal**	**Formal**
yakking	talking	discussing
kids	children	youth
a no-account	a problem child (or delinquent)	a delinquent (or social offender)
my guess is	I would guess	I would estimate

Such a list is arbitrary. Words considered informal by one generation may be considered appropriate formal terms by the next. (For example, contractions like *isn't* and *haven't* were once strongly rejected in a formal paper. Today, even conservative periodicals print essays using contractions.) Still, the contrast reveals that a significant choice is available to a writer—and also confirms that material written in one voice may be changed or translated into another voice.

Jim Brown, for example, must have felt comfortable writing in a conversational style. His ideas presumably came to him most readily in the voice closest to his speaking voice. But if his audience had been a convention of psychologists instead of the casual reader, Brown might have returned to his material and translated it into formal prose.

> I am disturbed at hearing that broken homes are blamed for 96.3 percent of American youth's difficulties. . . . I estimate that because of excessive discussion about broken homes, many young people have found a good excuse to become social offenders.

The point is clear: By writing in your natural voice, you allow your imagination to flow; your attention can be focused where it should be—on the subject. But later you can (and should) return to your first draft and double-check the *appropriateness* of the voice you have written in. Once your ideas and experiences are on the page, the voice can be adjusted to match the expectations and needs of your audience.

The Appropriate Voice

Every voice has its limitations. A *conversational* voice may be highly successful for entertaining a sympathetic, casual audience. It is appropriate for humor or light entertainment. But such a voice usually prevents you from discussing more serious material—that is, if you want to be taken seriously. An *informal* voice, however, may be considered a solid bridge between conversational and formal. It may be either entertaining or serious. E. B. White often shifts easily from pleasant memories into thoughtful reflections on human values. The informal voice is the most flexible of all styles: friendly, relaxed, familiar, yet at the same time more polished and edited than the conversational. The informal voice is especially appropriate for essays. Unless you are highly skilled, however, the audience for a research paper, critical analysis, or report will probably expect a more *formal* voice. The need for objective data, factual information, and logical analysis requires a tone of high seriousness to convince the reader.

Know your audience, then; know what it expects and needs. But also know yourself. If you write more freely and comfortably in one voice, use it to its best advantage, especially in your notebook or on the first draft. Write fast, keeping your subject vividly and imaginatively before your mind's eye. Use the most natural voice, then be willing to return later and make whatever adjustments are necessary for your ideas and experiences to be communicated effectively to your audience.

Exercises

1. Here is a series of paragraphs, each by a different author and each with a distinctive voice. Consider the audience for each voice, and suggest the type of character behind the voice. Discuss the limitations of each voice—that is, would it be effective for a convention of physicists or for an informal audience reading for pleasure? Are there any voices here

you find annoying to your ear? Any you feel you might like to emulate in your writing?

Among the most comprehensive of the existing synthetic models that do not use human-capital approach is that by Stiglitz, who integrates the distribution of income into its major sources, *viz.*, wages and profits. Stiglitz examines the distribution impact of nonlinear saving functions, heterogeneity of labor skills, material-capital inheritance policies, variable reproduction rates of different income classes, tax policies, and the nature of the stochastic elements in the accumulation process.

Gian Singh Sahota, "Theories of Personal Income Distribution"
Journal of Economic Literature

Just to paint is great fun. The colours are lovely to look at and delicious to squeeze out. Matching them, however crudely, with what you see is fascinating and absolutely absorbing. Try it if you have not done so—before you die. . . . One begins to see, for instance, that painting a picture is like fighting a battle; and trying to paint a picture is, I suppose, like trying to fight a battle.

Winston Churchill, *Painting as a Pastime*

Wednesday, Mr. and Mrs. Johnnie Gann went to Kansas City. Sure was a hot day but enjoyed our trip. Couldn't hardly sleep that night. They were gone but they came after we were there for some time. We took the lawn chairs, went out in the back yard to keep cool until James came. He took us over to Bobby's to get something to eat. We just got a hot dog when we got to the Bus Station. Bobby works late, comes home after dark. When James' wife came home they came to get us. Went over there for supper.

We saw several sight-seeing different places. Was close to an airplane. Went under several overhead bridges. The Bus Station sure is a nice large building, has nice seats, two lunch counters.

We saw the Kaw river going down it was full. Steamboats were sailing.

Mrs. Johnnie Gann, *Lily Grove News,*
Tri-County Weekly

Everybody in our family has different hair. My Papa's hair is like a broom, all up in the air. And me, my hair is lazy. It never obeys barrettes or bands. Carlos' hair is thick and straight. He doesn't need to comb it. Nenny's hair is slippery—slides out of your hand. And Kiki, who is the youngest, has hair like fur.

But my mother's hair, my mother's hair, like little rosettes, like little candy circles all curly and pretty because she pinned it in pincurls all day, sweet to put your nose into when she is holding you, holding you and you feel safe, is the warm smell of bread before you bake it, is the smell when she makes room for you on her side of the bed still warm with her skin, and you sleep near her, the rain outside falling and Papa snoring. The snoring, the rain, and Mama's hair that smells like bread.

Sandra Cisneros, *The House on Mango Street*

Darling, I'm weary, and there is no rest. I have been fighting in the hills around the city for days, in the snow and mud, against the enemy I do not hate because I do not know how to hate, an enemy that I regard like a monster in the fairy stories that must be hacked to pieces with the sword, the impenetrable forest around the castle of Sleeping Beauty. I believe with all my heart that I shall emerge from these shadows, and shall come to you, so delicate, luminous, dear, but the carelessness or tiredness of an instant, or even bad luck, could check me forever.

Pavel, *Voices from Sarajevo*

A tourist is an ugly human being. You are not an ugly person all the time; you are not an ugly person ordinarily, you are not an ugly person day to day. From day to day you are a nice person.

Jamaica Kincaid, *A Small Place*

a. To what extent does sentence length affect the voice in each piece?

b. Does the use of *I, we,* or *you* change the feeling in the voice?

c. Many writers have observed that the use of Anglo-Saxon words (simple three- and four-letter terms like *pig, man, live, hand*) creates a different reaction in the reader than the use of words of Latin origin *(heterogeneous, preterition, lactiferous)*. Do you find these writers using one or the other with any consistency? Does it affect their voice?

2. Here is a student writing about a personal experience. Has he chosen the right voice? What specific problems, if any, do you detect?

My most embarrassing moment was having the zipper of my pants split apart during church. Since church services traditionally demand one's attire to be elaborate, to see a person with his fly open must be quite striking to the observer and embarrassing to the observed. The abashment that followed the accident was humorous at the initial thought of the situation. Uncontrollably following was a nervous and very desperate search for the most logical path to use for an exit. The path hopefully would serve the purposes of a stealthy departure from the congregation and to allow unnoticed repairs to take place. Once repairs had taken place to fix the obvious defect, the feeling of complete isolation flooded my brain in order to contribute in dismissing all possibilities of the situation recurring. The end of the service was reached to find my body outside the church in the parking lot hastily waiting the departure home in the most inconspicuous manner possible. Consequently, when the time to dress for church services arrives in the future, a special precaution related to the strength and durability of zippers in pants will be unforgettably performed.

Practice

Experiment with voice. In your notebook or on a computer disk write three different letters in three different voices. Assume this is your first term at college and you've discovered a serious problem—perhaps you've discovered your roommate selling term papers and one of them is yours, or your tuition payment was not properly recorded, or the manager at your place of employment prevents you from attending one class a week with the toughest professor you have.

a. Send an e-mail to a good friend in a conversational voice describing the problem. Use concrete, specific details. Be yourself.
b. Write a second e-mail to someone who might be able to help—a senior dormitory assistant, a school counselor, or the manager at work. Assume you want to demonstrate maturity and tolerance here: Use an informal voice, but be specific and detailed about the problem.
c. Write a third e-mail to the highest reasonable authority—the college president, the professor himself, the district manager of your company. Use a firm voice and firmly request an immediate solution.

CHAPTER 4

Facing the Blank Page

The time arrives. You've been exploring various subjects; you've practiced several exercises. Perhaps your instructor has already assigned a subject and an audience. One way or another, the preparation stage is drawing to a close. You have to face the inevitable. You have to write a full-fledged paper. Oh, shudder and dread!

You spread out paper, pens, erasers, and dictionaries. You adjust the desk lamp over your computer. Perhaps you drink a Coke or doodle little circles inside of big circles. You punch a cassette into your tape deck, listen for a while to a new British singer, and remember good times in high school.

But the blank paper remains white and glaring; the cursor light on your word processor blinks on an empty screen. There is no escape. At some point you must face the single most difficult part of the writing process: beginning to write.

How the Process Works

One of the great misunderstandings about writing involves the concept of failure. We need to get it out of the way at the beginning. For the successful writer, failure is normal to the process. To say such a thing may sound like a paradox, but actually, without failure, most of us would never be able to say what we wanted to at all. In fact, most of us probably would not know what we truly think and feel without first saying what we did not think and feel. In the first version of this very paragraph I wrote a dozen sentences that did not express what I wanted to say. Why? Because until I saw the words in front of me, I could not be sure. I "knew" (like an unvoiced urge) that I should say something about failure. But I had never articulated the ideas before. The first two sentences of the paragraph appear here exactly as I wrote them. Success. But the third sentence did not come until I had first failed at several false starts. I had to work through some awkward, inaccurate, and actually misleading sentences until I came to the next one that seemed right to me. I wish I could say it wasn't necessary. I wish I could say that with practice each sentence will flow out upon the page. But, in reality, even the best writers know they must work through the failures to arrive at success.

In 1926, William Butler Yeats wrote "Sailing to Byzantium," a 31-line poem. The manuscript reveals that Yeats wrote nineteen pages of material in pencil, ink, and typescript, each page averaging about fourteen crossed-out, reworked, and abandoned lines. No line now in the final poem appears in the manuscript before the tenth page. In other words, Yeats wrote approximately 140 lines before he found even the first few rough images that satisfied him; and he still had another 126 lines to struggle through: a total of some 266 lines to achieve 31 lines of poetry.

Theodore Geisel wrote the famous Dr. Seuss books for children. Simple lines, simple rhymes. Nothing like the complex moral vision of William Butler Yeats.

> The sun did not shine
>
> It was too wet to play
>
> So we sat in the house
>
> All that cold, cold, wet day.

Yet Geisel admitted that *The Cat in the Hat,* a book of sixty-one pages (only 223 words), took ten months to write.

No one, of course, will expect you to spend ten months writing a college paper, but the more words you're willing to explore on any one writing project, the more likely you'll eventually discover what it is you want to say and how you want to say it. What you need to know is what the professional knows: that the first working copy will be only a sketch of the writer's ideas, of the facts and details of perception, and that much of it will be almost inevitably badly written. If you, too, can know in advance that you are never going to show that first awkward draft to any audience, if you can know that the first draft is *your* copy and that its sole purpose is to provide you with a worksheet, a place to sketch out in as much detail as possible your ideas in rough form, and that it is absolutely *normal* for your first draft to seem like a failure, you will probably find yourself less threatened, less fearful of the blank page. What you are about to do is to explore, and every explorer must chop through a lot of tangled underbrush to reach the crest of a hill. You must be willing to take wrong turns, to make mistakes. You cannot know the path in advance, nor can anyone else. So take a chance and start with the first word.

The Habits of Writing

Certain types of preparation and mental attitudes can make your approach to the first draft, if not easier, at least more productive.

1. **Make writing a habit.** As long as writing is an occasional thing, it will seem strange, even threatening. If you practice the piano or trumpet or guitar a little every day, it becomes a familiar instrument; you feel comfortable with it. Familiarity in any situation helps you relax. Better to write an hour a day, every day, than to postpone an assignment until the night before and attempt a twelve-hour marathon. Work for an hour a day in your journal, on a lab report, on two pages of a fifteen-page research paper—it really does not matter as long as you're writing every day.
2. **Find a regular time and place.** Try to write at approximately the same time each day. We are creatures of regularity. Football coaches know how important it is for a team to practice at the same hour, five days a week. The body—and the mind—has its rhythm. Whether you write best in the early morning or at midnight makes little difference so long as you find the tide of your personal rhythm and flow with it every day.

   Most successful writers have also discovered they need a special place in which to work. Some prefer absolute silence; others write well immersed in noise. Find what works for you and stick to it. Create your own nest. Surround yourself with books or paintings or bare walls—whatever makes you comfortable. The German writer Schiller claimed to work well only when he could smell rotten apples. Most of us aren't that eccentric, but having a special place helps establish a pattern for writing that almost all of us need.
3. **Do warm-up writing when necessary.** When Kurt Vonnegut was still employed by General Electric Company and not yet famous for his novels of fantasy and science fiction, a story was told about how he would arrive for work each morning, immediately sit down at his typewriter, and pound on it for about ten minutes, describing nothing more than the eggs he ate for breakfast, the rumbling of the subway that morning, and the feel of snow in the air. He called it his warm-up. To use the analogy of an athlete or musician again, trying to perform cold, without preparation, may be possible; but the performance will usually be halting and error-prone until the mind or senses are fully tuned in. The best preparation for beginning the first draft may be to write for ten minutes. A warm-up can never substitute for honest effort on the main writing project. But don't hesitate to play a little at first. Write about anything that comes into your head. If nothing comes, write Mary had a little lamb; then find a new rhyme to go with it, then another. Play. Exercise. But start writing fast. Time yourself and do not stop writing for at least ten minutes. If nothing at all seems effective, take a break. Work

on some other project or go to a movie. Let the incubation phase do its own thing in your subconscious. Try again later. But don't postpone the assignment until the night before it's due. Keep trying any and all exercises suggested so far, and if nothing works, start writing about anything. Remember, the act of writing itself is almost always more productive than merely worrying about or thinking about what to write.

4. **Write fast.** Once you begin work on your real subject, write with as much intensity and speed as possible. Because the mind usually moves faster than the hand, a word processor can prove valuable. You might even want to try dictating your ideas into a tape recorder. But work fast.

   Most successful writers have found that the more slowly they write the first draft, the more slowly ideas tend to come. The more words you get on the page, the more the words themselves seem to activate the imagination. Words call up words. Images call up images. Slow writing may allow time for you to become overly critical. You may consciously begin to challenge the sentence you've just completed. (Is it the best way to phrase what you want to say? Did you spell that word correctly? Should you be varying your sentence structures more?) Once this sort of self-criticism begins, you're no longer writing. You're editing. Writing and editing are different stages in the writing process. During the first draft, fast, intensive writing focuses your mind on the subject. Ideas will grow only out of an encounter with the subject, not out of concern for grammar or spelling. After you've finished a rough working copy, there will be time (and need) to revise, edit, and polish.

Form and the Personal Essay

Form refers to the shape of your experience, to the way you organize your material. In personal writing, form is usually subjective. It tends to develop from the natural sequence of events you are writing about (this happened and then this happened) or from subconscious "associations" (one word calls up a second; one image leads to another). I won't tell you not to outline or plan before you write. Many writers find it helpful. But because part of the aim of writing about personal experience is to explore yourself and your voice freely, for the time being you'll probably find that conscious concern for form should follow the first draft, not precede it. Yet two traditional elements of form tend to be associated with most personal essays. Knowing them in advance may help you focus even your rough draft more clearly.

First, although the whole range of human experience is open to you, you cannot successfully write about ten years of life, or even twenty-four hours, in only four or five pages. The personal essay may be organized around a single, unique experience, one that you develop in great detail, helping the reader to see, hear, smell, and touch. Or the personal essay may be organized around two or three smaller experiences that reveal some kind of pattern—a series of ordinary daily situations that are typical or that lead to general insight. Either way, you will need to *select* only the one major incident or the two or three typical incidents and to exclude all the millions of others that compose your life.

Second, the elements of experience you select to write about should show the reader how they led you to some type of growth, insight, or understanding, even if it is a humorous one. You do not necessarily need to explain the meaning of the experience in abstract, general terms (although you can do so), but the meaning must be evident or implied by the end of the essay. After all, why write about it if it has no meaning to you?

Practice

If you've been practicing regularly in a notebook or on the computer, you already have a number of strategies for beginning your first essay—and you may already have the subject for it. Making lists, webs, freewriting, exploring your memory, sharing stories and experiences with the blank page are all ways of getting started.

1. Look back through practice exercises you may have written on any personal experience. Select one that seems to have possibilities and make a list of ideas that might extend it into a longer essay. Perhaps you wrote a paragraph about your first meeting with your new roommate. Consider how the topic might be developed further.

   initial encounter in hallway

   luggage with airline tickets pasted on sides

   sweaty palms

   obnoxious parents

   father wearing tennis shorts and talking loud

   mother with sickly smile, left basket of overripe grapefruit

   roommate wouldn't talk for two days

   spent two more days moping about bad cafeteria food

   hated each other

   then found we were both on swim team

   first instinct: competitive, determined to beat each other out

   initial practice session

   water overheated; coach too demanding

   everybody seemed arrogant, everybody for themselves

   roommate only person who talked to me

   stuck together out of necessity

   asked for lockers together

   eye contact said we were both nervous

   cheered for each other in trial heats

stopped hating, started respecting each other's abilities

found we could be best friends

Now you've got the potential for a full essay, and it's already beginning to take shape. Sometimes you may find you won't even get to the end of your list before you'll have too many ideas. Instead of listing, you'll find you're already writing. Go ahead. Trust your instincts and trust the act of writing to generate more ideas.

2. If none of your previous entries seems to offer possibilities, or if a new listing doesn't stimulate the imagination this time, try a technique called "webbing." Begin with a key word, *any* word, and follow whatever comes to mind. Allow one word to create associations or memories. Trace them out; draw lines and circles that follow your ideas.

   If no ideas come, draw the line and circle first. The very act of showing the mind that it is supposed to fill in the blank often triggers an idea.

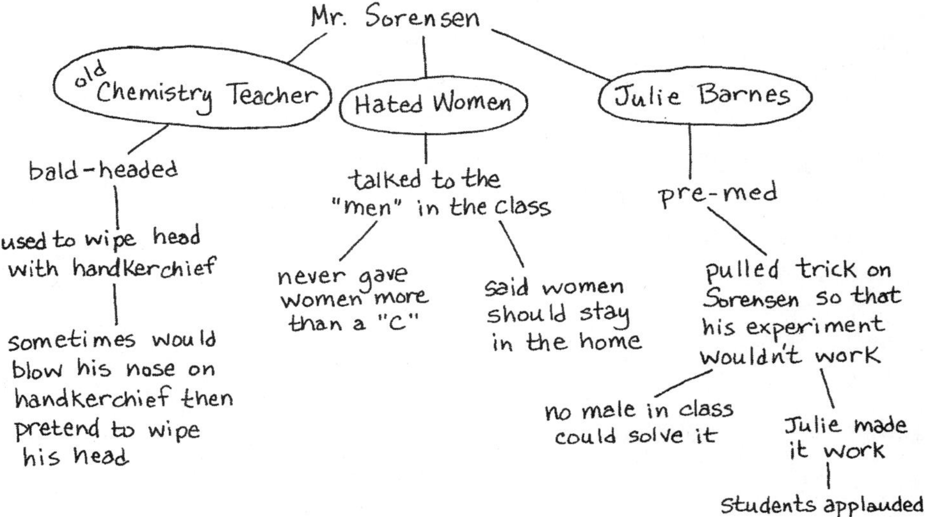

Group Inquiry

Write a letter (or send e-mail) to others in your class. Describe the essay you've been considering. Don't worry about structure, organization, or technical details; just get the ideas down. List some of the more important details as they come to you, in any order. "Talk" to your other reader, then let your peer group or partner respond. Very often, the informal letter format allows you to break through the mental shackles, loosens up the blockage, and—if nothing else—gets words on the page (or the computer screen). And that's a starting place.

CHAPTER 5

Precision and Feeling

Interviewer: *How much rewriting do you do?*

Hemingway: *It depends. I rewrote the ending of* Farewell to Arms *thirty-nine times before I was satisfied.*

Interviewer: *Was there some technical problem there? What was it that had stumped you?*

Hemingway: *Getting the words right.*

Paris Review

During the early drafting phase, many writers work in stop-and-go fashion, pausing over a single word, revising a sentence, perfecting a whole paragraph, moving on, slowing down. Other writers, especially when the juices are flowing, push quickly through the working draft, writing fast and exploring ideas with little hesitation for precision and accuracy of language. In fact, you may find, at any given time, that you'll alternate between these two methods, depending on the project and your state of mind. Either way, the real work of writing begins when you determine to make your prose say exactly what you want it to say, when some inner feeling suggests that the words you've used do not yet express what you hoped they would. This is the point where you cross out, rephrase, begin again, testing each new sentence against the old. Your focus, of course, must remain on the subject—on the ideas and feelings you're trying to express—while your effort struggles to find the right word, the most meaningful sequence of ideas or images, and the most unified effect.

Searching for the Right Meaning

Many take language for granted. In terms of influencing their lives, they tend to place words somewhere between sunshine and potato chips. But language has a remarkable, almost awesome power over us. Words spoken by someone you love on an autumn afternoon unite the two of you forever. Words written on a letter of application get you accepted to law school. Words spoken on television by a local car dealer campaigning for mayor make you slam a book on the table in anger. The power of language is such that almost two-thirds of the world's governments forbid newspapers to publish freely. Priests in many early cults and religions often were feared because people believed they knew magic words that summoned the gods. Telling stories, fables, and fantasies around the campfire led to complex mythologies that eventually became the cultural fabric of civilization. Indeed, without words, we would have no civilization. Language is inseparable from being human. As a beginning writer, you need at least a rudimentary understanding of some of the ways words affect you and your reader.

Here's how one first-year student (who had not yet developed a feeling for words) began an early draft of an essay about his grandfather:

> Royster R. Matting lived an immemorial life. He began as a surveyor in Montana, made and lost a fortune as a miner, once owned a railroad in Virginia, became a judge in Maryland, and raised thirteen children who honored his loins.

Well, maybe, but the writer seems to have encountered two kinds of language problems, both related to accuracy. One is a matter of denotation; the other, a matter of perception.

Denotation is the explicit (or dictionary) meaning of a word. Obviously, using a word with the correct denotation is essential to clear communication. *Immemorial,* for example, means reaching beyond the limits of memory, beyond even recorded history. As admirable a life as Royster R. Matting may have had, it surely wasn't beyond memory's scope. The student has clearly wanted to express the breadth and energy found in his grandfather's life, but the word *memorable* (something worth remembering) probably comes closer and expresses his feelings more exactly. Mark Twain's famous remark still applies: "The difference between the right word and the wrong word is the difference between lightning and a lightning bug." Words are symbols. Unless we use them with generally agreed-upon meanings, confusion and disorder result. In this case, the student has simply chosen the wrong word. Thirty seconds with any dictionary would have revealed the problem.

But dictionaries are not always the solution to achieving accuracy. Accuracy begins in clarity of perception. If you are not seeing your subject clearly, you obviously won't find clear and precise words to communicate it. The first-year student who wrote about his grandfather admitted that he felt uncomfortable with the phrase "thirteen children who honored his loins," but it had a biblical ring to it and he hoped it would work. The student accepted the first phrase that sounded good to his ear (something that's fine to do on a first draft), but that uncomfortable feeling should have signaled a need for challenging the phrase in the second draft. Surely, these thirteen children honored more than their father's prodigious sexual abilities. The problem here is not that the student has chosen a wrong word, but that he has not truly identified what it was about his grandfather the children honored. Was it his remarkable career? His achievements? His human compassion? We don't know and neither does the student. At this point, a dictionary won't help.

Revising the first draft often means re-seeing the subject (from the Latin for "looking again"). This student should have asked himself a series of questions: If I haven't found the precise word, is it because I haven't found the right insight? If I haven't found the right insight, is it because I haven't looked honestly, haven't struggled to find the small details that make up the total? What is it about my subject that I'm not yet seeing?

The answer in this case was not difficult.

> Royster R. Matting lived a memorable life. He began as a surveyor in Montana, made and lost a fortune as a miner, once owned a railroad in Virginia, became a judge in Maryland, and raised thirteen children who always honored the model of courage and discipline he established.

Before submitting a final typed version of his essay, the student reread it and again refined the accuracy by penciling in the term *self-* before "discipline." Now the reader can be convinced. Self-discipline and courage can indeed make for a memorable life. Precise words strike home more forcefully than a page full of words that only circle the subject. The "almost right" word is never the right word.

Searching for the Right Feeling

If you were hired to write menus for Top of the Town Restaurant, you might find that correct denotation was only half the problem. Here are two versions of the same menu, each conveying a similar denotative meaning.

> Succulent roast beef served in its own juice with tiny young peas and mashed potatoes . . . $12.50
>
> Bloody cow's flesh with tiny young *pisum sativum* seed and squashed tubers . . . 75¢

No doubt most of your customers would prefer to pay $12.50 for the first dish, even though the 75¢ meal is identical. Words do more than communicate messages. The *connotation* of a word is the feeling it suggests to us.

Nursing merely names a medical occupation, but the word has about it an aura of feelings: tenderness, care, sacrifice. The nature and intensity of feeling associated with a word may be peculiar to your individual relationship with it. If you appreciate athletics, *jock* might be a term you use with pride, but if you don't like sports, *jock* might be a term you use as an insult. Other words, however, seem to share a general *connotation* throughout a given culture—*snake,* for example.

Sometimes the feelings we have about words become so strong that they actually replace the original denotative meanings. In the Middle Ages, the word *mistress* meant a woman who had control of the house. Possession of numerous keys to pantries, cupboards, and wine cellars symbolized her control. The word was equivalent to the male appellation *master* and projected a similar positive connotation. During Shakespeare's time, *mistress* began to be used metaphorically, as in "mistress of my heart," suggesting the woman who possessed keys to, or control of, her lover's emotions. Apparently the metaphor seemed so right that a *mistress* began to be associated more with love than with home. By the seventeenth century, the denotation had actually changed to "an illicit lover" and the connotation had become negative.

Compare your emotional responses to each of the following words with similar denotations. The positive or negative feeling you experience is the connotation. Words that evoke no feelings are said to be connotatively neutral.

gay	homosexual	fag
female activist	feminist	women's libber
amour	love affair	making it
tumor	malignancy	cancer
restroom	powder room	john

Words evoke feelings, but communicating the *exact* feeling is not easy. Several years ago a student of mine, Kiki Nikoni, wanted to write about a painful moment from childhood. Kiki stumbled into what is probably the most common danger among beginning writers—overwriting, telling too much, using words that are too emotional or that suggest an inappropriate connotation. In listening to her first draft, Kiki's peer group argued that her essay sounded melodramatic. Kiki rewrote it several times to make it more genuine, but at the same time she wanted it to be forceful because the real experience had been important to her. Read the original version through before you read the revision.

Original

Where I used to live there was a train. I would hear it but I never really listened until after my father died. Once I was alone at night by the window. Frankenstein-shadows seemed as deathly cold as I felt inside. I heard the whistle like a moaning screaming animal somewhere far outside. The silence roared about me! Then the whistle blew again, this time closer but still painful and really lonely. I remember thinking for a moment that it was like I was out there and my heart was broken and torn out of me and lost, like a father's ghost crying out! It hurt my ears, it hurt my heart until the tears ran down my cheeks.

Revision

In Japan I used to live near a train. Each night I would hear its whistle but I never really listened until the night after my father's funeral. I was alone at the window and the shadows seemed thin and cold. Then I heard the whistle, high and far away, like a child's toy in the dark. The silence afterward seemed unsteady, as if something whole had been sliced. The whistle blew again, this time closer but still hollow and lonely. For a moment I felt some part of me was out there, like my father's ghost. Then the whistle again, but further away, faint and fading. After a while I couldn't hear it. There was just moonlight on empty fields.

Both versions reveal problems with connotations, but the first presents serious difficulties. Kiki's peer group objected especially to lines 13 through 20. Kiki's listeners felt she was crying out in abstractions *(painful, lonely, lost, hurt)* and that she was perilously close to clichéd melodrama *(a broken heart, a ghost, tears running down her cheeks).* Kiki had tried to select words and images she thought would convey an honest feeling of pain. The opposite effect resulted. The peer group doubted the sincerity of her description.

In the second version, Kiki tried to re-see the scene in her memory. She removed most of the abstractions and substituted concrete images, using words that might *suggest* the feelings of pain and loss *(a hollow whistle, a faint and fading whistle, moonlight on open fields).* She removed the reference to her broken heart, replacing it with the generalization: *some part of me.* The peer group agreed that this was a time when the generalization worked more successfully because it seemed less melodramatic. In the context (and connotation is always affected by context), *some part of me,* by its very abstractness, suggested emptiness and helped promote the appropriate feeling.

Kiki made a number of other changes you might want to consider.

1. Why did she add *Japan* to line 1? How does a specific place suggest feeling? Would the connotation have been different had she lived in Little Rock at the time?

2. Why did she change *after my father died* in lines 3 and 4 to *after my father's funeral?*
3. Why use *shadows seemed thin and cold* instead of *Frankenstein-shadows* in line 6?
4. What was gained or lost in changing *moaning screaming animal* in line 9 to *high and far away, like a child's toy in the dark?* How do the connotations of either one relate to the loss of a father, and which seems most appropriate for the mood Kiki wants to convey?
5. What kind of feelings does *moonlight on empty fields* in lines 20 and 21 connote for you? Why did Kiki think that it could substitute for the original *tears ran down my cheeks?*

As a writer you need to develop the confidence that words can be played with. Just because you've written a word on the page, you should not think it's sacred. Indeed, you may not know exactly what you want to say until you've tried to say it in several different ways. By understanding something about how language affects all of us, you learn how to discover and express your ideas with more force.

Exercises

1. *The Oxford English Dictionary* (usually called the *OED*) traces word histories, providing you with a thorough sense of a word's past and, by implication, its denotative and connotative developments.

   Investigate the histories of the following terms. In your own words, write up each history as you understand it, giving some of the examples listed in the *OED.*

science	nice
woman	humanities
sophisticated	text

2. Look up the following terms in a dictionary of synonyms. Find three synonyms for each, and in your own words suggest the differences in connotation. For example, *Roget's Thesaurus* lists *dowager* and *relict* among the synonyms for *widowhood.* To me, *widowhood* suggests loneliness, dark dresses, and silence, whereas *dowager* suggests strength in a woman's old age, a widow with power and authority, and something vaguely Elizabethan. Frankly, I'm surprised to find *relict* there at all. If *relict* is a synonym for *widowhood,* then it suggests a decrepit woman, the leavings of a man's life, a woman without value.

submission	regret
money	marriage
cool	truth
trust	student

3. Identify and discuss the positive, negative, or neutral connotations in each of the following sentences. In which sentences can an alternative word evoke a different emotional response?
   a. The Russians wanted to attack Afghanistan.
   b. Grandmama is selling her *objet d'art.*
   c. The president is proposing tax incentives for hog farmers.
   d. The ingredients on a can of cat food include fish by-products.
   e. Juan comes from a Chicano family.

Practice

Select one of your previous exercises and evaluate every sentence in light of what you now know about connotations and denotations. Does every word contribute to the precise meaning and feeling that you want? Are some words or phrases inappropriate? Rewrite the passage to make it more effective, to make it suggest the emotions you honestly feel. Would the rewritten version make it a stronger piece for you to share with an audience (a reader)?

CHAPTER 6

Cutting Unnecessary Words

The distinction between editing and revising is somewhat arbitrary. For more experienced writers, editing techniques blend naturally with the process of exploring the subject in second and third drafts. The goal of both stages in the writing process is to improve the effectiveness of writing so that you find the means of conveying your subject clearly and convincingly. But many necessary aspects of writing involve the mechanics of effective expression: sentence structure, sentence variety, paragraphing, logical order, and accurate documentation. When such qualities are emphasized too early in the learning process, beginning writers tend to be overwhelmed by what they perceive as rules and restrictions. The results can often create stillborn prose and the "I hate to write" attitude. It might be best (even if somewhat oversimplified) to think of rewriting as a phase in which your primary focus remains on developing the subject, and editing as a phase in which your attention shifts to achieving the most polished and effective form of expression.

The Editor's Job

Editing involves selecting, arranging, and correcting a manuscript. Your papers may not be intended for publication, but as most audiences are accustomed to thinking of "good writing" as that which they see published, your writing will usually be judged by similarly high standards. You must become your own editor. You must learn some essential skills of editing. Almost without exception, you'll find their application to every essay, report, or research paper will make the difference between average work and good work.

Editing requires an attitude almost opposite to the one you were urged to adopt in writing the first draft. Instead of spontaneous, fast writing and suspension of all concern for sentence structure and correctness, editing requires a cool, slow, self-critical act. Most writers find that they need to turn away from their writing for a while, distance themselves from it, and later return with a coldly skeptical attitude: Every word, every sentence, must prove its worth. As a student you may not have the ideal amount of time to pause between rewriting and editing, but you can still train yourself to approach your material with an editor's eye.

Because the sentence is the shortest complete unit of thought, it seems the best place to begin the practice of editing. The first step in forming a solid, readable sentence is to make it say only what it needs to say and nothing more: That means eliminating unnecessary words. Unfortunately, many students have been taught that short simple sentences should be avoided. Long, complex-compound sentences seem to get all the praise. Some students go out of their way to use as many words as possible in every paper. Editing down to simple, irreducible elements may seem in conflict with everything you've been taught. But a major misconception is at work here. Long sentences in themselves are neither better nor worse than short sentences, but extra words are deadly to all forms of writing. The first goal of sentence editing is to clear away clutter that distracts from meaning. *Every word or phrase that can be cut should be cut.*

Here's a typical early-draft sentence:

◆ Having just finished college myself, I can testify that mental discipline is the greatest asset a college student can have while he's in school.

Fair enough. But not good enough. The simplest editorial act strikes out excess.

Cut Having just finished college [~~myself~~], I can testify that mental discipline is the greatest asset a [~~college~~] student can have [~~while he's in school~~].

By eliminating six redundant words or phrases, we have a cleaner sentence that directly conveys its message.

Here's another example from a first-year student's paper:

- At an early stage in his career, Barry Bonds met a coach who kept urging him to go and analyze his motions while he was up at the plate.

No two editors would necessarily find the same weaknesses in this sentence. Right and wrong answers are seldom clear-cut in editing. But most editors would probably agree that almost half the words could be eliminated without losing the meaning of the sentence.

Cut [~~At an~~] early [~~stage~~] in his career . . .
("Early in his career" says the same thing.)

Cut . . . Barry Bonds met a coach who [~~kept~~] urg[~~ing~~] him to [~~go and~~] analyze . . .
(*Kept urging* adds little to the concept of *urge,* and *go and* simply distracts from the stronger word, *analyze.*)

Cut . . . his motions [~~while he was up~~] at the plate.
(As we seldom think of someone being *down* at the plate, *while he was up* contributes nothing to meaning.)

A final edited version might now read like this:

- Early in his career, Barry Bonds met a coach who urged him to analyze his motions at the plate.

We have eliminated ten words, made the sentence simpler, and, in the process, allowed the meaning to come through more clearly.

Sometimes prepositions are special offenders to wordiness.

- The federal government has sponsored several programs *to* assist *in* providing *for* funds *for* the college student.

Prepositions are essential to English grammar, but if you find them popping up like dandelions, do some weeding.

- The federal government has sponsored several programs to assist college students.

The Backward Sentence

In early drafts, we often tend to write about what something is not, rather than what it is. Again, the process seems normal. In trying to figure out what we want to say, we may need to circle and come in from behind. Editing can be the time when we reconsider and consciously reshape the sentence to strengthen its meaning.

◆ There is no doubt that Ellen looked as though she were not feeling well.

Cut	[~~There is no doubt that~~] Ellen looked as though she were not feeling well. (Introductory phrases that use the word *that* can almost always be eliminated.)
Tighten	as if she were sick Ellen looked [~~as though she were not feeling well~~]. (It is almost always more effective to say what something is instead of what it isn't. "He was not a weak man" suggests weakness by the very presence of the word; "he was a strong man" suggests strength that is actually there.)
Tighten again	sick Ellen looked [~~as if she were sick~~]. (Sometimes a short, blunt sentence is the most forceful of all.)

Here's the sentence before editing . . .

◆ There is no doubt that Ellen looked as though she were not feeling well.

and after editing . . .

◆ Ellen looked sick.

The editing process eliminated eleven unnecessary words and reversed the meaning of the sentence from what Ellen was not to what she was. The result is a simple, strong statement that leaves "no doubt"—the point the writer began with.

The word *not* should be a clue. When it shows up in a sentence, challenge the sentence. Obviously, there will be many times when *not* works well; but if you're a good editor, you'll probably find an equal number of times when the direction of the sentence needs reversing or when a single word will substitute for a phrase.

I did *not* remember.	I forgot.
I did *not* believe his statistics.	I distrusted his statistics.
It did *not* seem important.	It seemed unimportant.

Who, Which, and That

Like the word *not,* the words *who, which,* and *that* should be seen as clues. Every time they occur, challenge their necessity. About half the time they serve no function.

Cut I lived in a room [~~that was~~] over the garage.
("I lived in a room over the garage" says the same thing.)

Cut How could I know that her mother, [~~who was~~] short and dumpy, would oppose our marriage?
(Make it sound more like the spoken voice: "How could I know that her short, dumpy mother would oppose our marriage?")

Cut [~~I think that~~] we owe first responsibility to our moral conscience.
("We owe first responsibility to our moral conscience" is stronger and more direct.)

Adjectives

Adjectives modify nouns: a *red* house, a *grouchy* professor. They can be helpful at times. But the beginning writer often overuses them, sometimes attaching a string of adjectives to a single noun—or even an adjective to every noun—in a mistaken belief that "adjectives are colorful" or that in some way they will make up for weak writing. Successful writers have learned from experience that a strong noun in itself is more colorful than a weak noun propped up with one to six adjectives. Nouns, not adjectives, are the foundation blocks of every sentence. Use of an adjective should cause you to question the noun to which it's attached. Can the adjective be eliminated, either because it's unnecessary or because a stronger noun will supplant it?

Challenge I ate a [~~red apple~~].

Winesap might be a better noun ("I ate a *Winesap*") because a Winesap is both red and an apple. A concrete noun simplifies the sentence (one less word) while making it more sensuous. *Winesap* does more than suggest red; it suggests a shade of red (wine-colored) and a taste (sweet wine).

Challenge I studied a [~~small brown~~] insect that I found by an [~~old gray~~] rock.

Why not name the *insect?* A cricket, for example, is both *small* and *brown* (a two-word saving). And aren't all rocks *old?* In this case, we would know more if the adjective identified a less predictable quality. Was the rock covered with lichen or moss?

◆ I studied a cricket that I found by a mossy rock.

or better yet

◆ I studied a cricket by a mossy rock.

Challenge A [~~big, red, growling, thundering, incredible, bell clanging~~] fire engine came down the alley.

A string of adjectives attached to a single noun is called an adjective pileup. In this case, *fire engine* is a strong enough noun, but more than two adjectives in a row should cause the writer to think twice. Here are some steps we might go through to reconsider.

1. *Big* seems weak because of its vagueness. How big is big? In this context, *thundering* probably connotes bigness anyway.
2. *Red* is generally associated with fire engines and, therefore, adds nothing to the image.
3. *Growling* and *thundering* suggest similar sounds but with slightly different connotations. We need to choose between them. As both are stronger than the verb, one or the other might replace the verb.
4. *Incredible* might be valuable, but as it's used here, it seems lost amid the other adjectives.

5. *Bell-clanging* adds another dimension of sound and might be an adjective we want to retain.

Here, then, are several possible revisions.

- A bell-clanging fire engine thundered down the alley.
- A clanging fire engine growled down the alley.
- An incredible, bell-clanging fire engine thundered down the alley.

The context in which a sentence occurs, your purpose, and your ear will have to help you decide. But, in general, two or more adjectives in a row should be seen as a caution signal. Editing is probably called for.

Adverbs

What the adjective is to the noun, the adverb is to the verb: The legislator argued *endlessly*. Adverbs often end in *-ly* (*only, quickly, tightly*), and some have both long and short forms (*deep/deeply; slow/slowly*). The adverb helps, but often with only modest success.

Challenge I [really] felt strange and uptight.

The reader can only respond that *really* feeling is still feeling and hasn't added enough dimension to justify letting it live in this sentence.

Challenge Both of us ran [very] fast.

We can accept *fast* as an adverb (I suppose one could run slowly), but what does *very* add? What is the difference between *very fast* and *fast*? A smidgen at best, and not worth the extra word.

Maybe we can come up with a general principle. Adverbs and adjectives should be used so sparingly that their effectiveness is increased by the rareness of their appearance.

A Reminder

Each example in this chapter has been edited out of context. Obviously, in your own papers, word choice and sentence length must be evaluated within the flow and meaning of the whole essay (see Chapter 20). But remember that editing is usually considered the final stage of the writing process. For some, writing on the computer encourages almost simultaneous drafting, revising, and editing. It is simply too easy to type a paragraph, reread it, add or subtract material, change the verb, cut three extra words, and develop a whole new sentence. This turns out to be my personal way of working.

You'll need to discover your own best method. For some, editing too early may create problems. If you become consumed in perfecting a sentence, correcting grammar, studying over the use of a word, or honing the rhythm of a sentence, you may lose momentum and find it difficult to recover the stuff of your argument. You may lose your train of thought. For many, especially beginning writers, the best advice may be to get content on the page first, no matter how roughly written, and then shape and polish afterward. Content must precede form.

However, do not think that you can ever skip the editing phase. Content alone is never effective. The way you express yourself is as important as what you have to say. If your ideas are submerged in an ocean of unnecessary words, you'll find your reader unwilling to make the dive for fear of drowning. The best of writers—Hemingway, Fitzgerald, Thomas Wolfe—all had editors. The rest of us must learn to become our own.

Exercises

Although you must eventually learn to edit your own material, it may at first be easier to identify wordiness in someone else's sentences. Try some of the following games before you begin editing your own papers.

1. In each of the following sentences, eliminate every unnecessary word or phrase. Do not change the meaning of the sentence itself. When necessary, replace a cluttered phrase with a single word or with a more concrete and specific word.

   a. Owing to the fact that he was late, he missed seeing the president.

   Cut Because [~~Owing to the fact that~~] he was late, he missed seeing the president.

   b. I do not approve of the methods he employs.

   c. His tale is very old and strangely different.

   d. His brother, who is a member of the same firm, was indicted by the grand jury.

   e. This is a subject that has always interested me.

   f. Her sweater has a red glow to it.

   g. The question as to whether he succeeded has not been decided.

   h. The people who stood around outside in the street had a better view than those who stayed inside.

i. Mike was different from him. His face was quite round, and a pale white color. On his chin he had a beard which was thin and scraggy in some places. He wondered where he was at.

2. Here is a paragraph from E. L. Doctorow's *Ragtime,* a novel about America in the 1920s. The main character in this passage is "Mother's Younger Brother." He had no other name. I have rewritten the paragraph as it might have looked in a first-draft version. Edit out every word you feel is unnecessary. Then compare your edited version with Doctorow's, which follows. Don't cheat by looking ahead. Right and wrong answers are seldom available in editing. Context, purpose, and your inner ear must determine your answers. Test your ear against that of a professional writer.

    The air was very saltylike in your nose. Mother's Younger Brother, in his white linen suit and boater, had rolled his trousers up to almost his knees and taken off his shoes and was walking barefoot in the salt marshes. Sea birds were startled by his approach and flew up into the blue sky. This was the time in our history, which was before most of us were born, when Winslow Homer was doing his painting. A certain type of light was still available along the whole Eastern seaboard. Homer painted the light in his paintings. The light gave the sea a very heavy, dull menace and shone very coldly on the black rocks and rough shoals of the New England coast.

Here is Doctorow's edited version.

    The air was salt. Mother's Younger Brother in his white linen suit and boater rolled his trousers and walked barefoot in the salt marshes. Sea birds started and flew up. This was the time in our history when Winslow Homer was doing his painting. A certain light was still available along the Eastern seaboard. Homer painted the light. It gave the sea a heavy dull menace and shone coldly on the rocks and shoals of the New England coast.

Practice

1. Edit two of your previous practice writings. Eliminate every unnecessary word. Look especially for clutter words like *of, at, to,* and *the.* Try to eliminate or find single-word substitutes for unnecessary phrases like *the fact that, whether or not,* and *the question of.* Be careful of overusing *who* and *which;* they can be eliminated about half the time. It is possible to overwork a piece of writing. Sometimes your first instinct is best. If you feel yourself becoming angry or frustrated, stop for a while. Go over it again later when you feel cooler. For many people, the process works better in the back of the mind than on paper. For others, it's always a word-by-word battle, crossing out and starting over. Never think you are alone. Everyone from Thomas Jefferson to Toni Morrison has worked in exactly the same way.

2. Edit any one of your previous papers by making it at least one-third shorter than the original version.Do not cut anything that is essential to the meaning or feeling, but be brutal; throw away everything that doesn't contribute directly and concretely to the total effect.

Group Inquiry

Share your edited revision with others in your peer group. Each member of the group should edit someone else's paper. Mark the passage you are editing. Do your editing directly on the page(s) of the practice writing and sign your work. Then, on a separate page, write out your edited version so that you can see a clean copy of it. Discuss your version with your partner, noting the reasons you made changes. This exercise is not intended as a critical judgment, but as a way of seeing how others might edit your rough draft, as compared with the way you might edit it, and as a way of developing your own skills by editing someone else's draft material.

A Student Example from Drafting to Revision

Fred Cox wanted to major in sports medicine. He signed up for my class only because it was required. Fred dreaded "English" and sat in a back row where he could gaze longingly out the window. Early in the semester, I asked the class to list any past experience that began negatively and ended positively and then to write briefly on one item from the list. Here is what Fred wrote.

Chinatown on New Year's Eve

Patty Rogers' party

my first wrestling match

learning sign language

taking the SAT exam

I remember the first time I ever wrestled in high school and my dad came and saw me lose. He was the kind who you could tell was angry or something, but he never really talked to me, and when he did it was only to criticize. It was always the silent treatment. We had a real shouting match in the car on the way home, or at least I shouted at him because he wouldn't say anything, and then all he could do was tell me everything I had done wrong, but after we got home he put his arm around me and I've never forgot and I think I never really knew how he felt about me until then.

Later, I asked my students to select one excerpt from their practice writing and to develop it into a full essay. Everyone brought a draft copy to class for his or her peer group to read and react to. Our goal was to help each other by offering comments and questions. Here's the first page of Fred Cox's draft with some of the observations students wrote in the margins.

[Lots of generalizations but no details]

I remember the first time I ever wrestled and my dad came and watched. It was awful. Even though I had made the team in my freshman year I had to face a guy who had wrestled in the state state tournemnent the year before, and I lost badly. But the hard part was not losing because I had expected to. My dad was the hard part. After the match we drove home and he never said a word. The interior of the car was cold. Almost immediately a thin layer of ice formed on the inside of the windshield. Maybe it was from my hot, sweaty body which only a few minutes earlier had been badly beaten. My dad got into the car and you could tell he was angry. I thought to myself, this is what I really hate, the silent treatment. You could never tell what he was thinking, just nothing. I wondered whether he was proud of me or disappointed.

[Good concrete details here—we need more]

[Could we see him?]

[How? Show us instead of telling us]

Fred's peer group suggested that he was *telling* rather than *showing*. He needed to focus on the memory itself, to find concrete, sensory details that would bring it to life for the reader. Fred insisted he had done the best he could. "I just can't write," he complained.

A week later, he brought in a second draft. Even Fred felt he was making progress. The essay seemed richer and more fully developed. My suggestion that he could improve it even more was met with shocked silence. Fred left my office with a sigh. Here's a copy of his first page with some of my comments.

I remember the first time I ever wrestled and my dad came and watched. It was awful. Even though I had made the team in my freshman year I had to face a guy who had wrestled in the state tournemnent the year before, and I lost badly. But the hard part was not losing because I had expected to. My dad was the hard part. After the match we drove home and he never said a word. The interior of the car was cold. The red leather seat crackled as I slid acorss. Almost immediately a thin layer of ice formed on the inside of the windshield. Maybe it was from my hot, sweaty body. Only a few minutes earlier it had been badly beaten. It was the first match my dad had ever attended. I leaned my body up against the door, slumping in the seat in a tired way. Dad got into the car slamming the door. I could see the black outline of my dad's head from the dim light of the gym. Without a word, he turned the key in the ignition. The engine sputtered as it started. I thought to myself, this is what I really hate, the silent treatment. My dad never told me how he felt, what he was thinking, nothing. I wondered whether he was proud of me for making the team my freshman year. Was he disappointed in my losing tonight?

Still seems too general—do we actually need this?

Soph? Junior? Be specific

Perhaps should begin here(?) Isn't this where the incident itself begins?

What kind of car? Is it really "leather"?

I felt hot

simplify!

"Slumping" shows that you're tired

Nice images here—you begin to slow down and give reader concrete details

right word?

good verb

Three days later, after struggling through a third revision and some late-night editing, Fred presented another copy. The essay now begins with the actual experience. As readers, we participate in the sequence of events and learn about a father-and-son relationship from their own actions and words. Fred's selection of concrete details creates a sense of watching the memory unfold. By the end, we do not need to be told the meaning of the incident. The actions themselves inform us. Best of all, Fred discovered good writing isn't something magical or mysterious. Good writing is the result of a process involving drafting, revising, and editing. His later essays got better and better. And although I can't say Fred ever actually came to like writing, he did discover that with plain hard work, he could be proud of the quality of his effort.

Here's the final version of Fred's first college essay.

The Match

Fred Cox

The interior of our Chevy was cold. The red vinyl seat crackled as I slid across. Almost immediately, a thin layer of ice formed on the inside of the windshield. I felt hot and sweaty. Only a few minutes earlier I had been badly beaten in a wrestling match, the first match my dad had ever attended.

I leaned my body up against the door, slumping in the seat. Dad got into the car slamming the door. I could see the silhouette of my dad's head from the dim light of the gym. Without a word, he turned the key in the ignition. The engine sputtered as it started. I thought to myself, this is what I really hate, the silent treatment. My dad never told me how he felt, what he was thinking, nothing. I wondered whether he was proud of me for making the wrestling team my freshman year. Was he disappointed in my losing tonight?

We started home. The air whistled through the defroster. We passed the high school stadium, crossed the railroad tracks and were halfway through town. He still hadn't spoken. I blurted out, "What did you think, Dad?" He turned his head, glanced at me for a second and then turned his attention back to the road. "Did I do all right?" He only kept driving. The engine strained as we accelerated. I would have felt better if he had said anything, even if it was disheartening, at least I would know where I stood. "Did I do all right?" His hands tightened on the steering wheel.

After a long pause he answered. "He beat you. He was all over you, turning you over on your back, almost pinning you. You have to ask how you did? You were too slow and couldn't get away from him."

Wow! I thought. He's an expert and this was the first match he had ever seen. I didn't think he knew anything about wrestling.

"Are you glad I made the team?" There was a long pause like maybe he really had to think about it.

"You should've played football," he said.

Not this again, I thought. He had really been upset in the fall when I had refused to go out for football. I had tried it in the seventh grade and had not enjoyed playing, but I still enjoyed watching. The main reason I had gone out for wrestling was to try to make him proud of me. But it wasn't working.

"Did you know the guy I wrestled was a senior and went to the state tournament last year?"

No answer.

By this time the interior of the car was unbearably hot. I reached over and turned off the fan. My stomach felt queasy like the hot dog I had eaten earlier was about to come up. I could feel the hair on the back of my neck standing straight out.

My dad was not a cruel man. He had always given me what I needed plus some. Never had he beaten or abused me. He wasn't even overly strict. He let me come and go as I pleased. But he hardly ever talked, and when he did it was to criticize. Nothing I ever did was right. Even if I won the match, he would have said the opponent was a pushover or something.

We were halfway home. In desperation I screamed, "Damn it, say something." He glared at me. His nostrils flared and his jaw tensed. "Don't you ever talk to me in that tone of voice again if you know what's good for you." I pressed closer to the door. I had really made him mad now. Then he started talking about respect and then something about how I had inconvenienced him for the last fifteen years. How your kids never treat you right.

After a short time he seemed to calm down. "I'm sorry," I mumbled, but he didn't answer. By this time my stomach felt all knotted. My body was breaking into a cold sweat, but my face burned.

We were almost home, still riding in silence. "I'm sorry I didn't play football," I said. "I'm just no good at it. You know you're the only reason I went out for wrestling. It was to make you proud of me." Headlights from an oncoming car illuminated his face. He stared straight ahead.

We headed down Lattimore Street to our house, the only one with a porch light still burning. Dad swerved the car into the driveway and switched off the key. I got out slamming the door behind me and stood there in my baggy sweats shivering. I waited while Dad got out, watching as he walked around the front of the car. His breath ballooned in the cold as he walked toward me. I stared at my feet. Then, without saying a word, my dad did something he hadn't done since I was a little kid. He put both arms around me and hugged me hard.

To Catch a Thief

Rita Ann Christiansen

Rita Ann Christiansen wrote the following essay as a second-semester first-year student. She revised it several times, trying to capture the experience and the feeling with images and concrete details. The essay was almost a page longer in its original version, but in working with other students in class, she edited out unnecessary words and phrases, and sometimes whole paragraphs. "Trying to be honest," she said, "was the hardest part. I kept wanting to make the whole thing sound dramatic." In the end, the class felt she achieved the right balance.

At the age of sixteen, I began shoplifting. Small things like makeup or three-dollar plastic earrings. I did it with a couple of friends from high school. We giggled and smirked and thought the clerks were stupid. It sent a little thrill to the pit of the stomach for a few moments. Then for the rest of the afternoon we strutted around the mall in our tight Levis feeling superior to adults, and enjoying the way guys followed us around. We were pretty hot.

Daniels department store was our favorite: lots of fluorescent lights, chrome and mirrors, busy clerks looking the other way. On the Monday before the Fourth of July, my parents dropped me off to meet my friends, but no one showed up. I wandered about alone, running my fingers over the dresses, trying on belts, watching my face in all the various mirrors, until I came to the fifty-dollar silk scarves and the two-hundred-dollar Gucci purses. I was sixteen years old and I suddenly knew exactly what I was going to do. I was hot, after all, and I knew my friends would be impressed when I told them.

I held up the scarves to my face, the soft pinks, the blues and lavenders. Behind the counter in the brightly lit mirror, I watched the swirl of colors. I watched my own eyes. And I watched the gray-haired clerk turn her back on me and begin talking to another customer. She was complaining about her feet because she'd been standing around all day. Then I carefully folded up the scarf—one that pictured a green parrot on a background of dark blue leaves and fine veins of gold. The scarf folded into a neat little square, no bigger than my wallet in the bottom of my purse.

Every cell in my skin hummed with anticipation. My lungs felt as if I had inhaled the purest air from the top of Mt. Everest. I could feel my blood surging through veins, arteries, capillaries, like hot ice. I could feel it in my face and in my wrists. I strolled through Daniels. I had all the time in the world. I stopped and looked at swim suits. I tried on several pair of shoes. I took the escalator up. I rode it down. All the time my heart was hammering as if I'd just had a date with Tom Cruise.

Then in the lingerie department I saw a woman stuff a satin teddy in her shopping bag. I saw her because she seemed to accidentally knock several teddies to the floor. She bent over and pushed one into a woven bag while she picked up and brushed off the others, returning them to the table. She was in her early twenties, her hair still long and blond, pulled back away from her face. She wore a knee-length sun dress with thin straps and a square bodice. Her arms and shoulders looked tanned, soft, her face lovely and perfectly made up with blue eye shadow. She was stunning. I remember, just for a moment, feeling envious of her.

Then she looked at me. I can still see her eyes. It was like watching my own eyes in the mirror when I stole the silk scarf. Her eyes were as distant and metallic as a clear sky in winter. It was as if she had recognized me. She looked at me and defied me to tell. And I realized she probably wasn't in her early twenties at all. The makeup did not hide the lines around her eyes. It probably wasn't even her own hair; it was probably a wig. Her mouth looked tired, like the skin of an apple that has grown old from the inside. The tan on her shoulders was layered from too many afternoons in the sun, oiled and shiny but tough as cat's hide. Then she looked away, bored and no longer interested. She straightened up the counter of lingerie, picked up her straw bag, and strolled away, stopping here and there to run her hand over a silk nightgown, a pink chemise, fading into the other shoppers.

I wish I could say I learned something on the spot. I wish I could say I turned myself in or became a nun or devoted my life to the poor. Instead, I wandered on through the store, checking my face in every mirror. I was hot stuff. That woman had nothing to do with me. Later, just like I'd planned, I bragged about stealing the scarf to my friends. But when school started the next fall we drifted apart and I didn't see much of them anymore.

I still have the scarf buried deep in a bottom drawer at home. It's not the kind of thing I would ever wear. I came across it when I was packing for college. At first I thought of just throwing it away, but I didn't. I'm not sure why I'm saving it.

Shame

Dick Gregory

Dick Gregory was first known as a stand-up comedian whose political comedy encouraged supporters of the civil rights movement in the 1960s. His two major books, *From the Back of the Bus* (1962) and his autobiography, *Nigger* (1964), helped draw attention to the pain and injustice of racial prejudice. The following excerpt from his autobiography uses concrete details to help us experience the degradation of growing up poor and black in a segregated world.

I never learned hate at home, or shame. I had to go to school for that. I was about seven years old when I got my first big lesson. I was in love with a little girl named Helene Tucker, a light-complected little girl with pigtails and nice manners. She was always clean and she was smart in school. I think I went to school then mostly to look at her. I brushed my hair and even got me a little old handkerchief. It was a lady's handkerchief, but I didn't want Helene to see me wipe my nose on my hand. The pipes were frozen again, there was no water in the house, but I washed my socks and shirt every night. I'd get a pot, and go over to Mister Ben's grocery store, and stick my pot down into his soda machine. Scoop out some chopped ice. By evening the ice melted to water for washing. I got sick a lot that winter because the fire would go out at night before the clothes were dry. In the morning I'd put them on, wet or dry, because they were the only clothes I had.

Everybody's got a Helene Tucker, a symbol of everything you want. I loved her for her goodness, her cleanness, her popularity. She'd walk down my street and my brothers and sisters would yell, "Here comes Helene," and I'd rub my tennis sneakers on the back of my pants and wish my hair wasn't so nappy and the white folks' shirt fit me better. I'd run out on the street. If I knew my place and didn't come too close, she'd wink at me and say hello. That was a good feeling. Sometimes I'd follow her all the way home, and shovel the snow off her walk and try to make friends with her Momma and her aunts. I'd drop money on her stoop late at night on my way back from shining shoes in the taverns. And she had a Daddy, and he had a good job. He was a paper hanger.

I guess I would have gotten over Helene by summertime, but something happened in that classroom that made her face hang in front of me for the next twenty-two years. When I played the drums in high school it was for Helene and when I broke track records in college it was for Helene and when I started standing behind microphones and heard applause I wished Helene could hear it, too. It wasn't until I was twenty-nine years old and married and making money that I finally got her out of my system. Helene was sitting in that classroom when I learned to be ashamed of myself.

It was on a Thursday. I was sitting in the back of the room, in a seat with a chalk circle drawn around it. The idiot's seat, the troublemaker's seat.

The teacher thought I was stupid. Couldn't spell, couldn't read, couldn't do arithmetic. Just stupid. Teachers were never interested in finding out that you couldn't concentrate because you were so hungry, because you hadn't had any breakfast. All you could think about was noontime, would it ever come? Maybe you could sneak into the cloakroom and steal a bite of some kid's lunch out of a coat pocket. A bite of something. Paste. You can't really make a meal of paste, or put it on bread for a sandwich, but sometimes I'd scoop a few spoonfuls out of the big paste jar in the back of the room. Pregnant people get strange tastes. I was pregnant with poverty. Pregnant with dirt and pregnant with smells that made people turn away, pregnant with cold and pregnant with shoes that were never bought for me, pregnant with five other people in my bed and no Daddy in the next room, and pregnant with hunger. Paste doesn't taste too bad when you're hungry.

The teacher thought I was a troublemaker. All she saw from the front of the room was a little black boy who squirmed in his idiot's seat and made noises and poked the kids around him. I guess she couldn't see a kid who made noises because he wanted someone to know he was there.

It was on a Thursday, the day before the Negro payday. The eagle always flew on Friday. The teacher was asking each student how much his father would give to the Community Chest. On Friday night, each kid would get the money from his father, and on Monday he would bring it to the school. I decided I was going to buy a Daddy right then. I had money in my pocket from shining shoes and selling papers, and whatever Helene Tucker pledged for her Daddy I was going to top it. And I'd hand the money right in. I wasn't going to wait until Monday to buy me a Daddy.

I was shaking, scared to death. The teacher opened her book and started calling out names alphabetically.

"Helene Tucker?"

"My Daddy said he'd give two dollars and fifty cents."

"That's very nice, Helene. Very, very nice indeed."

That made me feel pretty good. It wouldn't take too much to top that. I had almost three dollars in dimes and quarters in my pocket. I stuck my hand in my pocket and held onto the money, waiting for her to call my name. But the teacher closed her book after she called everybody else in the class.

I stood up and raised my hand.

"What is it now?"

"You forgot me?"

She turned toward the blackboard. "I don't have time to be playing with you, Richard."

"My Daddy said he'd . . ."

"Sit down, Richard, you're disturbing the class."

"My Daddy said he'd give . . . fifteen dollars."

She turned around and looked mad. "We are collecting this money for you and your kind, Richard Gregory. If your Daddy can give fifteen dollars you have no business being on relief."

"I got it right now, I got it right now, my Daddy gave it to me to turn in today, my Daddy said . . ."

"And furthermore," she said, looking right at me, her nostrils getting big and her lips getting thin and her eyes opening wide. "We know you don't have a Daddy."

Helene Tucker turned around, her eyes full of tears. She felt sorry for me. Then I couldn't see her too well because I was crying, too.

"Sit down, Richard."

And I always thought the teacher kind of liked me. She always picked me to wash the blackboard on Friday, after school. That was a big thrill, it made me feel important. If I didn't wash it, come Monday the school might not function right.

"Where are you going, Richard?"

I walked out of school that day, and for a long time I didn't go back very often. There was shame there.

Now there was shame everywhere. It seemed like the whole world had been inside that classroom, everyone had heard what the teacher had said, everyone had turned around and felt sorry for me. There was shame in going to the Worthy Boys Annual Christmas Dinner for you and your kind, because everybody knew what a worthy boy was. Why couldn't they just call it the Boys Annual Dinner, why'd they have to give it a name? There was shame in wearing the brown and orange and white plaid mackinaw the welfare gave to 3,000 boys. Why'd it have to be the same for everybody so when you walked down the street the people could see you were on relief? It was a nice warm mackinaw and it had a hood, and my Momma beat me and called me a little rat when she found out I stuffed it in the bottom of a pail full of garbage way over on Cottage Street. There was shame in running over to Mister Ben's at the end of the day and asking for his rotten peaches, there was shame in asking Mrs. Simmons for a spoonful of sugar, there was shame in running out to meet the relief truck. I hated that truck, full of food for you and your kind. I ran into the house and hid when it came. And then I started to sneak through alleys, to take the long way home so the people going into White's Eat Shop wouldn't see me. Yeah, the whole world heard the teacher that day, we all know you don't have a Daddy.

It lasted for a while, this kind of numbness. I spent a lot of time feeling sorry for myself. And then one day I met this wino in a restaurant. I'd been out hustling all day, shining shoes, selling newspapers, and I had googobs of money in my pocket. Bought me a bowl of chili for fifteen cents, and a cheeseburger for fifteen cents, and a Pepsi for five cents, and a piece of chocolate cake for ten cents. That was a good meal. I was eating when this old wino came in. I love winos because they never hurt anyone but themselves.

The old wino sat down at the counter and ordered twenty-six cents worth of food. He ate it like he really enjoyed it. When the owner, Mister Williams, asked him to pay the check, the old wino didn't lie or go through his pocket like he suddenly found a hole.

He just said: "Don't have no money."

The owner yelled: "Why in hell you come in here and eat my food if you don't have no money? That food cost me money."

Mister Williams jumped over the counter and knocked the wino off his stool and beat him over the head with a pop bottle. Then he stepped back and watched the wino bleed. Then he kicked him. And he kicked him again.

I looked at the wino with blood all over his face and I went over. "Leave him alone, Mister Williams. I'll pay the twenty-six cents."

The wino got up, slowly, pulling himself up to the stool, then up to the counter, holding on for a minute until his legs stopped shaking so bad. He looked at me with pure hate. "Keep your twenty-six cents. You don't have to pay, not now. I just finished paying for it."

He started to walk out, and as he passed me, he reached down and touched my shoulder. "Thanks, sonny, but it's too late now. Why didn't you pay it before?"

I was pretty sick about that. I waited too long to help another man.

Living South of L.A.

Mike Rose

Mike Rose is associate director of UCLA Writing Programs. Author of a number of books and articles on language and literacy, he has received awards from the National Academy of Education, the McDonnell Foundation, and the National Council of Teachers of English. "Living South of L.A." is excerpted from *Lives on the Boundary* (1989), a moving account of the struggles and achievements of America's educationally underprepared.

Some nights, John and I and Roy the artist and a wild kid named Gaspo would drive into downtown L.A.—down to where my mother had waited fearfully for a bus years before—and roam the streets and feel the excitement of the tenderloin: The flashing arrows, the blue-and-orange beer neon, the burlesque houses, the faded stairwell of Roseland—which we would inch up and then run down—brushing past the photos of taxi dancers, glossy and smiling in a glass display. Cops would tell us to go home, and that intensified this bohemian romance all the more.

About four months after John moved in, we both entered Loyola University. Loyola is now coeducational; its student center houses an Asian Pacific Students Association, Black Student Alliance, and Chicano Resource Center; and its radio station, KXLU, plays the most untamed rock 'n' roll in Los Angeles. But in the early sixties, Loyola was pretty much a school for white males from the middle and upper middle class. It was a sleepy little campus—its undergraduate enrollment was under two thousand—and it prided itself on providing spiritual as well as intellectual guidance for its students: Religion and Christian philosophy courses were a required part of the curriculum. It defined itself as a Catholic intellectual community—promotional brochures relied on phrases like "the social, intellectual, and spiritual aspects of our students"—and made available to its charges small classes, a campus ministry, and thirty-six clubs (the Chess Club, Economics Society, Fine Arts Circle, Debate Squad, and more). There were also six fraternities and a sports program that included basketball, baseball, volleyball, rugby, soccer, and crew. Loyola men, it was assumed, shared a fairly common set of social and religious values, and the university provided multiple opportunities for them to develop their minds, their spirits, and their social networks. I imagine that parents sent their boys to Loyola with a sigh of relief: God and man strolled together out of St. Robert Bellarmine Hall and veered left to Sacred Heart Chapel. There was an occasional wild party at one of the off-campus fraternity houses, but, well, a pair of panties in the koi pond was not on a par with crises of faith and violence against the state.

John and I rattled to college in his '53 Plymouth. Loyola Boulevard was lined with elms and maples, and as we entered the campus we could see the chapel tower rising in the distance. The chapel and all the early buildings had been constructed in the 1920s and were white and separated by broad sweeps of very green grass. Palm trees and stone pines grew in rows and clumps close to the buildings, and long concrete walkways curved and angled and crossed to connect everything, proving that God, as Plato suspected, is always doing geometry. . . .

My first semester classes included the obligatory theology and ROTC and a series of requirements: biology, psychology, speech, logic, and a language. I went to class and usually met John for lunch: We'd bring sandwiches to his car and play the radio while we ate. Then it was back to class, or the library, or the student union for a Coke. . . . When I look back through notes and papers and various photographs and memorabilia, I begin to remember what a disengaged, half-awake time it really was. I'll describe two of the notebooks I found. The one from English is a small book, eight by seven, and only eleven pages of it are filled. The notes I did write consist of book titles, dates of publication, names of characters, pointless summaries of books that were not on our syllabus and that I had never read ("*The Alexandria Quartet:* 5 or 6 characters seen by different people in different stages of life"), and quotations from the teacher ("Perception can bring sorrow."). The notes are a series of separate entries. I can't see any coherence. My biology lab notes are written on green-tint quadrille. They, too, are sparse. There is an occasional poorly executed sketch of a tiny organism or of a bone and muscle structure. Some of the formulas and molecular models sit isolated on the page, bare of any explanatory discussion. The lecture notes are fragmented; a fair number of sentences remain incomplete.

By the end of the second semester my grades were close to dipping below a C average, and since I had been admitted provisionally, that would have been that. . . . Speech and Introductory Psychology presented no big problems. General Biology had midterm and final examinations that required a good deal of memorizing, and I could do that, but the textbook—particularly the chapters covered in the second semester—was much, much harder than what I read in high school, and I was so ill-adept in the laboratory that I failed that portion of the class. We had to set up and pursue biological problems, not just memorize—and at the first sign of doing rather than memorizing, I would automatically assume the problem was beyond me and distance myself from it. Logic, another requirement, spooked me with its syllogisms and Venn diagrams—they were just a step away from more formal mathematics—so I memorized what I could and squirmed around the rest. Theology was god-awful; ROTC was worse. . . . Freshman English was taught by a frustrated novelist with glittering eyes who had us, among other things, describing the consumption of our last evening's meal using the images of the battlefield.

I was out of my league.

Faculty would announce office hours. If I had had the sense, I would have gone, but they struck me as aloof and somber men, and I felt stupid telling them I was . . . well—stupid. I drifted through the required courses, thinking that as soon as these requirements were over, I'd never have to face anything even vaguely quantitative again. Or anything to do with foreign languages. Or ROTC. I fortified myself with defiance: I worked up an imitation of the old priest who was my Latin teacher, and I kept my ROTC uniform crumpled in the greasy trunk of John's Plymouth.

Many of my classmates came from and lived in a world very different from my own. The campus literary magazine would publish excerpts from the journals of upperclassmen traveling across Europe, standing before the Berlin Wall or hiking through olive groves toward Delphi. With the exception of one train trip back to Altoona, I had never been out of Southern California, and this translated, for me, into some personal inadequacy. Fraternities seemed exclusive and a little strange. I'm not sure why I didn't join any of Loyola's three dozen societies and clubs, though I do know that things like the Debate Squad were way too competitive. Posters and flyers and squibs in the campus newspaper gave testament to a lot of connecting activity, but John and I pretty much kept to ourselves, raging on the "Loyola man," reading the literary magazine aloud with a French accent, simultaneously feeling contempt for and exclusion from a social life that seemed to work with the mystery and enclosure of the clockwork in a music box.

It is an unfortunate fact of our psychic lives that the images that surround us as we grow up—no matter how much we may scorn them later—give shape to our deepest needs and longings. Every year Loyola men elected a homecoming queen. The queen and her princesses were students at the Catholic sister schools: Marymount, Mount St. Mary's, St. Vincent's. They had names like Corinne and Cathy, and they came from the Sullivan family or the Mitchells or the Ryans. They were taught to stand with toe to heel, their smiles were inviting, and the photographer's flash illuminated their eyes. Loyola men met them at fraternity parties and mixers and "CoEd Day," met them according to rules of manner and affiliation and parental connection as elaborate as a Balinese dance. John and I drew mustaches on their photographs, but something about them reached far back into my life.

Growing up in South L.A. was certainly not a conscious misery. My neighborhood had its diversions and its mysteries, and I felt loved and needed at home. But all in all there was a dreary impotence to the years, and isolation, and a deep sadness about my father. I protected myself from the harsher side of it all through a life of the mind. And while that interior life included spaceships and pink chemicals and music and the planetary moons, it also held the myriad television images of the good life that were piped into my home: Robert Young sitting down to dinner, Ozzie Nelson tossing the football with his sons, the blond in a Prell commercial turning toward the camera. The images couldn't have been more trivial—all sentimental phosphorescence—but as a child tucked away on South Vermont, they were just about the only images I had of what life would be without illness and dead ends. I didn't realize how completely their message had seeped into my being, what loneliness and sorrow was being held at bay—didn't realize it until I found myself in the middle of Loyola's social life without a guidebook, feeling just beyond the superficial touch of the queen and her princesses, those smiling incarnations of a television promise. I scorned the whole silly show and ached to be embraced by one of these mythic females under the muted light of a paper moon.

So I went to school and sat in class and memorized more than understood and whistled past the academic graveyard. I vacillated between the false potency of scorn and feelings of ineptitude. John and I would get in his car and enjoy the warmth of each other and laugh and head down the long strip of Manchester Boulevard, away from Loyola, away from the palms and green, green lawns, back to South L.A. We'd throw the ball in the alley or lag pennies on Vermont or hit Marty's Liquor. We'd leave much later for a movie or a football game at Mercy High or the terrible safety of downtown Los Angeles. Walking, then, past the *discotecas* and pawnshops, past the windows full of fried chicken and yellow lamps, past the New Follies, walking through hustlers and lost drunks and prostitutes and transvestites with rouge the color of bacon—stopping, finally, before the musty opening of a bar where two silhouettes moved around a pool table as though they were underwater.

PART 2

Writing About People and Places

Suggested Writing Projects

Writing about yourself offers an enormous amount of information: All your past experiences, emotions, activities, loves, and hates—the people you've known and the places you've been—are at your beck and call. Writing about other people or other places presents a different challenge. You might, of course, write about an important individual from your past or a special place where you've lived. This type of essay usually focuses on a single day or incident, revealing how a specific character or place has affected your values or life.

- Write an essay on someone who had a special influence on your life. Focus on one or two scenes or incidents in which you show selected details of action, physical qualities, speech, background, or environment. By the end of the essay, the reader should know the character so well that you will have little need to generalize upon what the person was like, or how he or she affected your life.

- Write about a special place: a treehouse you and your father built together, an urban basketball court where you played for hours every summer evening, or a shopping mall where you and your friends spent Saturday mornings. Help your reader see the place by using all the elements of scene. If possible, describe one or two specific times or incidents illustrating why the place was important to you. Focus on specific details of memory that draw your reader into the experience. Would the place be the same if you returned there today?

Group Inquiry

Determine whether you want to write about someone you know from the past or about a place that's been important to you. Make a list of reasons why you feel you want to write about that particular person or place. Review your list and add details and specific examples from your memory that make each point interesting. Then meet with three to five others from your class. Take turns reading your lists aloud and discussing each other's proposed topic. What details, examples, or ideas seem most interesting to the peer group? What have you left out that the group would like to know? Can you explain to the group what impact this individual or place has made on your life? Which sounds most interesting? Which would be most feasible? What details would you like to know? Would the group want background details, workplace details? What kinds of questions might be asked? Help each other to narrow the possible subject and to make a rough list of questions.

CHAPTER 7

Focusing on People

At one time I lived in a small village on the side of a mountain in South America. The village priest, Padre Bolanos, was also the mayor. A thin, almost gaunt man who wore a faded black cassock and drove a jeep, the padre seemed to be everywhere—organizing a festival, laying a water pipe from a spring to the village, building an electrical generator to light the church, petitioning for government funds to construct a small bridge, initiating a soccer game in the rain in which he ran wildly through the mud, his black cassock flaying the wind, his boots kicking the splattered ball high into the air. Everyone loved Padre Bolanos.

As I was one of the few outsiders ever to stay in the village, the padre invited me to live in his home behind the church. I had hardly settled in when I discovered that a young woman and her small son also lived with the padre. The very mention of the young woman to others in the village caused raised eyebrows and knowing smiles. "The padre is only human," one man told me. I quickly found a room with another family. For six months I felt contempt for the priest. That the villagers loved him made him only more hypocritical in my eyes. I avoided him, spoke coolly to him. And then once, in an emergency of sorts, I found I had to ask him to drive me to the nearest large town where I could find a doctor. Padre Bolanos acted without hesitation. Within minutes he had the jeep bouncing down the mountainside. On the way, he told me a story.

He told how a priest had once visited the capital city of his country and walked late at night through the poorest *barrio.* As he walked among the broken streets, the priest heard muffled cries from an alley and found there a young girl who had just given birth among the rags and ashes. The girl was fourteen. She had been a prostitute since she was eleven. The priest had taken the girl home with him, where for several years now she served as housekeeper. He knew many people felt horrified that a priest should have an ex-prostitute for a housekeeper; others, more cynical perhaps, felt certain the priest kept the girl as his mistress. In a few weeks she would be eighteen and leaving for the capital city again. She did not like living in a rural village. The priest would continue to raise the little boy, at least for a while, until the girl found a job. The priest's only regret was that the girl was still not a Christian. She did not believe in God.

I sat quietly, ashamed. How could I have misjudged him so badly? As we pulled up to the doctor's office, Padre Bolanos turned to me. "You know," he said, "for a long time I thought you were a sullen young man, perhaps even a little arrogant. But I apologize to you for my mistake. I see now that you are only shy." I had climbed out of the jeep. "Character," he said, "is a difficult thing. Too often I don't know what to look for, or I judge too quickly." He smiled at me and added in English, "I must learn to look most closely."

After two years in South America I returned home. I wanted to write about the economic consequences of a village market on sociological development—big words, big ideas. Most college writing deals with ideas and issues. But I found I could not separate my ideas from the people I had known. Ideas and issues do not exist in a vacuum. People with complex characters create ideas, cause events, stir up issues, invent machines, change the course of history, and indulge in little acts of human kindness. Describing people requires that we learn to look "most closely" and is perhaps the best training we can have for the development of writing skills. Good writing begins with perception of the subject. Teaching yourself to perceive people in all their complexities is a major step toward teaching yourself to perceive the complexity of the world people have created—and perhaps toward making us all a little more human.

Perception of Character

What exactly is "character"? What do we mean when we say (in the abstract) that "Gomez is a real character"? Or "Loretta has a super personality"? Even though you may not plan to write novels, novelists are one of the better sources to learn from, for a major tradition in the novel for 200 years has been the creation of character.

Here is David Copperfield describing (concretely) his stepfather's sister, whom he has never met and who has just arrived by stagecoach:

> It was Miss Murdstone who was arrived, and a gloomy-looking lady she was; dark, like her brother, whom she greatly resembled in face and voice; and with very heavy eyebrows, nearly meeting over her large nose, as if, being disabled by the wrongs of her sex from wearing whiskers, she had carried them to that account. She brought with her two uncompromising hard black boxes, with her initials on the lids in hard brass nails. When she paid the coachman she took her money out of a hard steel purse, and she kept the

purse in a very jail of a bag which hung upon her arm by a heavy chain, and shut up like a bite. I had never, at that time, seen such a metallic lady altogether as Miss Murdstone was. . . . Then she looked at me, and said:

"Is that your boy, sister-in-law?"

My mother acknowledged me.

"Generally speaking," said Miss Murdstone, "I don't like boys."

Charles Dickens is famous for his ability to create a sense of character within a short space, sometimes by exaggeration, but more often by seeing with an accurate eye the precise details that contribute to making a person unique. If we look closely at this description of Miss Murdstone, we find—either through direct concrete description or by implication—almost all of the major qualities that create in our minds an image of character.

Physical Description

As always, we begin with *seeing*. The way people look, the way they dress, the physical qualities of their person—all suggest something about character. Miss Murdstone is dark with heavy eyebrows that almost meet over her large nose (suggesting a perpetual scowl); she carries a hard steel purse in a jail of a bag with a heavy chain. Now, although it might be possible that Miss Murdstone is actually delicate, kind, happy, and charming, her physical appearance suggests the opposite. And although we have always heard we should not judge a book by its cover, we do. We tend to judge people, rightly or wrongly, by their physical appearance.

We can begin to distinguish between fact and inference. A *fact* is a direct observation of the senses that can be verified by someone else making the same observation. "John has a black eye." An *inference* is a conclusion about something that you cannot observe directly but that facts suggest to you. "John has probably been in a fight."

The facts of physical appearance lead us to inferences about character. If we see a teenage girl with purple lipstick, orange hair combed straight up, a safety pin stuck through one ear, and the name MARVIN tattooed on her bare shoulder, the facts, which all can be verified, lead to inferences about her character, inferences that may or may not be correct. Physical appearance, then, is our first contact with character. But we need more details of another nature to confirm our impressions.

Actions

Actions can overcome the impressions made by outward physical appearance, or they can confirm our impressions. In the paragraphs by Dickens, Miss Murdstone is seen performing only two significant acts: paying the coachman for her ride and speaking to David Copperfield's mother. We see her in more action later in the novel; but even at this stage, in our introduction to her, we begin to sense a quality of her personality by the way she takes her money from a steel purse (that shuts with a bite) and by the bluntness—could one say rudeness?—of her speech. Dickens tells us nothing in the abstract. He never says, "Miss Murdstone was greedy and cruel." But the *fact* of her actions causes us to *infer* that she is.

Look at the actions of people around you. Perhaps you have a grandfather who locks himself in a fruit cellar when your grandmother gets angry. Perhaps you have a college roommate who sticks wads of used chewing gum on the bottom of a desk. You've probably encountered the college instructor who is never in his or her office during posted office hours. You make inferences about all their characters. Neither physical appearance nor actions by themselves give a complete picture of character, but together they build impressions.

Speech

What we say and how we say it reveal an almost infinite number of qualities. Miss Murdstone's blunt dislike of children could not be made more stunning than by her single line, "Generally speaking, I don't like boys." Physical details and physical actions can suggest inner qualities, but speech has the potential of directly revealing values, ideas, rigor of intellect, attitudes, beliefs—even educational and cultural background. There is a striking difference between the character who says, "I ain't gonna put up with no more crap!" and another who says, "Your suppositions about me are highly distressing, and I refuse to tolerate further insinuations."

Yet speech, too, must be weighed against other perceptions. When you've just caught a man at midnight leaving your room with your TV set, and he says, "Gee, I guess I must be sleepwalking again," you may find yourself skeptical about the *fact* of his statement.

Self-Created Environment

The type of environment we surround ourselves with, the physical nature of the rooms we live in, the condition of our homes, the cars we drive—all contribute to perception of character. For example, Miss Murdstone apparently surrounds herself with metallic hardness. She carries her belongings in *hard* black boxes on which she has her initials pounded in *hard* brass nails. She even carries her money in a *hard* steel purse hung on her arm by a metal chain. Dickens would have created a different character in our minds had he described her as carrying a silk umbrella, a purse made of see-through wicker with wild straw flowers on top, and a trunk painted with fragile blue forget-me-nots.

Background

Background may or may not be important in creating a sense of character. We know nothing about Miss Murdstone's background when we first meet her, and we probably don't need to. At other times, background can be the single most vital quality in explaining why someone acts as he or she does—for example, an actress may have had a "stage mother" who drove her relentlessly to become famous, or the president of a giant corporation may have learned his dedication as a boy by getting up at 4 A.M. to milk cows on his parents' Missouri farm. But writers must be cautious about background details. If you tell us, "Mr. Harper was born on July 9, 1932. He lived in a small town until he was six, then he moved to a large city where he attended elementary school . . . ," you will bore all of us to death. Background details must be striking and essential to understanding current qualities of character, or they must be avoided altogether. Dickens, like other successful writers, uses background material with careful selectivity.

Others' Reactions

Finally, the way other people react to character helps to establish the validity of a writer's observations. Any writer may be biased in judgment. As we've already seen, it's possible to select only details with negative connotations or only those with positive connotations to sway the reader's impression. A second and third opinion can help us as readers to believe that the writer is reporting fairly and honestly. In the scene of Miss Murdstone's arrival, we have no reactions from other characters, but later in the novel we find that people tiptoe around Miss Murdstone, no one dares speak loudly to her, and others obey shamefacedly when she commands. Their reactions to her confirm our original impression of her character.

Although we could probably name several more aspects of life that shape our attitudes toward character, the following six attributes—balanced against each other—seem to be the most frequently observed and used by successful writers.

Physical description

Actions

Speech

Self-created environment

Background

Others' reactions

As Dickens shows, a writer need not present all six qualities to evoke a sense of character. Some writers have achieved solid, believable characters by using only dialogue or by using only action and speech without physical description. You must train yourself to look for the most interesting and important qualities in your subject, the unique elements of human nature that separate the person you're writing about from all others.

How Writing About People Relates to Other Forms of Writing

Of course, you're not going to write novels or short stories—at least not most of you. So why learn how to write about people?

First, any training in how to select factual details that lead to logical inferences is simply good training for every paper or report you'll ever write in college or in your career. But the suggestions for selecting those details that I've listed in this chapter are also crucial: It is one thing to say, "Learn how to select good factual details"; it is another to question, "How?" The strategy of looking for *physical details, actions, speech, environment, background,* and *others' reactions* provides you with a focus for selection that goes beyond "character." For example, with only slight modification, you might use the same criteria of selection for a history paper on the battle of Marathon.

1. What *physical details* were significant? What type of armament, protective shields, and supplies affected the outcome?
2. What *actions* were significant? Why did the Athenians form a battle line that was thin in the middle and heavy on the flanks?
3. What *speech* was significant? Who convinced the Greeks to meet the Persians on the plain of Marathon instead of awaiting battle at Athens?
4. What elements in the *environment* were significant? How did the shape of the hills and the narrow passes affect the outcome?
5. What elements of *background* are important? Why were the Plataeans willing to aid the Athenians? Where did the Athenian generals learn their tactics?
6. How have *others* reacted to the battle? To what good fortune does Herodotus attribute the victory?

In other words, the attributes a novelist looks for in "character" can be used as strategies any writer can look for in developing almost any subject. In later chapters, I'll develop this approach more fully.

But it must also be said that perception of character—and the ability to share that perception in writing—goes beyond a mere set of techniques. The need to extend our awareness, to sense and feel the qualities of another person's life, is one of the great steps out of self-centered adolescence and into adulthood. Only by training ourselves to sympathize (and ultimately to empathize) with other people in their fears, their ideals, their frustrations, and their convictions—only in developing the ability to project ourselves into others—can we begin to know and better evaluate our lives by contrast. As Padre Bolanos said, we "must learn to look most closely."

Practice

1. Try some thumbnail sketches—one- or two-line descriptions of people you observe. Try to reveal something about character by focusing on physical details, speech, or actions. Here are a few examples:

   He wore shorts and a white shirt and he was smoking a European cigarette out of a flat silver box.

   Student Journal of Sharon Grant

   The Arab nurse who nails down the coffin has a cyst on her nose and wears a permanent bandage.

   Notebooks of Albert Camus

   A horrid priest came to the back door of the mansion yesterday, raw, bright red face looked to have gone under a carrot scraper. Black coat, white neckband. . . . He chewed gum of some sort, harrumphed, rubbed some coins together.

   Journal of Sylvia Plath

   But it was my mother's and father's feet that I watched most. She was wearing low heels that needed mending and her feet were always swollen so that even from there I could see the shoe leather embedded, vanishing from that angle, into her ankles. There was more scuffle and noise and her feet disappeared into the hallway, after the stretcher, and she was cough-crying as my father's workboots followed close behind her, huge, with the laces thronged round the back.

   Reading in the Dark, by Seamus Deane

2. Write at least two full pages about an experience you had with someone important to you. Look deeply into your memory for actual details; don't depend upon clichés to express what you saw and felt. Focus on your memory. Show actions, physical details, speech, and any other details that re-create the character. Here is how Eva Figes described a child's perception of her grandmother and artist grandfather, Claude Monet, in her novel *Light.*

   Grandmama leaned forward and put her white plump hand on her arms, so she could smell the funny odour that always seemed to come from her.

"Is there something you want, child?" she asked kindly, but Lily just shook her head, pressing her lips together. It always seemed to come out of her clothes, thought Lily, sitting rigid, watching the brown flecks on the back of her grandmother's hand, and half the smell was sweet, like flowers, like the bottle which stood on her dressing table, but under it was something not so nice, something sharp and acrid, a mixture of skin and powder and sweat, and through it all something even more powerful, the pungent odour of mothballs. Her clothes smelt of years of folding, putting away, as though the fresh air could not get at them, however much she walked about.

Everything was different about old people, she thought, their shape under the clothes they wear, their colour, everything. Those little brown flecks on the skin, for instance, and something flaccid, soft and loose about grandmama's cheek when she was expected to kiss her. Soft and dry, not unpleasant: just different. But grandpapa, who also had brown flecks on the back of his hands, his skin was anything but soft, firm and bristling with beard, and from his clothes came an odour of tobacco, which she liked. Strong earth smells which came from out of doors, and sometimes tiny particles of colour caught round his fingernails, which she thought fun. As though he had come away with bits of river, field or sky clinging to him, after making such things. Like she and Jimmy after using plasticine. Everything about grandpapa, she thought, staring at his bearded head on the far side of the water jug, everything about grandpapa was on the surface, outside where you could see and hear and touch it, but grandmama was concealed in her black dress, in the folds of her gown and what she might wear underneath. It was buried in her face, too, in the slack mouth and soft white cheeks, and the pale eyes that said nothing. Only now and then one got a whiff of it, her secret, in the faint odour coming from her clothes.

3. Reveal the character of someone you don't know through his or her actions. Actions may be as small as gestures made by the hands or as large as decisions made in the face of a great crisis. Here is how historian and essayist Paul Horgan recorded in his journal a scene observed in passing on the street.

The man paralyzed from the waist down being wheeled on a winter afternoon in a small neat compact chromium wheelchair to his Rolls Royce limousine parked at the curb in 54th street. On his lap is balanced an attaché case. There is a young woman waiting at the car—a nurse?—in a winter overcoat. The man wheeling him turns him to the open front door of the car. The nurse takes away the left armrest of the chair and attempts to remove the attaché case. He slaps her away from it. With his right hand and arm he arranges his inert legs to a slanting position for moving. She sets a smooth board from the car's front seat to the raised footrest of the wheelchair. He turns himself to sit on the board. He then hunches and grubs himself along into the car. His movements are like those of a seal out of water. Finally he is in, the board removed, the chair is folded and stowed in the rear of the car, the attendants get into the car, she driving, and all the doors are shut. During the maneuver the slim, shiny, black attaché case has remained on his lap and as they drive away, he clutches it to his breast.

4. Interview your roommate or a friend. If possible, keep the interview going informally on-and-off for several days. Watch for gestures, actions, physical details, speech patterns, and so on. Look for anecdotes or elements from your subject's past that might be meaningful. Look for conflicts or contradictions and gently probe their origin or significance.
   Most important of all, find a central "idea" your subject believes in and make that the focal point of your paper. Let us *see* and *hear* your subject, but also let us *understand* his or her character as revealed through ideas or beliefs. Select only the most significant details to write about.

Copying

Sometimes it may be helpful to copy two or three paragraphs by different writers to see how they perceive and reveal a character in writing. Copy any of the following passages to see what you can discover about writing from these writers: Charles Dickens' paragraphs on Miss Murdstone, pages 75–76; Eva Figes' description of her grandmama pages 80–81; or Paul Horgan's observation of the man confined to his wheelchair, pages 81–82.

After copying the passage slowly, use it as a model and write your own passage about a person still alive in your memory

Group Inquiry

Pair up and conduct practice interviews. Take five minutes to find a controversial subject, one that—if possible—you disagree on. Question your partner about his or her views and beliefs, remaining as neutral as possible during the interview. Avoid arguing or interrupting. Take notes and use follow-up questions. When you finish, use your notes as reminders and try to paraphrase—or re-phrase—your partner's views. Does your partner feel you have heard and recorded them accurately, fairly, and without intrusion of your own attitudes? Were you able to capture his or her values or beliefs in such a way that you could write them without distortion in an essay?

CHAPTER

Focusing on Place

To describe is to picture, to create a scene in the reader's imagination.

> As I walk along the stony shore of the pond in my shirt sleeves . . . it is cool as well as cloudy and windy, and I see nothing special to attract me. . . . The bullfrogs trump to usher in the night, and the note of the whippoorwill is borne on the rippling wind from over the water. Sympathy with the fluttering alder and poplar leaves almost takes away my breath; yet, like the lake, my serenity is rippled but not ruffled. These waves raised by the evening wind are as remote from storm as the smooth reflecting surface. Though it is now dark, the wind still blows and roars in the wood, the waves still dash, and some creatures lull the rest with their notes.

This is how Thoreau described Walden Pond in a memorable chapter on solitude, and that is how many of us first think of description—as something associated with nature.

But this is also description:

> A distractingly pretty girl with dark brown eyes sat at the edge of our group and ignored both the joint making its rounds and the record player belching away just behind her. Between the thumb and middle finger of her left hand she held a pill that was blue on one side and yellow on the other; steadily, with the

> double-edge razor blade she held in her right hand, she sawed on the seam between the two halves of the pill. Every once in a while she rotated it a few degrees with her left index finger. Her skin was smooth, and the light from the fireplace played tricks with it, all of them charming. The right hand sawed on.

This paragraph, by Bruce Jackson, is taken from a magazine article on drug abuse. The article has nothing to do with rippling wind and whippoorwills, yet the same attention to specific details engages our imagination.

Here, too, is description:

> Squirrel monkeys with "gothic" facial markings have a kind of ritual or display which they perform when greeting one another. The males bare their teeth, rattle the bars of their cage, utter a high-pitched squeak, which is possibly terrifying to squirrel monkeys, and lift their legs to exhibit an erect penis. While such behavior would border on impoliteness at many contemporary human social gatherings, it is a fairly elaborate act and serves to maintain dominance hierarchies in squirrel-monkey communities.

Scientist Carl Sagan, writing about the evolution of human intelligence in *The Dragons of Eden,* is a long way from Thoreau writing about waves on Walden Pond. But both use an identical process of focusing on selected details. All three writers describe the ordinary world about us; yet each has sharpened his perceptions so that the reader's consciousness is heightened, magnified. The commonplace is no longer common when seen by a focused intelligence. We are made to experience the newness of our world.

Descriptive Focus

How does a beginning writer learn to select the best details from all those thousands of images registering on the senses every moment? Over the years, experienced writers have discovered some general principles that may help.

1. If a detail isn't interesting to you, you probably won't be able to make it interesting to your reader. Don't include it just to fill the page.
2. Sometimes you may fail to recognize the interest value of a detail because you haven't looked closely enough. If your senses have dulled or your mind has grown lazy from lack of challenge, you may never see the element in the detail that makes it significant. Look again. Focus your mind like a camera moving in for a close-up.
3. Use all your senses: listen, taste, touch, smell, look. Make mental or written lists of more details than you can ever use. From thirty visual details, select two or three that will help your reader *see.*

a. Look especially for light. Without light, other details remain in the dark.

b. Choose one detail that suggests the predominant character, atmosphere, or impression of the thing observed.

c. Select one detail that personalizes the subject or that seems to be the unique feature setting it apart from all others.

If I look about my office, for example, I see brick walls, a dull red carpet, shelves of books, a Chinese evergreen with yellowed leaves, an ashtray on the desk, a telephone, morning light through the window, stacks of unread student papers, and so on. What should I choose? Probably the morning light because, in addition to lighting the scene, the word *morning* gives us a type of light, an angle to the light, and a time of day—all of which open the scene to the mind's eye. Then I might select the rows of books or toppling piles of student papers; either would suggest the predominant atmosphere. Finally, I might focus on the milk-glass ashtray with red lettering stamped around the rim: COWBOY BAR—PINEDALE, WYO., U.S.A. The ashtray suggests something personal, something that sets me apart from other college instructors. (Do I spend my summers herding cattle in Wyoming? Could I have stolen it one wild and drunken night?)

4. Select the small detail most representative of the larger whole. Flyspecks on a water glass may be the only detail needed to suggest an unsanitary restaurant. A comb poking from the pocket of a teenage boy may suggest his pride or vanity. A hesitant pause before answering a question may give a clue to a congressman's use of slush money.

5. Look for details that reveal contradictions, conflict, or contrast, either in the subject itself or in what you anticipate the audience expects from the subject. A white picture is heightened by contrasting it with a dark matting. A man's strength may be emphasized by the tenderness with which he holds his six-month-old daughter. The character of a sixty-year-old woman may be revealed when she runs in the Boston Marathon.

Obviously, every subject may call for special treatment, yet these guidelines can suggest a starting point for observation. Here's part of an essay in which first-year student Gary Svoboda described an occurrence on a beach in North Carolina—before he had trained himself to select:

> Later on that night I went out to the beach and met several people who were hauling in a fishing net. One was named Jim and there was a woman whose name I didn't catch. I asked if I could help, just for the fun of it, and I worked with them for about an hour pulling fish and all kinds of sea life out of the net. They gave me a couple of fish for my help. We worked hard and I was tired by the end.

Gary has described, but he has failed to evaluate the effectiveness of his details. Both randomness and abstraction show that he hasn't yet disciplined his perceptions. A woman whose name he didn't catch creates no picture in our mind; neither does feeling tired after an hour's work of pulling "sea life" from a fishing net. Nothing here engages our imagination. After hearing a peer-editing group react indifferently to the essay, Gary complained that in his hometown this was just an ordinary event. How could he do more than write an ordinary description? As an experiment, we asked him to name twenty details from the experience. Here are only a few that Gary listed on the blackboard:

Gary's details	Peer response
a man named Jim	The detail lacks significance.
fish tossed in piles	What kind of fish?
croakers, sand sharks	Good, the names create images. What did they do with the sand sharks? Do croakers croak?
The fish got tangled in the net.	Fair. Keep going.
skates made a clapping noise	What are skates? How do they clap?
trying to escape	Why didn't you tell us this before?

The interest shown by his peer-editing group in certain types of details helped Gary rewrite:

> Later on I went out on the beach and walked along the sand in the moonlight. There was a small crowd gathered around some fishermen hauling in a net. I watched for a while and then asked if I could help. The rope felt like a steel cable cutting into my hands. When the net came out of the waves it sounded like someone clapping, like applause. At first I thought it was the bystanders, and then I realized it was the skates caught in the net and clapping their winglike bodies, trying desperately to escape. I put on a pair of gloves borrowed from one of the fishermen and knelt in the wet sand and helped them untangle the fish from the net. There were croakers and sea trout, sand sharks, and horseshoe crabs. The fish were tossed in a heaping pile on the sand. We heaved the skates and crabs back into the surf. We let the two-foot-long sand sharks die on the beach. They were still there the next morning. They had their mouths open and I felt like their eyes were staring at me.

Although the writing here needs editing, Gary's second version contains details that involve the reader in the experience. Gary has omitted dull points (surely a man "named Jim" did not stir interest, even in Gary), and he has replaced them with sensory details (moonlit beach, a cutting rope), with details that contrast with the reader's expectations (skates that clap their bodies in an effort to escape), and with small details that suggest a larger significance (their mouths gape open; eyes seem to stare at him).

A unique style, correct grammar, a large vocabulary—all are wasted unless you also develop a disciplined mind eager to encounter the realities of an ordinary world—the "fabulous realities" as Thoreau calls them. To describe with precision, you must see with precision.

Narrative Focus

In the process of re-seeing details in his subject, Gary Svoboda also discovered a natural, chronological ordering for presenting his experience. His description moves clearly from a nighttime setting to early the next morning; the rope is pulled; the net hauled onto the beach; the fish removed—all in the sequence in which they obviously occurred.

Few students experience any difficulty with narrative. Chronological sequence seems to come naturally to us: this happened; then this happened; then this happened. But good narrative—the ordering of events—requires a mental discipline similar to that required by description: To order or arrange, you must select. Some aspects of an event must be omitted in favor of other aspects. Time must be shortened here, dwelt on in more detail there.

Not all narrative is chronological, of course. Sometimes a writer begins with the present, moves to the past, then to the distant past and back to the present. This is the beginning of form: selection and ordering for the sake of emphasis, clarity, interest. All professional writers, writers of fiction as well as of nonfiction, know that the ordering of events affects the reader's ability to follow a story or essay logically, as well as the pace or speed with which the essay seems to flow.

Here is an example of superb ordering and pacing from *Black Elk Speaks* as recorded by John G. Neihardt. Black Elk describes the butchering at Wounded Knee.

> I had no gun, and when we were charging, I just held the sacred bow out in front of me with my right hand. The bullets did not hit us at all. . . .
>
> The soldiers had run eastward over the hills where there were some more soldiers, and they were off their horses and lying down. . . .
>
> We followed down along the dry gulch, and what we saw was terrible. Dead and wounded women and children and little babies were scattered all along there where they had been trying to run away. The soldiers had followed along the gulch, as they ran, and murdered them in there. Sometimes they were in heaps because they had huddled together, and some were scattered all along. Sometimes bunches of them had been killed and torn to pieces where the wagon guns hit them. I saw a little baby trying to suck its mother, but she was bloody and dead. . . .
>
> When we drove the soldiers back, they dug themselves in, and we were not enough people to drive them out of there. In the evening they marched off up Wounded Knee Creek, and then we saw all that they had done there. . . .

> Many were shot down right there. The women and children ran into the gulch and up west, dropping all the time, for the soldiers shot them as they ran. There were only about a hundred warriors and there were nearly five hundred soldiers. . . .
>
> It was a good winter day when all this happened. The sun was shining. But after the soldiers marched away from their dirty work, a heavy snow began to fall. The wind came up in the night. There was a big blizzard, and it grew very cold. The snow drifted deep in the crooked gulch, and it was one long grave of butchered women and children and babies, who had never done any harm and were only trying to run away.

Notice how the flow of this narrative is maintained by the first sentence in each paragraph.

> I had no gun, and when we were charging . . .
>
> The soldiers had run eastward over the hills . . .
>
> We followed . . .
>
> When we drove the soldiers back . . .
>
> Many were shot down right there . . .
>
> It was a good winter day when all this happened . . .

Of course, the power of Black Elk's story depends equally upon the descriptive details. Narration almost always works hand in hand with description. Practice in describing and narrating is practice in perceiving and shaping experience. Teaching yourself how to *select* and *order* is the first major step in disciplining the senses and in moving eventually toward logic and critical judgment.

Practice

1. Write about the worst place you ever spent a night—inside a tent that leaked; curled behind the steering wheel of a pickup truck; the Dreamland Motel where cockroaches and a lumpy mattress kept you awake; on the kitchen floor at Aunt Mildred's with twenty other relatives. Share the event in narrative or story form with focused selection of sensory details. (Sometimes the best way to discover the best details is through freewriting. Let the images flow. Then look back over your work, select the most striking images, and rewrite with more focus and order.)
2. Description should have a direction or purpose. A random listing of details has little interest even for the writer. The purpose may be

nothing more than creation of mood or feeling. Here is Joan Didion's opening paragraph from a short story. By focusing her perceptions on selected details, she creates an atmosphere that suggests the quality of life along a particular stretch of highway in California. Her purpose is to make you see and feel that quality.

> Imagine Banyan Street first, because Banyan is where it happened. The way to Banyan is to drive west from San Bernardino out Foothill Boulevard, Route 66: past the Santa Fe switching yards, the Forty Winks Motel. Past the motel that is 19 stucco tepees: SLEEP IN A WIGWAM—GET MORE FOR YOUR WAMPUM. Past Fontana Drag City and the Fontana Church of the Nazarene and the Pit Stop A Go-go; past Kaiser Steel through Cucamonga, out to the Kapu Kai Restaurant-Bar and Coffee Shop, at the corner of Route 66 and Carnelian Avenue. Up Carnelian Avenue from Kapu Kai, which means "Forbidden Seas," the subdivision flags whip in the harsh winds. HALF-ACRE RANCHES! SNACK BARS! TRAVERTINE ENTRIES! $95 DOWN. It is the trail of an intention gone haywire, the flotsam of the new California. But after a while the signs thin out on Carnelian Avenue, and the houses are no longer the bright pastels of the Springtime Home owners but the faded bungalows of the people who grow a few grapes and keep a few chickens out here, and then the hill gets steeper and the road climbs and even the bungalows are few, and here—desolate, roughly surfaced, lined with eucalyptus and lemon groves—is Banyan Street.

Write a paragraph describing a street that leads to your home or school. Focus your perceptions in such a way that you select only details that suggest what it would be like to live there. Do not *tell* through abstractions; *show* in carefully selected concrete images.

3. A change of scene may stimulate perceptions and awaken awareness. If you shop exclusively at large supermarkets, this week shop at a small Chinese grocery store; instead of eating at a fast-food restaurant, eat at a local Greek or Vietnamese restaurant. Make a list of your spontaneous observations before you leave the site; then, back at your desk, re-create a sense of place through a descriptive narrative focusing on selected details.

4. Describe and narrate the most important two or three scenes from some significant event in your childhood—perhaps the moment when your brother came home from the hospital, or the day your mother sat you down in the kitchen to tell you of your parents' divorce. Select carefully both descriptive details and the *chronological ordering* of events. Try to help the reader see and feel the flow of your experience. Write as if the whole of it were occurring in a story.

   Now rewrite the experience with a different narrative pattern. Begin at the end of the event, then flash back to the beginning. Narrate up to the same point you described in the first sentence of your version.

What is the difference in effect? Is one version stronger than the other? More effective?

Copying

Copying is an old technique first practiced by medieval monks but continued in our own time by writers as diverse as Tennessee Williams and Malcolm X. Benjamin Franklin copied paragraphs from writers he admired, then paraphrased the passage, and later wrote a paragraph or so in the same style exploring his own ideas. Ralph Ellison has acknowledged he taught himself to write by copying Dostoevsky. Like sketching, the act of copying requires you to slow down and to pay attention to details you might otherwise miss. You learn to see how others have used language to re-create experience. One writer's style—the lengths and rhythms of sentences, the choice of words, the gift for the unexpected—may encourage you to take more risks with your own writing. More important, it may gradually help you discover more and better choices for expressing just what it is you need to say.

Turn back to Dick Gregory's essay "Shame," and copy the paragraph on page 65 beginning "Now there was shame. . . ." Pay particular attention to Gregory's use of specific nouns and concrete details. What discoveries can you make? What word does Gregory repeat and what is its effect? Following Ben Franklin's method, can you use a similar style to describe in your journal the last time you experienced shame or embarrassment or humiliation?

CHAPTER 9

The Scene

That night Demirgian lay in his combat clothes—his steel helmet, the damp fabric of his shirt and trousers, his canvas boots—and Demirgian had a wet black rifle on the soil beside him as with intricate fingers he made himself a glass of grape juice. Slower than a caterpillar chews on a maple leaf his fingers tore a small paper packet of Kool-Aid and quieter than a dandelion loses its fluff his hand shook the light purple powder into his Army canteen. The cold stars above, the cool earth below him kept their complete silence as Demirgian tilted his rubber canteen to its left—right—left—right with the slow periodicity of a pendulum. One long minute of this and Demirgian took a quiet sip. And ah! Demirgian had come alive! He's in the grape-juice generation! He buried the torn paper packet quietly in six inches of Vietnam's soil.

This paragraph is not taken from a short story or a novel, although it seems to have all the qualities we expect in fiction. Actually, it was written by John Sack, a professional writer describing in an article for *Esquire* a true character involved in the Vietnam War. Sack writes nonfiction, but like many successful writers, he incorporates the techniques of fiction into his work to make it more interesting. In almost any type of personal writing and in many other kinds of writing, the various elements of perception, language, and form that have been covered in the first eight chapters of this book (especially in description and narration) can be drawn together into a fiction technique labeled *scene.* Understanding the components of scene can give you both an effective device for beginning an essay and a structural unit for shaping your first draft.

Elements of Scene

A prose scene usually consists of seven elements:

1. *Light.* The stage in a theater cannot be seen without light, nor can your reader see a prose scene in his or her imagination without some mention or implication of light.
2. *Time.* Light often suggests time: A "November dawn," for example, gives time of year, time of day, and type of light. We do not need time as given in detective novels ("it was 6:42 P.M. when the murder occurred") but we do need a general range of time like morning, evening, noon, or whatever.
3. *Place.* We all live in a real world, in a real setting, and we cannot imagine people functioning in a vacuum. A sentence or two can suggest the gates of a castle, a Victorian living room, or the path in a dark forest.
4. *Character.* Common sense tells us that character is the focal point of any scene. Light, time, and place are all background to the character who walks, talks, acts, and reveals for us the vital qualities of his or her life.
5. *Position.* Is the character standing or sitting? If the character gets up from sitting on the floor and stretches out on the couch, the scene and the experience will change because his or her position has changed.
6. *Purpose.* Nothing can be more dull than a scene that doesn't go anywhere. No scene in a play or in your writing should exist without some clear intention. Purpose can lie in demonstrating some aspect of character, in setting the mood for what is to follow, or in presenting a problem or conflict that will need to be solved.
7. *Five senses.* The theater can successfully suggest only sight and sound to the audience. Prose can involve as many of the five senses as possible or necessary to absorb the reader physically or emotionally in the scene.

If we go back for a moment to John Sack's opening paragraph about a soldier in Vietnam, we will find all of these qualities: The first sentence establishes time (night, stars out); we know immediately that a character (obviously a soldier wearing combat clothes and a steel helmet) is lying on the ground, a detail that indicates both his position and our first indication of place, which turns out to be Vietnam soil; the larger setting of the article will follow. In addition to sight, sensory details include touch (a wet rifle, cold earth) and sound (quieter than dandelion fluff). Sack's purpose here is not as immediately clear. We do gain some insight into the soldier's personal, human qualities as we see him mixing Kool-Aid grape juice in his canteen. Actually, it is not until the next paragraph (which I have not quoted) that the author makes his point: While a soldier is on ambush patrol, nothing ever happens. The scene becomes clear. The soldier is doing what soldiers have always done—lie in the mud, wait, and find some way to pass the time.

Scene is a literary device, but it is so only because we all live every day in a scene, as you are doing at this moment. Knowing the elements of scene gives you a method for observing and recording. Description and narration should not consist of random details. Selection should be made from those qualities most likely to convey to the reader's imagination the actual and most vivid elements of life itself. Thus scene: *light, time, place, character, position, purpose,* and *sensory experience.* Scene provides you with the first major step in creating form; a scene *is* form.

Organizing Within the Scene

The elements of scene can be organized into whatever pattern is most effective. There are no rules, but there are some conventional organizations that you should be familiar with and that might help you in your writing.

Zooming in

Because a reader needs orientation, it often helps to begin with a larger frame, a panoramic overview or setting, and then focus in step-by-step toward smaller, more-specific details. Here's how first-year student Caitlin Brubach began her essay on a special place she remembered:

> When I was fourteen, my father served as Director of the American Center in Thessoloniki, Greece. We had an apartment on the top floor of the center overlooking the ocean. Across the mirrored sea, in the far distance, we could sometimes make out Mount Olympus with its permanent clouds hiding the peak, dark and mysterious even in bright sunlight. The gods, we were told, no longer revealed themselves. The world had passed them by.
>
> Seven stories below our apartment, the boulevard formed a hot ribbon of asphalt around the margin of the bay, and almost weekly the old Communist Party would march back and forth in front of the center protesting something, usually no more than thirty or forty bald-headed men in worn black suits, or grandmothers in black scarves, tired revolutionaries with signs and banners so faded they could not be made out. One or two bored policemen would direct traffic into side streets. No one anymore paid attention to their rallies.
>
> Seven stories up we could hear the faint chants. And on some days, when the sun broiled down upon them, my mother would feel sorry and take down trays of ice cold water on a tea cart. I would lean out on the balcony and watch the old revolutionaries gather gladly around her, taking a break in the slim shade of the building. I could see my mother chatting with them, and after awhile, they would drift away in small groups of five or six to sit under umbrellas at nearby outdoor cafes, perhaps to talk about the old days. The policemen would re-open the boulevard and traffic would begin its ceaseless roar again.
>
> It all seemed rather sad. Mother always saved two special glasses of cold water for the policemen.

The student writer begins with a wider frame, sometimes called a panoramic scene, showing us a view of the sea and Mount Olympus, then narrowing to an observer leaning over a balcony seven stories above the street. The focus narrows again to a crowd of protesters below, then once more to her mother taking ice water to them. The pattern of moving from general to specific is valuable in that it locates the reader, placing us in a context or world where the specific event or happening then makes sense.

The panoramic technique may also be especially helpful for a writer during the first draft because the mind, too, needs orienting, needs to follow a process of focusing. By allowing yourself to begin with the general, you help the words flow. Writing about generalities is usually easier than writing about small details (easier to begin with "It was a July morning" or "All over Brooklyn the rain was falling") and then to lead into finer elements.

Zooming out

The alternative is obvious. John Sack's scene about Demirgian begins with the soldier lying in the mud. Not until the end do we find out he is in Vietnam. We move from the focused detail to the larger frame. Here is Billy Whitmore, a sophomore, following such a technique in an essay about his coach.

> His hand reached out and slapped my helmet. An explosion like a dull boom thundered inside my head. His shoulder clipped my shoulder and the pads made a vicious smack! I felt myself spinning for a moment off balance, the sun flashing past my eyes, blue sky, then the cold plastic grass coming up at my nose. I was reaching out to catch myself when something hit me from behind like three heavy mattresses falling on me at once, smashing me down. Then someone's knee drove itself into my kidneys and the pain arched across my back. My ribs poked into my lungs. For a moment everything was just still, only the sounds of several people panting. Huffing. Then the weight lifted off me and I heard the coach yelling, "Jesus H. Christ, Whitmore! Where's your head? You were out of position! Get yourself up before I kick your ass all the way to Rolf Hall!"
>
> It was the third day of practice. Coach Harley was standing over me, and between his legs I could see the afternoon sun dripping down over the empty bleachers. The dull thundering in my ears had not gone away. His voice sounded as if he were shouting at me through a cloud. I got to my knees and in spite of the pain burning in my back I pulled myself up. The other guys trying out for the team had drifted back over to the scrimmage line and were looking away from me, pretending not to notice. It was the third major mistake I had made that day and something in Coach Harley's face told me it would be my last.

Although the reader can quickly tell that the author is writing about football (the helmet and the shoulder pads appear in the first three sentences), we know nothing of the larger situation until the second paragraph. Only gradually do we perceive the more general setting (a sinking sun, empty bleachers, other football players, the coach). And not until the final sentence of the second paragraph do we get a suggestion of purpose or direction.

Beginning with selected details plunges the reader immediately into your writing. The audience is caught up in an event or a description without knowing exactly why and must keep reading to find out. Therein lies the risk. The reader will stay with you only so long—perhaps a few paragraphs or a page—before you must provide some general orientation. But either organizing technique—general to specific or specific to general—provides you with a relatively easy and sequential pattern to follow for getting the first few paragraphs of an essay flowing.

Drafting Scenes

As the first draft often presents the most difficult obstacle to overcome in writing, an understanding of scene and its components can provide you with an immediate place to begin writing: Create a scene in which you *show* us your subject; write a series of scenes showing different aspects of your subject. In early drafts, the scenes need not be logically connected. You can always return later and fill in the relationships, add commentary or personal reflection, and draw conclusions. *A scene or a series of scenes can be the organizing unit of a complete essay: It can serve as a sensory and dramatic introduction to an essay or it can provide an effective and often moving conclusion.* The readings collected at the end of this unit provide several examples.

The function of a scene is not to tell but to dramatize. A scene helps you select and order your details by focusing your attention on light, time, place, character, position, purpose, and sensory experience. It provides a manageable shape for organizing details, either from specific to general or general to specific. Ford Madox Ford, an early twentieth-century writer, said you must always write as if your subject were acting out its life before you on a stage. If you see nothing in your mind's eye, you can be sure your reader won't see anything either. Especially in writing about a character or in writing any form of description and narration, keeping the elements of scene in the back of your mind while keeping a picture of the thing you're describing in the front of your mind can help make words flow onto the page.

Exercises

Analyze the following scene by John Knowles, from his novel *A Separate Peace.* Identify each of the elements of scene. Has he left any out?

No one else happened to be in the pool. Around us gleamed white tile and glass brick; the green, artificial-looking water rocked gently in its shining basin, releasing vague chemical smells and a sense of many pipes and filters; even Finny's voice, trapped in this closed, high-ceilinged room, lost its special resonance and blurred into a general well of noise gathering up toward the ceiling. He said blurringly, "I have a feeling I can swim faster than A. Hopkins Parker."

We found a stop watch in the office. He mounted a starting box, leaned forward from the waist as he had seen racing swimmers do but never had occasion to do himself—I noticed a preparatory looseness coming into his shoulders and arms, a controlled ease about his stance which was unexpected in anyone trying to break a record. I said, "On your mark—Go!" There was a complex moment when his body uncoiled and shot forward with sudden metallic tension. He planed up the pool, his shoulders dominating the water while his legs and feet rode so low that I couldn't distinguish them; a wake rippled hurriedly by him and then at the end of the pool his position broke, he relaxed, dived, an instant's confusion and then his suddenly and metallically tense body shot back toward the other end of the pool. Another turn and up the pool again—I noticed no particular slackening of his pace—another turn, down the pool again, his hand touched the end, and he looked up at me with a composed, interested expression. "Well, how did I do?" I looked at the watch; he had broken A. Hopkins Parker's record by .7 seconds.

_____ light
_____ time
_____ place
_____ character
_____ purpose
_____ position
_____ sight
_____ touch
_____ sound
_____ taste
_____ smell

Practice

1. Glance through some of your past papers and select any paragraph you could now shape more powerfully by writing it as a complete scene. Begin by listing all the elements of scene that should have been in the passage—light, character details, position, time, place, and so on. Then select the most effective elements and revise the old entry.

2. Observe and create an indoor scene. Melinda Wilson, a first-year student, began by concentrating on the elements of scene as she woke up one morning.

"Cincinnati is playing Oakland tonight. The game is to be televised at 8:00 P.M. . . ."

Groaning I rolled over and turned down the volume on my radio to a low whisper. My eyes watered as I yawned and my back arched in a stretch. I opened my eyes and looked at the clock. All I could see was a red glow. I pulled my hands from under my pillow and rubbed my eyes. With one fingernail I scraped the hard crumbly mucus from the corners. My eyes stretched wide and I blinked the water away. The red glow had become numbers: 7:34. The door was open and the light from the kitchen illuminated the bedroom. I could see the remnants from my midnight snack on the floor near the foot of the bed. A bowl of milk with a few Cheerios still floating in it and half a box of Fig Newtons. I pulled my pillow against my chest and wrapped my arms around it. The sheet felt warm and smooth against my legs. I wet my lips with my tongue and grimaced as I realized I didn't brush my teeth last night. I pushed my feet from under the covers and over the side of the bed. Still hugging my pillow, I pushed myself upright. Everything went black as the blood rushed to my head. I pushed my face into my pillow and waited for the fuzziness to go away. The hardwood floor felt cool under my feet.

3. Practice writing a *panoramic scene*. Look out your window. Describe the general location; record the light (try to imply "time" through the light); then focus in, step by step, on a simple but important or characteristic detail selected from the whole. Here is how first-year student Mark Bostic attempted it.

General overview	It was another gloomy Monday, and the light was beginning to fade for the day. The clouds in the sky grew darker and darker. Then the rain began, lightly at first,
Focusing in	barely touching the leaves of the trees outside my house.
Smaller focus	I saw my neighbor in his driveway with his car hood up. Then the rain began to fall harder. I saw it bouncing furiously against the top of his car. He slammed down the hood with a disgusted look
Specific focus	on his face. As he ran around the side of his car he tripped over his tool box. "Damn," he yelled, "who in the hell set this here?" He raced into the house to get out of the rain.

4. Write a scene involving two characters. Do not fictionalize. Observe and listen to two secretaries as they go about their work, or two janitors leaning on their brooms in the hall, or two professors having a cup of coffee. Catch the actual dialogue, the gestures. Look especially for opposition. Select details about each character that reveal their personalities. Focus on actions and speech. Include all other elements of scene necessary to orient the reader: light, time, place, position, purpose, and the five senses. Writing about two characters is at least twice as difficult as writing about one. Ease the way by organizing either from the general to the specific or the reverse. Do not merely list details at random.

CHAPTER 10

Using Strong Verbs

As a student I remember *style* always seemed one of those vague things others "had" and I was supposed to "get." But no one could tell me how. For a long time, I thought that style meant being flowery or dramatic or writing like William Faulkner. Only gradually did I come to discover that it meant, among other things, using your most natural voice. Indeed, some professional writers insist that style is voice, the revelation of your spirit, your biases, your vitality as it speaks to us from the page. In an earlier chapter, I emphasized that you could probably discover your natural voice while writing spontaneously during the first draft. Another surprising way of finding that voice, of developing strength and vigor in your style, is through the conscious search for strong verbs during the revising or editing phase of the writing process.

Weak and Strong Verbs

You may think of verbs (if you think of them at all) as grammatical elements in a sentence, as words that connect subjects with objects. Verbs do much more. Successful writers have found verbs the most important element in creating lively prose.

We can divide verbs into two general categories:

1. Strong verbs create a sense of direct, specific action, and because they are often concrete words, they tend to create an image in the reader's mind (*slump, crackle, shove, roar*).
2. Weak verbs use some form of the construction "to be" (*is, was, were, am, are, has been,* and so on), or they use what is generally called

a"passive voice" (*The line was hit by the fullback,* instead of *The fullback hit the line*). Sometimes weak verbs are merely those vague little words like *get, do, make, come, have, had,* and *go* that fail to give statements a forceful impact because they are so innocuous.

Most of us tend to rely on weak verbs, especially in the early stages of writing. Yet an overdependency on weak verbs leads to dreary, styleless prose. Because only a dozen "to be" forms exist in the language, their repetition in sentence after sentence becomes predictable and monotonous. Just as you should train yourself to avoid clichés and generalities in your writing, you should train yourself to eliminate all weak verbs. Why?

Strong verbs create the image of an action:

jump, smile, whistle, swivel, dive, pivot, float

Strong verbs focus an idea:

narrate, condemn, expose, recount, argue, define, explore, criticize

Strong verbs tighten and strengthen a sentence:

(Good writers never use seventeen words when eleven will do.)

It was brought to my attention by Dr. Lewis that I had failed to define my terms. (seventeen words)

Dr. Lewis told me I had failed to define my terms. (eleven words)

The best writers know that strong, active verbs create a sense of imaginative, original prose. Notice how Annie Dillard uses verbs to evoke strength and emotional force in this simple passage describing a moth flying into a candle.

> I *looked* up when a shadow crossed my page; at any rate, I *saw* it all. A golden female moth, a biggish one with a two-inch wing-span, *flapped* into the fire, *dropped* her abdomen into the wet wax, *stuck, flamed, frazzled* and *fried* in a second. Her moving wings *ignited* like tissue paper, enlarging the circle of light in the clearing and creating out of the darkness the sudden blue sleeves of my sweater, the green leaves of jewelweed by my side, the ragged red trunk of a pine. At once the light *contracted* again and the moth's wings *vanished* in a fine, foul smoke. At the same time her six legs *clawed, curled, blackened,* and *ceased,* disappearing utterly. . . . And her antennae *crisped* and *burned* away and her heaving mouth parts *crackled* like pistol fire.

Writers make choices. As they work to revise and edit their writing, they search for the strongest nouns, the most accurate verbs. Contrast, for example, the almost infinite number of strong verbs available for the single sentence *A snake is under the porch.*

- A snake coiled under the porch.
- A snake rattled under the porch.
- A snake hissed under the porch.
- A snake died under the porch.

The list might go on for pages. Strong verbs offer you an almost unlimited number of choices. And strong verbs make writing more precise, more sensory. *A snake is under the porch* locates the snake but nothing more. It doesn't show us anything for the imagination to grab hold of. *Coiled, slithered, rattled, hissed,* and *died* convey concrete details about the snake. The specific choice you make gives your writing a voice that distinguishes it from the choice someone else makes, even for the same sentence on the same subject.

Professional writers, like journalists, must be especially conscious of verbs. Stories have to move; action must keep the reader interested. Few reporters could get away with a story that relied on weak verbs. Notice how the writer of this *Newsweek* article used strong verbs to make the event more concrete, more specific, more active, and more interesting.

> She *strolled* into a New Orleans motel, calmly *demanded* money in the cash register and *warned* the clerk: "I'm going to spill your guts." When the disbelieving clerk *resisted,* the teenage holdup girl *stepped* behind the reservations counter and *slashed* the clerk in the belly with a 3-inch knife.
>
> While he *lay* bleeding on the floor, several motel guests *walked* in. The girl *made* change for one of them from the stolen money, *handed* a room key to the second and *checked out* the third.

Even the newspaper-headline writer knows that verbs sell a story by capturing the reader's interest.

- PRESIDENT WRESTLES WITH DEFICIT
- BARRY BONDS BREAKS RECORD
- PROFITS SOAR ON WALL STREET
- AMERICANS UNITE

The value of adding strong verbs to your writing cannot be overemphasized. More active verbs make sentences more concrete and sensory. They eliminate extra words, they emphasize the most important facts in the sentence, they make details more precise, they make all forms of writing sound vigorous, and they offer you the opportunity to express your own voice, to make your writing stand out.

Editing for Strong Verbs

For the beginning writer, finding strong verbs is usually an editorial act. After several years of practice, such verbs may come to you as early as the first-draft stage: The weak passive voice may seem almost unnatural. But too much conscious effort at the first-draft stage may cause inhibitions as much as excessive concentration on proper punctuation. Unless you already write using active verbs, it would be better to work with them during the revising or editing phase of the process.

As in other forms of editing, there are few clear rights and wrongs. Some sentences may work successfully with a passive verb, and every effort to change it to an active verb will only distort or strain the flow. *Never force a strong verb into the sentence merely for its own sake,* but do test every sentence you have written.

1. In many cases, the strong verb is already in the sentence. Find the word that seems to carry any action at all and rebuild the sentence around it.

Original:
The truck was overloaded by the workmen with watermelons.

Find the action:
overloaded

Rebuild the sentence around the action:
Workmen overloaded the truck with watermelons.

Original:
His work shirt had dark rings where it had been stained with sweat.

Find the action:
stained

Rebuild the sentence around the action:
Dark rings of sweat stained his work shirt.

Note that in both of these examples, editing for the strong verb also eliminates several unnecessary words. In each case, the active sentence reads more smoothly, simply, and effectively.

2. Avoid especially the "to be" verb form at the beginning of sentences. Such constructions as *There are, There is, It is,* and *It was* can often be eliminated.

Original:
There are two basic types of verbs you may have studied in high school.
[a sentence taken from my first draft of this chapter]

Find the action:
studied

Rebuild the sentence around the action:
You may have studied two basic types of verbs in high school.

Original:
It was her decision to become a banker.

Find the action:
decision

Rebuild the sentence around the action:
She decided to become a banker.

Changing verbs may also change the meaning, of course. "It was her decision" may suggest that a question existed regarding *who* made the decision. "She decided" loses such an implication. You must make editorial changes within the context of your whole essay. If the passive construction is more accurate, then use it. But if a strong verb can be substituted without distorting the accuracy, or if it increases the accuracy, then by all means make the change.

Original:
The elderly are thought by some people to be a burden on society because wages are not earned by most of them.

Find the action:
thought . . . earned

Rebuild the sentence around the action:
Some people think the elderly burden society because they earn no wages.

3. Finally, certain active verbs in themselves remain dull and empty because they lack concrete imagery. *Got, have, come, go,* and *made* serve better than a passive form, but not much better. Usually, a more precise action can improve the sentence.

Original:
I got in late at night.

Revision (that is, re-seeing in more precise or sensory terms):
I tiptoed in late at night.
I slipped in late at night.
I stomped in late at night.
I thundered in late at night.
I crept in late at night.

Most readers consider Shakespeare the finest writer in English because of the combined breadth and depth of his perception into human nature, but also because of the superiority of his craftsmanship. Critics long ago identified his use of strong verbs as a major element in that craftsmanship. One scholar estimates that Shakespeare uses approximately four active verbs for every passive verb. In the following passage from *King Lear,* Shakespeare uses no passives at all.

Lear:

Blow, winds, and crack your cheeks! *rage! blow*!
You cataracts and hurricanes, *spout*
Till you have *drench'd* our steeples, *drown'd* the cocks!

You sulphurous and thought-executing fires,
Vaunt couriers to oak-cleaving thunderbolts,
Singe my white head! And thou, all-shaking thunder,
Smite flat the thick rotundity o' the world!

Crack nature's moulds, all germens *spill* at once,
That *make* ingrateful man!

It would be misleading to state that style or voice is nothing more than the use of strong verbs. Style is ultimately the reflection in language of your total personality. But the conscious search for vigorous, forceful verbs can be a major step in learning to control language so that it speaks for you and through you. The verb may be the key element in making your writing sound fresh, as well as energetic and exact.

Group Inquiry

1. In the following paragraph from *Ragtime,* E. L. Doctorow narrates Houdini's first flight in a biplane with boxed wings. Almost all verbs have been left out. First read the paragraph to grasp what's happening, then fill in every blank with a strong, vigorous verb. Don't try to guess what verbs Doctorow used; try to come up with your own. Compare your answers with those of two or three classmates. If you're like most people, you'll find that you overlap with someone else on no more than five or six out of the sixteen blanks. As a group, decide on the strongest verbs to use in the passage, and consider the reasons for your selection.

   Houdini __________ into the pilot's seat, __________ his cap backwards and __________ it down tight. He __________ the wheel. His eyes __________ in concentration, he __________ his jaw firmly and he __________ his head and __________ to the mechanic, who spun the wood propeller. The engine __________. It was an Enfield 80-horsepower job, supposedly better than the one the Wrights themselves were using.

Hardly daring to breathe, Houdini ________ the engine, ________ it, ________ it again. Finally he ________ up his thumb. The mechanic ________ under the wings and ________ the wheel chocks. The craft slowly ________ forward.

2. Editing verbs in context is more difficult. Working in pairs or trios, try to improve the following paragraph by changing at least 50 percent of the weak verbs into strong verbs. Collaboratively revise each sentence. Do you agree on how to revise, or on which verbs need to be made stronger, or which words need to be eliminated? Is your collaborative prose any better than what you would have written on your own?

   In the 1930s scientists were beginning to be suspicious of cigarettes as a cause of illness and death. One reason was an increase in lung cancer. Around 3000 people were listed each year as dying from lung cancer. Today there is an increase to 18,000 annually. Also, many smokers have got emphysema, a disease that is destructive of the wall of the air sacs of the lungs. All other related diseases, such as cirrhosis of the liver, pneumonia, bronchiectasis, and even stomach ulcers, are contributing factors to an even higher death rate. If all related diseases are combined, there is a 57 percent increase in the death rate among smokers over nonsmokers.

Practice

Read two of your earlier practice writings. Circle every weak verb. Rewrite both exercises, substituting strong verbs in every possible case (but don't make the sentence sound unnatural to your ear). Try to eliminate each case in which two or more passives appear in a single sentence or in which two or more sentences in a row use weak verbs. If Shakespeare used an average of four active verbs for every passive, set yourself a goal of using at least one active for every passive. If you fall below the 50–50 ratio, you're probably not seeing the potential for vigor and action in your own material.

Readings

Grandpa Was a Big Man

Charles S. Rathbone

Charles S. Rathbone was a returning adult student taking night classes to complete his bachelor's degree in management when he wrote the following sketch of his grandfather. Rathbone uses narration and description, as well as several focused scenes with sense details, dialogue, and action to express the fullness of his memories.

Grandpa's big hairy hand gripped my two wrists and I felt helpless. He had just locked the door of his little country store and stepped down the wobbly steps. I started poking and grabbing at him as usual when I wanted to scuffle.

I pulled and tugged, wrestled and jumped about on the hard packed dirt of the store yard trying to break his hold. In a few minutes I began to tire. I had no chance of getting loose. I was ten and I thought pretty strong, but all I had to show for my efforts were the heel marks and furrows my feet made in the store yard that Grandma kept swept as clean as her front porch.

Grandpa Harley was a big man, six feet three inches tall and two hundred and fifty pounds. He filled a door frame, and even the horses he occasionally shod seemed smaller when he stood next to them. The boys on Fines Creek liked to scuff with him and test his considerable strength. He was in his sixties, but he could hold all their hands with one of his.

Grandpa was the patriarch of the Methodist Church we went to every Sunday. I could not imagine sitting in that little church and seeing anyone else but

Grandpa standing up at the pulpit conducting the Sunday School and hymns. For this occasion each week he substituted his overalls for his old beige suit which looked good on him. Perhaps it was the contrast between it and his overalls. He stood erect before the congregation and even leaned back slightly to balance the tilting pull of his stomach. He wore his coarse, grey hair permanently parted down the center of his head. Tight stiff waves rose up from the part, then faded toward each side of his head. He wore his hair clipped short on the sides making his big ears look even bigger, especially the lobes. The wrinkles on his weathered face swelled in and out as he sang.

Any time a member or close friend of the church died, Grandpa rang the church bell the next day at noon, one ring for each year lived. "It's a tribute to the deceased," he once told me, "and the family knows we share their loss."

I remember walking the half mile or so with him to the church to ring the bell for an eighty-nine-year-old man who had died the day before. I jumped along and played as we walked up the gravel road, and occasionally picked up a rock and sailed it into the creek, but Grandpa walked in a quiet steady stride. He felt even the walk to and from the church was a solemn ritual.

Grandpa unlocked the church door and we walked in. Several days with the door and windows closed had left the air hot and stale. The quiet left by the absence of worshipers caused our every movement to echo off the walls. I opened the little belfry door and Grandpa, hat in hand, stooped through. He took hold of the plow rope hanging from the bell, and in a quiet somber manner he began pulling. As I stood next to him, I could hear the rope scuff against the ceiling hole. The clapper struck the bell interrupting the calmness of that summer afternoon. I imagined everyone within earshot silently contemplating the loss of Mr. Tom Kirkpatrick.

After about forty rings, beads of sweat covered Grandpa's brow. Some trickled down his cheeks. Sweat covered the bib of his overalls below the pocket where he carried the gold colored watch with a steam locomotive engraved on the back.

"Son," he said between breaths, "do you think you can help me for a while?"

I felt grown up. "Sure," I said.

"Now, before I stop you take hold of the rope and follow it up and down a few times so you can keep ringing at the same pace." I took the rope loosely in my hands; I could smell his sweaty body as his arms came up and down above my head. "Are you ready?" he said.

"I think so."

Slowly he turned the rope loose and backed away still counting the rings and keeping time with his hand. He leaned against the wall, and with his other hand, fanned his face with his old felt hat. I concentrated on every pull, being careful not to swing the bell over the top and cause two or three rings out of time. After a few minutes, the cords of the rope cut into my hands. My arms grew weak. My earlier enthusiasm and feeling of being grown up disappeared. To ease my aching arms, I pulled with my whole body, bending my knees at the bottom of each stroke. The bell no longer seemed to communicate a compassionate message but rather the deadening clang of heavy metal at the end of each exasperating tug. Grandpa knew I couldn't last much longer. He took the rope from my hand and I leaned back against the wall sweating and panting.

After eighty-nine rings, he put his hand on my shoulder and we walked out of the church. The bright sun and cool air felt good as the blood returned to my arms. As I walked down the road, perhaps a little slower than before, the bell continued to ring in my ears with the same cadence.

Grandpa and one or two men in the congregation dug all the graves in the church cemetery, sometimes taking three days in the winter if the ground was frozen deep, or if they hit rock. I often walked to the cemetery with him carrying the spade or shovel. It always amazed me how different the grave looked compared to other holes he dug on the farm. Perfectly shaped from top to bottom, the walls never varied more than a half inch. The spade marks on the sides were smooth and never gouged. Grandpa said the care taken in digging a grave, like ringing the church bell or taking off your hat as a funeral procession passed by, showed respect for the dead.

Grandpa talked once about the number of stray cats that had taken up out at the barn and how something had to be done. A day or two later I heard a shot out at the barn and ran to see what happened. I saw Grandpa coming out of the barn into the sunlight. He walked slowly, his head down, his face hidden by his hat. He carried his rifle loosely by his side as if he wanted to drop it. When he met me, he raised his head slightly. "What's wrong, Grandpa?" I asked as I looked up into his face. The wrinkles on his brow stood out.

"I shot the black and yellow spotted cat," he said.

The next day he discovered five kittens under a pile of boards in back of the barn. He knew the mama was the cat he had killed. Afterwards he carried milk to the kittens every day for two months.

When Grandpa died several years later some of the lining had to be removed from the casket to make room for him. On Sunday after Thanksgiving, his body was brought to Mom and Dad's home before the funeral. Family and friends passed in and out of the house offering condolences. The weather was particularly distressing that day. A cold wind blew and the naked maple trees swayed back and forth as their last leaves fell to the ground. Dark, thick clouds raced across the sky. The grass, the ragweed, and the plantain had withered and turned brown.

The day of the funeral, Jeff and Jim, his two other grandsons, two funeral home attendants, and Dad and I carried the big casket out of the hearse. As we struggled through the door and across the porch one of the attendants looked at me and said, "There lies much of a man." The brass handle felt heavy in my hand, but not as heavy as the weight I felt inside.

Sister Flowers

Maya Angelou

Maya Angelou might be called a "Renaissance woman." Beginning as a singer and dancer, she has starred in off-Broadway productions, acted in movies, written plays, published numerous volumes of poetry, produced a PBS-TV series on Africa, and served as coordinator for the Southern Christian Leadership Conference. Her autobiography, *I Know Why the Caged Bird Sings* (1970), from which the following excerpt is taken, received national acclaim. Two other volumes of autobiography have followed, as have numerous awards. Yet as the following piece illustrates, her life began in the poorest of circumstances. It took a special person to show her the way out.

For nearly a year, I sopped around the house, the Store, the school and the church, like an old biscuit, dirty and inedible. Then I met, or rather got to know, the lady who threw me my first life line.

Mrs. Bertha Flowers was the aristocrat of Black Stamps. She had the grace of control to appear warm in the coldest weather, and on the Arkansas summer days it seemed she had a private breeze which swirled around, cooling her. She was thin without the taut look of wiry people, and her printed violet dresses and flowered hats were as right for her as denim overalls for a farmer. She was our side's answer to the richest white woman in town.

Her skin was a rich black that would have peeled like a plum if snagged, but then no one would have thought of getting close enough to Mrs. Flowers to ruffle her dress, let alone snag her skin. She didn't encourage familiarity. She wore gloves too.

I don't think I ever saw Mrs. Flowers laugh, but she smiled often. A slow widening of her thin black lips to show even, small white teeth, then the slow effortless closing. When she chose to smile on me, I always wanted to thank her. The action was so graceful and inclusively benign.

She was one of the few gentlewomen I have ever known, and has remained throughout my life the measure of what a human being can be.

Momma had a strange relationship with her. Most often when she passed on the road in front of the Store, she spoke to Momma in that soft yet carrying voice, "Good day, Mrs. Henderson." Momma responded with "How you, Sister Flowers?"

Mrs. Flowers didn't belong to our church, nor was she Momma's familiar. Why on earth did she insist on calling her Sister Flowers? Shame made me want to hide my face. Mrs. Flowers deserved better than to be called Sister. Then, Momma left out the verb. Why not ask, "How are you, Mrs. Flowers?" With the unbalanced passion of the young, I hated her for showing her ignorance to Mrs. Flowers. It didn't occur to me for many years that they were as alike as sisters, separated only by formal education.

Although I was upset, neither of the women was in the least shaken by what I thought an unceremonious greeting. Mrs. Flowers would continue her easy gait up the hill to her little bungalow, and Momma kept on shelling peas or doing whatever had brought her to the front porch.

Occasionally, though, Mrs. Flowers would drift off the road and down to the Store and Momma would say to me, "Sister, you go on and play." As she left I would hear the beginning of an intimate conversation. Momma persistently using the wrong verb, or none at all.

"Brother and Sister Wilcox is sho'ly the meanest—" "Is," Momma? "Is"? Oh, please, not "is," Momma, for two or more. But they talked, and from the side of the building where I waited for the ground to open up and swallow me, I heard the soft-voiced Mrs. Flowers and the textured voice of my grandmother merging and melting. They were interrupted from time to time by giggles that must have come from Mrs. Flowers (Momma never giggled in her life). Then she was gone.

She appealed to me because she was like people I had never met personally. Like women in English novels who walked the moors (whatever they were) with their loyal dogs racing at a respectful distance. Like the women who sat in front of roaring fireplaces, drinking tea incessantly from silver trays full of scones and crumpets. Women who walked over the "heath" and read morocco-bound books and had two last names divided by a hyphen. It would be safe to say that she made me proud to be Negro, just by being herself.

She acted just as refined as whitefolks in the movies and books and she was more beautiful, for none of them could have come near that warm color without looking gray by comparison.

I was fortunate that I never saw her in the company of po-whitefolks. For since they tend to think of their whiteness as an evenizer, I'm certain that I would have had to hear her spoken to commonly as Bertha, and my image of her would have been shattered like the unmendable Humpty-Dumpty.

One summer afternoon, sweet-milk fresh in my memory, she stopped at the Store to buy provisions. Another Negro woman of her health and age would have been expected to carry the paper sacks home in one hand, but Momma said, "Sister Flowers, I'll send Bailey up to your house with these things."

She smiled that slow dragging smile, "Thank you, Mrs. Henderson. I'd prefer Marguerite, though." My name was beautiful when she said it. "I've been meaning to talk to her, anyway." They gave each other age-group looks.

Momma said, "Well, that's all right then. Sister, go and change your dress. You going to Sister Flowers's."

The chifforobe was a maze. What on earth did one put on to go to Mrs. Flowers' house? I knew I shouldn't put on a Sunday dress. It might be sacrilegious. Certainly not a house dress, since I was already wearing a fresh one. I chose a school dress, naturally. It was formal without suggesting that going to Mrs. Flowers' house was equivalent to attending church.

I trusted myself back into the Store.

"Now, don't you look nice." I had chosen the right thing, for once. . . .

There was a little path beside the rocky road, and Mrs. Flowers walked in front swinging her arms and picking her way over the stones.

She said, without turning her head, to me, "I hear you're doing very good school work, Marguerite, but that it's all written. The teachers report that they have trouble getting you to talk in class." We passed the triangular farm on our left and the path widened to allow us to walk together. I hung back in the separate unasked and unanswerable questions.

"Come and walk along with me, Marguerite." I couldn't have refused even if I wanted to. She pronounced my name so nicely. Or more correctly, she spoke each word with such clarity that I was certain a foreigner who didn't understand English could have understood her.

"Now no one is going to make you talk—possibly no one can. But bear in mind, language is man's way of communicating with his fellow man and it is language alone which separates him from the lower animals." That was a totally new idea to me, and I would need time to think about it.

"Your grandmother says you read a lot. Every chance you get. That's good, but not good enough. Words mean more than what is set down on paper. It takes the human voice to infuse them with the shades of deeper meaning."

I memorized the part about the human voice infusing words. It seemed so valid and poetic.

She said she was going to give me some books and that I not only must read them, I must read them aloud. She suggested that I try to make a sentence sound in as many different ways as possible.

"I'll accept no excuse if you return a book to me that has been badly handled." My imagination boggled at the punishment I would deserve if in fact I did abuse a book of Mrs. Flowers'. Death would be too kind and brief.

The odors in the house surprised me. Somehow I had never connected Mrs. Flowers with food or eating or any other common experience of common people. There must have been an outhouse, too, but my mind never recorded it.

The sweet scent of vanilla had met us as she opened the door.

"I made tea cookies this morning. You see, I had planned to invite you for cookies and lemonade so we could have this little chat. The lemonade is in the icebox."

It followed that Mrs. Flowers would have ice on an ordinary day, when most families in our town bought ice late on Saturdays only a few times during the summer to be used in the wooden ice-cream freezers.

She took the bags from me and disappeared through the kitchen door. I looked around the room that I had never in my wildest fantasies imagined I would see. Browned photographs leered or threatened from the walls and the white, freshly done curtains pushed against themselves and against the wind. I wanted to gobble up the room entire and take it to Bailey, who would help me analyze and enjoy it.

"Have a seat, Marguerite. Over there by the table." She carried a platter covered with a tea towel. Although she warned that she hadn't tried her hand at baking sweets for some time, I was certain that like everything else about her the cookies would be perfect.

They were flat round wafers, slightly browned on the edges and butter-yellow in the center. With the cold lemonade they were sufficient for childhood's lifelong diet. Remembering my manners, I took nice little lady-like bites off the edges. She said she had made them expressly for me and that she had a few in the kitchen that I could take home to my brother. So I jammed one whole cake in my mouth and the rough crumbs scratched the insides of my jaws, and if I hadn't had to swallow, it would have been a dream come true.

As I ate she began the first of what we later called "my lessons in living." She said that I must always be intolerant of ignorance but understanding of illiteracy. That some people, unable to go to school, were more educated and even more intelligent than college professors. She encouraged me to listen carefully to what country people called mother wit. That in those homely sayings was couched the collective wisdom of generations.

When I finished the cookies she brushed off the table and brought a thick, small book from the bookcase. I had read *A Tale of Two Cities* and found it up to my standards as a romantic novel. She opened the first page and I heard poetry for the first time in my life.

"It was the best of times and the worst of times . . . ." Her voice slid and curved down through and over the words. She was nearly singing. I wanted to look at the pages. Were they the same that I had read? Or were there notes, music, lined on the pages, as in a hymn book? Her sounds began cascading gently. I knew from listening to a thousand preachers that she was nearing the end of her reading, and I hadn't really heard, heard to understand, a single word.

"How do you like that?"

It occurred to me that she expected a response. The sweet vanilla flavor was still on my tongue and her reading was a wonder in my ears. I had to speak.

I said, "Yes, Ma'am." It was the least I could do, but it was the most also.

"There's one more thing. Take this book of poems and memorize one for me. Next time you pay me a visit, I want you to recite."

I have tried often to search behind the sophistication of years for the enchantment I so easily found in those gifts. The essence escapes but its aura remains. To be allowed, no, invited, into the private lives of strangers, and to share their joys and fears, was a chance to exchange the Southern bitter wormwood for a cup of mead with Beowulf or a hot cup of tea and milk with Oliver Twist. When I said aloud, "It is a far, far better thing that I do, than I have ever done . . ." tears of love filled my eyes at my selflessness.

On that first day, I ran down the hill and into the road (few cars ever came along it) and had the good sense to stop running before I reached the Store.

I was liked, and what a difference it made. I was respected not as Mrs. Henderson's grandchild or Bailey's sister but for just being Marguerite Johnson.

Childhood's logic never asks to be proved (all conclusions are absolute). I didn't question why Mrs. Flowers had singled me out for attention, nor did it occur to me that Momma might have asked her to give me a little talking to. All I cared about was that she had made tea cookies for *me* and read to *me* from her favorite book. It was enough to prove that she liked me.

Beneath My House

Louise Erdrich

Louise Erdrich is best known for *Love Medicine* (1984), *The Beet Queen* (1986), and *Tales of Burning Love* (1996), all novels of Native Americans in North Dakota. In the following excerpt from the essay "Foxglove," originally published in *The Georgia Review,* Erdrich uses all the qualities of "scene" (sights, smells, sounds, light, purpose, and so on) to narrate the simple experience of crawling under a house after a kitten. By focusing on the concrete details of her experience, she not only creates a vivid sense of place, she gains an insight into herself and her relation to the world about her. This is one of the best examples I've found to illustrate the philosophy behind *From Sight to Insight.*

It was as if the house itself had given birth. One day the floor cried where I stepped on it, and I jumped back. I was near a heating vent, and when I bent and pried the cover off and thrust my hand in, I briefly grabbed a ball of fur that hissed and spat. I heard the kitten scrambling away, the tin resounding like small thunder along the length of its flight.

I went down to the basement, looking for it with a flashlight, but, of course, at my step the untamed creature fled from the concrete-floored area and off into the earthen crawl space—draped with spiderwebs as thick as cotton, a place of unpeeled log beams, the underside of the house. I put out milk in a saucer. I crouched on the other side of the furnace, and I waited until I fell half-asleep. But the kitten was too young to drink from a dish and never came. Instead, she set up, from just beyond where I could catch her, a piteous crying that I could hardly stand to hear.

I went after her. The earth was moldy, a dense clay. No sun had fallen here for over two centuries. I climbed over the brick retaining wall and crawled toward the sound of the kitten. As I neared, as it sensed my presence was too large to be its mother, it went silent and scrabbled away from the reach of my hand. I brushed fur, though, and that slight warmth filled me with what must have been a mad calm because when the creature squeezed into a bearing wall of piled stones, I inched forward on my stomach. My back was now scraping along the beams that bore the weight of the whole house above me. Tons and tons of plaster, boards, appliances, and furniture. This was no crawl space anymore. I could hardly raise my shoulders to creep forward, could move only by shifting my hips up and down. On the edge of panic—I had never before been in a space so tight—one thought pressed in: if I heard the house creak, if it settled very suddenly upon my back, my last crushed words would be, "Shit! I don't even *like* cats." Because I *don't* like cats, just find their silken ways irresistible.

Its face popped out right in front of me, and vanished. How far back did the piled rock go? If I moved a rock, would the whole house fall on me? I reached for the kitten, missed, reached again, missed. I tried to breathe, to be patient.

Then, after a time, the kitten backed toward me, away from a clump of dirt I managed to throw at the far wall. Its tail flicked through a space in the rocks, and I snatched it. Held it, drew it toward me. Out it came with a squeak of terror, a series of panting comic hisses, and a whirl of claws and teeth, tiny needles it didn't yet know how to use.

She is a pretty cat, a calico marbled evenly with orange and black. Rocky. She sits near as I write, leaps into the warmth of my chair when I leave, and is jealous of the baby.

The night after I pulled her from the house, the darkness pressed down on me until I woke. I'd swum weightlessly into a smaller and smaller space. What the body remembers of birth it anticipates as death. In the house of my dreams the basement is the most fearful: *the awful place filled with water, the place of both comfort and death.* I fear in particular the small space, the earth closing in on me, the house like a mother settling its cracked bones and plumbing.

That afternoon, from underneath, I had heard the house all around me like an old familiar body. I hadn't told anybody else that I was going after the kitten, so nobody knew I was below. The normal sounds of my family's daily life were magnified. Their steps trailed and traveled around me, boomed in my ears. Their voices jolted me, their words loud but meaningless, warped by their travel through the walls and beams. Water flowed through invisible pipes around me, hitched and gurgled. It was like being dead, or unborn. I hadn't thought about it then, but now I could clearly see part of me, the husk of myself, still buried against the east wall: a person sacrificed to ensure the good luck of a temple, a kind of house god, a woman lying down there, still, an empty double.

Coming Home Again

Chang-rae Lee

Originally published in the *New Yorker,* Chang-rae Lee's essay blends dialogue, key sensory, and location details. The result is a sharply focused and perceptive revelation of a Korean mother. Lee was born in Seoul, Korea, in 1965 and immigrated with his family to the United States at the age of three. He currently serves as Director of the MFA Program at Hunter College of CUNY. He has published two award-winning novels, *Native Speaker,* and *A Gesture Life.*

When my mother began using the electronic pump that fed her liquids and medication, we moved her to the family room. The bedroom she shared with my father was upstairs, and it was impossible to carry the machine up and down all day and night. The pump itself was attached to a metal stand on casters, and she pulled it along wherever she went. From anywhere in the house, you could hear the sound of the wheels clicking out a steady time over the grout lines of the slate-tiled foyer, her main thoroughfare to the bathroom and the kitchen. Sometimes you would hear her halt after only a few steps, to catch her breath or steady her balance, and whatever you were doing was instantly suspended by a pall of silence.

I was usually in the kitchen, preparing lunch or dinner, poised over the butcher block with her favorite chef's knife in my hand and her old yellow apron slung around my neck. I'd be breathless in the sudden quiet, and, having ceased my mincing and chopping, would stare blankly at the brushed sheen of the blade. Eventually, she would clear her throat or call out to say she was fine, then begin to move again, starting her rhythmic *ka-jug;* and only then could I go on with my cooking, the world of our house turning once more, wheeling through the black.

I wasn't cooking for my mother but for the rest of us. When she first moved downstairs she was still eating, though scantily, more just to taste what we were having than from any genuine desire for food. The point was simply to sit together at the kitchen table and array ourselves like a family again. My mother would gently set herself down in her customary chair near the stove. I sat across from her, my father and sister to my left and right, and crammed in the center was all the food I had made—a spicy codfish stew, say, or a casserole of gingery beef, dishes that in my youth she had prepared for us a hundred times.

It had been ten years since we'd all lived together in the house, which at fifteen I had left to attend boarding school in New Hampshire. My mother would sometimes point this out, by speaking of our present time as being "just like before Exeter," which surprised me, given how proud she always was that I was a graduate of the school.

My going to such a place was part of my mother's not so secret plan to change my character, which she worried was becoming too much like hers. I was clever and able enough, but without outside pressure I was readily given to sloth and vanity. The famous school—which none of us knew the first thing about—would prove my mettle. She was right, of course, and while I was there I would falter more than a few times, academically and otherwise. But I never thought that my leaving home then would ever be a problem for her, a private quarrel she would have even as her life waned.

Now her house was full again. My sister had just resigned from her job in New York City, and my father, who typically saw his psychiatric patients until eight or nine in the evening, was appearing in the driveway at four-thirty. I had been living at home for nearly a year and was in the final push of work on what would prove a dismal failure of a novel. When I wasn't struggling over my prose, I kept occupied with the things she usually did—the daily errands, the grocery shopping, the vacuuming and the cleaning, and, of course, all the cooking.

When I was six or seven years old, I used to watch my mother as she prepared our favorite meals. It was one of my daily pleasures. She shooed me away in the beginning, telling me that the kitchen wasn't my place, and adding, in her half-proud, half-deprecating way, that her kind of work would only serve to weaken me. "Go out and play with your friends," she'd snap in Korean, "or better yet, do your reading and homework." She knew that I had already done both, and that as the evening approached there was no place to go save her small and tidy kitchen, from which the clatter of her mixing bowls and pans would ring through the house.

I would enter the kitchen quietly and stand beside her, my chin lodging upon the point of her hip. Peering through the crook of her arm, I beheld the movements of her hands. For *kalbi,* she would take up a butchered short rib in her narrow hand, the flinty bone shaped like a section of an airplane wing and deeply embedded in gristle and flesh, and with the point of her knife cut so that the bone fell away, though not completely, leaving it connected to the meat by the barest opaque layer of tendon. Then she methodically butterflied the flesh, cutting and unfolding, repeating the action until the meat lay out on her board, glistening and ready for seasoning. She scored it diagonally, then sifted sugar into the crevices with her pinched fingers, gently rubbing in the crystals. The sugar would tenderize as well as sweeten the meat. She did this with each rib, and then set them all aside in a large shallow bowl. She minced a half-dozen cloves of garlic, a stub of gingerroot, sliced up a few scallions, and spread it all over the meat. She wiped her hands and took out a bottle of sesame oil, and, after pausing for a moment, streamed the dark oil in two swift circles around the bowl. After adding a few splashes of soy sauce, she thrust her hands in and kneaded the flesh, careful not to dislodge the bones. I asked her why it mattered that they remain connected. "The meat needs the bone nearby," she said, "to borrow its richness." She wiped her hands clean of the marinade, except for her little finger, which she would flick with her tongue from time to time, because she knew that the flavor of a good dish developed not at once but in stages.

Whenever I cook, I find myself working just as she would, readying the ingredients—a mash of garlic, a julienne of red peppers, fantails of shrimp—and piling them in little mounds about the cutting surface. My mother never left me any recipes, but this is how I learned to make her food, each dish coming not from a list or a card but from the aromatic spread of a board.

I've always thought it was particularly cruel that the cancer was in her stomach, and that for a long time at the end she couldn't eat. The last meal I made for her was on New Year's Eve, 1990. My sister suggested that instead of a rib roast or a bird, or the usual overflow of Korean food, we make all sorts of finger dishes that our mother might fancy and pick at.

We set the meal out on the glass coffee table in the family room. I prepared a tray of smoked-salmon canapés, fried some Korean bean cakes, and made a few other dishes I thought she might enjoy. My sister supervised me, arranging the platters, and then with some pomp carried each dish in to our parents. Finally, I brought out a bottle of champagne in a bucket of ice. My mother had moved to the sofa and was sitting up, surveying the low table. "It looks pretty nice," she said. "I think I'm feeling hungry."

This made us all feel good, especially me, for I couldn't remember the last time she had felt any hunger or had eaten something I cooked. We began to eat. My mother picked up a piece of salmon toast and took a tiny corner in her mouth.

She rolled it around for a moment and then pushed it out with the tip of her tongue, letting it fall back onto her plate. She swallowed hard, as if to quell a gag, then glanced up to see if we had noticed. Of course we all had. She attempted a bean cake, some cheese, and then a slice of fruit, but nothing was any use.

She nodded at me anyway, and said, "Oh, it's very good." But I was already feeling lost and I put down my plate abruptly, nearly shattering it on the thick glass. There was an ugly pause before my father asked me in a weary, gentle voice if anything was wrong, and I answered that it was nothing, it was the last night of a long year, and we were together, and I was simply relieved. At midnight, I poured out glasses of champagne, even one for my mother, who took a deep sip. Her manner grew playful and light, and I helped her shuffle to her mattress, and she lay down in the place where in a brief week she was dead.

My mother could whip up most anything, but during our first years of living in this country we ate only Korean foods. At my haranguelike behest, my mother set herself to learning how to cook exotic American dishes. Luckily, a kind neighbor, Mrs. Churchill, a tall, florid young woman with flaxen hair, taught my mother her most trusted recipes. Mrs. Churchill's two young sons, palish, weepy boys with identical crewcuts, always accompanied her, and though I liked them well enough, I would slip away from them after a few minutes, for I knew that the real action would be in the kitchen, where their mother was playing guide. Mrs. Churchill hailed from the state of Maine, where the finest Swedish meatballs and tuna casserole and angel-food cake in America are made. She readily demonstrated certain techniques—how to layer wet sheets of pasta for a lasagna or whisk up a simple roux, for example. She often brought gift shoeboxes containing curious ingredients like dried oregano, instant yeast, and cream-of-mushroom soup. The two women, though at ease and jolly with each other, had difficulty communicating, and this was made worse by the often confusing terminology of Western cuisine ("corned beef," "devilled eggs"). Although I was just learning the language myself, I'd gladly play the interlocutor, jumping back and forth between their places at the counter, dipping my fingers into whatever sauce lay about.

I was an insistent child, and, being my mother's firstborn, much too prized. My mother could say no to me, and did often enough, but anyone who knew us—particularly my father and sister—could tell how much the denying pained her. And if I was overconscious of her indulgence even then, and suffered the rushing pangs of guilt that she could inflict upon me with the slightest wounded turn of her lip, I was too happily obtuse and venal to let her cease. She reminded me daily that I was her sole son, her reason for living, and that if she were to lose me, in either body or spirit, she wished that God would mercifully smite her, strike her down like a weak branch.

In the traditional fashion, she was the house accountant, the maid, the launderer, the disciplinarian, the driver, the secretary, and, of course, the cook. She was also my first basketball coach. In South Korea where girls' high-school basketball is a popular spectator sport, she had been a star, the point guard for the national high-school team that once won the all-Asia championships. I learned this one Saturday during the summer, when I asked my father if he would go down to the school yard and shoot some baskets with me. I had just finished the fifth grade, and wanted desperately to make the middle-school team the coming fall. He called for my mother and sister to come along. When we arrived, my sister immediately ran off to the swings, and I recall being annoyed that my mother wasn't following her. I dribbled clumsily around the key, on the verge of losing control of the ball, and flung a flat shot that caromed wildly off the rim. The ball bounced to my father, who took a few not so graceful dribbles and made an easy layup. He dribbled out and then drove to the hoop for a layup on the other side. He rebounded his shot and passed the ball to my mother, who had been watching us from the foul line. She turned from the basket and began heading the other way.

"Um-mah," I cried at her, my exasperation already bubbling over, "the basket's over *here!*"

After a few steps she turned around, and from where the professional three-point line must be now, she effortlessly flipped the ball up in a two-handed set shot, its flight truer and higher than I'd witnessed from any boy or man. The ball arced cleanly into the hoop, stiffly popping the chain-link net. All afternoon, she rained in shot after shot, as my father and I scrambled after her.

When we got home from the playground, my mother showed me the photograph album of her team's championship run. For years, I kept it in my room, on the same shelf that housed the scrapbooks I made of basketball stars, with magazine clippings of slick players like Bubbles Hawkins and Pistol Pete and George (the Iceman) Gervin.

It puzzled me how much she considered her own history to be immaterial, and if she never patently diminished herself, she was able to finesse a kind of self-removal by speaking of my father whenever she could. She zealously recounted his excellence as a student in medical school and reminded me, each night before I started my homework, of how hard he drove himself in his work to make a life for us. She said that because of his Asian face and imperfect English, he was "working two times the American doctors." I knew that she was building him up, buttressing him with both genuine admiration and her own brand of anxious braggadocio, and that her overarching concern was that I might fail to see him as she wished me to—in the most dawning light, his pose steadfast and solitary.

In the year before I left for Exeter, I became weary of her oft-repeated accounts of my father's success. I was a teenager, and so ever inclined to be dismissive and bitter toward anything that had to do with family and home. Often enough, my mother was the object of my derision. Suddenly, her life seemed so small to me. She was there, and sometimes, I thought, *always* there, as if she were confined to the four walls of our house. I would even complain about her cooking. Mostly, though, I was getting more and more impatient with the difficulty she encountered in doing everyday things. I was afraid for her. One day, we got into a terrible argument when she asked me to call the bank, to question a discrepancy she had discovered in the monthly statement. I asked her why she couldn't call herself. I was stupid and brutal, and I knew exactly how to wound her.

"Whom do I talk to?" she said. She would mostly speak to me in Korean, and I would answer in English.

"The bank manager, who else?"

"What do I say?"

"Whatever you want to say."

"Don't speak to me like that!" she cried.

"It's just that you should be able to do it yourself," I said.

"You know how I feel about this!"

"Well, maybe then you should consider it *practice,*" I answered lightly, using the Korean word to make sure she understood.

Her face blanched, and her neck suddenly became rigid, as if I were throttling her. She nearly struck me right then, but instead she bit her lip and ran upstairs. I followed her, pleading for forgiveness at her door. But it was the one time in our life that I couldn't convince her, melt her resolve with the blandishments of a spoiled son.

When my mother was feeling strong enough, or was in particularly good spirits, she would roll her machine into the kitchen and sit at the table and watch me work. She wore pajamas day and night, mostly old pairs of mine.

She said, "I can't tell, what are you making?"

"*Mahn-doo* filling."

"You didn't salt the cabbage and squash."

"Was I supposed to?"

"Of course. Look, it's too wet. Now the skins will get soggy before you can fry them."

"What should I do?"

"It's too late. Maybe it'll be O.K. if you work quickly. Why didn't you ask me?"

"You were finally sleeping."

"You should have woken me."

"No way."

She sighed, as deeply as her weary lungs would allow.

"I don't know how you are going to make it without me."

"I don't know, either. I'll remember the salt next time."

"You better. And not too much."

We often talked like this, our tone decidedly matter-of-fact, chin up, just this side of being able to bear it. Once, while inspecting a potato-fritter batter I was making, she asked me if she had ever done anything that I wished she hadn't done. I thought for a moment, and told her no. In the next breath, she wondered aloud if it was right of her to have let me go to Exeter, to live away from the house while I was so young. She tested the batter's thickness with her finger and called for more flour. Then she asked if, given a choice, I would go to Exeter again.

I wasn't sure what she was getting at, and I told her that I couldn't be certain, but probably, yes, I would. She snorted at this and said it was my leaving home that had once so troubled our relationship. "Remember how I had so much difficulty talking to you? Remember?"

She believed back then that I had found her more and more ignorant each time I came home. She said she never blamed me, for this was the way she knew it would be with my wonderful new education. Nothing I could say seemed to quell the notion. But I knew that the problem wasn't simply the *education;* the first time I saw her again after starting school, barely six weeks later, when she and my father visited me on Parents Day, she had already grown nervous and distant. After the usual campus events, we had gone to the motel where they were staying in a nearby town and sat on the beds in our room. She seemed to sneak looks at me, as though I might discover a horrible new truth if our eyes should meet.

My own secret feeling was that I had missed my parents greatly, my mother especially, and much more than I had anticipated. I couldn't tell them that these first weeks were a mere blur to me, that I felt completely overwhelmed by all the studies and my much brighter friends and the thousand irritating details of living alone, and that I had really learned nothing, save perhaps how to put on a necktie while sprinting to class. I felt as if I had plunged too deep into the world, which, to my great horror, was much larger than I had ever imagined.

I welcomed the lull of the motel room. My father and I had nearly dozed off when my mother jumped up excitedly, murmured how stupid she was, and hurried to the closet by the door. She pulled out our old metal cooler and dragged it between the beds. She lifted the top and began unpacking plastic containers, and I thought she would never stop. One after the other they came out, each with a dish that travelled well—a salted stewed meat, rolls of Korean-style sushi. I opened a container of radish kimchi and suddenly the room bloomed with its odor, and I revelled in the very peculiar sensation (which perhaps only true kimchi lovers know) of simultaneously drooling and gagging as I breathed it all in. For the next few minutes, they watched me eat. I'm not certain that I was even hungry. But after weeks of pork parmigiana and chicken patties and wax beans, I suddenly realized that I had lost all the savor in my life. And it seemed I couldn't get enough of it back. I ate and I ate, so much and so fast that I actually went to the bathroom and vomited. I came out dizzy and sated with the phantom warmth of my binge.

And beneath the face of her worry, I thought, my mother was smiling.

From that day, my mother prepared a certain meal to welcome me home. It was always the same. Even as I rode the school's shuttle bus from Exeter to Logan airport, I could already see the exact arrangement of my mother's table.

I knew that we would eat in the kitchen, the table brimming with plates. There was the *kalbi,* of course, broiled or grilled depending on the season. Leaf lettuce, to wrap the meat with. Bowls of garlicky clam broth with miso and tofu and fresh spinach. Shavings of cod dusted in flour and then dipped in egg wash and fried. Glass noodles with onions and shiitake. Scallion-and-hot-pepper pancakes. Chilled steamed shrimp. Seasoned salads of bean sprouts, spinach, and white radish. Crispy squares of seaweed. Steamed rice with barley and red beans. Homemade kimchi. It was all there—the old flavors I knew, the beautiful salt, the sweet, the excellent taste.

After the meal, my father and I talked about school, but of course I could never say enough for it to make any sense. My father would often recall his high-school principal, who had gone to England to study the methods and traditions of the public schools, and regaled students with stories of the great Eton man. My mother sat with us, paring fruit, not saying a word but taking everything in. When it was time to go to bed, my father said good night first. I usually watched television until the early morning. My mother would sit with me for an hour or two, perhaps until she was accustomed to me again, and only then would she kiss me and head upstairs to sleep.

During the following days, it was always the cooking that started our conversations. She'd hold an inquest over the cold leftovers we ate a lunch, discussing each dish in terms of its balance of flavors or what might have been prepared differently. But mostly I begged her to leave the dishes alone. I wish I had paid more attention. After her death, when my father and I were the only ones left in the house, drifting through the rooms like ghosts, I sometimes tried to make that meal for him. Though it was too much for two, I made each dish anyway, taking as much care as I could. But nothing turned out quite right—not the color, not the smell. At the table, neither of us said much of anything. And we had to eat the food for days.

I remember washing rice in the kitchen one day, and my mother saying in English, from her usual seat, "I made a big mistake."

"About Exeter?"

"Yes. I made a big mistake. You should be with us for that time. I should never let you go there."

"So why did you?" I said.

"Because I didn't know I was going to die."

I let her words pass. For the first time in her life, she was letting herself speak her full mind, so what else could I do?

"But you know what?" she spoke up. "It was better for you. If you stayed home, you would not like me so much now."

I suggested that maybe I would like her even more.

She shook her head. "Impossible."

Sometimes I still think about what she said, about having made a mistake. I would have left home for college, that was never in doubt, but those years I was away at boarding school grew more precious to her as her illness progressed. After many months of exhaustion and pain and the haze of the drugs, I thought that her mind was beginning to fade, for more and more it seemed that she was seeing me again as her fifteen-year-old boy, the one she had dropped off in New Hampshire on a cloudy September afternoon.

I remember the first person I met, another new student, named Zack, who walked to the welcome picnic with me. I had planned to eat with my parents—my mother had brought a coolerful of food even that first day—but I learned of the cookout and told her that I should probably go. I wanted to go, of course. I was excited, and no doubt fearful and nervous, and I must have thought I was only thinking ahead. She agreed wholeheartedly, saying I certainly should. I walked them to the car, and perhaps I hugged them, before saying goodbye. One day, after she died, my father told me what happened on the long drive home to Syracuse.

He was driving the car, looking straight ahead. Traffic was light on the Massachusetts Turnpike, and the sky was nearly dark. They had driven for more than two hours and had not yet spoken a word. He then heard a strange sound from her, a kind of muffled chewing noise, as if something inside her were grinding its way out.

"So, what's the matter?" he said, trying to keep an edge to his voice.

She looked at him with her ashen face and she burst into tears. He began to cry himself, and pulled the car over onto the narrow shoulder of the turnpike, where they stayed for the next half hour or so, the blank-faced cars droning by them in the cold, onrushing night.

Every once in a while, when I think of her, I'm driving alone somewhere on the highway. In the twilight, I see their car off to the side, a blue Olds coupe with a landau top, and as I pass them by I look back in the mirror and I see them again, the two figures huddling together in the front seat. Are they sleeping? Or kissing? Are they all right?

PART 3

Factual Reporting

Suggested Writing Projects

In college, and in most professions, you'll be called upon repeatedly to report your observations with detailed accuracy, to explain information, events, problems, experiments, or new concepts, and usually to evaluate your findings with as much objective reasoning as possible. In a biology class, you might be required to report the exact conditions and results of an experiment on epithelial cells. In sociology, you might be asked to report the step-by-step procedures used in investigating the effect of poverty on children's reading skills and to draw reasoned inferences from the evidence you've gathered. A management course might require you to investigate and evaluate two new software products for accounting and to report on which would be the most efficient. You can imagine how these same assignments might occur in professional careers as well.

Reporting uses many of the same strategies covered in earlier chapters: precise observation of details, the ability to select and organize material effectively and interestingly, the need to anticipate your audience's expectations, to find an appropriate voice, and more. But reporting and evaluating are significantly different because the goal of these activities does not embrace your personal feelings. Although you'll still be searching for interesting points—sometimes using first-hand observation—you'll seldom include anecdotes or quirky elements of character. The focus now shifts to discovering and presenting information, to describing and characterizing events, problems, or issues, and sometimes, to exploring the values or ideas that underlie the focus of your report. Each of these acts constitutes a movement toward objective reasoning, which is what most of your college career will be about.

Here are suggestions for where you might begin:

- Write a report on a controversial issue at your university. Consider the latest changes in general education requirements, or the lack of parking, or new federal policies affecting financial aid. Controversy usually involves an element of change (desired or undesired), an element of contrast (past, present, future), and almost always, some type of consequence (people affected positively or negatively). Assume you are writing a report for your student council at the university. Report the facts as you find them, interview those in the know as well as those affected. You may still include sensory details, especially dialogue and description, but only as part of characterizing the problem itself. Avoid inserting your personal feelings, but at the end, draw a reasonable inference based on your findings, or evaluate the evidence you've presented.

- Write an essay in which you look at a problem, event, or issue by contrasting the emotions involved with the factual evidence—if there is any. This assignment will present you with additional difficulties. It requires you to separate fact from opinion, to sort out bias, to distinguish stereotypes or ideologies from hard evidence. Consider the argument for abandoning (or retaining) affirmative action as a consideration for admission to college or a move to allow marijuana to be legally prescribed for medicinal use. Or report on your college's policy toward sexual harassment and whether male students evaluate it in the same light as female students. These types of issues will require numerous interviews on campus, as well as research into the larger issue itself, either in magazines, newspapers, books, or on the Internet. Avoid inserting your own opinions, even though you are almost bound to have some. Attempt to reach a reasoned judgment or evaluation of your findings.

- Factual reporting might also include a profile of someone you've never met, one that reveals some unique or interesting characteristic. For this type of work, you may need to research your subject, conduct interviews, observe and select details, and then organize and synthesize it all into an interesting form. For some subjects—an artist who works in ceramics, a NASA engineer, a mortician, or perhaps the mortuary itself—you might need to research background material to better understand the subject, to acquire at least a modest amount of technical language, or to give yourself (and eventually your reader) an added perspective.

- Write a profile on someone you've met only recently or on someone who interests you: a journalist in your hometown who has uncovered corruption in the school system; the stylist who cuts your hair and rides a Harley on weekends; a student in your class who led a gay pride march the first week of the semester. For this project, you'll not only want to interview your subject, you'll also want to show your subject in action in the place he or she works or in his or her interactions with others. This may require following the subject for a few hours or a whole day, gathering details that reveal character.

Group Inquiry

In small groups, discuss some of the controversial issues on your campus. Make a list of those issues that might fall into "local campus" concerns and another list of those that might be considered issues in society at large. Select from each list one controversy that seems provocative and interesting. Review each of those conflicts as a group. If you disagree among yourselves about the issues, so much the better. Discuss who is affected by each issue, who might have the strongest opinions, who might best be interviewed to obtain evidence or opinions. Gain an overview of possibilities here, and consider using your lists—and your discussion—as starting points for seeking the facts.

CHAPTER 11

The Objective Eye

Someone once said, "There is no such thing as a true generalization, including this one," but we can come pretty close to a true generalization when we say that every writer must first be a reporter.

JOHN DEWHITT MCKEE

Reporting is an act of informing. Before you can inform others, however, you must discover the facts for yourself. To do this requires you to explore a subject in detail, using a variety of methods. Many of the strategies you'll want to use have been introduced in earlier chapters. You'll want to continue exercising all your perceptive powers in a search for appropriate physical and environmental details, actions, background information, and reactions other individuals may have. You may find it necessary to interview an expert on your subject, or someone affected—positively or negatively—by the issue. And you'll often need to do field research, using your own observations and experience to advance your knowledge.

Each of these strategies must now be placed in a new context of objective reasoning, a concept many of my students seem to think implies something dreary and dull. Actually, it's quite the opposite. Only through continued use of your strongest imaginative powers will the search for factual details lead to insight and understanding—the ultimate goal. One of the best illustrations of this can be found in the experience of Charles Nicolle, a medical doctor in the early part of the twentieth century.

For thousands of years, no one understood how typhus spread. Some thought it spread by touch, others by air, still others speculated that typhus dropped from moon rays. Not until Charles Nicolle saw the relationship of several previously ignored facts did he discover the true carrier. All this happened when a typhoid epidemic struck Tunis in 1909. Nicolle noticed that patients already inside his hospital did not catch the disease from newly arrived victims. Nor did the nurses and doctors catch it. One day, in the act of stepping over a typhus victim who had collapsed on the hospital steps, Nicolle realized that something must be actually stopping the spread of typhus at the hospital doors. He traced procedures back to the admission process and found that new typhus victims were bathed and their clothing burned. The carrier obviously had to be something the patients carried on the outside of their bodies. Nicolle determined that it could be nothing but a flea.

> The fact that I had ignored this point, that all those who had been observing typhus from the beginnings of history . . . had failed to notice the incontrovertible and immediately fruitful solution of the method of transmission, had suddenly been revealed to me. I feel somewhat embarrassed about putting myself into the picture. If I do so, nevertheless, it is because I believe what happened to me is a very edifying and clear example. . . . I developed my observations with less timidity.

He developed his observations with less timidity. Perception of specific factual details that others had never bothered to investigate literally led to insight.

Heraclitus told us more than 2500 years ago:

> Men who wish to know about the world must learn it in its particular details.

Only by observing the details of a subject—and then only after observing them with imaginative concentration—does sight lead to fresh understanding or, more importantly, to discovery of new and previously unseen relationships. But there are many different ways of "observing." Charles Nicolle suspended his emotional reactions, ignored all previous opinions, and tried to see the facts—and their relationships—with an objective eye. The key word is *objective.*

In the first two units of this book, I have urged you to pursue sensory details to intensify awareness of yourself in relation to the world around you. The pursuit of objective detail requires the same type of concentrated effort and uses the same sense receptors: sight, hearing, taste, touch, and smell. But a search for factual detail requires a shift from emotional experience to reasoned experience, from an extension of emotional awareness to an extension of intellectual awareness.

Objectivity Versus Emotion

Objectivity requires the observation of phenomena uninfluenced by feelings. Now in reality, that's impossible. Feeling always comes first. We are human beings after all, and it is impossible for us to be totally objective. Our family background, our culture, our ethnic makeup, our economic status, the books we've read, and movies we've seen all influence our perception. Even scientists recognize that how we see reality is shaped to a great extent by how we have been trained to see reality. We are saturated with opinions, stereotypes, culturally implanted values, and enculturated beliefs about the nature of the world. But there is an equally important truth here: We do not have to be limited to those previously shaped sets of perception. As human beings, we have the power to retrain ourselves by understanding how all these operative factors influence us. In acquiring such an understanding, we cannot eliminate bias and emotion, but we can compensate for it.

The first step is understanding that we can adopt a *stance of objectivity,* one in which we consciously attempt to eliminate emotional influences and biases. This is the stance taken by Charles Nicolle. He first eliminated what others had thought and felt about typhus, then set out to observe as best he could what was happening factually, objectively, in front of his eyes.

Here are three examples of how the process works:

Subjective observation	**Objective observation**
That's a beautiful sunset.	The sunset has streaks of yellow and lavender in it.
This fried chicken tastes terrible.	This fried chicken has a burned, metallic taste.
Tiger Woods wears Nikes so they must be good.	Tiger Woods wears Nikes.

If all life were this simple, the distinction between objective and subjective observation would also be simple. Unfortunately, emotion may be subtle and may influence observation without our knowledge.

Abortion is murder	**Abortion is the removal of a fetus from a woman's womb**
(Here, an implied judgment based on some deep inner belief—on some inner feeling about what is good and what is evil—may cause the observation to *seem* like an objective fact to the observer, but the term *murder* has such negative connotations that we should be immediately alert to a subjective intrusion.)	(Here, a simple desription retains objectivity because no judgment about good or evil and no hidden emotion apparently influence the observation. The connotations are neutral.)

Industry has poisoned our air and water

(This observer may believe he or she has stated an objective fact, but again the connotations suggest a negative emotion underlying the observation.)

Industry has often disposed of its waste material and by-products through the air and water

(Without the word *poisoned,* the observation seems more readily acceptable as objective fact—no negative feelings intrude. The modifier *often* also qualifies the statement.)

The various emotional influences in our lives and how they affect observation and judgment can be a complex subject. The problem will be explored more fully in the later chapter on critical thinking in Part 6. In the meantime, two common forms of *subjective* influences need to be understood now.

Inference and Opinion

While walking across campus this morning, I noticed a student who wore shoes but no socks. Such a sight might have disgusted me, and I might have inferred that the student was lazy or dirty, or I might have felt sorry for him and inferred that he was poor, or I might have laughed and inferred that he was following the latest fad. A *fact* is a quality that can be verified by a second observer. A second person could easily have verified that the student I saw wore no socks. But an *inference* is a conclusion drawn from the fact. Inferences may be logical and true. Or, as my examples here show, an inference may be influenced by emotion; my disgust, my pity, my laughter, could each lead me to interpret the objective fact differently. *An inference is not a fact.* A second observer cannot verify which, if any, of my conclusions might be true. The first step in removing emotional elements from my observations is to suspend judgment, to withhold inference, until I am in possession of more facts.

As a beginning writer, you may observe facts accurately; but because of this confusion between fact and inference, you may report the inference (the judgment) as if it were the fact. Here is what one student wrote when sent out to interview a local official.

> The warden was unhappy when the noon whistle drowned out his conversation.

The student insisted this was a fact. Yet the term *unhappy* is an inference drawn from concrete details that the student observed with his senses but that he has not reported to the reader. Perhaps the warden stopped talking in midsentence and held his breath until his face turned red, or perhaps he chewed on his lower lip and pounded the table with his pistol butt until the whistle stopped blowing. Any or all of these concrete details may have led the student to infer that the warden was "unhappy." The student's judgment may have been accurate. But the facts, the concrete details, should have been presented to us so that, in our role as readers, we could also function as the second observer.

Here is another student, reporting on how college women feel about changing their last names after marriage:

> I surveyed one hundred and eleven women in Howard Hall. Forty-seven indicated that they desired to retain the use of their own names after marriage. Thirty-one desired to use a hyphenated version of their maiden name with that of their future husband, such as Smith-Jones or Harrison-Williams. The remaining thirty-three women had obviously not had their consciousness raised since they desired to exchange their names for their husbands'.

The first three sentences can be accepted as fact. A survey has been taken, and a specific number of answers has been collected. A second observer could verify the information. But to infer that the first two groups of women have a higher degree of consciousness is unwarranted. No information has been given as to why any of the women offered the answers they did. Individuals in the third group might have varying reasons for adopting their husbands' names—religious, legal, or traditional. Some of them might even have last names they dislike, such as Zarlostowhimp.

Although somewhat different from an inference, an *opinion* raises a similar problem. In an older, legal sense, an opinion represents a judgment based on available data and logical argument, as in "The judge delivered the court's opinion on the Harris case." But more current and popular use of the term reduces opinion to personal taste. "Henrique loves jazz." "Ann Marie thinks ankle-length skirts are ugly." Such opinions cannot be substantiated by another observer because they deal not so much with the thing observed as with personal feelings. In the most extreme use of the term, an opinion may not be drawn from any objective evidence at all, as in "I feel sure life exists in many galaxies besides our own" or "People are, by nature, loving and good." Although such opinions may be held with confidence, they're based on speculation or intuition, not on verifiable, objective facts. Yet because opinions, like inferences, are expressed as conclusions—as judgments—they often sound more forceful and convincing than facts.

- People who want gun control are un-American.
- Acid rain is a hoax created by environmentalists.

Such bold, declarative statements are simplistic and easy to grasp. An opinion stated or held with conviction uses language itself to obscure our perceptions, to make us think no more seeking of fact is necessary because we supposedly already possess the truth.

If you are to train yourself in objectifying perception, you must be aware of the difference between a fact observed, an inference drawn from it, and an opinion expressed about it.

Objective Fact	Inference or Opinion
Toadstools are growing in the forest today.	It must have rained last night. I think toadstools are pretty. The soil there is probably rich in humus.
Rembrandt once painted a picture only three inches by five inches.	Small paintings sell for much less. He was too poor to afford a large canvas. Rembrandt was the world's greatest painter.
The stock market fell fourteen points in April.	The stock market is for gambling fools. Investors are afraid of inflation. Now's the time to buy stock.

Objectivity and Abstraction

Finally, I've found that some students confuse being objective with being abstract. These qualities are not related. Objectivity is an attitude of the mind. It is a way of approaching a subject. The subject itself may be concrete (a scientist looks objectively at a very tangible frog; a medical doctor looks objectively at the specific colorations and flesh tone of his or her patient), or the subject may be general and abstract (a philosopher attempts to study the question of justice by withholding all personal bias; a sociologist studies the relationship between poverty and behavior by quantifying the data). To be objective does not require you to be abstract *or* concrete. It requires you to perceive the subject—whatever it is—with as little intrusion of your emotion as possible.

Training ourselves to observe and report with an objective attitude provides excellent mental schooling; it sharpens powers of observation; it clarifies the separation between self and non-self, strengthening the ability to think and argue with finer distinctions; and it improves linguistic awareness, helping us to recognize how language itself may influence observation and judgment. A sound objective stance continues to require all our sensory and perceptive powers.

Exercises

1. In the following conversation, identify which observations are influenced by emotion and which might be considered factual—that is, which could be verified by a second observer.

Bob: That drunk almost hit me.

Mary: What drunk?

Bob: The one in that weaving car. He drove right up over the curb and I had to leap out of the way.

Mary: What did he look like?

Bob: A big ugly guy. He was aiming at me. You could see in his eyes he wanted to kill someone.

Mary: The car had a license from Montana.

Bob: It was some cowboy who's never been in the city before.

Mary: Are you all right now? Your face looks pale.

Bob: I'm OK. I just don't like drunken cowboys.

Mary: I read in the paper that there are still 15,000 people who make their living as cowboys.

Bob: Boy! Are you gullible! Not everything in the paper is fact, you know.

2. Here is a statement containing both opinions and inferences. Rewrite it so that the same information is conveyed as objectively as possible.

   Grade-point averages are higher today than twenty years ago, but the fact is that kids aren't smarter; teachers are just easier. Twenty years ago, a C was considered a good grade in college. The average grade was 2.2 on a 4-point scale. Today anybody who goes to class can get a B. The average grade across the country is 3.7. Over 90 percent of the Harvard class of 1996 graduated with honors, which proves how low the standards have fallen. One report from the U.S. Office of Education stated that teachers blamed grade inflation on the Vietnam War. A lot of cowards who didn't want to fight for their country hid out in college and as long as they got good grades, they draft-deferred. But once the teachers started giving grades for reasons other than performance, there was no more objective standard to judge by, so everyone had to get A's.

3. Your instructor will select a particular incident or topic currently in the news. Your job is to find at least three news reports on it in your local newspaper or in news magazines such as *Time, Newsweek,* and *U.S. News & World Report.* How objective is each report? Underline all signs of emotion, opinion, or inference. Are opinions attributed to a source or presented as *if* they were objective? Consider whether even verifiable facts are slanted; that is, are they preselected or heightened to affect the reader in a calculated way? After carefully considering your findings, bring your material to class for discussion.

4. Study the photograph by Dorothea Lange. Based on the specific details portrayed in the photograph, draw a reasonable inference about what is happening. Now write a brief paragraph that begins with your inference and is then supported by a description of the photograph that can be verified by a second observer. Compare your paragraph with those written by others in your class. Were your inferences the same? Can more than one inference be supported by the same data?

Practice

Choose any early entry that you have written subjectively—one that you have deep personal feelings about—and write about it again objectively. Give no opinions; avoid all emotionally charged words. Present only facts that could be verified by a second observer.

Group Inquiry

Along with others in your peer group, take a notebook to a student meeting, a campus concert, or a large lecture or presentation where questions may be asked afterward. Pretend you are a journalist, and take notes on a single important incident. Do not discuss your choice with your peer group. Afterward, write up a rough draft of your notes. Avoid inserting your own opinions. Try to select the most interesting facts. From the facts you have observed and presented, draw what seems to be a reasonable inference. Now read your rough draft to your peer group, and compare it with the rough drafts of others. Did all group members select the same incident as "most important"? Did all members see it in the same way? Were all of you objective in your presentation? What kinds of difficulties are revealed here about observing and writing "objectively"?

CHAPTER 12

Finding and Selecting Facts

Until a few years ago I thought my job was complete once I had advised students to pursue facts objectively, once I'd established the proper "attitude." What more could I do? That the writer also needed to select only the most important facts about a subject was self-evident. How the writer was to separate the significant from the insignificant seemed more mysterious—something I could explain only by the words *intuition* or *experience.* Then I had the opportunity of spending several days with a reporter for a large city newspaper. I hurried after him through the corridors of a state government office as he pursued a story on alleged payoffs to several low-ranking bureaucrats. I stood to one side while he researched dusty files and ledgers. I watched in amazement as he flirted with secretaries, all the while drawing out fragments of information. I waited outside closed doors while he interviewed officials. As it turned out, no evidence for payoffs could be found. For my friend the story was a dead end, but for me it had been a revelation.

The 4 *C*'s of Observation

A reporter knows a great deal about how to seek and find facts that could benefit any writer in any career. Reporters know, for example, that whatever story they write has to be interesting because it has to sell papers, and to make it interesting, they need to search out facts that affect the largest number of readers. They know that details with the most impact tend to be found by training the mind to look for certain aspects of a subject that I've grouped under four headings: *change, conflict, consequence,* and *characterization.* Although my friend would wince to hear his methods so labeled, I've come to call them the 4 *C*'s of observation. They are guidelines only. Any subject may suggest its own unique approach, and audience requirements may place restrictions on any writer. But the 4 C's provide an effective *starting point* for developing an eye for factual observation.

Change

Events, ideas, values, and social customs can all be studied according to how they are changing (or sometimes failing to change). Here is how sophomore Larry Kinde approached the subject of childbirth.

> At the center of the delivery room was a soft, padded chair, something like a dentist's chair, only angled more, so that a woman in it would have been half-reclining, half-standing. Toward the bottom of the chair were stirrup-like contraptions for the woman's legs to rest in. The room was painted a soft blue and there was even a speaker on the wall for music. Where was the white sterility of the old-fashioned delivery room? Where was the flat table with leather straps that held the woman down? Where were the bright overhead lights?

We could study childbirth delivery rooms for many qualities other than change. But in this case change was the key element for entry into the subject. It provided the focus for selecting important facts about new developments, and even though Kinde's report is objective, there is nothing dull about it. The focus on change stimulates interest in the subject.

Conflict

People clash and so do ideas. Republicans battle Democrats; psychotherapists disagree with behaviorists; environmentalists fight industrialists. Forces in opposition provide a natural focal point around which a writer can approach a subject.

> . . . a basic contention developed from the whole philosophy behind prisons. Those who guard and manage the prison tend to believe that its function is to punish the prisoners. Those who counsel and serve as probation officers tend to believe that a prison should reform the prisoners. Both sides were able to provide me with statistics and facts supporting their position.

This student writer has stepped into the middle of controversy. Almost every issue or event stimulates an opposing view. Contrast, conflict, contradiction, and opposition are not only eternally interesting to readers, they also provide natural ways of selecting, shaping, and organizing factual information. Looking for conflict in every subject should become habitual as you develop a reporter's eye.

Consequence

Interesting facts are useful. Significant facts are vital. To find the significance in a subject, a writer must look for facts that have the most impact and consequence on the people directly involved. Here is how a student reporter for a college newspaper zeroed in on the consequences of an action:

> The faculty voted Wednesday to change from a "course system" meeting four days a week for an hour per day, to a "credit-hour system," meeting on Monday, Wednesday, and Friday for an hour a day. The majority of the faculty argued that the credit-hour system was used by most colleges and that we were out of step.
>
> However, it could also be considered that while faculty members would teach a lighter load under the credit-hour system, students would need to take five courses per semester instead of four in order to graduate in the same number of years.

On the surface, a change in the organization of credits and class hours is being carried out to increase conformity with other colleges. Those are the facts. But the significance is revealed only by questioning the consequences of those facts: Students will need to carry more courses per semester; instructors will teach fewer hours. Actions, ideas, events—all produce consequences. To describe the action, idea, or event objectively is important. By asking whom the consequences affect, the writer begins to focus his or her attention on what is most significant.

Characterization

In an earlier chapter, I described a number of ways for selecting details that would characterize a person. Because ideas, values, and issues seldom exist or have interest for us apart from the human beings whose lives are affected by them, knowing how to bring people—character—into almost any essay or report can increase the impact it has on the audience. But "characterization" has a larger potential: The same techniques that bring people alive on the page of a novel can be applied as guidelines for selecting details from other types of subjects. If you wanted to report on a business operation in the Bahamas, for example, or on current developments in nuclear reactors, you could look for the same categories you sought out in characterizing your grandfather: *physical details, actions, background, speech, environment,* and *others' reactions.* To characterize is to give a full, rounded view of a subject. Here is how Kathleen Mills characterized the physical education facilities at her high school:

Physical details	The gymnasium was drafty and cold. The old wooden floor had splinters in it and the windows at either end were broken out and boarded over. Lockers had no
Others' reactions	locks; the showers had only cold water. The basketball team from North High refused to dress in our locker rooms. They dressed on their bus and their
Speech	their coach was quoted as saying, "It was nothing personal." The students at Jefferson were part of
Actions	the problem. They had torn out the toilets two years before after losing a game. They ripped locker doors
A self-created environment	off the hinges. Three times during the four years I attended, the local PTA tried to raise funds for
Actions	restoring and painting but the neighborhood had
Background	deteriorated since the 1980s. Some apartments were empty and boarded up. A large percentage of the population was on welfare. The tax base no longer supported the school, we were told, and the remaining residents would no longer support the PTA.
Action	Finally, in my senior year, ten seniors took to the school board a petition signed by over two hundred students. They demanded better facilities. The school
Lack of action	board promised to look into the situation but nothing was ever done.

Using the 4 *C*'s of observation offers no guarantee you'll find the most important factual details in every subject, but if you encounter a subject you don't know how to write about or if you don't know how to begin a report, ask yourself the following:

1. Is there an element of *change*? Is it the most interesting or important point in the subject?
2. Does any element of the subject involve *conflict* or *contradiction*? Could the best details be organized around one of those categories?
3. What quality about the subject has led to significant *consequences*? To whom or to what aspect of the subject are the consequences important? Whose lives are affected?
4. How could this subject be *characterized*? Which of the elements of characterization seem most consequential? (physical description? action? background? speech?) Is a full, rounded view of the subject what the reader needs or expects?

Obtaining Facts from Others

Relying solely on personal experience suggests obvious inadequacies: We cannot be in all places at once; we cannot always separate our emotions from the facts observed; we cannot be experts in all subjects. Others' views are necessary to formulating an objective and balanced understanding of a subject. In careers outside the academic world, writing often depends on interviewing as a major source of information. Historians talk to those who were there; biographers talk to those who remember; technical writers talk to engineers; medical writers talk to researchers. Even within the university, a student of political science, social work, anthropology, psychology, or sociology will recognize that significant amounts of data, almost all in many cases, are derived from surveys or interviews. An interview often provides information unobtainable from any other source, and it offers the writer a natural way to introduce human interest—and a human voice—into an otherwise objective report.

Preparing

Almost everyone agrees that the more you already know about a subject, the better you can question someone else on it. The first step in interviewing begins with research into whatever subject you're investigating—the university parking problem, the success or failure of the anti-schoolbook committee in your locality, the farm crisis—it really doesn't matter. You need background details. If it's a campus controversy, begin with back issues of the student newspaper. If it's a local or national topic, search through city newspapers or national news magazines. Know as much as possible before you begin the interview, not to show off, but to seem reasonably well-informed and intelligent—and to make your questions more substantive.

The second step is to ensure a positive reception for the interview. Don't just "drop by." Make an appointment. Tell the person you want to interview what your subject is, why you want the interview, why you think he or she can be indispensable in helping you, and how much time you will need (fifteen minutes to half an hour is usually enough). All this is only courtesy. It makes you seem levelheaded and professional.

Third, before you go, create a list of five to ten questions. Be prepared, of course, to follow up new points or unexpected answers that arise during the conversation. Your prepared questions are only a guide, not something to stick to religiously.

Questioning

The value of the information acquired in an interview is determined in part by the type of question you ask. Avoid the question that requires only a yes-or-no answer.

- Do you believe we ought to have a better campus police force?

Such questions might be valid for a survey, but you want more depth from a personal interview. Always prepare a number of questions in advance based on what you already know and on what you need to know.

- Thirteen rapes were reported on the State University campus last year. What kind of problem do we face here?

- Recently a number of letters to the editor in the campus paper have complained about theft in the dormitories. Do you think the problem is "out of control," as one letter writer suggested?

The phrasing of each question is vital. If you reveal bias or seem to be attacking the person you are interviewing, you may bring the interview to an abrupt end.

- Campus security is obviously inadequate. What are you going to do about it?

The shape of such a question, the emotional tone, inhibits a free exchange of information. Take time in advance to compose wording that makes each question seem open-minded, fair, and objective.

- What measures are being taken to improve campus security, or do you feel current procedures are working effectively?

Follow up answers by asking for supporting facts or concrete examples.

- Can you give me statistics on that? Exactly how many cases of theft were reported to your office last year? Are records available to show whether crime on campus has increased or decreased?

Listening

Most professionals insist that learning how to listen is the most vital element in an interview. A good interview must flow like a good conversation. If you merely read off that prepared list of questions, or if you fail to follow up on answers, you might as well conduct the interview by mail. Here is the wrong way to go about it:

Question: Do you feel America has an evenhanded policy toward China?

Answer: We've had one of the most biased and misguided policies that could have been devised.

Question: How important is Saudi Arabian oil?

The second question ignores the previous answer. The person interviewed can only assume you haven't listened or that you're not genuinely interested. Future answers will become more perfunctory. You'll probably find it more helpful to repeat the central point of an answer (this helps you remember it while making clear to the person interviewed that you're listening) and then to ask for further clarification or explanation.

Follow-up Question: You say "biased and misguided." Could we look at each of these points separately? In what way has American policy been biased? In whose favor? And why?

Now you've engaged in a dialogue. Perceiving that you're alert and interested, the person being interviewed will freely expand on his or her ideas.

A dialogue, however, does not mean you should take sides. Even if you personally disagree or find a flaw in what you're hearing, avoid a direct argument.

- But you're contradicting yourself now. You don't have a single fact to prove your point.

Instead, phrase your follow-up in such a way that you press hard for the answer but seem to be attributing your aggressiveness or disagreement to what others might say when they read your report.

- I wonder if others would see this as a contradiction to a point you made earlier?

- Could you give me any evidence to support that point?

Listen intently. Follow up. Train your ear to select important facts from others' observations in the same way you train your eye to observe minute details from personal experience.

Taking Notes

Although you should feel perfectly comfortable taking notes during the interview, it can sometimes prove best to avoid writing notes until *after* the interview. Except for a few direct quotations when actual wording is important, plan to write the rest from memory. After all, most of any interview will be summarized, and what you really want is the essence of someone's view on your subject, not the whole of it. During the interview, select only a few important or colorful quotations to record. Then immediately afterward—in the hall, in the park across the street, on the bus going home—write out the whole interview. Use the techniques practiced in earlier assignments: Describe the place of the interview, the light, smells, and sounds. Show the character, the physical details, speech patterns, actions. Put all of it into a scene. Leave yourself out of it for the most part. Focus instead on the opinions, ideas, and attitudes of the person interviewed. Blend in the specific quotations you wrote during the interview. Summarize the rest in your own words. Be fair and honest. Present the person's position objectively and accurately.

Now you have *complete* notes, even if scrawled roughly in pencil. From them you will probably select only a small portion to use in your final essay, but the full record is down on paper, far more thoroughly than a tape recorder could have captured it. Even better, in the act of writing down a complete record of the interview, your mind will select, organize, and evaluate all that you saw and heard. The act of writing stimulates the act of evaluating.

Evaluating

Just as you cannot always separate your own emotions from external facts, neither can others. You must assume that many answers you hear will reflect some degree of self-interest or bias. It will always be your job, both during and after an interview, to distinguish facts from opinions or inferences. You must ask yourself: Does this answer show a hidden emotional element? What are the consequences of such an answer? Am I hearing an opinion or a verifiable fact?

Opinions may form a part of any objective report so long as they are attributed to your source ("Dr. Harrison believes . . ." "Captain Miller thinks . . .") and do not derive from your own bias. For some subjects, opinions may be as important as the facts themselves. But any interview that tends to be opinionated should be balanced with an interview providing another side of the issue. You have no control over others' opinions, but you must demonstrate your own objectivity by presenting a balanced and fair report that includes equal representation of every point of view.

Learning how to obtain information from others extends your range of observation. Combined with the 4-*C*'s approach, it provides you with a tool for moving outside the limitations of personal feelings and personal experience—as you must if you are to begin to explore and write about the world you live in.

Profiling

Writing a profile requires all the techniques I've just discussed and more. Even if you already know the person you want to focus on, you'll need to conduct at least one or more interviews, visit the individual in his or her most characteristic place (the kitchen of a beanery, the inside of a police car, the newsroom of a local TV studio), and in some cases, do library research to gather ideas, information, or background on the individual's occupation or life.

Anthropologists, historians, journalists, sociologists, folklorists, and many others know the importance of immersing oneself, at least temporarily, in the daily life of individuals who make up a small part of a larger, more complex culture. Studying people as they act in the natural course of their ordinary lives—through extended observation and the recording of their words—offers the opportunity for exploring culture on the micro level. Scholars refer to this kind of research as *fieldwork,* an activity that takes you into the community for direct contact, observation, and understanding. Fieldwork involves collecting raw material, recording it, and then using that material to reach an insight into the actual conditions, attitudes, and values of the individual studied. A telephone call or e-mail may provide you with some additional follow-up information, but neither of these will provide the rich information derived from a face-to-face, person-to-person interview.

Preparation

You may already have in mind the perfect individual to write about. Perhaps your grandmother came from Russia and bakes a traditional family dish each Christmas. Maybe your retired neighbor brews beer or spent his life repairing cable cars in San Francisco. Perhaps you know someone who works with victims of rape or sexual abuse. Young teenagers could speak to drugs or sexual pressures in middle schools, individuals standing in an employment line might be willing to talk about losing their jobs.

Begin by preparing a rough list of possible subjects. Share your ideas with others in class. Your peer group or other students might serve as good judges for testing the possibilities, or they may offer some leads to possible subjects.

Once you've chosen a subject, you'll want to do a "pre-interview" by telephone, well in advance of the actual interview, explaining carefully what you are doing and why. Honesty here is important. If you plan to use a tape recorder, you'll need consent. Some people may not want their stories recorded or written about. Others may not be available. Still others may find talking into a tape recorder inhibiting. Helping your subject understand the project, the type of questions you'll probably ask, and the uses to which the information will be put—all this can give your subjects assurance and confidence. In the long run, if you've done some preparatory work, the individual you choose will be more likely to speak easily and candidly with you, the information will be more detailed and the project more rewarding.

Finally, you'll want to make a broad list of prepared questions, ideas that can help you get started: *I wonder if you could tell me what it's like to work in the emergency ward,* or, *How did you get started as an oil worker,* or, *What it was like growing up in South Africa?* Continue your list with follow-up questions: work related, personal, biographical, or value oriented. During the actual interview, be flexible. Use the list to jog your memory about ideas you might want to pursue or to pick up the slack if an uncomfortable pause occurs. Prepare yourself well so that you can spend more time listening than looking at your notes. If you listen closely, each answer you hear may be enough to trigger more questions, ones that grow specifically out of the conversation you're having, rather than artificially from notes.

Fieldwork

For the actual fieldwork, you'll need a pen and notebook—and usually a small tape recorder. Even though you may not use all of it, a sixty-minute cassette is probably best. It will give you plenty of time for the unexpected: interruptions, planes flying overhead, a sudden fit of coughing. Expect the unexpected and you'll feel more relaxed throughout the interview. If you're not familiar with the tape recorder, practice with it first, taping your own voice or asking rehearsal questions of a roommate until you feel confident. Remember to ask permission before taping a conversation. Some individuals feel uncomfortable having their voices taped. In that case, listen carefully and rely on your pen and paper.

Most important, be flexible. Allow your subject to lead you into his or her world. The more interest you show—the more you follow up on the ideas, values, or emotions being expressed—the more the subject will usually offer. Avoid interruptions and avoid arguing, being judgmental, or confrontational. You're not required to agree or disagree with anything, only to gather information. Later, in your essay, you may want to insert your own perceptions, insights, and judgments; but during the interview, it's best to remain neutral. Above all, it is important to be courteous.

If it's not possible to take notes during the interview, write everything down as soon as possible afterward. Include details about the location, smells, sounds, and light. Record everything while it's fresh in your memory. Jot rough notes on how the individual looked, what clothing was worn, what gestures were made, and any other revealing details you observed.

Transcription

Transferring every word you hear on the tape to the written page may be the toughest part of the project. Every word should be captured verbatim. In general, you'll find it may take up to an hour to transcribe only ten minutes of tape. For that reason alone you should keep the interview short—no more than thirty minutes. Give yourself plenty of time for the transcription process. When you're finished, verify the accuracy of your transcription by simultaneously reading the typed copy while listening to the tape.

A written transcription of your tape is like saving a hard copy of something you've prepared on your computer. If something happens to one or the other, you'll still have a complete record.

Finding a Theme

When you write about a person or place from memory, personal experience guides and shapes the essay: Events will probably be told in the sequence they occurred. But a profile may require *reshaping* of your material around a dominant theme—perhaps the subject's hobby, quirky character, expertise, or values. Details unrelated to the theme will then be discarded. For example, if you are profiling a college faculty member because she has a passionate interest in researching sharks' bellies, details on her driving habits may not be related and should be omitted. However, if the faculty member tends to park on the sidewalks because she grows so passionate in discussing sharks' bellies that she becomes oblivious to everything around her, the detail would be essential. The theme will drive the essay and determine the kinds of details, actions, speech, and so on that you'll include. To find that theme, you may need to ask some important questions before you begin drafting.

- What was the most interesting point of the experience? The most unusual fact? The most dramatic event you were told about or observed?
- What was the dominant characteristic of the subject: energy? anger? a special talent? humor? passion?
- What one thing drives this person?
- What habits or quirks would seem most interesting to your reader (most intriguing, amazing, laughable)?
- What was the most humorous anecdote this person told?
- What contradictions or discrepancies showed up? How did others react to your subject?

Once you've picked a theme, the organization will usually follow a conventional essay form with an introduction (or lead: see Chapter 18), a description of the individual, physical details, gestures, actions, and elements of scene, all described in your own words. Edited excerpts of your transcribed interview would then be integrated into the essay as quotations. (See Chapter 15 for examples of integrating quotations taken during interviews.)

Reflection and Assessment

Reflecting on the material you've gathered will probably occur throughout the process. Without reflection, the profile is fairly meaningless. It isn't enough to collect information without assessing the meaning or value of what you've seen and heard. What have you learned? How might this person reveal something about our lives or the time in which we live? What is your final personal reaction? A conclusion doesn't need to be profound, but careful reflection should lead you to some understanding of the subjective beliefs, lifestyle, problems, or cultural values that are represented by this one individual—and perhaps show you how those might relate to society as a whole.

Group Inquiry

1. With others in your peer group, discuss how *change, conflict, consequence,* or *characterization* might be a way of finding the best factual details about the following. Which of the 4-*C*'s methods or which combination might be useful in investigating each topic?

   tuition increases
   the grading system at your college
   drinking or drugs on campus
   off-campus housing conditions
   censorship policy for the student newspaper
   parking regulations
   professional college athletes
   bookstore profits
   budget-cutting effects
   class attendance regulations
   coed dormitories
   campus security
   cafeteria food

2. With others in your peer group, make a list of people you might ask for information about three or four of the preceding topics.

Practice

In addition to your daily freewriting, challenge yourself to move outside your immediate self. Begin writing about broader issues.

1. Make a list of concerns you have now about problems on your campus—something you'd like to know more about. Perhaps you're annoyed by bookstore prices, by the limited availability of campus computers, or maybe a community issue has you worried. List your concerns in question form. Questioning often triggers more questions, more possibilities.

2. Select one issue from your list and begin writing about it spontaneously, voicing your concerns and your questions. What do you know about your subject? What do you need to find out about?

3. The first step in finding out is to ask someone who should be in a position to know. Think of anyone you might talk to who could provide more information.

   Before you talk to the person, create in your notebook an interview web to provide a quick visual reminder of what you need to know.

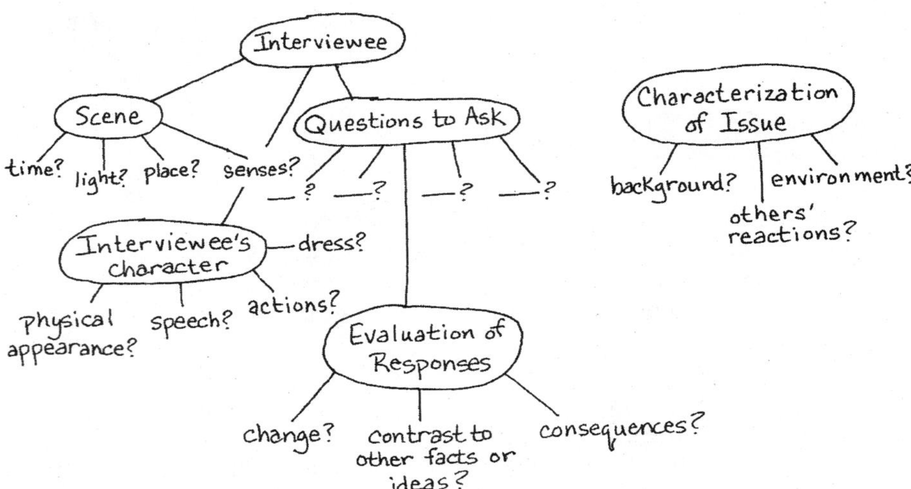

Take a notebook to the interview with you but don't fill it in until you've finished. Jot down material you want to quote and brief words and phrases that will jostle your memory later. Once you're back at your desk, and within an hour or so after the interview, fill in the web with specifics. Then write a rough draft of the interview in your notebook.

CHAPTER 13

Basic Forms in Factual Reporting

For most writers—not just beginning writers—finding the right order for the right content becomes a major stumbling block to success. To avoid the struggle and to save time, news reporters sometimes use a formula for organizing factual information. This formula gives them a ready form in which to shape their material. You should know it as well, because it is the simplest and easiest of all forms to learn and because it provides a natural starting point for objective reporting. It teaches you how to discipline facts, and it can be used for many other types of informative writing.

The 5-*W* Lead

As you develop your writing skills and become involved in complex interpretation and analysis of a subject, you will need to practice the art of creating an effective *thesis statement* (Chapter 23), but straight reporting of objective facts requires a simpler, although equally effective, type of introduction. Professional writers call it the *5-W lead.* A lead informs the reader of the five most important facts about the subject: *who, what, where, when,* and *why.* The facts may be organized in any sequence, according to which elements are most important.

The 5-*W* lead began as a journalistic device, and an experienced reporter can usually handle all five elements in the first sentence alone.

who ... *where* ... *when*
Sen. John McCain, R.-Arizona, said in Washington Saturday

what
he will introduce a major piece of legislation next week,

why
designed to upgrade parks, playgrounds, and other recreational areas in American cities.

where *when* *who* *what*
In Baltimore last week Sherry McCrystal, fifteen, broke the

why
world's chewing gum record just to win a ten-cent bet.

The 5-*W* lead groups and organizes information that might otherwise have appeared randomly throughout a news story. By shaping the material in this way, the reader receives all major facts immediately. Everything that follows the lead will support or elaborate on the major facts. But just as you probably don't plan to become a novelist who writes about character, you probably don't plan to become a journalist. How, then, does the 5-*W* lead apply to the type of writing you may be doing?

Here is how one student began a report for a sociology class:

who *where* *what*
A white, Anglo-Saxon Protestant in America is socially mobile

why
because achievement rather than background is the determining

who *what*
factor. For blacks and Jews, social mobility is restricted regardless

why
of achievement since color and religion are influencing factors.

By selecting all the important facts and organizing them according to the 5 *W*'s, the student has pulled together a surprisingly clear statement about her subject. The reader knows immediately what to expect in succeeding paragraphs—development or elaboration of details that support the statement and, depending on the type of report, perhaps an explanation of why such different patterns of social mobility exist.

Here is another example of the 5-*W* lead used for a political science course:

when *where* *who*
This morning at a Capitol Hill news conference, Senator Hillary Clinton (NY) joined

who *what*
Senators Edward M. Kennedy (MA) and Bill Frist (TN) in unveiling bipartisan plans

why
to combat bioterrorism.

This student has begun an informative essay by shaping his opening sentence around the most important facts. The reader is now prepared for succeeding paragraphs to provide evidence that supports the 5-*W* claim.

Even students of the humanities have found the 5-*W* lead effective. Here is how one sophomore began a report for a literature class.

> *where* *when* *who* *what*
> In *The Bell Jar,* first published in 1963, Sylvia Plath recounts the events of a young girl's twentieth year, her attempted suicide, and her struggle to avoid madness.

The 5-*W* lead is an all-around serviceable introduction for almost any kind of informative writing. It communicates the facts clearly and concisely. And because starting a first draft is often the point at which writers have the most difficulty, the 5-*W* lead offers a simple strategy for organizing information and getting the first sentence or first paragraph on the page.

Equally important, the lead can immediately suggest an organization for the rest of your report.

The Inverted Pyramid

Let's return one more time to how all this was developed by journalists. Because of the construction of space in a newspaper and because hurried readers often do not read to the end of a news story, the 5-*W* lead became a technique for presenting vital information as quickly as possible. But the nature of journalism also imposed another constriction on the reporter and predetermined the organization of remaining material. Until the final moments before a newspaper goes to press, neither the reporter nor the editor may know how much space is available for any one story. The writer must be prepared, then, for the editor literally to take scissors to a report (or more likely, to press the delete button on his or her word processor) so that it will fill the appropriate column. This means that all important supporting details must be presented early, followed by interesting details, and finally mere details. The editor can easily delete "mere" details without any great loss. The editor can even cut the story in half and remove the "interesting" details, still without damaging the important supporting information that follows the lead. The reporter has thus learned to envision the organization of his or her story in the form of an upside-down pyramid.

The technique is also used in laboratory and engineering reports as well as in formal business reports. A busy executive, for example, does not necessarily have time to read through twenty pages of details. The executive wants and needs to know important information immediately, at the beginning of the report. He or she does not want to be kept in suspense as to what it all means. But the inverted pyramid design also creates a problem because, by its nature, it fails to come to a conclusion. Other than in the field of journalism, few situations

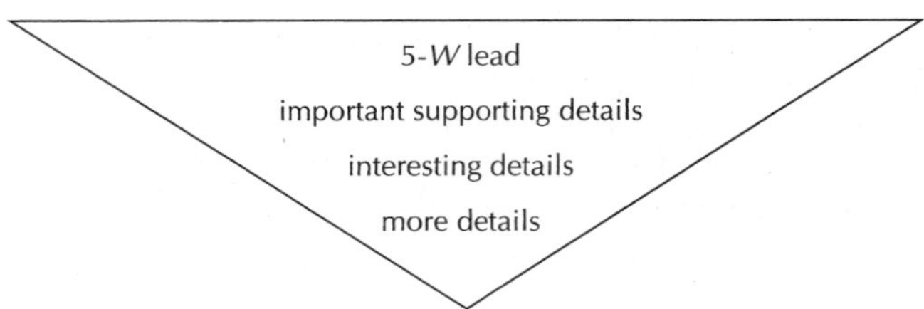

exist in which you will ever be allowed to drift off with "mere" details. On the assumption that you have engaged your intelligence with the subject at all, you will want to do more—and your reader will expect more. If nothing else, you must at least summarize your findings. Better, you must draw a reasonable inference from the facts you have gathered and come to a concluding generalization. Even the business executive will expect a final paragraph that at least restates or reinforces the 5-*W* lead. Here, then, is how three first-year students used such a form to organize a report assigned as part of a psychology class group project on teenage behavior. Louise Chappell, Cynthia Hall, and Kin Chang spent two weeks interviewing female students and campus medical personnel on condom use among college students. The following excerpts from their report illustrate the pattern.

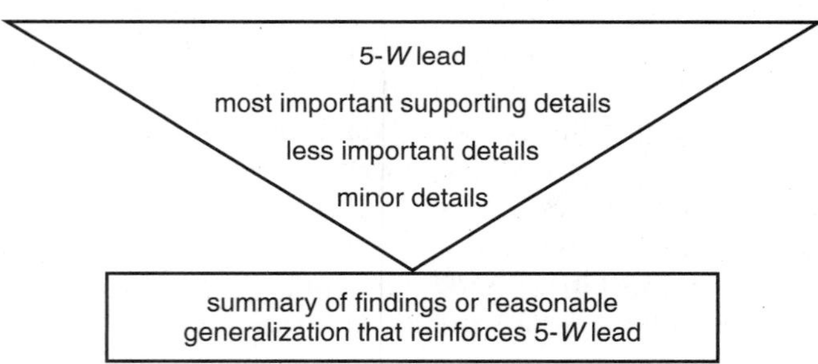

5-*W* lead

According to Tia Katz, Supervising Nurse at the University Medical Service, the distribution of condoms has increased 32 percent in the two years that condom machines have been available on campus, but the reported use of those condoms has changed little, in spite of the fact that one suspected case of the HIV virus has been identified among the student body. . . .

Most important supporting facts

We interviewed seven female students currently living in the residence halls, all of whom claimed to have had sexual relations within the past six months. Only two of the students reported the regular use of condoms. One claimed she "almost always" carried condoms with her (which she obtained on campus from the free vending machines). The other student indicated she requested the use of condoms from her partners.

Four other students reported that on no more than "one or two" occasions during the six-month period, had they either requested—or had their partner volunteered—the use of a condom. Of this group, none of the women obtained a condom in advance, relying on males to provide them. All four indicated they had in fact wanted their partners to use condoms, but each admitted that if the male was not in possession of one, it did not deter sexual activity.

One student, a sophomore, indicated she never carried or used condoms, and had never requested their use from a partner. . . .

Interesting details

Tia Katz indicates that national studies show college students obtain condoms from vending machines with good intentions, but then either fail to use them "because of embarrassment or the heat of the moment."

Least important

Condom machines on campus were requested by student government after two years of debate. . . .

Concluding generalizations

Our study seems to confirm the general national trend, at least among female students. College women are fully aware of the need for safe sex, and at least a majority would ideally like their partners to use condoms. But few make an effort on their own to obtain or provide condoms, and just as few request their partners to use them. As one student said, "They're awkward, they interrupt the moment, and no one has yet told me what I'm supposed to do while I wait. So I have to go on my instinct: If the guy seems nice enough, I just can't believe he'd have AIDS."

This most-important-to-least-important method of organizing is not the only pattern that can evolve from the 5-*W* lead. Any one element or combination of elements from the lead may form the focus of your organization. The lead for the student's paper on social mobility (p. 148), for example, might suggest that the *why* is the key question a reader would be interested in. The writer could supply supporting factual evidence to defend the lead, then move quickly into an interview with a sociologist on why such a social pattern exists. The lead might equally suggest that the report will be organized around the contrast between the two groups being discussed (in several later chapters I will develop the contrast design more fully). In turn, the lead for the student's political science paper (p. 148) implies that the what and why will be pursued: what the bipartisan plan is and why it is being created. In other words, the value of the 5-*W* lead lies in its potential for serving you and the reader with a concise, clear statement of your findings in the first sentence or paragraph and then in *suggesting* a possible organization to follow. The very act of looking for the 5-*W* lead in your material actually forces you to begin a process of discovering your purpose, selecting the most important facts, and organizing them concisely.

And Then There's *How*

I've left out a final but important element. To the 5 *W*'s reporters often add an *H*—for *how* an event happens, *how* an engine works, *how* the civil rights act was created, *how* the stock market reacts to interest rates. Obviously, a factual report for business, science, medicine, engineering, history—even advertising or a creative art—may be more concerned with *how* than almost any other approach to the subject. Yet because the "how" of something is often complex and detailed, it is seldom used as a lead. Instead, the lead may consist of some element of the 5 *W*'s plus the *H*.

> *what* *who*
> Industrial alcohol is produced by the Gehrneight Corporation for use
>
> *how*
> in antifreeze and industrial solvents. Through a process of fermentation, glucose and fructose (usually derived from cane sugar or beet-sugar molasses), alcohol, and carbon dioxide are created by a catalytic action of enzymes. The molasses is first distilled with water. . . .

And so on. The remainder of the report takes its own organic shape, that is, it follows the natural step-by-step process of *how* industrial alcohol is made. Chronological order, spatial order, and logical sequence, rather than a predetermined form, usually describes the organization of the report. Yet note that even when objectively describing *how* something works, or *how* it is created, or *how* it is accomplished, *what* happens, *when* and *where,* by *whom,* and *why* will often remain key elements.

The strategy of searching out 5 *W*'s and 1 *H* can therefore be one of the most valuable techniques you can train the mind to use. A word of caution, however: Your writing will quickly become dull if you use such formulas in everything. Be selective. When the subject–context–audience–purpose calls for a simple but factual presentation, the strategy will serve you well. Other audiences, other contexts, may be responsive only to fresher, more creative designs. Eugene O'Neill once said that "a man's work is in danger of deteriorating when he thinks he has found the best formula for doing it."

Exercises

1. Identify the 5 *W*'s in the following leads.

   A spokesman for the firefighter's union said Wednesday that negotiations with city hall have been broken off until the mayor is willing to be more flexible.

   Marketing conditions have remained unstable during the last six months because of inflationary pressures. The Federal Reserve Bank in Washington has increased prime interest rates three times. Investment conditions could not be worse.

   The English Advisory Board believes that current requirements in the English department are arbitrary and inflexible. A review of requirements at other colleges shows that students elsewhere have more opportunity to make selections from clusters of related-area courses.

   Professor Mike Kepple, chairperson of the chemistry department at Milligan College, has been elected chairperson of the National Honors Colloquium, to be held on the University of Southern California campus next fall.

2. Write three different 5-*W* leads based on the same set of facts.
   a. John Smith is director of public relations at Simkon Foundry.
   b. The foundry has decided to donate $5,000,000 to the United Appeal.
   c. United Appeal will divide the money among the Boy Scouts, the Children's Hospital, and Mothers for Peace.
   d. Bentley V. Cunningham is chairman of the board that made the decision.
   e. The stockholders voted last April on the issue.
   f. The vote passed by only 52 percent.
   g. Smith made the announcement public on Tuesday, August 7.
   h. Cunningham hopes the gift will create goodwill for the foundry.
   i. Simkon Foundry has been located in the city for twenty years.
   j. Claire Wilson, representative of a minority group of stockholders, spoke out against what she called a "giveaway" of stockholder profits.
   k. Cunningham personally delivered the check into the hands of Bennett Goodman, president of the United Appeal.

CHAPTER 14

Context, Purpose, and Voice

Unlike personal writing, for which you could expect a sympathetic audience, perhaps even a friendly audience that wants to share your feelings and experience, no such simple generalization can be made for informative writing. Too many variables exist. In certain situations, the audience for informative writing may want straightforward, no-nonsense facts. In other situations, your audience may appreciate a more informal voice, even a personal voice, while still reading for objective information. Everything depends on four interacting elements: the subject, the audience's needs, the context (or situation), and your own purpose.

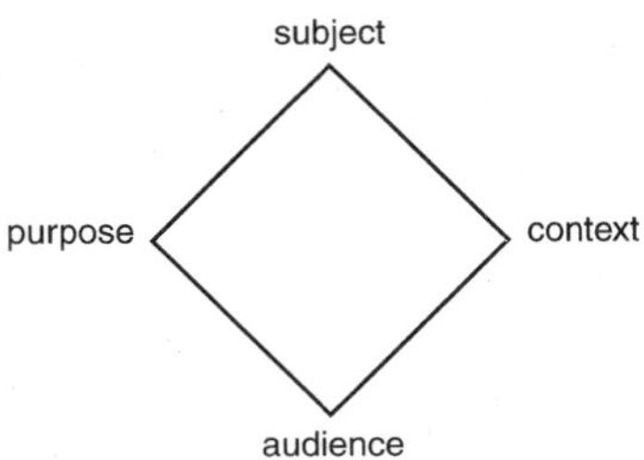

Most of the time these four factors are defined for you in advance. In college your instructor assigns an essay on the French Revolution (*subject*): your paper will be evaluated to determine how well you know the subject, and it will count as part of your final grade (*context*); your instructor alone will read it (*audience*); and in the process of investigating the subject, you determine which particular aspect you wish to explore and what you want to say about it (*purpose*). In the career world, a similar situation will usually influence your writing projects. Your supervisor will assign you to write a report on whether your company is meeting environmental regulations (*subject*); the report will be used by company officials to prepare for an upcoming federal inspection (*context*); your supervisor, the company vice president, and several government agents will read it (*audience*); and although the report must be accurate, it must also present the company's efforts in a positive light (*purpose*).

Once you make the leap from personal writing into more objective forms of writing, the demands on you increase rapidly. Yet this relationship of subject–audience–context–purpose does not necessarily make the act of writing as difficult as it may sound. In many cases, knowing the four points of influence actually simplifies your job by clearly defining what you need to write about and how you must approach it. All four points in combination also determine the voice and tone you will use. Because that voice can be significantly different from the voice you use in personal writing, we need to look at some of the options open to you.

Objective Reporting: The Formal Voice

The most objective writing is usually found in scientific work, where the voice must be formal and the tone objective. No element of your personality or inner feelings should be apparent. In scientific reporting, your audience will desire facts alone. Here is a report on Martian landing sites from *Scientific Results of the Viking Project:*

> Both sites are dominated by a variety of rocks among fine-grained material, and both have the brownish to orange color of the surface and the sky. Beyond this superficial similarity the sites are quite different in their appearance. The Chryse site topography is undulating and has a great range of rock size and type from rocks a few centimeters across to one nearby large rock almost 2 m across and others in the distance much larger. . . . No evidence of life has been found in the pictures at either site.

The tone here is factual and unemotional. The avoidance of either positive or negative connotations modulates the voice and creates a neutral effect. Even the last sentence shows no trace of personal emotion (although it may have stirred a feeling of regret in the scientists). Instead, we receive only a straightforward statement of observable fact—in this case, concrete, sensory details observed in a photograph.

The use of the pronoun *one* in place of *I* or *we* is sometimes associated with formal writing. The *one* creates a distance between writer and reader and may sometimes be necessary. But note that the NASA scientists who reported on the Viking Project avoided its use altogether. The use of *one* too often creates awkward sentences in which the pronoun tends to pile up in clusters that sound contrived. Here is how a university scholar misuses it in a book on poetry:

> When one begins writing poetry one tends to use language that convinces one that it is truly poetry that is being written. One uses a special voice . . .

Try reading such sentences aloud, and you find that the excessive repetition of *one* begins to feel like marbles in the mouth.

The use of *one* can be necessary at times, but it works best when it does not call attention to itself. Here is an objective report on Alaskan snow in which the *one* blends easily and unobtrusively:

> There are different kinds of snow. New-fallen snow yields almost silently underfoot. Midwinter snow is dry, and squeaks and crunches as one walks through it, while spring snow is tired and crackles as the crust resists, then breaks. Wind-driven snow is riffled like lace or like the whitecaps of the sea, and it sparkles with flashes of blue, yellow, orange, and green.

Tom Walker, writing in a book entitled *We Live in the Alaskan Bush,* has so skillfully blended the objective *one* into this passage that a reader might miss it entirely—which is what should happen.

Objective Reporting: The Informal Voice

In many situations, when context and audience are appropriate, the informal voice may be used quite successfully with objective writing. Naturally, the author must still avoid intrusion of personal feelings or emotions, but the notion that all objective writing must be dull is mistaken. The following is a report on the sloth bear from the *Audubon Society Book of Wild Animals:*

> Termites are a staple of the sloth bear (*Melurus ursinus*) of the Indian subcontinent and Sri Lanka, and to get at the insects this dim-sighted creature has evolved a snout that approximates a vacuum cleaner. The lips of the sloth bear are hairless and flexible and can be protruded like a tube a considerable distance from the mouth. The bear can close its nostrils whenever it wishes. After digging open a termite mound, the bear literally huffs and puffs to uncover and ingest its prey. Puckering its lips into a tube, with its nostrils shut to keep out dust, it blows away the loose dirt to expose the termites, then sucks them in, a process facilitated by a gap in its teeth resulting from the absence of two upper incisors.

Although the reporting here is objective—each fact can be verified by a second observer—the tone is lighter and more casual. The active verbs (more than ten in five sentences) and the humorous imagery (a snout like a vacuum cleaner, huffing and puffing, sucking termites between a gap in the teeth) make the writing lively and interesting. Yet no personal emotion, opinion, or bias appears. The Audubon Society has produced a book for informative reading but one meant to entertain at the same time. Context and purpose justify the informal voice.

Objective Reporting: The First Person

Writers for more popular magazines often use the first person while still reporting objective information. The admission that a human being is behind the observation tends, naturally, to create a more personal and informal tone. At one time, such reporting was avoided. Writers went to great lengths to objectify or disguise their presence, sometimes using such awkward phrases as "This reporter saw . . ." or "The writer has noticed that. . . ." Today the trend is toward an honest admission that the writer (using the pronoun *I*) exists as a person but that he or she also has the ability to report objectively. After all, the use of *one* or the neutral, objective tone in the scientific voice is only a subterfuge. A writer still is present. He or she is a human being, and because the writer has consciously selected some details to present while omitting others, we know that the writer's personal imagination is actively involved. Total objectivity is impossible.

Here, then, is how Jane Winslow Eliot reports for *The Atlantic* on winemaking in Spain in the 1930s:

> By the light of one candle I saw three men inside the vat. Their coats were off, their trousers rolled above the knees. They hung onto knotted ropes which were looped over the rafters, and, barefoot, they rhythmically stomped the slippery grapes. Sweating, faces distorted by candlelight, they shouted back and forth as friends came to watch. Fumes began to rise, and their footing became less sure, their laughter louder. A new basket of grapes was tipped into the vat. Twirling around and around, one man lost his grip. With a splash he fell into the richly reeking mash.

The concrete details make the scene rich and sensuous, perhaps even evoking emotion in the reader. Yet the writer herself injects no undue inferences or opinions. Eliot presents a verifiable report, but she uses a personal voice that candidly admits, "I was there, and I'm reporting what I saw." In a different context, of course, and for a different purpose and audience, this voice might be highly inappropriate. You must determine the subject–audience–context–purpose *before* you begin to write; otherwise, you will find yourself working in a vacuum and merely guessing or hoping that the way you treat your material will be successful.

Objective Reporting: The Authoritative Voice

Finally, no matter which of the "voices" you write with, solid reporting requires a tone of authority. The reader wants to know that the author feels confident about the facts, details, and information being presented. To feel confident, you must do your research well, and you must present your findings strongly and clearly—without being argumentative. Argument is often a valid approach for other types of essays, but the reporter wants the information to make the argument, factually and without appeal to an expression of emotion or bias. The tone should never be strident, never overbearing, but always quietly confident.

Exercises

1. Read each of the following selections. Then (a) identify the level of formality or informality, (b) describe a *context, purpose,* and *audience* for which each passage might be appropriate, and (c) describe a *context, purpose,* and *audience* for which the voice and tone would be highly inappropriate or less effective.

Some hermit crabs have developed a relationship with a group of anemones that benefits both creatures. Relations like these are called symbiotic relations. Once it has found a shell, the hermit crab finds a special kind of anemone that has tentacles which sting and irritate fish and other potential enemies. In some cases the anemone climbs on the hermit crab's shell and plants itself there. In other cases there seems to be some complex communication based on touch between the hermit crab and the anemone. They tap and touch each other, and the anemone then releases its grip on the rock it clings to and plants itself on the hermit crab's shell.

Judith and Herbert Kohl, *The View from the Oak*

The top of a maple leaf is dark green with green-yellow lines running through it. These lines are fairly straight and seem to branch off into smaller and smaller lines, which give the surface of the leaf a scale-like appearance. The leaf is thin, about the thickness of two sheets of paper. It is about four inches wide, measuring from tip to tip, and about four inches long. At the bottom of the leaf there is a thin, pliable tube which seems to connect with the largest of the green-yellow lines.

Student Report

The eel is a fish which believes in long journeys. It is spawned in the Sargasso Sea in the western Atlantic, and from there will travel back to its fresh water haunts in this country or in Europe to feed and grow up in the rivers and streams frequented by its parents. The young eel or elver is still only 2 or 3 inches longer after its immense journey, and is transparent and yellowish. . . . As with cats, there is more than one way to skin a fresh eel.

We prefer the following. Slip a noose around the eel's head and hang the other end of the cord on a hook, high on the wall. Cut the eel skin about 3 inches below the head all around, so as not to penetrate the gall bladder which lies close to the head. Peel the skin back, pulling down hard—if necessary with a pair of pliers—until the whole skin comes off like a glove.

Rombauer and Becker, *The Joy of Cooking*

Committing the mind to one approach for a long period of time with no evident prospect of success is a mistake. Of course, the length of time one should devote to any one approach cannot be stated in advance. It depends on the difficulty of the problem. But if one does not seem to be making any progress the thing to do is to try to break from that pattern of thought, though it is very hard to give up once one starts to think along that line. What one should do is probably forget the whole thing and come back to it sometime later when that mental groove has disappeared.

Morris Kline, *The Creative Experience*

2. Rewrite the following passage to make it more informal. Use the personal *I* instead of *one.* Try to find strong verbs to replace weak ones.

A decline in energy is observed as the team continues its workout. The gymnasts who are on the rings show fatigue early. One notices that the faces begin to turn red and the veins bulge in the throat. If one looks closely, one also sees a slight quivering in the biceps as the exercises continue. Even after the rings have been released and the student is back on the mat, the shoulder and back muscles often can be observed to twitch involuntarily.

Practice

1. Copy three different voices. Try the formal academic voice of the scientific work (p. 155), a more informal voice as in the passage on the sloth bear (p. 156), and the personal voice used to describe winemaking (p. 157).

2. Here is how the Brothers Grimm wrote about "Little Red Riding Hood."

"But Grandmother," she said, "what big eyes you have!"

"The better to see you with, my child," was the reply.

And here is humorist and journalist Russell Baker telling the same tale in the voice of exaggerated objectivity.

"Grandmother," she said, "your ocular implements are of an extraordinary order of magnitude."

"The purpose of this enlarged viewing capability," said the wolf, "is to enable your image to register a more precise impression upon my sight systems."

Retell a folk or fairy tale in a different voice. Use either a hyped-up, streetwise voice or the formal voice of an official government notice.

CHAPTER 15

Reshaping, Rearranging, Integrating

I can't understand how anyone can write without rewriting everything over and over again.

LEO TOLSTOY

The most serious error the beginning writer can commit is to write only a single draft and assume the writing process is complete. You might at first believe that objective reporting would require less rewriting than a personal essay. After all, you're dealing with facts, not struggling to express inner feelings. Although the problems seem different, the demands on you are similar: to find precise words, to discover the best arrangement of parts, to blend or join each part so that the whole of it reads clearly. If we consider the various needs for informative reporting, the complexities become more apparent.

1. Objective observation of factual detail
2. A focus on elements of change or contrast (if significant)
3. A focus on major consequences
4. Characterization of the subject as a whole (including actions, physical description, background, and so on)
5. Understanding of the subject–audience–context–purpose

6. A lead that clearly presents all major facts in a sentence or two
7. An organization that flows naturally out of the lead and serves the subject–audience–context–purpose

To do all of this well in a first draft would be impossible for most of us. Even when we feel we have a subject well in hand, some elements of a paper always seem to get muddled. Here are four paragraphs of a rough draft by first-year student Cathy Brooks. In the first paragraph, the 5-*W* lead shows she has found her purpose and made a clear statement that ought to lead her into an easy-flowing organization. But the following paragraphs present serious problems. (Comments in the left margin reflect responses from Brooks' peer group.)

Good 5-*W* lead

Darlene Grimes wants to ban smoking everywhere on the New South campus by next fall. Grimes is a senior majoring in Women's Studies whose mother and uncle both died from lung cancer attributed to smoking. "I have a right to be free from other people's smoke anywhere I go," Grimes claims. "Even if I'm sitting by the fountain or under a tree, no one has a right to harm my health," she said, strongly.

Immediate focus on conflict

But quote goes on too long

Student Government President Ronnie Phelan is equally determined to stop Grimes' proposal. Phelan has smoked Marlboros since he was in high school in New Jersey, and he argues that smoking is legal and therefore he has a right to smoke if he chooses to. "I support banning smoking indoors because in an enclosed environment others may be forced against their will to inhale someone else's smoke. But that is not true outdoors. If I sit on the fountain, then Grimes is not forced to sit next to me or even within a hundred yards of me, or any other smoker. She can claim she has a right to sit on the fountain, but she can't claim that her right supersedes other's. We all have rights."

Good to bring in authoritative source for evidence

The July 1997 issue of the *Journal of the American Medical Association* reports on a major study on second-hand smoking. The researchers found that second-hand smoke in closed areas provides almost as much nicotine, tar, and other additives to the non-smoker as it does to the smoker. Other studies, according to the article, have not found as much serious damage, but the control groups in

Speculation rather than evaluation	the other studies were often inadequately controlled. This may be a bias of the authors. How are we to know? Maybe they didn't like the other authors. I interviewed Benjamin Crown who said, "I sympathize with both sides in this argument, but at present, the university is not prepared to take action on the issue. A lot of students still smoke, of course, but more and more, it seems to me, have given it up. I doubt if it will ever go away entirely. A few years ago we recommended to the Board of Trustees that all university buildings should be smoke free, and the
Quote is too long	Trustees approved. But I'm not sure that the support is yet there for this next step. Even some of the Board smoke and the issue may be too difficult to find a consensus on at the present time."
His authority should come earlier **Characterization lacks details**	Benjamin Crown is dean of student affairs at New South College. He has a PhD in psychology from the University of Nebraska and has been dean here for nine years. He seemed very nice about it all but didn't seem to have the authority to make a decision. *Newsweek* and *Time* magazines both have September 1997 issues in which second-hand smoking is discussed.
Good research but seems out of place	Both mention the American Medical Association article and *Time* calls it the first definitive study. *Newsweek* reports that the movement "toward forcing smokers outdoors, may now be forcing them to hide in their cars in the parking lot."
Conclusion is personal opinion rather than evaluation of evidence	The problem with ever-increasing prohibitions against smoking may be that we will make smoking more attractive by making it more forbidden.

Brooks was aware of the problems encountered in her report as it moved along, but she felt unsure about how to solve them. For her, as for most of us—especially when working with facts and opinions collected from other sources—revising is often a process of selecting only the best statements for quotation, summarizing other parts, and integrating the two. We must sharpen the focus of our essays while being careful not to distort the meaning of the information provided by the source.

Summarizing

To summarize is to restate concisely in your own words the essence of a larger work or idea. A person you interview or material you read may provide more information than you need or material not directly relevant to your paper. The long quotation in Cathy Brooks' report is an example. Much of it could be selectively omitted; most of it can be summarized in a sentence or two.

Professional writers know that good quotations make writing seem lively. But lengthy quotations or too many quotations can become as tedious as none at all. The reader expects a balance between summary and direct quotation. In general, approximately 80 percent of material taken from other sources (through interviews or reading) should be summarized in your own words. You should summarize only the information or ideas that directly relate to your subject, while being careful not to distort, oversimplify, or in any other way change the meaning of the original. Only the most important element should actually be quoted.

Here is how Cathy revised Ronnie Phelan's statement, blending summary with quotation:

Original

Student Government President Ronnie Phelan is equally determined to stop Grimes' proposal. Phelan has smoked Marlboros since he was in high school in New Jersey, and he argues that smoking is legal and therefore he has a right to smoke if he chooses to. "I support banning smoking indoors because in an enclosed environment others may be forced against their will to inhale someone else's smoke. But that is not true outdoors. If I sit on the fountain, then Grimes is not forced to sit next to me or even within a hundred yards of me, or any other smoker. She can claim she has a right to sit on the fountain, but she can't claim that her right supersedes other's. We all have rights."

Revision

Student Government President Ronnie Phelan is equally determined to stop Grimes' proposal. A Marlboro smoker since high school, Phelan argues that smoking is legal and therefore he has a right to do so. Phelan agrees with prohibiting smoking indoors, but not outdoors where Grimes is not being forced to sit next to Phelan or any other smoker. Her rights do not supersede the rights of others, he claims.

The summary has shortened the original by almost half. By focusing on main points, the writer directs the reader's attention to key ideas while condensing a great deal of verbiage.

Brooks faced the same problem with the quotation from Dean Benjamin Crown. Here is how she blended summary and quotation. Note that the essence of Crown's ideas has not been changed, only condensed.

Original
I interviewed Benjamin Crown who said, "I sympathize with both sides in this argument, but at present, the university is not prepared to take action on the issue. A lot of students still smoke, of course, but more and more, it seems to me, have given it up. I doubt if it will ever go away entirely. A few years ago we recommended to the Board of Trustees that all university buildings should be smoke free, and the Trustees approved. But I'm not sure that the support is yet there for this next step. Even some of the Board smoke and the issue may simply be too difficult to find a consensus on at the present time."

Revision
I interviewed Benjamin Crown who said, "I sympathize with both sides in this argument." However, Crown pointed out that the Board of Trustees recently declared all campus buildings "smoke free," and consensus for additional action may be lacking. Crown believes the "university is not prepared to take action on the issue."

Quoting

To quote another person means to use the exact words you've heard or read. Although you have a great deal of flexibility in how you integrate those words into your text, you will seldom be forgiven even the smallest inaccuracy. A word omitted or a phrase inverted can change the total meaning of an idea. If you cannot be sure of the exact words, place the idea in your own terms and give credit to your source. Do not use quotation marks unless you can be precise.

But Brooks has not changed the original wording of Crown's final statement:

Crown believes "the university is not prepared to take action on the issue."

She has only chosen to move the quotation to the end because she felt it would conclude her own paragraph with decisiveness. Many students aren't aware that they have a right to alter a sequence of information from the way it appears in an original source. In fact, you have an obligation to your reader to reorganize whenever clarity is improved, *so long as no change in meaning or emphasis is created.* In this case, moving the quotation has distorted neither accuracy nor meaning.

Integrating

Reorganizing material from a single source may be valuable. Integrating and blending all the parts of your essay are essential. The great value of word processors is that you can "block" sentences, paragraphs, or whole pages and move them around easily, testing the most logical or effective location. Brooks' peer group identified two sections of her report that seemed misallocated. The information gathered from *Time* and *Newsweek* did not seem to have any justification for appearing after Benjamin Crown's statement. The news reports clearly responded to material taken from the *Journal of the American Medical Association,* and Brooks made the move.

In the process, she dropped the "speculative" material that ended the original paragraph so that she could devise a new transition to what would now be the following paragraph. This is how the two were blended:

> Other studies, according to the article, have not found as much serious damage, but the control groups in the other studies were often inadequately controlled.
>
> In September of 1997, both *Newsweek* and *Time* magazines reviewed the *American Medical Association* article, and *Time* even called it the first definitive study.

Now the reading flows smoothly between paragraphs, and the connection between related ideas is clearer.

The next step for Brooks was to identify Crown's authority to speak on the subject at the point where he is first introduced to the reader. In general, a speaker needs to be identified or described *before* his or her ideas are given. Brooks rewrote the opening of the Crown paragraph one more time.

> I interviewed Benjamin Crown, dean of student affairs at New South College. Crown spoke to me in his office, rocking back in his chair, relaxed and comfortable after nine years in the job. "I sympathize with both sides in this argument."
>
> However, Crown pointed out that the Board of Trustees recently declared all campus buildings "smoke free," and consensus for additional action may be lacking. . . .

Details describing character (leaning back in his chair and smiling) may be inappropriate for a more formal report. Cathy Brooks felt these few details placed Crown's decision not to take action on the issue in a human context.

The function of drafting is to explore ideas, to get facts on the page. One function of revision is to reshape, rearrange, integrate, and develop these facts and ideas. As Donald Murray, a Pulitzer prize–winning journalist, has said, "Rewriting is like rubbing a dirty window with a cloth. The more you rub, the clearer the vision on the other side becomes." The normal process for almost all of us is to move from awkward, stumbling prose toward a gradually emerging clarity.

Exercises

1. Summarize in class the following passage in no more than two sentences. A summary should be written in your own words and should constitute the essence of the original without distorting the central idea. Compare your summaries with those of others in class or in your peer group.

   The mentally healthy freshman comes with a basic sense of industry. Industry is the positive identification with those who know things and know how to do things, with workmanship and task mastery; it is the capacity to learn how to be, with skill, what one is in the process of becoming; it is the sure knowledge of personal competence. . . . This sense of industry is severely tested. Not necessarily because the academic tasks are too difficult or onerous, but because of the unimaginable number of distractions, temptations, annoyances, and interruptions that ensnare and drag one down to exhaustion. The student is surrounded by seducers, exploiters, entrepreneurs, manipulators, and many hedonists, and a few nihilists.

   Hal Crowley, *Forum for Honors*

2. Summarize Wendy Rose's poem on pages 400–401. In your own words, capture the feeling and tone of the poem as well as the reflective pattern of ideas.

3. Assume that you are writing a report on the community relations—or lack of relations—between your college and the surrounding neighborhoods. You obtain an interview with the mayor or borough representative. From the following exchange, select the most important statement for quotation, decide which material is irrelevant to your study, and summarize the remainder in no more than a couple of sentences. Share your results with the class or your peer group. Can you justify your choices? Is there a consensus?

   Interviewer: Do you feel Learning University has achieved satisfactory community relations?

   Mayor: We're very proud to have Learning University as a part of our great community.

   Interviewer: Some people have suggested that the university locks itself away in an ivory tower and ignores the concerns of the surrounding neighborhoods.

   Mayor: Well, you know, I am an alumnus of old Learning U. and it was a fine school. Class of 1975. We had a winning football season for the first time in a decade. Do you play a sport?

   Interviewer: No, sir. But I wonder if you might elaborate on how the community looks at the university. Are there specific problems that 10,000 students create? How do the merchants feel? Or the police force?

Mayor: Well, there are always problems, you know. I suppose that we are concerned about the off-campus parking. A lot of residents complain about cars blocking their driveways, that type of thing.

Interviewer: What about the tax base? The university pays no taxes as I understand.

Mayor: That's a particularly sore point with me. Everybody's taxes in this community are higher because of the university. There are four streets, fifteen light poles, a dozen sidewalks that all cut through the university, but the city has to maintain them. That means some little old lady on social security has to pay property taxes to repave streets for freshmen to ride their bicycles on. And then there's the cost of fire and police protection. Yet the university doesn't pay one cent for all the services we provide!

4. It is sometimes easier to identify faults in others' papers than to see them in your own. Here is a portion of a first draft. Rewrite it by rearranging whatever is necessary, omitting irrelevant detail, summarizing, and integrating related parts. The focus of the paper should be on the lack of social life at this student's college.

I did a survey of Milligan Hall and found that only 40 percent of the students remained on campus last weekend. One student, who shall remain nameless because he doesn't want to be identified, told me: "I just hate it around here. For kicks I go down and do my laundry or maybe watch the squirrels bury nuts in the south quadrangle. I mean, I think the school ought to bring in more movies or speakers. We were supposed to have a dance in February but only fifteen people showed up. Thirteen were girls." As I talked to this student, he told me that he came from a small farm in Iowa and that his father owned over one hundred milk cows. He is a freshman planning to major in economics.

Another comment I got came from a junior. She told me, "I think everyone complains because they don't have enough imagination to think of something on their own. I've never been bored a minute here. The school has a choral group, a theater club, a dance ensemble, a chess tournament, you name it, but everyone wants to be entertained instead of getting involved in something and entertaining themselves. Do you see what I mean?" Her name is Barbara Walker, and she is a chemistry major from Detroit. She also plays flute in the university symphony and paints for a hobby. The day I interviewed her, she wore patched Levis and an old paint-spotted sweatshirt.

Readings

Student Power

Rebecca Morris

Rebecca Morris was a second-term first-year student when she wrote the following short report. Hearing that the dining service had adopted dramatically new policies since the previous year, she let three of the 4 *C*'s (*change, conflict,* and *consequence*) guide her investigation.

Last year six students, led by Terri Shaw, decided they'd had enough of nuked hot dogs, corned beef hash, chipped beef on toast, rubbery Swiss steak smothered with tomato sauce, and macaroni and hamburger. Clark Dining Hall, they claimed, was serving the same kinds of meals it had served half-a-century ago to returning GI's after World War II. The six students first complained by writing a mimeographed letter to other students in the residence halls. "We know students have probably always complaned [*sic*] about cafeteria food, but the world has changed and the management of Clark has not." Where, they asked, were the options for people who didn't want to eat meat at every meal? They wanted to know why they couldn't have fresh fruit? Why couldn't the dining service install a yogurt machine? Why did everything have to be heavily salted? Did vegetables have to be over-cooked? Why not fresh vegetables instead of canned peas? They concluded their letter with a plea: "If you agree with us, then let the food service management know. After all, we're the ones who pay for this 'glop' and we're the ones who have to eat it."

Terri Shaw, who is now a senior theatre major, says she had no idea that their letter would have such an impact. "We were just really sick of having to spend fifteen dollars a week to buy our own groceries when our parents had already paid for us to eat at the dining hall." Terri is twenty-two and starred this winter in the university production of *A Mid-Summer Night's Dream*. But she's best known on campus as the girl who gets up at five every morning to run five miles before breakfast. "I come from a health-conscious family," she admits. "We ate yogurt and bananas for breakfast, not greasy eggs and bacon. My father was always playing golf or tennis, and my older brother was a long distance biker. I think it was just trying to keep up with them that made me health conscious."

Margaret Williams is the new food service manager. She remembers what happened next. She still has a copy of Terri Shaw's letter under a glass top on her desk. "Students do always complain. That's just part of the business. We don't prepare food like Mom does. But this time everyone was caught off guard by the size of the rebellion."

Mrs. Williams had been assistant manager of the college food service for only a week when Shaw's letter came out. She had previously worked for two other college cafeterias, first at Kent State and then at Virginia Tech. She has an Associate Degree in food preparation from a community college in Ohio.

For the next three weeks Terri Shaw and other students picketed the dining hall with signs and posters. Many of the faculty also complained, including Dorsey Leighton, the coach of the women's basketball team who joined the picket line. Then several students called for a boycott of weekend meals. On the first weekend only about fifty students stayed away, but on the second weekend several hundred students sat outside the entrance and sang songs and chanted.

"We had to throw away thousands of dollars worth of food," Mrs. Williams said. "And I think maybe a hundred other students blocked the hall in front of the Dean of Students' office." After that, the dean met with the former manager, Harry Bosworth, asking why the food service couldn't try some of the student suggestions. "But Harry resisted," Mrs. Williams said. "He had directed the food service for twenty years and he didn't want to change." Bosworth finally announced to an *Eagle* reporter that "if the health nuts are going to take over the world, I would rather retire and go fishing." Which he did.

Mrs. Williams then took over and met with both students and faculty for about six weeks to work out a new menu. Students now have choices, she pointed out during a tour of the kitchen. Every meal offers a traditional meat dish, a vegetarian dish, and simple snack food such as bagels and cream cheese, peanut butter sandwiches on whole wheat bread, or fresh fruit. Each offering has a "nutrition sign" which lists total calories, sodium count, cholesterol, and carbohydrates. Along with low-calorie dressings, the new salad bar offers bowls of raw vegetables such as chopped cauliflower, broccoli, and sliced carrots on ice. Yogurt is available at every meal from a shiny new machine. And for dessert, sugar-free brownies or some other low-calorie offering is prepared.

"I couldn't be happier," Terri Shaw says. "We haven't taken anything away from students who want to eat traditional Americana stuff like meat, potatoes and gravy. But everybody now has a choice." Shaw will graduate in two months, but she thinks students should be aware that they have more influence than they think. "They've been silent for so many years they don't know their own power."

Trouble for America's "Model" Minority

David Whitman

For this study, first published in *U.S. News & World Report* in 1987, David Whitman, a professional journalist, relies heavily on the 4 *C's* of observation. His opening paragraph uses all of the 5 *W's,* then contrasts their surface appearance with behind-the-scenes reality. As you read further, consider how Whitman continues to use *change, conflict,* and *consequences,* both to probe his subject and to organize the essay.

When 12-year-old Hue Cao shyly read her prize-winning essay at last year's nationally televised Statue of Liberty centennial celebration, she seemed the very model of a thriving Indochinese boat person. Only six years before, Hue, her mother, four brothers and two sisters fled Vietnam in a fishing boat, and now she was the center of national attention, having bested 2,000 other children in a highly competitive essay contest. "This nation has given my family a brand-new life," Hue recited proudly as tens of millions of equally proud Americans looked on.

Unfortunately, however, what they saw on their TV screens was something of a sham. Far from flourishing in the U.S., the Cao family turned out to be on welfare, unable even to accept the contest prize—a new automobile—because it would have meant surrendering their public-assistance benefits. "The girl's mother was in tears," recalls Reg Schwenke of the Aloha Liberty Foundation, sponsor of the essay contest. "She was both anxious and ashamed."

The problems of Hue Cao and her family illustrate a major but long-hidden difference in social backgrounds between the two groups that make up the more than 800,000 Indochinese who sought refuge in the U.S. in the past 11 years. The first wave of 130,000 refugees—those who arrived in the immediate aftermath of the fall of Saigon in 1975—was largely an elite group. They were officials of the deposed South Vietnamese government, employees of the American military, dependents of U.S. servicemen and upper-echelon staffers of multinational corporations. Given their experience and contacts, these refugees made a relatively easy transition to life in the U.S. and created a near mythic image of the Indochinese as brilliant students, flourishing entrepreneurs and altogether successful symbols of the American dream. After only four years in the U.S., the first wave of Indochinese refugees earned 18 percent more than the average American.

The story, however, is far different for the second wave, the 640,000 who arrived in the U.S. following Vietnam's invasion of Cambodia in 1978. For many of them, life in America has been far less satisfying and considerably more precarious. In contrast to those who preceded them, the second wave of refugees had little education and few skills to bolster them in their new homes. Instead of sophisticated city dwellers, they were mostly rural people—farmers, fishers, small merchants and mountain tribespeople—many unable to speak English and illiterate in their own language. Half came from Laos and Cambodia, nations considerably poorer and socially less developed than Vietnam. And unlike the earlier refugees, those in the second wave often suffered brutal physical and psychological traumas before arriving in the United States. Many had been imprisoned in Vietnamese re-education camps, nearly starved and tortured in Pol Pot's Cambodia, or raped, beaten and robbed by the Thai pirates who preyed on the boat people in the Gulf of Thailand.

"This was the largest nonwhite, non-Western, non-English-speaking group of people ever to enter the country at one time," says Peter Rose, a Smith College professor who has written widely on the refugees. "The public assumed they succeeded just because the first wave did." Adds Ruben Rumbaut, director of the Indochinese Health and Adaptation Research Project at San Diego State University: "The Southeast Asian success stories play well in Peoria. Those of the losers don't."

Even when compared with depressed minorities in the U.S., "second wave" Indochinese fare poorly. A staggering 64 percent of the Indochinese households headed by refugees who arrived after 1980 are on public assistance—three times the rate of American blacks and four times that of Hispanics. And among refugee groups as a whole, the newly arrived Indochinese are by far the most dependent upon the dole.

"In our old country, whatever we had was made or brought in by our hands," says Chong Sao Yang, 62, a former farmer and soldier who moved to San Diego from Laos. Yang and three family members have been on welfare for seven years. "We are not born on earth to have somebody give us food. Here, I'm sure we're going to starve, because since our arrival there is no penny I can get that is money I earn from work. I've been trying very hard to learn English, and at the same time look for a job. But no matter what kind of job—even a job to clean people's toilets—still people don't trust you or offer you such work. I'm not even worth as much as a dog's stool. Talking about this, I want to die right here so I won't see my future."

Many in the newer wave of refugees grew up in Laos and Cambodia without electricity, running water, clocks or stoves—much less banks, savings accounts and credit cards. And Hmong tribesmen like Yang from the highlands of Laos feel even more isolated because of their illiteracy and traditional beliefs in witchcraft and shamans. "What we have here are 16th-century people suddenly thrust into 20th-century life," says Ernest Velasquez of the welfare department in Fresno, Calif., home for an estimated 18,000 Hmong. . . .

Nao Chai Her was the respected head of a Hmong village of more than 500 people in Laos. Here, he is on welfare and shares a cramped three-bedroom apartment with 20 relatives. "We are just like the baby birds," says Nao, 61, "who stay in the nest opening their mouths, waiting only for the mother bird to bring the worms. When the government doesn't send the cash on time, we even fear we'll starve. I used to be a real man like any other man, but not any longer. The work I used to do, I can't do here. I feel like a thing which drops in the fire but won't burn and drops in the river but won't flow."

Many Indochinese experience similar sieges of depression but manage to carefully disguise the condition behind a mask of hard work and traditional courtesy. In one standardized psychological test given in San Diego, 45 percent of the adult refugees showed distress symptoms serious enough to require clinical treatment, four times the proportion among the population at large. Cambodian women, many left husbandless by Pol Pot's genocide, are especially troubled. Lay Plok, 34, of Arlington, Va., lost her husband in 1977 when they fled the famine in Cambodia. "I'm down," she says quietly, "and yet I don't know what would make life feel better."

Like U.S. veterans with painful memories of Vietnam, some Indochinese refugees suffer repeated nightmares and evidence a variety of stress-related disorders. Indeed, emotional trauma among the new arrivals is so extensive and little understood that Dr. Richard Mollica and social worker James Lavelle of St. Elizabeth's Hospital set up the Indochinese Psychiatry Clinic in 1981 in Boston just to assist refugees. One woman treated at the clinic wandered from city to city in the U.S., fearful that her Communist jailers were out to recapture her. She told clinic doctors a harrowing but not atypical story of having been repeatedly raped, tortured and given mind-altering drugs while imprisoned.

For all their problems, however, the newer refugees don't fully fit the underclass stereotype. Most cherish hard work and stress the value of family and education. Divorce and out-of-wedlock pregnancy are still taboo. Drug and alcohol abuse is minimal. Studies of the refugee children, including those with illiterate Hmong parents, indicate they do quite well in school. And even where most of the family gets public-assistance payments, at least one member has a paying job, sometimes off the books. "The refugees make exemplary use of the welfare system," argues Nathan Caplan of the University of Michigan, an expert on the second wave of refugees. "They tend to have large families, so they pool resources to finance education and training. And they rely on welfare less as time goes by."

In the end, however, whatever their cultural liabilities, the refugees' greatest asset may be simply that they are survivors. Puthnear Mom, 22, also of Arlington, lost her husband while crossing the Cambodian border to Thailand. She can't read or write, and has been unemployed for two years. "I'm unhappy to receive welfare," she says through a translator, "but life is better now than in Cambodia or the refugee camp. I can learn anything here I want. Freedom does matter."

Soup

Anonymous

The *New Yorker* is well known for its profile pieces, sometimes short and humorous, as this one is, sometimes long, serious, and highly insightful. The following originally appeared as part of a larger column titled, "Talk of the Town." The writer blends direct dialogue from an interview with the main figure, Albert Yeganeh, with key sensory details, location details, and comments from others. The result is a sharply focused revelation of character.

When Albert Yeganeh says, "Soup is my lifeblood," he means it. And when he says "I am extremely hard to please," he means that, too. Working like a demon alchemist in a tiny storefront kitchen at 259-A West Fifth Street, Mr. Yeganeh creates anywhere from eight to seventeen soups every weekday. His concoctions are so popular that a wait of half an hour at the lunchtime peak is not uncommon, although there are strict rules for conduct in line. But more on that later.

"I am psychologically kind of a health freak," Mr. Yeganeh said the other day, in a lisping staccato of Armenian origin. "And I know that soup is the greatest meal in the world. It's very good for your digestive system. And I use only the best, the freshest ingredients. I am a perfectionist. When I make a clam soup, I use three different kinds of clams. Every other place uses canned clams. I'm called crazy. I am not crazy. People don't realize why I get so upset. It's because if the soup is not perfect and I'm still selling it, it's a torture. It's *my* soup, and that's why I'm so upset. First you clean and then you cook. I don't believe that ninety-nine per cent of the restaurants in New York know how to clean a tomato. I tell my crew to wash the parsley *eight* times. If they wash it five or six times, I scare them. I tell them they'll go to jail if there is sand in the parsley. One time, I found a mushroom on the floor and I fired the guy who left it there." He spread his arms, and added, "This place is the only one like it in . . . in . . . the whole earth! One day I hope to learn something from the other places, but so far I haven't. For example, the other day I went to a very fancy restaurant and had borscht. I had to send it back. It was *junk*. I could see all the chemicals in it. I never use chemicals. Last weekend, I had lobster bisque in Brooklyn, a very well known place. It was *junk*. When I make lobster bisque, I use a whole lobster. You know, I never advertise. I don't have to. All the big-shot chefs and the kings of the hotels come here to see what *I'm* doing."

As you approach Mr. Yeganeh's Soup Kitchen International from a distance, the first thing you notice about it is the awning, which proclaims "Homemade Hot, Cold, Diet Soups." The second thing you notice is an aroma so delicious that it makes you want to take a bite out of the air. The third thing you notice, in front of the kitchen, is an electric signboard that flashes, say, "Today's Soups . . . Chicken Vegetable . . . Mexican Beef Chili . . . Cream of Watercress . . . Italian Sausage . . . Clam Bisque . . . Beef Barley . . . Due to Cold Weather . . . For Most Efficient and Fastest Service the Line Must . . . Be Kept Moving . . . Please . . . Have your Money . . . Ready . . . Pick the Soup of your Choice . . . Move to Your Extreme . . . Left After Ordering."

"I am not prejudiced against color or religion," Mr. Yeganeh told us, and he jabbed an index finger at the flashing sign. "Whoever follows that I treat very well. My regular customers don't say anything. They are very intelligent and well educated. They know I'm just trying to move the line. The New York cop is very smart—he sees everything but says nothing. But the young girl who wants to stop and tell you how nice you look and hold everyone up—*yah!*" He made a guillotining motion with his hand. "I tell you, I hate to work with the public. They treat me like a slave. My philosophy is: The customer is always wrong and I'm always right. I raised my prices to try to get rid of some of these people, but it didn't work."

The other day, Mr. Yeganeh was dressed in chefs' whites with orange smears across his chest, which may have been some of the carrot soup cooking in a huge pot on a little stove in one corner. A three-foot-long handheld mixer from France sat on the sink, looking like an overgrown gardening tool. Mr. Yeganeh spoke to two young helpers in a twisted Armenian-Spanish barrage, then said to us, "I have no overhead, no trained waitresses, and I have the cashier here." He pointed to himself theatrically. Beside the doorway, a glass case with fresh green celery, red and yellow peppers, and purple eggplant was topped by five big gray soup urns. According to a piece of cardboard taped to the door, you can buy Mr. Yeganeh's soups in three sizes, costing from four to fifteen dollars. The order of any well-behaved customer is accompanied by little waxpaper packets of bread, fresh vegetables (such as scallions and radishes), fresh fruit (such as cherries or an orange,) a chocolate mint, and a plastic spoon. No coffee, tea, or other drinks are served.

"I get my recipes from books and theories and my own taste," Mr. Yeganeh said. "At home, I have several hundreds of books. When I do research, I find that I don't know anything. Like cabbage is a cancer fighter, and some fish is good for your heart but some is bad. Every day, I should have one sweet, one spicy, one cream, one vegetable soup—and they *must* change, they should always taste a little different." He added that he wasn't sure how extensive his repertoire was, but that it probably includes at least eighty soups, among them African peanut butter, Greek moussaka, hamburger, Reuben, B.L.T., asparagus and caviar, Japanese shrimp miso, chicken chili, Irish corned beef and cabbage, Swiss chocolate, French calf's brain, Korean beef ball, Italian shrimp and eggplant Parmesan, buffalo, ham and egg, short rib, Russian beef Stroganoff, turkey cacciatore, and Indian mulligatawny. “The chicken and the seafood are an addiction, and when I have French garlic soup I let people have only one small container each,” he said. “The doctors and nurses love that one.”

A lunch line of thirty people stretched down the block from Mr. Yeganeh's doorway. Behind a construction worker was a man in expensive leather, who was in front of a woman in a fur hat. Few people spoke. Most had their money out and their orders ready.

At the front of the line, a woman in a brown coat couldn't decide which soup to get and started to complain about the prices.

“You talk too much, dear,” Mr. Yeganeh said, and motioned to her to move to the left. “Next!”

“Just don't talk. Do what he says,” a man huddled in a blue parka warned.

“He's downright rude,” said a blond woman in a blue coat. “Even abusive. But you can't deny it, his soup is the best.”

PART 4

Investigating Concepts

Suggested Writing Projects

An investigation into a concept or idea goes beyond reporting. It requires more active curiosity—a desire to learn—and at the same time, a healthy skepticism, a determination to probe conventional answers. You'll be required to research new types of sources, and you'll be faced with explaining, evaluating, and interpreting what you find. In academic writing, exploring an idea often involves looking into definitions, investigating origins, and sorting out conflicting opinions. The focus may be on abstract concepts that are central to understanding at least some *small* portion of a larger subject like physics, literature, philosophy, engineering, architecture, and so on.

In many ways, you'll find you can build upon strategies already practiced in reporting: personal observation or field research, an objective stance, interviews with experts, a search for important and revealing details, and avoidance of your own opinion. Reporting, however, usually limits its focus to events, issues, or conflicts where the writer arrives at a reasoned inference about the facts. An extended investigation or explanatory essay requires more analysis and insight, usually achieved by discovering relationships or patterns to the evidence. The reader expects a conclusion that goes beyond informing and moves toward understanding or insight. This is, indeed, how human knowledge has been formed in the past and is continuing to be formed today. As a college student, you are now expected to become engaged in the same intellectual activity.

Here are some suggestions on where you might begin.

- Explain an abstract concept or principle you've been studying in another class: "culture" in sociology, "bi-polar disorders" in psychology, "process" in history. Assume your audience will be fellow students who know little about the topic. For such readers, you'll want to use your first paragraph to stimulate interest. Then focus in on a clear definition, one that draws from various sources (interviews, a college text, library research, the Internet). Explain the concept (or a portion of it) in detail; survey its origin or history, or illustrate key points with examples. Lead your reader toward understanding of both the idea itself and why it's important to know about it.

- Consider the evolution of a value. Explain how the concept of "love" has evolved from, say, the medieval era to our own, exploring briefly the development of "Courtly Love" and the idealization of women. Or explore the meaning and origin of the "Puritan Work Ethic." Or attempt a definition of "The American Dream," a phrase we hear all the time which seems to have an endless number of meanings. Each of these general concepts has a direct effect on our lives, and yet we live with each of them without curiosity, accepting or rejecting them emotionally. To reach a fuller understanding, you may first need to narrow your focus to a small portion of the concept, then engage in library research or interviews with experts.

Group Inquiry

Working with another student, examine the "concepts" of cooperation and collaboration. Develop a definition of each term, and discuss how the meanings are both alike and different. You may need to refer to a library resource such as the *Oxford English Dictionary* to explore origins and use of the two words. Consider how the two concepts might be applied to your own work, for example, research and writing. Are there ways you might cooperate or collaborate on investigating and writing about an academic concept or the evolution of a value? What would be the dangers? What would be the benefits?

Oral Presentation of Research.

170-185

Choose a principal or concept that your interested in.

Defination Paper.

Bring in Friday. One possible topic for next paper.

Research + Define for others.

CHAPTER 16

Seeing Beyond the Surface

Albert Einstein once wrote that "Imagination is more important than knowledge. For knowledge is limited, whereas imagination embraces the entire world." And to some extent, he's right. But Einstein is also being disingenuous, because the most productive imaginations are usually founded on our understanding of prior forms and principles of knowledge. Einstein, if truth be told, first immersed himself in Newtonian physics, understood its basic concepts and principles, and then—with the aid of a brilliant imagination—moved our understanding of the universe in a totally new direction.

Two points are being made here: Human knowledge builds upon understanding ideas previously conceived and developed, then it expands through applying our own imagination to those ideas.

Much of your academic education at the undergraduate level is aimed at building a foundation in the first of these two points. You'll find, in almost every subject you study, that one of your primary responsibilities is to explore and reach at least a general appreciation of some concept, notion, idea, principle, or development—past or present—that is central to understanding that particular body of knowledge. A serious inquiry into any field of learning goes beyond mere reporting, beyond observing facts or listening to facts or gathering facts. To investigate means to pursue detail in such a way that you begin to perceive a pattern or association that suggests a reasonable meaning, a probable truth. The reporter's role is often complete when he or she has presented the evidence. The scholar's job demands a deeper immersion in definitions, historical patterns, stages of development, cultural influences, and more.

Narrowing the Focus

To investigate (and gain understanding) of a specific portion of an abstract concept can be complex and demanding. But your eye functions as the lens of your imagination. You have the ability to see the whole of something or to focus on minute detail. Successful writers—and successful students—have found that most effective and significant work has a narrow focus on one or two specific areas of a larger subject. The sharp focus allows you to avoid writing in clichés and vague generalities and, most important, to discover patterns and relationships—the first step toward insight.

The instructor may sometimes do the narrowing for you. For a course in botany, you might be asked to write a three-page explanation of photosynthesis. For a course in economics, you might be required to explain the concept of supply-side economics. In literature, you might be asked to explore the nature of the hero in Greek tragedy. Each of these carries with it the unspoken requirement to investigate sources, select details and illustrations, define terms, and sometimes to take into account competing theories or critical positions. You may find you'll want to take a particular angle on the topic: a historical approach, for example, or a look at the topic in light of recent perspectives. Here's where your imagination can play an active role. And here's where the instructor will recognize the difference between the writer who makes only a perfunctory recitation of facts (a reporting of facts) and the writer who becomes actively mentally engaged with the material.

On the other hand, an instructor may assign a paper on a general concept and *assume* you'll narrow the broader idea to a single aspect that can be explored in depth. It will be crucial for you to know whether this is the expectation, because a narrowly focused paper requires a totally different type of intellectual work.

Here's one example of how you might begin a focusing process for this type of paper: **Assignment:** *For a course in Western Civilization, write a four-page paper on Feudalism.* The topic of "feudalism" is an enormously broad subject, having developed over hundreds of years out of complex conditions during the medieval period. If you try to write on "feudalism" you'll end up producing a three-volume book.

The first step is to break down the topic into major categories, perhaps those you're already familiar with (assuming you've been studying something about the subject in your world civilization class), or into categories that represent common sense components of most historical subjects:

Feudalism {
- time frame
- geographical area covered
- historical conditions
- cultural conditions
- economic conditions
- human relations
- power and ownership of land

You may want to pause here and consider what you already know, if anything, about each of these various subcategories. Which topics are most interesting to you? Which do you already have some information on? Which would you find most stimulating to research? Which would be easiest to locate information on? Using these types of questions as a guide, select one category and again break it down into its own various components. Let's say, for example, that you really know nothing about any of the subcategories, but you find the idea of human relations most intriguing.

Human relations {
- relations between kings and other nobility
- relations between lords and their knights
- relations between lords and their serfs
- relations between the aristocracy and the Church
- relations between the Church and its followers
- relations between men and women
- relations between the community and individuals

The list might be longer, of course. But even these categories remain too broad. Each could still form the basis of a whole book. On the other hand, perhaps you've now found the one that stimulates your interest: *relations between men and women.* With additional focused research on this specific topic, you might find an enormous amount of information and decide once again that you need to break down the topic:

- economic relations between men and women
- marital relations
- women as property
- dowries
- female children versus male children
- religious influences on men versus women
- male–female stereotypes
- the relations between aristocratic women and men versus the relations between peasant women and men, and so on

My point here is to illustrate how broad "concepts" usually are. The process of narrowing may constitute a significant portion of your time, but it is crucial that you give it full intellectual attention. Only by finding the small, focused portion of a general concept can you begin to locate significant and interesting details. And only then can your imagination become engaged in considering differing interpretations of the facts and differing angles on the subject (historical, evolutionary, new developments, contrasting options, and so on). A topic narrowly and sharply focused allows the mind and the imagination to focus as well. When that happens, you increase the possibility of an exciting interaction with your material.

Investigating Abstract Concepts

In truth, what I've described so far is only a crude example of how abstract topics are focused. The steps I've listed form, at best, a starting point—some of the time. Several other methods need to be discussed, because as you enter into more formal research, you'll discover that "concepts" are remarkably slippery. The direction of your original interest will often shift when you encounter a new resource or a new explanation of the topic. All your early efforts to narrow the topic are valuable, but must be considered preliminary. Researching ideas requires constant flexibility and a tolerance for frustration. *Always* be prepared to modify the focus of your topic as you go along.

Consulting an Expert

Sometimes the best place to begin is with a knowledgeable individual who can help focus your study and perhaps direct you to the most important resources. The broad topic of "expressionism" in art, for example, obviously suggests that a professional painter or art instructor might be able to provide you with several good ideas, with recent articles or books, or a working definition, or an initial way to limit the subject and frame its potential for you. Such an expert might also be able to warn you about certain pitfalls: out-of-date texts, limited resources for research, and complexities that will need to be overcome.

At other times, you may want to save an interview with an expert for later in the research. By going straight to the Internet or to the library, you can begin to explore the information available to you, begin to look into several important sources and gather ideas (at this point, perhaps nothing more than random ideas) about the topic. By familiarizing yourself with the subject, you can approach your interview source with a more intelligent set of questions. Instead of asking merely for help where to begin, you can conduct a full-fledged interview on the topic itself, being honest about your limited background, but nonetheless showing that you already have ideas and information and that you want to pursue some of the problems or contradictions you've uncovered.

Either way, an interview with an expert on the topic can be helpful. And don't feel uncomfortable calling on such a person. Remember that most individuals feel flattered to be considered an expert, and most will talk to you just because you've shown an interest in something dear to their heart.

Incorporating Previous Strategies

Almost half of the previous chapters in this textbook have dealt with the pursuit or selection of specific details. Each method and technique discussed earlier may apply at some point during an investigation of any subject, including research into abstract concepts. It would probably be best to keep them all in the back of your mind, selecting from them as the topic itself seems to call them forth.

Look for the 5 *W*'s. Think of the 5 *W*'s as more than a technique used in writing a lead or reporting facts. *Who?*, *What?*, *Where?*, *When?*, and *Why?* are questions that apply to every subject as a whole.

Look for Change. Change may be the key element. What changes in the concept have occurred over time? Whom does the change affect? When did it occur? How was it brought about?

Look for Conflict. Contrast, conflict, contradiction, or opposition may lead to the center of a concept. Why is there a conflict? What does it grow out of? Who is involved? Where and when did it begin?

Look for Consequences. How does one fact, concept, or notion influence another? What elements of the concept have the most serious impact? Who is affected? Why?

Look for Characterization. Major actions, speeches or written documents, background, others' reactions or opinions, and physical description or environment (when appropriate) may all contribute to the evolution of almost any concept or idea.

Look for Elements of Scene. The concrete, sensory elements of a scene might not seem appropriate to understanding an abstract concept, yet these are the elements of life. All concepts exist in the real world, they begin in a "place," in a time frame, and with people who have purpose and motivation. An objective search for truth does not mean we abandon the concrete world for the sake of abstractions. See your subject in its real setting, in its world context. A selected "scene" may still be valuable as a lead paragraph for your essay (see Chapter 9), or as part of an anecdote, example or illustration in your essay.

Look for People Behind the Concept. Whether through observation, interviews, or library research, keep your eyes open to the human element, both to make your writing more interesting and to retain a human perspective.

John Ciardi, a poet and essayist, once wrote: "The fact is that anything significantly looked at is significant. And that is significant which teaches us something about our own life-capabilities. The function of detail when ordered by a human imagination is to illustrate the universe."

The Role of Feeling

To all these previous techniques, we should add a few points about mental and emotional attitudes during an inquiry. We've already seen that to reach even a probable truth, we need an objective approach. It seems self-evident that personal bias or an emotional attitude will only lead a person to prove what he or she already believes. Yet we face a paradox here. The best writing, and probably the more important discoveries, derive from intense involvement, from deep personal feelings about a subject. I began this book with two units on personal writing because my experience with students has led me to believe that the human voice speaking out of honest personal observation rings truest in the ear of the reader. Unless we are able to *feel* a subject as well as perceive it objectively, we have not truly explored it in all its fullness.

You must approach a subject with an open mind, but also with a sense of caring. That is what it means to be sensitive. Pierre Curie, a French scientist and the husband of Marie Curie, entered into a ten-year investigation of piezoelectric crystals because of their beauty. Beauty involves aesthetic appreciation. In other words, it was an emotion that motivated and sustained objective research. In Curie's case, the emotion and the objective facts complemented each other and enriched the inquiry process. On other occasions, you'll find that objective facts oppose inner feelings. You can never ignore the facts or slight them or distort them because of that. The facts must always be fairly and accurately presented, no matter how painful it may be. Emotion and objectivity may oppose or complement each other. Either way, your research and your writing will be enhanced by an intense commitment that effectively balances the two qualities.

Evaluating Sources

To *evaluate* is to judge the worth of something. Each fact, idea, or opinion you obtain during an investigation must be evaluated for its worth. A few years ago, a book was published claiming to have evidence that a human being had been cloned. Because cloning was a "hot" topic, the book sold well. But some individuals had their doubts. When the author of the book was discovered to have previously published science-fiction novels on cloning, even more doubts were raised. The evidence itself *might* have been valid, but the source of the evidence required that we accept an assertion of human cloning with great skepticism.

But what if the source is a distinguished physicist, the author of a textbook on physics you've located in your library? Surely a respected scientist can be believed. But if the date on the textbook is 1915, it too must be considered a doubtful source. The study of physics has been turned upside down in the twentieth century, and any views presented in 1915 are probably outdated.

All of this gets tricky. A radio commentator who often opposed the environmentalist movement recently claimed that the discovery of a "dangerous hole in the ozone" was a hoax perpetrated by environmentalists using scare tactics to raise funds and enlist supporters. The radio commentator argued that the ozone hole was in fact a natural phenomenon that allowed "bad gases" to escape the atmosphere. Should we believe environmentalists, who might indeed be influenced by self-interest? Or should we believe a radio commentator (with no scientific training) who had often expressed his bias against "radical" environmentalists?

The problem here is that your own bias might come into play. Your background, your parents' views, the attitudes of those in your neighborhood, church, or college might affect your judgment. You might have an inclination to accept one or the other of these *sources* because you already favor that particular *position*. Yet, in truth, both sources need to be evaluated. Self-interest, and even an announced position of bias for or against something, does not *in itself* preclude valid evidence. Nor do you need to be "an authority" or possess a fancy title or degree for the evidence to be meaningful. Each source must be tested, questioned, and evaluated. Consider the context, the time frame, and the cultural influences. In other words, be skeptical. Human nature is always involved. Withhold judgment until more facts or evidence can be obtained. No matter who or what your source is, attempt to verify all information from a second source.

Evaluating Evidence

All information must be weighed carefully *regardless of the source*. We have been taught to think of scientists as objective and to consider their findings as truth. Yet, after two respected university scientists announced that they had conducted successful "cold fusion" experiments in the laboratory, it was discovered the evidence did not stand up under further research by other scientists, which, if nothing else, may prove that even professional researchers make mistakes.

So do others who have the best of intentions. For example, evidence on the abuse of women is not necessarily valid merely because most of us may have strong moral feelings about the subject. A moral position does not sanctify facts and make them accurate. Questions must still be asked: Where did the information come from? Who did the research? How reliable is it? A few years ago, a national women's organization claimed that every sixty seconds a woman was being abused somewhere in America. The statistic was shocking, and because it was based on hospital research the data seemed valid. It turned out that the hospital that did the research was a single institution located in a poverty-stricken, inner-city neighborhood and that the information came from emergency room admissions. There are at least three problems here: First, the data may be unusually high because of social conditions prevalent in that particular neighborhood. Second, no determination was made as to how many of the patients being admitted were repeats (that is, a single individual battered six times in six months might well have been counted as six different individuals). Third, even if the data were accurate for that hospital in that setting, there was no additional research to confirm its validity nationwide. The women's organization that released the data was reputable. The hospital that did the study was reputable. But there was no evidence that we could generalize from conditions in a single neighborhood and call it true for an entire nation.

Data that is consistent, or that can be verified by separate independent sources, is probably accurate. Opinions and inferences may be valuable to understanding a subject even though they are not factual. As a beginning scholar, the primary thing to remember is that you should not accept the first information encountered, or the first definition of a concept, or the first opinion or theory of anything as "truth." Look for more information, additional definitions, and more interpretations and opinions. *Compare, contrast, question,* and *evaluate.*

Exercises

1. Because much of your college work will focus on understanding abstract concepts, principles, and "ideas," consider the following definition of "concept" by a noted psychologist, Lyle E. Bourne, Jr. Your instructor may want you to discuss, as a class, or with your peer group, other possible definitions of the term, as well as the ambiguities. Can you find even more complications than Bourne has found? More ways the term is used? Do you feel Bourne's definition is helpful, or does it remain vague and confusing? Is there any reason at all to explore the definition of a term in this much depth?

   The term "concept" has a multitude of meanings. Most of us have used or applied it in a myriad of ways, and among these uses there may not be a great deal of obvious similarity. For example, "concept" is commonly used as a synonym for idea, as when we say, "Now he seems to have the concept," in reference to someone who has finally caught onto a message. Or we may talk of an abstract state of affairs, such as freedom, and call it a concept. On other occasions, a concept seems to be akin to a mental image, as in the case of trying to conceptualize (visualize) an unfamiliar object or event from a verbal description. Undoubtedly, each of these examples captures in part the meaning of "concept." But clearly, it would be difficult (or impossible) to formulate an unambiguous definition from them.

   In experimental psychology the term "concept" has come to have a rather specialized meaning, which may not encompass all its various ordinary uses. Psychology is the scientific investigation of the behavior of organisms, which includes as a sub-area the study of how organisms (human beings and lower animals) learn and use concepts. In such an undertaking, explicitly, communicable definitions of terms are an absolute necessity. "Concept" is no exception.

   As a working definition we may say that a concept exists whenever two or more distinguishable objects or events have been grouped or classified together and set apart from other objects on the basis of some common feature or property characteristic of each. Consider the class of "things" called dogs. Not all dogs are alike. We can easily tell our favorite Basset from the neighbor's Great Dane. Still all dogs have certain features in common and these serve as the basis for a conceptual grouping. Furthermore, the grouping is so familiar and so well defined that few of us have any difficulty calling a dog (even an unfamiliar dog) by that name when we encounter one.

There is then the concept "dog"; similarly, the class of all things called "house" is a concept, and the class of things called "religion."

Lyle E. Bourne, Jr., *Human Conceptual Behavior*

2. Select a concept, value, notion, idea, or principle that you might be interested in investigating. Make a list of everything you know (or assume you know) about the topic. From the list, consider how you might begin to narrow the focus and what types of additional resources you'll need to explore it further. Use some of the strategies reviewed in this chapter to consider the types of questions that might be valuable in exploring the concept: *Who* is involved in this concept? *What* are the primary issues or conflicts (if any)? *Where* did the concept come from? *Why* is it important? *When* was it first conceived? Is there a standard definition of it, or is it ambiguous and difficult to pin down? Has it evolved or changed over time? Answer as many of your own questions as possible in rough form. Some answers may lead you to more questions. Once you've seemingly reached an end, consider whether you need to narrow the focus of your investigation and how both your questions and your answers might suggest the next step.

3. Evaluating sources and information are crucial steps you'll need to undertake in any investigation. The following are three sources providing information about a student's application to join a college honors program. Evaluate each of the sources and the information provided by each. Look for patterns or relationships. Draw a reasonable inference about the student's qualifications for honors work.

Excerpts from Student Application Form

a. Describe the most important book you've read this year.

   The best book I've read this year was *Einstein's Dreams*. Usually I read biographies.

b. What are your goals and ambitions?

   I plan to open my own successful law office and go into politics. I'd like to be a congressman or senator someday.

c. Describe an accomplishment of which you are particularly proud.

   Last spring my father had a stroke while running our family's business—a dry cleaners. My brother and I kept the store open and profitable for two months by ourselves until my father recovered.

d. Why do you want to participate in an honors program?

   I am applying for honors because it would be a personal accomplishment. It also might help me get into law school.

Excerpts from Letters of Reference

I have known Randolph for several years. I once treated him for hyperactivity when he was younger. Throughout the years he has matured and turned out to be a fine young man. I understand from his mother that he has applied for your honors program, and I feel he would be a welcome addition.

John L. Morando, M.D.

It is a pleasure for me to recommend Randolph as a candidate for your honors program. As his guidance counselor I have known him for three years. I also taught him in a class on interpretative dance, for which he received an A plus. He is an excellent student whose chief areas of interest are history, psychology, and political science. We would be very proud here at Easter High School for Randolph to be selected for such a fine program.

Kathleen Spangler, Counselor

Excerpts from High School Transcript

National Test Scores: SAT Verbal 601/SAT Math 545

Grades in Senior Year: English . . . A
Algebra II . . . C
History . . . A
Physical Education . . . B
Psychology . . . A
Social Studies . . . A
French II . . . A

Activities: Debating Club, Young Men's Republican Club, Chess Club, President of Senior Class, Honors Society.

Awards: Junior Chamber of Commerce Award for Business Competition—Youth Class, Wisconsin High School Chess Tournament Honorable Mention, Junior Achievement Award, Honorable Mention in the "I Speak for Democracy" competition, delegate to the Midwest United Nations Conference.

CHAPTER 17

Primary and Secondary Sources

No writer who is any good writes solely from the contemplation of his navel. He must know, either through personal experience or through research.

JOHN DEWITT MCKEE

We're now ready to put together the process by which writers set out to research an abstract concept or idea. We might describe this as a triangular process involving first, your personal observation (when possible or applicable); second, the extension of observation by using others' eyes and experience as reported directly to you in an interview or as recorded in an original document; and third, the exploration of secondary sources—the use of knowledge and insight accumulated throughout history by other authors.

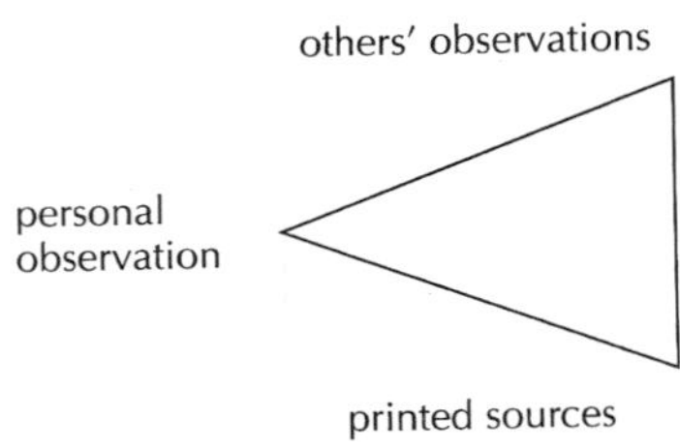

Primary Materials

A primary source provides information to you in some direct way—through a personal interview, telephone conversation, e-mail message, letter, diary, journal, ledger, memo, manuscript, or book that presents a first-hand account. Even your own personal experience might be considered a primary source if it directly involves the subject of investigation. This may not be as limited as it first appears. For example, if you were writing about the concept of the "American Dream," your experience and observation is absolutely appropriate. At some level, almost all abstract concepts or ideas have a concrete element to them. "Minority rights" can be discussed as an abstract notion, but it has a direct, real-world application, and you may have been intimately involved in some part of it. The same would be true of "love," or "child abuse," or "capitalism."

I once had the opportunity of living in an eastern European country that had been under the influence of the former Soviet Union. Although I had previously studied the ideas of Karl Marx, until I lived the experience, talked with workers in the "worker state," and was invited into the homes of the "middle class" (which supposedly did not exist in a "classless society"), I did not truly understand all the implications, contradictions, and complexities of an abstract concept called "Communism."

Even if you haven't had first-hand knowledge of the concept you're investigating, others may have. Interviews, phone calls, letters, and biographical accounts may provide you with insights, with the human element behind the abstraction.

Secondary Materials

A secondary source provides information, analysis, interpretation, and perhaps most important, the broad overview that takes into account patterns and organization of knowledge. Secondary sources will probably constitute the largest body of material available to you on most topics. Obviously, your personal ability to observe is limited, as are the number of interviews you might conduct. And "concepts" or ideas are always more comprehensive than any single individual's personal experience.

Students sometimes feel that investigation of secondary material is somehow taxing, more duty than pleasure—all those hours in the library taking notes or sitting in front of a computer screen searching a database. But every subject is interesting when pursued imaginatively, critically, and skeptically. If you bring a dull mind to the work, it will indeed seem dull. If you involve yourself with some sort of personal commitment, even the evolution of the aardvark can become fascinating. What is always necessary is a focused question—the question that grows out of the narrowing of your topic: Does this fact or opinion relate to others? Does it conflict with others? How is it significant? Whom does it affect? Does it constitute part of a larger pattern? Does it fit the definition you've been working with? Is it true?

Researching Secondary Sources

Some students arrive at college with extensive experience at computer searches; others have barely learned to use the traditional print index. All of us, however, must face the fact that the world of research is undergoing a profound change. Some information is still found in print, in books and journals; other information is located on various types of microfilm; still more is available electronically. Libraries themselves can barely keep up with developments.

The best attitude to take is the paradoxical one of "calm excitement." You'll need to accept the revolution going on about you with calmness. Nothing will stop it. You *will* be a part of it, but you also need to enjoy the excitement of it. Change always causes problems, but it also brings incredible opportunities.

For a short essay on an abstract concept or idea, you need not feel overwhelmed by the research portion. Begin where you are most comfortable. That might mean looking up the term in an encyclopedia. Encyclopedias give good broad overviews for nonspecialists, and some provide further suggestions for research. Other, more specialized encyclopedias may be even more valuable. Here's a short list to suggest the types of specialized works available to you:

Dictionary of American History
Encyclopedia of Environmental Science
Encyclopedia of Chemistry
Encyclopedia of Human Biology
Encyclopedia of Religion
Encyclopedia of the American Constitution
Encyclopedia of World Cultures
New Grove Dictionary of Music and Musicians
Women's Studies Encyclopedia

The list could fill pages. Reference works like these will offer you more technical data, more specialized information and opinion, and usually, lists of other major resources to follow up on.

You may also want to consult one of numerous disciplinary guides that identify the important journals, bibliographies, and handbooks in a given field of study. Here's a very brief sampling:

Education: A Guide to Reference and Information Sources
Political Science: A Guide to Reference and Information Sources
Library Use: A Handbook for Psychology
Visual Arts Research

Some topics may be current news, in which case you'll want to concentrate your early search on newspapers and news magazines. Periodical guides (*The Reader's Guide* or various electronic databases, such as *InfoTrac*) searched by topic or keywords, will give you immediate help. Additional information, and step-by-step strategies for research, can be found in Part 8, Scholarly Research, pages 408–461. Most college libraries will assist you in finding reference materials (that is, those sources organized by subject matter that inform you of where you can find specific information on your topic). Many libraries also offer classes on how to use the online catalog and how to do more extensive electronic searches.

The best advice, at this stage, is this: Don't let yourself feel overwhelmed by it all. Begin with strategies you know and feel comfortable with. Then, on each further paper you write, extend your knowledge of resources and research techniques. Add at least one new method or one new resource opportunity each time.

This also can be an excellent time to work with a partner. Even if you are researching different topics, you will bring different backgrounds and ways of thinking to the search. What puts off one of you may be familiar territory to the other. Working with a partner also tends to enhance perseverance because, by sharing, you can halve the frustration and double the pleasure of the research process.

Documentation of Sources

Because the source of any information you obtain affects the value of the information, a writer must always provide complete and accurate documentation. In formal papers, you'll want to provide identification of sources within the text and in a separate listing of "Works Cited" at the end. In a report or short essay, however, identification of sources within the text is usually enough.

Both primary and secondary sources need to be documented. Some instructors may provide you with a preferred method; some businesses and institutions may provide a "style sheet" that lists a prescribed form. Without such guidance, you can rely on any number of methods for integrating the documentation into your material so long as it provides, in general, *who, what, where,* and sometimes *when.*

Primary Sources

Who? The first time information from a source is used, give the full name of the source. In addition, give the source's full title or a description of his or her authority to speak on the subject.

What? If a manuscript, original document, or book is used, give the full title (or a description if it doesn't have a title). If the source is an individual, give his or her location.

Where? Tell where the source is located, should the reader wish to verify the information. (If the source is a published book, you would not, of course, want to say that it is located in the library. Instead, provide the same in-text documentation described next under *Secondary Sources.*)

what *who* *where* *authority*
A letter from Roger T. Jerome, California state assemblyman and self-professed expert on aardvarks, claims that aardvarks have become an uncontrolled problem near the campus area.

when *what* *who* *where*
In a June 3, 1998 e-mail interview message, Horace Greene, San Diego Zoo-
authority
keeper and noted aardvark specialist, dismissed the notion that the species could constitute an uncontrolled threat. He cited the relatively low aardvark population numbers throughout California.

who *where*
Bud Walker, University of Missouri freshman, claims he had never heard of aardvarks until he became mixed up with a bad crowd.

authority
Today, however, Walker raises aardvarks in his basement.

Secondary Sources

For secondary sources (or published primary sources), the same general information is necessary, although *when* the information was published must be added.

who
Former President George Bush declared, "There were no aardvarks in my
where *when*
administration" (*Time,* December 2, 1993).

who *authority* *where*
Dr. Harold Bley, professor of zoology, Arizona State University, asserts in his
when *what*
classic 1931 study on aardvarks, *Cognitive Configurations of Snout Development,* that aardvarks will inherit the earth (231).

where *who*
In her *Save Our Aardvarks* advocacy website, Sarah Summers, animal
authority *what*
behavior psychologist, adds that aardvarks are remarkably peaceful and non- aggressive creatures (2000, para. 3).

Direct quotations, paraphrases, and summaries all need to be attributed to a fully documented source. Statistics, facts, ideas, inferences, and opinions should all be attributed to a fully documented source.

The reader needs to know specifically *who* your source is, *what* information you obtained from that source, *what* authority the source had to speak on the subject, *where* the subject can now be found (if primary material), or *where* and *when* the information was printed.

You should recognize that this demand for accurate documentation exists not only so that material can be verified by a second observer but also because the stronger the source of information, the stronger the facts will seem to your reader and the more thorough your investigation will appear.

(For other examples, and for an explanation of the "Works Cited" format, see pages 451–455.)

The Full Investigation

Even as a first-year student, Barry Kolodny had a serious interest in art. Simultaneously with taking first-year writing, he had enrolled in a 300-level art history class, and although he liked it, he confessed to sometimes feeling in over his head. He was especially interested in Gothic art, but after looking up the term in an encyclopedia, he felt lost. The encyclopedia had given him a seemingly endless number of definitions. His next step was to interview the instructor of his art history class, who helped him limit his topic to stained-glass windows, which the instructor said would "reflect the primary thrust of Gothic art in general."

Over the next week, Barry surveyed numerous art books with photos of various famous Gothic windows. He read selections from three different art history texts: Emile Males' *The Gothic Image,* Henry Adams' *Mont-Saint-Michael and Chartres,* and Otto Simson's *The Gothic Cathedral.* After writing his essay, he tested it on his peer group for clarity, effectiveness, and interest.

Here are the first four paragraphs of Barry's essay:

Provocative lead (see Chapter 18)	"If you can learn to read the symbolism of Gothic stained-glass windows," Professor Sheryl Dickinson says, "you can understand Gothic, and you can understand the soul of the middle ages."
Authority	Dickinson is assistant professor of art at MiddleValley State College. This is her first year teaching after completing a Ph.D. in art history, with
Primary source (interview with expert)	a special emphasis on Gothic cathedrals. "Art always reflects the spirit of an age," Dickinson observes, "and that was never more true than the Gothic period."
Overview of concept	She defines the Gothic age as "the dominant aesthetic mode in Western Europe between the 12th and 16th centuries." Dickinson describes it as full of contradictions, "intoxicated" with energy, mysticism, religious hysteria, and even a type of philosophy called "scholasticism."
	Dickinson also argues that stained-glass windows in Gothic cathedrals were in fact intended to be the

books of their time, books for otherwise illiterate serfs and peasants. If that is true, then the soul of the era was entirely Christian.

Secondary source

The windows are a replacement for the Bible itself. They tell the story of Christianity, and, according to Emile Males, much that was apocryphal as well (15). One finds side by side in the windows, images of Old and New Testament figures, along with later saints and historical figures such as Charlemagne, Clovis,

Illustration

and crusaders, sometimes surrounded by images of stone masons, carpenters, and a bishop or two, all crowded together in a *"Summa* of encyclopedic knowledge," including moral, natural, and historical, as well as spiritual (27).

Contrast

To our mind, at the turn of the second millennium, stained-glass Gothic windows seem darkly mysterious, a kaleidoscope of colors, faces, Biblical figures, dying saints, bleeding hearts, and Kings with uplifted faces. But to a 13th-century peasant in France, the same window must have seemed like a ray of light,

Evaluation of evidence to this point

a revelation of the meaning of existence and an explanation of his cultural heritage. It turns out that "Gothic" is not just art, it is history, philosophy, mysticism, and culture.

In his research, Barry eventually realized the only kind of paper he could write on "Gothic" was one that continually attempted to explain and define the concept itself. The reason the encyclopedia he had first looked into offered so many different definitions was clear: The concept of "Gothic" is so complex, no single meaning can express it all. Even in narrowing his focus to stained-glass windows, Barry found the topic remained broad enough to write a book on and that many previous scholars had done just that. But as a starting point for exploration, he was pleased that the focus on windows gave him concrete visual illustrations of the concept and of the richness of cultural and historical values it encompassed.

Group Inquiry

After selecting a concept, value, notion, idea, or principle you might be interested in investigating, pair up with another student for mutual interviews. In order to sharpen your focus, ask each other questions from the 5 *W*'s and 4 *C*'s as well as questions about people and context associated with your concept. Take copious notes or tape-record your conversation. When each of you has discovered a manageable topic, change the focus of the interview to audience concerns. At this point, the person planning to write on a particular topic should question the other about what information needs to be included in the essay to make it both convincing and compelling for a reader.

Exercises

1. For each of the following "concepts," discuss types of resources you might consider researching. For example, are any of them open to "personal observation" or experience? If so, under what circumstances would it be possible, appropriate, or valuable to bring yourself into it? Consider the types of experts who might be interviewed—in person or even by telephone—on any given topic. Who would constitute being an expert for these topics? What type of printed or electronic resources can you use as a starting point for your investigation?

   Grade inflation (education)
   Virtual reality (computers, psychology)
   Zero-based budgeting (management)
   Utopias (literature, philosophy)
   Recovered memory (psychology, law)
   Recycling (environmental studies)
   Method acting (theater, film)
   Form versus function (architecture)
   Special interest groups (politics)
   Bilingual education (foreign languages, politics)

2. Here are four "documented" sources taken from student papers. Consider which are complete and informative and which have omitted essential elements needed for verification.

   a. Samuel B. Goldman, commission chairman, indicated in a speech to the accounting class on Friday that Minneapolis business conditions were unstable.

   b. As part of my study, I wrote to North Carolina's Republican congressman, Bill Hendon. In a letter from his Washington office, dated January 3, 1997, he claimed to support the college-tuition tax credit for the following reasons: . . .

   c. Bilingual programs were begun nationwide in all cities with more than a 5 percent Chicano population, according to a *Time* magazine interview with Dr. Kenneth Kriester, Title VII coordinator for the U.S. Department of Health, Education and Welfare (*Time,* September 23, 1998).

   d. CBS News reported that the divorce rate had risen again in the 1990s, but so had the marriage rate.

3. In a sentence or two, provide all necessary documentation and the main facts for each of the following notes.

a. "I believe the Charismatic Christian movement is just reaching its peak," *Religion Today,* Reverend Charles Mathews, Jr., page 21, June 1981, Church of the Good Pastor, Baltimore.

b. Dr. Cameron Kelly, from an e-mail interview message, "There's a trend in popular culture toward growing suspicion of the U.S. government and an increasing belief in conspiracy theories," lecturer and Doctor of Philosophy at Swarthmore University, March 7, 1999, discussed mass hysteria and paranoia while on a guest lecturing tour of 12 campuses.

c. p. 369, *The Origins of Evolutionary Theory,* P. Samuel Wyndcotyl, "Darwin was not the first to propose the concept of evolution," professor of biology, chairperson of the biology department at the University of Toronto, has published six books on evolution since 1955, copyright 1972.

d. "We are approaching an ecological disaster," Boston, Mass., John Pittston, Staley Lecture series, Thursday, March 5, 1993, Boston University, editor of the *Ecological Drift,* a collection of essays, spokesman for the Sierra Club.

e. Looked up and found Nov. 11th, 2001, from The Brady Campaign to Prevent Gun Violence Website, "There is one critical need that Congress has failed to address—weak federal firearm laws that terrorists exploit to stockpile deadly weapons," in an unsigned article, researching gun control for social issues class, http://www.brady campaign.org/.

CHAPTER 18

Imaginative Leads

It was a pleasant summer day—warm with just a hint that it would grow hot and humid later on. Doctors moved quietly among a score of patients at the Jewish Chronic Disease Hospital in Brooklyn, giving them injections under the skin of one thigh. It was just a test of their immunity, the patients had been told. There was no real danger, though they "might feel a little discomfort and perhaps see a lump for a while." But there was one thing the patients weren't told: that the injections contained live cancer cells.

William Barry Furlong wrote the above paragraph as an introduction to an article in *Good Housekeeping.* Furlong might have written, "The subject of my report is about doctors who are experimenting with cancer on live human beings." He might have, but he didn't. Few professional writers begin an informative article or essay or even a business report with such a dull statement of purpose. As a writer you want to tell your reader the subject of your paper. But why be boring when you can be interesting?

You've already studied the 5-*W* lead in Chapter 13. Knowing other types of imaginative leads can give you a surprising range of alternatives for effective introductions. Imaginative leads may be anything from a sentence to a page or more (depending on the length of the total writing project). Their intent is to involve the reader directly in some concrete element of the subject while also directly or indirectly presenting the underlying idea. The imaginative lead attempts to catch the reader's interest through the use of quotation, a question, a dramatized conflict, suspense, humor, or shock—and then to lead clearly and logically into the subject itself. The lead should set the tone, provide the underlying idea of your paper, and even suggest to the reader the organization of the essay that follows. A lot for a few sentences to accomplish, but perhaps it explains why professional writers put so much emphasis on the value of the lead. Donald M. Murray, essayist, novelist, journalist, Pulitzer prize winner, and teacher, says that many writers spend 85 percent of their effort on the lead—not just to catch the reader's attention, but because of its focusing and organizing potential (Chapter 19 will go into more depth on how the lead suggests an organization).

The Provocative Lead

A bold, provocative statement may be the easiest way to grab your reader's attention.

> The feminist movement was a spectacular failure. Instead of freeing women to find the best qualities in themselves, it condemned them to adopt the very worst qualities found in men.

Here, a student writer has used a strong, declarative first sentence. It is actually a conclusion based on his investigation. The author does not present the facts, only the meaning he has interpreted from them. The result, standing by itself as the first sentence, can seem striking, challenging, opinionated. The reader may be in full support or may be offended. Either way, one feels compelled to continue reading. Will the author be able to support such boldness with concrete factual evidence or with logical argument?

A provocative lead may come from the situation itself rather than from a judgment about the situation. Here's the best example and probably the most famous lead of all time:

> In the beginning God created Heaven and earth.

Hard to stop reading at this point. The audience is almost trapped into continuing to see how God did it.

The Contrast or Conflict Lead

Aldous Huxley was a master of the contrast lead.

> The most distressing thing that can happen to a prophet is to be proved wrong; the next most distressing thing is to be proved right. In the twenty-five years that have elapsed since *Brave New World* was written, I have undergone both these experiences. Events have proved me distressingly wrong; and events have proved me distressingly right.

The paradox of this lead is so intriguing that the reader's interest is immediately captured. At the same time, Huxley clearly implies his topic (events confirmed or denied since the writing of his novel) as well as the probable design of the essay (half on events that proved to be right, half on events that proved wrong).

For some reason human beings have an eternal interest in conflict: cops and robbers, Luke Skywalker and Darth Vadar, girls and boys. Find a conflict or a clearly defined contrast, especially an unexpected one, and you'll probably have a natural lead paragraph.

> The process of cloning may be one of the most beneficial discoveries ever made by humankind.
>
> But cloning may also lead to loss of individual rights and freedom, political dictatorship, and a more frightening world than even George Orwell imagined in *1984.*

This student writer has emphasized conflicting opinions by using two one-sentence paragraphs. Many teachers dislike the one-sentence paragraph, and rightly so when it is used to make a random statement without further development, evidence, or support. In general, such paragraphs should be avoided. But when a strong emphasis is desired, the one-sentence lead may be the perfect way to catch the reader's attention.

The Question Lead

The question lead can fail miserably if it seems to be a substitute for a more thoughtful or imaginative introduction. Try to avoid the rhetorical or dead-end question: *Can human beings live without love? What is the meaning of life? Should disease be wiped out?* A truly thoughtful question, however, can stimulate interest if it raises the reader's curiosity or seems to suggest an impact on the reader's values, beliefs, or the like. Here is a student lead that raises legitimate issues:

> The American Psychiatric Association once held that homosexuality was a category of mental illness. About twenty years ago, at a convention where there was extensive gay lobbying, the members of the association voted to adopt a new definition called "sexual orientation disturbance." Today, most psychologists apparently believe that homosexuality is in fact caused by biological or genetic factors and is not related to any kind of psychological "disturbance." The APA has therefore removed it entirely from its list of abnormal psychological conditions.
>
> This decision may be correct, but all this raises serious questions about the field of psychology. The APA seems to be acting more out of political correctness than science. If medical doctors decided that because of

> pressure by lobbying groups, a ruptured appendix was not an illness, would we accept the decision? Do psychologists have no other method for distinguishing emotional problems from normal conditions, except by voting? Can psychiatry really be called a science if it can so easily redefine the nature of a supposed illness into a "disturbance" and then into an apparently "normal" condition?

In an age dominated by psychology, such questions have direct impact on us all. The question lead also sets up a natural organization for your paper: You have to answer your own question.

The Cumulative-Interest Lead

> Seven dead of wounds. A twenty-one-year-old woman paralyzed from the neck down. Four widows. Twelve children left without fathers. Over $158,000 in medical and funeral expenses. Two hundred and six robberies. These were the statistics for one city—Los Angeles—during a single month without gun-control legislation.

The cumulative-interest lead attempts to overwhelm the reader with a "pileup" of facts, sometimes without attaching the facts to any specific subject until several sentences into the essay. Dramatic lists or statistics seem to stimulate interest automatically.

The preceding lead comes from a student report. Even though it does not directly state the subject of the report, the tone and focus—even the conclusion—are implied. The author has presented a series of objective facts, yet each fact has been carefully selected for its impact. And the final sentence suggests the remainder of the paper will deal in more detail with gun-control legislation. If, for some reason, the paper actually focused on robberies committed with guns, the lead would be a failure because the last sentence implies a larger issue.

Here is a cumulative-interest lead from an essay in *Smithsonian:*

> For years now the stuff has been insidiously creeping into the nooks and crannies of our lives, firmly but unobtrusively shouldering aside the traditional materials of which our world is made. Cars are constructed of it, and boats and even airplanes, to say nothing of computer housings and camera bodies and fishing rods and watch cases and suitcases and cookware and roller skates and toothpaste tubes. It has replaced the glass in our spectacles, the

> paper in our grocery bags, the wood in our tennis rackets, the cotton in our clothing and, in an especially pernicious peanut-shaped form used for packing material, it has exploded from a million cardboard appliance cartons to lodge under our couches and drive us to intemperate language.
>
> It can be brittle or brutishly strong, dirt cheap or astonishingly expensive, fragile or virtually indestructible. It can go anyplace from outer space to the depths of the sea, and once there it will do just about any job it is called upon to do. For decades, as a society we have denigrated it even as we have consumed more and more of it. If in our fanciful moments many of us imagine ourselves in a world free of it, in fact most of us would sorely miss its extraordinary versatility and usefulness. By now the stuff has—literally—found its way into our hearts.
>
> The stuff is, of course, plastic.

Like all leads, this one establishes a tone and a sense of direction. Although the lead begins with negatives, the clear suggestion is that a positive essay on plastic will follow.

The Descriptive Lead

The descriptive lead might also be called the literary lead because it takes as its model the concept of the scene (see Chapter 9). Human beings have a natural interest in hearing stories. A scene, in effect, presents a story in miniature and is, therefore, one of the most popular and most effective means of concretely involving the reader.

> For more than half an hour thirty-eight respectable, law-abiding citizens in Queens watched a killer stalk and stab a woman in three separate attacks in Kew Gardens. Twice the sound of their voices and the sudden glow of their bedroom lights interrupted him and frightened him off. Each time he returned, sought her out, and stabbed again. Not one person telephoned the police during the assault; one witness called after the woman was dead.

The horror of this news story is intensified by *The New York Times* writer who takes us step-by-step through the event. We hear the voices, we see lights in bedroom windows, and perhaps in our imagination we see the killer's shadow stalking the young woman. Not until the final word of the paragraph do we learn the result. The emphasis we placed on sensory perception in earlier chapters can be used with dramatic effectiveness in a descriptive lead. Here is student Laura Stone's opening paragraph for a sociology report on aging. She began by visiting a nursing home.

The old woman sat with her hunched back to me. Her wheelchair faced the window that looked out on a Sunoco gas station. Greasy barrels and stacks of used rubber tires and cardboard boxes of worn-out auto parts lined the back of the station. The light coming through the window seemed greasy and faded. The old woman's hair was curled in ringlets and the light shone through giving her a halo effect. From the next room a TV voice announced *As the World Turns.* I made a halfhearted attempt at saying hello but the old woman did not move an inch. Over her bed hung a crucifix with a plastic rose taped to it. On a nightstand there were several bottles of green pills, pink false teeth soaking in a glass of water, and several worn copies of *Reader's Digest.* I tried again. "Hello!" This time louder. "Hello!" Still the woman sat unmoving. The tile floors were polished, the white walls were newly painted. The bed was made. It was not a bad place. But the hunched old woman sat staring out through the window at the rear of a gas station, at the worn-out tires and generators and dead batteries.

Actually, the various types of leads are limited only by your own imagination. Furlong's lead, used at the beginning of this chapter, describing doctors injecting cancer cells into live patients, is a combination of the literary lead and the surprising statement. You could easily combine a question lead with a contrast lead or a literary lead with conflict, and so on.

It should be emphasized that a lead is not necessary. You can write an adequate informative investigation or essay without one or by using a factual 5-*W* lead. Most students and beginning writers never use leads. Yet a lead establishes a feeling of professionalism from the first sentence; it catches our imagination and makes us think, "Now here's a writer who seems to have something to say." Leads can do for you what almost no other writing technique can: capture the audience, set the mood or tone, suggest the focus and organization of your essay, and psychologically prepare the reader to be more receptive to your ideas—all at the same time.

Finding the Lead

Few professional writers wait until they have gathered all details on a subject before writing the lead. They train themselves to search out leads at the same time they are investigating the subject. Leads, therefore, directly relate to the exploration phase as well as to form and the first draft. If you come across a good quotation, an element of conflict, a dramatic change, a sensuous scene, or some startling fact, test it immediately in your mind: Would this make a good lead? If you can come up with a lead *before* you ever sit down to write, you will have solved one of those inhibitions to writing: facing the blank page. There won't be a blank page. Instead, you'll already have a sentence or a paragraph in mind. Leads thus are vital to the writer as well as the reader. Knowing in advance that you've got the first sentence or first paragraph helps release tension, helps to release the flow of ideas so that writing gets off to a good start.

Never trust yourself, however, to accept the first lead that comes along. Keep looking. A better one may turn up as you further explore your subject. Always try to write out several leads before you settle on the best. Try them on friends. Read several leads aloud to a roommate. Find out which one the listener would be most responsive to, which would make him or her want to hear more. Some professional writers admit that they spend as much time on the lead as on all the rest of their essay.

On the other hand, if you haven't been able to identify a good lead during the investigation of the subject, go ahead and begin your first draft. You may find that in writing the paper a lead will appear in the middle of it or even in the last sentence. Many a writer has discovered that his or her conclusion made a better lead than it did a final paragraph. Don't be afraid to move sentences and paragraphs around. Remember that drafting is only a process of discovery, and what you may discover is that a scene, fact, or detail you hadn't recognized as striking makes a natural introduction around which the rest of your ideas logically group themselves. In other words, let the lead work for you. Try to find it while studying the subject, but if you can't, don't panic. Let it find you during the writing process itself.

Exercises

1. Read each of the following leads. Discuss the technique the writer seems to be using. What type of tone or mood, if any, is established? From the brief sentence or paragraph provided, what probable design or organization of the material would you expect to follow? What specific quality in each lead makes it interesting or makes you want to read on?

   All happy families resemble one another, but each unhappy family is unhappy in its own way.

   Leo Tolstoy, *Anna Karenina*

   George Kastrides said it was like "being in the eye of a tornado with a high wind blowing." The passengers aboard TWA Flight 840 from Rome to Athens last week heard a loud bang. Then there was a flash of light. Oxygen masks dropped. A woman screamed. Several Arabs began chanting "*Al hamdu lil lah*" ("God be praised"). In the sudden swirl of wind and dust and flying particles, pilot Richard Peterson did not realize that four people, all Americans, had been blown out of the gaping hole in the Boeing 727. But Janet Chaffee looked behind her and saw sky where seat 10F had been. And on the ground, construction worker Alberto Ospina was still strapped into seat 10F when it hit the earth in a terrible tangle of blood and metal.

   Newsweek

Some hold that sports are childish, at best adolescent. "When one becomes a man, one ought to put aside the things of childhood." But what if participation in sports is the mark of a civilized person? What if it deepens and mellows the soul?

Michael Novak, "The Metaphysics of Sport"

I was born a white girl in Puerto Rico but became a brown girl when I came to live in the United States.

Judith Ortiz Cofer, "The Story of My Body"

In the past few decades, man has become capable of controlling almost every aspect of life through modern equipment and increased knowledge and insight into and about the human body. But these medical and technical advances are having a dual effect. True, in many instances, they are prolonging life. But in many other cases, they are, more accurately, prolonging death.

Student Research Paper

Once upon a time and a very good time it was there was a moocow coming down along the road and this moocow that was coming down along the road met a nicens little boy named baby tuckoo. . . .

His father told him that story: his father looked at him through a glass: he had a hairy face.

He was baby tuckoo. The moocow came down the road where Betty Byrne lived: she sold lemon platt. . . .

When you wet the bed first it is warm then it gets cold. His mother put on the oilsheet. That had the queer smell.

James Joyce, *A Portrait of the Artist as a Young Man*

When in the Course of human Events, it becomes necessary for one People to dissolve the Political Bands which have connected them with another, and to assume among the Powers of the Earth, the separate and equal Station to which the Laws of Nature and of Nature's God entitled them, a decent Respect to the Opinions of Mankind requires that they should declare the causes which impel them to the Separation.

Thomas Jefferson, *Declaration of Independence*

2. Create three different types of leads based on the following collection of material. Assume that this material represents the core of observations and research you have made on your subject. Which elements would be most interesting to begin with? Which elements might suggest a way of organizing the rest of the material?
   a. Marietta Bowker has lived in Bay's End, Maine, for her whole life, some ninety-three years.
   b. She raises strawberries, cabbage, corn, and tomatoes.

c. She now walks with a cane.
d. When she was sixteen, she married Harold Bowker and gave birth to thirteen children in the next fifteen years.
e. "I drink a nip of whiskey every day, and sometimes I smoke a cigar," she says, laughing.
f. She wears a red dress with white lilies on it.
g. The ocean breezes blow through the open window of her house.
h. Her six books of poetry have never sold more than fifty copies apiece.
i. There are geraniums on her windowsill.
j. She has outlived her husband and seven of her children, but she has thirty-two grandchildren and nine great-grandchildren.
k. She last went to the movies in 1952.
l. She walks five miles a day.
m. She doesn't know why she has lived so long.
n. "I just regret I didn't write more poetry," she says.

3. Return to one of your earlier assignments and write at least three different leads for it. For example, if you wrote a factual report for Part 3, try to come up with three new ways of beginning the same paper. Write a descriptive lead, a contrast lead, and a bold statement.

4. Audience and intention make a difference in how you begin anything you write. Choose a previous assignment or exercise and write new leads addressed to several different audiences. For example, if you wrote a profile for Part 3, use the same material to create three new leads: one for an essay to be published in a psychological journal; another for an essay to be distributed anonymously to your peers in a sociology class; a third for an essay to be included in a new anthology, titled *Interesting Americans,* intended for sale to a general audience.

Practice

1. Write about a time you bought something you desperately wanted but later regretted. Describe the object, sharing details that made it so enticing to you. Include your feelings about it before you bought it and after. What made you regret the purchase? How did your feelings and attitude change?

2. Write about a haunting agony: a sister who was accidentally killed; the day you were fired from your first job; being kicked off the soccer team your senior year; the time you discovered your younger brother was doing drugs. Focus sharply on a single specific scene and include characters and dialogue.

Copying

1. Practice copying leads (which may vary from one sentence to full paragraphs). Copy at least three different kinds of leads from this chapter. Watch for particularly striking leads while reading newspapers or magazines and be sure to copy them into your notebook or your computer file
2. Write three different leads for one of your previous papers.

CHAPTER 19

Visual Forms

Aldous Huxley has stated that the writer must have the urge "first of all, to order the facts one observes and to give meaning to life." To discover the pattern formed by a series of facts is to find order and meaning. Your audience shares that need with you. It cannot see meaning in your work without form or pattern. Random facts are like those disconnected dots on the page of a child's coloring book. Only when the dots are connected, and only when they are connected in recognizable shapes, is meaning communicated. Without order, without form or design or plan, we have only chaos, and chaos is not meaningful.

The most simple example proves the point. Try mixing up the sequence for a butterscotch brownies recipe:

Bake for 20 minutes.
Stir into the butter mixture.
Sprinkle flour on the dates and figs.
Cut into bars and serve.
Sift 1/2 cup of flour.
Pour the batter into a greased pan.
Chop the dates and figs.
Grease pan.
Melt 1/2 cup of butter in a saucepan.
Cool the ingredients.
Preheat oven to 350°.
Beat in one egg.

Without the proper arrangement, nothing makes sense.

Just as there is no one recipe that serves all types of cooking, you should not expect any one pattern or method of organization to serve all types of writing. In a personal essay, the arrangement of the parts usually grows organically out of the experience you've had with the subject. In more objective writing, form may sometimes grow out of the complex subject–audience–context–purpose or it may be based on an imitation of a traditional design. In a formal research paper, organization is usually constructed around a conventional thesis design. The frustrating part about "ordering the facts" is that for every set of facts there always seems to be a different order.

How the Lead Suggests Form

In many cases the organization of a paper can be discovered in the process of searching out the best lead. We've already noted how the 5-*W* lead suggested a natural sequence for an objective report. As the 5-*W* structure provides all major information in the first few sentences, it follows logically that less and less important information must trail behind. The visual design illustrates the form.

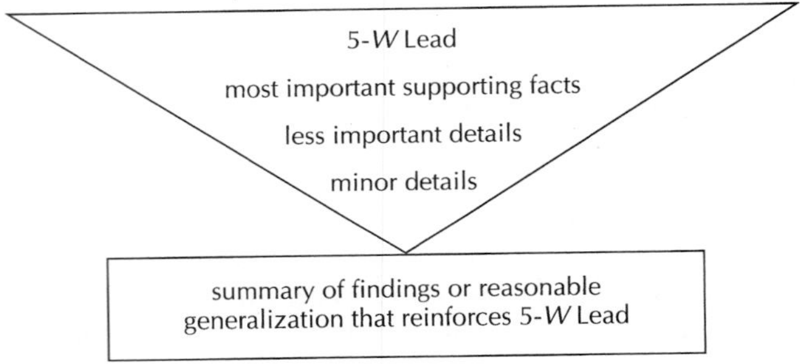

Note, however, that the lead does not create form. Rather, in the process of searching for a lead, you find that you must sift through all the information you have gathered; you must question the value, meaning, and worth of it; and you must consider your audience, purpose, and context. Each of these factors affects your choice of a lead. But these are the same factors that influence overall organization. In the process of looking for a lead, the mind wrestles with the shape of the subject itself. Just as the 4-*C*'s method of investigation gives you a strategy for finding potential meaning in a subject, so the lead gives you a strategy—a method—for finding an effective form. A lead is never something patched onto the beginning of an essay merely to make the introduction interesting. A lead is integral to the whole body of material you are working with.

Because we are visually oriented creatures, professional writers have developed several specific diagrams to help themselves envision forms that often grow out of the imaginative leads discussed in the previous chapter. Remember, however, that these patterns of organization are only suggestions, not rules.

The Provocative Lead Design

Because the provocative lead is usually a bold generalization of some sort—and usually judgmental—the nature of the lead demands that it be supported with objective evidence.

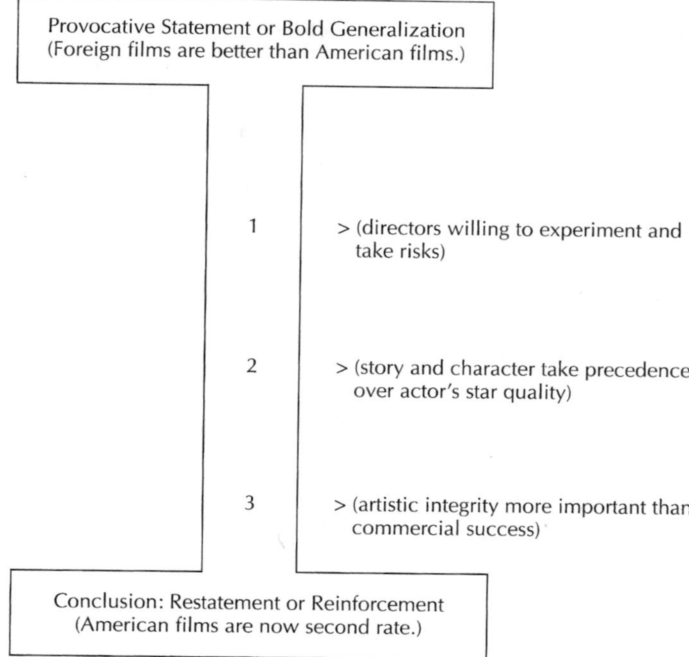

Once the facts and data have been given, the strength of the lead is then reinforced by repeating it as the conclusion, usually with different wording.

The sequence of facts in the middle of the paper may be organized either from most important to least important or the reverse. Good arguments have been presented for both methods. By starting with your weakest facts and building to your strongest, you raise the intensity of your paper as you progress and hope to sweep the reader along with you. On the other hand, by beginning with your strongest points, you hope to demonstrate immediately the truth of your bold generalizations by providing overwhelming evidence. In the preceding example, I've organized from "least to most." To me, artistic integrity is the final and most important critical judgment. Either organizational method may be effective. But do have a method: Don't jump randomly from strong point to weak point. Begin forcefully, present your facts in a planned sequence, and end forcefully.

The Contrast Design

A lead that calls attention to some type of opposition implies to the reader that you will deal equally and fairly with both sides of the conflict. For example, if you investigated the latest increase in tuition, you would find many students opposed; but you would also find explanations in support of it, perhaps from administrators. On a larger scale, an investigation of welfare costs might turn up many who would justify a large federal budget and others who would oppose it. The easiest way of organizing such information is to group all facts supporting one position in the first half of your paper and all facts supporting the other position in the second half. This organization has the benefit of simplicity for both you and the reader.

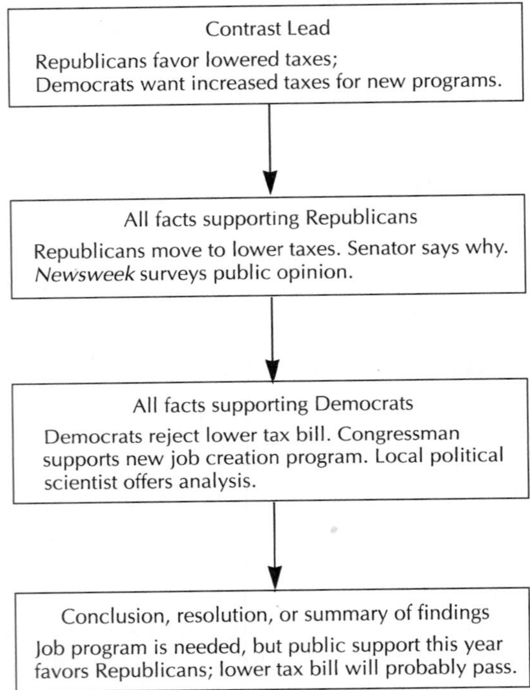

But this is not the only way to contrast material. A second method reveals the conflict more directly by alternating facts supporting one position with facts supporting the other (this is usually done by giving a paragraph or a page to each in alternating sequence). Most of us like a good debate. A back-and-forth exchange creates the tension and interest of two good debaters.

A word of caution, however. The alternating method of organization is more difficult for both reader and writer. Unless clear transitions are used at each changeover, the reader can easily become lost. Gather a good supply of transitions before you begin: *however, by contrast, in opposition to that view, but, on the other hand,* and so on.

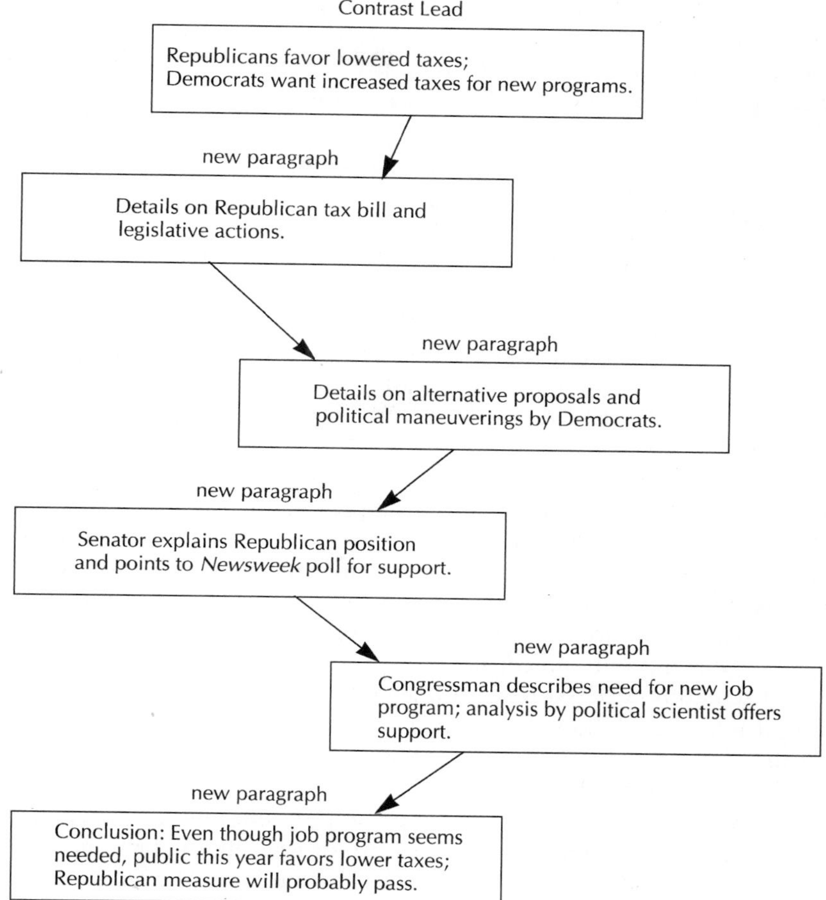

The Literary Design

Both the *cumulative-interest lead* and the *descriptive lead* suggest the possibility of moving from the specific details with which each begins toward a more general or abstract understanding of the details. The conclusion, as in a work of literature, remains in suspense until the final page. This type of organization is the opposite of the inverted pyramid.

The literary-lead design has several major advantages for the objective investigation or personal essay written in a humanities or social science course. The nature of the lead captures the reader's interest immediately; the ever-increasing importance of the details maintains interest and builds step-by-step toward what you hope will be seen as an inevitable conclusion. The form suggests a logical mind at work and tends to lead the reader toward accepting the concluding generalization. As in reading a mystery novel, the reader continues to the end in order to discover the fullest realization of facts you've perceived.

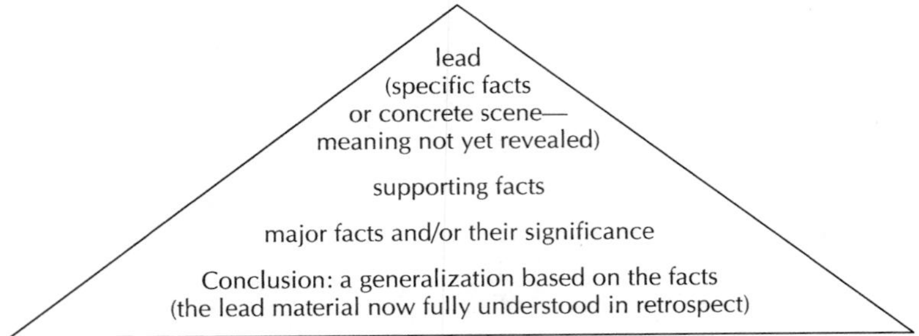

If we now consider the *lead* in retrospect, we see that its role in writing can be central both for reader and writer. For the reader, a lead creates interest and captures attention. It suggests tone, mood, and direction. For the writer, it provides an excellent method of getting started on the first draft. And it suggests a design or organization for the report as a whole.

Finding order in your subject need not be quite as overwhelming if, in the process of selecting the best lead, you also discover an organizational pattern for all that follows. Perhaps that's why professional writers willingly spend so much time on leads. They know that once the lead is set, the remainder of the paper will flow more easily.

Ultimately, of course, form grows out of content, not out of a predetermined diagram. Visual designs are not a substitute for engaging your mind with the subject. They offer only outlines that may help you "see" the content and discover its potential.

Group Inquiry

Three sets of facts are collected below. In your peer group, study the relationship within each set, and determine which of the visual designs discussed in this chapter might be best for organizing the facts. Draw the design on a full sheet of paper and test your proposal by filling in the appropriate spaces.

a. Trucking should not be regulated, according to Congressman Smith.

   Government statistics show higher costs owing to regulation.

   Trucking owners want regulations to continue.

   Some costs are double because of regulations.

Economic analysts in Washington say that industry fears competition if regulations are removed.

Regulations allow small companies to survive, according to the secretary of commerce.

b. The price of gold has gone down.

Oil nations want more dollars for oil.

Unemployment is increasing.

The president announces, "I will support the dollar."

A local economist fears a depression.

The danger to our economy was never greater.

c. The board of regents is concerned about a balanced budget.

Six men have gathered in the board-of-regents room; afternoon light filters in; coffee cups clank; discussion is heated; voices rise.

Board members agree to reinvest the funds in an Angolan gold mine.

Outside the windows two hundred students with signs march in a circle.

The return on the investment is enough to pay for five faculty salaries.

The students are concerned about moral values.

Students are protesting having university funds invested in a foreign country.

A student leader says the funds support racism and dictatorship.

An investigation of the financial statement reveals that 10 percent of the funds are invested in foreign countries.

Exercises

1. Study the readings included at the end of this unit. What relationship between the lead and overall design can you identify?

2. Draw a visual outline of the last paper you wrote for this or any other class. It does not need to look like any of the designs discussed in this chapter, but it should reveal the organization—or lack of organization—in your essay.

CHAPTER 20

Rhythm, Variety, and Emphasis

Have you ever "listened" to your writing? Here's a paragraph from a student who hasn't.

> Professor Shirley Baxton is in the English department. The interview was held in her office. She told me that she believed writing should be required in the whole university. She didn't believe it should be just required for English. She has a reputation for having high standards. She says writing is an expression of the inner self. She says it should be part of the experience we have in every class.

These are perfectly correct sentences, but not the sentences of real life. This student has not listened with his inner ear, and the result is Dick-and-Jane monotony. People don't talk this way. And even though good writing is not identical to speech, it should sound like speech. Good writing should reflect all the variety and points of emphasis found in the best conversation; it should express the rhythms of the human voice.

Rhythm

Rhythm means flow. Effective writing has a flow to it that suggests the sound patterns of living speech. And yet rhythm involves more than sound; it is inseparable from clarity, coherence, unity, order, and all the other elements of style as they work together within a specific context. Prose with little meaning is almost always accompanied by weak rhythms, and, in turn, weak and awkward rhythms signal that meaning may not yet be clearly expressed. Many of our best writers insist that one must develop an ear for the silent rhythm of the printed page. The best method for doing so, and the one least likely to be attempted by most students, is to listen to good prose as it's read aloud. The ear is more sensitive to rhythm than the eye.

Read aloud the following passage from Abraham Lincoln's *First Inaugural Address.* Listen to the voice you hear.

> I am loath to close. We are not enemies, but friends. We must not be enemies. Though passion may have strained it must not break our bonds of affection. The mystic chords of memory, stretching from every battlefield and patriot grave, to every heart and hearthstone, all over this broad land, will yet swell the chorus of the Union, when again touched, as surely they will be, by the better angels of our nature.

Lincoln begins with a short sentence, followed by another short sentence lengthened only slightly by a second clause. He returns to the short pattern and then moves on to what might be considered a sentence of medium length. The final sentence begins a long sweeping roll where clause after clause delays the most important words, like a symphony building toward a final musical statement. Read it aloud and the passage sings. But did you? I've taken surveys of my students and found that when I give this exercise, two-thirds continue to read silently. Yet rhythm, which is so essential to effective prose, cannot be learned in silence. If you would learn to play the drum, you must bang on it and listen to the sounds; if you would learn to write well, you must read aloud both good prose by professional writers and your own prose. And you must listen to the rhythms. If, out of laziness or shyness or whatever, you choose not to read aloud, you ignore one of the primary techniques our best authors have found successful. Quite simply, the student who reads aloud will have an advantage over the one who doesn't.

Let's return to the Lincoln passage and see what can be learned. Perhaps most important, we discover that rhythm is not a part of any one sentence. Rhythm is always found in context. That is why neither I nor anyone else can establish a "correct" or "model" sentence for you to imitate. There are none. A sentence is not a static or rigid absolute. A perfectly good sentence in one context will fail miserably in another. The *subject–audience–context–purpose* and your own voice must all be considered—consciously at this stage, where you may feel unsure of yourself, intuitively at a later stage, when practice and experience can be supported by the ear of your imagination. Lincoln's prose reflects his personality, his voice. We know that to be true because, in this particular instance, we have not only the four drafts that Lincoln worked on but also a first draft written by William H. Seward, who was to become Lincoln's secretary of state. Here are Seward's words.

> I close. We are not, we must not be, aliens or enemies, but fellow countrymen and brethren. Although passion has strained our bonds of affection too hardly, they must not, I am sure they will not, be broken. The mystic chords which proceeding from so many battlefields and so many patriot graves, pass through all the hearts and hearths in this broad continent of ours, will yet again harmonize in their ancient music when breathed upon by the guardian angel of the nation.

Seward's proposal has its own rhythm, but Lincoln improved on it. Compare Seward's blunt and unsatisfactory first sentence with Lincoln's still brief but more melodious version. In turn, compare the simplicity of Lincoln's second sentence with Seward's choppy (and somewhat clichéd) second sentence. Read both versions aloud. What other changes in the next three sentences improve the flow? Can you determine how changes in rhythm parallel the clarification (and simplification) of meaning?

If we represent Lincoln's sentences with graph lines, we might diagram the paragraph as follows.

Sentence 1: __________.
Sentence 2: __________, _____.
Sentence 3: __________.
Sentence 4: ____.
Sentence 5: _____, _____, _____, ________________________________,
__________, __________, __________.
________________________________.

Obviously, variety of sentence structure and length are key elements. In art, music, dance, and language, rhythm is always achieved by theme and variation, by establishing a pattern and then varying the pattern.

Editing for Variety in Sentence Patterns

Sentences can be simple, compound, complex, or even compound-complex. If you're unsure of the differences, you might want to look into a handbook on grammar. Yet knowing definitions for sentence structure is not as important as knowing that every sentence ought to organize a thought into a clear, coherent pattern that flows well within the larger context of your essay. Two editing steps discussed in earlier chapters (omitting needless words and using strong verbs) should help you begin. Return to the student example on page 214. If we graph-lined that paragraph, it would look something like this.

Sentence 1: ______________________.
Sentence 2: ______________________.
Sentence 3: __________________________.
Sentence 4: ______________________.
Sentence 5: ______________________.
Sentence 6: __________________________.
Sentence 7: __________________________.

The variation here is slight at best. Each sentence makes a simple statement with a subject–verb–object sequence; each is approximately the same length as its neighbor. The monotony is deadening. But through careful editing, we can combine some of those Dick-and-Jane constructions into sentences of varying lengths and rhythms.

Circle unecessary or repetitive words. Find the action and rebuild around it:

Professor Shirley Baxton (is) (in) (the) English department. (The) *action* interview (was) held in her office.

Result:

I interviewed English Professor Shirley Baxton in her office.

Two sentences reduced to one saves six words and eliminates choppiness.

Again, circle unnecessary or repetitive words. Find the action and rebuild around it:

She (told) (me) (that) (she) believed writing should be required in the whole university. She (didn't) (believe) (it) should be just required for English.

Result:

She believes writing should be required throughout the university curriculum, not just in English classes.

Even though I've added new words for clarity, we still save eight words and improve the flow.

Circle unnecessary or repetitive words. Find the action and rebuild around it:

(She) (has) (a) reputation for having high standards. (She) *action* says writing is a expression of the inner self. (She) (says) (it) should be part of the experience we have in every class.

Result:

Baxton, who has a reputation for high standards, says writing is an expression of the inner self and should therefore be a part of every classroom experience.

In the process of performing this type of editorial act, we not only clarify meaning, but also enhance it by creating a more natural rhythm. Yet when I read these new sentences aloud as a complete paragraph, the second sentence still jars my ear. It seems out of place. Because I'm at a loss on how to change the sentence further, my "ear" suggests that the second sentence might exchange places with the third. A fortunate discovery. When this is done, the logic itself proves more convincing.

> I interviewed English Professor Shirley Baxton in her office. Baxton, who has a reputation for high standards, says writing is an expression of the inner self and should therefore be a part of every classroom experience. She believes writing should be required throughout the university curriculum, not just in English classes.

Now I think we have a more precise statement supported by a rhythm that, without calling attention to itself, suggests a natural, if somewhat formal, speech pattern. *The first step in editing for variety in sentences, then, is not deliberately to make sentences longer or shorter, but to make them better.* Almost inevitably, the rhythms will begin to flow.

Here is the process.

1. Circle unnecessary and repetitive words.
2. Locate the action.
3. Combine or rebuild around the verb.
4. Read aloud.

The Parallel Sentence

Effective writing needs more than just a mixture of long and short sentences, however. Rhythm does not exist for its own sake but to heighten clarity and emphasize important or related elements. For that reason, you must develop a familiarity with the concept of *parallelism*—a method of shaping sentences so that a series of related ideas is expressed in a related grammatical structure. What that grammatical structure might be does not matter—a series of similar verb forms, a series of similar prepositional phrases, a series of nouns—so long as each follows a parallel pattern on the page.

Let's begin with a single idea.

- Roger's dad promised to buy him a new bicycle.

But what if Roger's dad made two promises, and the two promises were related?

- Roger's dad promised to buy him a new bicycle *and* that he would let him ride it before Christmas.

Now we have two related ideas, but the sentence structure does not show that relationship. The promised idea before the *and* is expressed differently from the promised idea after the *and*. Here's how we could make each clause show the relationship.

> Roger's dad promised to buy him a new bicycle and to let him ride it before Christmas.

In this case, infinitives have been made parallel (*to buy, to let*). The result forms a closer psychological relationship in the mind of the reader. The ideas seem to cohere more closely.

We can create the same parallelism with other grammatical structures.

> The company wants a new taxi driver who knows the city and who has a good safety record. (adjective clauses are parallel) Chinita believes in God, motherhood, and country. (nouns are parallel)

Parallelism is not merely a grammatical device made fetish by English teachers. Parallel structure is one of the oldest techniques in our language, existing long before English grammar itself was ever set down in rule books. We can trace its importance in English to the influence of the Bible, where parallelism was a basic element of Hebrew poetry.

> Blessed are the meek, for they shall inherit the earth; Blessed are those who thirst for righteousness, for they shall be satisfied.

The effectiveness of parallel structure can be most clearly emphasized if we take such a well-known passage and rewrite it out of parallel.

- Blessed are the meek, for they shall inherit the earth; And we should also bless those who thirst for righteousness so satisfaction can be obtained by them as well.

What we discover is that a failure to provide parallel structure not only makes relationships between ideas less clear but also weakens the forcefulness of writing in general.

Poets and politicians have long used parallel structure for the sense of dignity and strength it creates in the ear of the reader.

> Let the word go forth from this time and place, to friend and foe alike, that the torch has been passed to a new generation of Americans, born in this century, tempered by war, disciplined by a hard and bitter peace, proud of our ancient heritage, and unwilling to witness or permit the slow undoing of those human rights to which this nation has always been committed, and to which we are committed today at home and around the world.
>
> Let every nation know, whether it wishes us well or ill, that we shall pay any price, bear any burden, meet any hardship, support any friend, oppose any foe to assure the survival and the success of liberty.

John F. Kennedy, *Inaugural Address*

In every case, the rhythm emphasizes and clarifies a relationship. The result is a coherence that can seldom be more effectively achieved.

The Balanced Sentence

A *balanced sentence* is related to parallelism, but the emphasis is achieved through the equal "weight" of each clause, not necessarily through grammatical structure.

Both parallel and balanced structures tend to be found more often in formal prose than in informal writing, but even the most casual essay may reach a point where the relationship of ideas needs to be stressed clearly, and an otherwise informal style can often increase its impact on the reader by using carefully selected balanced sentences. Such symmetry not only is appealing to the ear but also suggests an almost irrefutable logic and can be especially effective in clarifying contrasts or in ending an essay with dramatic finality.

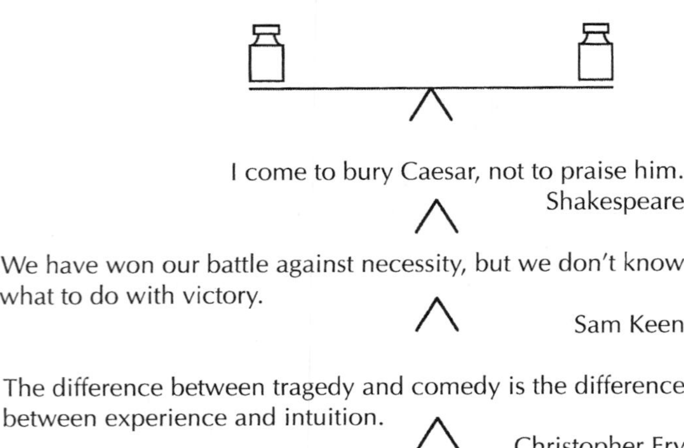

Do writers create balanced sentences or parallel structure on a first draft? No doubt, some do. After becoming familiar with the technique, you might do so as well. But the place to teach yourself such forms is in the revising or editing phase. Any series of related ideas can be expressed in similar grammatical form, whereas contrasting ideas can be expressed in a balanced style. Do not be afraid to rearrange the parts of a sentence or to combine several sentences to achieve the desired emphasis.

The Periodic Sentence

Emphasis can be achieved in other ways. The most amateurish way is to add an exclamation mark! Or worse, to underline important words just to make sure your reader gets the point!!!! Both exclamation marks and underlining have a place, but they quickly grow tiring, and in the long run they are merely external punctuation. A truly good sentence should achieve its emphasis from within. By arranging word order to fall at exactly the right point in a sentence, you can control the reader's reaction. When a sentence delays the most important words for last through the use of several interior clauses, we call it a *periodic sentence.* The trick is to postpone the important words, as Lincoln did in the final sentence of his *First Inaugural Address,* to delay and create suspense, to build the reader's anticipation, and then to fulfill it with a bang.

Simple sentence:
Beverly decided to run for president.

Periodic sentence:
Beverly, who had so often thought of herself only as a housewife, a servant of others, and a woman of no special talents, decided to run for president.

The order should follow the natural intensity of the details. Build from the least important to the most important, and the rhythms as well as the suspense will create a sense of controlled tension.

> The dictator exploited his country's resources, stole from the common people, executed those who opposed him, and trampled over their corpses.

Sentences have movable parts and you should feel free to experiment with their arrangement. Move the parts about. Combine and recombine. Read each of your experiments aloud and test it with your ear.

> We have a responsibility to look further into how we were drawn into war. A nation like ours has a high moral tradition. Perhaps what we find will teach us a lesson about the future.

Try an experiment. Combine and rearrange the parts:
To learn what lessons it will teach us about the future, we have a responsibility, as a nation with high moral traditions, to know how we became drawn into war.

Experiment again. Recombine the parts:
A nation like ours, with its high moral tradition, has a responsibility to discover how we were drawn into war and to learn what lessons it will teach us about the future.

By attempting several versions and by reading each aloud, you will quickly detect the difference in emphasis and rhythm. Of course, if you turned every sentence into a periodic sentence or a balanced sentence, you would not have theme and variation. Lincoln used three relatively short, simple sentences and one medium-length sentence before building to a crescendo in a final periodic sentence. The short rhythms made the long rhythms more effective. A blunt sentence can often be the best way to emphasis, especially at the beginning or end of an essay. Short sentences have force. They make a point. Use them. But use them with recognition that they must be rhythmically varied with other types of sentences for the total effect to seem natural to our human patterns of speech.

Emphasis Through Word Order

The components of even a simple sentence may be arranged to affect emphasis. Your purpose determines what is placed at the beginning of each sentence.

Purpose: to emphasize Eisenhower's leadership
Dwight D. Eisenhower directed the Normandy invasion from a small base in England.

Purpose: to describe the invasion
The Normandy invasion was directed by Dwight D. Eisenhower from a small base in England.

Purpose: to recount England's role in the invasion
It was from a small base in England that Dwight D. Eisenhower directed the Normandy invasion.

But the traditional point for emphasis in the sentence (as well as in the paragraph) is at the end.

Weak emphasis:
The concept of "giving until it hurts" derives from an irrational guilt, in my opinion.

Strong emphasis:
In my opinion, the concept of "giving until it hurts" derives from irrational guilt.

By arranging your words so that they build toward the most forceful term or phrase, you lead the reader toward the most important idea. Your purpose is more effectively achieved.

Weak emphasis	Strong emphasis
Our neighborhoods are still unsafe and dirty, Councilman Moody told me.	Councilman Moody told me our neighborhoods are still dirty and unsafe.
My father remained a widower for twenty years. The women he met always lost out, and Dad lost out, too, because he compared them with my mother.	For twenty years my father remained a widower. Because he compared the women he met with my mother, the women always lost, but Dad lost, too.

In some ways, all of this is only common sense. The order of words affects the meaning. Writers and speakers knew that long before textbooks were dreamed of. And, no doubt, you already know it and make use of it in your everyday speech, especially when trying to be forceful or "make a point." Rhythm, variation, and emphasis are natural to speech. You must make them equally natural to your prose. During the editing phase, read aloud, *listen* to what you have written, and be willing to combine, rearrange, or rewrite until each sentence sounds strong and natural, as if spoken in your own voice.

Exercises

1. Identify the method by which each of these sentences achieves its effectiveness.

a. There is an appointed time for everything, and
a time for every affair under the heavens.
A time to be born, and a time to die;
a time to plant, and a time to uproot the plant.

Ecclesiastes

b. In proportion as men delight in battles, bullfighting, and combats of gladiators, will they punish by hanging, burning, and the rack.

Herbert Spencer

c. The best writing, both prose and poetry, as Shakespeare preeminently shows, makes use, with condensation and selection, of playful, impassioned, imaginative talk.

Sidney Cox

d. Consider what had happened to me: I had thought myself lost, had touched the very bottom of despair; and then, when the spirit of renunciation had filled me, I had known peace.

Antoine de Saint Exupéry

2. Rewrite the following passages to achieve a more natural rhythm. First, circle unnecessary and repetitive words. Second, find the action. Third, combine sentences or rebuild sentences around the verb.

   a. The *College Chimes* is the campus newspaper. I interviewed Tony Rosenblatt, who is the editor of the *Chimes.* The interview was conducted in the *Chimes* office located in the basement of the student union. Tony Rosenblatt is a senior majoring in English. Tony was dressed in faded jeans and a wrinkled shirt that said "Country Time Lemonade" on the front.

   b. Brown's family was not a particularly religious one at all. His grandmother made him attend a religious revival that was taught by a man with particularly narrow views about the Bible and religious areas. He was a traveling evangelist. The man's name was LeRoy Jedson. His sermon was filled with hellfire and brimstone and threats of what would happen to sinners.

3. Make each of the following sentences parallel. First identify areas that need to be related. Then choose a pattern of expression and rewrite each idea to fit the pattern.

   a. The ballerina is light, very agile, and moves with grace.

   Identify related ideas:

   light
   very agile
   moves with grace

   Choose one pattern:

   light
   very agile
   moves with grace

   Express each idea in the same pattern:

   light
   agile
   graceful

   Rewrite the sentence in parallel form:

   The ballerina is light, agile, and graceful.

   b. Henry advised him forget time and to forge ahead for victory.

   c. All work and not playing makes life dull.

   d. Julio promised to bring a copy of the play and that he would not be late.

   e. A few generations ago children learned early in life to obey their parents without question, to consider all adults their superiors until told differently, and they had much better table manners.

   f. It was a time not for words but action.

   g. The French, Italians, the Spanish, and Portuguese all speak a form of language that derives from the Romans.

h. A perfect croissant is tender, flaky, and, of course, good tasting.

i. My objections are, first, the injustice of the measure; second, that it is unconstitutional; and third, an inhumaneness.

j. Each room in the dorm is complete with little closet space, no air conditioning, bedroom and living room combined in one room, no appliances, and the sharing of bathroom facilities with forty other students.

k. We shall not always expect to find them supporting our view; but their freedom is something they have to put their support behind.

4. Edit your last writing assignment for rhythm, variation, and emphasis. Do not make changes merely to make changes. Read each passage aloud. Rewrite only those sentences that need to be improved so that the whole of it sounds natural to your ear.

Copying

As you've already learned, because it slows down the eye, copying is one of the best ways to learn about composing. At the same time, it helps develop style. Many rhythms and varieties of sentence structure that seem new to you become assimilated through copying and will resurface at some future time in your own writing.

1. Copy Abraham Lincoln's paragraph on page 215 or John F. Kennedy's on page 220. Turn back to Louise Erdrich's essay and copy the final paragraph on page 113, or to the paragraph of Jane Winslow Eliot on page 157.

2. Over the period of a week, copy each of the following passages. You'll find the rhythms become infectious.

> For everything there is a season, and a time for every purpose under heaven: a time to be born, and a time to die; a time to plant, and a time to pluck up that which is planted; a time to kill, and a time to heal; a time to break down, and a time to build up; a time to weep, and a time to laugh; a time to mourn, and a time to dance; a time to cast away stones, and a time to gather stones together. . . .
>
> **The Bible, King James Version**

> Persons attempting to find a motive in this narrative will be prosecuted; persons attempting to find a moral in it will be banished; persons attempting to find a plot will be shot.
>
> **Mark Twain**

> She was very old and small and she walked slowly in the dark pine shadows, moving a little from side to side in her steps, with the balanced heaviness and lightness of a pendulum in a grandfather clock.
>
> **Eudora Welty**

It was the best of times, it was the worst of times, it was the age of wisdom, it was the age of foolishness, it was the epoch of belief, it was the epoch of incredulity, it was the season of Light, it was the season of Darkness, it was the spring of hope, it was the winter of despair, we had everything before us, we had nothing before us, we were all going direct to Heaven, we were all going direct the other way—in short, the period was so far like the present period, that some of its noisiest authorities insisted on its being received, for good or for evil, in the superlative degree of comparison only.

Charles Dickens

When I awoke in the morning she was already at her machine, or in the great morning crowd of housewives at the grocery getting fresh rolls for breakfast. When I returned from school she was at her machine, or conferring over *McCall's* with some neighborhood woman who had come in pointing hopefully to an illustration. . . . When my father came home from work she had somehow mysteriously interrupted herself to make supper for us, and the dishes cleared and washed, was back at the machine. When I went to bed at night, often she was still there, pounding away at the treadle. . . .

Alfred Kazin

Readings

Do You Speak American? Sí Señor!

Holly Paterno

Holly Paterno was a first-year student majoring in French and Spanish when she investigated one of the principal controversies in her future profession, one that centers on the concept of "bilingual education." After beginning with an imaginative lead, Holly blends primary and secondary sources. Notice how her conclusion is strengthened by using various rhythmic devices including parallel structure.

Let's say you move to Portugal because you want more opportunity for you and your family. Prices are low, the chance to make a fortune is great. Along with your wife and children, you take your grandmother, three cousins, and an aging uncle. When you arrive you join other Americans living in a small colony. Later, even more Americans follow. But the children have trouble in school. It seems that school teachers conduct classes in Portuguese. So you and the other Americans go on a public campaign to require schools to teach all subjects in English as well as Portuguese. That way your children won't fall behind. What surprises you is that the Portuguese get angry. They claim that if you choose to live in Portugal, raise your children there, earn your income there, you ought also to learn their customs and language. Are the Portuguese right? Or are they prejudiced against Americans and merely trying to deny your children an equal opportunity to compete?

All this would be hypothetical and silly if it weren't happening here and now in America.

In 1968, to assist students of immigrants who couldn't speak English, the United States government approved of funding bilingual education—instruction given in a child's native language while he or she also learns English. According to Woodrow Wilson University's Associate Professor of Spanish, Peter Valdez, the attempt had a noble aim: to prevent foreign-speaking children from being denied an equal opportunity because of language difficulties. *U.S. News* reports in its March 31, 1986, issue that many of the bilingual programs have been successful. In such places as Spring Valley Elementary School in San Francisco's Chinatown, three-fourths of the school's 580 pupils speak little or no English. They come from homes where not only is English not spoken, literacy itself often does not exist. "Such disparity between home life and school demands this type of instruction," says [Principal Lonnie] Chin. "It is incumbent on schools to bridge that gap, and that is the real purpose of bilingual education" (20). Test scores often support the claim. In Houston and Michigan, national scores in such subjects as math and science show that students (both native Americans and immigrants) who participate in multi-lingual programs have test scores at least equal to those in regular programs, and often better (21). In other words, there seems to be no particular evidence that the program has been educationally unsound.

But Professor Valdez is now concerned that the effort has been taken over by members of his own discipline (foreign language teachers) and by ethnic politicians for self-serving ends. "We now have several thousand teachers employed in bilingual programs, and several thousand government administrators, all who want the program to grow even bigger," Valdez says. "It means more job security. And we have street-corner councilmen who want to stay in office by arousing racial and ethnic emotions over the issue because it means more votes and more local power." Valdez claims that any opposition to the aims of these groups has been labeled as racist. And there is evidence on both counts. The same issue of *U.S. News* indicates that by 1986 the government was spending $139 million on only 210,000 students involved in bilingual classrooms (20). The list of languages taught has spread from only a handful to hundreds. Describing "The Case Against Bilingual Education," Tom Bethell, writing in *Harper's* (February 1979), offers a partial list of the languages the U.S. government now provides. The list includes Central Yup'ik, Aleut, Gwich'in, Athabascan, Tagalog, Pima, Plaute, Ilocano, Punjabi, Keresian, Tewa, Chamorro, Trukese, Paluna, Ulithian, Yapese, and many others (32).

Not only does such evidence suggest the concept has grown topsy-turvy, Bethell claims that the original intention has become lost in the process. Students apparently are not being moved through the programs—from native speaking to English speaking and out—but being retained in the native speaking portions of the program by teachers and administrators who claim it is necessary for "maintenance" of the native language and customs. According to Bethell, a government report showed that 85% of the students are kept in bilingual programs after they are capable of learning English (32), and that fewer than one-third of the students now in the programs are there because they have not yet acquired sufficient English (34).

Yet this in itself might cause little controversy. Professor Valdez indicates that the real problem is that because of Cuban refugees and legal and illegal aliens from Mexico, the Spanish language dominates 80% of the bilingual programs. The number of Latin-speaking immigrants in the South and Southwest is now so large that Valdez believes they no longer feel they have a need to blend into the dominant culture. That is, they no longer need to learn English as part of the traditional melting pot, because their numbers are so large that in those areas Spanish is the dominant culture. *Newsweek* (June 30, 1986) provides evidence as support. It reports how in Miami, Florida, commercial signs, as well as radio and TV broadcasts, are often entirely in Spanish. Two women in Florida recently sued and won because they were actually turned down for jobs because they could not speak Spanish (24).

The consequence seems to be a creation of racial, ethnic, and cultural divisiveness. Backlash proposals to make English the official language are causing emotional and political tensions in numerous states, most recently in California. According to an editorial in *The Atlanta Constitution* (Oct. 4, 1986), proponents such as California Senator S. I. Hayakawa fear that bilingual culture will create a divided nation where Hispanic politicians will keep Spanish-speaking people in ghettos for a power base. Opponents such as Los Angeles Mayor Tom Bradley charge that trying to make English compulsory is "evil," "unjust," and "prejudiced" (4).

An objective look at other countries shows that language conflicts repeatedly cause this kind of political and cultural divisiveness. In Belgium, a long-standing conflict between those who speak Dutch and those who speak French has so divided the people into warring camps that a "language border" was actually drawn across the country in 1963. And in Canada, the province of Quebec has repeatedly raised the issue of secession as a separate French-speaking nation. Quebec currently requires French as its "official" language even though it is surrounded by an English-speaking culture. The fact would seem to be that bilingual education in itself is not bad. The study of multiple languages has repeatedly proven to be a valuable educational exercise that increases intellectual acumen while creating broader understanding of differing cultures. The danger seems to arise when any group begins to think that multiple languages can exist side by side as part of a single culture. America may be a multi-racial, multi-ethnic society with only minor conflicts because of it, but a true multi-language culture may not be possible to create. Professor Peter Valdez claims that "language *is* culture." The clear implication is that separate language-speaking groups will always form separate cultures, and hence eventually want separate governments. George Will, writing in *Newsweek* (July 8, 1985), points out that language is the primary link between citizenship and a shared culture. "Immigrants, all of whom came here voluntarily, have a responsibility to reciprocate the nation's welcome by acquiring the language that is essential for citizenship" (78).

Children should not be denied the opportunity to succeed because of language difficulties. That is why they might be better off in intensive English language programs than in bilingual programs. No one in America should be forced to lose contact with their original culture. Mine is Italian, and it is a rich and valuable heritage. But neither should immigrants fail in their obligation to become a part of their new culture. America, too, as a varied multi-ethnic nation is rich and rewarding. I believe that all of us should be bilingual if we want to be well educated. But evidence would seem strongly to support the contention that our first language must be English if we want to be American.

Dumpster Diving

Lars Eighner

Unable to support himself by writing stories, Lars Eighner became a homeless itinerant traveling the country with his Labrador retriever, Lizbeth. His work became more widely appreciated when the *Threepenny Review* published two of his essays on the homeless including "Dumpster Diving." *Travels with Lizbeth: Three Years on the Road and on the Streets* was published in 1993.

Long before I began Dumpster diving I was impressed with Dumpsters, enough so that I wrote the Merriam-Webster research service to discover what I could about the word *Dumpster.* I learned from them that it is a proprietary word belonging to the Dempsey Dumpster company. Since then I have dutifully capitalized the word, although it was lowercased in almost all the citations Merriam-Webster photocopied for me. Dempsey's word is too apt. I have never heard these things called anything but Dumpsters. I do not know anyone who knows the generic name for these objects. From time to time I have heard a wino or hobo give some corrupted credit to the original and call them Dipsy Dumpsters.

I began Dumpster diving about a year before I became homeless.

I prefer the word *scavenging* and use the word *scrounging* when I mean to be obscure. I have heard people, evidently meaning to be polite, use the word *foraging,* but I prefer to reserve that word for gathering nuts and berries and such which I do also according to the season and the opportunity. *Dumpster diving* seems to me to be a little too cute and, in my case, inaccurate because I lack the athletic ability to lower myself into the Dumpsters as the true divers do, much to their increased profit.

I like the frankness of the word *scavenging,* which I can hardly think of without picturing a big black snail on an aquarium wall. I live from the refuse of others. I am a scavenger. I think it a sound and honorable niche, although if I could I would naturally prefer to live the comfortable consumer life, perhaps—and only perhaps—as a slightly less wasteful consumer, owing to what I have learned as a scavenger.

While Lizbeth and I were still living in the shack on Avenue B as my savings ran out, I put almost all my sporadic income into rent. The necessities of daily life I began to extract from Dumpsters. Yes, we ate from them. Except for jeans, all my clothes came from Dumpsters. Boom boxes, candles, bedding, toilet paper, a virgin male love doll, medicine, books, a typewriter, dishes, furnishings, and change, sometimes amounting to many dollars—I acquired many things from the Dumpsters.

I have learned much as a scavenger. I mean to put some of what I have learned down here, beginning with the practical art of Dumpster diving and proceeding to the abstract.

What is safe to eat?

After all, the finding of objects is becoming something of an urban art. Even respectable employed people will sometimes find something tempting sticking out of a Dumpster or standing beside one. Quite a number of people, not all of them of the bohemian type, are willing to brag that they found this or that piece in the trash. But eating from Dumpsters is what separates the dilettanti from the professionals. Eating safely from the Dumpsters involves three principles: using the senses and common sense to evaluate the conditions of the found materials, knowing the Dumpsters of a given area and checking them regularly, and seeking always to answer the question "Why was this discarded?"

Perhaps everyone who has a kitchen and a regular supply of groceries has, at one time or another, made a sandwich and eaten half of it before discovering mold on the bread or got a mouthful of milk before realizing the milk had turned. Nothing of the sort is likely to happen to a Dumpster diver because he is constantly reminded that most food is discarded for a reason. Yet a lot of perfectly good food can be found in Dumpsters.

Canned goods, for example, turn up fairly often in the Dumpsters I frequent. All except the most phobic people would be willing to eat from a can, even if it came from a Dumpster. Canned goods are among the safest of foods to be found in Dumpsters but are not utterly foolproof.

Although very rare with modern canning methods, botulism is a possibility. Most other forms of food poisoning seldom do lasting harm to a healthy person, but botulism is most certainly fatal and often the first symptom is death. Except for carbonated beverages, all canned goods should contain a slight vacuum and suck air when first punctured. Bulging, rusty, and dented cans and cans that spew when punctured should be avoided, especially when the contents are not very acidic or syrupy.

Heat can break down the botulin, but this requires much more cooking than most people do to canned goods. To the extent that botulism occurs at all, of course, it can occur in cans on pantry shelves as well as in cans from Dumpsters. Need I say that home-canned goods are simply too risky to be recommended.

From time to time one of my companions, aware of the source of my provisions, will ask, "Do you think these crackers are really safe to eat?" For some reason it is most often the crackers they ask about.

This question has always made me angry. Of course I would not offer my companion anything I had doubts about. But more than that, I wonder why he cannot evaluate the condition of the crackers for himself. I have no special knowledge and I have been wrong before. Since he knows where the food comes from, it seems to me he ought to assume some of the responsibility for deciding what he will put in his mouth. For myself I have few qualms about dry foods such as crackers, cookies, cereal, chips, and pasta if they are free of visible contaminants and still dry and crisp. Most often such things are found in the original packaging, which is not so much a positive sign as it is the absence of a negative one.

Raw fruits and vegetables with intact skins seem perfectly safe to me, excluding of course the obviously rotten. Many are discarded for minor imperfections that can be pared away. Leafy vegetables, grapes, cauliflower, broccoli, and similar things may be contaminated by liquids and may be impractical to wash.

Candy, especially hard candy, is usually safe if it has not drawn ants. Chocolate is often discarded only because it has become discolored as the cocoa butter de-emulsified. Candying, after all, is one method of food preservation because pathogens do not like very sugary substances.

All of these foods might be found in any Dumpster and can be evaluated with some confidence largely on the basis of appearance. Beyond these are foods that cannot be correctly evaluated without additional information.

I began scavenging by pulling pizzas out of the Dumpster behind a pizza delivery shop. In general, prepared food requires caution, but in this case I knew when the shop closed and went to the Dumpster as soon as the last of the help left.

Such shops often get prank orders; both the orders and the products made to fill them are called *bogus*. Because help seldom stays long at these places, pizzas are often made with the wrong topping, refused on delivery for being cold, or baked incorrectly. The products to be discarded are boxed up because inventory is kept by counting boxes: A boxed pizza can be written off; an unboxed pizza does not exist.

I never placed a bogus order to increase the supply of pizzas and I believe no one else was scavenging in this Dumpster. But the people in the shop became suspicious and began to retain their garbage in the shop overnight. While it lasted I had a steady supply of fresh, sometimes warm pizza. Because I knew the Dumpster I knew the source of the pizza, and because I visited the Dumpster regularly I knew what was fresh and what was yesterday's.

The area I frequent is inhabited by many affluent college students. I am not here by chance; the Dumpsters in this area are very rich. Students throw out many good things, including food. In particular they tend to throw everything out when they move at the end of a semester, before and after breaks, and around midterm, when many of them despair of college. So I find it advantageous to keep an eye on the academic calendar.

Students throw food away around breaks because they do not know whether it has spoiled or will spoil before they return. A typical discard is a half jar of peanut butter. In fact, nonorganic peanut butter does not require refrigeration and is unlikely to spoil in any reasonable time. The student does not know that, and since it is Daddy's money, the student decides not to take a chance. Opened containers require caution and some attention to the question "Why was this discarded?" But in the case of discards from student apartments, the answer may be that the item was thrown out through carelessness, ignorance, or wastefulness. This can sometimes be deduced when the item is found with many others, including some that are obviously perfectly good.

Some students, and others, approach defrosting a freezer by chucking out the whole lot. Not only do the circumstances of such a find tell the story, but also the mass of frozen goods stays cold for a long time and items may be found still frozen or freshly thawed.

Yogurt, cheese, and sour cream are items that are often thrown out while they are still good. Occasionally I find a cheese with a spot of mold, which of course I just pare off, and because it is obvious why such a cheese was discarded, I treat it with less suspicion than an apparently perfect cheese found in similar circumstances. Yogurt is often discarded, still sealed, only because the expiration date on the carton had passed. This is one of my favorite finds because yogurt will keep for several days, even in warm weather.

Students throw out canned goods and staples at the end of semesters and when they give up college at midterm. Drugs, pornography, spirits, and the like are often discarded when parents are expected—Dad's day, for example. And spirits also turn up after big party weekends, presumably discarded by the newly reformed. Wine and spirits, of course, keep perfectly well even once opened, but the same cannot be said of beer.

My test for carbonated soft drinks is whether they still fizz vigorously. Many juices or other beverages are too acidic or too syrupy to cause much concern, provided they are not visibly contaminated. I have discovered nasty molds in vegetable juices, even when the product was found under its original seal; I recommend that such products be decanted slowly into a clear glass. Liquids always require some care. One hot day I found a large jug of Pat O'Brien's Hurricane mix. The jug had been opened, but it was still ice cold. I drank three large glasses before it became apparent to me that someone had added the rum to the mix, and not a little rum. I never tasted the rum, and by the time I began to feel the effects I had already ingested a very large quantity of the beverage. Some divers would have considered this a boon, but being suddenly intoxicated in a public place in the early afternoon is not my idea of a good time.

I have heard of people maliciously contaminating discarded food and even handouts, but mostly I have heard of this from people with vivid imaginations who have had no experience with Dumpsters themselves. Just before the pizza shop stopped discarding its garbage at night, jalapeños began showing up on most of the discarded pizzas. If indeed this was meant to discourage me it was a wasted effort because I am a native Texan.

For myself, I avoid game, poultry, pork, and egg-based foods, whether I find them raw or cooked. I seldom have the means to cook what I find, but when I do I avail myself of plentiful supplies of beef, which is often in very good condition. I suppose fish becomes disagreeable before it becomes dangerous. Lizbeth is happy to have any such thing that is past its prime and, in fact, does not recognize fish as food until it is quite strong.

Home leftovers, as opposed to surpluses from restaurants, are very often bad. Evidently, especially among students, there is a common type of personality that carefully wraps up even the smallest leftover and shoves it into the back of the refrigerator for six months or so before discarding it. Characteristic of this type are the reused jars and margarine tubs to which the remains are committed. I avoid ethnic foods I am unfamiliar with. If I do not know what it is supposed to look like when it is good, I cannot be certain I will be able to tell if it is bad.

No matter how careful I am I still get dysentery at least once a month, oftener in warm weather. I do not want to paint too romantic a picture. Dumpster diving has serious drawbacks as a way of life.

I learned to scavenge gradually, on my own. Since then I have initiated several companions into the trade. I have learned that there is a predictable series of stages a person goes through in learning to scavenge.

At first the new scavenger is filled with disgust and self-loathing. He is ashamed of being seen and may lurk around, trying to duck behind things, or he may try to dive at night. (In fact, most people instinctively look away from a scavenger. By skulking around, the novice calls attention to himself and arouses suspicion. Diving at night is ineffective and needlessly messy.)

Every grain of rice seems to be a maggot. Everything seems to stink. He can wipe the egg yolk off the found can, but he cannot erase from his mind the stigma of eating garbage.

That stage passes with experience. The scavenger finds a pair of running shoes that fit and look and smell brand-new. He finds a pocket calculator in perfect working order. He finds pristine ice cream, still frozen, more than he can eat or keep. He begins to understand: People throw away perfectly good stuff, a lot of perfectly good stuff.

At this stage, Dumpster shyness begins to dissipate. The diver, after all, has the last laugh. He is finding all manner of good things that are his for the taking. Those who disparage his profession are the fools, not he.

He may begin to hang on to some perfectly good things for which he has neither a use nor a market. Then he begins to take note of the things that are not perfectly good but are nearly so. He mates a Walkman with broken earphones and one that is missing a battery cover. He picks up things that he can repair.

At this stage he may become lost and never recover. Dumpsters are full of things of some potential value to someone and also of things that never have much intrinsic value but are interesting. All the Dumpster divers I have known come to the point of trying to acquire everything they touch. Why not take it, they reason, since it is all free? This is, of course, hopeless. Most divers come to realize that they must restrict themselves to items of relatively immediate utility. But in some cases the diver simply cannot control himself. I have met several of these pack-rat types. Their ideas of the values of various pieces of junk verge on the psychotic. Every bit of glass may be a diamond, they think, and all that glistens, gold.

I tend to gain weight when I am scavenging. Partly this is because I always find far more pizza and doughnuts than water-packed tuna, nonfat yogurt, and fresh vegetables. Also I have not developed much faith in the reliability of Dumpsters as a food source, although it has been proven to me many times. I tend to eat as if I have no idea where my next meal is coming from. But mostly I just hate to see food go to waste and so I eat much more than I should. Something like this drives the obsession to collect junk.

As for collecting objects, I usually restrict myself to collecting one kind of small object at a time, such as pocket calculators, sunglasses, or campaign buttons. To live on the street I must anticipate my needs to a certain extent: I must pick up and save warm bedding I find in August because it will not be found in Dumpsters in November. As I have no access to health care, I often hoard essential drugs, such as antibiotics and antihistamines. (This course can be recommended only to those with some grounding in pharmacology. Antibiotics, for example, even when indicated are worse than useless if taken in insufficient amounts.) But even if I had a home with extensive storage space, I could not save everything that might be valuable in some contingency.

I have proprietary feelings about my Dumpsters. As I have mentioned, it is no accident that I scavenge from ones where good finds are common. But my limited experience with Dumpsters in other areas suggests to me that even in poorer areas, Dumpsters, if attended with sufficient diligence, can be made to yield a livelihood. The rich students discard perfectly good kiwifruit; poorer people discard perfectly good apples. Slacks and Polo shirts are found in the one place; jeans and T-shirts in the other. The population of competitors rather than the affluence of the dumpers most affects the feasibility of survival by scavenging. The large number of competitors is what puts me off the idea of trying to scavenge in places like Los Angeles.

Curiously, I do not mind my direct competition, other scavengers, so much as I hate the can scroungers.

People scrounge cans because they have to have a little cash. I have tried scrounging cans with an able-bodied companion. Afoot, a can scrounger simply cannot make more than a few dollars a day. One can extract the necessities of life from the Dumpsters directly with far less effort than would be required to accumulate the equivalent value in cans. (These observations may not hold in places with container redemption laws.)

Can scroungers, then, are people who must have small amounts of cash. There are drug addicts and winos, mostly the latter because the amounts of cash are so small. Spirits and drugs do, like all other commodities, turn up in

Dumpsters and the scavenger will from time to time have a half bottle of a rather good wine with his dinner. But the wino cannot survive on these occasional finds; he must have his daily dose to stave off the DTs. All the cans he can carry will buy about three bottles of Wild Irish Rose.

I do not begrudge them the cans, but can scroungers tend to tear up the Dumpsters, mixing the contents and littering the area. They become so specialized that they can see only cans. They earn my contempt by passing up change, canned goods, and readily hockable items.

There are precious few courtesies among scavengers. But it is common practice to set aside surplus items: pairs of shoes, clothing, canned goods, and such. A true scavenger hates to see good stuff go to waste, and what he cannot use he leaves in good condition in plain sight.

Can scroungers lay waste to everything in their path and will stir one of a pair of good shoes to the bottom of a Dumpster, to be lost or ruined in the muck. Can scroungers will even go through individual garbage cans, something I have never seen a scavenger do.

Individual garbage cans are set out on the public easement only on garbage days. On other days going through them requires trespassing close to a dwelling. Going through individual garbage cans without scattering litter is almost impossible. Litter is likely to reduce the public's tolerance of scavenging. Individual cans are simply not as productive as Dumpsters; people in houses and duplexes do not move so often and for some reason do not tend to discard as much useful material. Moreover, the time required to go through one garbage can that serves one household is not much less than the time required to go through a Dumpster that contains the refuse of twenty apartments.

But my strongest reservation about going through individual garbage cans is that this seems to me a very personal kind of invasion to which I would object if I were a householder. Although many things in Dumpsters are obviously meant never to come to light, a Dumpster is somehow less personal.

I avoid trying to draw conclusions about the people who dump in the Dumpsters I frequent. I think it would be unethical to do so, although I know many people will find the idea of scavenger ethics too funny for words.

Dumpsters contain bank statements, correspondence, and other documents, just as anyone might expect. But there are also less obvious sources of information. Pill bottles, for example. The labels bear the name of the patient, the name of the doctor, and the name of the drug. AIDS drugs and antipsychotic medicines, to name but two groups, are specific and are seldom prescribed for any other disorders. The plastic compacts for birth-control pills usually have complete label information.

Despite all of this sensitive information, I have had only one apartment resident object to my going through the Dumpster. In that case it turned out the resident was a university athlete who was taking bets and who was afraid I would turn up his wager slips.

Occasionally a find tells a story. I once found a small paper bag containing some unused condoms, several partial tubes of flavored sexual lubricants, a partially used compact of birth-control pills, and the torn pieces of a picture of a young man. Clearly she was through with him and planning to give up sex altogether.

Dumpster things are often sad—abandoned teddy bears, shredded wedding books, despaired-of sales kits. I find many pets lying in state in Dumpsters. Although I hope to get off the streets so that Lizbeth can have a long and comfortable old age, I know this hope is not very realistic. So I suppose when her time comes she too will go into a Dumpster. I will have no better place for her. And after all, it is fitting, since for most of her life her livelihood has come from the Dumpster. When she finds something I think is safe that has been spilled from a Dumpster, I let her have it. She already knows the route around the best ones. I like to think that if she survives me she will have a chance of evading the dog catcher and of finding her sustenance on the route.

Silly vanities also come to rest in the Dumpsters. I am a rather accomplished needleworker. I get a lot of material from the Dumpsters. Evidently sorority girls, hoping to impress someone, perhaps themselves, with their mastery of a womanly art, buy a lot of embroider-by-number kits, work a few stitches horribly, and eventually discard the whole mess. I pull out their stitches, turn the canvas over, and work an original design. Do not think I refrain from chuckling as I make gifts from these kits.

I find diaries and journals. I have often thought of compiling a book of literary found objects. And perhaps I will one day. But what I find is hopelessly commonplace and bad without being, even unconsciously, camp. College students also discard their papers. I am horrified to discover the kind of paper that now merits an A in an undergraduate course. I am grateful, however, for the number of good books and magazines the students throw out.

In the area I know best I have never discovered vermin in the Dumpsters, but there are two kinds of kitty surprise. One is alley cats whom I meet as they leap, claws first, out of Dumpsters. This is especially thrilling when I have Lizbeth in tow. The other kind of kitty surprise is a plastic garbage bag filled with some ponderous, amorphous mass. This always proves to be used cat litter.

City bees harvest doughnut glaze and this makes the Dumpster at the doughnut shop more interesting. My faith in the instinctive wisdom of animals is always shaken whenever I see Lizbeth attempt to catch a bee in her mouth, which she does whenever bees are present. Evidently some birds find Dumpsters profitable, for birdie surprise is almost as common as kitty surprise of the first kind. In hunting season all kinds of small game turn up in Dumpsters, some of it, sadly, not entirely dead. Curiously, summer and winter, maggots are uncommon.

The worst of the living and near-living hazards of the Dumpsters are the fire ants. The food they claim is not much of a loss, but they are vicious and aggressive. It is very easy to brush against some surface of the Dumpster and pick up half a dozen or more fire ants, usually in some sensitive area such as the underarm. One advantage of bringing Lizbeth along as I make Dumpster rounds is that, for obvious reasons, she is very alert to ground-based fire ants.

When Lizbeth recognizes a fire-ant infestation around our feet, she does the Dance of the Zillion Fire Ants. I have learned not to ignore this warning from Lizbeth, whether I perceive the tiny ants or not, but to remove ourselves at Lizbeth's first pas de bourrée. All the more so because the ants are the worst in the summer months when I wear flip-flops if I have them. (Perhaps someone will misunderstand this. Lizbeth does the Dance of the Zillion Fire Ants when she recognizes more fire ants than she cares to eat, not when she is being bitten. Since I have learned to react promptly, she does not get bitten at all. It is the isolated patrol of fire ants that falls in Lizbeth's range that deserves pity. She finds them quite tasty.)

By far the best way to go through a Dumpster is to lower yourself into it. Most of the good stuff tends to settle at the bottom because it is usually weightier than the rubbish. My more athletic companions have often demonstrated to me that they can extract much good material from a Dumpster I have already been over.

To those psychologically or physically unprepared to enter a Dumpster, I recommend a stout stick, preferably with some barb or hook at one end. The hook can be used to grab plastic garbage bags. When I find canned goods or other objects loose at the bottom of a Dumpster, I lower a bag into it, roll the desired object into the bag, and then hoist the bag out—a procedure more easily described than executed. Much Dumpster diving is a matter of experience for which nothing will do except practice.

Dumpster diving is outdoor work, often surprisingly pleasant. It is not entirely predictable; things of interest turn up every day and some days there are finds of great value. I am always very pleased when I can turn up exactly the thing I most wanted to find. Yet in spite of the element of chance, scavenging more than most other pursuits tends to yield returns in some proportion to the effort and intelligence brought to bear. It is very sweet to turn up a few dollars in change from a Dumpster that has just been gone over by a wino.

The land is now covered with cities. The cities are full of Dumpsters. If a member of the canine race is ever able to know what it is doing, then Lizbeth knows that when we go around to the Dumpsters, we are hunting. I think of scavenging as a modern form of self-reliance. In any event, after having survived nearly ten years of government service, where everything is geared to the lowest common denominator, I find it refreshing to have work that rewards initiative and effort. Certainly I would be happy to have a sinecure again, but I am no longer heartbroken that I left one.

I find from the experience of scavenging two rather deep lessons. The first is to take what you can use and let the rest go by. I have come to think that there is no value in the abstract. A thing I cannot use or make useful, perhaps by trading, has no value however rare or fine it may be. I mean useful in a broad sense—some art I would find useful and some otherwise.

I was shocked to realize that some things are not worth acquiring, but now I think it is so. Some material things are white elephants that eat up the possessor's substance. The second lesson is the transience of material being. This has not quite converted me to a dualist, but it has made some headway in that direction. I do not suppose that ideas are immortal, but certainly mental things are longer lived than other material things.

Once I was the sort of person who invested objects with sentimental value. Now I no longer have those objects, but I have the sentiments yet.

Many times in our travels I have lost everything but the clothes I was wearing and Lizbeth. The things I find in Dumpsters, the love letters and rag dolls of so many lives, remind me of this lesson. Now I hardly pick up a thing without envisioning the time I will cast it aside. This I think is a healthy state of mind. Almost everything I have now has already been cast out at least once, proving that what I own is valueless to someone.

Anyway, I find my desire to grab for the gaudy bauble has been largely sated. I think this is an attitude I share with the very wealthy—we both know there is plenty more where what we have came from. Between us are the rat-race millions who nightly scavenge the cable channels looking for they know not what.

I am sorry for them.

American Dreamer

Bharati Mukherjee

Born in Calcutta, India, Bharati Mukherjee came to the United States where she attended the University of Iowa and received her M.F.A. in creative writing. In 1963 she married and became a U.S. citizen. She is currently on the faculty at the University of California at Berkeley. Most of her novels, *Jasmine* (1989), *The Holder of the World* (1993), *Leave it to Me* (1997), and her anthology *The Middleman and Other Stories* (1998)—winner of the National Book Critics Circle Award—deal with the conflicts of Indian immigrant experience in America. Her latest novel is *Desirable Daughters* (2002).

The United States exists as a sovereign Nation. "America," in contrast, exists as a myth of democracy and equal opportunity to live by, or as an ideal goal to reach.

I am a nationalized U.S. citizen, which means that, unlike native-born citizens, I had to prove to the U.S. government that I merited citizenship. What I didn't have to disclose was that I desired "America," which to me is the stage for the drama of self-transformation.

I was born in Calcutta and first came to the United States—to Iowa City, to be precise—on a summer evening in 1961. I flew into a small airport surrounded by cornfields and pastures, ready to carry out the two commands my father had written out for me the night before I left Calcutta: Spend two years studying creative writing at the Iowa Writers' Workshop, then come back home and marry the bridegroom he selected for me from our caste and class.

In traditional Hindu families like ours, men provided and women were provided for. My father was a patriarch and I a pliant daughter. The neighborhood

I'd grown up in was homogeneously Hindu, Bengali-speaking, and middle-class. I didn't expect myself to ever disobey or disappoint my father by setting my own goals and taking charge of my future.

When I landed in Iowa 35 years ago, I found myself in a society in which almost everyone was Christian, white, and moderately well-off. In the women's dormitory I lived in my first year, apart from six international graduate students (all of us were from Asia and considered "exotic"), the only non-Christian was Jewish, and the only nonwhite an African-American from Georgia. I didn't anticipate then, that over the next 35 years, the Iowa population would become so diverse that it would have 6,931 children from non-English-speaking homes registered as students in its schools, nor that Iowans would be in the grip of a cultural crisis in which resentment against immigrants, particularly refugees from Vietnam, Sudan, and Bosnia, as well as unskilled Spanish-speaking workers, would become politicized enough to cause the Immigration and Naturalization Service to open an "enforcement" office in Cedar Rapids in October for the tracking and deporting of undocumented aliens.

In Calcutta in the '50s, I heard no talk of "identity crisis"—communal or individual. The concept itself—of a person not knowing who he or she is—was unimaginable in our hierarchical, classification-obsessed society. One's identity was fixed, derived from religion, caste, patrimony, and mother tongue. A Hindu Indian's last name announced his or her forefathers' caste and place of origin. A Mukherjee could *only* be a Brahmin from Bengal. Hindu tradition forbade intercaste interlanguage, interethnic marriages. Bengali tradition even discouraged emigration: To remove oneself from Bengali was to dilute true culture.

Until the age of 8, I lived in a house crowded with 40 or 50 relatives. My identity was viscerally connected with ancestral soil and genealogy. I was who I was because I was Dr. Sudhir Lal Mukherjee's daughter, because I was a Hindu Brahmin, because I was Bengali-speaking, and because my *desh*—the Bengali word for homeland—was an East Bengal village called Faridpur.

The University of Iowa classroom was my first experience of coeducation. And after not too long, I fell in love with a fellow student named Clark Blaise, an American of Canadian origin, and impulsively married him during a lunch break in a lawyer's office above a coffee shop.

That act cut me off forever from the rules and ways of upper-middle-class life in Bengal, and hurled me into a New World life of scary improvisations and heady explorations. Until my lunch-break wedding, I had seen myself as an Indian foreign student who intended to return to India to live. The five-minute ceremony in the lawyer's office suddenly changed me into a transient with conflicting loyalties to two very different cultures.

The first 10 years into marriage, years spent mostly in my husband's native Canada, I thought of myself as an expatriate Bengali permanently stranded in North America because of destiny or desire. My first novel, *The Tiger's Daughter,* embodies the loneliness I felt but could not acknowledge, even to myself, as I negotiated the no man's land between the country of my past and the continent of my present. Shaped by memory, textured with nostalgia for a class and culture I had abandoned, this novel quite naturally became an expression of the expatriate consciousness.

It took me a decade of painful introspection to put nostalgia in perspective and to make the transition from expatriate to immigrant. After a 14-year stay in Canada, I forced my husband and our two sons to relocate to the United States. But the transition from foreign student to U.S. citizen, from detached onlooker to committed immigrant, has not been easy.

The years in Canada were particularly harsh. Canada is a country that officially, and proudly, resists cultural fusion. For all its rhetoric about a cultural "mosaic," Canada refuses to renovate its national self-image to include its changing complexion. It is a New World country with Old World concepts of a fixed, exclusivist national identity. Canadian official rhetoric designated me as one of the "visible minority" who, even though I spoke the Canadian languages of English and French, was straining "the absorptive capacity" of Canada. Canadians of color were routinely treated as "not real" Canadians. One example: In 1985 a terrorist bomb, planted in an Air-India jet on Canadian soil, blew up after leaving Montreal, killing 329 passengers, most of whom were Canadians of Indian origin. The prime minister of Canada at the time, Brian Mulroney, phoned the prime minister of India to offer Canada's condolences for India's loss.

Those years of race-related harassments in Canada politicized me and deepened my love of the ideals embedded in the American Bill of Rights. I don't forget that the architects of the Constitution and the Bill of Rights were white males and slaveholders. But through their declaration, they provided us with the enthusiasm for human rights, and the initial framework from which other empowerments could be conceived and enfranchised communities expanded.

I am a naturalized U.S. citizen and I take my American citizenship very seriously. I am not an economic refugee, nor am I a seeker of political asylum. I am a voluntary immigrant. I became a citizen by choice, not by simple accident of birth.

Yet these days, questions such as who is an American and what is American culture are being posed with belligerence, and being answered with violence. Scapegoating of immigrants has once again become the politicians' easy remedy for all that ails the nation. Hate speeches fill auditoriums for demagogues willing to profit from stirring up racial animosity. An April Gallup poll indicated that half of Americans would like to bar almost all legal immigration for the next five years.

The United States, like every sovereign nation, has a right to formulate its immigration policies. But in this decade of continual, large-scale diasporas, it is imperative that we come to some agreement about who "we" are, and what our goals are for the nation, now that our community includes people of many races, ethnicities, languages, and religions.

The debate about American culture and American identity has to date been monopolized largely by Eurocentrists and ethnocentrists whose rhetoric has been flamboyantly divisive, pitting a phantom "us" against a demonized "them."

All countries view themselves by their ideals. Indians idealize the cultural continuum, the inherent value system of India, and are properly incensed when foreigners see nothing but poverty, intolerance, strife, and injustice. Americans see themselves as the embodiments of liberty, openness, and individualism, even as the world judges them for drugs, crime, violence, bigotry, militarism, and homelessness. I was in Singapore in 1994 when the American teenager Michael Fay was sentenced to caning for having spraypainted some cans. While I saw Fay's actions as those of an individual, and his sentence as too harsh, the overwhelming local sentiment was that vandalism was an "American" crime, and that flogging Fay would deter Singapore youths from becoming "Americanized."

Conversely, in 1994, in Tavares, Florida, the Lake County School Board announced its policy (since overturned) requiring middle school teachers to instruct their students that American culture, by which the board meant European-American culture, is inherently "superior to other foreign or historic cultures." The policy's misguided implication was that culture in the United States has not been affected by the American Indian, African-American, Latin-American, and Asian-American segments of the population. The sinister implication was that our national identity is so fragile that it can absorb diverse and immigrant cultures only by recontextualizing them as deficient.

Our nation is unique in human history in that the founding idea of "America" was in opposition to the tenet that a nation is a collection of like-looking, like-speaking, like-worshiping people. The primary criterion for nationhood in Europe is homogeneity of culture, race, and religion—which has contributed to blood-soaked balkanization in the former Yugoslavia and the former Soviet Union.

America's pioneering European ancestors gave up the easy homogeneity of their native countries for a new version of utopia. Now, in the 1990s, we have the exciting chance to follow that tradition and assist in the making of a new American culture that differs from both the enforced assimilation of a "melting pot" and the Canadian model of a multicultural "mosaic."

The multicultural mosaic implies a contiguity of fixed, self-sufficient, utterly distinct cultures. Multiculturalism, as it has been practiced in the United States in the past 10 years, implies the existence of a central culture, ringed by peripheral cultures. The fallout of official multiculturalism is the establishment of one culture as the norm and the rest as aberrations. At the same time, the multiculturalist emphasis on race- and ethnicity-based group identity leads to a lack of respect for individual differences within each group, and to vilification of those individuals who place the good of the nation above the interests of their particular racial or ethnic communities.

We must be alert to the dangers of an "us" vs. "them" mentality. In California, this mentality is manifesting itself as increased violence between minority, ethnic communities. The attack on Korean-American merchants in South Central Los Angeles in the wake of the Rodney King beating trial is only one recent example of the tragic side effects of this mentality. On the national level, the politicization of ethnic identities has encouraged the scapegoating of legal immigrants, who are blamed for economic and social problems brought about by flawed domestic and foreign policies.

We need to discourage the retention of cultural memory if the aim of that retention is cultural balkanization. We must think of American culture and nationhood as a constantly reforming, transmogrifying "we."

In this age of diasporas, one's biological identity may not be one's only identity. Erosions and accretions come with the act of emigration. The experience of cutting myself off from a biological homeland and settling in an adopted homeland that is not always welcoming to its dark-complexioned citizens has tested me as a person, and made me the writer I am today.

I choose to describe myself on my own terms, as an American, rather than as an Asian-American. Why is it that hyphenation is imposed only on nonwhite Americans? Rejecting hyphenation is my refusal to categorize the cultural landscape into a center and its peripheries; it is to demand that the American nation deliver the promises of its dream and its Constitution to all its citizens equally.

My rejection of hyphenation has been misrepresented as race treachery by some India-born academics on U.S. campuses who have appointed themselves guardians of the "purity" of ethnic cultures. Many of them, though they reside permanently in the United States and participate in its economy, consistently denounce American ideals and institutions. They direct their rage at me because, by becoming a U.S. citizen and exercising my voting rights, I have invested in the present and not the past; because I have committed myself to help shape the future of my adopted homeland, and because I celebrate racial and cultural mongrelization.

What excites me is that as a nation we have not only the chance to retain those values we treasure from our original cultures but also the chance to acknowledge that the outer forms of those values are likely to change. Among Indian immigrants, I see a great deal of guilt about the inability to hang on to what they commonly term "pure culture." Parents express rage or despair at their U.S.-born children's forgetting of, or indifference to, some aspects of Indian culture. Of those parents I would ask: What is it we have lost if our children are acculturating into the culture in which we are living? Is it so terrible that our children are discovering or are inventing homelands for themselves?

Some first-generation Indo-Americans, embittered by racism and by unofficial "glass ceilings," construct a phantom identity, more-Indian-than-Indians-in-India, as a defense against marginalization. I ask: Why don't you get actively involved in fighting discrimination? Make your voice heard. Choose the forum most appropriate for you. If you are a citizen, let your vote count. Reinvest your energy and resources into revitalizing your city's disadvantaged residents and neighborhoods. Know your constitutional rights, and when they are violated, use the agencies of redress the Constitution makes available to you. Expect change, and when it comes, deal with it!

As a writer, my literary agenda begins by acknowledging that America has transformed me. It does not end until I show that I (along with the hundreds of thousands of immigrants like me) am minute by minute transforming America. The transformation is a two-way process: It affects both the individual and the national-cultural identity.

Others who write stories of migration often talk of arrival at a new place as a loss, the loss of communal memory and the erosion of an original culture. I want to talk of arrival as gain.

Earth's Eye

Edward Hoagland

Best known for his essays on wild animals and natural phenomena, Edward Hoagland's writing is marked by honesty and attention to the details of life. Hoagland is the author of five works of fiction and numerous essay collections including *The Courage of Turtles, Red Wolves, Black Bears,* and *Tigers and Ice.*

Water is our birthplace. We need and love it. In a bathtub, or by a lake or at the sea, we go to it for rest, refreshment, and solace. "I'm going to the water," people say when August comes and they crave a break. The sea is a democracy, so big it's free of access, often a bus or subway ride away, a meritocracy, sink or swim, and yet a swallower of grief because of its boundless scale—beyond the horizon, the home of icebergs, islands, whales. Tears alone are a mysterious, magisterial solvent that bring a smile, a softening of hard thoughts, lend us a merciful and inexpensive respite, almost like half an hour at the beach. In any landscape, in fact, a pond or creek catches and centers our attention as magnetically as if it were, in Thoreau's phrase, "earth's eye."

Lying on your back in deep meadow grass facing a bottomless sky is less focusing, but worth a drive of many hours, as weekend traffic will attest. Yet the very dimensions of the sky, which are unfathomable after the early surge of pleasure that they carry, cause most of us to mitigate their power with preoccupations such as golf or sunbathing as soon as we get outdoors. That sense of first principles can be unnerving, whereas the ground against our backs—if we lie gazing up into the starry night or a piebald day—is seething with groping roots and sprouting seeds and feels like home, as the friendliest dappled clouds can't be. Beyond the prettiest azure blue is black, as nightfall will remind us, and when the day ends, cold is the temperature of black.

A pond, though, is a gentle spot (unless you are Ophelia). Amber- or pewter-colored, it's a drinking fountain for scurrying raccoons and mincing deer, a waterbugs' and minnows' arena for hunting insect larvae, a holding pen for rain that may coalesce into ocean waves next year. Mine flows into the St. Lawrence River. I live in Vermont and spent a hundred dollars once to bulldoze a tadpole pond next to my little stretch of stream. A silent great blue heron, as tall as a Christmas tree, and a castanet-rattling kingfisher, a faster flier and brighter blue, showed up to forage for amphibians the next year. Garter snakes also benefited from the occasional meal of a frog, and a red-tailed hawk, cruising by, might grab a snake or frog. More exciting, a bull moose began using it as a hot-weather wallow, soaking for half an hour, mouthing algae, munching sedges, and browsing the willows that lean from the bank. A beaver cut down some poplar saplings to gnaw and stitch into a dam for creating a proper flow, but the depth remained insufficient to withstand a New England winter, so he retreated downstream to a wetland in my woods.

I bought this land for eighty-five dollars an acre in 1969, and today a comparable hideaway would probably still cost no more than about the price of a good car. We're not talking luxury: As with so much of life, your priorities are what count, and what you wish to protect and pay attention to. I've been a sinner in other ways, but not in this respect.

Remoteness bestows the amenity of uninterrupted sleep. No telephone or electric line runs by, and the hikers and pickups are gone by sunset. When the season of extravagant daylight shortens so I can't simply sleep from dusk to dawn, I light candles or kerosene, but in balmy weather I can nap with equal ease at any hour in the meadow too, or watch the swallows and dragonflies hawk after midges, as the breezes finger me and a yellowthroat hops in the bushes to eat a daddy long-legs. At dark the bats hawk for bugs instead, or an owl hunts, all wings, slow and mothlike, till it sees a rodent. The trees hang over a swimming hole nearby, with a dovish or a moonlit sky showing beyond the leaves like a kind of vastly enlarged swimming hole, until I feel I was born floating in both the water and the air. It's a hammock all the more beguiling because if you relax too much while swimming and let yourself sink, you might conceivably drown. Similarly, in the meadow, if you lazed too late into the fall, woolgathering, snow could fill your mouth.

Nature is not sentimental. The scenery that recruits our spirits in temperate weather may turn unforgiving in the winter. It doesn't care whether we love it and pay the property taxes to save it from development, having walked over it yard by yard in clement conditions. When the birds flee south and other creatures, from bears to beetles, have crawled underground to wait out the cold, we that remain have got to either fish or cut bait: burn some energy in those summer-lazy muscles cutting wood, or take some money out of the bank.

A mountain can be like that all at once. Summer at the bottom, winter at the top; and you climb through all the climates of the year as you scramble up. In the past half-century I've climbed Mount Jefferson in Oregon (a cousin died there in a fall soon afterward) and Mount Washington in New Hampshire, Mount Katahdin in Maine and Mount Etna in Sicily. I've clambered a bit in Wyoming's Wind Rivers and in the Absaroka Range; also in British Columbia and North Yemen; in the Western Ghats in southern India and the Alpes Maritimes in the south of France; and have scrambled modestly in the High Sierras, Alaska's Brooks Range, and on the lower slopes of Mount Kinyeti in the Imatong Massif in southern Sudan. More particularly, I climbed all of Vermont's firetower mountains, back when Vermont still used towers to locate fires, instead of planes.

This feast of variety is part of a writer's life, the coin of the realm you inhabit if you sacrifice the security of Americans used to think they'd have if they weren't freelance in their working lives. In reality, everybody winds up being freelance, but mountains telescope the experience. During a weekend you climb from flowery summer glades to the tundra above treeline, slipping on patches of ice, trudging through snowdrifts; the rain turns to sleet. The view is rarefied until a bellying, bruise-colored sky turns formidable, not pretty. Like climbing combers in a strong surf, there's no indemnity if you come to grief. You labor upward not for money but for joy, or to have *been somewhere*, closer to the mysteries, during your life. Finding a hidden alpine col, a bowl of fragile grassy beauty, you aren't just gleeful; you are linked differently.

Leaving aside specific dangers like riptides, vertigo, or terrific cold, I found I was comfortable on mountainsides or in seawater or in caves or wilderness swatches. In other words, I was fearful of danger but not of nature. I didn't harbor notions of any special dispensation, only that I too was part of it. I'd fought forest fires in the Santa Ana Mountains of southern California when I was twenty and had discovered that moderate hardship energized yet tempered me, as it does many people, just like the natural sorties for which one puts on hiking shoes and ventures where barefoot peoples used to go. In central Africa I've walked a little with tribesmen like the Acholi and the Didinga, who still tend to be comfortable when nearly naked, and have seen that the gap between us seems not of temperament or of intuitions but only acculturation.

As virtual reality captures our time and obsessive attention, some of the pressures that are killing nature may begin to relent. Not the primary one of overpopulation, which is strangling the tropics; but as people peer more and more into computer screens and at television, the outdoors, in affluent countries, may be left in relative peace. This won't stop the wholesale extinction of species, the mauling of the ocean, or other tragedies, but close to home may give a respite to what's left of nature.

Where I live alone each summer, four families lived year-round eighty years ago. The other new landowners don't choose to occupy their holdings even in warm weather because of the absence of electricity. An unusual case, yet I think indicative, and supported by the recent return of numbers of adaptive sorts of wildlife, like moose and fisher, to New England—though, in contrast, along the lake a few miles downhill, cottages perch atop one another, motorboats and water-skiers buzz around, and trollers use radar fish-finders to trace the final sanctuaries of the schools that the lake still holds.

Just as habitat is the central factor in whether birds and animals can survive, what *we* are able to do in the woods will be determined by land regulation or taxing policy and public purchases. Maine's private timberlands have remained unpopulated because of America's lavish need for toilet paper—as Vermont's trees too make paper, cotton-mill bobbins, cedar fencing, and yellow-birch or maple dowels that become furniture legs. Any day, I watch truckloads of pulpwood go by. And in the California Sierras above Lake Tahoe, or on the pristine sea island of Ossabaw, off Savannah, Georgia, I've devoted lovely, utterly timeless hours to exploring refuges that seem quite empty of people but are actually allotted in careful fashion by state or federal agencies for intensive recreational use. The animals hide while the sun is up and feed when it's down. This is the way it will have to work. Levels of life on the same acreage. Or else it won't work at all.

I can be as jubilant indoors, listening to Schubert or Scott Joplin, as when sauntering underneath a mackerel sky on a day striped yellow, red, and green.

Indeed, the density of sensations in which we live is such that one can do both—enjoy a virtuoso pianist through a headset outside. We live two lives or more in one nowadays, with our scads of travel, absurd excesses of unread informational material, the barrage of Internet and TV screens, wallpaper music, the serializing of polygamy and the elongation of youth blurring old age. A sort of mental gridlock sometimes blocks out the amber pond, the mackerel sky, the seething leaves in a fresh breeze up in a canopy of trees, and the Walkman's lavish outpouring of genius too. Even when we just go for a walk, the data jam.

Verisimilitude, on computer screens or in pictorial simulation, is carrying us we don't entirely know where. I need my months each year without electricity and a telephone, living by the sun and looking down the hill a hundred times a day at the little pond. The toads sing passionately when breeding, observing a hiatus only at midmorning when the moose descends from the woods for his therapeutic wallow, or when a heron sails in for a meal. I see these things so clearly I think our ears have possibly changed more than our eyes under the impact of civilization—both the level of noise and subtleties of sound are so different from hunter-gatherer whisperings. I'm a worrier, if not a Luddite. The gluttonies that are devouring nature are remorseless, and the imbalances within the human family give me vertigo. The lovely old idea that human life is sacred, each soul immortal, is in the throes of a grand mal seizure; overpopulation is doing it in. I didn't believe that anyway, but did adhere to the transcendental idea that heaven is right here on earth, if we perceive and insist on it. And this faith is also becoming harder to sustain.

"Religion is what the individual does with his own solitariness," as A. N. Whitehead said. ("Thus religion is solitariness; and if you are never solitary, you are never religious," he added.) I fall back on elemental pleasures like my love of ponds, or how my first sight of any river invariably leaves me grinning. And the sheen of rainwater on a bare black field in March. The thump of surf, combed in the wind and foaming, glistening, yet humping up again like a dinosaur. Yet fish don't touch me as much as animals, perhaps because they never leave the water. Frogs *do;* and I seem to like frog songs even more than bird songs, maybe because they're two-legged like us but can't fly either and were the first vertebrate singers. But I especially respond to them because they live a good deal more than we do in the water.

Frogs are disappearing worldwide in a drastic fashion, perhaps because of ultraviolet rays or acid rain; and I may finally cease to believe that heaven is on earth, if they do. Water without dolphins, frogs, pelicans, cormorants will not mean much to me. But in the meantime I like to search out springs in the high woods where brooks begin—a shallow sink in the ground, perpetually filling. If you carefully lift away the bottom covering of waterlogged leaves, you'll see the penny-sized or pencil-point sources of the groundwater welling up, where it all originates—the brook, the pond, the stream, the lake, the river, and the ocean, till rain brings it back again.

PART 5

Strategies for Academic Writing

Suggested Writing Projects

Academic writing is the method by which scholars talk to each other. Yet critical thinking through writing is obviously not limited to universities. Scientists share their experiments and evaluate the work of others through an ongoing written conversation. So do medical doctors when they write a report on a new surgical procedure, or Supreme Court justices when they issue a decision on a constitutional question. Engineers evaluate design failures and compare or contrast them with earlier problems. Investors depend each day on articles in *The Wall Street Journal* that analyze the cause and effects of an increase in interest rates or the process by which the Federal Reserve controls monetary policy.

The point is the type of mental activity most often required of you in college—the kind that requires a complex interplay of thinking, analyzing, evaluating, and writing—is clearly not limited to the ivory tower. When we report, explain, assess, summarize, and investigate critically, we are doing the world's work. The following unit offers an array of additional tools you'll find necessary: the skills of analyzing, comparing and contrasting, classifying, defining, and illustrating.

Here are some suggestions on where you might begin:

- Select a subject, perhaps a seminal event in history (the assassination of Martin Luther King, Jr., the stock market crash of 1929, the terrorist attack on the World Trade Center) or select a subject that provokes national debate (gay marriages, the quality of public education, religion and politics, political correctness). Narrow your subject to a focused portion of that topic, perhaps by considering such questions as these: **Who** is affected? **Who** is responsible? **Why** are people concerned? **What** are the causes? **Why** did it happen? Initiate the necessary research: interviews, books, journals, and electronic sources. With such questions in mind, consider whether **comparison and contrast** might be an appropriate strategy to help you focus in on the topic or to help you organize the essay itself. Another method might be to **classify** the subject according to the purpose you have for studying it. Consider whether it will be necessary to **define** the broader topic or to define the narrow aspect you've focused on. (Definitions in academic papers may take a full paragraph or may constitute the entire essay.) Keep a look out for interesting **illustrations** or examples that will clarify a point. **Analyze** your findings and assess the evidence or opinions you've uncovered. This final step is essential. Remember that the best student papers go beyond description, narration, and reporting. They evaluate and make judgments.

Group Inquiry

Working in small groups, select a topic that has relevance to your campus as well as to other American colleges and universities (general education requirements for first-year students, affirmative action, college tuition costs, special treatment for athletes). Exchange what you each already know about the issue—your experiences as well as perceptions formed through readings or discussions. How is the issue being addressed at your institution? Are other students on campus aware of it? Consider who is affected, who is responsible, why people might (or might not) be concerned, and so on. What would you or other students need to know to understand and form an intelligent opinion about the issue? Based on your discussion, decide whether you could now focus the topic or whether some exploratory research might be required. Make a list of possible ways to focus or possible sources to begin your research, and then present an overview of your findings to your class. Have other groups come to similar conclusions? Found interesting problems you overlooked? Or interesting solutions you had not thought of?

CHAPTER 21

Classical Patterns of Thought

The voice of the intellect is a soft one, but it does not rest until it has gained a hearing. Ultimately, after endless rebuffs, it succeeds. This is one of the few points in which one may be optimistic about the future of mankind.

SIGMUND FREUD

Good old Aristotle. The more we need to confront the complexities and issues of our time, the more often we turn to ancient Greeks for advice. From them we have inherited a number of valuable tools for thinking about difficult problems, for ways of organizing our thought processes and of inspecting ideas. It was Aristotle's notion that through close perception we could find order and pattern in the world. His work demonstrated that we must first learn to see a thing—a fact—as it really is. In itself, that was a radical concept for its time. But Aristotle went beyond facts. He demonstrated that by looking at relationships and categories, we could infer facts from general principles.

Good writing and clear thinking, then, are united in the same way. We begin with intense perception, with learning how to see the thing, the detail. Then we learn to go beyond our senses—or rather to build upon them.

More and more, that which catches our attention should be a detail or fact illuminated by an idea or an idea incarnated in a fact. We must now further develop techniques that help us identify relationships and form judgments. And that takes us back to Aristotle again. From his work, we've also inherited a number of strategies for accomplishing all of this: *comparison and contrast, classification, definition,* and *illustration.* Each of these, alone or in combination, provides a valuable method for exploring ideas in our minds—and for organizing them in our essays.

If you haven't done this type of thing before, it may at first seem confusing. Be patient. Activities of the mind are not separate from your inner life. All truly valuable intellectual work grows from spiritual strength. The merit of the mind lies in its ability to adapt to new principles and new techniques, even when they're hard to come by. Remember that the goal is not the technique in itself, but the excitement, the nourishment the mind and soul derive from mastering deeper intellectual insights.

Comparison and Contrast

To *compare* is to show similarities. To *contrast* is to show differences. Note that in both cases I've used the phrase *to show.* Because the use of comparison and contrast enables the writer to be specific, it has proved to be one of the most successful methods of writing about abstractions. But to use it in writing, you must first see it in your subject.

Do you want to understand the feminist movement? One way might be to compare it with other social revolutions, perhaps the effort of African Americans to achieve civil rights.

Comparison

Both women and blacks have been arbitrarily limited to certain occupations and social roles because of inherited characteristics: sex and color.

Both have been considered less intelligent than white males, and both at times have been denied the right to education.

Both have been "honored" for stereotyped qualities: blacks, for physical ability and cheerfulness; women, for virginity and motherhood. As a consequence, both blacks and women have often attempted to live up to the stereotype.

Aristotle said that to see relationships is one of the highest acts of human intelligence. By comparing, we draw together similar qualities from things or concepts that previously may have seemed dissimilar.

Contrast often proves equally instructive. Again consider the feminist and black movements for equal rights.

Contrast

Although often disagreeing on means, blacks have tended to support the goals of equal rights; women, however, have been divided, and some have even formed groups to oppose equal rights.

> The black movement produced a charismatic leader in Martin Luther King, Jr., an individual who singularly represented and expressed the highest ideals; the women's movement has tended to remain fragmented.
>
> Pressure for change has always begun first among blacks and been followed shortly thereafter by women. (Is there a cause-and-effect relationship?)

Here's a brief example from professional writer Robert Pirsig describing why he travels cross-country on a motorcycle rather than in a car.

> You see things vacationing on a motorcycle in a way that is completely different from any other. In a car you're always in a compartment, and because you're used to it you don't realize that through that car window everything you see is just more TV. You're a passive observer and it is all moving by you boringly in a frame.
>
> On a cycle the frame is gone. You're completely in contact with it all. You're *in* the scene, not just watching it anymore, and the sense of presence is overwhelming. That concrete whizzing by five inches below your foot is the real thing, the same stuff you walk on, it's right there, so blurred you can't focus on it, yet you can put your foot down and touch it anytime, and the whole thing, the whole experience, is never removed from immediate consciousness.

Through contrasting paragraphs loaded with concrete specifics, Pirsig recreates the sensations of travel in two different modes. The contrast heightens our awareness and clarifies understanding.

The following is another example from an essay titled "Football Red and Baseball Green" by Murray Ross. Although at first one might think Ross is merely exploring nostalgic memories, his real goal is to reveal new insights into the American psyche.

> Football, especially professional football, is the embodiment of a newer myth, one which in many respects is opposed to baseball's. The fundamental difference is that football is not a pastoral game; it is a heroic one. One way of seeing the difference between the two is by the juxtaposition of Babe Ruth and Jim Brown, both legendary players in their separate genres. Ruth, baseball's most powerful hitter, was a hero maternalized (his name), an epic figure destined for a second immortality as a candy bar. His image was impressive but comfortable and altogether human: round, dressed in a baggy uniform, with a schoolboy's cap and a bat which looked tiny next to him. His spindly legs supported a Santa sized torso, and this comic disproportion would increase when he was in motion. He ran delicately, with quick, very short steps, since he felt that stretching your stride slowed you down. This

sort of superstition is typical of baseball players, and typical too is the way in which a personal quirk or mannerism mitigates their awesome skill and makes them poignant and vulnerable.

There was nothing funny about Jim Brown. His muscular and almost perfect physique was emphasized further by the uniform which armored him. Babe Ruth had a tough face, but boyish and innocent; Brown was an expressionless mask under the helmet. In action he seemed invincible, the embodiment of speed and power in an inflated human shape. One can describe Brown accurately only with superlatives, for as a player he was a kind of Superman, undisguised.

Brown and Ruth are caricatures, yet they represent their games. Baseball is part of a comic tradition which insists that its participants be humans, while football, in the heroic mode, asks that its players be more than that. Football converts men into gods, and suggests that magnificence and glory are as desirable as happiness.

In this excerpt, Ross focuses on specific players in baseball and football, looking at each in detail, then draws a general conclusion about the two sports from what he sees in their most famous players. Comparison and contrast, together or separately, then, can lead to insight. You'll recall that *contrast, opposition,* and *contradiction* are some of the qualities reporters seek out in any subject. The same could probably be said of a State Department analyst studying military spending in China or a business executive studying market trends. Comparison and contrast are perceptual strategies that clarify, as the concept of male is clarified by female, and female by male.

Classification

To *classify* is to arrange persons, places, ideas—almost anything—in groups or categories according to certain common characteristics. The goal of classification is to understand the whole of something by understanding an arrangement of its parts.

Actually, classification is something you do almost every day without much conscious thought. When you trudge down to the laundromat to wash your clothes, you sort bright colors into one pile, white clothes into another, or you make a separate grouping for synthetic fibers and another for cottons. Whatever your categories, you do it because to mix them randomly might mean that some clothes would be ruined. The purpose determines the way you classify, and you can apply the same principle to complex questions and issues. A concept won't be "ruined" by mixing all the parts, but any attempt to understand it may be confused.

When we classify, then, we determine the qualities that any particular item or concept must have to fall within a particular *class.* The items in the class, selected according to purpose, constitute a *subclass*. If you decide to write a humorous essay on the sexual attractiveness of males to college females, you might come up with the following.

class: potential college lovers
subclass: frat boys, jocks, geeks, punks

On the other hand, if you wanted to write a serious essay on the same subject, your subclass might be quite different.

class: potential college lovers
subclass: those who are afraid of commitments; those who are chauvinistic; those who need mothers; those who possess maturity

A further step in classification occurs when you identify the distinguishing characteristics of any new item in the subclass.

subclass: those who possess maturity
distinguishing characteristics: respect for self, openness to the needs of others, spontaneity, numerous interests, sense of humor, creativity

But how does all this help in working with abstract subjects? First, it offers you a means of narrowing any broad subject to a more specific and manageable topic. Second, the classes or subclasses you arrive at may form various portions of your paper (in other words, all this helps organize the body of the essay). In a work titled "Propaganda Techniques in Today's Advertising," professional writer Ann McClintock uses classification to accomplish both of these aims. McClintock begins by pointing out that propaganda is not simply something governments use to retain the loyalty of citizens. Advertisers, she argues, bombard us daily with claims and persuasive techniques intended to sell us products. McClintock then divides the propaganda of advertising into seven categories: name calling, glittering generalities, transfer techniques, testimonials, plain folks, card stacking, and bandwagoning. Each category serves as a natural division for her essay.

For example, McClintock discusses how "transfer techniques" work by associating a product with something else that we already know, such as associating beer with cold mountain streams or suburban vans designed to carry children to soccer games with race cars. Such a technique can totally change our attitude toward the product. But this is only a single method. In your own work, you might find that you could organize an essay according to the various sub-classes of transfer techniques. The testimonial, for example, is one of the advertisers' most-loved and most-used propaganda methods. As a subcategory of the transfer device, the testimonial uses the admiration people have for a celebrity to make the product shine more brightly—even though the celebrity is not an expert on the product being sold. Print and television ads offer a non-stop parade of testimonials: on any given night we might see Michael Jordan selling hot dogs and underwear; Daisy Fuentes promoting folic acid; 'N Sync celebrating Burger King; Jerry Seinfeld losing his American Express card; and Britany Spears singing for Pepsi. Testimonials can sell movies, cars, even books—see the blurbs by celebrities and critics on the backs of paperbacks. Political candidates—as well as their ad agencies—know the value of testimonials. Barbara Streisand endorses Al Gore; Charlton Heston lends his star appeal to George W. Bush.

For both writer and reader, the world is a swarm of images and conflicting messages. By breaking advertising techniques into the various classes and subclasses, one can then begin to focus on examples and details within each class. Dividing your topic into separate units or categories, then focusing on each category individually, allows us to concentrate our minds and further our understanding.

Classification can also serve as a method of introducing a subject. Here is how business major Sheri Martin introduced a paper on economic systems:

> The relationship between the economic system of a country and the amount of government regulation of that system depends upon five different organizational structures: communism, socialism, fascism, regulated capitalism (as in the United States), and pure capitalism. In a short paper of this nature, I cannot treat all of these. Instead, I will attempt to outline the contrasting functions of government in two seemingly similar systems: regulated capitalism and pure capitalism. I will try to show that those functions are actually as unlike as day and night.

Economics (a difficult, abstract subject) has been classified into five methods of organizing the economic structure of a society. Sheri then narrows her proposed topic to two of those structures. By attempting to *see* (intellectually) a subject's various subclasses according to a defined purpose, you can clarify the resulting order and begin the process of understanding. For both writer and reader, classification focuses perception.

Definition

Classification may reduce a subject from a general concept to more specific categories, but unless we all agree on the meaning of those categories, they still may not be clear. You've probably all had the experience of arguing with someone, perhaps in a heated and emotional exchange, only to discover you were using the same word to mean different things.

Without definition, communication may not occur. *Capitalism,* for example, is still a general term. *Regulated capitalism* is a rather specialized term, one that may not be familiar to many readers. Here's how Sheri Martin continued the second paragraph of her paper on economic systems.

Capitalism is one of the oldest economic systems in the world. In essence, it is characterized by a free market with private ownership of production and means of distribution. When two tribal farmers in West Africa meet in a market to sell and exchange goods based on their own needs and desires, without regulation by any other authority, they are engaging in a primitive form of capitalism. But regulated capitalism is very different. It is characterized by private ownership and imposed government restrictions. The restrictions theoretically prevent any one person or company from dominating the free market or prevent monopolies, like utilities, from earning an unfair profit. By contrast, socialism means that the government not only regulates the market, it may actually own much of the production and means of distribution, retaining all profits for itself.

Sheri has used several conventional methods of defining. She has *described* the basic qualities of both systems. She has given a specific *illustration* of one system and an *example* of the other. And she has *contrasted* the second system to something it is not.

As senses shape experience, so words shape our thoughts. Failure to define words leads to faulty thinking. But we are dealing here with something more than mere definition of specialized terms (as important as that is). Definition is inherent in the very notion of understanding ideas in themselves. Concepts such as *liberalism, imagination, faith, human nature,* as well as *capitalism,* may require extended definition—the pursuit of meaning through a complete essay. Here's an extended definition of "The American Dream," by Betty Anne Younglove, originally published in *U.S. News & World Report.*

The American Dream

Betty Anne Younglove

The lament for the death of the American dream grows ever louder. And although the verses may vary, the chorus is the same: The American dream is out of reach, unattainable.

Some of the verses I hear most often:

- Young families cannot afford a three-bedroom house in the suburbs because the prices or interest rates or taxes are too high.
- The average family cannot afford to send its sons and daughters to "a Harvard" because the cost is equivalent to the total family income before taxes; moreover, there is not enough money to send the kids to a prep school to insure they can get into "a Harvard" even if they can come up with the money.
- Why, oh why, can't the young people of today be guaranteed the dreams their parents had?

First, let us get this dream business—and business it now seems to be—straight. The word *dream* is not a synonym for *reality* or *promise.* It is closer to *hope* or *possibility* or even *vision.* The original American dream had only a little to do with material possessions and a lot to do with choices, beginnings and opportunity. Many of the original American dreamers wanted a new beginning, a place to choose what they wanted and a place to work for it. They did not see it as a guarantee of success but an opportunity to try.

The dream represented possibilities: Get your own land and clear it and work it; if nature cooperates, the work might pay off in material blessings. Or the dream represented the idea that any citizen with the minimum qualifications of age and years of citizenship could run for President even if he were born in a humble log cabin. He had no guarantee he would win, of course, no more than the man clearing his land was guaranteed a good crop.

The preamble to the Constitution does not promise happiness, only the right to pursue it.

This new elegy, however, seems to define the American dream as possessions and to declare that material things, power and money are our rights; we not only deserve them but maybe a free lunch as well.

Whatever verse we have been listening to in this new song about the dream, we should recognize it as nothing more than a siren song leading us with Pied Piper promises. Let's go back to the original idea—a tune we can whistle while we work to achieve the goal of our choice.

Younglove contrasts two definitions of the American dream. Her essay might have been extended by adding more detailed illustrations of each version, or by contrasting both versions to the promises of the good life made by Marxist nations, or by quoting from others whose words from the past may have contributed to our perception of the American dream—from Abraham Lincoln or John F. Kennedy or Martin Luther King, Jr. In other words, if the concept of definition is extended to its limits, the material available to you is almost inexhaustible. And each additional piece of information, in turn, extends our understanding of the subject.

Definition means clarification through precision; it means uncovering the nature or basic qualities of a concept. The need for definition, then, begins inside ourselves as we first approach a subject. Later, as we begin to write, the need becomes public, to communicate and explain what we have learned.

Illustration

The traditional rhetorical methods of exploring ideas, issues, and values can sometimes seem overly abstract. *Comparing* and *contrasting, classifying,* and *defining* may be brilliant exercises of the mind, but without concrete details, they often seem fuzzy to readers. When using such strategies in our papers, we can sometimes forget that *showing* is more immediately effective than *telling.* One way to enrich every classical strategy (indeed, it is a classical strategy in itself) is to illustrate our thinking with concrete examples, anecdotes, or specific evidence.

Here's an example from first-year student Charles Bonnette. Charles is writing about individual responsibility—an abstract concept that he needs to illustrate if the reader is to understand fully.

> In the United States we have long abandoned personal responsibility in favor of placing that responsibility on others—on "society," or our "parents," or the "government." But in other countries, individual responsibility still counts. For example, when I was traveling with my parents in Spain last summer, we stayed at a small hotel in the mountains. Outside our window, a winding narrow road made a sharp turn, dropped sharply, then began to climb again. Road crews had dug a deep hole in the right lane just beyond the sharp turn. At night, a single warning lantern and sign on a barricade indicated that cars coming down the hill should pull into the left lane. The barricade was placed thirty feet or so from the hole. For three nights in a row I watched car after car, plus several motorcycles, roar down the hill, speed around the sharp turn, crash through the barricade and drop into the hole.
>
> In the United States, we would claim that the government was at fault—not enough warning, only one lantern, find a lawyer and sue. But in Spain, the hotel workers and a few guests would help the driver pull out his car, straighten out the fender, wipe away the nose bleed, and wave goodbye as the driver sped away. Then they would replace the barrier, re-light the lantern, and wait for the next accident. In Spain, it was clear that a driver assumed responsibility for his own actions. If he was going too fast to stop, that was not the government's fault. Not one driver seemed to feel that someone else should have done something to protect him or his car. No one even dreamed about suing someone else.

Charles uses a traditional strategy here. He first makes a generalization, then signals the use of an illustration to support or clarify the generalization with the words *for example.* The example itself, in this case, uses *comparison and contrast* to illuminate the differences in the way two cultures might respond to a specific incident.

Professional writers especially rely on illustrations. In an essay titled "College Pressures," William Zinsser first divides college pressure into four categories, then uses an anecdote, followed by personal examples, to illustrate one of those categories.

> Peer pressure and self-induced pressure are almost intertwined, and they begin almost at the beginning of freshman year.
>
> "I had a freshman student I'll call Linda," one dean told me, "who came in and said she was under terrible pressure because her roommate, Barbara, was much brighter and studied all the time. I couldn't tell her that Barbara had come in two hours earlier to say the same thing about Linda."

> The story is almost funny—except that it's not. It's symptomatic of all the pressures put together. When every student thinks every other student is working harder and doing better, the only solution is to study harder still. I see students going off to the library every night after dinner and coming back when it closes at midnight. I wish they could sometimes forget about their peers and go to a movie.

It should be clear that *illustration* is not a strategy that exists apart from other techniques. Using specific examples supports and clarifies other classical methods of thinking discussed in this chapter. Perhaps I can best illustrate that myself by offering a brief excerpt of an essay by Desmond Morris called "Territorial Behavior." Morris argues that human beings have evolved as tribal animals. For millions of years our home base was a protected hunting territory. In general, his essay analyzes ways in which contemporary humans continue to act as tribal units—by forming small subgroups such as teenage gangs, college fraternities, political parties, and local clubs.

Morris begins by *defining* the concept of "territory." He then divides the concept into categories, an act of *classification.*

> A territory is a defended space. In the broadest sense there are three kinds of human territory: tribal, family and personal.

To explain each category, and to make it vivid for the reader, Morris then uses paragraph-long examples that *illustrate* by making a *comparison* of a modern human activity with more primitive "tribal" activities.

> Each of these modern pseudo-tribes sets up its own special kind of home base. In extreme cases non-members are totally excluded, in others they are allowed in as visitors with limited rights and under a control system of special rules. In many ways they are like miniature nations, with their own flags and emblems and their own border guards. The exclusive club has its own "customs barrier": the doorman who checks your "passport" (your membership card) and prevents strangers from passing in unchallenged. There is a government: the club committee; and often special displays of the tribal elders: the photographs or portraits of previous officials on the walls. At the heart of the specialized territories there is a powerful feeling of security and importance, a sense of shared defense against the outside world. Much of the club chatter, both serious and joking, directs itself against the rottenness of everything outside the club boundaries—in that "other world" beyond the protected portals.

The effective use of *illustration* grows directly out of the earliest stages of the writing process. Training yourself to see details, to become aware of specifics, to use concretions—enriches and clarifies even the most abstract forms of thought and analysis.

Synthesis and the Writing Process

Which of all the mental processes reviewed in this chapter is best? Which will be most important to you in academic writing? Which will serve you well in a career? The answer is all of them. Like other teachers of writing, I have divided these mental processes into separate strategies for the sake of discussion and clarity. It is easier to learn one method at a time. But in a very real sense, everything I've said is a distortion of the way the mind actually works. The experienced writer does not sit down and say to himself or herself, "Now I'm going to write a 'compare and contrast' article for *National Review.*" Instead, the writer begins with a subject—with prison reform in California or the psychological effect of terrorism on first graders. In the process of studying the subject, the writer uses not only the methods described in this chapter—*comparison and contrast, classification, definition, illustration*—but all other methods covered in this book. He or she looks for *who, what, where, when, why,* and *how;* for the human examples that will make the subject come alive and seem relevant; for *change, conflict, characterization;* and for possible leads that will make an imaginative introduction. The writer *evaluates* and *interprets.* Each of these, alone or in combination, may be used as part of a formal essay. Each is a means to an end—to explain a subject to an audience. *Synthesis* is the act of combining separate parts to form a whole. In writing, one does not so much "combine" as move through a process of back-and-forth interaction with all possible strategies, a testing of the subject against all the varying capacities of the mind.

But remember, in themselves, each of these methods is only that—a method. Even when combined they do not constitute knowledge. For that you must turn to personal experience, interviews, and reading, where you will *use* such methods to seek out the facts, the details, and the substance that all lead to understanding. Vitality in writing comes from the immersion of your energies, from a commitment to the experience you are writing about. Ideas, issues, and values—abstractions—will be significant only insofar as you do experience them, only insofar as you make them concrete, feel them, care about them. The fully synthetic essay, then, draws together everything you are, everything you've learned; it is the whole process working together. Don't expect it to come easily. Starts and stops, confusion, and wasted paper are normal. This will be the most demanding work you've attempted. But persist. Take on the challenge. Commit the whole self, the whole mind. Begin the act of synthesizing all that you have now studied and practiced.

Here's an outline of steps you might want to take in approaching an idea, issue, or value and the various methods that might be useful in preparing to write about it.

Exploration process	Method
1. Begin with an overview of the subject as a whole.	*Define* the terms of the concept with a dictionary. Use an encyclopedia or general article to explore the background if necessary. Consider various ways the subject can be *classified.* What are its major categories? How can you narrow the subject to one specific component or subclass that might be treated in a short essay?
2. Form a question or series of questions on the narrowed subject.	Further *define* the specific terms and components you plan to write about. If possible, use the techniques of *comparison and contrast* to bring your purpose more clearly into focus and to form specific questions for inquiry.
3. Investigate for details. If possible, locate original sources to interview. Read several articles or a relevant chapter from a book.	Look for the 5 *W*'s and 4 *C*'s. Collect specific illustrations to make the subject as concrete as possible. *Interpret* and *evaluate* what you discover.

Chapter 23 will show how a professional writer has used many of these techniques in a formal essay, but it must be remembered that the *product* you'll see there evolved from a *process* much like the one described here.

Practice

1. As part of a class or small-group discussion, study the following excerpt from Trey Ellis, writing in *The Village Voice.* Is Ellis using definition? Comparison and contrast? Classification? Or is his essay a synthesis of several methods? Be sure. Consider each paragraph as a unit, as well as how the whole of it works together.

> *African-American* is merely a more specific, more formal, and less powerful synonym for *black. Afro-American,* like *Italo-American,* is simply a more wieldy, slightly less formal version of its longer brother.
>
> The change from *colored* to *black* was an important linguistic battle for our self-determination; our own Russian revolution into good Soviets. While the terms *black* and *African-American* both predate this century, *black* was the one my parents fought for from the wrong end of a fire hose. Why throw it away? It is equal in importance and weight (and, while we're at it, number of letters) to *white* and graphically demonstrates how divided we still are.

African-American, though more specific, relegates us to just another hyphenate satellite around WASP America. Yet no matter what you call it or how you capitalize it, today's world is not divided between African-American and white, but still, unfortunately, between black and white.

Black unifies all people of African descent across national borders. Africans themselves are blacks. Whether Senegalese, Brazilian, Jamaican, Haitian, or Alabaman, *black* integrates us all. In England, Africans and Afro-Caribbeans call themselves *blacks.* Aboriginal Australians are black and call themselves just that. Many Polynesians are black, and there are even black Mexicans called *morenos* (blacks).

Before the '60s, *black* meant something very different to black people: *If you're white you're all right, if you're yellow you're mellow, if you're brown stick around, if you're black stay back.* Unlike Brazil's encyclopedia of skin-tone and hair-texture gradations, *black* unified the rainbow coalition of African-Americans. After the term was coined here, whether yellow or chocolate or pitch, we all rallied around the very word that had been a shameful insult for decades.

2. *Classify* one of the following items. Assume your purpose is to write a humorous essay.

   rap videos

   horror films

   TV advertisements for toilet paper

   fraternities or sororities

   roommates

3. *Classify* the same subject again with a serious purpose: to write an essay critical of the subject.

4. Although no *definition* may be totally adequate, consider the following. In what way is each extract satisfactory (if it is), and in what ways is each unsatisfactory? What methods of definition are used? What additional methods might extend the definition and make it more complete?

   Americans seem to live and breathe and function by paradox; but in nothing are we so paradoxical as in our passionate belief in our own myths. We truly believe ourselves to be natural-born mechanics and do-it-yourselfers. We spend our lives in motor cars, yet most of us—a great many of us at least—do not know enough about a car to look in the gas tank when the motor fails. Our lives as we live them would not function without electricity, but it is a rare man or woman who, when the power goes off, knows how to look for a burned-out fuse and replace it. We believe implicitly that we are the heirs of the pioneers; that we have inherited self-sufficiency and the ability to take care of ourselves, particularly in relation to nature. There isn't a man among us in ten thousand who knows how to butcher a cow or a pig and cut it up for eating, let alone a wild animal. By natural endowment, we are great rifle shots and great hunters—but when hunting season opens there is a slaughter of farm animals and humans by men and women who couldn't hit a real target if they could see it. Americans treasure the knowledge that they live close to nature, but fewer and fewer farmers feed more and more people; and as soon as we can afford to we eat out of cans, buy frozen TV dinners, and haunt the delicatessens. Affluence means moving to the suburbs, but the American suburbanite sees, if anything, less of the country than the city apartment dweller with his window boxes and his African violets carefully tended under lights. In no country are more seeds and plants and equipment purchased, and less vegetables and flowers raised.

John Steinbeck, *America and Americans*

Being an artist means, not reckoning and counting, but ripening like the tree which does not force its sap but stands, confident in the storms of spring, without fear that after them may come no summer. It does come, but only to the patient, who are there as though eternity lay before them so unconcernedly still and wide. I learn it daily, learn it with pain to which I am grateful. Patience is everything.

Rainer Maria Rilke, *Letters to a Young Poet*

Scientific knowledge is not knowledge of Being. This means that scientific knowledge is particular, not general, that it is directed toward specific objects, and not toward Being itself. Through knowledge itself, science arrives at the most positive recognition of what it does *not* know.

Scientific knowledge or understanding cannot supply us with the aims of life. It cannot lead us. By virtue of its very clarity it directs us elsewhere for the sources of our life, our decisions, our love.

Karl Jaspers, *Is Science Evil?*

CHAPTER 22

The Analytical Mind

Whether Aristotle invented analysis is unclear. But Aristotle did use analysis with such success that—after its rediscovery in the Renaissance—it became the dominant thought pattern of the Western mind. To analyze means to divide a subject into parts for individual study, much as you would for classification. But where classification may stop with identifying and describing the parts, analysis proceeds to evaluate their relationship.

Here, in simple outline, is the analytic process.

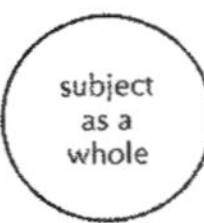

Consider the subject as a whole, as an idea, argument, issue, or whatever in its full context. General definition is essential at this point.

Divide the subject into its various components as you would in classification (that is, as determined by your purpose).

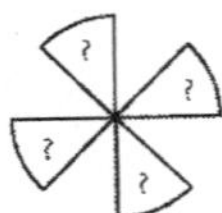

Consider each part separately. If each subject is too large, this is when to narrow your focus and deal primarily with only one or two components (as Sheri Martin did in her essay in Chapter 21). Each component may need further definition.

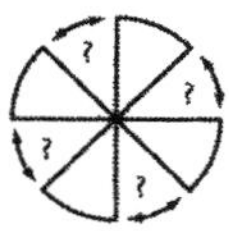

Evaluate the relationship of each part to every other part. The compare-and-contrast strategy will often prove helpful at this stage.

or

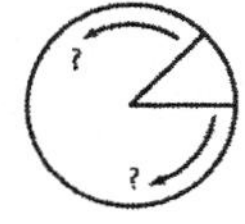

If you've narrowed your focus to a single component, consider how it relates to the subject as a whole.

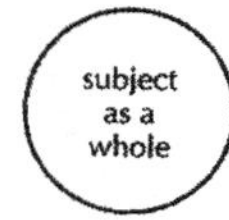

Interpret your findings. What do you know about the subject from having studied the parts and their relationships? (Inexperienced writers often omit this final phase, but analysis is of little value unless you draw the subject together again and form an overall assessment.)

Obviously, analysis incorporates other conventional methods: *classification, comparison and contrast,* and *definition.* By drawing them all together and by discovering relationships, you'll find that analysis becomes one of the single most important intellectual strategies you can learn. For further clarification, analysis is traditionally divided into two related but somewhat different approaches.

Process Analysis

If you wanted to understand relationships that are part of a chronological sequence, you could trace and evaluate the process. This textbook is an attempt to work with the process of writing. In preparing it, I first spent a number of years mulling over actual phases the mind goes through as it explores a subject, as words are put on paper for the first time, and as the mind reshapes and refines those words. I attempted to break down my own process into separate activities. I read about how others had described such phases in their writing. I attempted to see how each related in sequence. I have to admit that no new discovery resulted. *Exploring, drafting, organizing, revising,* and *editing* turned out to be a process long known by professional writers and many teachers of writing. But for me it was an invaluable insight. By identifying individual activities in the process and their relationship, I found the subject of writing as a whole clarified. Analysis helped me understand why some strategies in teaching writing might have disastrous consequences when taught out of sequence. It helped me see that the expository methods I'm discussing in this chapter are actually ways of looking at and thinking about a subject that can later become ways of organizing the same subject on paper. To analyze a process, then, is to explore the way the mind and the world works—in its actual sequence.

Here's an example from a book by John McPhee describing and narrating the simple process of turning fresh oranges into frozen concentrate.

> As the fruit starts to move along a concentrate plant's assembly line, it is first culled. In what some citrus people remember as "the old fresh-fruit days," before the Second World War, about forty percent of all oranges grown in Florida were eliminated at packinghouses and dumped in fields. Florida milk tasted like orangeade. Now, with the exception of the split and rotten fruit, all of Florida's orange crop is used. Moving up a conveyor belt, oranges are scrubbed with detergent before they roll on into juicing machines. There are several kinds of juicing machines, and they are something to see. One is called the Brown Seven Hundred. Seven hundred oranges a minute go into it and are split and reamed on the same kind of rosettes that are in the centers of ordinary kitchen reamers. The rinds that come pelting out the bottom are integral halves, just like the rinds of oranges squeezed in a kitchen. Another machine is the Food Machinery Corporation's FMC In-line Extractor. It has a shining row of aluminum jaws, upper and lower, with shining aluminum teeth. When an orange tumbles in, the upper jaw comes crunching down on it while at the same time the orange is penetrated from below by a perforated steel tube. As the jaws crush the outside, the juice goes through the perforations in the tube and down into the plumbing of the concentrate plant. All in a second, the juice has been removed and the rind has been crushed and shredded beyond recognition.
>
> From either machine, the juice flows on into a thing called the finisher, where seeds, rag, and pulp are removed. The finisher has a big stainless steel screw that steadily drives the juice through a fine-mesh screen. From the finisher, it flows on into holding tanks.

In McPhee's *Oranges,* a relatively simple mechanical process is divided into each phase of the operation. The author traces the step-by-step process, using concrete detail to show us the oranges tumbling along the conveyor belt, almost as if we were watching a film. McPhee wants to help us understand the process. His intention is clearly not to instruct us in how to run such an operation, although by making the language more formal and directive, he could easily do so.

> First, cull all split and rotten fruit as it moves along the assembly belt. Second, scrub the oranges with detergent using spray-jet machinery. Third, insert the oranges into the Brown 700 De-Juicer. . . .

And so on. As in other types of writing, the purpose and audience help determine vocabulary, tone, and style. In either case, a relationship is illustrated by the natural narrative sequence of the process: first this, then this. A process analysis makes heavy use of transitions: *next, following, afterward, then, beyond this point, later, finally.*

But a process analysis can do much more than focus on simple sequential steps such as tying your shoes or making orange juice. It can give us insight into ideas and values. Here's a brief excerpt from sophomore Cray Steward's essay titled "Romantic Love":

> Today we tend to see falling in love as a natural human right, and I would guess that most of us think of it also as a natural step toward marriage. There aren't many of us who would want to marry someone just for their money or their power. We want love, too. And we will marry people without money or power, without anything at all except love. But "sweep-me-off-my-feet" love is actually something new in human history. Marriage was once considered a property right that had little or no relation to love. As late as the Victorian period, upper class marriages were organized by families to preserve property, or even better to increase property, and to preserve blood lines. In the Western world, the bride was considered as belonging to her father, in the same way that a horse or good piece of furniture belonged to the father, and the father alone had the right to dispose of her. That's why in our marriage ceremony, we still ask the question, "Who gives this woman?" at which point the father steps forward and says "I do." The ceremony is recognizing that the woman herself has no right to enter into marriage on her own without permission from the father. In fact, even a woman from a "good family" was not really very desirable if she didn't have some property to go with her. A beautiful lady who might be charming, loving, generous, and devoted was not enough in herself unless a dowry could be offered. Women were merely part of the exchange system concerned primarily with material values.
>
> According to Ernst Van Den Haag, in "Marriage vs. Love," our concept of romantic love originated in the Middle Ages. Romantic love was at first a poetic idea sung about by court entertainers who turned women into an ideal image of beauty and delicacy rather than see them as property. In these poems, knights would "fall in love" with a woman who was already married (already somebody else's property) and who was therefore unattainable. In such a way, their value to the knight could not be materialistic, but purely idealistic. The knights would do great deeds for their adored lady, such as slay dragons or set off in quest of some magic potion, but the knights did not expect to "win" their ladies because they were already possessed, and the lady was not expected to submit to expressions of love, although some did I guess. Instead, the two were united only by the bond of romantic love which was a new concept.
>
> In *The Origins of Love,* Catherine Calloway states that idealized romance, which she terms a new "invention," led to two new developments in the way men and women saw their relationship to each other. . . .

Cray Steward's essay does not merely narrate a sequence of events. In fact, Cray moves back and forth between different types of human experience at different periods of history. But the overall pattern is clear by the third paragraph:

In tracing the development of a new form of emotional bond between men and women, Cray hopes to explain the process by which we now believe in marrying for love rather than for property. By analyzing a contemporary value according to the historical process by which we arrived at that value, we discover more about who we are and why we act and think as we do.

In addition to analyzing a process, analysis may also look at causes and effects. Where process concerns itself primarily with *how* something occurs, a cause-and-effect analysis concerns itself with *why* something occurs.

Cause-and-Effect Analysis

Whenever events occur in sequence, the possibility exists that one may have caused the other. But this type of potential relationship is fraught with danger. We must always distinguish between necessary factors and incidental factors. If *X* precedes *Y*, is it necessarily the *cause* of *Y*?

I had relatives, for example, who were living in Kansas when the first atomic bomb was dropped on Hiroshima. They heard the announcement on the radio and moments later the sky turned greenish black, the winds howled, and a tornado swept down upon them, barely missing their house. My relatives were convinced that what they were experiencing was caused by the atomic bomb. It was not an unnatural fear, nor was it an unnatural link for the mind to make. Tolstoy described how serfs on his estate believed that spring winds were caused by new buds on oak trees. Yet, in both cases, either a coincidence or an incidental relationship was incorrectly perceived as a cause. This type of fallacy has been so common throughout history that logicians have given it a fancy name—*post hoc, ergo propter hoc*. It simply means "after this, therefore because of this"—after my cat ate raw liver, she climbed a tree; therefore, my cat climbs trees because she eats raw liver. These examples may seem silly, but when a doctor is confronted with a symptom, a cause must be determined and the consequences of error could be fatal.

How then can we be reasonably sure of a cause-and-effect relationship? In the scientific laboratory, two rules have been devised as tests.

1. Without *X*, there would be no *Y*.
2. Whenever we find *X*, we will find *Y*.

One or the other of these two conditions (some would say both) must be met for a cause to be considered reasonably certain. Yet in dealing with the complexities outside the laboratory, such a formula, valid as it may be, can lead to distortion and oversimplification. Without Osama bin Laden, there might not have been a war against terrorism, but we cannot therefore say that bin Laden was the sole cause of the war. Hundreds of other factors played significant roles. Causal analysis, then, requires caution and a concern for finding both the *necessary factors* (as opposed to incidental ones) and a *sufficient number of factors* (as opposed to a single or simplistic one).

When anthropologist Margaret Mead asked, "Can the American Family Survive?" she was fully aware of the danger of blaming a problem on a single cause.

> In recent years, various explanations have been suggested for the breakdown of family life.
>
> Blame has been placed on the vast movement of Americans from rural areas and small towns to the big cities and on the continual, restless surge of people from one part of the country to another, so that millions of families, living in the midst of strangers, lack any continuity in their lifestyle and any real support for their values and expectations.
>
> Others have emphasized the effects of unemployment and underemployment among Blacks and other minority groups, which make their families peculiarly vulnerable in life crises that are exacerbated by economic uncertainty. This is particularly the case where the policies of welfare agencies penalize the family that is poor but intact in favor of the single-parent family.
>
> There is also the generation gap, particularly acute today, when parents and their adolescent children experience the world in such very different ways. The world in which the parents grew up is vanishing, unknown to their children except by hearsay. The world into which adolescents are growing is in many ways unknown to both generations—and neither can help the other very much to understand it.
>
> Then there is our obvious failure to provide for the children and young people whom we do not succeed in educating, who are in deep trouble and who may be totally abandoned. We have not come to grips with the problems of hard drugs. We allow the courts that deal with juveniles to become so overloaded that little of the social protection they were intended to provide is possible. We consistently underfund and understaff the institutions into which we cram children in need of re-education and physical and psychological rehabilitation, as if all that concerned us was to get them—and keep them—out of our sight.
>
> Other kinds of explanations also have been offered.
>
> There are many people who, knowing little about child development, have placed the principal blame on what they call "permissiveness"—on the relaxing of parental discipline to include the child as a small partner in the process of growing up. Those people say that children are "spoiled," that they lack "respect" for their parents or that they have not learned to obey the religious prohibitions that were taught to their parents, and that all the troubles plaguing family life have followed.
>
> Women's Liberation, too, has come in for a share of the blame. It is said that in seeking self-fulfillment, women are neglecting their homes and children and are undermining men's authority and men's sense of responsibility. The collapse of the family is seen as the inevitable consequence.
>
> Those who attribute the difficulties of troubled families to any single cause, whether or not it is related to reality, also tend to advocate panaceas, each of which—they say—should restore stability to the traditional family or, alternatively, supplant the family. Universal day care from birth, communal

> living, group marriage, contract marriage and open marriage all have their advocates.
>
> Each such proposal fastens on some trouble point in the modern family—the lack of adequate facilities to care for the children of working mothers, for example, or marital infidelity, which, it is argued, would be eliminated by being institutionalized. Others, realizing the disastrous effects of poverty on family life, have advocated bringing the income of every family up to a level at which decent living is possible. Certainly this must be one of our immediate aims. But it is wholly unrealistic to suppose that all else that has gone wrong will automatically right itself if the one—but very complex—problem of poverty is eliminated.

Mead recognizes that complex issues and ideas almost always have complex causes. Her review of possible causes for the deterioration of traditional family life establishes the context for her own understanding of the problem, and as readers, we now know that simple cause-and-effect relationships will not be forthcoming, nor would they be accurate. And we also know that identification of so many causes may force us to consider broader and more imaginative solutions than we had at first thought necessary.

If the first rule of cause-and-effect analysis is to avoid oversimplification, the second is to avoid settling for clichés and stereotypes. For example, it would be easy to say—and has been said—that fewer females enter the fields of physics and chemistry because they do not have analytical minds. But when Sheila Tobias studied the situation for her book *Overcoming Math Anxiety,* here is what she found:

> Although fear of math is not a purely female phenomenon, girls tend to drop out of math sooner than boys, and adult women experience an aversion to math and math-related activities that is akin to anxiety. A . . . survey of the amount of high school mathematics taken by incoming freshmen at Berkeley revealed that while 57 percent of the boys had taken four years of high school math, only 8 percent of the girls had had the same amount of preparation. Without four years of high school math, students at Berkeley, and at most other colleges and universities, are ineligible for the calculus sequence, unlikely to attempt chemistry or physics, and inadequately prepared for statistics and economics.
>
> Unable to elect these entry-level courses, the remaining 92 percent of the girls will be limited, presumably, to the career choices that are considered feminine: the humanities, guidance and counseling, elementary school teaching, foreign languages, and the fine arts.

Tobias has uncovered causes that challenge our biases and force us to reconsider the standard answers. First-year student Melinda Holt tried to do the same thing when she studied causes and effects of television on family life.

But is it really that bad? Are we really all such sheep that we sit mindless in front of the tube letting the blue glow hypnotize us? In my family, the TV actually brought us *together,* and we didn't sit passively either. We talked to each other about what was happening. Sometimes we poked fun at banalities of situation comedies. Other times we laughed and argued with the news-casters. In other words, I think that in my family, the TV was more like a guest in our home who for an hour or so each evening drew us all together. We talked *to* the TV just as we talked to each other, and when we grew bored, we didn't sit around and flip channels; my dad would turn it off and all of us went our separate ways. Wagoner's idea that TV has "isolated us from each other and destroyed our abilities to act like social animals" (130), or that it has taken away time that would have been spent doing things like playing basketball with our fathers and baking cakes with our mothers, is simply not true in my household. Watching television was the one time in the evening, other than dinner itself, when the whole family sat down together. It was no different than if we'd all got in the car and gone to the movies together (which by the way, is something I can never remember us doing). Thus in my case, TV had the opposite effect usually attributed to it.

Like other forms of writing, cause-and-effect analysis requires you to provide concrete or specific evidence. Merely asserting a cause or an effect convinces no one. Examples, facts, personal experience, or logical argument are all essential. Melinda, of course, has only demonstrated that the effect of television on her family was positive. She has not yet proven that television has a positive effect on other families. To do that, she will have to broaden her study and find evidence that suggests whether her family is typical or the exception.

Cause-and-effect analysis, then, is a process of beginning with a whole problem, issue, or concept, dividing it into parts (according to your purpose), and then studying the cause-and-effect relationship of those parts. But such an analysis often requires you to gather supporting data, investigate other sources and authorities, and explore numerous possibilities to avoid oversimplifying.

Practice

For in-class discussion of *analysis,* consider the problem of "alcohol abuse in college." Begin by defining the problem. Then break it down into component parts (see pages 357–360). Decide which two parts might serve for an effective comparison-and-contrast essay and what kinds of insights you might gain. Consider which single part might be investigated for itself and what insight might be derived. What kinds of results could a "process analysis" lead to? What could a "cause-and-effect" analysis lead to? How could the 5-*W* method or the 4-*C* method play a role in your analysis?

CHAPTER 23

Shaping the Formal Essay

Formal essays have no prescribed form. Too bad. It would be so much easier if I could tell you to write first this, then that, or the other. But as in most other types of writing, *subject, audience, context,* and *purpose* must guide you. In writing about ideas, issues, or values, your purpose may be varied, but in one fashion or another, it will usually include the concept of explaining, of leading the reader toward some insight into the subject. Over the years, a number of traditions have evolved regarding how best to achieve that end. Many instructors will expect you to adhere fairly closely to them, at least in the beginning.

Audience and Context

Formal essays may be written for national audiences in national magazines, they may take the form of specialized studies for scholarly journals, or they may be written—as they often are—for a college assignment. Obviously, the needs and expectations of all those varying audiences will differ. It is exactly these differences you must keep in mind. Specialized terms and professional jargon may be satisfactory in many circumstances, whereas simple terms and careful definitions of abstract concepts may be the crux of your paper for another audience. *You* must be the one who asks yourself the needed questions: What experience does my audience have with the subject? What level of vocabulary can I expect my audience to recognize? What terms and concepts should I be sure to define? What, exactly, does my audience need to know?

A recognition of your audience also forces you to consider the tone of your paper. Tone was earlier defined as the attitude an author takes toward his or her material. Sarcasm may be effective in some cases. Anger or hostility may work in others. But for most essays, you will be expected to write in a straightforward, serious, and impartial tone. You should at least give the impression of objectivity. As Erich Fromm expressed it, "Objectivity does not mean detachment, it means respect; that is, the ability not to distort and falsify things, persons and oneself." A tone that shows "respect" will probably be the most convincing of all.

Finally, like tone, the voice you write in will be determined in part by audience and context. Some college instructors may want a strictly formal voice with complete absence of the personal "I." Others may feel the personal voice should be used in a paper dealing with values or in one that tries to persuade a reader to accept a certain argument. When context, however, is outside the college classroom, voice may be prescribed by a company's individual policy or by the journal to which you plan to submit your essay. Again, *you* are responsible for knowing your audience and making the determination in advance.

The Introduction

As in earlier forms of writing, the imaginative lead may be an effective means of capturing your reader's attention while creating a sense of immediate involvement. Professional writers almost always use a lead. But a college essay may also require a formal introduction. Such an introduction may contain any or all of the following elements.

1. A general overview of the subject, usually in one or two sentences:

   > The United States has been in the foreign-aid business since the end of World War II. Last year alone we spent more than $600 billion, supposedly in an attempt to help underdeveloped nations.

   The overview presents the reader with a broad picture so that more focused details of the essay can be seen in perspective.
2. A brief review of the historical or cultural context:

   > . . . [T]wo national commissions have studied the effects on children of televised violence. Both commissions came to the same conclusion: Televised violence can teach, influence, and legitimatize antisocial behavior. The U.S. Surgeon General has presented testimony to the United States Senate that "the overwhelming consensus and the unanimous Scientific Advisory Committee's report indicate that televised violence, indeed, does have an adverse effect on certain members of our

> society. . . ." Yet ten years after the report NBC presented a prime-time film, *Born Innocent,* that depicted an explicit rape of a young girl with a broom handle. Three days later in San Francisco, three girls, ages ten to fifteen, committed a similar attack on a nine-year-old child.

As no idea, issue, or value exists in a vacuum, the historical context prepares us to understand attitudes or events that influence the subject you plan to write on.

3. A definition of the concept that will be elaborated upon in the essay:

> In 1886 Thomas Henry Huxley defined education as "the instruction of the intellect in the laws of Nature, under which name I include not merely things and their forces, but men and their ways. . . ." Today, however, we define education as a process requiring compulsive attendance at an institution for twelve years. Only a fool believes that education means learning.

By beginning with a definition, you immediately begin to focus the subject.

4. A classification of the subject:

> There are two kinds of happiness. First is the happiness based on consumption and possession. The second, by contrast, is based on giving and sharing.

Classification directs the reader's attention to the specific categories or components you plan to discuss. The example given here also has the happy advantage of comparing and contrasting.

The Thesis

A formal essay may also require a *thesis statement,* usually as the concluding sentence of the introduction. This concept sometimes sounds inhibiting, but it simply requires you to summarize the dominant idea of your findings in one or two sentences. It should be a simple, unadorned statement of the argument you plan to support with evidence and reason. Traditionally, a thesis statement focuses and further restricts the subject, it states the purpose or direction of the paper in precise words, and, if possible, it indicates something about the writer's attitude toward the subject.

> The pollution problem in Lake Angelo can be solved only through the combined efforts of the city government and the Forystal Mining Company.

Subject of paper: the pollution problem in Lake Angelo
Restriction of subject: how the problem can be solved
Purpose of argument: to demonstrate that a combined effort of two organizations can solve it
Attitude of writer: This is the only way the problem can be solved.

In many ways a formal thesis statement is similar to a 5-*W* lead (see Chapter 14), except that instead of merely gathering together important facts, it shapes those facts and gives them a purpose or direction or meaning. A weak thesis will usually be caused by a failure to narrow the subject, by a failure to use precise language, by a failure to suggest a single dominating purpose for the paper, or by a sentence structure that is too complex and therefore confusing.

Subject too broad: Pollution must be solved.
Imprecise language: The pollution problem around here can be solved in a couple of good ways.
No clear purpose: Lake Angelo is full of pollution from the Forystal Mining Company because of years of chemical dumping, even though the city has been aware of it.
Too complex: Although it is now evident that only by working together can progress be made, the Forystal Mining Company, having spent twenty years dumping chemical waste in Lake Angelo without a sense of guilt, has been made recently aware of the bad public relations and wants to solve the problem, the same problem the city itself wants to solve, although to date conflicting proposals and bureaucratic bungling have prevented them from joining forces.

Here are four guidelines to keep in mind as you shape a thesis statement.

1. Use one or two simple declarative sentences.
2. Use language with precise denotations.
3. Narrow the subject to the single most important idea in your paper.
4. Clearly indicate the purpose or argument of the essay.

The Working Thesis

So far so good. But when should you develop a thesis? Many argue that a working thesis must be formulated *before* you begin a first draft. It may take several hours of thinking, writing, and rewriting. You've already studied your subject and acquired a general idea about what you want to explore. Jotting down various forms of a thesis at this point can help you clarify or even discover your focus. Don't assume the first sentence you scribble out will be satisfactory. This is not a time to put pressure on yourself, but a time to play with ideas that interest you. Be willing to try five or ten versions. Test various efforts on a friend or roommate for clarity. Ultimately, discovering a focus means narrowing the subject to a manageable limit and that means making your essay easier to write. An hour at this stage can save you many hours of agony and frustration later.

Keep in mind, however, that as you begin drafting your essay, your working thesis is not carved in marble. Don't let it loom over you like a tombstone. If new ideas occur, or the direction you've taken seems unproductive, the thesis can always be rewritten, refined, or redirected; it should guide you, not inhibit you.

The Revision Thesis

On the other hand, not everyone's mind works alike. I have to confess I've seldom been able to devise a thesis in advance of a first draft. I usually don't know what my argument is until I've reached my conclusion. And at times I've been fortunate to find new insights only because I allowed myself to follow an "irrelevant" byway. Although it will not be true for all, the effort to compose a thesis in advance may block creativity and inhibit the potential for discovering ideas in the course of writing. So here's the result: If you find you can't come up with a "working thesis" before the first draft, you *will* probably wander around and write a disorganized essay, and you *will* be envious of those who seem to have more structured minds. But if that's the kind of person you are, don't worry about it. Just don't submit your first draft (which you shouldn't be doing anyway). Use that draft as a time for exploration and discovery. Afterward, look over what you have written and force yourself at *that* point to identify your thesis. Write it up in a simple statement that has a restricted, narrow focus. Then reorganize and rewrite your essay to correspond to your newly perceived purpose.

For the writer, a thesis written after the first draft serves the same function as one written before the first draft. It defines and clarifies. It helps you organize and give purpose to the essay. For the reader, it doesn't matter at all what your working methods are. The reader doesn't care *when* you organize, only *that* you organize.

The Formal Introduction

Any combination of the following:

- General overview of the subject
- Review of the historical or cultural context
- Definition of the basic concept
- Classification of the subject

Plus:

- A thesis statement
  - Restriction to one narrow component
  - Purpose or argument made clear
  - Attitude of writer suggested
  - All in a simple focusing sentence or two

The Body of the Essay

Obviously, the rest of your paper will be shaped by subject and purpose. No single example can illustrate the variety of forms open to you, but the following excerpt—from a student essay—demonstrates how some of the methods I've discussed can be combined into an interesting article that deals with an abstract concept. The author, Dragi Ancevski, was a twenty-four-year-old student whose parents had immigrated from Yugoslavia ten years earlier. Dragi was deeply concerned about the collapse of Yugoslavia into civil war, and he set out to analyze some of the causes.

The Death of a Nation

Thesis

Contrast to conventional expectations

The civil war in Bosnia was no accident. It was in fact a planned campaign on the part of several individuals to seize political power. It was a war for personal aggrandizement far more than an inevitable conflict between ethnic groups, as it has been portrayed by television and the press.

Analysis begins with overview of the subject as a whole

Yugoslavia, of which Bosnia was originally a part, was an artificial nation created after World War I out of more than fifty ethnic groups. After the rise to power of Josip Broz (Tito) in 1945, it was shaped into a Communist nation of eight "republics," some of which were dominated by single ethnic groups. For example, Serbia was the home of Serbs, while Croatia was dominated by Croatians. But some states contained mixed ethnic cultures. Macedonia, for example, held Turks, Bulgarians, Greeks, Albanians, Gypsies, and Serbians, as well as Macedonians.

Bosnia was dominated by two groups, Serbs and Croatians, but approximately half the Serbs in Bosnia were Moslem, while the other half were Catholics. In actual fact, then, Bosnia contained three cultural groupings with two ethnic identities. And for more than fifty years, under a fairly benevolent Communist dictatorship, all of these groups lived at peace.

Comparison used to clarify complex situation

As in some American states where blacks, Mexican-Americans, and whites live side by side, sometimes with minor tensions but always thinking of themselves as part of a single nation, so the Bosnians occupied the most beautiful mountain region in all of south-central Europe—until the collapse of the Communist dictatorship.

First major point begins cause-and-effect analysis

It is possible that these peoples might have continued to live peacefully together. The world has blamed the Serbs for provoking a three-way civil war that has essentially destroyed the country, and in the process murdered thousands of innocent civilians. But the Serbs did not simply rise up spontaneously. They were led into this disaster by a small-time bureaucrat named Slobodan Milosovic, who is now being held for trial by the World Court.

Supporting evidence

In 1993, however, U.S. News (Mar. '93) reported that Milosovic was the Communist leader of Serbia who felt it was his duty to prevent the illegal immigration of Albanians into Kosovo. Albanians lived under such poor conditions that they fled their country by the millions, seeking a better life. In the process, they drove out most of the original Serb population from Kosovo. Milosovic found that by appealing to the base instincts of man—fear of foreigners, the desire for dominance, and the hatred aroused by loss of power and position—he could rouse the Serbs of Kosovo into denying the immigrant Albanians their civil rights, guaranteed them by the then-Communist government. Milosovic became so successful at stirring up hate and appealing to base emotions that he saw the opportunity for increasing his own power on a national basis.

Comparison strengthens analysis

Milosovic used the confusion and uncertainty that arose after the fall of Communism in Yugoslavia in 1990 to seize power, much as Hitler had used the same methods to take over Germany in the 1930s. By appealing to the Germans' former glory, their supposed racial superiority, and their desire for future greatness, and by blaming all their woes on the Jews and others of "lesser races," Hitler stirred up a nation into actions that horrified the world. I do not know that Milosovic consciously modeled his own campaign on Hitler's, but like Hitler, he was legally elected the president of Serbia and then used his position to play on centuries-old fears

Comparison supports cause-and-effect analysis

and anger to turn the Serbs into a Nazi-style war machine. Like Hitler, he convinced a confused populace that they deserved to enlarge their homeland, to "reclaim" territories stolen in the past by other ethnic groups (in this case, Albanians in Kosovo, and Croats and Muslims in Bosnia).

Second major point begins

> A long essay in the February 1992 issue of *Vanity Fair* points out none of this could have been accomplished by Milosovic alone. A second factor was necessary. . . .

Dragi Ancevski was fortunate to have previous knowledge about Yugoslavia. Much of the background for this essay came from having lived there until he was fourteen. Yet Dragi also gathered information from several outside sources, ranging from *U.S. News & World Report* to *Vanity Fair.* Research itself is not a requirement for the typical formal essay, but student writers have seldom studied long enough, thought deeply enough, or known enough life experiences to sit down and write about an abstract idea, issue, or value off the top of their heads. Much bad writing in college occurs for the simple reason that the writer has nothing to say. If the body of a short essay is to have substance, then you might be best advised, like Dragi, to investigate two or three sources at a minimum, if for no other reason than to stimulate your thinking on the subject, and to gain a more balanced viewpoint.

The Conclusion

As the conclusion is the last contact you'll have with a reader, you'll want to leave a strong impression. The following are some of the ways to *fail.*

- Don't have a conclusion at all; let the reader guess.
- Apologize for not having done better.
- Repeat everything you've said in the same words.
- Ignore the evidence in your own paper.
- End by saying, "In conclusion . . ."

But it's easier to say what you should not do than to clearly state what you should. A good conclusion grows naturally out of the argument or evidence of your paper. In that sense, every good conclusion is in some way original and cannot be demonstrated to you in advance. If you're not feeling very original, however, here are some tried-and-true methods you might consider.

1. Evaluate the significance of the evidence you've presented. Don't merely list all your points; rather, reflect on the meaning of them. Draw reasonable inferences from the overall pattern of information or ideas you've worked with.
2. If it is called for, offer a solution. Be modest and admit that it may not be the only answer, but at the same time, be firm and assert that it represents a good start toward resolving the issue.

3. Use an analogy.
4. Consider the consequences and suggest who may be affected or what the future will hold (but beware of overgeneralizations such as "Humankind will destroy itself if . . .").
5. Use a striking quotation that reinforces your ideas but do not substitute the quotation for your own assessment. The final paragraph must still be written in your words and reflect your judgment. A quotation should be used only to add strength or support.
6. If the paper is long, make an emphatic restatement of your central idea. Don't, however, merely repeat your thesis statement word for word from the introduction.

No matter what method you use, base your final paragraph on the evidence presented in your essay. If possible, try to relate your conclusion to your opening, to some element of your lead, to your general introduction, to your thesis statement, or to your title. And be especially conscious of word order in the final sentence. A short, emphatic statement or an especially strong phrase will be most effective.

At this point you may be questioning the value of all this work. Just what does it have to do with you or with your interests in becoming an engineer or a dietician or a biologist? As surprising as it may sound, however, training in the formal patterns of perception and organization are proven methods of helping you discover and set forth *your* ideas. Such training demands that your mind engage all its resources in a self-disciplined effort at understanding not only the concrete world about you but also the ideas and values abstracted from that world. The ability to narrow a subject to a single quality, classify it, analyze it, and clarify it is one of the most valued abilities in any profession or career. Indeed, it is this type of self-disciplined intelligence that we most clearly associate with an educated man or woman.

If by this point you feel self-expression has become lost amid the jargon, the forms, and the various techniques, it may be good to remind yourself again that all of it is only a means to an end. "One must, of course, master technique," Pablo Casals has said, but "at the same time, one must not become enslaved by it. One must understand that the purpose of technique is to transmit the inner meaning, the message of the music."

Group Inquiry

1. With others in your peer group, consider the following thesis statements. In what way is each too broad for a 1,000-word essay? Suggest ways each could be rewritten to narrow the focus and make it more precise.
   a. Dumping chemicals is dangerous to human health.
   b. Saving the environment is the number one problem in the world.

c. The Supreme Court has ignored the wishes of the American people.
d. Drug laws reflect the interests of drug companies.
e. Terrorism is justified when Westerners attempt to impose their will on other cultures.

2. Consider which of the following thesis statements are effective. Which would give the reader a clear indication of what to expect in the essay that follows? If you find one that is inadequate, identify the problem.
   a. Limited opportunities for entrance into medical schools cause pre-med students to cheat for the sake of higher grades.
   b. Gays should have equal opportunities.
   c. I believe there are six types of students in college today.
   d. Effective comedy requires an element of surprise and a sense of timing.
   e. The central idea of an essay should be expressed in a single opening sentence.
   f. Because of its cathartic effect, art can be a central tool in the treatment of mental illness.

Practice

1. Read one of the essays included at the end of this unit. Consider the following questions:
   a. What methods does the writer use to shape the introduction?
   b. How does the writer organize the body of the essay?
   c. What combination of formal methods is used in the body of the essay to clarify and explain?
   d. Is the conclusion effective? Can you identify any particular method discussed in this chapter as part of the conclusion, or is it unique to the particular way the writer has treated the subject?
2. What method of analysis have you used in studying the end-of-unit essay?

Copying

A good conclusion often echoes the beginning of an essay by reminding the reader of the focus. Such a technique seems especially satisfying to a reader. It creates a sense of wholeness and completeness. The introduction and conclusion work together like bookends to support and contain the body of the argument.

One way to get a feeling for how this is accomplished is to copy several introductions and conclusions by hand. Select some of the professional essays in this textbook or in a high-quality magazine such as *The Atlantic* or *Harper's.* Copy introductory paragraphs, followed immediately by concluding paragraphs. Study the relationships, the techniques by which the authors echo introductions in their conclusions and, in those essays that present an argument or analysis, by which they integrate a forceful summation or judgment.

Here are the introductory and concluding paragraphs of a student essay by Sherry Shelly. Copy each paragraph into your journal and consider the various methods Sherry has used to pull them together.

Introduction:
My father. Withered and silent, he looms before me. This is the same image of the father I find in Richard Rodriguez's intellectual autobiography, *Hunger of Memory.* In a series of six essays, Rodriguez, a Mexican-American, takes a firm stand on affirmative action and bilingual education. He shares the effect formal education has had on his life. The pain and sadness of losing his past while gaining his education is conveyed to us as he progresses from elementary school to college. Although his father is mentioned scarcely throughout the essays, his presence is deeply felt. In a world where the English language is dominant, his Spanish-speaking father changes from a steady, confident man, to a silent, withdrawn man. Rodriguez's confidence in his father is shaken and the image the young boy once held for his father is shattered. The connection he feels to his father, one that goes back to his father's own youth, is forever lost.

Conclusion:
Throughout *Hunger of Memory* Richard Rodriguez shares the changes he endured through formal education. These changes draw him away from his father as his father gives in to English, the alien language that enters his home and bears him down. While reaching out to better understand his father's life, Rodriguez comes to the recognition that this very English language which gave him success and fame in an English-speaking world separated him forever from one who, ironically, had encouraged him to learn it. I was moved by his need to share with his father. Losing the ability to touch and communicate with a person who affected such a great part of his life was something I could identify with, a loss I too have known. How odd that education which our parents so encourage is the culprit which distances us irrevocably from their world. I suspect that all of us must admire the courage it takes to look closely at one's life and relationships. There is, perhaps in all of us, a part of our past that is lost forever. Finding out what part, and why, is truly courageous.

CHAPTER 24

The Challenge of Simplicity

Making the simple complicated is commonplace; making the complicated simple, awesomely simple, that's creativity.

MARVIN BELL

Theodore M. Bernstein, a former editor of *The New York Times,* recounted the story of a plumber who cleaned drains with hydrochloric acid and wrote to a chemical research bureau inquiring about its safety. The bureau wrote back, "The efficacy of hydrochloric acid is indisputably established, but the corrosive residue is incompatible with metallic permanence." The plumber, impressed by such a response, thanked the bureau for its approval. Another letter arrived: "We cannot assume responsibility for the production of a toxic and noxious residue with hydrochloric acid. We beg leave to suggest to you the employment of an alternative procedure." More proud than ever, the plumber again expressed his appreciation. In desperation the bureau called in an older scientist, who wrote a third letter to the plumber: "Don't use hydrochloric acid. It eats the hell out of pipes."

Jargon

Jargon has its rightful place in the language: It communicates specialized concepts to other specialists. Every profession and occupation needs a specialized vocabulary. Linguists must talk of *deep structures;* mechanics need to discuss *carbon buildup;* government officials must consider *systems management.* Yet it is not just a matter of knowing your audience. Most audiences, even those trained in the specialties you may be writing about, usually prefer clear, concrete communication. Einstein was admired for his ability to write about scientific complexities with simplicity. Freud, who probably contributed more jargon to the twentieth century than any other individual, at least had the courtesy in his own writing to define his terms.

Pretentiousness

The problem with jargon arises when we use it pretentiously for the sake of impressing rather than communicating, or when it is used to obscure meaning, to hide ignorance through lack of precision. Yet all of us want others to think we are intelligent and wise. We seek praise and reputation. We sometimes believe that if our writing sounds obscure, others will think us profound. We may fear simplicity. Only dullards are simple. Those who are knowledgeable, we believe, impress us with their vocabulary. Why, all we need to do is listen to our professors.

> . . . the most basic problems that arise in connection with knowledge utilization may be those that stem from the social and organizational character of educational institutions. . . . Public schools display a myriad of normative and other regulatory structures that promote predictability, as well as a host of adaptive mechanisms that reduce external uncertainties.

Quite impressive. But sad, nevertheless. Sad because this professor (of education, no less) is not honestly trying to inform us of anything. His real subject is himself. "Look at me," he says. "Just look at all the big words I know." And too often it happens to us all, especially when we begin to write formal prose about abstract issues or values. We shift to a serious tone, we adopt a pompous voice, and before the old computer even begins to warm up, we're writing as this student did.

> The choice of exogenous variables in relation to multicollinearity is contingent upon the derivations of certain multiple correlation coefficients.

Pretentiousness, affection, overabstraction, circumlocution—the many names for such gobbledygook could fill a small dictionary. Those who admire language, those who respect it, have been railing for generations against the pseudointellectual misuse of it. Here is Sir Arthur Quiller-Couch writing in 1923:

> If your language be jargon, your intellect, if not your whole character, will almost certainly correspond. Where your mind should go straight, it will dodge: the difficulties it should approach with a fair front and grip with a firm hand it will be seeking to evade or circumvent. For the style is the man, and where a man's treasure is, there his heart, and his brain, and his writing will be also.

And a woman's too, we might add.

Writing is a social act. Like other social acts it imposes obligations. In the case of formal prose, our responsibility is to explain or set forth clearly so that the reader understands. The use of jargon or other outlandish abstraction becomes an evasion of that responsibility. That is why Quiller-Couch makes language a moral issue. The use of clear, straightforward prose means that you face up to your responsibilities, your obligation to communicate what you know.

Some of the most famous—or infamous—uses of language to avoid responsibility came from government officials during the Vietnam War. American generals described weapons that were intended to kill people as *antipersonnel devices. Protective reaction* became a military phrase meaning that we bombed "them" before they bombed "us." Concentration camps were termed *relocation centers.* Each of these is an example of a *euphemism,* that is, of a substitute for a straightforward, simple term. Certainly not all euphemisms are immoral. We call undertakers *morticians,* and we substitute *passed away* for death; we elevate janitors to *maintenance engineers,* and we promote old people to *senior citizens.* But euphemisms do lead us astray from reality in the same way that jargon obscures reality through inflated words.

Circumlocution

Unfortunately, we can sometimes lead ourselves astray just by using too many words, by circling about a subject without ever quite touching upon it. Here is a student example of *circumlocution.*

> The actualization of an objective decision to follow the rules was not something they really felt was something compelled by their hearts. Oftentimes, a person agrees with the legal legitimacy of something but it is against his ethical values to go ahead with it. Having been confronted with these postulates and their modifications or contingencies, it soon becomes difficult determining exactly what our response should be.

The consequence of inflated language is now apparent. When we substitute jargon, pretentious abstractions, euphemisms, and circumlocutions for precision, we run the risk of concealing our meaning—or lack of meaning—even from ourselves.

When Thoreau wrote his famous advice, "Simplify, simplify," he was speaking of our lives, but the advice applies no less to our writing. Most social issues and moral values are complex. To explain complexity in simple prose is not a fault; it is a mark of achievement. Yet few of us can sit down to the first draft and say, "Now I am going to write a coherent, simple sentence." What we can do is return to those first rough scribblings and ask, "Do I know what I'm trying to say?" and "Can the reader follow it?" Both questions are important. Unless you have discovered and fully explored your ideas, demanding exactness of yourself, all the tinkering in the world will fail to patch over your confusion. Once you feel confident that you do understand your own ideas, then you are obligated to question whether the reader can.

Your goal should be to find the simplest language possible while still conveying the seriousness and full weight of your intentions. Neither of the following examples would serve.

- The high-level government representative indulged in a special purchase of verdurous flora for a close relative.
- The guy got his mom some flowers.

The first is pretentious; the second sounds like Dick and Jane. Somewhere in the middle we might try:

- The senator bought roses for his mother.

If you have plowed your way through earlier chapters in this book on revising and editing, you should be fully prepared to handle the extra demands complex ideas may put upon your writing: Eliminate extra words; whenever possible, use concrete images instead of abstractions; trust the simple sentence; build paragraphs around a logical purpose; and so on. To simplify essentially means to be straightforward (avoiding circumlocutions and overblown abstractions) and to be exact (to convey a precise meaning, usually through concrete nouns or active verbs). But to that list of techniques, we must add an earlier concept: *honesty*. Not just honesty of perception, but honesty in the manner of presentation. Your goal should be to present what you know in your own voice as an expression of your imagination and intellect, avoiding the temptation to write as you think others are praised for writing—profoundly, elegantly—choosing instead to be responsible above all for clarity and precision.

Practice

1. Each of the following is taken from a published source. Consider the actual meaning, and try writing a simple alternative version.
   a. "He established an objective and pursued the ultimate achievement of success with diligence."

      Example: *He set a goal and worked hard to achieve it.*
   b. From the director of the CIA: "I wish to restrict lateral input of outside retirees into positions that could be filled within our own ranks. Therefore, effective immediately, the further hiring of annuitants is prohibited."
   c. From an essay on capitalism: "The neoclassical postulate of rationality and the concept of the entrepreneur as the profit-maximizing individual should, I think, be replaced by a sociological analysis of the goals of the firm in relation to its nature as an organization within the sociopolitical system."
   d. "Thirdly, the aim [of this book] is not to set forth a list of abstract properties of human knowledge but to assist the reader in effecting a personal appropriation of the concrete, dynamic structure immanent and recurrently operative in his own cognitional activities. . . ."
   e. From a student paper: "Legalization of euthanasia is, retrospectively, a barbaric liability hung upon the corporate neck of civilized society today. It manifests our egocentrical natures and ignores our inherent rights constitutionalized in 1884."

2. The following words and phrases have become the overused, empty, pretentious, or jargonish vocabulary found in almost everybody's writing. Find a simple word or phrase as a replacement for each.

utilize	in today's society
Example: *use*	**Example:** *today*
subject area	come in contact with
in the last analysis	in accordance with
fully recognize	absolutely essential
input/output	in the case of
the end result	in the field of
the final solution	factor
parameters	maturation
wholly justifiable	socioeconomic considerations
bottom line	delivery system
down the road	at this point in time

Readings

America's Emerging Gay Culture

Randall E. Majors

Randall E. Majors' essay, taken from *Intercultural Communication: A Reader* breaks down a complex cultural identity into simple categories of human experience: neighborhoods, safety, political power, symbols, and so on. Consider how clearly and simply each is identified, and how each is followed by various subcategories with simple, concrete descriptions or illustrations.

A gay culture, unique in the history of homosexuality, is emerging in America. Gay people from all walks of life are forging new self-identity concepts, discovering new political and social power, and building a revolutionary new lifestyle. As more people "come out," identify themselves as gay, and join with others to work and live as openly gay people, a stronger culture takes shape with each passing year.

There have always been homosexual men and women, but never before has there emerged the notion of a distinct "culture" based on being gay.[1] A useful way to analyze this emerging gay culture is to observe the communication elements by which gay people construct their lifestyles and social institutions. Lesbians and gay men, hereafter considered together as gay people, are creating a new community in the midst of the American melting pot.[2] They are building social organizations, exercising political power, and solidifying a unique sense of identity—often under repressive and sometimes dangerous conditions. The following essay is an analysis of four major communicative elements of the American gay culture: the gay neighborhood, gay social groups, gay symbols, and gay meeting behavior. These communication behaviors will demonstrate the vibrancy and joy that a new culture offers the American vision of individual freedom and opportunity.

The Gay Neighborhood

Most cultural groups find the need to mark out a home "turf." American social history has many examples of ethnic and social groups who create their own special communities, whether by withdrawing from the larger culture or by forming specialized groups within it. The utopian communities of the Amish or Shakers are examples of the first, and "ghetto" neighborhoods in large urban areas are examples of the latter.

This need to create a group territory fulfills several purposes for gay people. First, a gay person's sense of identity is reinforced if there is a special place that is somehow imbued with "gayness." When a neighborhood becomes the home of many gay people, the ground is created for a feeling of belonging and sharing with others. Signs of gayness, whether overt symbols like rainbow flags or more subtle cues such as merely the presence of other gay people on the street, create the feeling that a certain territory is special to the group and hospitable to the group's unique values.

How do you know when a neighborhood is gay? As with any generality, the rule of thumb is that "enough gay people in a neighborhood and it becomes a gay neighborhood." Rarely do gay people want to paint the streetlamps lavender, but the presence of many more subtle factors gives a gay character to an area. The most subtle cues are the presence of gay people as they take up residence in a district. Word spreads in the group that a certain area is starting to look attractive and open to gay members. There is often a move to "gentrify" older, more affordable sections of a city and build a new neighborhood out of the leftovers from the rush to the suburbs. Gay businesses, those operated by or catering to gay people, often develop once enough clientele is in the area. Social groups and services emerge that are oriented toward the members of the neighborhood. Eventually, the label of "gay neighborhood" is placed on an area, and the transformation is complete. The Castro area in San Francisco, Greenwich Village in New York, New Town in Chicago, the Westheimer district in Houston, and West Hollywood or Silver Lake in Los Angeles are examples of many emergent gay neighborhoods in cities across America.[3]

A second need fulfilled by the gay neighborhood is the creation of a meeting ground. People can recognize and meet each other more easily when a higher density of population is established. It is not easy to grow up gay in America; gay people often feel "different" because of their sexual orientations. The surrounding heterosexual culture often tries to imprint sexual behaviors and expectations that do not suit gay natures. Because of this pressure, gay people often feel isolated and alienated, and the need for a meeting ground is very important.[4] Merely knowing that there is a specific place where other gay people live and work and play does much to anchor the psychological aspect of gayness in a tangible, physical reality. A gay person's sense of identity is reinforced by knowing that there is a home base, or a safe place where others of a similar persuasion are nearby.

Gay neighborhoods reinforce individual identity by focusing activities and events for members of the group. Celebrations of group unity and pride, demonstrations of group creativity and accomplishment, and services to individual members' needs are more easily developed when centralized. Gay neighborhoods are host to all the outward elements of a community—parades, demonstrations, car washes, basketball games, petition signing, street fairs, and garage sales.

A critical purpose for gay neighborhoods is that of physical and psychological safety. Subcultural groups usually experience some degree of persecution and oppression from the larger surrounding culture. For gay people, physical safety is a very real concern—incidences of homophobic assaults or harassment are common in most American cities.[5] By centralizing gay activities, some safeguards can be mounted, as large numbers of gay people living in proximity create a deterrence to violence. This may be informal awareness of the need to take extra precautions and to be on the alert to help other gay people in distress or in the form of actual street patrols or social groups, such as Community United Against Violence in San Francisco. A sense of psychological safety follows from these physical measures. Group consciousness raising on neighborhood safety and training in safety practices create a sense of group cohesion. The security inspired by the group creates a psychic comfort that offsets the paranoia that can be engendered by alienation and individual isolation.

Another significant result of gay neighborhoods is the political reality of "clout."[6] In the context of American grassroots democracy, a predominantly gay population in an area can lead to political power. The concerns of gay people are taken more seriously by politicians and elected officials representing an area where voters can be registered and mustered into service during elections. In many areas, openly gay politicians represent gay constituencies directly and voice their concerns in ever-widening forums. The impact of this kind of democracy-in-action is felt in other institutions as well: police departments, social welfare agencies, schools, churches, and businesses. When a group centralizes its energy, members can bring pressure to bear on other cultural institutions, asking for and demanding attention to the unique needs of that group. Since American culture has a strong tradition of cultural diversity, gay neighborhoods are effective agents in the larger cultural acceptance of gay people. The gay rights movement, which attempts to secure housing, employment, and legal protection for gay people, finds its greatest support in the sense of community created by gay neighborhoods.

Gay Social Groups

On a smaller level than the neighborhood, specialized groups fulfill the social needs of gay people. The need for affiliation—to make friends, to share recreation, to find life partners, or merely to while away the time—is a strong drive in any group of people. Many gay people suffer from an isolation caused by rejection by other people or by their own fear of being discovered as belonging to an unpopular group. This homophobia leads to difficulty in identifying and meeting other gay people who can help create a sense of dignity and caring. This is particularly true for gay teenagers who have limited opportunities to meet other gay people.[7] Gay social groups serve the important function of helping gay people locate each other so that this affiliation need can be met.

The development of gay social groups depends to a large degree on the number of gay people in an area and the perceived risk factor. In smaller towns and cities, there are often no meeting places, which exacerbates the problem of isolation. In some small towns a single business may be the only publicly known meeting place for gay people within hundreds of miles. In larger cities, however, an elaborate array of bars, clubs, social groups, churches, service agencies, entertainment groups, stores, restaurants, and the like add to the substance of a gay culture.

The gay bar is often the first public gay experience for a gay person, and the gay bar serves as a central focus in gay life for many people. Beyond the personal need of meeting potential relationship partners, the gay bar also serves the functions of entertainment and social activity. Bars offer a wide range of attractions suited to gay people: movies, holiday celebrations, dancing, costume parties, live entertainment, free meals, boutiques, and meeting places for social groups. Uniquely gay forms of entertainment, such as drag shows and disco dancing, were common in gay bars before spreading into the general culture. Bars often become a very central part of a community's social life by sponsoring athletic teams, charities, community services, and other events as well as serving as meeting places.

The centrality of the bar in gay culture has several drawbacks, however. Young gay people are denied entrance because of age restrictions, and there may be few other social outlets for them. A high rate of alcoholism among urban gay males is prominent. With the spread of Acquired Immune Deficiency Syndrome (AIDS), the use of bars for meeting sexual partners has declined dramatically as gay people turn to developing more permanent relationships.[8]

Affiliation needs remain strong despite these dangers, however, and alternative social institutions arise that meet these needs. In large urban areas, where gay culture is more widely developed, social groups include athletic organizations that sponsor teams and tournaments; leisure activity clubs in such areas as country-and-western dance, music, yoga, bridge, hiking, and recreation; religious groups such as Dignity (Roman Catholic), Integrity (Episcopal), and the Metropolitan Community Church (MCC); volunteer agencies such as information and crisis hotlines and charitable organizations; and professional and political groups such as the Golden Gate Business Association of San Francisco or the national lobby group, the Gay Rights Task Force. A directory of groups and services is usually published in urban gay newspapers, and their activities are reported on and promoted actively. Taken together, these groups compose a culture that supports and nourishes a gay person's life.

Gay Symbols

Gay culture is replete with symbols. These artifacts spring up and constantly evolve as gayness moves from being an individual, personal experience into a more complex public phenomenon. All groups express their ideas and values in symbols, and the gay culture, in spite of its relatively brief history, has been quite creative in symbol making.

The most visible category of symbols is in the semantics of gay establishment names. Gay bars, bookstores, restaurants, and social groups want to be recognized and patronized by gay people, but they do not want to incur hostility from the general public. This was particularly true in the past when the threat of social consequences was greater. In earlier days, gay bars, the only major form of gay establishment, went by code words such as "blue" or "other"—the Blue Parrot, the Blue Goose, the Other Bar, and Another Place.

Since the liberalization of culture after the 1960s, semantics have blossomed in gay place names. The general trend is still to identify the place as gay, either through affiliation (Our Place or His 'N' Hers), humor (the White Swallow or Uncle Charley's), high drama (the Elephant Walk or Backstreet) or sexual suggestion (Ripples, Cheeks, or Rocks). Lesbians and gay men differ in this aspect of their cultures. Lesbian place names often rely upon a more personal or classical referent (Amanda's Place or the Artemis Cafe), while hypermasculine referents are commonly used for gay male meeting places (the Ramrod, Ambush, Manhandlers, the Mine Shaft, the Stud, or Boots). Gay restaurants and nonpornographic bookstores usually reflect more subdued names, drawing upon cleverness or historical associations: Dos Hermanos Women and Children First, Diana's, the Oscar Wilde Memorial Bookstore, and Walt Whitman Bookstore. More commonly, gay establishments employ general naming trends of location, ownership, or identification of product or service similar to their heterosexual counterparts. The increasing tendency of businesses to target and cater to gay markets strengthens the growth and diversity of gay culture.

A second set of gay symbols are those that serve as member-recognition factors. In past ages such nonverbal cues were so popular as to become mythic: the arched eyebrow of Regency England, the green carnation of Oscar Wildes' day, and the "green shirt on Thursday" signal of mid-century America. A large repertoire of identifying characteristics have arisen in recent years that serve the functions of recognizing other gay people and focusing on particular interests. In the more sexually promiscuous period of the 1970s, popular identifying symbols were a ring of keys worn on the belt, either left or right depending upon sexual passivity or aggressiveness, and the use of colored handkerchiefs in a rear pocket coded to desired types of sexual activity. Political sentiments are commonly expressed through buttons, such as the "No on 64" campaign against the LaRouche initiative in California in 1986. The pink triangle as a political symbol recalls the persecution and annihilation of gay people in Nazi Germany. The lambda symbol, an ancient Greek referent, conjures up classical images of gay freedom of expression. Stud earrings for men are gay symbols in some places, though such adornment has evolved and is widely used for the expression of general countercultural attitudes. The rainbow and the unicorn, mythical symbols associated with supernatural potency, also are common signals of gay enchantment, fairy magic, and spiritual uniqueness by the more "cosmic" elements of the gay community.

Another set of gay symbols to be aware of are the images of gay people as portrayed in television, film, literature, and advertising. The general heterosexual culture controls these media forms to a large extent, and the representations of gay people in those media take on a straight set of expectations and assumptions. The results are stereotypes that often oversimplify gay people and their values and do not discriminate the subtleties of human variety in gay culture. Since these stereotypes are generally unattractive, they are often the target of protests by gay people. Various authors have addressed the problem of heterosexual bias in the areas of film and literature.[9] As American culture gradually becomes more accepting of and tolerant toward gay people, these media representations become more realistic and sympathetic, but progress in this area is slow.

One hopeful development in the creation of positive gay role models has been the rise of an active gay market for literature. Most large cities have bookstores which stock literature supportive of gay culture. A more positive image for gay people is created through gay characters, heros, and stories that deal with the important issues of family, relationship, and social responsibility. This market is constantly threatened by harsh economic realities, however, and gay literature is not as well developed as it might be.[10]

Advertising probably has done the most to popularize and integrate gay symbols into American culture. Since money making is the goal of advertising, the use of gay symbols has advanced more rapidly in ad media than in the arts. Widely quoted research suggests that gay people, particularly men, have large, disposable incomes, so they become popular target markets for various products: tobacco, body-care products, clothing, alcohol, entertainment, and consumer goods. Typical gay-directed advertising in these product areas includes appeals based upon male bonding, such as are common in tobacco and alcohol sales ads, which are attractive to both straight and gay men since they stimulate the bonding need that is a part of both cultures.

Within gay culture, advertising has made dramatic advances in the past ten years, due to the rise of gay-related businesses and products. Gay advertising appears most obviously in media specifically directed at gay markets, such as gay magazines and newspapers, and in gay neighborhoods. Gay products and services are publicized with many of the same means as are their straight counterparts. Homoerotic art is widely used in clothing and body-care product ads. The male and female body are displayed for their physical and sexual appeal. This eroticizing of the body may be directed at either women or men as a desirable sexual object, and perhaps strikes at a subconscious homosexual potential in all people. Prominent elements of gay advertising are its use of sexuality and the central appeal of hypermasculinization. With the rise of sexual appeals in general advertising through double entendre, sexual punning, subliminal seduction, and erotic art work, it may be that gay advertising is only following suit in its emphasis on sexual appeals. Hugely muscled bodies and perfected masculine beauty adorn most advertising for gay products and services. Ads for greeting cards, billboards for travel service, bars, hotels, restaurants, and clothing stores tingle to the images of Hot 'N' Hunky Hamburgers, Hard On Leather, and the Brothel Hotel or its crosstown rival, the Anxious Arms. Some gay writers criticize this use of advertising as stereotyping and distorting of gay people, and certainly, misconceptions about the diversity in gay culture are more common than understanding. Gay people are far more average and normal than the images that appear in public media would suggest.

Gay Meeting Behavior

The final element of communication in the gay culture discussed here is the vast set of behaviors by which gay people recognize and meet one another. In more sexually active days before the concern for AIDS, this type of behavior was commonly called cruising. Currently, promiscuous sexual behavior is far less common than it once was, and cruising has evolved into a more standard meeting behavior that helps identify potential relationship partners.

Gay people meet each other in various contexts: in public situations, in the workplace, in gay meeting places, and in the social contexts of friends and acquaintances. Within each context, a different set of behaviors is employed by which gay people recognize someone else as gay and determine the potential for establishing a relationship. These behaviors include such nonverbal signaling as frequency and length of interaction, posture, proximity, eye contact, eye movement and facial gestures, touch, affect displays, and paralinguistic signals.[11] The constraints of each situation and the personal styles of the communicators create great differences in the effectiveness and ease with which these behaviors are displayed.

Cruising serves several purposes besides the recognition of other gay people. Most importantly, cruising is an expression of joy and pride in being gay. Through cruising, gay people communicate their openness and willingness to interact. Being gay is often compared to belonging to a universal—though invisible—fraternity or sorority. Gay people are generally friendly and open to meeting other gay people in social contexts because of the common experience of rejection and isolation they have had growing up. Cruising is the means by which gay people communicate their gayness and bridge the gap between stranger and new-found friend.

Cruising has become an integral part of gay culture because it is such a commonplace behavior. Without this interpersonal skill—and newcomers to gay life often complain of the lack of comfort or ease they have with cruising—a gay person can be at a distinct disadvantage in finding an easy path into the mainstream of gay culture. While cruising has a distinctly sexual overtone, the sexual subtext is often a symbolic charade. Often the goals of cruising are no more than friendship, companionship, or conversation. In this sense, cruising becomes more an art form or an entertainment. Much as the "art of conversation" was the convention of a more genteel cultural age, gay cruising is the commonly accepted vehicle of gay social interaction. The sexual element, however, transmitted by double meaning, clever punning, or blatant nonverbal signals, remains a part of cruising in even the most innocent of circumstances.

In earlier generations, a common stereotype of gay men focused on the use of exaggerated, dramatic, and effeminate body language—the "limp wrist" image. Also included in this negative image of gay people was cross-gender dressing, known as "drag," and a specialized, sexually suggestive argot called "camp."[12] Some gay people assumed these social roles because that was the picture of "what it meant to be gay," but by and large these role behaviors were overthrown by the gay liberation of the 1970s. Gay people became much less locked into these restraining stereotypes and developed a much broader means of social expression. Currently, no stereotypic behavior could adequately describe gay communication style—it is far too diverse and integrated into mainstream American culture. Cruising evolved from these earlier forms of communication, but as a quintessential gay behavior, cruising has replaced the bitchy camp of an earlier generation of gay people.

The unique factor in gay cruising, and the one that distinguishes it from heterosexual cruising, is the level of practice and refinement the process revives. All cultural groups have means of introduction and meeting, recognition, assessment, and negotiation of a new relationship. In gay culture, however, the "courtship ritual" or friendship ritual of cruising is elaborately refined in its many variants and contexts. While straight people may use similar techniques in relationship formation and development, gay people are uniquely self-conscious in the centrality of these signals to the perpetuation of their culture. There is a sense of adventure and discovery in being "sexual outlaws," and cruising is the shared message of commitment to the gay life style.[13]

Conclusion

These four communication elements of gay culture comprise only a small part of what might be called gay culture. Other elements have been more widely discussed elsewhere: literature, the gay press, religion, politics, art, theater, and relationships. Gay culture is a marvelous and dynamic phenomenon. It is driven and buffeted by the energies of intense feeling and creative effort. Centuries of cultural repression that condemned gay people to disgrace and persecution have been turned upside down in a brief period of history. The results of this turbulence have the potential for either renaissance or cataclysm. The internalized fear and hatred of repression is balanced by the incredible joy and idealism of liberation. Through the celebration of its unique lifestyle, gay culture promises to make a great contribution to the history of sexuality and to the rights of the individual. Whether it will fulfill this promise or succumb to the pressures that any creative attempt must face remains to be seen.

Notes

1. Several good reviews of "famous homosexuals" include the following: Barbara Grier and Coletta Reid, *Lesbian Lives* (Oakland, Calif.: Diana Press, 1976); Noel I. Garde, *Jonathan to Gide: The Homosexual in History* (New York: Nosbooks, 1969); and A. L. Rowse, *The Homosexual in History* (Metuchen, N.J.: Scarecrow Press, 1975).
2. The relative differences and similarities between gay men and lesbians is a hotly debated issue in the gay/lesbian community. For the purposes of this paper, I have chosen to speak of them as a single unit. For an introduction to this issue, see Celia Kitzinger, *The Social Construction of Lesbianism* (Newbury Park, Calif.: Sage Publications, 1987).
3. An excellent analysis of the role of the Castro in California's gay culture is in Frances FitzGerald, *Cities on a Hill* (New York: Simon and Schuster, 1986). An entertaining source that discusses gay neighborhoods across America is Edmund White, *States of Desire: Travels in Gay America* (New York: E. P. Dutton, 1980).
4. For more information on the problems of gay self-identity, see Don Clark, *(The New) Loving Someone Gay* (Berkeley: Celestial Arts, 1987) and George Weinberg, *Society and the Healthy Homosexual* (New York: Doubleday, 1973).
5. A discussion of violence and its effects on gay people is in Dennis Altman, *The Homosexualization of America: The Americanization of Homosexuality* (New York: St. Martin's Press, 1982), pp. 100–101.
6. For a discussion of emerging gay politics, see Peter Fisher, *The Gay Mystique* (New York: Stein and Day, 1972) and Laud Humphreys, *Out of the Closets: The Sociology of Homosexual Liberation* (Englewood Cliffs, N.J.: Prentice-Hall, 1972).
7. Problems of young gay people are discussed in Mary V. Borhek, *Coming Out to Parents* (New York: Pilgrim Press, 1983) and in story form in Mary V. Borhek, *My Son Eric* (New York: Pilgrim Press, 1979) and Aaron Fricke, *Reflections of a Rock Lobster* (New York: Alyson, 1981).
8. Gay relationships are discussed in Betty Berzon, *Permanent Partners: Building Gay and Lesbian Relationships That Last* (New York: E. P. Dutton, 1988) and David P. McWirter and Andrew M. Mattison, *The Male Couple* (Englewood Cliffs, N.J.: Prentice-Hall, 1984).
9. The treatment of gay people in literature is discussed in Barbara Grier, *The Lesbian in Literature* (Iowa City, Iowa: Naiad, 1988); George-Michel Sarotte, *Like a Brother, Like a Lover* (New York: Doubleday, 1978); Ian Young (Ed.), *The Male Homosexual in Literature: A Bibliography* (Metuchen, N.J.: Scarecrow Press, 1975); and Roger Austen, *Playing the Game: The Homosexual Novel in America* (Indianapolis: Bobbs-Merrill Press, 1977). Gay people in films are discussed in Parker Tyler, *Screening the Sexes: Homosexuality in the Movies* (New York: Holt, Rinehart, & Winston, 1972) and Vito Russo, *The Celluloid Closet: Lesbians and Gay Men in American Film* (New York: Harper & Row, 1980).
10. The emergence of positive roles is discussed in Betty Berzon, *Positively Gay* (Los Angeles: Mediamix Associates, 1979).
11. An excellent reference source for more information on gay communication research is Wayne R. Dynes, *Homosexuality: A Research Guide* (New York: Garland, 1987). He covers nonverbal communication in his section on "Social Semiotics," pp. 372 ff.
12. Camp is discussed in Susan Sontag, "Notes on Camp," *Against Interpretation* (New York: Dell, 1969). For a dictionary of antique camp language, see Bruce Rodgers, *The Queen's Vernacular: A Gay Lexicon* (New York: Simon and Schuster, 1972).
13. Altman discusses cruising in *The Homosexualization of America,* p. 176.

The Arab World

Edward T. Hall

The following excerpt from Edward T. Hall's classic study, *The Hidden Dimension,* illustrates how blending comparison, contrast, and illustration illuminates a subject, encouraging us to rethink our attitudes and preconceived biases. Few other strategies could have been as effective or as clarifying.

In spite of over two thousand years of contact, Westerners and Arabs still do not understand each other. Proxemic research reveals some insights into this difficulty. Americans in the Middle East are immediately struck by two conflicting sensations. In public they are compressed and overwhelmed by smells, crowding, and high noise levels; in Arab homes Americans are apt to rattle around, feeling exposed and often somewhat inadequate because of too much space! (The Arab houses and apartments of the middle and upper classes which Americans stationed abroad commonly occupy are much larger than the dwellings such Americans usually inhabit.) Both the high sensory stimulation which is experienced in public places and the basic insecurity which comes from being in a dwelling that is too large provide Americans with an introduction to the sensory world of the Arab.

Pushing and shoving in public places is characteristic of Middle Eastern culture. Yet it is not entirely what Americans think it is (being pushy and rude) but stems from a different set of assumptions concerning not only the relations between people but how one experiences the body as well. Paradoxically, Arabs consider northern Europeans and Americans pushy, too. This was very puzzling to me when I started investigating these two views. How could Americans who stand aside and avoid touching be considered pushy? I used to ask Arabs to explain this paradox. None of my subjects was able to tell me specifically what particulars of American behavior were responsible, yet they all agreed that the impression was widespread among Arabs. After repeated unsuccessful attempts to gain insight into the cognitive world of the Arab on this particular point, I filed it away as a question that only time would answer. When the answer came, it was because of a seemingly inconsequential annoyance.

While waiting for a friend in a Washington, D.C., hotel lobby and wanting to be both visible and alone, I had seated myself in a solitary chair outside the normal stream of traffic. In such a setting most Americans follow a rule, which is all the more binding because we seldom think about it, that can be stated as follows: as soon as a person stops or is seated in a public place, there balloons around him a small sphere of privacy which is considered inviolate. The size of the sphere varies with the degree of crowding, the age, sex, and the importance of the person, as well as the general surroundings. Anyone who enters this zone and stays there is intruding. In fact, a stranger who intrudes, even for a specific purpose, acknowledges the fact that he has intruded by beginning his request with "Pardon me, but can you tell me . . .?"

To continue, as I waited in the deserted lobby, a stranger walked up to where I was sitting and stood close enough so that not only could I easily touch him but I could even hear him breathing. In addition, the dark mass of his body filled the peripheral field of vision on my left side. If the lobby had been crowded with people, I would have understood his behavior, but in an empty lobby his presence made me exceedingly uncomfortable. Feeling annoyed by this intrusion, I moved my body in such a way as to communicate annoyance. Strangely enough, instead of moving away, my actions seemed only to encourage him, because he moved even closer. In spite of the temptation to escape the annoyance, I put aside thoughts of abandoning my post, thinking, "To hell with it. Why should I move? I was here first and I'm not going to let this fellow drive me out even if he is a boor." Fortunately, a group of people soon arrived whom my tormentor immediately joined. Their mannerisms explained his behavior, for I knew from both speech and gestures that they were Arabs. I had not been able to make this crucial identification by looking at my subject when he was alone because he wasn't talking and he was wearing American clothes.

In describing the scene later to an Arab colleague, two contrasting patterns emerged. My concept and my feelings about my own circle of privacy in a "public" place immediately struck my Arab friend as strange and puzzling. He said, "After all, it's a public place, isn't it?" Pursuing this line of inquiry, I found that an Arab thought I had no rights whatsoever by virtue of occupying a given spot; neither my place nor my body was inviolate! For the Arab, there is no such thing as an intrusion in public. Public means public. With this insight, a great range of Arab behavior that had been puzzling, annoying, and sometimes even frightening began to make sense. I learned, for example, that if *A* is standing on a street corner and *B* wants his spot, *B* is within his rights if he does what he can to make *A* uncomfortable enough to move. In Beirut only the hardy sit in the last row in a movie theater, because there are usually standees who want seats and who push and shove and make such a nuisance that most people give up and leave. Seen in this light, the Arab who "intruded" on my space in the hotel lobby had apparently selected it for the very reason I had: it was a good place to watch two doors and the elevator. My show of annoyance, instead of driving him away, had only encouraged him. He thought he was about to get me to move.

Another silent source of friction between Americans and Arabs is in an area that Americans treat very informally—the manners and rights of the road. In general, in the United States we tend to defer to the vehicle that is bigger, more powerful, faster, and heavily laden. While a pedestrian walking along a road may feel annoyed he will not think it unusual to step aside for a fast-moving automobile. He knows that because he is moving he does not have the right to the space around him that he has when he is standing still (as I was in the hotel lobby). It appears that the reverse is true with the Arabs who apparently *take on rights to space as they move.* For someone else to move into a space an Arab is also moving into is a violation of his rights. It is infuriating to an Arab to have someone else cut in front of him on the highway. It is the American's cavalier treatment of moving space that makes the Arab call him aggressive and pushy.

The experience described above and many others suggested to me that Arabs might actually have a wholly contrasting set of assumptions concerning the body and the rights associated with it. Certainly the Arab tendency to shove and push each other in public and to feel and pinch women in public conveyances would not be tolerated by Westerners. It appeared to me that they must not have any concept of a private zone outside the body. This proved to be precisely the case.

In the Western world, the person is synonymous with an individual inside a skin. And in northern Europe generally, the skin and even the clothes may be inviolate. You need permission to touch either if you are a stranger. This rule applies in some parts of France, where the mere touching of another person during an argument used to be legally defined as assault. For the Arab the location of the person in relation to the body is quite different. The person exists somewhere down inside the body. The ego is not completely hidden, however, because it can be reached very easily with an insult. It is protected from touch but not from words. The dissociation of the body and the ego may explain why the public amputation of a thief's hand is tolerated as standard punishment in Saudi Arabia. It also sheds light on why an Arab employer living in a modern apartment can provide his servant with a room that is a boxlike cubicle approximately 5 by 10 by 4 feet in size that is not only hung from the ceiling to conserve floor space but has an opening so that the servant can be spied on.

As one might suspect, deep orientations toward the self such as the one just described are also reflected in the language. This was brought to my attention one afternoon when an Arab colleague who is the author of an Arab–English dictionary arrived in my office and threw himself into a chair in a state of obvious exhaustion. When I asked him what had been going on, he said: "I have spent the entire afternoon trying to find the Arab equivalent of the English word 'rape.' There is no such word in Arabic. All my sources, both written and spoken, can come up with no more than an approximation, such as 'He took her against her will.' There is nothing in Arabic approaching your meaning as it is expressed in that one word."

Differing concepts of the placement of the ego in relation to the body are not easily grasped. Once an idea like this is accepted, however, it is possible to understand many other facets of Arab life that would otherwise be difficult to explain. One of these is the high population density of Arab cities like Cairo, Beirut, and Damascus. According to the animal studies described in the earlier chapters the Arabs should be living in a perpetual behavioral sink. While it is probable that Arabs are suffering from population pressures, it is also just as possible that continued pressure from the desert has resulted in a cultural adaptation to high density which takes the form described above. Tucking the ego down inside the body shell not only would permit higher population densities but would explain why it is that Arab communications are stepped up as much as they are when compared to northern European communication patterns. Not only is the sheer noise level much higher, but the piercing look of the eyes, the touch of the hands, and the mutual bathing in the warm moist breath during conversation represent stepped-up sensory inputs to a level which many Europeans find unbearably intense.

The Arab dream is for lots of space in the home, which unfortunately many Arabs cannot afford. Yet when he has space, it is very different from what one finds in most American homes. Arab spaces inside their upper middle-class homes are tremendous by our standards. They avoid partitions because *Arabs do not like to be alone.* The form of the home is such as to hold the family together inside a single protective shell, because Arabs are deeply involved with each other. Their personalities are intermingled and take nourishment from each other like the roots and soil. If one is not with people and actively involved in some way, one is deprived of life. An old Arab saying reflects this value: "Paradise without people should not be entered because it is Hell." Therefore, Arabs in the United States often feel socially and sensorially deprived and long to be back where there is human warmth and contact.

Since there is no physical privacy as we know it in the Arab family, not even a word for privacy, one could expect that the Arabs might use some other means to be alone. Their way to be alone is to stop talking. Like the English, the Arab who shuts himself off in this way is not indicating that anything is wrong or that he is withdrawing, only that he wants to be alone with his own thoughts or does not want to be intruded upon. One subject said that her father would come and go for days at a time without saying a word, and no one in the family thought anything of it. Yet for this very reason, an Arab exchange student visiting a Kansas farm failed to pick up the cue that his American hosts were mad at him when they gave him the "silent treatment." He only discovered something was wrong when they took him to town and tried forcibly to put him on a bus to Washington, D.C., the headquarters of the exchange program responsible for his presence in the U.S.

◆ ◆ ◆

In summary, proxemic patterns differ. By examining them it is possible to reveal cultural frames that determine the structure of a given people's perceptual world. Perceiving the world differently leads to differential definitions of what constitutes crowded living, different interpersonal relations, and a different approach to both local and international politics. . . .

Debating Moral Questions

Vincent Ryan Ruggiero

Vincent Ryan Ruggiero, Professor of Humanities at State University of New York at Delhi, is author of eight books on critical thinking. The following excerpt from *The Art of Thinking* relies almost entirely on the use of illustration to bring clarity to a complex issue.

Nowhere is modern thinking more muddled than over the question of whether it is proper to debate moral issues. Many argue it is not, saying it is wrong to make "value judgments." This view is shallow. If such judgments were wrong, then ethics, philosophy, and theology would be unacceptable in a college curriculum—an idea that is obviously silly. As the following cases illustrate, it is impossible to avoid making value judgments.

Raoul Wallenberg was a young Swedish aristocrat. In 1944 he left the safety of his country and entered Budapest. Over the next year he outwitted the Nazis and saved as many as 100,000 Jews (he was not himself Jewish) from the death camps. In 1945 he was arrested by the Russians, charged with spying, and imprisoned in a Russian labor camp. He may still be alive there. Now, if we regard him as a hero—as there is excellent reason to do—we are making a value judgment. Yet if we regard him neutrally, as no different from anyone else, we are also making a value judgment. We are judging him to be neither hero nor villain, but average.

Consider another case. In late 1981 a 20-year-old mother left her three infant sons unattended in a garbage-strewn tenement in New York City. Police found them there, starving, the youngest child lodged between a mattress and a wall, covered with flies and cockroaches, the eldest playing on the second-floor window ledge. The police judged the mother negligent, and the court agreed. Was it wrong for them to judge? And if we refuse to judge, won't that refusal itself be a judgment in the mother's favor?

No matter how difficult it may be to judge such moral issues, we *must* judge them. Value judgment is the basis not only of our social code, but of our legal system. The quality of our laws is directly affected by the quality of our moral judgments. A society that judges blacks inferior is not likely to accord blacks equal treatment. A society that believes a woman's place is in the home is not likely to guarantee women equal employment opportunity.

Other people accept value judgments as long as they are made *within* a culture, and not about other cultures. Right and wrong, they believe, vary from one culture to another. It is true that an act frowned upon in one culture may be tolerated in another, but the degree of difference has often been grossly exaggerated. When we first encounter an unfamiliar moral view, we are inclined to focus on the difference so much that we miss the similarity.

For example, in medieval Europe animals were tried for crimes and often formally executed. In fact, cockroaches and other bugs were sometimes excommunicated from the church. Sounds absurd, doesn't it? But when we penetrate beneath the absurdity, we realize that the basic view—that some actions are reprehensible and ought to be punished—is not so strange. The core idea that a person bitten by, say, a dog, has been wronged and requires justice is very much the same. The only difference is our rejection of the idea that animals are responsible for their behavior.

Is it legitimate, then, for us to pass judgment on the moral standards of another culture? Yes, if we do so thoughtfully, and not just conclude that whatever differs from our view is necessarily wrong. We can judge, for example, a culture that treats women as property, or places less value on their lives than on the lives of men. Moreover, we can say a society is acting immorally by denying women their human rights. Consider the following cases.

In nineteenth-century Rio de Janeiro, Brazil, a theatrical producer shot and killed his wife because she insisted on taking a walk in the botanical gardens against his wishes. He was formally charged with her murder, but the judge dismissed the charge. The producer was carried through the streets in triumph. The moral perspective of his culture condoned the taking of a woman's life if she disobeyed her husband, even in a relatively small matter. A century later that perspective had changed little. In the same city, in 1976, a wealthy playboy, angry at his lover for flirting with others, fired four shots into her face at point-blank range, killing her. He was given a two-year suspended sentence in light of the fact that he had been "defending his honor."

Surely it is irresponsible for us to withhold judgment on the morality of these cases merely because they occurred in a different culture. It is obvious that in both cases the men's response, murder, was out of all proportion to the women's "offenses," and therefore demonstrated a wanton disregard for the women's human rights. Their response is thus properly judged immoral. And this judgment implies another—that the culture condoning such behavior is guilty of moral insensitivity.

The Insufficiency of Honesty

Stephen L. Carter

After attending Yale Law School, Stephen L. Carter served as law clerk for Supreme Court Justice Thurgood Marshall. Carter has written numerous essays, articles and books, including *Reflections of an Affirmative Action Baby* (1992) and *Civility: Manners, Morals, and the Etiquette of Democracy* (1998). The following essay first appeared in *Integrity* in 1996. Consider how Carter begins by establishing a definition and a clear distinction between honesty and integrity, supporting his definition with examples and illustrations. He then sets up an argument about how these two distinctions function in daily life, and how they lead to certain "virtues" and "political values." You might want to compare and contrast Carter's position with Vincent Ryan Ruggerio's essay (pages 301–302). In what ways, if any, are the two arguments compatible? How do they differ? Is either more convincing than the other? And if so, why?

A couple of years ago I began a university commencement address by telling the audience that I was going to talk about integrity. The crowd broke into applause. Applause! Just because they had heard the word "integrity": that's how starved for it they were. They had no idea how I was using the word, or what I was going to say about integrity, or, indeed, whether I was for it or against it. But they knew they liked the idea of talking about it.

Very well, let us consider this word "integrity." Integrity is like the weather: everybody talks about it but nobody knows what to do about it. Integrity is that stuff that we always want more of. Some say that we need to return to the good old days when we had a lot more of it. Others say that we as a nation have never really had enough of it. Hardly anybody stops to explain exactly what we mean by it, or how we know it is a good thing, or why everybody needs to have the same amount of it. Indeed, the only trouble with integrity is that everybody who uses the word seems to mean something slightly different.

For instance, when I refer to integrity, do I mean simply "honesty"? The answer is no; although honesty is a virtue of importance, it is a different virtue from integrity. Let us, for simplicity, think of honesty as not lying; and let us further accept Sissela Bok's definition of a lie: "any intentionally deceptive message which is *stated.*" Plainly, one cannot have integrity without being honest (although, as we shall see, the matter gets complicated), but one can certainly be honest and yet have little integrity.

When I refer to integrity, I have something very specific in mind. Integrity, as I will use the term, requires three steps: discerning what is right and what is wrong; acting on what you have discerned, even at personal cost; and saying openly that you are acting on your understanding of right and wrong. The first criterion captures the idea that integrity requires a degree of moral reflectiveness. The second brings in the ideal of a person of integrity as steadfast, a quality that includes keeping one's commitments. The third reminds us that a person of integrity can be trusted.

The first point to understand about the difference between honesty and integrity is that a person may be entirely honest without ever engaging in the hard work of discernment that integrity requires; she may tell us quite truthfully what she believes without ever taking the time to figure out whether what she believes is good and right and true. The problem may be as simple as someone's foolishly saying something that hurts a friend's feelings; a few moments of thought would have revealed the likelihood of the hurt and the lack of necessity for the comment. Or the problem may be more complex, as when a man who was raised from birth in a society that preaches racism states his belief in one race's inferiority as a fact, without ever really considering that perhaps this deeply held view is wrong. Certainly the racist is being honest—he is telling us what he actually thinks—but his honesty does not add up to integrity.

Telling Everything You Know

A wonderful epigram sometimes attributed to the filmmaker Sam Goldwyn goes like this: "The most important thing in acting is honesty; once you learn to fake that, you're in." The point is that honesty can be something one *seems* to have. Without integrity, what passes for honesty often is nothing of the kind; it is fake honesty—or it is honest but irrelevant and perhaps even immoral.

Consider an example. A man who has been married for fifty years confesses to his wife on his deathbed that he was unfaithful thirty-five years earlier. The dishonesty was killing his spirit, he says. Now he has cleared his conscience and is able to die in peace.

The husband has been honest—sort of. He has certainly unburdened himself. And he has probably made his wife (soon to be his widow) quite miserable in the process, because even if she forgives him, she will not be able to remember him with quite the vivid image of love and loyalty that she had hoped for. Arranging his own emotional affairs to ease his transition to death, he has shifted to his wife the burden of confusion and pain, perhaps for the rest of her life. Moreover, he has attempted his honesty at the one time in his life when it carries no risk; acting in accordance with what you think is right and risking no loss in the process is a rather thin and unadmirable form of honesty.

Besides, even though the husband has been honest in a sense, he has now twice been unfaithful to his wife: once thirty-five years ago, when he had his affair, and again when, nearing death, he decided that his own peace of mind was more important than hers. In trying to be honest he has violated his marriage vow by acting toward his wife not with love but with naked and perhaps even cruel self-interest.

As my mother used to say, you don't have to tell people everything you know. Lying and nondisclosure, as the law often recognizes, are not the same thing. Sometimes it is actually illegal to tell what you know, as, for example, in the disclosure of certain financial information by market insiders. Or it may be unethical, as when a lawyer reveals a confidence entrusted to her by a client. It may be simple bad manners, as in the case of a gratuitous comment to a colleague on his or her attire. And it may be subject to religious punishment, as when a Roman Catholic priest breaks the seal of the confessional—an offense that carries automatic excommunication.

In all the cases just mentioned, the problem with telling everything you know is that somebody else is harmed. Harm may not be the intention, but it is certainly the effect. Honesty is most laudable when we risk harm to ourselves; it becomes a good deal less so if we instead risk harm to others when there is no gain to anyone other than ourselves. Integrity may counsel keeping our secrets in order to spare the feelings of others. Sometimes, as in the example of the wayward husband, the reason we want to tell what we know is precisely to shift our pain onto somebody else—a course of action dictated less by integrity than by self-interest. Fortunately, integrity and self-interest often coincide, as when a politician of integrity is rewarded with our votes. But often they do not, and it is at those moments that our integrity is truly tested.

Error

Another reason that honesty alone is no substitute for integrity is that if forthrightness is not preceded by discernment, it may result in the expression of an incorrect moral judgment. In other words, I may be honest about what I believe, but if I have never tested my beliefs, I may be wrong. And here I mean "wrong" in a particular sense: the proposition in question is wrong if I would change my mind about it after hard moral reflection.

Consider this example. Having been taught all his life that women are not as smart as men, a manager gives the women on his staff less-challenging assignments than he gives the men. He does this, he believes, for their own benefit: he does not want them to fail, and he believes that they will if he gives them tougher assignments. Moreover, when one of the women on his staff does poor work, he does not berate her as harshly as he would a man, because he expects nothing more. And he claims to be acting with integrity because he is acting according to his own deepest beliefs.

The manager fails the most basic test of integrity. The question is not whether his actions are consistent with what he most deeply believes but whether he has done the hard work of discerning whether what he most deeply believes is right. The manager has not taken this harder step.

Moreover, even within the universe that the manager has constructed for himself, he is not acting with integrity. Although he is obviously wrong to think that the women on his staff are not as good as the men, even were he right, that would not justify applying different standards to their work. By so doing he betrays both his obligation to the institution that employs him and his duty as a manager to evaluate his employees.

The problem that the manager faces is an enormous one in our practical politics, where having the dialogue that makes democracy work can seem impossible because of our tendency to cling to our views even when we have not examined them. As Jean Bethke Elshtain has said, borrowing from John Courtney Murray, our politics are so fractured and contentious that we often cannot reach *disagreement.* Our refusal to look closely at our own most cherished principles is surely a large part of the reason. Socrates thought the unexamined life not worth living. But the unhappy truth is that few of us actually have the time for constant reflection on our views—on public or private morality. Examine them we must, however, or we will never know whether we might be wrong.

None of this should be taken to mean that integrity as I have described it presupposes a single correct truth. If, for example, your integrity-guided search tells you that affirmative action is wrong, and my integrity-guided search tells me that affirmative action is right, we need not conclude that one of us lacks integrity. As it happens, I believe—both as a Christian and as a secular citizen who struggles toward moral understanding—that we *can* find true and sound answers to our moral questions. But I do not pretend to have found very many of them, nor is an exposition of them my purpose here.

It is the case not that there aren't any right answers but that, given human fallibility, we need to be careful in assuming that we have found them. However, today's political talk about how it is wrong for the government to impose one person's morality on somebody else is just mindless chatter. *Every* law imposes one person's morality on somebody else, because law has only two functions: to tell people to do what they would rather not or to forbid them to do what they would.

And if the surveys can be believed, there is far more moral agreement in America than we sometimes allow ourselves to think. One of the reasons that character education for young people makes so much sense to so many people is precisely that there seems to be a core set of moral understandings—we might call them the American Core—that most of us accept. Some of the virtues in this American Core are, one hopes, relatively noncontroversial. About 500 American communities have signed on to Michael Josephson's program to emphasize the "six pillars" of good character: trustworthiness, respect, responsibility, caring, fairness, and citizenship. These virtues might lead to a similarly noncontroversial set of political values: having an honest regard for ourselves and others, protecting freedom of thought and religious belief, and refusing to steal or murder.

Honesty and Competing Responsibilities

A further problem with too great an exaltation of honesty is that it may allow us to escape responsibilities that morality bids us bear. If honesty is substituted for integrity, one might think that if I say I am not planning to fulfill a duty, I need not fulfill it. But it would be a peculiar morality indeed that granted us the right to avoid our moral responsibilities simply by stating our intention to ignore them. Integrity does not permit such an easy escape.

Consider an example. Before engaging in sex with a woman, her lover tell her that if she gets pregnant, it is her problem, not his. She says that she understands. In due course she does wind up pregnant. If we believe, as I hope we do, that the man would ordinarily have a moral responsibility toward both the child he will have helped to bring into the world and the child's mother, then his honest statement of what he intends does not spare him that responsibility.

This vision of responsibility assumes that not all moral obligations stem from consent or from a stated intention. The linking of obligations to promises is a rather modern and perhaps uniquely Western way of looking at life, and perhaps a luxury that the well-to-do can afford. As Fred and Shulamit Korn (a philosopher and an anthropologist) have pointed out, "If one looks at ethnographic accounts of other societies, one finds that, while obligations everywhere play a crucial role in social life, promising is not preeminent among the sources of obligation and is not even mentioned by most anthropologists." The Korns have made a study of Tonga, where promises are virtually unknown but the social order is remarkably stable. If life without any promises seems extreme, we Americans sometimes go too far the other way, parsing not only our contracts but even our marriage vows in order to discover the absolute minimum obligation that we have to others as a result of our promises.

That some societies in the world have worked out evidently functional structures of obligation without the need for promise or consent does not tell us what *we* should do. But it serves as a reminder of the basic proposition that our existence in civil society creates a set of mutual responsibilities that philosophers used to capture in the fiction of the social contract. Nowadays, here in America, people seem to spend their time thinking of even cleverer ways to avoid their obligations, instead of doing what integrity commands and fulfilling them. And all too often honesty is their excuse.

The Fear of Losing a Culture

Richard Rodriguez

Richard Rodriguez attracted national attention with his controversial autobiography, *Hunger of Memory* (1981), in which he portrayed the difficulties of growing up as a Mexican American in a culture that wanted to reward him for being a minority. In the following essay, originally published in *Time,* Rodriguez again challenges our established perceptions of the role minorities can and will play in American life, this time using a synthesis of all the major strategies: comparison and contrast, illustration, and cause and effect.

What is culture?

The immigrant shrugs. Latin American immigrants come to the United States with only the things they need in mind—not abstractions like culture. Money. They need dollars. They need food. Maybe they need to get out of the way of bullets.

Most of us who concern ourselves with Hispanic-American culture, as painters, musicians, writers—or as sons and daughters—are the children of immigrants. We have grown up on this side of the border, in the land of Elvis Presley and Thomas Edison; our lives are prescribed by the mall, by the DMV and the Chinese restaurant. Our imaginations yet vacillate between an Edenic Latin America (the blue door)—which nevertheless betrayed our parents—and the repellent plate glass of a real American city—which has been good to us.

Hispanic-American culture is where the past meets the future. Hispanic-American culture is not an Hispanic milestone only, not simply a celebration at the crossroads. America transforms into pleasure what America cannot avoid. Is it any coincidence that at a time when Americans are troubled by the encroachment of the Mexican desert, Americans discover a chic in cactus, in the decorator colors of the Southwest? In sand?

Hispanic-American culture of the sort that is now showing (the teen movie, the rock song) may exist in an hourglass; may in fact be irrelevant to the epic. The U.S. Border Patrol works through the night to arrest the flow of illegal immigrants over the border, even as Americans wait in line to get into "La Bamba." Even as Americans vote to declare, once and for all, that English shall be the official language of the United States, Madonna starts recording in Spanish.

But then so is Bill Cosby's show irrelevant to the 10 o'clock news, where families huddle together in fear on porches, pointing at the body of the slain boy bagged in tarpaulin. Which is not to say that Bill Cosby or Michael Jackson are irrelevant to the future or without neo-Platonic influence. Like players within the play, they prefigure, they resolve. They make black and white audiences aware of a bond that may not yet exist.

Before a national TV audience, Rita Moreno tells Geraldo Rivera that her dream as an actress is to play a character rather like herself: "I speak English perfectly well . . . I'm not dying from poverty . . . I want to play *that* kind of Hispanic woman, which is to say, an American citizen." This is an actress talking, these are show-biz pieties. But Moreno expresses as well the general Hispanic-American predicament. Hispanics want to belong to America without betraying the past.

Hispanics fear losing ground in any negotiation with the American city. We come from an expansive, an intimate culture that has been judged second-rate by the United States of America. For reasons of pride, therefore, as much as of affection, we are reluctant to give up our past. Hispanics often express a fear of "losing" culture. Our fame in the United States has been our resistance to assimilation.

The symbol of Hispanic culture has been the tongue of flame—Spanish. But the remarkable legacy Hispanics carry from Latin America is not language—an inflatable skin—but breath itself, capacity of soul, an inclination to live. The genius of Latin America is the habit of synthesis.

We assimilate. Just over the border there is the example of Mexico, the country from which the majority of U.S. Hispanics come. Mexico is mestizo—Indian and Spanish. Within a single family, Mexicans are light-skinned and dark. It is impossible for the Mexican to say, in the scheme of things, where the Indian begins and the Spaniard surrenders.

In culture as in blood, Latin America was formed by a rape that became a marriage. Due to the absorbing generosity of the Indian, European culture took on new soil. What Latin America knows is that people create one another as they marry. In the music of Latin America you will hear the litany of bloodlines—the African drum, the German accordion, the cry from the minaret.

The United States stands as the opposing New World experiment. In North America the Indian and the European stood apace. Whereas Latin America was formed by a medieval Catholic dream of one world—of meltdown conversion—the United States was built up from Protestant individualism. The American melting pot washes away only embarrassment; it is the necessary initiation into public life. The American faith is that our national strength derives from separateness, from "diversity." The glamour of the United States is a carnival promise: You can lose weight, get rich as Rockefeller, tough up your roots, get a divorce.

Immigrants still come for the promise. But the United States wavers in its faith. As long as there was space enough, sky enough, as long as economic success validated individualism, loneliness was not too high a price to pay. (The cabin on the prairie or the Sony Walkman.)

As we near the end of the American century, two alternative cultures beckon the American imagination—both highly communal cultures—the Asian and the Latin American. The United States is a literal culture. Americans devour what we might otherwise fear to become. Sushi will make us corporate warriors. Combination Plate #3, smothered in mestizo gravy, will burn a hole in our hearts.

Latin America offers passion. Latin America has a life—I mean *life*—big clouds, unambiguous themes, death, birth, faith, that the United States, for all its quality of life, seems without now. Latin America offers communal riches: an undistressed leisure, a kitchen table, even a full sorrow. Such is the solitude of America, such is the urgency of American need, Americans reach right past a fledgling, homegrown Hispanic-American culture for the real thing—the darker bottle of Mexican beer; the denser novel of a Latin American master.

For a long time, Hispanics in the United States withheld from the United States our Latin American gift. We denied the value of assimilation. But as our presence is judged less foreign in America, we will produce a more generous art, less timid, less parochial. Carlos Santana, Luis Valdez, Linda Ronstadt—Hispanic Americans do not have a "pure" Latin American art to offer. Expect bastard themes, expect ironies, comic conclusions. For we live on this side of the border, where Kraft manufactures bricks of "Mexican style" Velveeta, and where Jack in the Box serves "Fajita Pita."

The flame-red Chevy floats a song down the Pan American Highway: From a rolled-down window, the grizzled voice of Willie Nelson rises in disembodied harmony with the voice of Julio Iglesias. Gabby Hayes and Cisco are thus resolved.

Expect marriage. We will change America even as we will be changed. We will disappear with you into a new miscegenation.

Along the border, real conflicts remain. But the ancient tear separating Europe from itself—the Catholic Mediterranean from the Protestant north—may yet heal itself in the New World. For generations, Latin America has been the place—the bed—of a confluence of so many races and cultures that Protestant North America shuddered to imagine it.

Imagine it.

PART 6

Analysis and Argument

Suggested Writing Projects

By this point in your life, you've been shaped by an almost uncountable number of influences: parents, schools, religion, ethnic background, television, movies, books, friends, teachers, and the culture and history of which you are a part. You hold opinions; you have values, beliefs, and principles. It is not the role of college to change any of that. It is, however, the role of higher education to involve you in the larger debates of your society. Part of that involvement may very well require you to reconsider previously formed positions, to accept them with new insights or to modify them—and, at times, abandon them. All this will constitute one of the larger challenges you face.

In earlier papers, you've described experiences from your past, perhaps interviewed others to gather opinion, reported on facts, or researched and evaluated evidence. You've probably explored abstract concepts, ideas, and values: explaining them, tracing their origins or histories, and perhaps assessing some aspect of them. Now you must go one final step. You must investigate contemporary societal issues and controversies, some of which may be based on competing ideologies or values, some of which may challenge your own basic beliefs. You will find it necessary to analyze the arguments you read with special care, making yourself aware of the various ways arguments are constructed, and the various methods by which appeals are made to emotion (because emotion is always inherent in the most important issues). You will find that facts and evidence are central, but sound reasoning may be more so, and most vital of all may be unmentioned or even unrecognized principles and values. The argumentative paper, or position paper, constitutes your entry into the ongoing debate.

Here are some suggestions where you might begin:

- Several argumentative essays have been collected at the end of this unit. The first two argue for and against the current feminist stand on sexual harrassment. The third essay argues for "interreligious dialogue," and the final essay presents a stand against political correctness on college campuses. Each essay in turn uses numerous elements of logical analysis, as well as varying degrees of emotional appeal. Your instructor may want to select one or two of them for you to analyze and discuss in class or to stimulate further research into the subject. Use the library, contemporary magazines and journals, or the Internet to do any other research on the topic that might be valuable. Then write your own essay, as objectively as possible, characterizing the argument as a whole as you understand it, and then developing your own argument using sound reasoning and evidence, or by appealing to your readers' emotions in such a way that the appeal might unite your readers around a common value.

- *Time, Newsweek, Saturday Review, The New York Times,* and many other journals and newspapers run argumentative essays in almost all issues. Choose one that angers you, and write your own essay in which you demonstrate that the author is wrong. Use evidence, reasoning, and an evaluation of values or principles. Consider any objections that might be made to your own position, and rebut them in advance.

- Select one of the following controversies. Locate two or three current positions on the topic (in sources such as current magazines, newspapers, or Internet sites) and critique the reasoning you encounter. Consider where the arguments are strong and where they are weak. If the sources disagree, come to a conclusion in which you clearly identify the most effective argument.

  diversity
  euthanasia
  animal rights
  gay marriages
  terrorism as political action

Group Inquiry

Collaboration in argumentation can be very helpful. If your partner disagrees with your position, you have a built-in source of information on the opposite point of view. If you happen to agree, you can explore your individual assumptions in more depth, and the two of you can work together to question other points of view.

Divide into groups of twos and read several of the argumentative essays at the end of this unit. Choose one to analyze and discuss with your partner. Begin to develop an understanding of your individual and joint strengths as well as noticing any weaknesses. If it turns out that you both share similar thoughts, feelings, and ways of thinking, be especially careful not to underestimate the power in the position of the other side of the issue. Deliberately devise and anticipate an argument that counters your own. If, on the other hand, you disagree with each other, listen closely to the other's position. Weigh strengths and weaknesses. As an exercise, write a brief counterpoint essay to the other's position.

CHAPTER 25

Critical Thinking

In good speaking, should not the mind of the speaker know the truth of the matter about which he is to speak?

PLATO

The winter sun had almost set, and my office was growing dark when he knocked. I had been holding conferences with first-year students for several hours, and their faces had begun to blur. He was a young African-American man who had just received an *F* on a literature exam. He sat across the desk, twisting the paper in his hands. "All you want us to do is repeat what you think," he began. "My ideas are just as good as yours."

Outside my window the lights came on in the gymnasium across the street. My wife would be expecting me home for dinner. I took a deep breath and tried to explain that his ideas might indeed be as valid as mine but that he must demonstrate their validity. He could not simply assert, as he had, that Robert Frost's poem "Stopping by Woods on a Snowy Evening" dealt with a ghost. That might be true, I said, but he must point to specific evidence in the poem that would show me how he had come to such a conclusion.

"That's how I felt," he said. "That's what the poem made me feel."

I spent fifteen minutes going over the poem with him. Where did he find evidence that the speaker of the poem was a ghost? Where did he find "church bells tolling for the dead"? (A line that did not appear in the poem.) His anger grew. My frustration increased. I was beginning to think that first-year students in general were hopeless, when he suddenly blurted out, "It's the same ol' thing. The white man tells you what to do and think, and I'm supposed to say, 'Yes suh.' Well, I got a different message than you did—I felt it, and that makes it true."

I was furious that race had been brought into the issue. It was a direct blow to my self-image. I handed back his exam and told him to leave. I even suggested several places he might take his truth. Afterward, I regretted my anger, but I knew that in both of us emotion had won out over reason.

The nature of truth has long presented us with one of our most complex intellectual challenges. Are all ideas equally true? Is there such a thing as truth at all? If so, how can we know it? If not, by what method can we determine even the probable truth of anything? Those who are most confident about the existence of something called Absolute Truth (a truth that is eternally undeniable and undebatable) usually depend on intuition and faith for their conviction. The problem is that Absolute Truth known through faith cannot be demonstrated to others. You either believe or you don't believe. By contrast, when we use *reason,* we ask that the truth of something be demonstrated through evidence or argument. In its simplest form, I might make a comparison with the concepts of *telling* and *showing* that have been emphasized in earlier chapters. You may tell me you perceive or possess the truth, but logic requires that you *show* me both the evidence and the method of reasoning you used to arrive at your conclusion.

Reason or logic, then, becomes a method of seeking probable truth through inference or interpretation of observable facts—something you began working with in earlier chapters. Before we pursue it further, however, we need to identify some of the problems that interfere with reasoning. The incident with my student reveals several. I was tired and quick to anger. I had begun to classify all first-year students as the same. He was convinced that all professors were the same and that racial bias had influenced my judgment. I felt that he must use logic to demonstrate the truth; he felt that emotion evoked by poetry contained its own truth. Both of us ended up *feeling* we were in the right. But sometimes feelings can be seriously wrong.

Emotional Blocks to Reason

Several years ago, I listened to a speaker talking to an all-male audience of college students on the surprising growth of women's athletic abilities. Among dozens of other facts, the speaker pointed out that thirty years earlier, in the 100-meter dash, the fastest woman in the world was 11.88 percent slower than the fastest man. By the end of the 1990s, this margin had been reduced to 6 percent and was continuing to decrease as more women entered physical training earlier. In fact, the women's marathon record today would have won every gold medal in the men's marathon at the Olympic games through 1982. In other words, all evidence tends to show that with better training and positive encouragement, women can and will close the gap on such male bastions as physical strength and endurance. Many in the all-male audience seemed to accept this as progress. But one young man sitting in front of me leaned over and whispered to his friend, "Yeah, but women will never be able to play football!"

When we are emotionally committed to something, contradictory data are easily ignored. The emotional support we attach to our gender, race, ethnic group, culture, or religion will often overpower the logic of mere reason. It seems normal in human nature to believe that *our* way of living makes sense, whereas others have funny habits. It seems normal to believe in our own superiority. The Indian word *Cheyenne* means "the people," a term that obviously suggests that other tribes, such as the Sioux and Blackfeet, were something less than people. Hitler manipulated just such an attitude to persuade a nation that Jews were an inferior "race" deserving barbaric treatment. Americans, too, are not immune. Racist attitudes separating African Americans from whites, or Chicanos from whites, can cause people to act in ways that they would normally condemn in others. We can create such strong stereotypes in our minds that when presented with facts to the contrary, we may tend to assume the facts are inaccurate and the stereotype true.

For example, after Al Qaeda terrorists attacked the twin towers in New York and the Pentagon in Washington, D.C., there were numerous incidents of harassment and threats made to innocent American citizens who happened to be of Arabic or Muslim heritage. In the anger and grief of the moment, stereotypes won easily over reason and conscience. Even on the most everyday level, we tend to see our city or neighborhood as better than others; we tend to believe that the way we eat or the clothing styles we wear are "normal." Once we become emotionally committed to our private or cultural truths, logical reasoning is blocked. Yet for some 2500 years, logic has been the primary method accepted by the Western world for determining truth. If we are to function successfully in such a world, we must recognize how emotion—as necessary as it is for human behavior—can nevertheless sometimes cloud our thinking and distort our judgment.

Consider the various types of oversimplifications you find in the following. Consider how an oversimplification might disguise hidden bias or culturally trained (but unrecognized) attitudes.

1. The U.S. Congress refused to grant statehood to Utah until the Mormons ceased their immoral practice of polygamy.
2. Baby girls should be dressed in pink; boys, in blue.
3. From a radio talk show announcer: "The problem with trying to deal with Afghans is that you can never trust them. The 'truth' about anything depends on which tribal leader you talk to."

4. Do you know who won the Polish beauty contest? Who? No one.
5. A wife should be subordinate to her husband. As St. Paul writes in Ephesians 5:23–4, "Wives, submit yourselves unto your husbands . . . for the husband is the head of the family, even as Christ is the head of the church."
6. The proper way to cut your meat is to hold your fork in your left hand and your knife in your right hand. Cut off a single bite. Place your knife at the top of the plate. Shift your fork to your right hand and eat. Repeat the process for the next bite.

Intellectual Laziness

Some obstacles to clear reasoning derive less from emotional blocks than from lazy thinking. We prefer simple ideas to complex ideas. Truth always seems more evident if we don't bother to consider details or consequences.

An *oversimplification* is caused when we fail to investigate an idea thoroughly. In the 2000 election, for example, a Southern governor ran for reelection after more than one-third of the state's public school systems faced bankruptcy. Many schools had actually closed their doors. The governor campaigned on a banner of "no new taxes." He argued that by cutting taxes on the rich, the economy would be stimulated, consumers would spend more money, and the state, through the collection of increased sales taxes, would be able to fund the school system. The argument may sound complicated, but it had actually been oversimplified. For one thing, the governor ignored evidence showing that it is the poor and middle classes who generate the most state revenue through sales taxes, not the rich. Cutting taxes on the rich might in fact eventually stimulate extra investment in business and industry, but such investment tends to take years, if not decades, to translate into "sales taxes." The oversimplification appealed to voters, however, and the governor was reelected.

Simplification may be a valuable approach to any subject if by simplifying we clarify. But when we oversimplify, we distort and mislead. Instead of telling the truth, we lie. Here are several types of oversimplifications that sound logical and convincing but ignore the complexities of human nature.

Faulty cause and effect:

- Alcoholism is caused by the availability of alcohol.
- Rome fell after the introduction of Christianity; therefore, Rome fell because of Christianity.

Naturally, if alcohol did not exist, we would not have alcoholism, but the fact that it *does* exist does not make it the singular cause of the disease. Not everyone who drinks alcohol becomes an alcoholic. Nor does the fact that Christianity preceded the fall of Rome mean that it caused such a fall. In fact, the notion that "Rome fell" is itself an oversimplification.

Overgeneralizations:

- Democracy is the best form of government.
- People on welfare are lazy.
- Poor students are a result of poor teachers.

Overgeneralizations usually depend on a stated or implied *always, never, greatest, best,* or on other superlatives that claim a truth without exception. We can criticize the preceding examples by observing that for nations with no heritage of self-government, democracy may *not* be the best form of government, that *all* welfare recipients are not necessarily lazy, that *not all* poor students are the product of poor teachers. In each case, the writer should qualify his or her assertion: Democracy is *often* (or *usually* or *sometimes*) the best form of government; *some* people on welfare are lazy; poor students *may* be a result of poor teaching.

Hasty conclusions:

- My friend scored 100 on an I.Q. exam. It's obvious his abilities are merely average and he should become an auto mechanic.
- Alpha Pi was suspended for holding another drunken brawl. They ought to end the whole fraternity system.

When a judgment is made too early in the reasoning process or before all evidence has been examined, it is called a *hasty conclusion,* or *hasty generalization.* An I.Q. of 100 indicates the score on a single type of examination. Your friend may be a creative genius in music, painting, or sculpture, but none of those is tested on I.Q. exams. And just because one fraternity fails to police itself does not necessarily mean that *all* fraternities should be banished.

Undefined abstractions:

- Coke is it!
- Sam Smith is neurotic.

But what exactly does the word "it" mean? The answer seems to be that "it" can mean anything or nothing. And for that matter, what is "neurotic"? This word is often used to imply that someone acts in a "strange" manner—but according to whose standards? So many mental conditions have been grouped under "neurotic" that the American Psychological Association no longer recognizes the term as describing a meaningful medical condition. Like the word "it," neurotic seems to mean whatever we want it to mean. Without precise definition, the reader can rightly suspect that we don't really know what we're talking about.

Clear reasoning requires hard work, time, and careful attention to details. Some people are upset by complexity and leap at the first solution or easiest answer. But the successful writer builds an argument slowly, with arduous attention to word choice and concrete evidence. He or she works to clarify and simplify, not to oversimplify.

Consider the various types of oversimplifications you find in the following:

1. From the Hartford, Connecticut, sheriff: "Marijuana should never be legalized. Of twenty heroin addicts now in my jail, eighteen of them started on marijuana. That's 90 percent!"
2. Miss USA for 2002 ate Campbell's Tomato Soup when she was a little girl. Look at her today!
3. Two hospital studies have shown that for pain other than headaches, Excedrin is more effective than aspirin.
4. Why, I would never promote fluoridation. Fluoridation was tried in Cleveland in 1843, and not *one* of those people who drank the water is alive today.
5. The Marines will make a man of you.
6. From a student paper: "The issue of interracial marriages is frequently judged by today's society. But times are changing and each generation should accept new ideas. When society is against a couple's marriage, they will have a closer bond of love between themselves. They won't argue as much. If all marriages were interracial, there wouldn't be any discrimination."
7. Without a college education, you can't find a good job.
8. If guns are outlawed, only outlaws will have guns.
9. The governor was reelected in 2000 because he oversimplified the school-tax issue.

Modes of Argument

An argument is a course of reasoning aimed at convincing an audience to believe in the truth of something. Obviously, the various modes of arguing are many. Knowing them and using them can serve you well. At the same time, many strategies are dual-edged swords: They can serve to enhance an argument and to persuade a reader while in fact constituting a fallacy in themselves. In other words, arguing well, and separating a good argument from a false one, is tricky business.

Analogies

In logical reasoning, an analogy is a good way to show a relationship. Analogies lead a reader from something known to something unknown. If I tell you that learning to write is like learning to swim because both require practice and repetition, you may understand more about writing *if* you already know something about swimming. And my reasoning may be accurate if the likeness is close enough to make my conclusions "highly probable." But, by definition, an analogy contains differences as well as similarities. If we decide that the differences are greater than the likenesses, we must call it a *false analogy*. Several years ago the Shell Oil Company ran a commercial on television that concluded with the analogy: "If Shell Oil Company can make such high-quality components for airplanes, think how good its gasoline must be." The problem, of course, is that even if Shell does build quality airplane parts, there is no guarantee that another branch of the same company, a thousand miles away, under different management, and pursuing a different manufacturing process in refining gasoline from oil, will also make a quality product. The only valid connection is the corporate name, not the quality of the product; therefore, the analogy is false.

Even when an analogy is successful in clarifying or explaining, it is still only a comparison. In itself, it does not *prove* anything.

Appeals to Authority

Calling on authority can form an essential component to a sound argument. When you claim that America needs universal health care, a citation of support from the president of the American Medical Association would strengthen your argument. Most of us cannot be expected to understand the complexity of such topics. Calling upon someone recognized for extensive study of a subject, or for extensive experience, will often be more persuasive than logical argument alone.

On the other hand, one still needs to determine whether the authority being cited has a hidden stake in the argument. A weak argument can be disguised, its falsity hidden, or its shaky reasoning overwhelmed by the use of a famous name. For example, citing Madonna as one who supports foreign aid to Nigeria should carry no weight. Madonna may be an authority in music, and her interests in helping the people of Nigeria should be praised, but it's doubtful she knows more about foreign aid policy than you or I. Beware also of the generalized citation: "Religious leaders everywhere oppose cloning," or "Scientists tell us of the many dangers . . ." How many religious leaders? What kind? Which scientists? Where and when? And finally, always be suspicious of the appeal to authority for vague emotional reasons: "John F. Kennedy believed in a world where each man was free to worship in his own way. Unless we abandon the teaching of evolution, we will never live up to Kennedy's dream."

Appeals to Emotion

A false appeal to authority is only one way of calling up emotions. In September 2001, at the beginning of the war against the Taliban in Afghanistan, a few individuals, including some college professors and students, spoke out against war: They argued that a peaceful resolution should be found. Some asserted that America itself was responsible because of repressive policies and acts of economic aggression. Their voices, however, were quickly repressed by the sweep of overwhelming emotions after the loss of so many innocent American lives. A few outspoken professors were actually dismissed from their jobs. Pacifist students were often attacked in newspaper editorials as disloyal to America. In the stunning anguish of the moment, the desire for revenge was far stronger—and almost universal in the United States. Appeals for reason were scoffed at or declared treasonous. I confess, at the time, I too felt swept up in the emotion. Yet at the same time, I felt appalled that in America we could so quickly abandon our constitutional tradition of free speech. Waving patriotic flags and calling our adversaries "evil" seemed to trigger automatic reactions in most of us. The danger is that a skilled writer or speaker can sway whole nations by such tactics, even though logic and evidence might demonstrate that such appeals distort our judgment.

Yet we are, after all, human. Our feelings cannot and should not be ignored. The moral codes of all great civilizations are based as much on emotion as on reason, perhaps more so. When we learn that a twelve-year-old girl has been raped in our own neighborhood or when we read that six million Jews were murdered in the Holocaust, our response is shock and horror. A mother committing suicide in the Bronx because her welfare check was stolen by two teenage boys to buy drugs, or children starving in Africa, or nuns tortured in Nicaragua, or a man executed in Texas for a crime he didn't commit—all of these can provoke our sense of outrage and injustice. An argument to end such abuses would almost of necessity enlist a degree of emotional support. Arguments that are totally cold and dry, totally rational, may be essential in many cases. But supplementing reason with an appeal to emotion can often be a legitimate support strategy.

The question here is always "How much emotion?" and "For what purpose?" Is an appeal to emotion used as *support* for a well-reasoned argument or is it used to avoid reason or to repress evidence? The answer may not be easy, but the danger in not asking the question is even greater. Emotion must be tested against reason, reason against emotion.

Using Statistics

In an age when presidents carry Gallup polls in their pockets to demonstrate the popularity of their policies, the danger of arguments founded on statistics needs to be especially noted. Because mathematics seems "scientific," we tend to be swayed by numbers, any kind of numbers, as if numbers in themselves always constituted proof. A college professor recently talked about how a committee he served on had reached a deadlock and could not decide whether to include a proposed course in the new curriculum. The professor broke the deadlock by announcing that 62 percent of the students favored such a course. The committee immediately voted its approval. Later, the professor admitted that the statistic was invented; yet it had exercised more influence than all the previous arguments.

Even if the statistic had been taken from a valid survey of student opinion, we would still need to know when the poll was taken, the size of the sampling (just how many students were actually questioned), the wording of the questionnaire, any biases it may have contained, and how the statistic was mathematically determined. Without such data, even valid statistics may be misleading. A famous example occurred in the 1950s when the surgeon general of the United States announced that the average American smokes a pack of cigarettes a day. But what exactly does average mean? If only two of your ten best friends smoked five packs of cigarettes apiece each day, the average for all your friends would be a pack a day, even though eight of them did not smoke at all.

Can such a statistic have the weight of proof? No. It *can* be offered as evidence, but it must always be evaluated as carefully as any other form of evidence or argument.

Reasoning Well

The heart of reasoning lies in clear relationships. It requires that we examine evidence from as many sources as possible, that facts be distinguished from mere assertions or unchallenged emotion, that causes do in fact lead to effects, and that our conclusions be directly related to our premise.

The use of analogies, citations of authority, valid statistics, and even emotional support, are all helpful strategies for argument. The point is to distinguish between the valid use of such methods and their invalid use. A well-reasoned argument demonstrates how relationships are sound, whereas a weak argument either blurs relationships or attempts to establish or disguise a questionable relationship.

Inductive and Deductive Reasoning

The surest kind of reasoning is usually considered *inductive:* moving from the specific to the general, from facts and evidence to a conclusion about the facts. A belief in the value of inductive reasoning is built into this book, which from the first page has argued that you must train yourself to see, to search out the concrete specific details, to investigate, and then to draw inferences or to interpret your findings based solely on the evidence, evidence that a second observer can verify.

> William Shakespeare used more active verbs than passive verbs.
> John Donne used more active verbs than passive verbs.
> Mark Twain used more active verbs than passive verbs.

Virginia Woolf used more active verbs than passive verbs.
Alice Walker uses more active verbs than passive verbs.
Therefore, good writers use more active verbs than passive verbs.

As in all inductive reasoning, the connection between specific facts and the generalization may be proven wrong. Inductive reasoning does not guarantee truth. It works to establish a probable truth based on an accumulation of verifiable facts, observations, or experiences that form a clear relationship—a pattern—that seems to support a general conclusion.

Deductive reasoning works in the opposite manner. It reasons from the general to the specific, from broad abstractions to particular truths. In its simplest form, it includes three divisions of argument, which compose a *syllogism:* a proposition (called a major premise), a second proposition (called the minor premise), and then a conclusion deduced from the relationship.

All men are mortal.	(major premise)
John is a man.	(minor premise)
Therefore, John is mortal.	(conclusion, deduced from the relationship between the major and minor premises)

The initial generalization (major premise) must be either self-evident or of such a nature that we can agree on its truth without need for further evidence. The second (minor premise), and any following premise in the chain, must be more specific and verifiable. If the conclusion illustrates a proper relationship between or among the premises, we can then claim that the conclusion is true. But this pattern of argument can still create problems.

All voters are good citizens.
John votes.
John is a good citizen.

Here all the requirements seem to have been met. We can say that this syllogism is valid insofar as it follows the prescribed form. Yet the conclusion is false. For it to be true, each step in the chain must be true; but the major premise, or generalization in this case, cannot be accepted as self-evident. All voters are not necessarily good citizens. A Mafia hit man is not a good citizen, even though he may have voted for George W. Bush. Therefore, the fact that John votes does not necessarily make him a good citizen.

Another danger occurs when the form of the syllogism is distorted in such a way that it makes the logical process look like nonsense.

All dogs have four legs.
My cat has four legs.
Therefore, my cat is a dog.

All men have facial hair.
My mother has a moustache.
Therefore, my mother is a man.

The complexity and subtlety of deductive reasoning are best left to a philosophy course. But you should be aware that reasonable-sounding argument may not be reasonable at all. Each component of the argument and each relationship must be tested and held accountable in its own right for the conclusion to be true.

Emotional blocks, lazy thinking, syllogisms that seem logical but are not—the list begins to seem endless. Yet if we want to write clearly and persuasively, to think clearly and soundly, we need at least an elementary grounding in the all-too-human problems that interfere. Our hope must be that even if such problems cannot be eliminated, by knowing they exist we can triumph over them. Ultimately, a sensitive perception of facts, details, emotions, and ideas is not enough for the writer. The successful writer must also perceive reasonable relationships among those facts, details, emotions, and ideas.*

Consider the various problems found in the following arguments:

1. Seventy-one percent of all business transactions today occur via fax or computer. Businesspeople don't need to write letters anymore; therefore, colleges ought to cease requiring composition courses.
2. From a student paper: "To be a science-fiction writer you have to be a little wacko, for the science portrayed in such works is usually fantastic and without a sound basis in fact."
3. King James of England said that as the monarch is the head of the state, democracy is demonstrably false. James argued that if you cut off the head of a body, the other organs cannot function, and the body dies. Similarly, if you cut off the head of a state, the state may flop around for a while, but it is due to perish in time or become an easy prey to its neighbors.

Practice

1. Because the emotional attachment to values learned through our family, our ethnic group, our social class, and our culture is so strong and so prevalent, politicians and advertisers often appeal directly to emotions.

*You may wish to study or review Chapters 21 and 22 for additional information on steps to logical reasoning, especially on developing the ability to see relationships through such conventional strategies as comparison and contrast, classification, definition, illustration, and process and cause-and-effect analysis.

Consider the type of emotion each of the following seeks to arouse. Why is it so powerful? Why wouldn't logic be better? What is illogical in each statement?

a. A vote for Governor Brown is a vote for freedom, integrity, and efficiency in government.

b. From an ad for 7-Up: "It's the same thing, only different."

c. From a speech by an individual running for city coroner: "I was born here and have lived here all my life. I went to Abraham Lincoln High School, and some of you probably still remember the home run I hit in the Medfield game."

d. A man running for state senator attacks his opponent: "Senator Hale has supported legislation that would encourage voter fraud. If I am elected, I promise to oppose any new attempt at online voter registration."

e. In a 1939 *Saturday Evening Post:* "Thousands of physicians smoke Luckies."

2. The following paragraphs were written in first-year composition classes at one of the nation's largest universities. Evaluate each for its logical problems.

a. College is a beneficial experience to everyone who attends it. It is a start of a better life that gives a person an opportunity to pursue a meaningful and challenging career. A college graduate does not have to take a job he won't enjoy just for the purpose of money. College also enhances a person's personality in that one meets many different types of people with varying personalities. College also puts a person into a position of responsibility by making a person learn how to take care of himself.

b. All the emotion over the death of Princess Diana was wasted emotion because she was, after all, incredibly rich. She had been born into a noble family with servants, nannies, chauffeurs, and tutors. She married the heir to the throne of England and lived for fifteen years with the title "Her Royal Highness" in castles and on yachts. She travelled around the world. Others took care of her children, others washed her clothes and her sheets, others prepared her meals and dusted her furniture and mowed her lawn(s). She was bowed to and curtsied to wherever she went. She was applauded and admired and photographed. She had various lovers and spent her time at polo matches and tennis matches and art galleries. She lived in luxury that most of us can't even conceive of. And she was unhappy. Well my position is that it is a lot easier to be unhappy rich than unhappy poor.

c. You should not wear a watch if you are honestly concerned about your health. A survey was conducted by the American Heart

Association to relate the incidence of heart attack to personal actions or qualities. It was found that people who wore watches had a higher rate of heart attacks than those who did not. Time is important to fast-paced, high-pressured people, where promptness is a must to be successful. A high-pressured lifestyle also raises blood pressure, which leads to an increase in the chances of heart attack and slows the pace of life down to a new, healthier level.

d. The fact is, we are all sexual hypocrites. My parents pounded into me the need to avoid sex until after I was married, but this came from two people who had to get married when they were nineteen because my mother was pregnant with my older sister. When I lived in North Dakota, I liked a rather special girl in high school who told me she was a virgin who wanted to get married before she had sex. That really attracted me to her, and I respected her for it. A few months later she ran away with a football jock and they lived together in Texas for three months before their parents found them and brought them home. The first week of classes here, my roommate spent the night with a girl in our room who told me the next morning that she was engaged to someone else, and still intended to marry the guy. She asked me not to say anything about this. The fact is, human beings don't even admit to ourselves that our standards and morals are meaningful only until the next sexual opportunity.

3. Consider each of the following statements. Which contain deductive reasoning? Which lead to a valid conclusion?

a. The University of Southern California defeated Oregon State in football by the score of 31 to 7. UCLA defeated that same Oregon State team, 14 to 7. The University of Southern California can obviously defeat UCLA.

b. All teenagers have pimples. My sister has pimples. Therefore, my sister is a teenager.

c. A student should not be required to take classes he or she is not interested in when he or she gets to college. College students are legal adults and should be allowed to choose their own curriculum.

d. Most professors have Ph.D.s. If all students were required to stay in college until they obtained the Ph.D., we would no longer need professors.

e. The last heroes we had, like Martin Luther King, Jr., and John F. Kennedy, ended up getting shot. Since then, America has not really had any identifiable national heroes. The fact is that we seem to have outgrown our need for such role models.

4. Consider the following dialogue and determine its relationship to logical thinking. Does it express the limits of logic?

   Master Joshu was asked: "What is the ultimate principle of Zen Buddhism?"

   He replied: "The cypress tree in the courtyard."

   "You are talking," another monk said, "of an objective symbol."

   "No, I am not talking about an objective symbol."

   "Then what is the ultimate principle of Zen Buddhism?"

   "The cypress tree in the courtyard," answered Joshu again.

CHAPTER 26

Critical Reading

Pretend for a moment, that you've just picked up an essay—an argument—on ethnic plurality in America. The author contends that when a African-American woman in Los Angeles desires to find her "roots," she is searching for something "that isn't there." He asserts that when a Polish American in Chicago campaigns to save Polish neighborhoods, he is promoting group conformity. The author even argues that when a Mexican American in Houston wants a bilingual school system, he is furthering inequality of the races.

Is the author right or wrong? How you respond to his arguments might range from enthusiastic support to hostility, depending on your own ethnic background. But can you separate your emotions from the argument in the essay? Can you evaluate it for logic and evidence? Can you determine its validity or find its fallacies through a fair and objective analysis?

Serious reading goes beyond entertainment. A chemist reads a scholarly journal to learn about a new discovery in organic neurology. An engineer reads about developments in architectural glass for sun control. A mother reads about a psychiatrist who claims children under five must be disciplined with gentle, but nonetheless, physical punishment. How can any of them evaluate what they read except by considering it logically, analyzing its content, and judging its validity? Such a process requires *critical analysis*—a formal strategy that is both a method for perceiving and evaluating as well as a technique for writing. This chapter deals with analysis as a method that develops critical reading skills. The next chapter offers a traditional structure used for writing an analysis.

The Strategy of Reading Critically

Analysis is a process by which you divide a subject into its various parts. By studying each of the parts and their relationship, you hope to understand more about the subject as a whole (see Chapter 22). But before you can actually analyze something you read, you must learn a particular method of reading that prepares you for each of the steps analysis will demand.

Understand the Content

The need to comprehend content sounds self-evident, but it is neither as easy nor as commonly accomplished as we might like to believe. Every college instructor is aware that perhaps one-fourth of the problems on essay exams can be traced to a student's failure to read or understand the question. Critical reading is a strategy—a method of approaching your reading so that you increase comprehension.

1. Underline key sentences and circle key words. Read each paragraph as a unit of thought. Look for the most important sentences and underline them, especially those that express the theme and the major points used to support the theme. Circle words used in special ways, words you don't know, or words repeated for emphasis.
2. Take notes in the margins. Try to summarize each major point in a few words directly beside the key sentence that makes the point. Try to use your own words for your summary. Being able to put an idea into your own words helps you understand and remember it. Number the notes in the margin so that at a glance you can tell how many major points the writer has made.
3. For every major word you don't know, use a dictionary. (Alas, how many times have you heard that commandment. But you live in a world of words. Ideas are expressed in words. If you don't know the language, you are a prisoner of ignorance.) Write a brief definition in the margin by the word you've circled. Writing the definition helps you remember it.
4. Finally, once you've completed the reading, write a brief summary in your own words, *objectively* and *fairly* restating the author's theme, major points, and conclusion. (Do not interpret or make hasty judgments.) Use your marginal notes to aid you in writing your summary. The summary helps draw together the author's ideas. Until you've written the summary, you may *think* you know what you've read but you can't be sure. The summary is excellent mental work for preparing to take an exam or to write a paper as well as to reinforce comprehension.

Evaluate the Content for Logic

Once you've objectively understood the content, you're in a good position to scrutinize the author's theme more critically. When you read about Japanese buying up American hotels and businesses, does the author appeal to your logic or to your emotions? Is more than one side of the issue presented? Are both sides given fair and equal treatment? Is the content based on opinion? Evidence? Logic? Are the Japanese presented as stereotypes? Is the author's argument based on overgeneralizations? Cultural or racial bias? Is the conclusion based on evidence or logical argument presented in the body of the work?

Here is where you'll want to challenge each major point separately, then compare each point with others, then with the basic theme itself—all to determine logical relationships. If you've numbered each point in the margins, your work will proceed quickly.

Evaluate Yourself for Emotional Blocks

If you find you are easily convinced by the author's position, is it because you're already biased in favor of such ideas? If you are unconvinced, is it because you have a closed mind? In addition to considering the author, the audience, and the work, you must consider *your* relationship to it. If an author proposes a socialistic form of government for the United States, do you disagree because of fear of change or because of unexamined values and beliefs adopted from your parents? Is it possible you have misjudged the work because of a hasty conclusion, or do the ideas sound perfectly logical to you because they conform to the values you want to believe in regardless of their logic? You cannot be sure you have considered your author's material fairly and objectively until you can be sure of your emotional biases.

Consider the Author and the Historical Context

Although it will not always be possible to find out who the author is or to discover what audience the work was originally intended for, every effort should be made to see the work in its original historical context.

1. Who is the author and what is his or her authority to speak on the subject? Sometimes the author's experience and credentials will be identified on the dust jacket or last page of a book. Articles in magazines may identify the author at the bottom of the title page or on the last page of the essay. In some cases, you'll need to do a little research. Almost all libraries contain reference books that identify authors and provide a guide to their background.

   Why do you need to know about the author? Because evaluation of source affects the worth of the information. A few years ago, for example, a book was published claiming to document an authentic account of cloning: An actual human being had been cloned from the cells of another human being and was alive and well. The author asserted that this story was true. But who was the author? He turned out to be a science-fiction writer who had previously written fictional accounts of cloning. Could his claim for truth now be taken seriously? Perhaps. But his authority to document a scientific experiment of such magnitude had to be considered somewhat less reliable than had he been a noted scientist.

2. What is the historical context? Where and when was the work originally published, and who was the probable audience? No poem, essay, or book exists in a vacuum. It grows out of that complex relationship of *subject–audience–context–purpose.* The more you can know about each element, the better you can make reasonable judgments. Every era, for example, tends to promote its generally accepted assumptions. A writer may echo the values of his or her day or may attack them. Either way, an understanding of those cultural values would help you evaluate the argument. And if you can discover the audience or purpose for which a work is written, you can often understand why it takes the form it does, why it uses emotion or logic or a complex or simple vocabulary, and so on.

Reading and critical reading are different acts. Most reading is done for pleasure—a process of absorbing information without serious thought. But critical reading is an intense, concentrated form of evaluating what the author tells you. Here is an outline summary of the critical reading process.

Understand the Content

- Underline key sentences; circle key words.
- Take notes in the margin.
- Use a dictionary.
- Write a brief summary of the main idea, major points, and conclusions.

Evaluate the Content

- Look for logic; look for appeals to emotion.
- Look for both sides of an argument.
- Look for evidence, logical analysis, reasoning.
- Look for meaningful sources to support claims of fact. (If an author claims that 8,000 people died last year from air bags, where did he or she find this information? From U.S. government research? Or from a pamphlet left on his or her doorstep by the "Freedom from Air Bags Society"?)

Evaluate Yourself

- Beware of your biases for and against certain ideas.
- Evaluate whether your reactions are caused by enculturated attitudes.
- Look for immediate denials or approvals; then evaluate whether you've made a hasty conclusion or reacted according to the cultural assumptions of your era.

Consider the Author and Historical Context

- What is the author's authority to speak on a subject? (Personal experience? Scholarly study? Research?)
- What is the motive behind the author's essay? (Self-serving? Results of scientific inquiry? Propaganda?)
- Who was the original audience for the work? (Where was it first published? In a book? In a magazine? As a lecture?)
- What were the biases of the original audience?
- Do any elements in the historical period in which it was written explain elements of the work itself?

The Strategy at Work

Here is how you might apply these guidelines to a specific reading.

Hidden Dangers in the Ethnic Revival

Orlando Patterson

Main thesis
Emphasis upon ethnic revival is retreat from traditional value of equality

The ethnic revival sweeping the United States is another example of this nation's retreat from its constitutional commitment to the ideal of equality.

seemingly liberal, actually reactionary

The fact that the movement has the strong support of many so-called liberals and minority activists makes it all the more insidious and disturbing. The harmless, if vain, search for ancestral roots and communal solidarity is the tip of an ideology that is both reactionary and socially explosive.

① Early ethnic groups were transitory; actually aided assimilation

The ethnic communities that developed in early 20th-century America were essentially transitory. They developed to buffer the economic and cultural shock of adjusting to a new host society. They were aids to assimilation, not barriers. And they succeeded.

What is remarkable about 20th-century America is the rapid rate of assimilation of immigrant groups into the mainstream of social life.

Chauvinism: zealous and belligerent patriotism; prejudiced devotion to a cause →

Chauvinistic intellectuals, by emphasizing those who remain "unmelted," shift the focus from the vast majority who assimilated to those few still remaining in ethnic neighborhoods, although the actual behavior of the majority of those remaining is in the direction of assimilation.

Examples of 1st point:
- Jews becoming assimilated
- black majority wants assimilation

The Jews, often regarded as among the most ideologically and socially cohesive of modern ethnic groups, exhibit increasing rates of out-marriage and secularism and tend more and more to live in non-Jewish neighborhoods. The same is true of all those of Eastern European origin. And despite the talk about black "soul" and separatism, every poll of the black community indicates that the great majority of blacks favor assimilation and would prefer to live in integrated neighborhoods.

Ideology: body of doctrines or beliefs that guide an individual or group

Demagogue: leader who arouses emotion & prejudices →

② Ethnic revival is alliance between conservative demagogues and disenchanted intellectuals—basically ideological

This ethnic revival then is largely an ideological revival wrought by alienated and disenchanted intellectuals and activists in a dangerous alliance with conservative political demagogues. It is the *idea* of ethnicity that is being celebrated, in much the same way that the much talked-about religious revival is largely a commitment to the *idea* of religion.

It is an increasing of awareness about the need for roots. But the ideology has no content, for the roots are simply not there.

③ Ideological rise of ethnicity is compensation for behavioral decline

Paradoxically, the single most important factor accounting for the doctrinal revival of ethnicity is the behavioral decline of ethnicity. Doctrinal intensity is a reaction to, and a compensation for, the actual social indifference of ordinary, decent men and women who have other things on their minds.

④ Civil rights movement is another cause of revival

Other factors account for the ideological revival of ethnicity. One of these is the climax of the black civil rights movement in the mid-1960s. To heal the low self-image created by centuries of racial discrimination, blacks felt obliged to glorify their race, history and culture.

– led to acceptance of chauvinism

The acceptance of black people's right to use ethnic chauvinism as a means of psycho-social liberation revived ethnicity in American political and popular intellectual life.

– but political chauvinism became a two-edged weapon

Soon conservative politicians and other leaders of the white backlash began to use the blacks' own weapon against them. A telling example of the way in which ethnicity became, for blacks, a viper biting its own tail, is the strange career of the principle of community control of neighborhoods.

Example: Community control of neighborhoods first raised by blacks later used by whites to keep blacks out

It was black chauvinists who first made this demand during the 1960s under the mistaken belief that it was an effective means of social and economic independence. Today, the call for community control of schools and the ethnic integrity of neighborhoods comes no longer from blacks but from white reactionaries wishing to keep blacks out of their neighborhoods.

⑤ Ethnic revival (a) damages social fabric

Ethnic pluralism, however dressed up in liberal rhetoric, has no place whatever in a democratic society based on the humanistic ideals of our Judeo-Christian ethic. It is, first, socially divisive. However much the more liberal advocates of the revival may proclaim the contrary, the fact remains that the glorification of one's heritage and one's group always implies its superiority, its "chosenness" over all others.

(b) obscures real issues like poverty and racism

Second, the ethnic revival is a dangerous form of obfuscation. There are indeed many severe problems in our society but interpreting them in psychocultural terms immediately obscures the real issues such as poverty and unemployment in the midst of affluence, racism, sexism and environmental assault. These are tough issues requiring tough-minded and rational solutions as well as unswerving commitment to equality and human fraternity. We do not solve them by idle talk about "the twilight of authority" or by searching for largely fanciful roots.

Ethnicity: an ethnic mentality
(c) obscures common human heritage
(d) supports concept of inequality

Ethnicity emphasizes the trivialities that distinguish us and obscures the overwhelming reality of our common genetic and human heritages as well as our common needs and hopes. By emphasizing differences, ethnicity lends itself to the conservative belief in the inevitability of inequality. It is no accident that the neoconservative thinkers have all hailed the revival.

Once again the vicious dogma "separate but equal" has resurfaced; only now it is phrased in the pseudoliberal language of pluralism—we are plural but equal—and, even more tragically, it now has the sanction of misguided leaders and intellectuals of the very groups that hardly a few decades ago were savagely repressed and segregated in the name of this dogma.

(6) Ethnic revival is anti-individualistic; promotes conformism

Profoundly anti-American in its anti-individualism, the ethnic revival celebrates diversity, not however of individuals but of the groups to which they belong. It is a sociological truism that the more cohesive an ethnic group, the more conformist or the more anti-individualistic are its members. Thus the call for a diversity of cohesive, tightly knit groups actually amounts to an assault on the deeply entrenched principle of individualism.

Ideology of ethnic pluralism is dangerous – shows parallels to fascist movement

The fact that the ethnic revival is largely ideological should not lead us to underestimate it. We know from the history of ethnic movements that ideology, under the right circumstances, can transform reality. European fascism was first and foremost an ideological movement, and, in a disturbing parallel with modern America, fascist ideology had its roots in the romantic revolt against the enlightenment—a revolt that, in its early phases, was generally liberal, very concerned with the social and human costs of "progress," and espoused the principle of ethnic pluralism.

Conclusion
all humanists should support constitutional ideal of equality

The time has come when all genuine humanists who cherish the great ideal of the Constitution—that all human beings are created equal—must awake from their slumber and meet head on the challenge of the chauvinists.

At this point, several questions, perhaps even several challenges, to Orlando Patterson's argument may have arisen, but the first step in critical reading is to make sure we have objectively and fairly comprehended the author's ideas. We must suspend for the moment our questions and criticism. Now is the time for jotting down notes or summarizing the essay as a whole.

Here is how you might write a brief summary.

> Orlando Patterson, in his essay "Hidden Dangers in the Ethnic Revival," argues that an emphasis upon ethnic pluralism is a retreat from the constitutional ideal of equality, "both reactionary and socially explosive." He contends that early ethnic groups were transitory. Today's revival of ethnicity comes from an alliance of conservative demagogues and disenchanted liberal intellectuals. Patterson contends that the decline of interest in things ethnic is actually the most important factor in an ethnic revival, although it was the climax of the black civil rights movement that brought about what he calls the acceptance of "ethnic chauvinism," which was then turned against blacks. Patterson asserts that ethnicity is "socially divisive": it obscures our common human heritage, is used by conservatives to support their belief in inequality, celebrates group conformity, and it is anti-individualistic. He sees many parallels to the ideological rise of fascism which, among other similarities, also supported ethnic plurality. Finally, he calls for humanists to support the constitutional ideal of equality.

Now we are ready to analyze the content. Analysis is a process of dividing the essay into its major parts, questioning each part for its logic and validity, and then evaluating the relationship of the parts to the whole. Here are the types of questions you would want to ask about Orlando Patterson's arguments. (Do not confuse this stage with the writing stage—that will come later.)

Major Point 1: How did early ethnic groups actually aid assimilation? Is there statistical evidence to support Patterson's contention that a majority of blacks and other minorities want to be assimilated?

Major Point 2: Is there any support for the assertion that the ethnic revival is an ideological movement? Does Patterson resort to name calling when he uses such terms as "alienated intellectuals" and "conservative demagogues"? And who, specifically, are these people? Patterson compares the belief in ethnic *ideas* with the belief in the *idea* of religion. Is this a good analogy? What is he getting at?

Major Point 3: Isn't Patterson appealing to emotion when he speaks of "ordinary decent men and women" as having other things on their mind? If he is, does that in itself invalidate the argument that it is the *behavioral* decline in ethnic matters that caused the *ideological* rise?

Major Point 4: Patterson observes that "ethnic chauvinism" was accepted as a means to "psycho-social liberation." Why all the big words? Is this a resort to jargon just to make us think his argument is highly intelligent, or is there some justification for his use of such terms? How effective is the analogy about the viper biting its own tail? What are the connotations of the analogy? Whom are they aimed at?

Major Point 5: The movement toward Patterson's main thesis—that ethnic pluralism lends support to conservatives who believe in the "inevitability of inequality"—seems to begin in these three paragraphs. Trace each step in the argument here. Is it well made? Are there gaps? How can these so-called conservatives make the leap from "differences" to "unequal"?

Major Point 6: Are the phrases "profoundly anti-American" and the later analogy to fascism meant to be factually descriptive, are they appeals to emotions, or both?

Conclusion: The concluding sentence refers directly back to point 5, where Patterson stated, "By emphasizing differences, ethnicity lends itself to the conservative belief in the inevitability of inequality." But if conservatives do indeed believe in inequality, is it the same kind of inequality the Constitution was designed to overcome? Is it possible that two kinds of "equality" or "inequality" are being blurred here into a single point? And if they are, can an argument still have a probable truth even if there is a flaw in the method of arriving at the conclusion?

No analysis is complete at this point. You must still consider your emotional relationship to the argument as well as to the author and the historical context. Some of Patterson's ideas may seem convincing; some may seem illogical. They may even anger you. But to what extent are your feelings the result of your biases or of the cultural assumptions of your particular generation? Can reasons be found outside the reading itself that might help us to judge more temperately the overall worth of Patterson's argument?

That it was originally published in *The New York Times* may help establish part of the context. The *Times* is one of the world's major newspapers, read by both liberal and conservative intellectuals, but usually considered to have a strong liberal slant. Many of Patterson's contentions would oppose the beliefs of liberal readers. He may be arguing that they are unwittingly playing into the hands of neoconservatives. But the timing is also important. The ever-increasing demands of various ethnic groups, religious groups, and other marginal movements, all demanding recognition and "rights" (often supported by professors at distinguished universities) may have convinced Patterson that a heightened, even emotional, rhetoric was needed to combat the swell of opinion.

But who is Patterson? The newspaper indicates, in a small box at the end of the essay, that he teaches sociology at Harvard. A quick check in the social and behavioral science volume of *American Men and Women of Science* (available in most libraries) gives us more information. Patterson was born in Jamaica and received a Ph.D. in sociology at the London School of Economics. He has held several postdoctoral fellowships and served as consultant both to the World Bank and to the prime minister of Jamaica. More importantly, his field of study is social change, and he has published widely on slavery and its social effects. Clearly, we're dealing with an expert on the subject, but one who disagrees with the trends of his time and with many other experts in the same field.

Having now considered the man and the historical context, having accounted for our prejudices, if any, and having scrutinized each part of the essay for logic and evidence, we can feel reasonably confident that an overall assessment can be made: What are the strong and weak points? Where is Patterson's argument most convincing? Where does this argument appear to fail and why? What is the ultimate value and worth of the essay in terms of the ideas it offers for consideration?

The critical voice is sometimes mistaken as a negative voice. Actually, to be critical means to discriminate with exactness. Hence a critical analysis must discriminate between good and bad. It praises as well as condemns. If we are exacting, we will usually discover that an author is seldom wholly right or wholly wrong. We will not slant our judgment to one side or the other, but toward fair and balanced understanding. The conclusion of a critical analysis should assess the work in its fullness.

By its nature the critical reading process is slow and methodical. It takes effort and self-discipline. But when objectivity is maintained, the close scrutiny of detail pursued, and relationships evaluated, it can lead to insight that is balanced, rewarding, and reasonable.

Exercises

1. Consider the following editorial that appeared in a college newspaper. In what ways are the arguments logical? Illogical? Does the author appeal to reason or emotion to support his or her position?

Alcohol Laws Won't Achieve Goal

Underdog Productions is sponsoring another dance in the Highsmith Center this weekend. This time, it's Sleaze Factor, a well-known band which has played in many regional cities. UP is doing a good job—the word has it that they're pretty good—but if the turnout Friday night is anything like the "droves" who mobbed the Highsmith Center during the first dance this semester, they'd better plan to hold the next one in the gym.

Some have said one reason that first dance was a flop is because of the new alcohol laws. Of course, no one officially maintains that point of view, but given the facts, it's a logical conclusion.

By practically banning alcohol consumption on campus, the state has effectively closed off what was once a relatively safe way to party.

Forbidding someone under 21 to drink is a crock, anyway. An 18-year-old can get married, drive a car, cast a vote to help choose our leaders, beat up on his/her spouse, go to jail, be sent to Afghanistan to fight and possibly die—all before he/she is 21 and legally able to buy a beer. Talk about a paradox.

In our opinion, the new law will make little difference in the long run. About the only end outlawing booze in the 1920s accomplished was making a select group of daring Mafia-type bootleggers very wealthy. Then, as now however, it was a handy hook for hapless politicians to grab.

Meanwhile, maybe Sleaze Factor will give UNCA students a chance to rock the Highsmith Center, even if cracking open a Bud Light is now illegal.

2. Study the following paper written by a first-year student in a political science course. Because the essay was written in class, no opportunity was available for bringing in concrete evidence. Analyze it only for the logic and soundness of the argument.

We owe allegiance to the state, namely the United States of America, because we live here. We are part of the country. People can choose where they want to live and we have chosen to live here. The nation protects each person's individual liberties and thus demands certain duties from its people. Everyone has human rights—freedom of speech, religion, and the press. We can choose what area we want to live in and how we want to live our life. The list goes on and on. As our country gives us so much, we should be loyal to it.

In past years, many times when war was announced, that was it. A person's responsibility was now to the state and no one could take time to do what they wanted unless, of course, it was for the good of the war. When farmers fought during the war, their responsibility was often to themselves as well as to the state. They worked the land and it was theirs. The land was their life. They fought to protect it and to keep it free. People were impassioned during these wars to fight with all they had, in hopes that future generations would be free. It was an honor to go into battle and something that men and boys often looked forward to. There wasn't much of a question whether or not a person would go to war at that time, like there was during the Vietnam War—it was a person's privilege and responsibility.

Responsibilities that are greater than our responsibilities to the state are to yourself, your family and friends and your religion. You have to think of yourself because if you don't, no one else will. If you don't save yourself, you won't be any good to yourself or to anyone else. If your family and friends were killed, and you could have helped prevent it but didn't, what good would it be to be free? What would be the use of winning a war if you had nothing to live for?

A country grants each person certain civic rights that he possesses from the day he is born. It offers its citizens protection when they are away from it and privileges when they are at home. In turn, each citizen owes allegiance to his country. It is his duty to support his government, obey its laws, and defend his country.

Practice

Use your journal to record reactions to your reading. Write whatever is important to you. Be honest. Record interesting facts, quotations, observations. Ask questions and attempt to answer them even if you find yourself stumbling around. Make maps, lists, webs, anything that involves you with the work and leads to a clearer understanding. Writing about your reading helps you absorb ideas.

In addition to keeping you alert as you read, recording your responses helps you remember. As you write, you begin the act of selecting; patterns emerge and fresh insights surface. Your reactions are sharpened and preserved.

Look up definitions for words you don't know. (In addition to some thirty-two-odd journals kept during his lifetime, Walt Whitman filled fifteen notebooks with words and definitions he wanted to remember.) If you are confused about a particularly difficult reading, talk your thoughts to the paper until your thinking clarifies. Copy passages that are difficult to understand. Sometimes what begins as confusion turns into startling insights. You may write pages of seemingly worthless meanderings before you experience the kind of illumination that becomes its own reward for all this effort—to see and understand for yourself just what it is you think and feel. You may also find that when it comes time to write a paper, you'll have much of your work already completed.

CHAPTER 27

The Structure of Analysis and Argumentation

Some of your best arguments probably take place in the residence hall or sorority house late at night. You may enjoy a good debate. You may like finding flaws in your opponent's logic and the emotional heat that begins to build. You may find yourself holding opinions on numerous topics you've never investigated with any thoroughness. Perhaps you feel strongly about Democrats, vegetarianism, or abortion. And based on opinions formed by family and friends, you may even come up with a decent, rational argument.

But almost all formal argument in college requires a more detached, reflective attitude, and most of the time it emerges from your careful reading rather than from oral debate. Your skill at analyzing and evaluating someone else's writing, as well as your ability to organize your counterargument, becomes an essential ingredient of the education process. That's because the world of scholarship is a print-centered culture. We trust the written word more than the spoken word, if for no other reason than because we can reflect upon a printed argument with more cool deliberation. We can consider the very points of reasoning and evidence I've been talking about in previous chapters. We can more easily detect appeals to emotion or other fallacies. In turn, we write out our critiques and rebuttals for the same reason. The act of writing clarifies our thoughts and our argument for ourselves. And it gives others the chance to test our words and ideas against the highest standards. Written argument is thus a type of dialogue, an engagement of ideas between writer and reader, and if you write back, between reader and writer.

A good argument, of the type I'm describing here, requires both a good analysis and a thoughtful presentation of evidence and logic. To accomplish that, readers may expect you to follow a rather traditional form that has proven successful since Aristotle first began his studies on rhetoric. I'm going to describe that organization here, and it may well sound as if I've fallen into my own trap: naming the ten elements of beauty or whatever. But there are no rules, only method. A conventional form is not like a glass bottle into which you pour the milk of your observations. It's more like a dance step. At first you may feel as if you're being asked to follow cut-out footprints pasted on the floor. Your movements may seem awkward. You may feel inhibited. But with practice and experience you'll find that organization is merely a mental guideline. You may continue to follow it mechanically and dully, or you may bring to it your own spirit and liveliness, investing it with style, grace, and originality.

The Formal Introduction

In Chapter 26 you needed an objective understanding of the essay by Orlando Patterson before you could analyze it. So, too, does your reader need an objective overview of a subject before you plunge into finer points of argument. A formal introduction usually includes three elements.

Name of Author and Work

Give the full name of the author and the essay or book you plan to discuss. (You'd be surprised at how many inexperienced writers forget to do this.)

- Orlando Patterson, in his essay "Hidden Dangers in the Ethnic Revival," argues that . . .
- According to Sandy Crawford's "The Bashing of Michael Jackson" (*Harper's*, May 2001), contemporary attitudes toward public figures have turned away from . . .
- Martin Luther King's "Letter from Birmingham Jail" (April 16, 1963) is a major document explaining the nonviolent philosophy behind King's campaign for . . .

Each of these examples identifies author and title, then leads the reader toward the next step.

Characterization of the Whole

Although your audience may have read the work you are analyzing, you should not expect others to have memorized it or to have studied it as closely as you. You'll want to provide a brief summary of the article or book in its historical context. Knowledge about the author and his or her qualifications to speak—or about the cultural era out of which the work arose—can sometimes contribute to a general understanding. You may even want to note briefly the publishing history of a work if it is especially interesting or perhaps the reaction of critics when the work first appeared.

The summary itself is most important. No matter what your ultimate judgment is, give fair hearing to the author at this point. Present his or her ideas accurately and without bias. As briefly as possible, give at least the basic theme and the author's conclusion. If the work is long and complicated, you may want to go into more detail and review some of the major points as well.

This combination of historical context and brief summary is common courtesy to the reader. It provides us with a context in which to follow your more detailed analysis. Here is how sophomore Ann Max introduced her subject, using a rather full characterization.

Identification of author and her credentials	Ellen Harris is a freelance journalist and reviewer for such major publications as the *New Yorker* and the *New York Review of Books.* She recently attacked
Overview of author's argument	the conventional understanding of the consumer as a victim of the sellers and the advertisers.
Title and source of publication	In "Women and the Myth of Consumerism," first published in *Advance,* Harris argues that the theory of the advertisers using depth psychology to
Summary of the essay	convince women to buy a product is not only a false theory, but one that confuses cause and effect. The true purpose behind advertising, she claims, is merely capitalistic exploitation, which she finds
Basic theme	normal and inoffensive in a capitalist society today. What does disturb her is that advertising creates images that reflect "women as they are forced by
Judgment (must be supported later)	men in a sexist society to behave." But her presentation is marred by an angry, bitter tone in the essay. *Advance* was a semirevolutionary magazine that grew out of the cultural upheaval after Vietnam.
Historical context	Harris obviously assumed that her readers already held anticapitalist, antisexist, anti-just-about-
Focusing thesis	everything attitudes. The result is interesting but contains serious oversimplifications and unsupported assumptions.

Ann Max has taken the time to find out about both the author and the magazine in which the author published. Ann then summarizes the basic thesis, and moves toward a focusing statement that indicates how she plans to critique the work.

The Focusing (or Thesis) Sentence

If you plan to analyze an entire essay, you must first focus on how you propose to do it. If the subject is too complex to analyze the whole, then the focusing sentence should indicate how you've narrowed your subject. The reader also needs to move from the general overview of the work to the more specific argument you plan to make in your paper.

- Virginia Smith's essay is logical and effectively argued, but she fails to account for a great number of scientific studies that provide evidence on the other side of the issue. For example . . .
- Professor Harris' thesis is flawed by several dramatic breakdowns in clear reasoning. First . . .
- John Binder's book is especially important to the young person seeking direction and meaning to life. Perhaps his most important point is . . .

You might think of a formal introduction as following the same pattern used in the panoramic scene (described in Chapter 9). Begin with a broad overview that provides a general background; then move in closer, looking at major details—the theme and the conclusion; and finally, focus in (or narrow the subject) on the elements you find most important for analysis or argument.

Analysis and Argument

Much of your paper should present a detailed analysis of the single theme or major components of the work you have focused on.

1. *Describe* the specific portion of the work you plan to deal with. Your formal introduction gives only an overview. Here we need details. What is the major point the author is making? Use your own words to summarize. Back up your summary with a short but significant quotation.
2. *Analyze* the idea for its logic, evidence, soundness, and relationship to other ideas.
3. *Interpret* your findings. Argue the soundness of the reasoning, or offer a counterargument with clear reasoning of your own.

Do not assume that your paper must follow the sequential organization of the original essay. Do not assume that you should discuss every argument in the original. In Chapter 26, I found six major elements in Orlando Patterson's essay on ethnic revival. For the sake of understanding Patterson's logic, I needed to question each point in my mind. But I would not want to write on each point. As in any other paper, the subject must be narrowed and only the most significant elements discussed. A formal critique on "Hidden Dangers in the Ethnic Revival" might focus on only one or two of Patterson's concepts. Your analysis will almost always seem more effective if you go into detail on a single but significant theme rather than attempt to discuss each phase of the original.

However, for each theme or argument that you do discuss, repeat the three steps listed here: *describe, analyze, interpret.* Be sure to include quotations and examples from the work itself to make your paper as concrete as possible—that is, to provide evidence that supports your own analysis. Here is an excerpt from first-year student Tony Ludlum's critique of a single portion of John Locke's "Second Treatise of Civil Government." In a brief introduction, Tony narrows his subject to the section of Locke's argument that deals with establishment of government. Then he begins the body of his essay.

Description of the author's major point

After proposing that the natural condition of man is one of freedom and equality, Locke argues that freedom is limited by the "law of Nature" which is, as he defines it, "reason." This law teaches us that our liberty is not absolute. We may not, for example, kill or steal, unless it is to punish an offender of this law of Nature.

For the law of Nature would, as all other laws that concern men in this world, be in vain if there were nobody that in the state of Nature had a power to execute that law. . . . Locke then decides that in the perfect state of Nature, since all are equal, each of us has the right to prosecute the law, although punishment too must be guided by reason. Locke concludes this portion of his essay by saying that it is not his intention to describe the "particulars of the law of Nature" but "it is certain there is such a law," one that is clearly understandable to rational creatures.

Student integrates summary in his own words with selected quotations from the author

But is there? Apparently reasonable men in the eighteenth century believed there was. The Declaration of Independence mentions the same phrase. If a whole culture believed something to be true, maybe you can get away with such a statement so that there is not any need to go into detail or define it. But even if for the time being we suspend our twentieth-century doubts and accept such a law, how can it be so clear that Nature's law is reasonable? Or that it is so reasonable that it can be clearly "executed" by men even when it is not defined? However, Locke doesn't claim that the law is reasonable. He claims that the law *is* reason. I guess my problem with this is that I end up going in a circle: the law of nature is certain, the law is reason; if we are

Analysis begins by questioning—in this case, student focuses on a key term

Student recognizes that historical factors may influence even reasoned belief

Student focuses on logical relationships in author's argument

Challenge to author's logic

> reasonable we will understand the law; if we are not reasonable we will supposedly not understand it nor even know that it is certain. Locke's use of the term cleverly says, in effect, if you believe me and accept what I say, you are a reasonable man, but if you don't accept what I say, or doubt my "certainty," you are unreasonable. Also, since the rest of his argument in the essay depends upon this one concept, the reader is placed in a bind. Believe and you will be saved. Don't believe and you are not worth saving. For a reasonable man, this sounds like a strangely unreasonable argument.

Refutation and Rebuttal

A major element of the argumentative essay is the anticipation of those arguments or challenges that might be thrown back at you. By answering them in advance, you take away from your reader the opportunity for criticism. You also add further persuasion and force to your work by showing how thoughtful and careful you've been in building your argument. It suggests you have an informed perspective, a balanced rational view, which in itself gives additional force to your other contentions. Even if you can't absolve yourself of some inconsistency or potential flaw in your argument, it remains better to show your good faith and to admit it.

Here's how Greg Knopke, a business major, handled this part of his paper on economic losses caused by auto imports. (Greg has been arguing that because 175,000 jobs may be lost due to imports and robotics, government intervention and legislation are required.)

First refutation given fair hearing

Student's rebuttal

> True, the purest form of capitalism would lead us to the conclusion that competition ought to be allowed full reign and that those companies which are less efficient should be allowed a peaceful death. All those unemployed workers will eventually find other jobs in areas where America is more competitive. So the argument goes. But what we are hearing here is only partly true. Seventy-five thousand unemployed are not the only ones affected. For every worker in the auto industry who loses his job, *Business Week* (March 2000) estimates that three others in subsidiary industry or in small business indirectly supported by those workers will also lose their jobs. And that army

of 300,000 will require unemployment benefits which you and I will pay. There will also be a loss of local, state, and federal taxes which will cause retrenchment in everything from schools to road repair. The social cost is too great to adhere to free-market capitalism for its own sake.

Second refutation

Finally, one could also argue that government intervention is only a short-term solution, that it will merely forestall an eventual collapse of the auto industry. And that the government will be required to pour more and more subsidy, more and more tax dollars, into a lost cause. This is the strongest argument against my own position. And I would say it will prove to be true unless the government also initiates a limited partnership with the auto industry to insure that the subsidy is contingent upon modernization and gradual retraining of workers. The truth is that my argument for intervention is doomed to failure without this additional commitment.

Admission that argument has truth to it

Student's rebuttal

Conclusions

Conclusions are sometimes difficult to generalize on, for every good conclusion flows naturally from the evidence or argument presented in the body of the paper. But several important points about the conclusion to a formal analysis can be made. Analysis is meaningful only when the parts are joined together again with the whole. To have looked in detail at a single theme or even at each major argument is not enough. You must show your reader how it all relates to the whole.

Do the parts depend on rational arguments? On emotion or unclear thinking? On a historical or cultural value? Where is the work sound and meaningful? Where is it less effective?

As I noted earlier, the point of critical analysis is not to attack everything you read with a negative voice. The goal is to discriminate between that which is valuable and that which is not and then to persuade the reader to accept your reasoning. Although the examples I've given in this chapter have focused on weaknesses, a good critical argument may focus on strengths to which you add your own voice.

Finally, it is equally important that you take care not to allow your conclusion to reflect a personal bias, stereotype, or emotional argument of your own. Judgment must be based on reason and on critical thinking, not on personal opinions, such as "I don't like this book on cats because I don't like cats."

Here is how we might informally outline the structure of analysis and argument.

Introduction

- Name of author and work
- General overview of the subject, historical background, or summary of the argument
- Thesis (your position, focused and narrowed)

Evidence

- Objective description of major point
- Detailed analysis of logic and relationships
- Interpretation followed by supportive argument or counterargument
- Repetition of description, analysis, and interpretation if more than one major concept is covered
- Refutation and rebuttal

Conclusion

- Overall summary of findings
- Relationship of findings to the subject as a whole
- Critical assessment of the value, worth, or meaning of your findings, both negative and positive

Critical analysis does not guarantee you will discover the truth. Yet it can provide the concrete evidence that permits you to demonstrate (to *show*) you have used logical reasoning to arrive at a conclusion. Should your reasoning be faulty, the process also allows someone else to pinpoint precisely where you have erred. Thus, analysis and argument is a method that permits verification by a second observer. In that sense, both you and the reader can feel more confident about the probable truths revealed by the process.

Writing the First Draft

Did Tony Ludlum or Ann Max write a successful analysis in their first draft? The answer is simply no. For almost all of us, drafting remains a time of exploration, a time of crossing out and starting over. As E. M. Forster once said, "How do I know what I think until I see what I say?"

By studying the subject and taking notes before you begin to write (as described in Chapter 26) and by using the guideline described here as "the traditional structure of analysis and argument," you might make your first draft flow more simply and clearly than if you plunge in without preconceived direction. But for some students, obsessive concern with form will actually block ideas. The form must be thought of as a guideline only, not a God-given standard. Your personal experience with the subject, filtered now through reason, must still be the main focus as you face the blank page. You must be willing to follow new ideas as they occur, not force ideas to fit the form. Write the first draft as quickly as possible, absorbed in the subject. Use the form in the rewriting phase as a check against what you have written. For example, you may find you have failed to describe certain parts of the essay before you analyzed the detailed points. The formal guideline should remind you that your reader needs that description. Go back and work it in. In other words, use the drafting stage as you have in the past—to experiment and explore. Use the formal guideline to clarify and organize, either before or after the drafting, depending on your personal needs. But do use it because the audience for critical writing will expect a clear and logical form.

Readings

Sexual Harassment and Sexual Politics

Catharine MacKinnon

Catharine MacKinnon has been one of the leading activists in providing legal remedies for women from the harms of sexual harassment and from pornography. A Yale Law School graduate, she has taught at Yale, Harvard, Stanford, and Osgoode Hull (Canada). She is Professor of Law at the University of Michigan and the University of Chicago. The following excerpt is taken from *Feminism Unmodified: Discourse on Life and Law.* (Numerous footnotes supporting MacKinnon's argument have been omitted.)

The legal claim for sexual harassment marks the first time in history, to my knowledge, that women have defined women's injuries in a law. Consider what has happened with rape. We have never defined the injury of rape; men define it. The men who define it, define what they take to be this violation of women according to, among other things, what they think they don't do. In this way rape becomes an act of a stranger (they mean Black) committed upon a woman (white) whom he has never seen before. Most rapes are intraracial and are committed by men the women know. Ask a woman if she has ever been raped, and often she says, "Well . . . not really." In that silence between the well and the not really, she just measured what happened to her against every rape case she ever heard about and decided she would lose in court. Especially when you are part of a subordinated group, your own definition of your injuries is powerfully shaped by your assessment of whether you could get anyone to do anything about it, including anything official. You are realistic by necessity, and the voice of law is the voice in power. When the design of a legal wrong does not fit the wrong as it happens to you, as is the case with rape, that law can undermine your social and political as well as legal legitimacy in saying that what happened was an injury at all—even to yourself.

It is never too soon to worry about this, but it may be too soon to know whether the law against sexual harassment will be taken away from us or turn into nothing or turn ugly in our hands. The fact is, this law is working surprisingly well for women by any standards, particularly when compared with the rest of sex discrimination law. If the question is whether a law designed from women's standpoint and administered through this legal system can do anything for women—which always seems to be a good question—this experience so far gives a qualified and limited yes.

It is hard to unthink what you know, but there was a time when the facts that amount to sexual harassment did not amount to sexual harassment. It is a bit like the injuries of pornography until recently. The facts amounting to the harm did not socially "exist," had no shape, no cognitive coherence; far less did they state a legal claim. It just happened to you. To the women to whom it happened, it wasn't part of anything, much less something big or shared like gender. It fit no known pattern. It was neither a regularity nor an irregularity. Even social scientists didn't study it, and they study anything that moves. When law recognized sexual harassment as a practice of sex discrimination, it moved it from the realm of "and then he . . . and then he . . . ," the primitive language in which sexual abuse lives inside a woman, into an experience with a form, an etiology, a cumulativeness—as well as a club.

The shape, the positioning, and the club—each is equally critical politically. Once it became possible to do something about sexual harassment, it became possible to know more about it, because it became possible for its victims to speak about it. Now we know, as we did not when it first became illegal, that this problem is commonplace. We know this not just because it has to be true, but as documented fact. Between a quarter and a third of women in the federal workforce report having been sexually harassed, many physically, at least once in the last two years. Projected, that becomes 85 percent of all women at some point in their working lives. This figure is based on asking women "Have you ever been sexually harassed?"—the conclusion—not "has this fact happened? has that fact happened?" which usually produces more. The figures for sexual harassment of students are comparable.

When faced with individual incidents of sexual harassment, the legal system's first question was, is it a personal episode? Legally, this was a way the courts inquired into whether the incidents were based on sex, as they had to be to be sex discrimination. Politically, it was a move to isolate victims by stigmatizing them as deviant. It also seemed odd to me that a relationship was either personal or gendered, meaning that one is not a woman personally. Statistical frequency alone does not make an event not personal, of course, but the presumption that sexual pressure in contexts of unequal power is an isolated idiosyncrasy to unique individual victims has been undermined both by the numbers and by their division by gender. Overwhelmingly, it is men who sexually harass women, a lot of them. Actually, it is even more accurate to say that men do this than to say that women have this done to them. This is a description of the perpetrators' behavior, not of the statisticians' feminism.

Sexual harassment has also emerged as a creature of hierarchy. It inhabits what I call hierarchies among men: arrangements in which some men are below other men, as in employer/employee and teacher/student. In workplaces, sexual harassment by supervisors of subordinates is common; in education, by administrators of lower-level administrators, by faculty of students. But it also happens among coworkers, from third parties, even by subordinates in the workplace, men who are women's hierarchical inferiors or peers. Basically, it is done by men to women regardless of relative position on the formal hierarchy. I believe that the reason sexual harassment was first established as an injury of the systematic abuse of power in hierarchies among men is that this is power men recognize. They comprehend from personal experience that something is held over your head if you do not comply. The lateral or reverse hierarchical examples suggest something beyond this, something men don't understand from personal experience because they take its advantages for granted: Gender is also a hierarchy. The courts do not use this analysis, but some act as though they understand it.

Sex discrimination law had to adjust a bit to accommodate the realities of sexual harassment. Like many other injuries of gender, it wasn't written for this. For something to be based on gender in the legal sense means it happens to a woman as a woman, not as an individual. Membership in a gender is understood as the opposite of, rather than part of, individuality. Clearly, sexual harassment is one of the last situations in which a woman is treated without regard to her sex; it is because of her sex that it happens. But the social meaning attributed to women as a class, in which women are defined as gender female by sexual accessibility to men, is not what courts have considered before when they have determined whether a given incident occurred because of sex.

Sex discrimination law typically conceives that something happens because of sex when it happens to one sex but not the other. The initial procedure is arithmetic: Draw a gender line and count how many of each are on each side in the context at issue, or, alternatively, take the line drawn by the practice or policy and see if it also divides the sexes. One by-product of this head-counting method is what I call the bisexual defense. Say a man is accused of sexually harassing a woman. He can argue that the harassment is not sex-based because he harasses both sexes equally, indiscriminately as it were. Originally it was argued that sexual harassment was not a proper gender claim because someone could harass both sexes. We argued that this was an issue of fact to be pleaded and proven, an issue of did he do this, rather than an issue of law, of whether he could have. The courts accepted that, creating this kamikaze defense. To my knowledge, no one has used the bisexual defense since. As this example suggests, head counting can provide a quick topography of the terrain, but it has proved too blunt to distinguish treatment whose meaning is based on gender from treatment that has other social hermeneutics, especially when only two individuals are involved.

Once sexual harassment was established as bigger than personal, the courts' next legal question was whether it was smaller than biological. To say that sexual harassment was biological seemed to me a very negative thing to say about men, but defendants seemed to think it precluded liability. Plaintiffs argued that sexual harassment is not biological in that men who don't do it have nothing wrong with their testosterone levels. Besides, if murder were found to have biological correlates, it would still be a crime. Thus, although the question purported to be whether the acts were based on sex, the implicit issue seemed to be whether the source of the impetus for doing the acts was relevant to their harmfulness.

Similarly structured was the charge that women who resented sexual harassment were oversensitive. Not that the acts did not occur, but rather that it was unreasonable to experience them as harmful. Such a harm would be based not on sex but on individual hysteria. Again shifting the inquiry away from whether the acts are based on sex in the guise of pursuing it, away from whether they occurred to whether it should matter if they did, the question became whether the acts were properly harmful. Only this time it was not the perpetrator's drives that made him not liable but the target's sensitivity that made the acts not a harm at all. It was pointed out that too many people are victimized by sexual harassment to consider them all hysterics. Besides, in other individual injury law, victims are not blamed; perpetrators are required to take victims as they find them, so long as they are not supposed to be doing what they are doing.

◆ ◆ ◆

The question seems to be whether a woman is valuable enough to hurt, so that what is done to her is a harm. Once a woman has had sex, voluntarily or by force—it doesn't matter—she is regarded as too damaged to be further damageable, or something. Many women who have been raped in the course of sexual harassment have been advised by their lawyers not to mention the rape because it would destroy their credibility! The fact that abuse is long term has suggested to some finders of fact that it must have been tolerated or even wanted, although sexual harassment that becomes a condition of work has also been established as a legal claim in its own right. I once was talking with a judge about a case he was sitting on in which Black teenage girls alleged that some procedures at their school violated their privacy. He told me that with their sexual habits they had no privacy to lose. It seemed he knew what their sexual habits were from evidence in the case, examples of the privacy violations.

◆ ◆ ◆

Most victims of sexual harassment, if the incidence data are correct, never file complaints. Many who are viciously violated are so ashamed to make that violation public that they submit in silence, although it devastates their self-respect and often their health, or they leave the job without complaint, although it threatens their survival and that of their families. If, on top of the cost of making the violation known, which is painful enough, they know that the entire range of their sexual experiences, attitudes, preferences, and practices are to be discoverable, few such actions will be brought, no matter how badly the victims are hurt. Faced with a choice between forced sex in their jobs or schools on the one hand and forced sexual disclosure for the public record on the other, few will choose the latter. This cruel paradox would effectively eliminate much progress in this area.

Put another way, part of the power held by perpetrators of sexual harassment is the threat of making the sexual abuse public knowledge. This functions like blackmail in silencing the victim and allowing the abuse to continue. It is a fact that public knowledge of sexual abuse is often worse for the abused than the abuser, and victims who choose to complain have the courage to take that on. To add to their burden the potential of making public their entire personal life, information that has no relation to the fact or severity of the incidents complained of, is to make the law of this area implicitly complicit in the blackmail that keeps victims from exercising their rights and to enhance the impunity of perpetrators. In effect, it means open season on anyone who does not want her entire intimate life available to public scrutiny. In other contexts such private information has been found intrusive, irrelevant, and more prejudicial than probative. To allow it to be discovered in the sexual harassment area amounts to a requirement that women be further violated in order to be permitted to seek relief for having been violated. I also will never understand why a violation's severity, or even its likelihood of occurrence, is measured according to the character of the violated, rather than by what was done to them.

It's a Jungle Out There

Camille Paglia

Camille Paglia is a nationally known campaigner against current trends in the feminist movement. The following essay is not a direct response to the preceding essay by Catharine MacKinnon, but to the general attitude that college-aged women must be protected—either by law, as MacKinnon argues, or by the college itself *in loco parentis* (in place of the parents). However, you might want to consider the differences between the emotional tone of MacKinnon and the tone Paglia uses. Which is more convincing? Which is more dangerous? Are there times when emotion, satire, scoffing might be more effective than an objective stance? Or does such a tone make it easier to discount the argument?

Rape is an outrage that cannot be tolerated in civilized society. Yet feminism, which has waged a crusade for rape to be taken more seriously, has put young women in danger by hiding the truth about sex from them.

In dramatizing the pervasiveness of rape, feminists have told young women that before they have sex with a man, they must give consent as explicit as a legal contract's. In this way, young women have been convinced that they have been the victims of rape. On elite campuses in the Northeast and on the West Coast, they have held consciousness-raising sessions, petitioned administrations, demanded inquests. At Brown University, outraged, panicky "victims" have scrawled the names of alleged attackers on the walls of women's rest rooms. What marital rape was to the '70s, "date rape" is to the '90s.

The incidence and seriousness of rape do not require this kind of exaggeration. Real acquaintance rape is nothing new. It has been a horrible problem for women for all of recorded history. Once fathers and brothers protected women from rape. Once the penalty for rape was death. I come from a fierce Italian tradition where, not so long ago in the motherland, a rapist would end up knifed, castrated, and hung out to dry.

But the old clans and small rural communities have broken down. In our cities, on our campuses far from home, young women are vulnerable and defenseless. Feminism has not prepared them for this. Feminism keeps saying the sexes are the same. It keeps telling women they can do anything, go anywhere, say anything, wear anything. No, they can't. Women will always be in sexual danger.

One of my male students recently slept overnight with a friend in a passageway of the Great Pyramid in Egypt. He described the moon and sand, the ancient silence and eerie echoes. I will never experience that. I am a woman. I am not stupid enough to believe I could ever be safe there. There is a world of solitary adventure I will never have. Women have always known these somber truths. But feminism, with its pie-in-the-sky fantasies about the perfect world, keeps young women from seeing life as it is.

We must remedy social injustice whenever we can. But there are some things we cannot change. There are sexual differences that are based in biology. Academic feminism is lost in a fog of social constructionism. It believes we are totally the product of our environment. This idea was invented by Rousseau. He was wrong. Emboldened by dumb French language theory, academic feminists repeat the same hollow slogans over and over to each other. Their view of sex is naive and prudish. Leaving sex to the feminists is like letting your dog vacation at the taxidermist's.

The sexes are at war. Men must struggle for identity against the overwhelming power of their mothers. Women have menstruation to tell them they are women. Men must do or risk something to be men. Men become masculine only when other men say they are. Having sex with a woman is one way a boy becomes a man.

College men are at their hormonal peak. They have just left their mothers and are questing for their male identity. In groups, they are dangerous. A woman going to a fraternity party is walking into Testosterone Flats, full of prickly cacti and blazing guns. If she goes, she should be armed with resolute alertness. She should arrive with girlfriends and leave with them. A girl who lets herself get dead drunk at a fraternity party is a fool. A girl who goes upstairs alone with a brother at a fraternity party is an idiot. Feminists call this "blaming the victim." I call it common sense.

For a decade, feminists have drilled their disciples to say, "Rape is a crime of violence but not of sex." This sugar-coated Shirley Temple nonsense has exposed young women to disaster. Misled by feminism, they do not expect rape from the nice boys from good homes who sit next to them in class.

Aggression and eroticism are deeply intertwined. Hunt, pursuit, and capture are biologically programmed into male sexuality. Generation after generation, men must be educated, refined, and ethically persuaded away from their tendency toward anarchy and brutishness. Society is not the enemy, as feminism ignorantly claims. Society is woman's protection against rape. Feminism, with its solemn Carry Nation repressiveness, does not see what is for men the eroticism or fun element in rape, especially the wild, infectious delirium of gang rape. Women who do not understand rape cannot defend themselves against it.

The date-rape controversy shows feminism hitting the wall of its own broken promises. The women of my '60s generation were the first respectable girls in history to swear like sailors, get drunk, stay out all night—in short, to act like men. We sought total sexual freedom and equality. But as time passed, we woke up to cold reality. The old double standard protected women. When anything goes, it's women who lose.

Today's young women don't know what they want. They see that feminism has not brought sexual happiness. The theatrics of public rage over date rape are their way of restoring the old sexual rules that were shattered by my generation. Because nothing about the sexes has really changed. The comic film *Where the Boys Are* (1960), the ultimate expression of '50s man-chasing, still speaks directly to our time. It shows smart, lively women skillfully anticipating and fending off the dozens of strategies with which horny men try to get them into bed. The agonizing date-rape subplot and climax are brilliantly done. The victim, Yvette Mimieux, makes mistake after mistake, obvious to the other girls. She allows herself to be lured away from her girlfriends and into isolation with boys whose character and intentions she misreads. *Where the Boys Are* tells the truth. It shows courtship as a dangerous game in which the signals are not verbal but subliminal.

Neither militant feminism, which is obsessed with politically correct language, nor academic feminism, which believes that knowledge and experience are "constituted by" language, can understand pre-verbal or non-verbal communication. Feminism, focusing on sexual politics, cannot see that sex exists in and through the body. Sexual desire and arousal cannot be fully translated into verbal terms. This is why men and women misunderstand each other.

Trying to remake the future, feminism cut itself off from sexual history. It discarded and suppressed the sexual myths of literature, art, and religion. Those myths show us the turbulence, the mysteries and passions of sex. In mythology we see men's sexual anxiety, their fear of women's dominance. Much sexual violence is rooted in men's sense of psychological weakness toward women. It takes many men to deal with one woman. Woman's voracity is a persistent motif. Clara Bow, it was rumored, took on the USC football team on weekends. Marilyn Monroe, singing "Diamonds Are a Girl's Best Friend," rules a conga line of men in tuxes. Half-clad Cher, in the video for "If I Could Turn Back Time," deranges a battleship of screaming sailors and straddles a pink-lit cannon. Feminism, coveting social power, is blind to woman's cosmic sexual power.

To understand rape, you must study the past. There never was and never will be sexual harmony. Every woman must take personal responsibility for her sexuality, which is nature's red flame. She must be prudent and cautious about where she goes and with whom. When she makes a mistake, she must accept the consequences and, through self-criticism, resolve never to make that mistake again. Running to Mommy and Daddy on the campus grievance committee is unworthy of strong women. Posting lists of guilty men in the toilet is cowardly, infantile stuff.

The Italian philosophy of life espouses high-energy confrontation. A male student makes a vulgar remark about your breasts? Don't slink off to whimper and simper with the campus shrinking violets. Deal with it. On the spot. Say, "Shut up, you jerk! And crawl back to the barnyard where you belong!" In general, women who project this take-charge attitude toward life get harassed less often. I see too many dopey, immature, self-pitying women walking around like melting sticks of butter. It's the Yvette Mimieux syndrome: Make me happy. And listen to me weep when I'm not.

The date-rape debate is already smothering in propaganda churned out by the expensive Northeastern colleges and universities, with their overconcentration of boring, uptight academic feminists and spoiled, affluent students. Beware of the deep manipulativeness of rich students who were neglected by their parents. They love to turn the campus into hysterical psychodramas of sexual transgression, followed by assertions of parental authority and concern. And don't look for sexual enlightenment from academe, which spews out mountains of books but never looks at life directly.

As a fan of football and rock music, I see in the simple, swaggering masculinity of the jock and in the noisy posturing of the heavy-metal guitarist certain fundamental, unchanging truths about sex. Masculinity is aggressive, unstable, combustible. It is also the most creative cultural force in history. Women must reorient themselves toward the elemental powers of sex, which can strengthen or destroy.

The only solution to date rape is female self-awareness and self-control. A woman's number one line of defense is herself. When a real rape occurs, she should report it to the police. Complaining to college committees because the courts "take too long" is ridiculous. College administrations are not a branch of the judiciary. They are not equipped or trained for legal inquiry. Colleges must alert incoming students to the problems and dangers of adulthood. Then colleges must stand back and get out of the sex game.

Join Hands Across the Divide of Faith

Cardinal Francis Arinze

The following essay is excerpted from a commencement address, delivered by Cardinal Francis Arinze at Wake Forest University in May, 1999. The cardinal was born in Nigeria and serves as president of the Pontifical Council for Interreligious Dialogue. Look carefully at the language the cardinal uses in his speech. Reflect on how it might appeal to our emotions as well as to our sense of reasoning. Consider also how the need for "definition" of concepts and ideas informs the whole of the essay.

There is not only one organized religion in the world. There are many. There are Christians and Muslims. There are Jews. But there are also Hindus, Buddhists, followers of traditional religions, Sikhs, Zoroastrians, and so on. Religious plurality is a fact.

Collaboration between the followers of the various religions is necessary both for theological and sociological reasons. Theologically, we consider that all human beings were created by the same God, they have the same human nature and, according to the Christian faith, they have all been redeemed by the same Savior, Jesus Christ.

Sociological reasons for interreligious collaboration come from considerations of joint promotion of the good of humanity and also of mutual enrichment. If citizens of the same country, for example, adhere to differing religions, it is better for them and their country that they accept and respect one another and that they join hands to seek solutions to major problems of their society.

Many problems and challenges do not respect religious frontiers. There is no Catholic hurricane or Baptist drought. There is no Jewish inflation or Muslim unemployment. There is no Buddhist drug addiction or Hindu AIDS.

Interreligious collaboration therefore calls on the followers of the various religions to join hands—for example, to defend the family and its positive values, to promote a society where the individual is appreciated, respected and cared for in case of need, to defend life in all its stages from conception right up to natural death, to tackle problems of unemployment, drug addiction and AIDS, and to defend religious freedom for citizens, not only in some countries but everywhere.

Religions are expected to contribute to a more just economic, social and political order. If the free play of market forces means that a few big companies stifle or snuff out the smaller industries, if an over-liberal economic and social system makes very acute the gap between rich and poor, so that a few over-rich people banquet every day as if in an oasis of opulence and enjoyment while others languish in a desert of misery, if the pitiless political system evolves into full-blown dictatorship that ridicules individual freedom, then the religions are definitely called upon to come all out and help to produce a solution.

The moral virtue of solidarity teaches us to share with others. Solidarity is interdependence accepted, loved and lived. And respect for the dignity of the human person means that democracy is no empty word, but that every citizen has the right, and the duty, of participation in public affairs, in ways to be worked out in each country and cultural area.

When, therefore, we talk of interreligious collaboration, we are referring to everyday needs and not to an elitist entertainment. When we say interreligious dialogue, we do not mean necessarily an international conference in which learned theologians and professors read their paper's 40 pages with 20-page bibliography. We need such professors, but most people are not of that level. They just want to interact at the level of daily life.

This plea for interreligious collaboration is not support for the foundation of more religions. We already have far too many. Nevertheless, much as it might be beautiful if there were only one religion, we should not deny any human being the exercise of the right to religious freedom, within due limits.

To argue in favor of interreligious collaboration, on the other hand, does not aim at depriving any religion of its identity. It is not an effort to persuade the various religions to cast their various beliefs, rites and moral codes into a melting pot for the brewing of a syncretistic product. We are not trying to make an omelet of the religions. Such a religion would be the religion of nobody. Meant to fit anybody, it could not offer anyone a dynamic and satisfactory philosophy of life, a clear enough road map. It would not stand anyone in good stead in a moment of great moral crisis.

Interreligious cooperation presumes that the participating believers belong each to a religion with clear self-identity. Such a genuine religion should be one that has clear beliefs, ritual and code of conduct. It should equip the believer with a unified view of life. It should present a vital synthesis of the details that make up a person's daily life.

We must not ignore the objection raised by some people who fear that in the seeking of harmony, religions may be part of the problem rather than part of the solution. Some even argue that along the corridors of history, religions have caused tension, violence and war. For them, discussion on interreligious collaboration is so much pious but unrealistic talk.

Let us begin by admitting that prejudices generated or occasioned by religions, and handed on from generation to generation, are not easy to discard. And de facto in history, and even at present, some people have alleged or tried to hijack religious considerations to justify or motivate tension, violence or even war.

But it must be asserted that every religion worthy of the name teaches the golden rule: Do unto others as you would have them do to you. Genuine religion is about love of God and consequent love of neighbor. "Anyone who says, 'I love God,' and hates his brother, is a liar," St. John tells us, "since a man who does not love the brother that he can see cannot love God, whom he has never seen."

The promotion of hatred, violence and war is the opposite of what true religion is all about. When a careful analysis is made of a particular case of tension, violence or war, it will be found that often considerations that are racial, political and economic have contributed to the disaster. There may also be the burden of history, unhealed memories of past injustices, real or merely perceived. Religion has sometimes been abused and exploited and blamed in order to hide these motivations and explain outbursts of violence, economically oppressive measures, massacres, so-called ethnic cleansings or other acts of injustice which fallen human nature is all too prone to perpetrate.

A true believer, on the other hand, is known by love of neighbor, readiness to admit guilt where there has been any, openness to reconciliation and positive promotion of solidarity between peoples, cultures and religions. Give us such people in large numbers, and our societies will be able to look to the future, to the forthcoming millennium, with a sense of renewed hope that greater harmony is not impossible.

Academia Goes to War

William Forstchen

William Forstchen has published several studies on the American Civil War, and over thirty novels. He holds a Ph.D. in nineteenth-century American military history. The following essay appeared in *The Asheville Tribune,* 2001. Identify the strengths and weaknesses of the argument. Consider especially the tone and how it might affect the reader. Would the essay have been stronger if Forstchen had argued his case more "objectively," or does the underlying emotion make the piece more persuasive?

America is geared up for war and where does academia fit in?

We who teach in the universities and colleges once had a proud tradition when our nation faced times of peril. It was the great intellectuals of this country who helped frame the moral and political arguments of our fight for Independence. During the Civil War, on both sides, entire university classes filled the ranks and college professors won undying glory for their heroism and self-sacrifice. In both World Wars campuses trained officers, did crucial research, and above all else were centers of intellectual support for our national effort.

So what about today?

The answer, in short . . . gutless silence, or worse, borderline treason.

It's the new tradition in American academia to demonstrate, at best, a cool disdain for military action and our government in times of military crisis, or to display outright hostility which quickly escalates to open hatred of America, its armed forces, and any who dare to voice support for that military effort.

I've heard a lot in the last month about the need to respect freedom of speech on college campuses, no matter how loathsome and heinous the statements, such as the barbaric spewings of women's studies professor Thobani from the University of British Columbia who, at a conference in Ottawa, expressed a fervent wish for our complete and utter defeat and received a standing ovation from her peers.

Freedom of Speech? Don't kid yourself, there is no such thing as freedom of speech in today's academic world. For thirty years college campuses have been dominated by a Leftist Thought Police that would have been the envy of McCarthy or Hitler. The wreckage left in its wake, careers terminated, careers which never were allowed to start, the damage inflicted upon our culture due to half-baked theories and outright lies is incalculable.

The system of faculty hiring, promotion, and tenure is tied, above all else, to never saying "the wrong thing," never displaying insensitivity to the politically correct doctrines and commandments, and never going against the herd of collective group think. Freedom of Speech is a river that moves in only one direction at most of our universities . . . downhill and to the left.

That is why our college campuses have been stunningly silent, why you have seen few if any news reports both locally and around the nation of organized student groups showing support, and why you have yet to see a single noted academic on television voicing strong support for military action against the viper nests of terrorism.

If he did, he would be hounded when he returned to his office, harassed by students following aging anti-war profs, smeared when it came time for tenure review, slammed with the indelible stink of being a racist, sexist, fascist, and dead ended in his career.

As a grad student a decade ago who dared to choose military history as a major I faced unending harassment from peers and faculty. I often said that if I could but change two words, military history to "gender studies," "feminist studies," or "racial studies" I could have sued and won half a hundred cases of harassment and sold a best selling book in the process exposing bias in our system. But then again, bias is never displayed against the conservatives, no we are getting what we deserve and freedom of speech doesn't apply to us.

You see as well the inane charade of anti-war and anti-American agitators crying out that college students will rally to the cause and somehow shape our national policy by their whining outcries. God forbid. It is a perverse logic which is yet another hangover myth from the Baby Boom generation. Sure, the kids are good at some mindless chants (which sound like recycled Vietnam era chants to me), but have you ever talked to a college freshman about the complexities of foreign policy in the Middle East, let alone where Afghanistan is on the map or what the Federalist Papers are all about.

No insult intended, I love the kids I teach, some of them display remarkable insight and brilliance, but they are still kids and they are in college to learn some facts, and to learn how to intelligently apply those facts, not to dictate national policy on the streets. To use them to advance cynical agendas is obscene. The indoctrination they receive at the hands of some alleged professors bears a semblance, in some ways, to the same type of indoctrination that Taliban clerics give to their youth . . . be self-righteous, hate anyone who disagrees, and silence all opposition.

For thirty years traditional views, traditional scholarship in academia, and above all else the true upholding of freedom of speech on college campuses has been dead. Isn't it time that at least a few professors got air time, a few stood up in the campus square and spoke out, a heroic few defied the cowardly silence, or outright anti-American propaganda and raised a challenge?

Who knows, it might even trigger a revolution long overdue, a return to balanced dialogue, a return to honest debate, a return to true academic excellence instead of the politically correct dribble that is cranked out in the quest for tenure . . . and it might even restore freedom of speech for real.

PART 7

Critiquing the Arts

Suggested Writing Projects

Ralph Waldo Emerson advised people to go into Nature and "read" it. By reading, Emerson meant paying concentrated, deliberate attention to detail, to the total experience in front of you—as well as to the emotional reaction inside you—from which you would then be able to interpret a meaning. Yet nature is ambiguous. It offers multiple "readings" because it provides multiple experiences. In the same way, all major art forms are ambiguous, often subtle and self-contradictory. How do you "read" a painting? How do you "read" a symphony? Or even a short story?

When we read and analyze a written argument, we usually confront an author who has attempted to make clear, logical points. If we can identify the points accurately, and fairly objectively, we can trace the logic, evaluate the conclusion, and reach a judgment. But a poet expresses feelings, not logic. A dancer shapes his or her body to sound and rhythm, not to abstract ideas. A sculptor usually wants to move you with an image, not convince you of an argument. Because art is almost always suggestive or symbolic rather than literal, it raises the level of intellectual challenge. You can no longer adopt an "objective stance" because the emotion you feel is central to the artistic effort.

The study of art, then, requires even more heightened attention, alertness, and questioning. When we study art, we bring our critical skills to the total life experience. We learn how to read with intense closeness; we learn how to become more discriminating, how to detect subtleties, how to interpret complexity, and how to evaluate our own emotional response. Indeed, we learn how to make meaning out of the swamp of feeling and experience in which most of us live every day. In that sense, the study of art is the study of ourselves and one in which every college student must engage.

Here are some suggestions on where you might begin:

- Critiquing and interpreting any work of art bears a similarity to making an argument: You must make a claim and support it with specific evidence, details, or examples from the art. But you must take into account that your reader may have come away from the same work of art with a totally different experience than you did. Your job is to assume your audience may have read the same book or looked at the same painting but that you brought to bear on it different backgrounds and different levels of sensitivity. Only with careful attention to detail, solid evidence, and careful reasoning will you persuade. Begin by selecting one of the poems or stories in this unit. Focus on a single element or aspect. Trace its development, looking for patterns, variations, or changes. What is the relationship of that single element to the larger work? To the emotional effect of the work? What kind of "meaning" can you draw from the whole by considering the development of a single aspect?

- Read Sherwood Anderson's "Book of the Grotesque" (page 378), followed by Diane Key's essay on it (page 396). If you disagree with Key, write a paper in which you analyze the story in your own terms. Show where Diane's interpretation may be right, but also where you think it may be weak or misleading.

- Attend an art exhibit, symphony performance, rock concert or foreign film. Assume your audience has not had the opportunity to experience the event. Write an essay in which you first summarize or provide an overview of the art under consideration. Then critique the experience, considering both strengths and weaknesses, providing specific details, patterns, or examples that support your view, and conclude with a strong assessment of the whole.

Group Inquiry

Share an experience with your class by attending a performance or exhibit together or by bringing a movie to class. Spend an entire class session conversing, first about the emotional experience evoked by the work of art, then about any intellectual questions the experience raises. Consider how the experience of art might help us define or give meaning to our own experience as human beings.

CHAPTER 28

Awareness of the Arts

Thomas Carlyle, one of the major nineteenth-century men of letters, once wrote that "the tragedy of life is not so much what men suffer, but rather what they miss." Unfortunately, what seems so often missing from our twenty-first-century world is an appreciation of the arts. In a technological age where value seems determined by what can be measured and weighed or bought and sold, the intangible, the imaginative, the dreamlike, or what exists solely because of its beauty, seems at best of secondary importance. But psychologist, Carl Jung, has pointed out that our overemphasis on rationality has resulted in a dangerous moral and spiritual disintegration.

It may sound odd at first to insist that feelings need to be developed and educated with as much attention as we give to the mind. Yet training that focuses exclusively on analysis of objective facts and on logic is training that educates the intellect while leaving emotional and moral development in a primitive state, rather like an athlete who concentrates his attention on developing a single set of muscles, his biceps, perhaps, until they bulge and ripple—all in grotesque proportion to the rest of his body. Through much of this book, we have been exercising our perception in objective ways, attempting to hold back private emotions, to suppress personal feelings. In dealing with fact and reason, that is the traditional way probable truth can be found. But there are other kinds of truths.

The Education of Emotion

Over three hundred years ago, Pascal wrote that "the heart has its reasons which reason cannot know." Most of us live most of our lives in a world dominated by emotion that we seldom understand: We fall in love, we pursue each other sexually, we hate, we are horrified by the evil we think we detect in others, we admire nobleness in some, we weep at loss, and we celebrate—sometimes just because we are alive. It is exactly this chaos of emotion that logic teaches us to avoid. By contrast, the artist attempts to deal with it, not by avoiding it, but by giving it shape and form. All art is primarily an expression of feelings structured according to the private vision of the artist. This ordering of feeling is the key to the way art educates our emotions.

Through art we experience feelings we might not otherwise encounter: the tragic fall of a great man, the sacrifices of idealistic lovers, the spiritual soaring of magnificent music. Through art we have the opportunity to reflect on those feelings, and to contemplate how they relate to the artist's vision. Because the mind finds meaning only in form, not in chaos, the shaping of art encourages us to interpret our experience, to explore its significance to our individual lives, to question whether we are led to new insights. By translating feelings into ordered patterns, art offers us the opportunity to understand emotions better and to refine and heighten our sensibilities.

The Creation of Meaning

The sad truth, however, is that many students are afraid of art, or at least made uncomfortable by it. For too long, we have approached art as we approach the study of physics or biology. We've been led to think that a work of art—a poem, a painting, even a symphony—contains a single specific "meaning" cleverly inserted by the artist. ("What is the 'meaning' of *Hamlet?*" "What is the 'theme' of Beethoven's Fifth Symphony?") Our job has been to study art like a specimen under a microscope, uncovering truth in the words, the paint, the musical notes, as something unrelated to our own experience with it. What we must realize, however, is that although objectivity remains important in numerous fields of study, an objective approach to art defies the very nature of the medium. The primary function of art is to stimulate our emotions. Art demands our personal interaction with it.

The "meaning" or "truth" we find in art cannot be separated from our experience of it. How we respond will be influenced by who we are: our age, gender, education, family background, culture—even by the era we live in with all its fads and fashions. In the same way, those same influences have shaped each individual artist, and to some extent, consciously or unconsciously, they find their way into the work of art itself. Every work of art is clearly an expression of complex mental, emotional, historical, and cultural factors, and each member of the audience is equally complex. Finding "meaning," then, is an interactive process, one in which you (as the individual audience to a work of art) explore a variety of influences and responses in the work as well as in yourself. Reading a novel or studying a piece of sculpture in this manner locates both you and the art in a human world, acknowledging that both of you are immersed in the goldfish bowl of your experience.

Study the photos of two famous works of sculpture on page 364.

Donatello, *David,* Alinari Art Resources, NY.

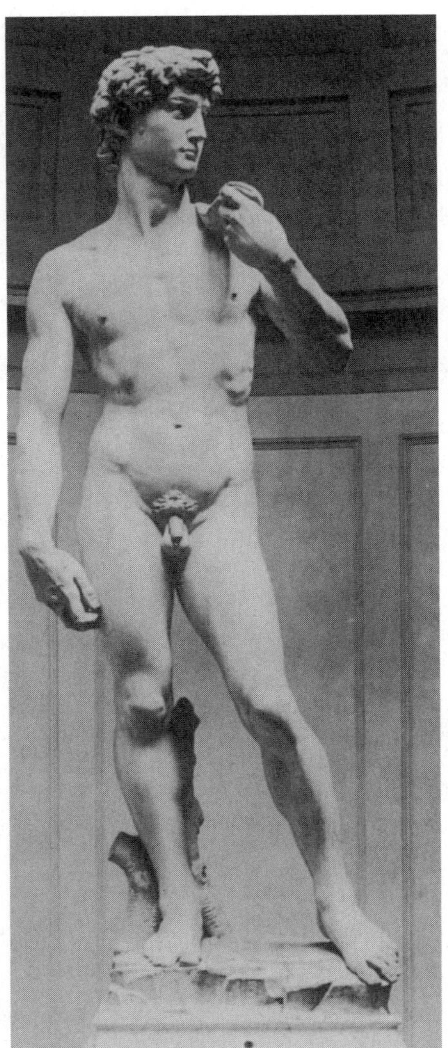

Michelangelo, *David,* Alinari Art Resources, NY.

You see them, of course, but *what* do you see? Take your time. Slow down. Reach out to both your sense of sight and to your emotions, but in different ways, for each artist has formed his material differently. Each is the product of an artist's interpretation of his own experience and emotions, as well as his personal vision of a biblical hero. What do *you* see, and what different kinds of responses do you feel?

Here is how two students responded in their journals:

Student A

My first reaction is to feel a little puzzled. I've seen pictures of Michelangelo's *David* before, and I think it probably distorts my reaction. He is probably beyond even the most ideal image of a man's body. Every muscular line is there, not overdone but perfectly carved. The face is serene, composed, confident, yet not arrogant, youthful but still masculine. His hands are incredibly large and heavy, weighted with power. The pose suggests great calmness and a lack of self-consciousness. He gazes into the future, to the next challenge. But Donatello's *David* is feminine. The hat (helmet?) looks like an Easter bonnet, the long curls flow over the very young boy's shoulders. The face has strength, but the lips are curved and full, like a girl's. In one sense the body is clearly pre-puberty: it lacks pubic hair, it's softer and less muscular, even though firm and beautiful in its own way. The pose is feminine, with one hip thrust out a little too much, the wrist curved in.

But he stands on the head of an angry Goliath. Sure. That's it. Donatello is showing us the young David, the shepherd boy who no one could expect to overcome a giant. He carries a sword almost as big as his body. It is the *contrast* that makes the point. Donatello is showing us a different kind of truth. David *was* an innocent young boy who played a lyre and tended sheep. He is the unexpected hero. He gazes down at what he's just done. He is absorbed in the act, not yet thinking about what is to come. On the other hand, Michelangelo's *David* is how we want our heroes to look. He is the god-like image we make of ourselves. He is the hero we created out of a young shepherd boy.

Student B

The statue on the right looks like a pretty athletic guy but the other one, to me, looks a little gay, it's probably by one of those fag artists who use tax dollars to promote gay rights. It turns my stomach if you want to know. The one on the right, however, has been working out and looks ok.

Student *A* has an advantage. Even though feeling confused at the beginning, by focusing on the sensory details of each work, she begins to perceive a "meaning," or "interpretation." She engages her perceptions fully, not just scanning the surface, but studying lines and forms in each figure. Various concrete details then *suggest* ways in which the art might be made meaningful. By looking closely and asking questions, she decides both statues may be heroic. The supposed "feminine" figure may even be more realistic, an image of the adolescent shepherd boy. The "masculine" figure, however, is an idealized hero, a vision of our individual and collective dreams.

But is student *B* entirely wrong? In one sense, yes. By rejecting Donatello's work out of hand because it appears to be the work of a "fag," student *B* allows a negative stereotype to end further consideration. If student *B* makes no further effort, he is trapped like a prisoner in Plato's cave, staring at shadows on the wall and accepting them as the only truth. Only if student *B* pursues his experience further can he discover more about the work of art—and more about himself. Psychologist Frank Smith has observed that comprehension is a matter of "relating what we attend to in the world around us . . . to what we already have in our heads." We have no other starting place. Smith goes on to point out that *learning* "is a process of modifying what we have in our heads as a consequence of attending to the world around us." Learning occurs only when we *add* to what we already have in our heads.

I have been arguing that the experience of art, and the "meaning" of art, is an interactive process. Student *B* brings to these Renaissance statues the information already in his head, which is all any of us can do. But to learn more about the art, and about himself, he must begin a process of questioning. He must pursue questions about each work of sculpture and about his own reaction. He may be right. Donatello may have been a gay artist, and it may be possible that Donatello intentionally created a "gay" David. But why? To defend the beauty of the feminine elements in man? To make a political statement? To express a new vision of that which constitutes the "heroic"? It may be possible that student *B,* through further study of his initial reaction, would identify the sources of his response. "Why do I have such an immediately negative feeling?" "What has formed my own values here?" "Are they justifiable?" Through deeper investigation, art offers us the opportunity to better understand emotions—and thus our humanness.

From the Literal to the Suggestive

All works of art begin with a literal, sensory experience. The first step in developing an increased appreciation of the arts is to become *sensitive* to the actual picture or sound or shape the artist has created. The sense experience evokes our physical emotions. This is where feeling begins.

But a good work of art, through any number of techniques, may also suggest something larger than itself—may *suggest* something more than the literal sense experience. Michelangelo's *David* is literally a stone figure of a man. It may suggest to us certain "heroic" qualities. But no sign on the pedestal tells us we should see these attributes. We infer them from the shape of the stone and from our emotional response. (As student *A* said, "He is the god-like image we make of ourselves.") To put it another way, the details of the carving can be thought of as similar to the "facts" you have been searching for in other types of writing. From the facts you *infer* certain conclusions. The process of interpretation from facts or from artistic forms is almost identical, except that in art the forms may seem more ambiguous and your response may be more emotionally heightened. You may need to pursue art with an even greater sense of a question.

Study the following poem by William Stafford. What do you see in it literally? What is the actual sense picture the poet draws for us in words? What types of feelings do the images evoke for you? Again, slow down. Take your time.

Traveling Through the Dark

William Stafford

Traveling through the dark I found a deer
dead on the edge of the Wilson River road.
It is usually best to roll them into the canyon:
that road is narrow; to swerve might make more dead.

By glow of the tail-light I stumbled back of the car
and stood by the heap, a doe, a recent killing;
she had stiffened already, almost cold.
I dragged her off; she was large in the belly.

My fingers touching her side brought me the reason—
her side was warm; her fawn lay there waiting,
alive, still, never to be born.
Beside that mountain road I hesitated.

The car aimed ahead its lowered parking lights;
under the hood purred the steady engine.
I stood in the glare of the warm exhaust turning red;
around our group I could hear the wilderness listen.

I thought hard for us all—my only swerving—
then pushed her over the edge into the river.

Here are two responses from student journals:

Student A

It describes a scene where he has found a dead deer on a narrow river road. He stops his car and in the light from the tail lights he discovers that the deer is pregnant. By touching the doe's stomach, he can feel the live fawn inside but knows that it will never be born. For a moment he hesitates but knows that if he doesn't push the deer off the road into the river, another car might swerve to miss it and plunge into the river, killing the people. After thinking about all involved, he chooses human life and pushes the deer off the edge of the road.

So much is happening here that I don't know where to begin. It's like two kinds of death and two kinds of life are being considered. "I thought hard for us all—" he says. The doe is dead, but the fawn is alive. Life *inside* death. But someone else driving along the road might be killed. The wilderness listens for his answer. What kind of life will he choose? The pain is enormous, like why do you have to choose at all? Maybe the title sums it all up. He has been traveling through the dark on the side of the mountain. Also in a different way through his whole life. Now he is confronted with a choice that seems terrible to him, but he makes the choice—human life over animal life. The poem leaves me with an empty feeling, as if such choices should not have to be made.

Student B

OK. This didn't make sense the first time, but the second time I realized a doe has been hit by a car or truck and the unborn fawn is still alive. I grew up in Montana and this kind of thing happened all the time. No one ever wants to kill a deer like this. A slaughter for no purpose. But it happens. Two forms of life confront each other, a man driving a truck at night and a deer leaping across a road at night. Neither one can know the outcome of their sudden meeting. How can I say this? This is what life is all about. *Both* of them are traveling through the dark. A chance circumstance might lead to something good. Another time might lead to death. And also two forms of life, here—the deer, natural and free, the man in the truck trapped inside his mechanical armor of rubber tires and steel pistons.

I never knew anyone in Montana that didn't feel bad about it. The man who hit the deer has gone on. The one who finds her, however, is not really any different. His car "purrs," its headlights are lowered like eyes that are ashamed or saddened, the warm exhaust is read in the taillights, like blood. His mechanical world has become his living world, the one we can't escape from. Only when we are forced to confront the wilderness like this are we forced to think hard about what we have become. But we still chose our own world. The guy in the poem pushes the deer over the side because our two worlds, the natural world and the mechanical world, are not compatible. He has to choose like the ranchers I knew in Montana. It isn't easy. They love the land and they love the deer. But we can't escape who we are. Humans survive only because of our mechanical armor, our machinery, our cars and planes and trains. The wilderness pays the price.

Student *A* first describes the touch, sound, and sight images she sees in each line. Having considered the details, she goes on to contemplate various ideas and feelings they suggest. She considers the paradox of life-in-death. She observes that we travel through life in darkness until confronted by such paradoxes. For her, the dilemma of the poem therefore lies in the line "I thought hard for us all." And she questions why we should be faced with such choices. Throughout her comments, student *A* continues to keep in mind the emotions stirred by such problems: pain, emptiness, terrible choices. Student *A* looks at the actual ordering of the images, considers her feelings and the questions they evoke, and allows the details to suggest several levels of significance.

The approach of student *B* is more personal. He recalls his past and relates the poem directly to feelings he and his neighbors have shared in a western state. For him, the deer as well as the man are traveling through the dark—literally—in that both are traveling through the night, and figuratively, in that neither can understand or predict the consequences of their confrontation. Student *B* is also aware that out of humankind's genius for mechanization, we have created a shield that further separates us from the wilderness. We feel the pain and the separation, but the purring car waits for us. Our cars and trucks have now become our living things, and when we confront the wilderness we must ultimately choose our own kind.

The Humanistic Heritage

Which student has the "right answer" to the poem? Which has found the "true meaning"? Obviously, such questions are misleading. Both students have found significance in the poem. Both have read details in the poem closely. And the artist's vision has presented them with a context for raising questions of real value: Does the work clarify an aspect of the human condition? Does it show the consequences of human choice and behavior? Do we know more about ourselves than we did before? For these students, intelligence and emotion now interact. Through art, they discover a unity between knowledge of fact and feeling about the fact. They participate in the education of the whole person, not just the mind. By interacting imaginatively with the author's words and images, they have immersed themselves in a process of exploration, opening their hearts to opportunity for growth in perception, and reaching a fuller understanding of who they are and what they believe.

In turn, by having an opportunity to share in both student readings, you and I also benefit. The poem grows larger; our sensitivity is deepened. As a result, we find ourselves linked to a great humanistic heritage, no longer limited to an isolated narrow world of here and now, but joined in spirit to ever-enlarging circles of human experience.

Practice

1. Study the two eighteenth-century paintings on page 370. Jot down your first general response to each painting. Next, search out the details in each, making two lists. What is the focal point of each artist? In Hogarth's work, look closely at the fashions, the decor in the room, the expressions on the faces. Compare these same details with those in the painting by Greuze. In what ways are they alike? In what ways different? Write a brief interpretation of what you have found, including any emotional response to the works. What can you learn about two different visions of the world?

William Hogarth, *The Marriage Transaction,* from the "Marriage à la Mode" series, 1742–1746. Engraving. Reproduced by courtesy of the Trustees of the British Museum, London.

Jean-Baptiste Greuze, *Village Betrothal,* 1761. Oil on canvas, 3 ft. 10 ½ in. × 3 ft. Louvre, Paris. Alinari/Art Resource, New York.

2. Study Marc Chagall's *Self-Portrait with Seven Fingers* above. Record your initial thoughts and feelings as honestly as possible. Do not be afraid of having a "wrong" response. Next, study the painting closely, recording the details and exaggerations you perceive: lines, shapes, facial expression, posture, dress. Count the fingers. Consider the images in the background. Write down what you see as you go along. When you're done, explore your thoughts and feelings about the painting. If the work seems "distorted," can you suggest any reasons for it? What is the artist trying to suggest about himself or about artists in general? What is more important here, the vision of the painter or the actual likeness of his self-portrait? What role do your personal feelings play as you interact with the details of the work? Can the painting be related to any aspect of your own background? Do we learn anything about ourselves from such a work?
3. Here is a well-known poem by Ezra Pound. The simplicity of it may be deceiving. Read it slowly.

The River-Merchant's Wife: A Letter
Ezra Pound

While my hair was still cut straight across my forehead
I played about the front gate, pulling flowers.
You came by on bamboo stilts, playing horse,
You walked about my seat, playing with blue plums.
And we went on living in the village of Chokan:
Two small people, without dislike or suspicion.

At fourteen I married My Lord you.
I never laughed, being bashful.
Lowering my head, I looked at the wall.
Called to, a thousand times, I never looked back.

At fifteen I stopped scowling.
I desired my dust to be mingled with yours
Forever and forever and forever.
Why should I climb the look out?

At sixteen you departed,
You went into far Ku-to-yen, by the river of swirling eddies,
And you have been gone five months.
The monkeys make sorrowful noise overhead.
You dragged your feet when you went out.
By the gate now, the moss is grown, the different mosses.

Too deep to clear them away!
The leaves fall early this autumn, in wind.
The paired butterflies are already yellow with August
Over the grass in the West garden;
They hurt me. I grow older.
If you are coming down through the narrows of the river Kiang,
Please let me know beforehand,
And I will come out to meet you
As far as Cho-fu-Sa.

In a few sentences record your initial response to Pound's poem. What do you think and feel on a first reading? Don't try to be profound. Write simply and honestly.

5. Copy Pound's poem out by hand. Copying is a way of getting inside the words. It can sharpen your perception. When you've finished copying, check a dictionary for words and names you are unsure of. Then write about the literal scene, the images you respond to. Consider how the various sensory images build toward and contribute to the feeling achieved by the end. Describe that feeling. What ideas and values are suggested by the poem?

6. Telling stories is one of the most natural things people do. Stories can be as long as *War and Peace* or as short as a few paragraphs. Here's a short one by Ann Beattie that may surprise you with its brevity and simplicity.

Snow

Ann Beattie

I remember the cold night you brought in a pile of logs and a chipmunk jumped off as you lowered your arms. "What do you think *you're* doing in here?" you said, as it ran through the living room. It went through the library and stopped at the front door as though it knew the house well. This would be difficult for anyone to believe, except perhaps as the subject of a poem. Our first week in the house was spent scraping, finding some of the house's secrets, like wallpaper underneath wallpaper. In the kitchen, a pattern of white-gold trellises supported purple grapes as big and round as Ping-Pong balls. When we painted the walls yellow, I thought of the bits of grape that remained underneath and imagined the vine popping through, the way some plants can tenaciously push through anything. The day of the big snow, when you had to shovel the walk and couldn't find your cap and asked me how to wind a towel so that it would stay on your head—you, in the white towel turban, like a crazy king of the snow. People liked the idea of our being together, leaving the city for the country. So many people visited, and the fireplace made all of them want to tell amazing stories: the child who happened to be standing on the right corner when the door of the ice-cream truck came open and hundreds of Popsicles cascaded out; the man standing on the beach, sand sparkling in the sun, one bit glinting more than the rest, stooping to find a diamond ring. Did they talk about amazing things because they thought we'd turn into one of them? Now I think they probably guessed it wouldn't work. It was as hopeless as giving a child a matched cup and saucer. Remember the night, out on the lawn, knee-deep in snow, chins pointed at the sky as the wind whirled down all that whiteness? It seemed that the world had been turned upside down, and we were looking into an enormous field of Queen Anne's lace. Later, headlights off, our car was first to ride through the newly fallen snow. The world outside the car looked solarized.

You remember it differently. You remember that the cold settled in stages, that a small curve of light was shaved from the moon night after night, until you were no longer surprised the sky was black, that the chipmunk ran to hide in the dark, not simply to a door that led to its escape. Our visitors told the same stories people always tell. One night, giving me a lesson in storytelling, you said, "Any life will seem dramatic if you omit mention of most of it."

This then, for drama: I drove back to that house not long ago. It was April, and Allen had died. In spite of all the visitors, Allen, next door, had been the good friend in bad times. I sat with his wife in their living room, looking out the glass doors to the backyard, and there was Allen's pool, still covered with black plastic that had been stretched across it for winter. It had rained, and as the rain fell, the cover collected more and more water until it finally spilled onto the concrete. When I left that day, I drove past what had been our house. Three or four crocus were blooming in the front—just a few dots of white, no field of snow. I felt embarrassed for them. They couldn't compete.

This is a story, told the way you say stories should be told: Somebody grew up, fell in love, and spent a winter with her lover in the country. This, of course, is the barest outline, and futile to discuss. It's as pointless as throwing birdseed on the ground while snow still falls fast. Who expects small things to survive when even the largest get lost? People forget years and remember moments. Seconds and symbols are left to sum things up: the black shroud over the pool. Love, in its shortest form, becomes a word. What I remember about all that time is one winter. The snow. Even now, saying "snow," my lips move so that they kiss the air.

No mention has been made of the snowplow that seemed always to be there, scraping snow off our narrow road—an artery cleared, though neither of us could have said where the heart was.

What feelings did you have as you read Ann Beattie's story? Explore them honestly without worrying whether you are reacting "correctly" to the work. Let your own personal experience come into play. Then try exploring some of the following:

a. Select a key sentence or passage in the story that seems important to you. Copy it out and write about why it seems important and how it might suggest an interpretation or insight that would apply to the story as a whole
b. Consider the following quotation from the story and write about it, relating your personal experience to it and, in turn, using your experience to interpret the story.
c. People forget years and remember moments. Focus in on details of the story as a way of relating it to something meaningful in yourself. Consider why the author gives two versions of the story in the first two paragraphs; or why a whole paragraph is devoted to visiting Allen's widow when Allen himself seemed to have only a minor role; or how and why the imagery of the snow changes.
d. Why doesn't the author tell us directly what the meaning of her experience was, rather than trying to evoke our emotions? How are we supposed to know the meaning if she doesn't tell us?

Group Inquiry

Divide into groups of four. Using the questions and guidelines from Practice exercise 1 (pages 369 and 371), two members of the group should argue the merits of Hogarth's painting, and two should argue the merits of Greuze's. Each group must use details from the paintings to support thoughts, feelings, and impressions. The argument is not intended to "prove" that one is better than the other, but to illustrate the values (or perhaps weaknesses) of both paintings.

CHAPTER 29

Literary Significance

There is creative writing, and
there is creative reading.

RALPH WALDO EMERSON

As a sophomore in college, I enrolled in a Victorian literature class. I was fascinated by my professor's enthusiasm for poetry and equally enthralled by his gymnastics. I remember how he once climbed upon a windowsill and sat precariously balanced, waving one arm and reading poems by Christina Rossetti. On another occasion, he bounded up the center stairs of the classroom, reciting and acting out "The Charge of the Light Brigade." But the day I remember most clearly is the day I decided not to become an English major.

I had spent the night before looking over poems by Gerard Manley Hopkins. Although none of them made much sense to me, I pushed my way through half a dozen and went to class confident I had fulfilled the assignment. Then the lecture began. My professor perched himself cross-legged on a table and announced, quite to my discomfort, that the sweeping flight of a bird in Hopkins' "Windhover" was a symbol for Christ. Image by image, line by line, he worked his way happily through the poem pointing out metaphors, subtle connotations, and historical allusions. By the end of the hour his face was red and puffed with pleasure, while I sat crushed by my own inadequacies. I had seen no Christ symbol. Indeed, I wasn't even sure I had seen a bird. It was obvious that others "saw things" in poetry that I didn't.

Not until I began graduate studies seven years later did I return to English literature, knowing then that what had happened to me was not all that unusual with students. I had looked at Hopkins' poems, all right, but I had not really read—not for significance and insight. I had skimmed hurriedly in much the same way one glances through a newspaper, looking for information, willing to be entertained if that should happen, hoping the "meaning" would leap out at me. Admittedly, I felt puzzled by strange language and odd sentences, but not so much that I was willing to reread. I had not even looked up in a dictionary the term *windhover.* How could I have known the poem was about a bird if I didn't know the title named the bird? Nor had I paid attention to the dedication, "*To Christ Our Lord,*" printed in bold italics directly under the title. After all, who reads dedications? The fact was I hadn't read at all.

The process of critical reading outlined earlier in Chapter 26 should give you the advantage over me. The strategy of reading described there is similar to the one you must use in reading for more than surface effects. Because a poem or novel or play may deal with so many complex levels (with emotion, fantasy, reality, myth, and alas, yes, with symbols), we cannot outline the same straightforward steps we used for reading prose essays. Each work of art is unique, and each may present us with new demands. But we can illustrate a similar approach that at least introduces the essential concept of reading with an engaged imagination.

The First Reading

Almost all art forms, and especially literary forms, must be experienced more than once. You should not expect to appreciate fully a poem or play or even a novel the first time you read it. A poem must be read many times. A play should be read at least twice, with parts of it several more times. And although a novel may be too long, or your time too limited, to read it twice through, key sections will often require rereading. There is no escape from this fact: Art demands your participation, your committed involvement. Because art forms are often subtle or ambiguous, because they often work on more than one level of understanding, because indeed they are often obscure, you must be willing to *study* the work. The most serious mistake young people make about art is to believe it does not require at least as much study and attention as a good problem in geometry.

Here are ten primary steps to serious reading:

1. **Read slowly.** If you rollerskate through an art museum, you won't see the paintings. Literature must be read at a slower pace than other forms of writing. Do not "speed-read" or skim. An author uses words as his or her basic tools. Every word counts for the author, as every color and line are meaningful for the painter. To feel the full effect, you must be conscious of the words themselves; you must allow sounds, images, and connotations to set up reverberations. If you have been trained to look only for facts, you must slow down and be willing to experience feelings.

2. **Read with pen in hand.** Underline key phrases, key speeches by major figures, key statements by the narrator. Take notes on ideas or questions (do not trust your memory). Circle words used in special ways or repeated in significant patterns. Look up in the dictionary words you do not know or words you think you know but that seem to have special weight or placement—the author may be using them in new ways. *You cannot expect to understand literature if you do not know the meaning of the words.*
3. **Be willing to read aloud.** Words have sounds, and sound is a sensory experience. Poetry, especially, needs to be listened to as well as read. Drama is by its nature a spoken medium. Even key passages from novels may become clear only when read aloud. James Joyce's *Finnegans Wake,* for example, looks like nonsense on the page; yet when listened to, its words become transformed into a hilarious, sensuous, flowing Irish brogue.
4. **Begin each new novel, play, or poem without predetermined bias.** If you decide in advance that all good art uses realistic settings and promotes your personal moral values, you close out the possibility of new experiences. You do not have to, nor should you, enjoy every work of literature you read. But you should be willing to recognize that the imagination is limitless. No matter how comfortable you may be with certain traditional forms and ideas, a new form or experiment in writing may offer you as much or more imaginative pleasure than the old. A first reading is almost never the time to pronounce final judgment.
5. **Ask silent questions of the material as you read.** Do not read passively, waiting to be told the "meaning." Most authors will seldom pronounce a moral. Even if they do, a work of literature is always more than its theme. Use the questions devised by reporters: *who?*, *what?*, *where?*, *when?*, *why?*, and *how?* You should usually be able to answer the first four questions after one reading—they form the surface of the work. *Why* and *how* may take more study—such questions probe the inner levels.
6. **Look for those qualities that professional writers look for in real life:** *conflict, contrast, contradiction, and characterization.* Most fiction and drama are built around one or all of these elements. Poetry, too, may use such devices, but in more subtle ways.
7. **Keep a reading journal.** Record first impressions, explore relationships, ask questions, write down quotations, copy whole passages that are difficult or aesthetically pleasing.
8. **Look for rhythm, repetition, and pattern.** Successful works of literature incorporate such structural devices in the language, in the dialogue, in the plot, in the characterization, and elsewhere. Pattern is form, and form is the shaping the artist gives to his or her experience. If you can identify the pattern and relate it to the content, you'll be on your way to insight.

9. **Listen to your own feelings, your own instincts.** They may often change as you read further or as you reread, but nonetheless they must serve you as a guide. Ask questions of yourself: Why does this make me feel this way? Why do I get angry? Why do I find this work appealing? What kind of values or experiences in me is this affecting? Is some kind of truth coming at me here? A truth I want to believe in? One that goes against everything I've ever believed?
10. **Finally, do not force an interpretation.** Because of the Western world's tradition of "interpreting" art, we often feel pressured to find instantaneous meaning: We search desperately for moralistic tags or simplistic messages or profound symbols. The truth is that a good work of literature comes to us by indirection, implication, suggestion, and feeling. The good author finds life too rich and complex for simplistic "messages." The good reader will wait patiently for understanding to grow out of various readings and rereadings. Keeping a reading notebook will help you explore the work and discover ideas.

The first reading must be thoughtful, but you must resist the temptation to plunge ahead with analysis. Read for the total feeling; read for an understanding of the work as a whole, before you return for more in-depth considerations.

Here is a very short story by Sherwood Anderson on which you might try applying some of these ten basic steps.

The Book of the Grotesque

Sherwood Anderson

The writer, an old man with a white mustache, had some difficulty in getting into bed. The windows of the house in which he lived were high and he wanted to look at the trees when he awoke in the morning. A carpenter came to fix the bed so that it would be on a level with the window.

Quite a fuss was made about the matter. The carpenter, who had been a soldier in the Civil War, came into the writer's room and sat down to talk of building a platform for the purpose of raising the bed. The writer had cigars lying about and the carpenter smoked.

For a time the two men talked of the raising of the bed and then they talked of other things. The soldier got on the subject of the war. The writer, in fact, led him to that subject. The carpenter had once been a prisoner in Andersonville prison and had lost a brother. The brother had died of starvation, and whenever the carpenter got upon that subject he cried. He, like the old writer, had a white mustache, and when he cried he puckered up his lips and the mustache bobbed up and down. The weeping old man with the cigar in his mouth was ludicrous. The plan the writer had for the raising of his bed was forgotten and later the carpenter did it in his own way and the writer, who was past sixty, had to help himself with a chair when he went to bed at night.

In his bed the writer rolled over on his side and lay quite still. For years he had been beset with notions concerning his heart. He was a hard smoker and his heart fluttered. The idea had got into his mind that he would some time die unexpectedly and always when he got into bed he thought of that. It did not alarm him. The effect in fact was quite a special thing and not easily explained. It made him more alive, there in bed, than at any other time. Perfectly still he lay and his body was old and not of much use any more, but something inside him was altogether young. He was like a pregnant woman, only that the thing inside him was not a baby but a youth. No, it wasn't a youth, it was a woman, young, and wearing a coat of mail like a knight. It is absurd, you see, to try to tell what was inside the old writer as he lay on his high bed and listened to the fluttering of his heart. The thing to get at is what the writer, or the young thing within the writer, was thinking about.

The old writer, like all of the people in the world, had got, during his long life, a great many notions in his head. He had once been quite handsome and a number of women had been in love with him. And then, of course, he had known people, many people, known them in a peculiarly intimate way that was different from the way in which you and I know people. At least that is what the writer thought and the thought pleased him. Why quarrel with an old man concerning his thoughts?

In the bed the writer had a dream that was not a dream. As he grew somewhat sleepy but was still conscious, figures began to appear before his eyes. He imagined the young indescribable thing within himself was driving a long procession of figures before his eyes.

You see the interest in all this lies in the figures that went before the eyes of the writer. They were all grotesques. All of the men and women the writer had ever known had become grotesques.

The grotesques were not all horrible. Some were amusing, some almost beautiful, and one, a woman all drawn out of shape, hurt the old man by her grotesqueness. When she passed he made a noise like a small dog whimpering. Had you come into the room you might have supposed the old man had unpleasant dreams or perhaps indigestion.

For an hour the procession of grotesques passed before the eyes of the old man, and then, although it was a painful thing to do, he crept out of bed and began to write. Some one of the grotesques had made a deep impression on his mind and he wanted to describe it.

At his desk the writer worked for an hour. In the end he wrote a book which he called "The Book of the Grotesque." It was never published, but I saw it once and it made an indelible impression on my mind. The book had one central thought that is very strange and has always remained with me. By remembering it I have been able to understand many people and things that I was never able to understand before. The thought was involved but a simple statement of it would be something like this:

That in the beginning when the world was young there were a great many thoughts but no such thing as a truth. Man made the truths himself and each truth was a composite of a great many vague thoughts. All about in the world were the truths and they were all beautiful.

The old man had listed hundreds of the truths in his book. I will not try to tell you of all of them. There was the truth of virginity and the truth of passion, the truth of wealth and of poverty, of thrift and of profligacy, of carelessness and abandon. Hundreds and hundreds were the truths and they were all beautiful.

And then the people came along. Each as he appeared snatched up one of the truths and some who were quite strong snatched up a dozen of them.

It was the truths that made the people grotesques. The old man had quite an elaborate theory concerning the matter. It was his notion that the moment one of the people took one of the truths to himself, called it his truth, and tried to live his life by it, he became a grotesque and the truth he embraced became a falsehood.

You can see for yourself how the old man, who had spent all of his life writing and was filled with words, would write hundreds of pages concerning this matter. The subject would become so big in his mind that he himself would be in danger of becoming a grotesque. He didn't, I suppose, for the same reason that he never published the book. It was the young thing inside him that saved the old man.

Concerning the old carpenter who fixed the bed for the writer, I only mentioned him because he, like many of what are called very common people, became the nearest thing to what is understandable and lovable of all the grotesques in the writer's book.

Beginning with the Literal

If you're like most of us, you probably read Anderson's story too quickly. I point no finger of guilt here because in searching for a story to print as an example, I, too, read it hurriedly. "Ah," I said to myself, "here's a short, simple story with few complications. Just the thing for a brief example." Had you asked me about the story after my first reading, I probably would have said something like, "Well, it's about an old man who sees everyone as grotesque." But I would have felt uncomfortable in my answer. Something about my first reading left an ache about the old man, about something lost and something gained—vague feelings I could not identify. My summary-type statement about the story would have seemed strangely inadequate for the feelings it aroused in me. Was there more to it than I had noticed? Had I really understood it at all? I began asking questions of myself, trying not to make hasty interpretations or judgments, but to *see* the literal level of the story.

Who? Who is the main character? The old man or the narrator? What is the role of the carpenter? What qualities about characterizing does Anderson use: physical details? actions? speech? background? others' responses? a self-created environment? And which are important in this particular story?

What? What actually happens in the story? Is there anything that could be called a plot? Is there a turning point or crisis? Any real conflict within the old man? With others? Any contrast between beliefs and actions? Is there a key scene where the action seems most revealing or important?

Where? Where does the story take place? A large city? A small town? Can we tell? Is it important? Does the old man's bedroom have any significance?

When? Do we know the time period in which the events occur? Should we ask when this particular event occurs during the old man's life? Would it make a difference?

Why? In some works, like *Hamlet,* the question "why" may be the central focus of the story: Why does Hamlet delay in killing his uncle? Is there a "why" in Sherwood Anderson's story? Does it relate to the old man? Or to the narrator?

How? How is the work put together? It may be too soon to answer this question. A second reading will probably be necessary to consider how each of the main elements relate—narrator, characters, plot, language, sense details, and so on.

Did I really ask myself such questions? Yes and no. Even after years of experience at reading literature, the questions hover in the back of my mind, although most of them have become more intuitive than conscious. For the beginning student, however, it seems to me that these questions do need to be consciously considered. Many will be rejected as inapplicable to any one particular work, but those that suggest possibilities must be followed up. And if you do not consciously work with such questions, chances are you'll forget some, perhaps the very ones that might have been most important.

The point is to understand the literal story. It makes no sense to pursue a "deeper" meaning if you haven't understood the surface. In Chapter 26, I encouraged you to write a brief summary after reading an essay. You may want to perform a similar act after reading a literary work. Or you may want to begin by writing down inner feelings about the reading—your initial response. The key to this, however, is to keep that response pointed at the work. Anderson's story may remind you of your grandfather. Write about it. But bring your writing and your thinking back to the story. How does the memory of your grandfather *relate* to the story of the old man? Use your personal experience (movies you've seen, books you've read, family events, travel, religion, and so on) as a starting point for questioning and exploring the story in front of you. Let the act of writing itself stimulate ideas and relationships.

The Second Reading

After you've noted your initial feelings or completed a summary—or both—it's time for a second reading. All serious reading is a process of vision and revision. If the first reading involves "seeing" or experiencing the story or poem or play on its literal level (what does it seem to say with the actual words, and what does it make me feel?), then the second reading involves exploring that surface with harder questions, with probing. You must question the details (the facts, the sensory images, the key actions or repeated words or phrases). Why do these particular points stand out for you? You must question how the details you feel relate to each other—and how they relate to the story as a whole.

Here are three strategies that might guide you.

Identify Patterns or Repetitions

All art is formed through patterns and repetitions—of colors, lines, and forms in painting, of musical phrases and themes in songs, of movements in dance, and so on. Look at a plaid shirt where stripes of blue alternate with smaller stripes of dark red and black, then repeat. Variations on a pattern in any art form confirm and heighten the pattern. Good writers may repeat key words or phrases to reinforce ideas and emotions, to establish rhythm (which is a form of pattern). Sometimes they repeat images, or modify earlier images with variations. Often they will present, like the contrasting smaller lines in a plaid shirt, contrasting minor characters to clarify the primary characters and their decisions or actions. On other occasions, authors may create a series of events or scenes to challenge a character. The manner in which the hero accepts or runs from these repeated challenges reveals aspects of character.

As readers, we may respond to repetition unconsciously. Like the rhythms of a song, we may be moved emotionally without awareness of how or why such an effect has been created. The word "blood" is repeated more than a hundred times in Shakespeare's *Macbeth.* The word "truth" appears more than a dozen times in Anderson's two-page short story. Like the beat of a drum, the pounding of these images or words affects us. On a first reading, we may only absorb their power. On a second reading, we must begin the act of bringing them to consciousness; we must begin to question their significance.

Identify Opposition and Conflict

Because most human experience evolves around opposition and conflict, most literature does as well, sometimes boldly, as in Tolstoy's novel *War and Peace,* and sometimes subtly, as in Ann Beattie's short story "Snow," printed at the end of Chapter 28. Conflict in art can be expressed as "tension" between musical ideas in a symphony or as opposing forces in painting (light and dark images). In literature it may take the form of men against women, cops and robbers, virtue and temptation, love and death, and so on. It may even exist only in the mind of a character—an inner psychological battle, like Huck Finn's conflict between acting according to the values of society or according to the dictates of his heart. Opposition and conflict form the substance of every "situation comedy" on television, every movie at your local theater, every play on Broadway.

Identifying the components, movements, and patterns for this basic structural element can provide you with a strategy for gaining insight into almost any work of art. Yet identifying the pattern is not enough. You must ask what the pattern reveals. What do we learn from it? Has any quality of human experience been illuminated? The goal here is to discover whatever meaning the work of art generates in you, and if it has none, or if it oversimplifies or lies about human experience, then to broadcast the truth and reveal its shallowness.

Identify a Key Passage

Sometimes a single sentence, or perhaps a single scene in a novel or story, will trigger a deep emotional response. And because the best way into any work of art is often to follow your instincts, digging deep into the passage you've identified may illuminate the work as a whole. Focusing in on such a passage—because it angers you, puzzles you, confirms your beliefs, stirs deep feelings of pain or joy, whatever—may stimulate the deepest insights of all.

But key passages can be tricky. By their nature, they constitute those points in a work of literature where you find yourself most moved or involved or where you suddenly acquire an insight. The tendency may be to wax philosophical or to generalize from the text to your own experience, forgetting that your job is to use the key passage as a method for negotiating meaning. It is the relationship between you, the passage, and the text that is central. You must always show how the passage opens up an understanding of the story or novel or play as a whole. A key passage, charged with possibilities, may become a focus for an extended exploration. The goal is to probe ways in which the sentence or passage reaches forward or back in the text, to discover how it relates to other actions, scenes, ideas, or feelings, and how, by seeing such relationships, we come to know the work better.

At this point, let me urge you to turn back and read Anderson's "The Book of the Grotesque" one more time. If you didn't underline and take notes the first time, do so now, watching for patterns and repetitions, opposition and conflict, or identifying a key sentence or passage. As you read, be willing to modify your initial views. The second reading may turn up details you missed the first time. You may sense new connections, ideas, or feelings that contradict the first reading. Allow yourself to change and grow into the story.

A reproduction of my own notes can be found on page 384, exactly as I took them on my own second reading of Anderson's story.

relationship

Writer – old – young inside — "pregnant w/ youth"

carpenter — is he example of grotesque? How?

Dream not a dream? Key event?

— the young in him drove grotesques before him

Narrator's statement

— many thoughts, no truths

— many made truths out of the thoughts

— all were beautiful until adopted by individuals as their truths

→ which turned them into grotesques

Writer in danger of becoming a grotesque

— the young in him saves him

← 3rd tag of this idea

What is there about the young that saves the old man?

— youth has innocence? no fixed truths?

— open to experience?

Relationship to truth??

— are all truths beautiful until they become obsessions? My truth vs. your truth?

Makes each of us grotesque

Your notes might look quite different. Yours might include webs, lists, definitions, more questions, whole paragraphs detailing your observations, or even a whole paragraph from the story, copied word for word to catch the feeling and rhythms of the prose. You may have focused on different points or perceived ideas that I missed. But from my notes you can tell I was beginning to consider the details of the story and their relationship. A number of repetitions stood out and I was forced to ask questions about them. A clear opposition between several elements arose, especially between "youth" and "age." By the end, I was striving to find connections and relationships.

I confess I was genuinely surprised at how much more complex and richly textured the story was than I had first thought. After a second reading I could *not* say, "Here's a story about an old man who sees others as grotesque." Such a shallow response would be seriously inadequate.

With a head full of feelings and ideas, a page full of notes, and a text underlined and marked, I would now be reading to write. Only by engaging in this type of thorough involvement with art can you expect to develop a written essay with any depth. The next chapter will discuss the actual job of getting it down on paper.

A Summary of Basic Activities in Reading for Significance

Read Fiction, Drama, and Poetry More than Once

- Read first for the total experience of the work.
- Read slowly for the words, feelings, emotions, and ideas.
- Underline key passages, repetitions, phrases, and words. Make marginal notes.
- Keep a reading notebook: Explore questions, ideas, and feelings.
- Look up important words in the dictionary.
- In poetry and drama, especially, read aloud.
- Be open to new possibilities; do not reject that which cannot be understood instantly on first reading.

Ask Silent Questions

- Who? What? Where? When? Why? How?
- Is there a pattern? A significant repetition?
- Is there conflict, contrast, or opposition?
- Is there a key sentence or passage that seems especially important to you?

Contemplate Relationships

- How do the details, the parts, relate to the whole?
- What feelings does the work evoke in you? How does it relate to your own experience? Your past reading? Your values?

Practice

1. Read the following poem by Robert Hayden. Use the strategies discussed in this chapter. Read it once for the total impression, for the feeling. Then reread it aloud, slowly.

Those Winter Sundays

Robert Hayden

Sundays too my father got up early
and put his clothes on in the blueblack cold,
then with cracked hands that ached
from labor in the weekday weather made
banked fires blaze. No one ever thanked him.

I'd wake and hear the cold splintering, breaking.
When the rooms were warm, he'd call,
and slowly I would rise and dress,
fearing the chronic angers of that house,

Speaking indifferently to him,
who had driven out the cold
and polished my good shoes as well.
What did I know, what did I know
of love's austere and lonely offices?

a. Copy the poem thoughtfully in your reading journal, giving your full attention to each word, each image. Use a dictionary for any word you're unsure of. Consider both denotations and connotations within the overall context.

b. Explore your feelings about the work. How does the poem affect you? Is there a key line or passage that strikes you especially hard? Does it stir memories or call up images from your past? How might your responses relate to the poem? That is, do they confirm it? Or do they make you want to challenge the poem?

c. What do you know about the speaker of the poem? About *his* feelings, his sensitivity, his present attitude, as well as his past experience?

d. Can you draw together your various ideas and emotions? Consider the details in the poem as well as your own experience. What kind of significance, if any, does this poem seem to have for you?

2. Here are two poems for close reading. Move slowly through the steps that might apply to each poem. Use the strategies discussed in this chapter. Do not rush to judgment. Remember that it may take time for a poem to grow on you.

This Is Just to Say

William Carlos Williams

I have eaten
the plums
that were in
the icebox

and which
you were probably
saving
for breakfast

Forgive me
they were delicious
so sweet
and so cold

Remember

Joy Harjo

Remember the sky that you were born under,
know each of the star's stories.
Remember the moon, know who she is. I met her
in a bar once in Iowa City.
Remember the sun's birth at dawn, that is the
strongest point of time. Remember sundown
and the giving away to night.
Remember your birth, how your mother struggled
to give you form and breath. You are evidence of
her life, and her mother's, and hers.
Remember your father. He is your life, also.
Remember the earth whose skin you are:
red earth, black earth, yellow earth, white earth
brown earth, we are earth.
Remember the plants, trees, animal life who all have their
tribes, their families, their histories, too. Talk to them,
listen to them. They are alive poems.
Remember the wind. Remember her voice. She knows the
origin of this universe. I heard her singing Kiowa war
dance songs at the corner of Fourth and Central once.
Remember that you are all people and that all people are you.
Remember that you are this universe and that this
universe is you.
Remember that all is in motion, is growing, is you.
Remember that language comes from this.
Remember the dance that language is, that life is.
Remember.

3. The Parable of the Good Samaritan is familiar to most readers. Look at it again in light of some of the ideas on reading discussed in this chapter.

The Parable of the Good Samaritan

And Jesus said, A certain man went down from Jerusalem to Jericho, and fell among thieves, which stripped him of his raiment, and wounded him, and departed, leaving him half dead.

And by chance there came down a certain priest that way; and when he saw him, he passed by on the other side.

And likewise a Levite, when he was at the place, came and looked on him, and passed by on the other side.

But a certain Samaritan, as he journeyed, came where he was; and when he saw him, he had compassion on him.

And went to him, and bound up his wounds, pouring in oil and wine, and set him on his own beast, and brought him to an inn, and took care of him.

And on the morrow when he departed, he took out two pence, and gave them to the host, and said unto him, Take care of him: and whatsoever thou spendest more, when I come again, I will repay thee.

Which now of these three, thinkest thou, was neighbor unto him that fell among the thieves?

And he said, he that showed mercy on him. Then said Jesus unto him, Go, and do thou likewise.

New Testament, Luke 10:30–37

a. Explore any initial feelings stimulated by this parable. Probe their origins. Are they generated by the work itself? By your cultural or religious background?

b. Consider the pattern or repetitions that may suggest significance here. If you changed the story so that no repetition occurred, would it have the same impact?

c. If the story were told from a different point of view (from the Samaritan's or the victim's), what would be the effect on the overall significance?

Imitating

You've already learned that copying is one way you can help yourself become a better reader and writer. Now you're ready to go one step farther. Try deliberately imitating a passage by another author. Select a topic to write about that is completely different from the passage you're working with, but imitate the author's sentence structure, rhythms, and types of words. If the first sentence has ten words, you write approximately ten words. If the writer begins with a fragment, you begin with one, too. Match noun to noun, verb to verb, adjective to adjective—but let the rhythms carry you in new directions when your imagination is stimulated.

Writers imitate, not to write like someone else, but to discover all the possibilities open to them. Robert Louis Stevenson, Richard Yates, Somerset Maugham, and countless others have admitted this exercise helped them become better writers. Poet Dylan Thomas has told how he "wrote endless imitations . . . of anything [he] happened to be reading at the time: de Quincey, Blake, the Bible, Poe, Keats, Lawrence, and Shakespeare." Thomas confessed that it was "a mixed lot," but raised a question that any would-be writer must ask: "How can I learn the tricks of the trade unless I try to do them myself?"

You may not plan to become a professional writer, just as you may not plan to become a professional tennis player. But you can learn a lot about improving your forehand by imitating a tennis pro, and you can—with work and patience—improve your writing by imitating a successful author.

Here is the lead sentence from "The Magic Barrel," a short story by Bernard Malamud:

> Not long ago there lived in uptown New York, in a small, almost meager room, though crowded with books, Leo Finkle, a rabbinical student in Yeshiva University.

And here is how first-year student Alice Reed imitated it:

> On the outskirts of Plain City, a small Mormon town just west of the Wasatch Mountains and nearly edging the great salt desert, lived Ordella Tippetts, a polygamist's wife who raised guineas and muscovy ducks.

Imitating is a way of freeing yourself to become the writer you want to be. You will become more proficient. As you play with language, you discover its structure and rhythms. You discover new words and old words used in a new way. You absorb craft and technique, freeing yourself from safe, monotonous patterns. You learn to take risks with language. By imitating, you teach yourself to write.

Try copying and then imitating any of the professional passages on pages 80–82.

CHAPTER 30

The Formal Critique

Until now I have discussed your audience as someone outside yourself, as a reader real or imagined, to whom you wanted to communicate. In studying art, however, you, too, form a part of the audience. First, you are audience to the creative work of someone else—to a symphony, a poem, a painting—before you are a writer about that work. Second, even though the paper you produce will be nominally addressed to a reader other than yourself, you'll find that during the actual process of writing, you continue to respond and react to the art. The writing process becomes a method of clarifying and discriminating for yourself, for your own understanding, not just for your imagined reader. In other words, writing about literature or music or art becomes, in a genuine sense, an exploration of your own experience, both emotional and intellectual. As the artist has given form to his or her feelings, so too must you give form to yours, for your own benefit as well as the benefit of another reader.

The Other Reader

What does the audience for a formal critique want and expect? The concept of a *literary critique* does not include the notion of fixed form so much as the idea of a serious examination of a specific work of art, including an assessment of its value or significance. The form is flexible, but your reader will expect more than just a "review," more than just a retelling of the plot.

The best critique may analyze only a portion of a work in some detail or will demonstrate how some element (a key passage, a repeated image or word, a striking pattern) might illuminate the whole. Your reader will probably expect you to use a personal voice, yet also expect that you will not drift away into mere recollections or emotions. For that reason, a literary critique presents added complications. If you're too cold and analytical, you may lose the human feeling art generates. If you're too subjective, your own experience may overshadow the story or poem. Keep in mind that the reader of your critique wants to know about the feelings rendered by the art, but also wants to know how your individual reading leads to understanding or insight.

The Critical Process

Although no specific form exists for a critique, you might want to follow a conventional pattern. First, look at the whole; then look more closely at the details that seemed important to you in your reading; then interpret or shape meaning from what you have discovered; and finally, form a judgment.

Many students mistakenly believe that if a story or a poem has been read by a class as a whole or even discussed in class, they need not guide the reader through each of these steps. Instead, they plunge immediately into analysis; or, worse, having completed the analysis in their minds, they plunge directly into interpretation. Even though the reader may have knowledge of the work being discussed, such abrupt leaps create a sense of disjointed confusion. You should not assume your reader has experienced the work as you have, even on the literal level. You have used your eyes; the reader has used his or hers. When studying a work of art and when writing about it, demand of yourself the discipline required to move the mind through each phase of the critical process.

The Formal Introduction

The introduction to a formal critique should provide the reader with an essential overview before you focus in on smaller details or interpretation.

1. Name the author and the work.
2. Survey the literal level—what the work is about as a whole.
3. Provide a focusing or narrowing of your approach.
4. Give the reader a general indication of the larger significance you plan to lead the reader toward.

Here is an example from a paper by Michelle Sheppard:

Provocative lead
Author and title

His whole life had been a lie. Of all the characters John Ehle introduces in his novel *The Winter People,* only Gudger, the eldest son of the Wright clan, undergoes a complete transformation. Set in the North Carolina mountains during the Depression, *The Winter People*

Student briefly summarizes the story as a whole	tells a story of the feuding Wright and Campbell clans in an atmosphere fraught with tension and mystery. The feud intensifies when Cole Campbell, father of Collie Wright's illegitimate son Jonathan, drowns in a creek on Collie's property. His death eventually brings about not only a truce between the clans but also Gudger's meta-
Begins to focus	morphosis. In the beginning, Gudger sees himself as a bear: "A bear fights back. No lamb about him." But is he really strong and forceful, a power to be respected? Or is
Subject narrows and significance suggested	he a coward, a lamb in bear's clothing who does not know the truth about himself? And do these questions about Gudger suggest John Ehle's larger theme?

Although an introduction *can* be written without including a sentence that suggests the ultimate significance or judgment you plan to arrive at, by including it, you establish an element of interest at the beginning—you say, "Here, reader, is why this whole thing is important"—and you prepare the reader for your conclusion. In doing so, you will make the critique seem more unified and complete. Introductions often can't be written until you've completed your first draft. If you're like me, you'll need to explore ideas in a rough form before you can return and write a clear introduction of the kind I've presented here.

The Body of the Critique

Most of your essay should present a detailed analysis of the work or of the major elements of the work you have focused on. Each step of your discussion should repeat the analytic process:

1. *Describe* a specific aspect of the story, poem, or play you plan to focus on. Use your own words to introduce your point; then provide a quotation, paraphrase, or description directly from the work.
2. *Analyze* that particular component. Show how the image works, what the character says, or how the plot turns. This is the place for details.
3. *Interpret* your findings. Limit your interpretation to the single element you are dealing with or show how it relates to other elements, but save your overall assessment for the end.

Repeat the three steps for each phase of the work you deal with: *describe, analyze, interpret.* Be sure to include quotations and examples from the work as evidence to support your ideas.

Here is Jim Havens, a first-year student, writing about a long poem, "Stages on a Journey Westward," by James Wright. In reading the poem, Jim discovered a pattern of repeated images, all of which he felt suggested death. His introduction, then, narrowed his focus to those images and suggested that by exploring such a pattern, we would discover the poem's significance: the dying of the American dream.

In the body of his paper he looks in detail at each of the images.

Description of the literal level in student's own words

In the first stage of Wright's work, he recalls the start of his trip westward by painting for the reader a scene of horses wandering into a barn to relax and eat.

Quotation to reinforce student's description

I began in Ohio
I still dream of home
Near Mansfield, enormous dobbins enter dark
  barns in autumn,
Where they can be lazy, where they can munch
  apples
Or sleep long.

Analysis begins—in this case by considering how individual words suggest a particular feeling

Student admits that interpretation must await more evidence

But if we probe further in Wright's word choice, we discover a possible foreshadowing of death. A "dobbin" is a term that is used for old workhorses that are really no longer of use for labor, a horse that is ready for the glue factory. The use of the word *dark* itself suggests death. *Autumn* is the figurative season for dying. *Apples* are the biblical symbol that calls to mind the death of paradise for mortal man. Nothing at this point in the poem confirms this image of death. But as we move toward the next lines in the poem, the dark foreshadowing seems to continue.

Description of literal level again: blend of paraphrase and quotation

Analysis of various images

Interpretation shows relationship of images to earlier points

Wright describes his memories of his father (or perhaps night dreams of his father) prowling, waiting in bread lines, wearing blue rags, leading a blind horse. He recalls how in 1932, "grimy with machinery," his father sang to him of a goosegirl while outside the house slag heaps were piled. In German folk tales the goosegirl was a Cinderella figure. Nineteen-thirty-two was the time of the Great Depression: poverty, hunger and degradation. The slag heap suggests the plight of the common worker. It was a pile of waste material that was separated during the smelting of iron. All of these negative images reinforce the foreshadowing of death we saw in the first lines. The suggestion is

Transition: student will repeat same process for second stage of poem

> that the American dream of justice and individual dignity seemed to be coming to an end, as it surely must have seemed in 1932. Like the goosegirl story, the American dream was only a fairy tale.
>
> In the second stage of his journey, Wright moves further west, to Minnesota, where a series of new images build upon this theme of death. . . .

Jim Haven's interpretation might be disputed by another reader who saw no death images at all in the poem. But by demonstrating that a repetition (a pattern) of words and images suggests death or dying, Jim hopes to lead even the unconvinced reader to his conclusion. Does that mean his interpretation is "right" and someone else's is "wrong"? No. It means that an effective work of art may have various interpretations, so long as each provides specific, concrete evidence from the work and so long as the overall context of the work supports it.

The Conclusion

Because assessment is part of the critical process, you must arrive at a final judgment. Like all conclusions, yours must grow out of evidence, ideas, and feelings you've developed in your paper. If the work has been poorly executed, your analysis should demonstrate it, and your conclusion should be strong, but it should be based on the argument you've presented.

> In *A Farewell to Arms,* Hemingway's hero hasn't really learned very much at all. If all the old values are no longer meaningful, we are left with the question, "How can I lead my life?" But Hemingway's vision is incomplete, for it fails to give us any answers. Hemingway implies, as I've tried to show, that values can be found in a return to sensations. But sensations are structureless, like a bunch of building blocks without any foundation. In terms of my generation, *A Farewell to Arms* tells us what we already know, but it ends where it should begin.

If the poem or story or play has been successful, however, your conclusion should note it with equal forcefulness.

> The unity of the poem depends on the recurrence of light and dark images, to which Tennyson has given particular attention. Throughout the poem, the words *day* and *dark* have appeared again and again. The light and dark contrasts become symbolic of man's belief or doubt in God. They create a

tension of opposites until they are brought together and seen as a balancing rather than a conflicting force. Tennyson's brilliance has been in leading us to see that faith swells not from "the light alone" but from the "darkness and the light."

A study of literature goes beyond merely increasing our appreciation of an art form. It increases our sensitivity to emotions and to the shades of human experience. It heightens our awareness of subtlety and ambiguity, of form and symbol, of line and color, of language itself. It develops our hearts and our minds.

The Structure as Outline

Introduction

- Name of author and work
- Brief overview of the work as a whole
- Focusing sentence
- General indication of overall significance

Body

- Literal description of first major element or portion of the work
- Detailed analysis
- Interpretation
- Literal description of the second major development
- Detailed analysis
- Interpretation (including, if necessary, the relationship to the first major point)
- And so on

Conclusion

- Relationship to the work as a whole
- Critical assessment of the value, worth, meaning, or significance of the work, both positive and negative, as you have seen and felt it

Practice

Study the student critique that follows. In it, Diane Key, a sophomore biology major, has attempted to analyze Sherwood Anderson's story. The approach she has used is only one of many; you may have seen the story in a different light. Consider where Diane's effort is successful and where it might be strengthened.

Analyze the components of Diane's introduction

intro

Truth in the Grotesque

The title of a short story by Sherwood Anderson, "The Book of the Grotesque," appropriately depicts the overall significance of the story. At first glance, the plot seems bizarre. Anderson takes his readers through the story by introducing us to a writer, an old man past sixty. The writer employs the services of a carpenter to raise the writer's bed so that he can see out the window. As the writer lies in his elevated bed one night, many strange thoughts and feelings overtake him. Although the old man has a weak heart and would not be alarmed if death came to him in the near future, he feels at odds with death; he feels as if a youth or young woman lived within him. Even though awake, the writer experiences a dream or vision caused by the young thing inside his body. An hour-long procession of grotesque figures appears before the old man's eyes. Because he is a writer, the old man later writes a book describing his dream and its significance. The book contains hundreds of truths and describes how these truths can turn people into "grotesques." The narrator of the story foresees the possibility that the old man may also become grotesque if the old man becomes obsessed with his book, but the young thing inside him saves him from such an outcome.

Consider how Diane moves from concrete details to what they suggest and how they may relate to the larger theme

Body

Anderson puts a great deal of stress on the writer's age. Besides using the word *old* to describe him, Anderson indicates that he has a "white mustache," he has "some difficulty in getting into bed," he is "past sixty," "he would some time die unexpectedly," and "his body was old and not of much use any more." Old age suggests brittleness, conformity, death, and finality. In a sense, these words and images are like truths. A truth according to its dictionary definition is fact or actuality. A fact is rigid, incapable of being changed, and is clearly defined. A truth is an absolute—there is no gray between the black and white.

What traditional technique does Diane use here?

In conflict with the finality of his age, however, the writer senses a contrasting feeling:

> . . .something inside him was altogether young. He was like a pregnant woman, only that the thing inside him was not a baby but a youth. No, it wasn't a youth, it was a woman, young, and wearing a coat of mail like a knight.

The word *pregnant* holds special significance, as does the observation that the sensation felt like a young

Discuss how the student moves through description, analysis, and interpretation in this paragraph

woman, someone capable of giving new life. We can even note that a coat of mail is *flexible armor.* These three concepts suggest birth, newness, and pliability. In fact, they are antonyms of the connotations of old age. Old age can be equated with rigidity and truth. Youth, on the other hand, is equated with flexibility, with that which is not absolute and can be changed. How does this all relate to the procession of grotesques that passes before the writer's eyes? It could be possible that as each person seizes a truth and tries to live his or her life according to its standards, he or she becomes cast into a mold that is unnatural and restricting. He or she is distorted into something other than human. "The grotesques were not all horrible. Some were amusing, some almost beautiful," states the narrator. But the grotesques are like the truths they embrace. Some of the grotesques are hideous when people try to live accordingly, like the truths of poverty and carelessness. Others are handsome, such as the truths of courage and thrift. The word *old,* therefore, suggests the inflexibility of "truth" and the "truth's" distortion of people. As the writer is old, he is in danger of becoming a grotesque, as his acquaintances have. But the old writer embodies the conflicting force of youth. "It was the young thing inside him that saved the old man."

Did you see the carpenter's role as Diane does? If not, is her interpretation convincing?

One begins to wonder when the writer first realized the young force within himself. I feel that the old man's discovery began soon after the carpenter's visit. Here, again, words and images suggest that the carpenter aided the writer in seeing his vision of the grotesques and in finding the youth within him. By means of the carpenter, who is a builder, the old man's bed was raised. The carpenter brought the man's bed to the level of the window so the old man could see the tree, which might suggest life, growth, and youth, or, at the very least, something outside the confines of the old man's age. The carpenter is a grotesque himself because he is obsessed with the truth of war and death. Unknowingly, by serving as an example, the carpenter stimulates the old man to see the procession of grotesques later. This is not to say that the carpenter enlightened the writer. On the contrary, Anderson writes, "The plan the writer had for the raising of his bed was forgotten and later the carpenter did it in his own way and the writer, who was past sixty, had to help himself with a chair when he went to bed at night." It was the writer's plan to raise the bed and it was the writer who had to help himself.

Active participation on the part of the writer was required if he was to recognize the youthful element in his life.

Consider how Diane assesses the overall value of the story

Perhaps Sherwood Anderson's story suggests that we should keep our youthful attitudes along with their flexibility. We should not be rigid and unbending; we should not try to live our lives solely by a single truth. A single truth, no matter how appealing, is always a distortion. We must not accept only the black and white, but live and experience the vast area of gray also. Yet there is a danger of excess in following this vision too. Without some kinds of truths, our lives would be meaningless. What we need is to live somewhere between an unyielding framework and total license. Sherwood Anderson's old writer has found that middle ground and is all the more human because of it.

Readings

Trinity

Pattiann Rogers

I wish something slow and gentle and good
Would happen to me, an easy and patient
And prolonged kind of happiness coming
In the same way evening comes to a wide-branched
Sycamore standing in an empty field; each branch,
Not succumbing, not taken, but feeling
Its entire existence a willing revolution of cells;
Even asleep, feeling a decision of gold spreading
Over its ragged back and motionless knots of seed,
Over every naked, vulnerable juncture; each leaf
Becoming a lavender shell, a stem-deep line
Of violet turning slowly and carefully to possess exactly
The pale and patient color of the sky coming.

I wish something that slow and that patient
Would come to me, maybe like the happiness
Growing when the lover's hand, easy on the thigh
Or easy on the breast, moves like late light moves
Over the branches of a sycamore, causing
A slow revolution of decision in the body;
Even asleep, feeling the spread of hazy coral
And ivory-grey rising through the legs and spine
To alter the belief behind the eyes; feeling the slow
Turn of wave after wave of acquiescence moving

From the inner throat to the radiance of a gold belly
To a bone-center of purple; an easy, slow-turning
Happiness of possession like that, prolonged.

I wish something that gentle and that careful
And that possessive would come to me. Death
might be that way if one knew how to wait for it;
If death came easily and slowly,
If death were good.

Three Thousand Dollar Death Song

Wendy Rose

Nineteen American Indian Skeletons from Nevada . . .
valued at $3000 . . .—Museum invoice, 1975

Is it in cold hard cash? the kind
that dusts the insides of men's pockets
lying silver-polished surface along the cloth.
Or in bills? papering the wallets of they
who thread the night with dark words. Or
checks? paper promises weighing the same
as words spoken once on the other side
of the grown grass and dammed rivers
of history. However it goes, it goes
through my body it goes
assessing each nerve, running its edges
along my arteries, planning ahead
for whose hands will rip me
into pieces of dusty red paper,
whose hands will smooth or smatter me
into traces of rubble. Invoiced now,
it's official how our bones are valued
that stretch out pointing to sunrise
or are flexed into one last foetal bend,
that are removed and tossed about,
catalogued, numbered with black ink
on newly-white foreheads.
As we were formed to the white soldier's voice,
so we explode under white students' hands.
Death is a long trail of days
in our fleshless prison.

From this distant point we watch our bones
auctioned with our careful beadwork,
our quilled medicine bundles, even the bridles
of our shot-down horses. You: who have
priced us, you who have removed us: at what cost?
What price the pits where our bones share
a single bit of memory, how one century
turns our dead into specimens, our history
into dust, our survivors into clowns.
Our memory might be catching, you know;
picture the mortars, the arrowheads, the labrets
shaking off their labels like bears
suddenly awake to find the seasons have ended
while they slept. Watch them touch each other,
measure reality, march out the museum door!
Watch as they lift their faces
and smell about for
us; watch our bones rise
to meet them and mount
the horses once again!
The cost, then, will be paid
for our sweetgrass-smelling having-been
in clam shell beads and steatite,
dentalia and woodpecker scalp, turquoise
and copper, blood and oil, coal and uranium,
children, a universe of stolen things.

The Peace of Wild Things

Wendell Berry

When despair for the world grows in me
and I wake in the night at the least sound
in fear of what my life and my children's lives may be,
I go and lie down where the wood drake
rests in his beauty on the water, and the great heron feeds.
I come into the peace of wild things
who do not tax their lives with forethought
of grief. I come into the presence of still water.
And I feel above me the day-blind stars
waiting with their light. For a time
I rest in the grace of the world, and am free.

I Wash the Shirt

Anna Swir

For the last time I wash the shirt
of my father who died.
The shirt smells of sweat. I remember
that sweat from my childhood,
so many years
I washed his shirts and underwear,
I dried them
At an iron stove in the workshop,
He would put them on unironed.

From among all bodies in the world,
animal and human,
Only one exuded that sweat.
I breathe it in
for the last time. Washing this shirt
I destroy it
forever.
Now
only paintings survive him
which smell of oils.

Love Poem

Denise Levertov

'We are good for each other.'
    —X

What you give me is

the extraordinary sun
splashing its light
    into astonished trees.

A branch
of berries, swaying

under the feet of a bird.
I know

other joys—they taste
bitter, distilled as they are
from roots, yet I thirst for them.

But you—
you give me

the flash of golden daylight
in the body's
midnight.
warmth of the fall noonday
between sheets in the dark.

The Ones Who Walk Away from Omelas

Ursula K. Le Guin

With a clamor of bells that set the swallows soaring, the Festival of Summer came to the city Omelas, bright-towered by the sea. The rigging of the boats in harbor sparkled with flags. In the streets between houses with red roofs and painted walls, between old moss-grown gardens and under avenues of trees, past great parks and public buildings, processions moved. Some were decorous: old people in long stiff robes of mauve and grey, grave master workmen, quiet, merry women carrying their babies and chatting as they walked. In other streets the music beat faster, a shimmering of gong and tambourine, and the people went dancing, the procession was a dance. Children dodged in and out, their high calls rising like the swallows' crossing flights over the music and the singing. All the processions wound towards the north side of the city, where on the great water-meadow called the Green Fields boys and girls, naked in the bright air, with mud-stained feet and ankles and long, lithe arms, exercised their restive horses before the race. The horses wore no gear at all but a halter without bit. Their manes were braided with streamers of silver, gold, and green. They flared their nostrils and pranced and boasted to one another; they were vastly excited, the horse being the only animal who has adopted our ceremonies as his own. Far off to the north and west the mountains stood up half encircling Omelas on her bay. The air of morning was so clear that the snow still crowning the Eighteen Peaks burned with white-gold fire across the miles of sunlit air, under the dark blue of the sky. There was just enough wind to make the banners that marked the racecourse snap and flutter now and then. In the silence of the broad green meadows one could hear the music winding through the city streets, farther and nearer and ever approaching, a cheerful faint sweetness of the air that from time to time trembled and gathered together and broke out into the great joyous clanging of the bells.

Joyous! How is one to tell about joy? How describe the citizens of Omelas?

They were not simple folk, you see, though they were happy. But we do not say the words of cheer much any more. All smiles have become archaic. Given a description such as this one tends to make certain assumptions. Given a description such as this one tends to look next for the King, mounted on a splendid stallion and surrounded by his noble knights, or perhaps in a golden litter borne by great-muscled slaves. But there was no king. They did not use swords, or keep slaves. They were not barbarians. I do not know the rules and laws of their society, but I suspect that they were singularly few. As they did without monarchy and slavery, so they also go on without the stock exchange, the advertisement, the secret police, and the bomb. Yet I repeat that these were not simple folk, not dulcet shepherds, noble savages, bland utopians. They were not less complex than us. The trouble is that we have a bad habit, encouraged by pedants and sophisticates, of considering happiness as something rather stupid. Only pain is intellectual, only evil interesting. This is the treason of the artist: a refusal to admit the banality of evil and the terrible boredom of pain. If you can't lick 'em, join 'em. If it hurts, repeat it. But to praise despair is to condemn delight, to embrace violence is to lose hold of everything else. We have almost lost hold; we can no longer describe a happy man, nor make any celebration of joy. How can I tell you about the people of Omelas? They were not naïve and happy children—though their children were, in fact, happy. They were mature, intelligent, passionate adults whose lives were not wretched. O miracle! but I wish I could describe it better. I wish I could convince you. Omelas sounds in my words like a city in a fairy tale, long ago and far away, once upon a time. Perhaps it would be best if you imagined it as your own fancy bids, assuming it will rise to the occasion, for certainly I cannot suit you all. For instance, how about technology? I think that there would be no cars or helicopters in and above the streets; this follows from the fact that the people of Omelas are happy people. Happiness is based on a just discrimination of what is necessary, what is neither necessary nor destructive, and what is destructive. In the middle category, however—that of the unnecessary but undestructive, that of comfort, luxury, exuberance, etc.—they could perfectly well have central heating, subway trains, washing machines, and all kinds of marvelous devices not yet invented here, floating light-sources, fuelless power, a cure for the common cold. Or they could have none of that: it doesn't matter. As you like it. I incline to think that people from towns up and down the coast have been coming in to Omelas during the last days before the Festival on very fast little trains and double-decker trams, and that the train station of Omelas is actually the handsomest building in town, though plainer than the magnificent Farmers' Market. But even granted trains, I fear that Omelas so far strikes some of you as goody-goody. Smiles, bells, parades, horses, bleh. If so, please add an orgy. If an orgy would help, don't hesitate. Let us not, however, have temples from which issue beautiful nude priests and priestesses already half in ecstasy and ready to copulate with any man or woman, lover or stranger, who desires union with the deep godhead of the blood, although that was my first idea. But really it would be better not to have any temples in Omelas—at least, not manned temples. Religion yes, clergy no. Surely the beautiful nudes can just wander about, offering themselves like divine soufflés to the hunger of the needy and the rapture of the flesh. Let them join the processions. Let tambourines be struck above the copulations, and the glory of desire be proclaimed upon the gongs, and (a not unimportant point) let the offspring of these delightful rituals be beloved and looked after by all. One thing I know there is none of in Omelas is guilt. But what else should there be? I thought at first there were no drugs, but that is puritanical. For those who like it, the faint insistent sweetness of *drooz* may perfume the ways of the city, *drooz* which first brings a great lightness and brilliance to the mind and limbs, and then after some hours a dreamy languor, and wonderful visions at last of the very arcana and inmost secrets of the Universe, as well as exciting the pleasure of sex beyond all belief; and it is not habit-forming. For more modest tastes I think there ought to be beer. What else, what else belongs in the joyous city? The sense of victory, surely, the celebration of courage. But as we did without clergy, let us do without soldiers. The joy built upon successful slaughter is not the right kind of joy; it will not do; it is fearful and it is trivial. A boundless and generous contentment, a magnanimous triumph felt not against some outer enemy but in communion with the finest and fairest in the souls of all men everywhere and the splendor of the world's summer: this is what swells the hearts of the people of Omelas, and the victory they celebrate is that of life. I really don't think many of them need to take *drooz.*

Most of the processions have reached the Green Fields by now. A marvelous smell of cooking goes forth from the red and blue tents of the provisioners. The faces of small children are amiably sticky; in the benign grey beard of a man a couple of crumbs of rich pastry are entangled. The youths and girls have mounted their horses and are beginning to group around the starting line of the course. An old woman, small, fat, and laughing, is passing out flowers from a basket, and tall young men wear her flowers in their shining hair. A child of nine or ten sits at the edge of the crowd, alone, playing on a wooden flute. People pause to listen, and they smile, but they do not speak to him, for he never ceases playing and never sees them, his dark eyes wholly rapt in the sweet, thin magic of the tune.

He finishes, and slowly lowers his hands holding the wooden flute.

As if that little private silence were the signal, all at once a trumpet sounds from the pavilion near the starting line: imperious, melancholy, piercing. The horses rear on their slender legs, and some of them neigh in answer. Sober-faced, the young riders stroke the horses' necks and soothe them, whispering, "Quiet, quiet, there my beauty, my hope. . . ." They begin to form in rank along the starting line. The crowds along the racecourse are like a field of grass and flowers in the wind. The Festival of Summer has begun.

Do you believe? Do you accept the festival, the city, the joy? No? Then let me describe one more thing.

In a basement under one of the beautiful public buildings of Omelas, or perhaps in the cellar of one of its spacious private homes, there is a room. It has one locked door, and no window. A little light seeps in dustily between cracks in the boards, secondhand from a cobwebbed window somewhere across the cellar. In one corner of the little room a couple of mops, with stiff, clotted, foul-smelling heads, stand near a rusty bucket. The floor is dirt, a little damp to the touch, as cellar dirt usually is. The room is about three paces long and two wide: a mere broom closet or disused tool room. In the room a child is sitting. It could be a boy or a girl. It looks about six, but actually is nearly ten. It is feeble-minded. Perhaps it was born defective, or perhaps it has become imbecile through fear, malnutrition, and neglect. It picks its nose and occasionally fumbles vaguely with its toes or genitals, as it sits hunched in the corner farthest from the bucket and the two mops. It is afraid of the mops. It finds them horrible. It shuts its eyes, but it knows the mops are still standing there; and the door is locked; and nobody will come. The door is always locked; and nobody ever comes, except that sometimes—the child has no understanding of time or interval—sometimes the door rattles terribly and opens, and a person, or several people, are there. One of them may come in and kick the child to make it stand up. The others never come close, but peer in at it with frightened, disgusted eyes. The food bowl and the water jug are hastily filled, the door is locked, the eyes disappear. The people at the door never say anything, but the child, who has not always lived in the tool room, and can remember sunlight and its mother's voice, sometimes speaks. "I will be good," it says. "Please let me out. I will be good!" They never answer. The child used to scream for help at night, and cry a good deal, but now it only makes a kind of whining, "eh-haa, eh-haa," and it speaks less and less often. It is so thin there are no calves to its legs; its belly protrudes; it lives on a half-bowl of corn meal and grease a day. It is naked. Its buttocks and thighs are a mass of festered sores, as it sits in its own excrement continually.

They all know it is there, all the people of Omelas. Some of them have come to see it, others are content merely to know it is there. They all know that it has to be there. Some of them understand why, and some do not, but all understand that their happiness, the beauty of their city, the tenderness of their friendships, the health of their children, the wisdom of their scholars, the skill of their makers, even the abundance of their harvest and the kindly weathers of their skies, depend wholly on this child's abominable misery.

This is usually explained to children when they are between eight and twelve, whenever they seem capable of understanding; and most of those who come to see the child are young people, though often enough an adult comes, or comes back, to see the child. No matter how well the matter has been explained to them, these young spectators are always shocked and sickened at the sight. They feel disgust, which they had thought themselves superior to. They feel anger, outrage, impotence, despite all the explanations. They would like to do something for the child. But there is nothing they can do. If the child were brought up into the sunlight out of that vile place, if it were cleaned and fed and comforted, that would be a good thing, indeed; but if it were done, in that day and hour all the prosperity and beauty and delight of Omelas would wither and be destroyed. Those are the terms. To exchange all the goodness and grace of every life in Omelas for that single, small improvement: to throw away the happiness of thousands for the chance of the happiness of one: that would be to let guilt within the walls indeed.

The terms are strict and absolute; there may not even be a kind word spoken to the child.

Often the young people go home in tears, or in a tearless rage, when they have seen the child and faced this terrible paradox. They may brood over it for weeks or years. But as time goes on they begin to realize that even if the child could be released, it would not get much good of its freedom: a little vague pleasure of warmth and food, no doubt, but little more. It is too degraded and imbecile to know any real joy. It has been afraid too long ever to be free of fear. Its habits are too uncouth for it to respond to humane treatment. Indeed, after so long it would probably be wretched without walls about it to protect it, and darkness for its eyes, and its own excrement to sit in. Their tears at the bitter injustice dry when they begin to perceive the terrible justice of reality, and to accept it. Yet it is their tears and anger, the trying of their generosity and the acceptance of their helplessness, which are perhaps the true source of the splendor of their lives. Theirs is no vapid, irresponsible happiness. They know that they, like the child, are not free. They know compassion. It is the existence of the child, and their knowledge of its existence, that makes possible the nobility of their architecture, the poignancy of their music, the profundity of their science. It is because of the child that they are so gentle with children. They know that if the wretched one were not there snivelling in the dark, the other one, the flute-player, could make no joyful music as the young riders line up in their beauty for the race in the sunlight of the first morning of summer.

Now do you believe in them? Are they not more credible? But there is one more thing to tell, and this is quite incredible.

At times one of the adolescent girls or boys who go to see the child does not go home to weep or rage, does not, in fact, go home at all. Sometimes also a man or woman much older falls silent for a day or two, and then leaves home. These people go out into the street, and walk down the street alone. They keep walking, and walk straight out of the city of Omelas, through the beautiful gates. They keep walking across the farmlands of Omelas. Each one goes alone, youth or girl, man or woman. Night falls; the traveler must pass down village streets, between the houses with yellow-lit windows, and on out into the darkness of the fields. Each alone, they go west or north, towards the mountains. They go on. They leave Omelas, they walk ahead into the darkness, and they do not come back. The place they go towards is a place even less imaginable to most of us than the city of happiness. I cannot describe it at all. It is possible that it does not exist. But they seem to know where they are going, the ones who walk away from Omelas.

PART 8

Scholarly Research

Suggested Writing Projects

Research lies at the heart of most professional life. Lawyers research legal decisions, government workers research community problems, corporations research marketing failures, doctors research the safety of new drugs, and scientists research everything. The nature of the modern world is constructed on such exploration and discovery.

To many students, of course, a research project sounds foreboding. For those who have been through the experience, the excitement of discovery, of learning, of creative play with ideas more than compensates for the hard work. Research papers written in college tend to remain in memory long after classes and exams are forgotten. These are the papers to which the whole self is given for days or even months. These are the papers that help you discover that the merit of the mind lies not so much in what it knows, but in that it knows how to learn.

Here are some suggestions on where you might begin:

- Consider every research project a matter of inquiry. If possible, begin with a question that interests you personally. Even if that's not possible, remember this: Anything looked at closely and imaginatively becomes interesting in itself. Begin by conducting an overview of the subject using encyclopedias or specialized dictionaries, then use indexes, the Internet, and your library's online catalog to locate possible sources. Do all of this step by step, knowing in your heart that each step helps clarify and sharpen your focus.

- Locate and evaluate sources carefully, and take notes even more carefully, knowing that research is not merely a recording process but a thinking process. Find patterns, relationships, and contradictions, then make use of them in your essay; they are the keys to making knowledge. Perhaps most important, enter every research project with the recognition that knowledge has the power to transform and enrich the mind. Research that expands knowledge is at the heart of the human enterprise.

Group Inquiry

Research is often conducted by a lone individual working late at night in the library or in front of a computer. This is usually the method of the scholar in history, philosophy, literature, the arts, or other humanistic fields. But in many academic areas, especially the sciences and some social sciences—and perhaps most often in commercial research—you'll find researchers working in teams. If your instructor approves, you might want to explore a research project with a partner. Use your first meetings to discover a topic of mutual interest and to construct a task list. Decide which tasks can be accomplished individually and which will need both of you to work together. Meet regularly and keep good records of what you are discovering, both in term of materials and ideas about the materials. Expect your exploration and discovery stage to take more time than your writing stage, and expect the collaboration to take more time than working alone. A collaboration's investment in time is well rewarded in the final richness of the research report; two minds, debating, brainstorming, and challenging each other can often provoke new insights that neither alone would have discovered. Begin talking early about the writing, and schedule your writing sessions well in advance of the due date. Stay flexible and be prepared for unexpected setbacks as well as unanticipated insights.

CHAPTER 31

The Preliminary Stages of Research

Whether he is an archaeologist, chemist, or astronomer, at the heart the researcher's goal is very much the same. Basically, he looks for facts that interest him and then tries to arrange them in meaningful sequence. . . . He defines what happens, then figures out where, when, how, and why it happens. His adverbial search for cause and effect, for the basic ordering in things, is primal, compelling, and satisfying, quite apart from practical considerations.

JAMES H. AUSTIN

You came to college because you wanted to know something. You wanted to learn, to grow, to change. Maybe it's turned out to be more difficult than you thought. But here and there, in a biology class perhaps, or in your personal contacts with a professor or an advisor, you've found yourself challenged and excited. Perhaps you've had the opportunity to read philosophy or to explore new techniques in electronic music. Or your philosophy instructor assigned you to write a library paper on existentialism, and you thought it would be boring but it turned out to be fascinating. Or, after taking a course in accounting, you've begun to doubt whether you really want to pursue it further. To your parents' grief, you've started thinking you might want to go into stage design.

Intellectual excitement stimulates personal growth. I suspect that's what undergraduate years are really all about. And one of the key ways such opportunity opens up for you is—of all things—through research, that old bugbear you may always have dreaded. Yet research is really the only way (other than personal experience) that we explore and discover new ideas and values. Research is the work of the mind. When approached with a lively spirit and a sense of inner order, it is an investment in intellectual growth and well-being. And because knowledge always moves from the known to the unknown, research in the undergraduate years is a way of helping you discover what is already known, so that you can spend the rest of your life, if you choose to do so, exploring the frontiers of knowledge.

Research need never be dull and tedious. Your personal interest and involvement may often be the only basis for pursuing it. A "personal" search emanates from your own questions: How can I overcome math anxiety? How can I help my alcoholic father? Do I really want to become a physical therapist? Is abortion a realistic possibility? A more objective search may be assigned in a particular class, such as Sociology 101, but usually you'll have a wide range of topics or avenues to follow: Is teenage suicide related to stress? Genetics? Cultural changes? Is it higher among bright students? Are incidents of suicide among youth rising, or are reporting methods merely more accurate? Are there distinct differences in urban and rural levels of suicide? Racial differences? Gender differences?

The personal search may reach out toward a more extensive use of primary sources such as interviews, letters, and e-mail; but like the more objective library search, it will require hours of solid reading in journals, magazines, and books. The differences may appear more in the final product (in tone or voice or the intended audience) than in method, because even the most seemingly intellectual research into the highest plane of ideas involves a commitment of the individual, of the self, of the personal "I."

Research as Inquiry

You may be asked to choose a topic suited to your personal interests or you may be asked to explore a subject related to some particular aspect of a course. Either way, you'll need to keep in mind that the whole of research is the asking of questions (and the search for answers).

Here are questions you need to start with. They ought to guide you from your earliest stages to the last sentence you revise.

1. What do I want to know? And why is it important?
2. What do I already know?

3. How do I find new information? Through personal interviews? Books? Field research? The Internet?
4. How do I evaluate what I find? Is it accurate? True? Meaningful? Pertinent?
5. What have I learned? Is it significant? How is it related to the subject as a whole? Is it related to myself in any way?

Preparing a Work Schedule

Research cannot be rushed. Interviews must be arranged, websites consulted, books studied, notes gathered, outlines constructed, citations recorded, and bibliographies suffered through. It all takes time, self-discipline, and planning. The first step is to organize a day-by-day schedule for yourself, as in the example on page 413.

You might need more or less time, depending on the length of the paper and on your personal working habits, but never underestimate the time it will take. A necessary book may turn up missing, information you've requested from a government agency may not arrive, or your roommate may accidentally unplug your computer while you're out of the room and obliterate three day's work. Build in time for the unexpected.

And build in time for relaxation. Numerous studies of the creative process show that most original ideas tend to appear in the mind when long periods of concentrated study are alternated with short periods of diversion and rest. Most documented cases of inspiration reveal that it seems to happen *between* intense work and play. No one knows why, but the unconscious elements of our mind need time to sort out and organize information. If your schedule is too tight or you find yourself working day and night, you may also find yourself overwhelmed by the material, unable to evaluate it, merely stringing ideas together without thought. French scholar Jean Guitton has described the golden rule for intellectual work: "Tolerate neither half-work nor half-rest. Give yourself totally or withhold yourself absolutely. Never allow the two to overlap."

Psychologist Rollo May argues strongly that you must schedule one other element: *solitude.* Some of my students tell me they write with music from their latest CD turned up full blast. They claim it is the only way they can work. But clinical studies show that the *distraction* from concentration remains, even if it is unconscious. Your best work may never occur. Rollo May points out that it is, in fact, "a characteristic of our time that many are afraid of solitude: to be alone may be a sign one is a social failure." Yet to find that deep inner voice, May argues, requires that "we be able to retire from a world that is 'too much with us,' that we be able to be quiet, that we let solitude work for us and in us." The individual who lives continuously "amid [a] constant din of radio and TV" may not be aware that "insights from unconscious depths" are being repressed. Rollo May observes that "if we are to experience" such "insights," we may need to retrain ourselves to hear the voice of solitude.

Tentative Work Schedule

Days 1–3

- Select a subject.
- Evaluate what you already know.
- Prepare a general question on what you want to learn.
- Begin preliminary reading—an overview of the subject.
- Narrow the subject based on overview.
- Raise specific questions for specific inquiry.

Days 4–5

- Locate topic in indexes, abstracts, and online catalogs.
- Select candidates for interviews, if any.
- Prepare a working bibliography.

Days 6–11

- Investigate sources.
- Gather data, ideas, facts, observations, and information.

Day 12

- Organize notes.
- Develop a specific focus or thesis to guide your writing.

Days 13–17

- Begin drafting and revising, revising and drafting.

Days 18–19

- Leave unscheduled days for the unexpected or to allow time for cooling off before final editing.

Day 20

- Prepare all bibliographic materials.

Day 21

- Print out your last draft and read with a critical eye.
- Make final revisions, line-by-line editing.

Day 22

- Prepare final draft and proofread. Do not depend solely on a computer spell check.

Day 23

- Celebrate!

Conducting an Overview

Once you've outlined a tentative schedule, set to work immediately. Whether you've selected a subject or received an assigned subject as part of a class project, you'll need to obtain a general overview of the topic as a whole. You cannot plunge into research on educational innovations without knowing some background about, and history of, education. You cannot analyze a proposal for a guaranteed annual wage without knowing the cultural and economic context that has brought about such a proposal. Even if you already feel you have a background in the subject, you will need to verify your understanding of terms and concepts you plan to deal with.

Reference Tools

One of the primary goals is to seek information while wasting as little time as possible in the actual search. Reference works such as encyclopedias and dictionaries (printed and electronic) exist for exactly that purpose. They not only provide facts, statistics, definitions, biographical information, historical chronologies, and geographical data, they also often list major sources for, and authorities on, a subject, saving you hours of random searching.

Encyclopedias and Dictionaries. Encyclopedias are valuable for general information, but they are written for non-specialists and should be used only to gain an overview of a topic. *The Encyclopedia Britannica* is usually the best source for an introduction to topics in humanities and social sciences. The information is authoritative and often provides references to other more specialized sources. The *Encyclopedia Americana* is less exhaustive but is in some ways a better general work on the sciences. The final volume offers a comprehensive index and is a good place to begin a search. Numerous specialized encyclopedias and dictionaries can provide even more detailed coverage as well as information on major authorities and sources.

You might think of dictionaries as merely offering simple definitions, but in fact, a number of major dictionaries offer complete histories of words, something that can be especially valuable in providing an overview of a topic. The *Oxford English Dictionary,* for example, is a multivolume work detailing how meanings have evolved over the centuries. Other kinds of dictionaries and encyclopedias focus on specialized academic subject areas, offering broad definitions, histories, and explanations of complete topics in the field. These works are written by specialists and will provide you with more detailed information, analysis, and competing views. Here are just a few you might want to know about:

Dictionary of the Middle Ages
Encyclopedia of Bioethics
Encyclopedia of Philosophy
Encyclopedia of Psychology
Encyclopedia of Religion

Encyclopedia of World Art
McGraw-Hill International Encyclopedia of the Social Sciences
New Grove Dictionary of Music and Musicians
New Palgrave Dictionary of Money and Finance
Women's Studies Encyclopedia

All of these can be located in your library by finding the call number in the library catalog. For a complete range of specialized dictionaries and encyclopedias, consult the *ARBA Guide to Subject Encyclopedias and Dictionaries,* or *First Stop: The Master Index to Subject Encyclopedias.*

In addition to the preceding possibilities, most individual disciplines also have specialized guides that identify important bibliographies, encyclopedias, computer databases, journals, and periodical indexes in that particular discipline. Here are just a few:

A Student's Guide to History
Introduction to Library Research in Anthropology
Introduction to Library Research in Women's Studies
Harvard Guide to American History
Music: A Guide to the Reference Literature
Reference Works in British and American Literature
Visual Arts Research: A Handbook

For topics currently in the news, you'll probably find it valuable to begin with *NewsBank Index,* a listing of current events from five hundred important newspapers. *NewsBank* is available in most libraries online (or on CD-ROM). *InfoTrac,* also available online, covers over two thousand general periodicals and newspapers such as *The New York Times,* the *Wall Street Journal,* the *Los Angeles Times,* and others, including most news magazines.

Research and the Writer's Journal. If you've been maintaining a journal throughout this course, you'll probably find it essential to continue with it. Most writers divide their computer journal into various files: One file for a working bibliography, another file for notes, another for interviews, and still another for ideas and explorations. When you sit down to write the essay itself, you'll do so with more confidence and a sense of having your material under control. You may find that as much as 50 percent will already be drafted in a computerized journal. In other words, the journal should remain integral to all your writing habits.

Focusing the Subject in Question Form

You cannot write a successful paper on the whole of World War II. You could not even do a satisfactory job on the role of women in World War II. You *might* be able to go into some detail on the role of women in the labor force during World War II *if* you were planning to write a master's thesis. But if you are considering a smaller research paper, you must find a single element of your subject that is appropriate both for the size of paper required and for the amount of research time available to you. Failure to narrow your topic may leave you awash in a sea of general information.

This is not the time to form an actual thesis statement that might lock you into an idea you can't prove or into a subject on which information is unavailable. But it is the time to ask questions. All the different techniques you're familiar with should now come into play. Begin with the 5 *W*'s: *who? what? where? when?* and *why?* Consider the 4 *C*'s of observation: *change, conflict* (or *opposition*), *consequence,* and *characterization* (in the full sense of that term—*physical details, actions, speech, background, others' reactions*). And finally, recognize that all of the formal patterns of perception may also need to be included: *comparison and contrast, definition, classification, illustration,* and *analysis.*

That may seem like a lot to keep in your head at once, but you've already practiced using most of those techniques in earlier papers. What you'll need now is time—lots of it. You cannot rush this phase or postpone it. It may be the single most crucial step you perform in preparing to engage in effective research.

Here is how you might consider the subject of women's entrance into the labor force during World War II. Begin with a general approach that has some personal interest to you. Let's say that in this case you're curious about the origins of the current feminist movement. Perhaps you could begin with one or two broad questions: Did women's entrance into the wartime labor force create new expectations and demands from women? Did it bring about any change in male attitudes? This may be a satisfactory start, but still too general. Even more focused questions must be found:

- Before the United States' entry into the war, what percentage of the workforce consisted of women?
- What were men's and women's attitudes toward "working women" before the war?
- What percentage of women were working by the end of the war?
- Why did this movement occur?
- What kinds of jobs did women take?
- Was there any opposition to women's entry into male jobs at that time?
- Was the working woman viewed as a temporary wartime phenomenon? By women? By men?
- Was it a temporary phenomenon? Evidence?
- Can specific consequences be determined?
- What were men's and women's attitudes after the war?
- Did opposition arise against women who continued to work? Evidence?

- What kind of evidence would be satisfactory? Did women speak out? Were new labor laws passed?
- Where could such evidence be found?

This is only a small beginning. But notice already how raising questions about the subject has led to raising questions about evidence. If the initial subject is a poor one or too complex, such questions will begin to identify the dangers of pursuing it further. No need wasting several weeks on a topic if evidence is not available. Only by considering in advance the types of evidence you may need, and where you may have to look to find it, can you begin to be somewhat confident that your research will prove successful.

One final suggestion: Don't try all of this in your head. Sit down in a quiet location and write out questions as you think of them. Seeing the words on paper will stimulate more questions, and it will also help you begin early to find an order or pattern to your research. Related questions can be grouped. Questions that seem to lead nowhere can be struck out. Only by doing this will you be prepared for the next two steps in the process: finding and investigating sources of information.

Locating Primary and Secondary Sources

Because most students do not attempt to locate and use primary sources, you can often impress your reader by showing a little initiative and imagination. A letter to a congressman or a company president, a telephone call to a local journalist or director of a social agency may bring in unexpected and fresh information. An interview with the curator of the local art gallery or a scientist at a major university may provide new ideas as well as human interest. In your journal, make a list of the potential primary sources, and attempt to locate at least one or two, if possible.

- authorities on the topic
- local or national organizations
- people involved in or affected by the issue
- letters, journals, diaries, e-mail
- movies, television, records, radio
- original documents

A personal investigation may focus more on primary sources, but much of your effort will still focus on the library. Because of that, some students head directly for their library's online catalog. But the experienced researcher knows that other reference tools can be far more helpful at this early stage.

Indexes and Databases

Not all information can be found in books, especially if your topic deals with current issues and ideas. An "index" offers a list of articles in everything from newspapers to magazines to specialized academic journals (usually classified together in library jargon as "periodicals"). Periodicals are especially valuable because they contain the most recent thinking on your topic. The newest interpretations, the latest facts and statistics, and the most current controversies will usually be found here. But because there are literally thousands of newspapers, journals, and magazines, you'll need to begin with an index or database to locate articles and book reviews on your individual topic. The term "index" is used to refer to printed volumes (or a printed volume located on microfiche) organized alphabetically by subject or author.

An electronic (or computerized) database is an index available online, or sometimes on CD-ROM. Databases can be especially valuable because they often offer more information, including brief summaries of an article's contents, something that can clue you immediately on whether you want to read the whole of it. Some specialized databases also offer access to the full-text article contents online, which obviously can save a great deal of time finding your information. One drawback is that many electronic databases do not cover materials before the 1980s. Some important electronic exceptions include *ERIC (Educational Resources Information Center)* and *MLA (Modern Language Association) Bibliography,* which index articles dating back to the 1960s, while still other specialized databases such as *Historical Abstracts* cover back as far as 1450. Printed versions of indexes may still be necessary for doing more historical type scholarly research.

The following are some of the most important printed and online indexes with which you should be familiar.

The *Applied Science and Technology Index* lists articles in highly specialized journals and may provide you with more depth on subjects like forestry, biology, chemistry, and the environment.

The *Business Periodicals Index* covers over three hundred different magazines and journals that deal with economics, finance, management, and so on.

InfoTrac Expanded Academic ASAP is a general electronic index that covers two thousand journals, popular magazines, and newspapers in a broad range of topics from current events, law, history, religion, psychology, and sociology, to women's studies and the sciences. Though coverage is not in-depth, it provides an excellent starting point and offers abstracts, images and some full-text article coverage since 1980.

The *Humanities Index* will be the primary place to begin a study on the arts, literature, languages, music, and philosophy.

The *New York Times Index* is indispensable for research on people, events, and organizations in the news since 1951. It even offers a brief summary of the information contained in each article so that you can quickly determine whether you need to pursue it further.

The *Reader's Guide to Periodical Literature* lists articles published since 1900 in popular magazines like *Time, Sports Illustrated,* and *Rolling Stone.* Obviously, you probably won't find in-depth coverage in such sources. But the *Reader's Guide* also lists many superior periodicals: *Atlantic, New Republic, Commonweal, Harper's,* and *National Review.* If you use this index selectively, you can often find excellent material, especially on current issues.

The *Social Sciences Index* provides author and subject headings for hundreds of magazines and scholarly journals in psychology, sociology, political science, and similar fields.

Searching the Library Catalog

Only now (after a preliminary search through indexes, databases, and bibliographies) should you turn to the library's online catalog for books. I make this suggestion because too many students who begin their search at the library catalog never seem to get past it. No doubt, information from books will constitute a major portion of your research, but relevant websites, journals and magazine articles should not be omitted. By discovering what current material is being published in periodicals and by having studied the various classifications of books on the subject as listed in a bibliography, you are in a more credible position to make meaningful selections from the library catalog.

Books are generally searchable in a library catalog in four ways: under author, under title, under subject, and under keyword searches. If you've obtained some names of authorities from your previous overview of the subject, you'll want to check their work under author headings. Otherwise, subject headings will group all works on a topic, and you'll probably find it a productive place to begin. But note that any topic may have several related subject headings. If your subject involves changing attitudes toward marijuana, you might begin your search under the heading of *marijuana,* but find few books because most of the information you need may fall under the headings of *drugs, drug abuse,* or *drugs—laws and legislation.* If you are unsure of the exact subject heading to use, or when you do not know specific titles or exact spellings of an author name, you should try *keyword searching.* A keyword search is widespread and typically best for broad initial research concepts. Keyword searches find and retrieve your search words from the title, subject heading, or contents sections of materials recorded in an online catalog or database. Examining a few results found with a keyword search will provide clues to correct name spellings, exact subject headings, and related search terms you might use to find more information. Remember that doing good research takes time, so give yourself several hours, and be willing to explore.

Searching the Internet

The Internet began in the 1960s as a network of computers linked by telephone, connecting universities, government agencies, and businesses around the world and providing for a free flow of information, including online catalogs, in-house databases, electronic mail, and electronic journals. Today, you have access to millions of sources of information, making it a "virtual library" with such things as full texts of books, articles, manuscripts, medical information, weather bulletins, stock market reports, scripts of old Beatles movies, government documents, and the *Journal of Postmodern Culture.* The resources available are almost unlimited. The result can be exciting or daunting. A first-time user may feel overwhelmed by the seeming chaos of the "system." But with practice and patience, the Internet can become an important research option.

You can access the Internet through a direct network connection, available on almost all college campuses, or through a private server such as America Online, CompuServe, or Prodigy. Both methods will charge you a fee. In some cases, your library or university may absorb some of the cost or charge you directly for time used. Browsing may be expensive. To conduct an online search, you may be required to work with a librarian. If you have already focused your topic, this can be productive, but without specific key words describing the subject (called "descriptors") you may receive too much data, and the time and cost may be prohibitive. Before you begin an Internet search, check with your librarian for information on fees and advice regarding whether such service would be worthwhile for your particular topic. You may find that for a small research paper, more conventional resources will prove adequate.

Boolean Searching

It's important to make the most of your online browsing time by using efficient search strategies. The last section covered author, title, subject and keyword searches. Another important concept for searching is the use of *Boolean operators* (*AND* or *OR*) to combine search words or phrases. If you wanted to find information about the *benefits of meditation,* it's unlikely you'll find this concept listed as an exact subject heading. Performing a keyword search for *benefits OR meditation* in your favorite search engine will result in a very broad set of websites that mention either *meditation* or *benefits,* but will not necessarily contain information about *both* search terms. A website that discusses *benefits* could involve anything from insurance plans to an online journal with the word "benefits" in the title, while websites that mention *meditation* range from religious organizations to those selling yoga instructional videos. Combining search terms with *OR* always broadens your search and increases your results, and is best used to expand an overly specific and narrow research topic.

Doing a keyword search for *meditation AND benefits* tells the search engine or database that the results found must contain *both* search terms. Such a search is more specific and should produce a set of websites for you to explore that provide information about the range of *meditation benefits* (whether physical, social, or psychological). Combining search terms with *AND* always narrows your search and decreases your set of results, and is best used to focus an overly broad and open research topic. In a popular search engine such as *Yahoo!* or *AltaVista,* a Boolean *AND* search will produce a smaller and more relevant number of websites for you to browse. You should be aware that certain on-line catalogs, databases and search engines such as *Google* now automatically place an *AND* between your search terms.

Truncation

One final important search technique is known as *truncation.* Truncation allows you to search for variations of a word such as its plural form or different endings. Truncation symbols can vary in different types of databases, but are most commonly an asterisk (*) or a question mark (?). If you are writing a paper on the *African economy,* performing a search for *Africa* AND econom** would find all results with the following variations: *Africa, Africa's,* or *African, AND economy, economic, economies,* or *economical.* Truncation symbols can also be used within your search words as well. Searching for *wom*n AND stud** means the same thing as searching for *woman* or *women, AND study, studies,* or *studied.* These truncated searches thoroughly expand your set of results and save you time and keystrokes.

Evaluating Traditional Sources

All ideas, insights, data, quotations, paraphrases and so on taken from a book, a document, a newspaper article, or other source located during your search must be evaluated for its quality, accuracy, and reliability. The process begins the moment you identify an item as a "possible source." Not all material may be current; some may present data in a slanted or biased way, and still other materials may reveal faulty reasoning or draw conclusions from inadequate data. *Before* you ever take a note, you must determine whether the evidence before you is trustworthy and valuable. Here are some points to consider.

Who Is the Author? Does he or she have credentials or authority to speak on the subject (a university scientist, a researcher associated with an established medical facility, a prize-winning newspaper reporter). Having credentials does not guarantee the information or argument is "truth," but it does mean it's probably worth your consideration.

You'll also want to question whether the author is associated with an organization that might have an announced agenda or political position (the National Right to Life movement, the National Organization for Women, the AFL–CIO, the Sierra Club). All of us have a position or stance—a cultural, religious, or professional bias. The point is not to discount it, but the opposite: to take it into account, to consider whether the argument or information may be valid, well reasoned, or slanted. Either way, it may be useful to support your own position or to argue against it.

If your source is an article from a newspaper or magazine, no author may be listed. Consider whether the source itself is trustworthy, whether it has an agenda of its own, a political stance, or whether it might be propaganda for a particular organization. *National Review* will always provide a highly intelligent, conservative position on an issue. The *Atlantic* may provide an opposing liberal slant. *Consumer Reports* will try to take an "unbiased" position. And a newsletter for the *National Arab League* will provide information and opinion favorable to its cause.

When Was the Material Published? It seems self-evident that a book on stock market investments must be up-to-date, but if you don't check the date, you may not know you're reading advice from the 1950s. In the same way, technical and scientific information must be current. New theories or perspectives on almost any subject may be valuable—and sometimes essential. But older views must be considered individually. Arguments for a certain moral position or certain basic principles may never be outdated. In other words, always check the date, and make a judgment about relevance.

What Kind of Material Is Being Offered? If you're working with a published book, begin by checking the table of contents or index. Is your focused topic listed? Skim the introduction, looking for any key elements of your topic. If you are considering material from a periodical, skim several paragraphs and the conclusion. Are you being presented a reasoned argument? Statistics and graphs? Does the material seem complete? Does the material offer citations for specific claims? Is a bibliography of sources used? Personal experience? Can you determine the stance or bias of the author? Will the ideas presented contribute to, or illuminate, some aspect of your topic? Five minutes glancing over a work to ensure that it is one you can feel confident about—and effectively use—can save an hour or two of wasted time later.

Evaluating Internet Sources

You may find your very best material on the Internet, something absolutely original and unavailable in your library, but you must also be aware that the Internet is unpoliced and unregulated. It contains vast networks of information resources that vary in quality and credibility. Many websites do not provide author or publisher credentials, or do not include enough information to insure the content or currency of the site. Often the reason for placing the information on the Web in the first place is not given. Much like evaluating traditional resources, you should consider specific *criteria* and ask yourself important questions to help you with website evaluation.

Examine the URL. To learn more about the type of website you are exploring and where the information comes from, begin by examining a website's URL (its uniform resource locator, commonly called its web address). The components of a URL include the host computer, or the host name of the computer server where a website is located. The computer name follows the "www," and this information is important for determining where the web page originates (for instance www.CNN.com is the Cable News Network website). *Domain Name* is the final few letters that follow the host computer name.

Some common domains include

- *.edu*—educational institution, which ranges from professional research to student pages
- *.net*—network provider, which usually provides services to subscribing customers
- *.gov*—government agency, which provides official government information
- *.org*—non-profit organization, which may promote a specific point of view
- *.com*—commercial enterprise, which may be trying to sell products.

Who Is the Publisher or Sponsoring Agency? Identify and evaluate the credentials of the organization or people responsible for maintaining a website. Does the site clearly identify the organization responsible for the information found on it? Does the document have consistent headers, footers, or wallpaper that imply an association with a larger website? Is there a link provided back to information about the website's publisher or sponsoring agency? Can you determine if the page is part of someone's personal account or part of an official site? A tilde (~) in the URL usually indicates a personal web page rather than an institutional website. Can you find the sponsoring organization's homepage by deleting all the information in the URL after the website's domain name? Can you determine if the information has been published in a respected journal?

Is the Material Objective? Identify any biases and determine whether or not such a point of view will influence your decision to use the information. What is the author's point of view? Is this point of view clearly stated by the author or editor of the information? Is the document trying to influence your opinion? Is this a commercial site? Is the purpose of the site to promote or sell products? Does the document come from a site sponsored by an organization with a specific agenda (political, commercial, or philosophical)? A web document with an obvious bias does not necessarily mean the information lacks value. Various sources of information are appropriate for use in different research situations. You must determine whether subjective information matches your requirements.

Does the Material Seem Accurate or Reliable? The information contained within a web document must be carefully examined for errors and misleading information. Is there a way to verify any background information provided in the document? Does the document contain any spelling or grammar errors? Is the site cluttered with advertisements, photos, or fancy graphics? If the document quotes or refers to other sources, does it include a bibliography or link to the sources mentioned? If you are looking at a research article, is the source of the information clearly identified? Does the article include data and explain the research methods used to gather and interpret it?

How Current Is the Information? If your topic involves recent events or developments, determine the currency of the information on the website. Is the page dated? Is it regularly maintained? Are specific data or events referenced? Do sources used in the bibliography provide dates or clues? Does the document refer to current news or recent discoveries? Have any of the links expired or moved?

Preparing a Working Bibliography

Every student develops his or her best method of working. You will probably find it easiest to develop a working bibliography in a separate computer file. However, as you know, it's essential to maintain a back-up file on a separate disk. The loss of a working bibliography can prove fatal. Some students will always prefer using a spiral notebook because they feel the information can't be erased. However, notebooks can be lost on busses and subways, or eaten by the cat. No matter your method, make the listing thorough, complete, and detailed the first time you take the note. You will discover that it is far faster than having to return to an online search because you forgot to record all the information.

Some instructors may require you to keep a formal listing of every possible source, recording author and publication data in the exact form later required for your "Works Cited" page (see pages 451–455). Others may argue that all you need at this point is *complete* information, believing that after you actually find that you have used material from a source is it necessary to organize it in the appropriate format.

I tend to agree with the latter point of view. Your time might be better spent at this stage making judgments about the content of books and articles rather than worrying about the mechanics of a bibliography. An informal working list, however, must be as complete and accurate as possible. Here's the information you'll need for every source you think you may use. Take it all down the first time, tedious as it may seem.

All this preliminary work may sometimes seem tedious and frustrating, but without it, your research phase will consist of random guesswork and hope work. Take the necessary time now to assure yourself that your actual investigation will be focused and productive.

Sample Working Bibliography

Name the index or source of information in case you must return to check entry.	Social Science Index
Record name of author, title, name of magazine or source, date, page numbers.	Forbes, Allyn, "The Disaster of CIA Involvement in Afghanistan," Harper's (June, 01). 15–21.

For journals, record both volume number and page number.	Greenbaum, R. A. "Who Really Controlled Afghanistan War Policy?" *Foreign Policy.* Vol 29, June 29, 2002, 62–3.
For newspapers, include page and column numbers.	Fishburn, Stanley. "The Decline of American Influence in Pakistan," *NY Times,* Dec. 21, 2001, Op/Ed page 1, col. 1.
For books, include call numbers.	Lisko, Christopher. *The War Against Evil,* N.Y.: Peabody Press, 2002 [DS558. B41].
For Internet, record author, article, page, and/or date you accessed website and/or site title, date accessed and URL (web address).	Afari, Mohammed. The Muslim Vision: photos & text. 15 November 2001 <http://afghanistan.com/text/20011080602.html>.

An Outline of Preliminary Steps in Research

1. *Prepare a work schedule.*
   - Do not underestimate the time needed.
   - Build in unscheduled days for rest or to gain perspective on the topic.
2. *Clarify and define the subject.*
   - Obtain an overview and historical background.
   - Check encyclopedias, bibliographies, electronic indexes, and databases.
3. *Narrow the subject and place in question form.*
   - Formulate your questions in impartial terms.
   - Consider kinds of evidence that will be needed.
4. *Locate primary and secondary sources.*
   - Consider potential organizations or authorities to contact for interviews.
   - Search indexes, bibliographies, Internet, and library catalog.
   - Evaluate sources as you go.
5. *Prepare a working bibliography.*
   - Obtain two to three times as many sources as you think you'll need.
   - Record all information available on each source in your journal or computer file.

Practice

Here are several questions for class discussion:

1. What type of search in the library catalog (author, title, subject, or keyword) would you perform to find the following:
   a. An edition of Dickens' *Great Expectations*
   b. Criticism of *Great Expectations*
   c. General criticism of Dickens' work
   d. Dickens' letters
   e. Fiction featuring Dickens as a character
   f. The role of women in Dickens' work
   g. Dickens and Romanticism
2. What would you expect to find if you used *InfoTrack Expanded Academic ASAP*?
3. How would you find articles published in *The New York Times* on terrorist attacks against the World Trade Center?
4. What is a specialized dictionary, and what can it do for you besides define a word?
5. If you wanted a general overview of a topic, what reference tools might be useful?
6. To find material on social aspects of computer technology, what index would you check?
7. What search technique allows you to find plural and different forms of a word?
8. If a website document doesn't have a clear author, how can you identify who's responsible for providing the information content?
9. If you can't find the material you're looking for, to whom should you turn?

CHAPTER 32

Thoughtful Note Taking

Once you learned to hold a pencil and scrawl your alphabet in shaky letters across the lined page. Each uncertain movement of the pencil was consciously made. Yet with time, the instrument in your hand and the words on the page became an extension of yourself. In the following chapters, detailed steps of formal note taking, outlining, and documenting may at first seem equally foreign and awkward. We all know it is not knowledge of such mechanics in itself that will bring the rewards of scholarship, yet with time the mechanics become second nature—like holding a pencil. Each technique becomes only another extension of yourself, freeing you for more concentrated attention to those qualities of intellectual endeavor that do bring satisfaction.

Preliminary Skimming

A scholarly approach to a subject requires a selective approach. You'll not want to waste time reading unrelated material. Before sitting down to a twenty-page essay, quickly study the opening paragraph and the conclusion. If you find nothing that points toward the narrowed questions you've posed for study, skim the remainder of the essay. Usually, this can be done by reading only the first and last sentences of each paragraph. If you find even a single idea that might be valuable, go back and read the whole essay more closely. Otherwise, in only a few minutes, you can determine that the essay has nothing of relevance, and you can move on to something more important.

Skimming a book requires several additional steps. If you've already obtained an overview of your subject, you'll seldom need to read complete works; after all, you need specific information on only a narrow portion of a topic. Begin with the *table of contents.* Select from it those chapters that seem relevant, and skim each chapter in the same way you would a magazine article. Do not take notes until you are certain the chapter offers something worth your time. If none of the chapter titles seems pertinent, quickly read the *preface* and *introduction.* That's where most authors summarize their intentions, their basic thesis, and their approach to a subject. Finally, turn to the *index* at the back of the book. Search out several different headings or terms that relate to your specific topic, and check those individual pages. If nothing meaningful shows up, you've spent only a few minutes with a book that would have proved of little value in the first place. But if you find even a single potentially valuable idea, read the whole chapter in which it occurs. See the idea in the full context in which the author intended it. Then, if it proves useful, take notes.

Preliminary skimming allows you to investigate far more material than the average student, who checks out a few large books and reads them cover to cover. You will be able to research five times as much material with less effort and less wasted time.

The Preliminary Reference List

If, after skimming an essay or book, you decide it will probably contain useful information or ideas on your topic, the first step—before you begin critical reading and certainly before you begin taking actual notes—is to create a bibliographic entry. You must train yourself to take this simple step first because no matter how good your intentions, generations of experience prove that students who jot down notes first may forget to record the full bibliographical data. The failure will not be apparent until you reach the final stage of writing your paper and suddenly find yourself needing a references-cited page. That's when your friends will see you at midnight pounding on the library door.

Don't take a chance. Write down all necessary information *before* you take a single note.

From the title page of a book, record the following.

1. Full name(s) of author(s) or editor(s) (last name first)
2. Full title of book, including subtitle (underlined)
3. Place of publication
4. Full name of publisher
5. Date of publication (use the last date given because later printings may contain revised material or new page arrangements)
6. The library call number (if appropriate)

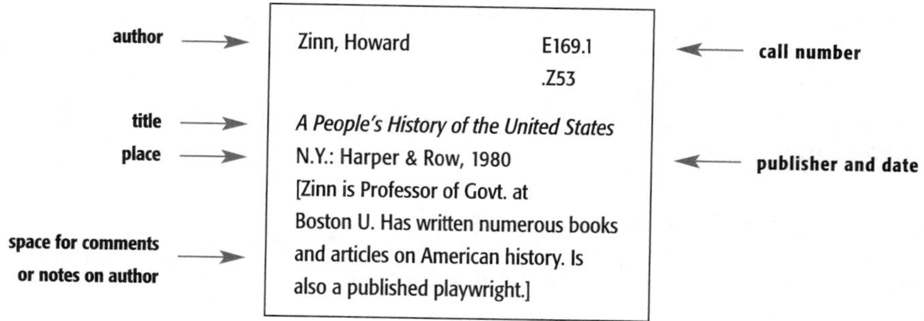

For an article from a magazine or journal, record the following.

1. Full name(s) of author(s) (last name first)
2. Title of the article (in quotation marks)
3. Full name of magazine (underlined)
4. Volume number (usually located on table of contents page)
5. Date of the magazine
6. Inclusive pages (for example: 125–152)

Although these two formats should serve for most sources, from time to time you'll encounter a source that creates special problems in both bibliographic entries. That's when you'll need to consult a style manual. Two of the most widely used are the *MLA Handbook for Writers of Research Papers* and the *Research Manual for the American Psychological Association.* Both offer hundreds of examples and details on in-text citations and bibliographic forms. Both are available in college bookstores or libraries.

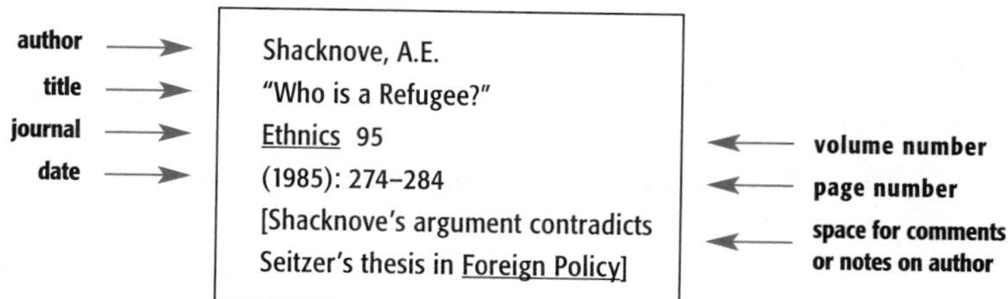

Critical Reading

Once you've found material directly relevant to your narrowed topic, you'll want to apply all the mental steps of critical reading covered earlier in Chapter 26. Approach the material as objectively as possible. Attempt to understand the author's ideas on his or her terms. Know your own biases as best you can, and avoid making hasty judgments. Do take notes with careful evaluation of the content: Make an effort to discover who the author is and what his or her authority to speak on the subject might be; try to consider the historical and cultural context in which the work was written; and, most important, look for logic, look for appeals to emotion, look for evidence supported with valid sources, and look for sound reasoning.

Note Taking: The Wrong Way

Learning how to take proper and meaningful notes requires more skill than student writers may first realize—and more effort. Here are three ways you should *not* take notes:

1. Do not copy an author's ideas word for word. A note that consists of nothing but a long quotation taken directly from a secondary source may give you the impression you're busy working hard—after all, it takes a long time to copy down a page of print in longhand. With few exceptions, however, you'll seldom need a page-long quotation from anyone. If you do, a photocopy machine can do it faster. But that leads to negative warning number two.
2. Do not photocopy passages from secondary sources as a substitute for taking a note. Photocopying machines are wonderful inventions. Yet they obviously do not *digest* or *contemplate* information as you should be doing. The time saving may be dangerously misleading.
3. Perhaps equally wasteful is the method of avoiding all note taking by underlining important passages in books or marking them with slips of paper and trying to write the first draft by spreading a dozen books about you on your desk and typing the paper as you go. Again, no assimilation or understanding of the material occurs. Such a writer is not really writing, only collating.

None of these methods will accomplish your purpose. No real thinking occurs. A machine can copy; the human brain has more potential. Unless you are summarizing or paraphrasing ideas in your own words, you are not really exerting intellectual effort; you are not grasping the meaning of ideas, evaluating, or interpreting. Note taking must be a thinking process, not merely a recording process. As your research progresses, you must continually reassess and refine your subject. You must be alert for areas of exploration that you might not have anticipated earlier. It may be possible that the direction established by your main question will prove unfruitful. New questions will almost always appear as you move from source to source. Unless you are actively engaged in thinking about the material, questioning the material, challenging the material as you take notes, you are not truly engaged in research at all.

Note Taking: The Right Way

Correct note taking involves a two-phase process. First comes the thinking phase. You must make repeated judgments about the worth and meaning of each idea you encounter. You must be involved in a constant process of evaluating the relationship of that idea or fact to all others you have uncovered. Train yourself to be highly selective. Correct note taking should accompany intellectual activity, not overshadow it. If you find yourself recording piles of information, it may be a signal that you're depending too heavily on your sources and not assimilating or digesting material. Too many notes also have a way of pressuring you to use each and every one of them. All that effort expended on writing them down makes you feel guilty if they aren't used, whether they're needed or not. The first phase in note taking, then, involves the careful screening of information. You'll want to select only the most significant ideas for recording.

The second step involves the actual recording of the note. Here, too, the most effective method requires experience, but it is one that can be more easily illustrated. Consider the following passage by Paul Zweig taken from a *Saturday Review* essay on heroes.

> Which is not to say that the contemporary world does not have its "heroes." For I doubt that human beings can live without some expanded ideal of behavior, some palpable image of the spaciousness of man. We want to know that our personal limitations are only a special case, that somewhere there is someone who can translate his words, thoughts, and beliefs into acts, even if we can't. Heroes in this sense represent a profoundly humanistic ideal.

Here are two different student notes taken during an in-class exercise.

Student A

Zweig believes that the contemporary world has its "heroes." He doubts that human beings can get along without some expanded ideal of behavior. All of us want to know that our personal limitations are special and that somewhere there will be someone else who can turn words, thoughts, and beliefs into acts. Heroes thus represent a profoundly humanistic ideal.

Student B

Heroes still seem necessary today according to Paul Zweig. Although each of us personally may feel small and limited, we require the knowledge that somewhere out there someone can put our ideals into action.

Student *A* has seemingly rephrased Zweig's material in his own words, but a closer look reveals a serious problem. Although a phrase or two have been omitted, the expression of ideas is almost identical to the original. Only a few minor words have been shifted out. The student thinks he has *paraphrased* correctly, but should this note end up in his final paper, it would be considered plagiarism. Student *B*, on the other hand, has succeeded in taking a valid note that is accurate to the sense of the original while actually *rephrasing* the ideas in her own words.

A *paraphrase* expresses the sense of a passage *in your own terms.* Technically, a paraphrase is a rewording of the *whole.* In practice, it may be handled like a summary: You may condense information or extract selected ideas, so long as you rephrase them. Any time you present information from another source, the words themselves must be yours, or the words must be enclosed in quotation marks. If the words are not in quotation marks and are as similar to the original material as student *A*'s example is, plagiarism will be charged.

Plagiarism involves the appropriation of someone else's words or ideas as your own. The sad thing is that plagiarism may be accidental. Students may believe that because they have changed a word or two, they have written a proper note. Or students may believe that because they have documented the material by saying, "Zweig believes . . . ," they have precluded plagiarism, no matter how close their phrasing is to the original. Ignorance, however, should not be an excuse. *Even when you give credit to the source in text or footnote, the words of a paraphrase must be yours.*

Fortunately, you can almost guarantee yourself a proper note (one that is not plagiarized), as well as an accurate note, by following a traditional procedure developed by generations of students and scholars. And although the doing requires concentrated effort, the method is surprisingly simple: *Do not look at the original material when writing your note.* Inexperienced writers tend to write their notes by keeping one finger in the book, pointing to the original sentences while writing the note with their other hand. Their eyes move back and forth between the two. But words printed in a book, especially words you've selected as important, have a way of psychologically dominating your own vocabulary. "How can I say it better—or differently?" you ask yourself. You may find yourself changing small, insubstantial words while retaining the author's principal phrases.

Instead, once you've chosen a passage as relevant to your study, *turn completely away from it.* Either close the book, turn the book upside down, or move your notepaper so that the book is out of your line of sight. Now write down the idea that struck you as important. This will set in motion a train of meaningful intellectual consequences. What you'll discover is that your brain is suddenly required to recall the idea. Without the direct influence of the author's words, your vocabulary will be all you can depend on. Psychological studies have repeatedly shown that unless you can say something in your own words, you cannot be certain of having understood it. Once you've phrased it for yourself, you not only know that the idea is understood, you have also made it more permanently a part of you. Recall implants the idea in your memory. Finally, you have in a sense forced yourself to think through the idea in order to phrase it, and you're in a sounder position to evaluate it or to compare it to others. Ideas of your own are likely to develop. Relationships and interpretations become possible. In other words, by the simple act of turning away from the original to write down your note, you discipline your mind and demand that it deal with the idea on its own terms. You engage yourself in the actual process of what we call "study."

One final step remains. Once you've completed your note, you must turn back and check its accuracy against the original (see Chapter 35 for a full discussion of accuracy). Again, an important train of consequences is set in motion. In the act of checking for accuracy, you assure yourself that your understanding of the author's idea is correct. If your note is in error, you are in an immediate position to clarify the mistake. If the note is accurate to the sense of the original, you can proceed with your reading, confident that when the time comes for writing your paper, you will be able to include the author's information accurately, thoughtfully, in your own words—because it already *is* in your own words.

This process of successful note taking does not seem to come naturally to many of us. We must train ourselves, and the training is demanding. Turning away and writing an idea in your own words requires an incredible amount of concentration. You may constantly find yourself tempted to do it in the old way. What you are faced with is the question of means and ends. If your "ends," your goal, is nothing more than to slide through college and life with the least possible effort, the old method will serve you. But if you have higher goals, if training your mind is important to you, then the "means" begins with the first step. It cannot be leaped over. *Note taking must be a thinking process, not merely an act of recording.*

Practice

1. The following three paragraphs express fairly complex ideas. Write a paraphrase of each (or a summary-type paraphrase in which you select the most important elements to put in your own words). Use the techniques described in this chapter: (a) Do not look at the original material when writing your note; (b) Attempt to recall the most important elements of the idea and express them in your own words; (c) Reread the original and check the author's expression against your own to determine whether your understanding is accurate and correct to the sense of the original.

   In theory, computers should be able to reflect an artist's sensibilities as validly as a brush and canvas; if the result seems banal or mechanical, it's the fault of the artist and not the medium. But can computer art convey the wealth of feelings that great art conveys? Can a program incorporate the quirks and flashes of inspiration that go into a masterpiece? And do the computer's immense capabilities somehow diminish the role played by the man at the controls? A similar question was raised during the early days of photography, when critics wondered how much of the final product was due to the nature of the camera and how much to the eye of the photographer. "Computer art is going through the same evolution as photography," says computer scientist Chuck Csuri of Ohio State University. "But when you look at the impact of photography today, it's absurd to question its artistic value."

   Time Magazine

The emphasis on equality within our social system has led to an almost dogmatic conviction that society can and must eradicate all differences between individuals. But a series of studies by Alexander Thomas, Stella Chess, and Herbert Birch has conclusively demonstrated what all mothers know: Babies are innately different. Infants only one to two weeks old possess clearly defined temperamental predispositions; they show measurable differences in activity levels, irritability, responsiveness, and general mood. In these studies, it was found that the key to a child's development over time lies in the interaction between the temperament of the caregiver and that of the child. An efficient, quick-moving parent, for example, may have to learn not to become exasperated with a daydreaming, dawdling offspring.

Diane McGuinness, *Human Nature*

In this final conception of conscience, Freud continued to be impressed with the importance of guilty fear and the internalized parent, but in addition he postulated that there is an internalized ideal of behavior by which we, our actual selves (our egos), judge our own behavior—and in our failures experience true guilt. Guilt, then, is a form of self-disappointment, a sense of anguish that we did not achieve our standards of what we ought to be. We have fallen short. We have somehow or other betrayed some internal sense of potential self. This is why guilt is the most internalized and personal of emotions. You-against-you allows no buffer, and no villains except yourself. Even when guilty fear is internalized, it is as if someone else were there. But guilt is like tearing apart our internal structure. This is why guilt is so painful to endure.

Willard Gaylin, *The Atlantic*

2. Make up three sample reference citations from the publication data that follows. The information is listed in a jumbled sequence, and, in some cases, more information is given than you'll actually need.

   a. Holmes & Meier Publishers, New York
      473 pages
      Printed in Great Britain
      Eda Sagarra, author
      A Social History of Germany: 1648–1914
      copyright, 1977
      Library call number: 301.143 Sal8

   b. Bruce E. Nickerson, author
      The Journal of American Folklore
      Published for the American Folklore Society by the University of Texas Press
      "Is There a Folk in the Factory?"
      Vol. 87, April–June, 1990
      pp. 133–140
      Journal Editor, Barre Toelken

c. "Facing the Lions"
Aug. 25, 1997
Newsweek
Published weekly by Newsweek, Inc. NY, NY.
Editor, Richard M. Smith
pp. 38–39

3. Consider the hypothetical research project described below. Following the description is a passage that offers ideas and information on the project. First, prepare a complete reference citation based on the data provided. Second, prepare one or two sample notes on which you select, summarize, or paraphrase relevant material. You should include only a few direct quotations. Your note cards must be both complete and accurate, but the notes themselves should be highly selective, with only one main idea per note. Be sure to choose only information directly relevant to your project.

Project: You are researching natural childbirth and decide to investigate the early uses of anesthesia. You are specifically interested in why it became popular even though many doctors and clergy condemned its use. You discover the following passage in an essay on nineteenth-century attitudes toward childbirth.

Publication data: "Temple and Sewer: Childbirth, Prudery, and Victoria Regina" by John Hawkins Miller in *The Victorian Family: Structure and Stresses* edited by Anthony S. Whol St. Martin's Press, New York, 1978.

Relevant passage (pp. 24–25): On 7 April 1853, Queen Victoria gave birth to her eighth child, Leopold, Duke of Albany. Present in the lying-in room with the Queen were Mrs Lilly (the Queen's monthly nurse), Mrs Innocent, and Dr John Snow. This nominally spiritual and immaculate trinity might well have helped the Queen to overcome her distaste for the 'animal' and 'unesthetic' aspects of childbirth so well-represented in the confinements attended by Mrs Bangham and Sarah Gamp of Victorian fiction. During this confinement, moreover, the Queen did not have to endure the 'sacred pangs' of labour, for, as she wrote later, Dr Snow 'gave me the blessed Chloroform and the effect was soothing, quieting, and delightful beyond measure.' Her personal physician, Sir James Clark, wrote to James Young Simpson, the Edinburgh obstetrician who first used chloroform in midwifery, that the anaesthesia 'was not at any time given so strongly as to render the Queen insensible, and an ounce of chloroform was scarcely consumed during the whole time. Her Majesty was greatly pleased with the effect, and she certainly never has had a better recovery.'

While the Queen testified to the heavenly benison bestowed by the drug in relieving women of the ancient curse upon Eve (that 'in sorrow shall she bring forth'), there were members of the clergy who considered chloroform a 'decoy of Satan, apparently offering itself to bless women; but in the end, it will harden society, and rob God of the deep earnest cries which arise in time of trouble for help.' The more puritanical and abstemious also inveighed against chloroform because of its well-known intoxicating effects: 'To be insensible from whisky, gin, and brandy, and wine, and beer, and ether and chloroform, is to be what in the world is called Dead-drunk,' wrote Dr Meigs, in his *Obstetrics: The Science and the Art.* 'No reasoning—no argumentation is strong enough to point out the 9th part of a hair's discrimination between them.'

This debate was largely resolved by the women themselves—including the Queen, a lady not known for irreligion or drunkenness. It was the Queen, as Head of the Church, who effectively silenced the objections of religious leaders by legitimizing the use of anaesthesia through her own use of it in 1853, and again in 1857 for the birth of her last child. It has even been claimed by Elizabeth Longford that her 'greatest gift to her people was a refusal to accept pain in childbirth as woman's divinely appointed destiny.'

According to a story current at the time, many of the Queen's subjects were eager to learn of Her Majesty's reactions to the use of anaesthesia. John Snow, the anaesthetist, was besieged with requests from his patients for such information. One woman, to whom Snow was administering anaesthesia while she was in labour, refused to inhale any more chloroform until told exactly what the Queen had said when she was breathing it. Snow replied: 'Her Majesty asked no questions until she had breathed very much longer than you have; and if you will only go on in loyal imitation, I will tell you everything.' The woman obeyed, soon becoming oblivious of the Queen. By the time she regained consciousness, Dr Snow had left the hospital.

While we too may be curious about what the Queen said at the time, we do know that she heartily approved of the effects of the anaesthesia, and many of her subjects were persuaded, in loyal imitation, to demand it during their confinements. What was technically called 'intermittent chloroform analgesia,' became more commonly known as 'chloroform *à la Reine.*'

CHAPTER 33

Organizing Complex Material

As your research continues, you will usually reevaluate and reformulate your questions about the subject. Your insight will change and grow as unexpected ideas enter the picture. By the time you near the end of your project, you may feel overwhelmed with possibilities. How can it all be pulled together?

Categorizing Notes

Begin by reviewing and sorting your notes according to categories. All notes with similar or related ideas should be grouped together. For example, a study of how superstition continues to influence our lives might be broken down into three groups: customs, ceremonies, and gestures. Or you might see other possibilities: fear, sexuality, and anger. The same topic might be organized around one of the 4 *C*'s: change, conflict, consequence, and characterization. Causes and effects—or comparisons and contrasts—might be grouped separately. Commonly mistaken views of superstitions might be sorted into one pile, whereas more accurate interpretations (that you've discovered) are collected in another. Or you might arrange note cards according to a historical sequence: the continuing evidence of superstition into the twentieth century. The possibilities are endless.

Unfortunately, no one can give you a simple formula. The subject itself, your powers of reasoning, and a little intuition must all interact. But the organizing is essential. Form may be "discovered" in the first-draft stage of personal writings, reports, and even expository essays. The research paper is decidedly

different. Complex ideas, dozens of sources, conflicting views—the research paper *must* be organized before you begin the first draft. Indeed, as you think through your ideas and consider your material, change those questions you began with into a thesis.

The Thesis

The concept of a *thesis statement* (or focusing statement) was introduced in Chapter 23. Essentially, it is a brief statement, usually in a sentence or two, that summarizes the dominant idea of your findings. If you're not yet sure what the dominant idea is, all the more reason for pausing at this point and working on it. Indeed, you may not be able to sort those notes at all until you have a clearly defined thesis. More than likely, however, you began to develop a thesis in your head while you were reading your sources—although you may not have called it such. You may simply have thought, "Here's a fascinating angle on the subject," or "Look at how all of these points are pulling together." Now's the time to shape those vague feelings into an exactly worded statement that will guide you in organizing your paper and eventually guide the reader in reading it.

1. Narrow your topic to the *single* most important element of your subject.
2. Start writing about the one or two significant points you've discovered about that element. Use your own voice. Don't worry about being formal or writing for an audience at this stage. This one's for you.
3. Be forceful. State what you know now in such a way that if someone asked you to prove it, you could begin offering evidence from that pile of note cards you've collected.
4. Get your attitude or opinion into it. If you think something is wrong, say so. If you think something needs to be changed, say so. Don't worry about bias; you can return later and make it sound more objective. At this point it's more important to get yourself involved with the subject.

And what if nothing happens? You stare at a blank computer screen, and you have all this information, but nothing seems to shape up. Then try another tactic. Pretend you're sitting in a coffee bar with a group of friends interested in the subject you've been studying. Someone asks you to tell them about it—only the catch is, the coffee bar closes in fifteen minutes. You have time only to summarize. Everyone looks at you, waiting. Start talking. Tell your friends about the most important ideas you've found. Talk out loud. Most of us are a lot more relaxed talking out loud than writing silently on paper. So talk. Your friends are waiting, and you've got to summarize what you now know as briefly as possible but as forcefully as possible. Try to find the three or four most important points. Then, if you can, narrow it to the one or two most important points. *Talk out loud.* Finally, sit down at your computer and type out the single most important point you've discovered. Sometimes you may have to write down all four, but that's OK, too, because now you've got four ideas on paper and you can begin working on how to generalize about them in a single focused thesis.

All of this is only to suggest that although most of us think of the thesis as a formal (and perhaps somewhat inhibiting) statement, it is actually only a *means,* not an end in itself—a means of helping you come to precise understanding of your study before you begin to organize and write. Later, it may form a portion of your introduction and will serve the reader as a means of getting into the same ideas.

Here are some good and bad thesis statements. The bad ones are bad only because they couldn't help either the writer or the reader get a focus on what the material is about.

Effective Thesis Statement	**Weak Thesis Statement**
Professional baseball has been destroyed by the players' greed for multi-million-dollar salaries.	Robert Frost writes poems that reveal moral values. [*Which poems? Which moral values? And is that good or bad? What is the purpose of telling us?*]
From 1995 to 2000, Bill Clinton's foreign policy was guided more by pragmatism than ideology.	America needs energy. Atomic power may be the answer although it has failed in Russia. [*Where's the focus? Energy? Or atomic power?*]
America's health care costs are continuing to inflate because three special interest groups—the physicians, the politicians, and the HMOs—are all making a profit. The patient is the only one who pays, and no change is in sight.	Today's society is composed of a phenomenon in which we find ourselves afraid to be individuals or to be willing to challenge the conformity imposed upon us. [*Too broad. Individualism and conformity are abstract subjects that need narrowing to specific components.*]

Notice that the last example of an effective thesis (in the left column) uses more than one sentence. Try as you might, sometimes you'll find that a complex subject needs two sentences, or three, or even a paragraph to state the thesis fully. The single-sentence ideal is not a holy commandment that can't be broken. The point is to design a statement that helps you organize your paper, not to terrorize yourself with a rule that can't possibly anticipate every situation. Make the thesis statement work for you; don't become its slave.

Developing a Design

No one can predict at what stage in the process a design will begin to take shape. By this point, you may already have a solid feel for how you're going to organize. If not, here's a quick review of all the different possibilities.

1. As in narration and description, almost all organizations move from either the general to the specific or the specific to the general, from most important to least important or from least important to most important (see Chapter 8 for a review).
2. An imaginative lead is effective for both reader and writer and can help the writer envision an organization. A provocative statement, a dramatic scene, a statement of contrast or conflict, a question, or a pileup of statistics that intrigue the reader—each can suggest a pattern for the rest of the paper to follow (see Chapters 18 and 19 for a review).
3. Definition, classification, comparison and contrast, illustration, process analysis, or cause-and-effect analysis may also give an almost automatic shape to the material (see Chapters 21 and 22).

Here is what you must remember: The methods you used to "see" your subject, whether sensory or intellectual, are almost always productive methods around which to design your paper. If, to understand Confucianism, you study its historical and cultural development, then it follows that a narrative presentation may be the most effective organization. But if you compare Confucianism with Christianity, it only makes sense that you will probably use one of the two contrast designs. And if you analyze the rise of terrorism in the early part of the twenty-first century among certain middle-eastern nations, then of necessity you must break the subject into parts and move step by step through each one, showing how each relates and whether or not there was a related cause and effect.

Before you move to the outline stage, take a few minutes and draw some visual designs—boxes, pyramids, circles, or whatever. Try to visualize the pattern your material may fit into. We are visually oriented creatures. Scientists tell us that some 90 percent of all information we gather comes through our eyes. The direction and organization of your paper may become more clear if you can design a visual statement of it—if you can see the pattern you're about to follow.

The Working Outline

Some instructors who want to make sure you've thought through your project may require you to submit a formal topic outline, as in this example.

Thesis Statement: *The decision by Harry S. Truman to drop the atom bomb on Japan was expedient but immoral.*

I. Summary of historical events leading up to Hiroshima
II. Truman uninformed of atomic experiments
  A. Secrecy under Roosevelt
  B. Truman puzzled by Stimson's account
III. The alternatives as perceived by Joint Chiefs of Staff
  A. Invasion of Japan
  B. Public threat of invasion by all allies jointly
  C. Show of power with atomic bomb
IV. How Truman made his decision
  A. Military considerations
  B. Political considerations
  C. Moral considerations
V. Evaluation of his final decision
  A. Consequences in terms of military effectiveness
  B. Consequences in terms of political effectiveness
  C. Consequences in terms of human life
VI. Overall assessment
  A. Politically and militarily correct
  B. Morally wrong
  C. The dilemma of choice

The assumption behind a conventional topic outline is that, at the very least, you will divide your subject into main ideas and subideas, as in the preceding example. Some writers may go further and fill in examples or perhaps even specific details and facts.

I. Main idea
  A. Subidea
    1. Example
    2. Example
  B. Subidea
    1. Example
      a. Specific fact
      b. Specific statistic
      c. Specific quotation
    2. Example

How much detail you go into depends on your personal needs and methods of working. Some students are best advised to omit nothing: Only in such a way will gaps in information or logical flaws be revealed. Others work well from general subheadings or even from a casual outline that does not use Roman numerals.

- Wartime pressures, national debt, and rationing put pressure on Truman to end war.
- The alliance between the Soviet Union and the West was weakening.
- Chiang Kai-shek was more interested in consolidating his own gains in mainland China.
- After Roosevelt's death, Truman discovered he was totally unprepared for all the complexity.
- Stimson's information about a new secret weapon was more puzzling than helpful.
- The Joint Chiefs of Staff presented Truman with several alternatives but could not agree among themselves.

And so on.

An outline is a working tool. Don't be afraid of it. Use your notes to shape each step. Be willing to revise several times. And recognize that no matter what method you use or how thorough you are, new ideas may still occur during the first draft that will cause you to break the pattern of your outline. After you finish the first draft, a second or third outline may be needed before you begin rewriting.

CHAPTER 34

Drafting and Documenting

You've conducted your interviews, read magazines and books, organized your ideas, and drawn up a design to follow. But certain components of a research paper tend to create problems you may not encounter in other forms of writing. The introduction, the handling of documentation, and the final organization of a "Works Cited" page all require extra attention.

Leads and Introductions

Although a research paper may begin with a formal introduction, an imaginative lead always adds interest and spark. The two can sometimes be combined. Here's how Terrie Clinger, a first-year nursing major, drew together various elements from her research to organize an effective, unified lead and introduction.

An Undignified Death

Lead consists of three examples

In New Freedom, Pennsylvania, George McGraw, a fifty-eight-year-old construction worker, rushed to the hospital after being involved in an automobile accident, was released because he appeared to only suffer from a scraped elbow. No X-rays were taken. On the way home, fragments of bone from a fractured neck and skull "sliced" into McGraw's brain and spinal cord, paralyzing him for life (*Time* 33).

In New York, a thirty-five-year-old printer who had been released from an emergency room with only painkillers for a stomach ache died at home with massive hemorrhaging of stomach ulcers (*Harvard Law* 461–468).

In Dallas, an accident victim brought in "appearing" to be dead on arrival was ignored for several hours until he caught someone's attention when he coughed. The patient survived but because of delay in treatment he suffered severe brain damage (*Dallas News* 1).

Formal introduction begins with overview

These three cases are almost insignificant when compared to the more than one million lives annually lost in crisis situations, with approximately sixty thousand of those being preventable deaths. These losses and tragedies are a result of mishandlings due to either inadequate emergency facilities or inadequate emergency treatment.

Historical context established

Fifteen years ago, the American Academy of General Practice listed a membership of 95,526 doctors, but today the list contains only 68,326 members (NBC). Although more and more doctors are turning to specialization, more and more people are turning to the emergency room for treatment. According to Scudder Winslow, M.D., and head of New York's Roosevelt Hospital Emergency Service, the emergency room has "simply become a substitute for the family doctor" because there are only a few general practitioners for people to turn to (*Time* 33).

Specific focus takes shape

Yet 90 percent of the seven thousand accredited hospitals in the United States provide emergency rooms that are poorly equipped and understaffed (NBC).

Thesis stated

This failure of hospitals and medical associations to deal with—or at times even to recognize—the emergency-room crisis has led to a frightening situation that shows no signs of early solution. As a future nurse, I'm vitally concerned.

Obviously, an introduction can take other shapes, but Terrie has followed a fairly conventional and traditionally successful method.

1. An imaginative lead (provocative statement, literary scene, contrast, question, quotation, and so on).
2. General overview of what the paper is about as a whole (in a sentence or two).
3. A brief summary of the background or historical context to orient the reader and establish the foundation for evidence that follows.

4. A focusing sentence (usually the thesis statement) that narrows the topic or presents the dominant idea that will be explored and supported by the body of the paper.

It might be misleading, however, to leave the impression that Terrie's introduction looked like this on a first draft. Actually, it went through hours of work. For most of us, the introduction remains the most difficult element of any paper to write. In fact, some writers avoid it entirely until the rest of the first draft is complete. If the introduction becomes hopelessly bogged down, give it up. Go straight to the body of the paper. Begin with your first example or quotation and write as fast as possible. You can return later and decide how to introduce the whole. As Ezra Pound put it, "It doesn't matter which leg of your table you make first, so long as the table has four legs and will stand up solidly when you have finished it."

Composing versus Collating

I want to stress one final time that during the drafting phase, you should see the subject with your mind's eye; concern yourself only with ideas; and save spelling, punctuation, correct usage, and all other necessary mechanics for later revisions. But research papers traditionally raise another problem. You'll find yourself concerned not only with your own ideas but also with those taken from others. You may be tempted to "sew together" your notes, moving slowly from one to the next and merely transcribing information from note card to paper, adding here and there a transition like *also* or *therefore*. Any personal understanding of the subject gained during research may be overwhelmed by all those facts gathered from authorities. You may find yourself repressing your own views and merely collating the views of your sources. It's at that point you'll need to call up again the whole purpose of research. You'll need to remind yourself that your imagination, memory, and reasoning must form a major part of your writing. All those notes and facts from others exist to support what you've discovered. They are never a substitute for your own insights.

Preliminary Documentation

A second problem—and one that used to be far more difficult when you were required to use footnotes—involves documentation of material taken from other sources. More and more disciplines now use a parenthetical form of documentation, with footnotes reserved only for additional commentary or for reference to additional sources that aren't directly cited in your paper.

Unfortunately, the information and the style used for in-text documentation and for "Works Cited" or "Reference" pages varies among disciplines and among professions. In the following, I've provided examples derived from two different "style sheets," one by the Modern Language Association (used throughout the humanities) and one by the American Psychological Association (used throughout the natural and social sciences). Your instructor may provide you with a different format or guideline. Your employer might require yet another. All this may seem confusing, but it is actually only a matter of knowing your audience and learning to adapt to varying expectations.

For research papers in most writing classes, you'll be expected to document sources in two ways. First, when a quotation or direct paraphrase is used, you must parenthetically identify your source at that point, directly in the text. The parenthetical information should be condensed enough not to interfere with reading the text, but full enough to refer the reader to complete bibliographic information provided at the end of your paper under the heading "Works Cited" or "References." During the drafting phase, all you need to do is insert in parentheses a brief note referring to your source. You should not worry at that time whether it fulfills all technical requirements. Just insert a note so that as you continue drafting and revising, the note remains with the material. Perhaps it will look something like this.

> Studies have shown that at some colleges up to 90% of so-called student athletes have not been graduating (*Chron. for Higher Ed.*, Carroway 9). Even worse is the attitude of many coaches. The story is told of a Texas A&M coach who is supposed to have glanced over the report card of one of his basketball players who received four F's and one D. The coach reportedly commented, "Son, looks to me like you're spending too much time on one subject" (Gluck, *Time* 97).

At this stage, parenthetical notes serve to help you clarify where you found the material. Later, you'll want those notes to conform to an approved format so that your reader can also identify your sources with ease. Obviously, it would be better if preliminary documentation were absolutely accurate. But in early drafting, perfecting your ideas is more important than perfecting your documentation. One way or another, when you reach a final revision, you'll still have to double-check each citation to assure conformity to proper style. As long as you have basic information from your source in early drafts, you can then edit it prior to final printing.

Parenthetical Citations

Once you've reached your final revision, you'll want to follow the essential principles found in the MLA or APA guidelines.

MLA Guidelines

1. If you are citing a *complete* work, and if you use the author's name or the title of the work in your sentence, you need not provide any further information.

Guitton encourages students to commit themselves to a life of the mind.

or

A Student's Guide to Intellectual Work encourages students to commit themselves to a life of the mind.

2. If you are citing a specific portion of a work, you have the option of including the author's name in the sentence or in the parenthetical reference along with the page numbers.

William James has observed that any attempt to define the concept has proven illusive for it takes us into a discussion about "fundamental properties of matter" (33).

or

Attempting to define the concept has proven illusive for it takes us into a discussion about "fundamental properties of matter" (James 33).

I recommend that the first time you use a *new* source in any paper, especially if quoting, you include the author's full name and, if possible, some identification of the author or the work you are citing in the text itself. To do so gives a sense of authority and authenticity to the information. It may mean little to a reader if you write:

Campaigning for President "has a tendency to change one's sense of values" (Stevenson 1980).

But it can be quite persuasive if you write:

Adlai Stevenson, Democratic presidential candidate in 1952 and 1956, observed that campaigning for the presidency "has a tendency to change one's sense of values" (1980).

The reader now knows that the source you're citing has authority. Your evidence is more convincing, and the quotation is attached to a real human being, not just to a bibliographical citation.

3. If you are using a quotation longer than four or five lines, it should be indented, usually five extra spaces. Again, you have two choices for citing the material: You may include the author's name in the introductory information (and all quotations should be introduced), followed by the page number at the end, or you may place all reference data in the parenthetical citation following the quote.

Another author, Virginia Woolf, writing about herself in the third person, describes pressures that interfere with a female artist's imagination when she tries to be both personal and honest.

The imagination had dashed itself against something hard. . . . She was indeed in a state of most acute and difficult distress. Men, her reason told her, would be shocked. The consciousness of what men will say of a woman who speaks the truth about her passions had roused her from her artist's state of consciousness. She could write no more. . . . Her imagination could work no longer. (16)

or

Another author, writing about herself in the third person, describes pressures that interfere with a female artist's imagination when she tries to be both personal and honest.

> The imagination had dashed itself against something hard. . . . She was indeed in a state of most acute and difficult distress. Men, her reason told her, would be shocked. The consciousness of what men will say of a woman who speaks the truth about her passions had roused her from her artist's state of consciousness. She could write no more. . . . Her imagination could work no longer. (Woolf 16)

4. You should follow the same guidelines for citing Internet resources in parenthetical citations that you would for citing print resources. Use paragraph, screen, or chapter numbers rather than page numbers to identify electronic text.

   No evidence was found to uphold the previous case study findings (Byers, screens 3–4).

   If no paragraph, screen, or chapter numbers are available, it is preferable to use the name of the author, editor, or performer *in the text* rather than in parenthetical citation. The reader can refer to the named source in the list of Works Cited for further information.

   Robert Byers' 2001 case study found sufficient evidence lacking to support its initial thesis.

APA Guidelines

The APA style sheet offers the following guidelines for correct parenthetical citations.

1. If you are citing a *complete work,* or a general element of that work, or the conclusion it reaches, the APA method recommends citing only the author's last name, followed by the date of publication, or the title of the work followed by the date of publication.

   Guitton (1948) encourages students to commit themselves to a life of the mind.

   or

   A Student's Guide to Intellectual Work (1948) encourages students to commit themselves to a life of the mind.

2. When citing a specific portion of a work, you have two options. You may include the author's name in the sentence, followed by the publication

date, with a specific page number listed at the end. Or you can place all documentation in the parenthetical reference.

> James (1899) has observed that any attempt to define the concept has proven illusive for it takes us into a discussion about "fundamental properties of matter" (33).
>
> *or*
>
> Another observer has argued that any attempt to define the concept has proven illusive for it takes us into a discussion about "fundamental properties of matter" (James, 1899, 33).

3. For Internet resources, use the same guidelines that you would for print resources. Use paragraph or chapter numbers rather than page numbers to identify electronic text.

> No evidence was found to uphold the previous case study findings (Byers, 1999, para.7).

If no chapter or paragraph numbers are visible, use the heading so that the reader may retrieve this information.

> The case study found sufficient evidence lacking to support its initial thesis (Byers, 1999, Conclusion section).

Common Forms of In-Text References

A Work by a Single Author:

MLA Janovy writes lyrically about nature: "One can never get enough of a falling star" (174).

APA Janovy (1994) writes lyrically about nature: "One can never get enough of a falling star" (p. 174).

A Work by Two or Three Authors:

MLA Darrow and Hicks have studied the problem but conclude that generational distrust is normal (132–133).

or

Later research by a team of psychologists failed to support the data (Darrow and Hicks, 1972, 132–133).

APA Darrow and Hicks (1972) have studied the problem but conclude that generational distrust is normal (pp. 132–133).

or

Other researchers have studied the problem but conclude that generational distrust is normal (Darrow & Hicks, 1972. pp. 132–133).

A Work by Three or More Authors:

MLA Smite, Weston, and Dickinson have assembled remarkable statistics on the age groups affected by this syndrome (415–419).

APA Smite, Weston, and Dickinson (1998) have assembled remarkable statistics on the age groups affected by this syndrome (pp. 415–419).

Subsequent References

Other researchers have assembled remarkable statistics on the age groups affected by this syndrome (Smite et al., 1998, pp. 415–419).

Same Author, Different Work:

MLA On the one hand, Heldman argues, "Painting is an act of life itself available to all who have the courage to risk failure" (*Memories* 44). But later she returns to her earlier thesis that the artist's life is unavailable to the common man, no matter his degree of courage (Art 110).

APA On the one hand, she argues, "Painting is an act of life itself available to all who have the courage to risk failure" (Heldman, 1927, p. 44). But later she returns to her earlier thesis that the artist's life is unavailable to the common man, no matter his degree of courage (Heldman, 1909, p. 110).

Works without an Author:

MLA The pamphlet Judaism Under Siege claims that Israel is threatened by twenty million hostile neighbors (3).

or

The claim has been made that Israel is threatened by twenty million hostile neighbors (Judaism, 3).

APA The pamphlet claims that Israel is threatened by twenty million hostile neighbors (*Judaism,* 1991, p. 3).

Literary Works:

MLA With little money left from what he inherited from his father, George Webber goes to Europe where once more "the hoof and the wheel came down the streets of memory" (Wolfe 328; ch. 17, bk. 4).

[Literary works may occur in numerous editions. The MLA recommends that in addition to page numbers, you indicate chapters, sections, and parts to help readers with different editions locate the reference. For poetry, plays, and biblical citations, omit page numbers altogether and indicate only acts, scenes, lines, or verses.]

Hamlet's soliloquy, "To be, or not to be . . . ," provides our first interior view of his dilemma (3.1.56–89).

[The reference is to Act 3, Scene 1, lines 56–89 of *Hamlet.* The periods distinguish act from scene and line. An alternative version is to use Roman numerals for act and scene, with Arabic numerals for line numbers: (III, I, 56–89).]

The "Works Cited" or "Reference" List

Each parenthetical reference in your paper must be supported at the end with full documentation in the form of an alphabetical list of "Works Cited" (for those following MLA format) or on a "Reference" page (for those following APA). The following offers only a small selection of the most common entries. For hundreds of other possibilities, with more detailed and exact guidelines, see either the *MLA Handbook for Writers of Research Papers,* fifth edition, 1999, or the *Publication Manual of the American Psychological Association,* fifth edition 2001.

Book by a Single Author:

MLA Page, Russell. The Education of a Gardner. New York: Random, 1983.

APA Page, R. (1983). *The education of a gardner.* New York: Random.

Book by Two or More Authors:

MLA Crews, Frederick, and Sandra Schor. The Borzoi Handbook for Writers. New York: Knopf, 1985.

APA Crews, F., & Schor, S. (1985). *The Borzoi handbook for writers.* New York: Knopf.

Two or More Books by the Same Author:

MLA Rhys, Jean. After Leaving Mr. Mackenzie. New York: Harper, 1927.
______ . Wide Sargasso Sea. New York: Norton, 1995.

APA Rhys, J. (1927). *After leaving Mr. Mackenzie.* New York: Harper.
Rhys, J. (1995). *Wide Sargasso sea.* New York: Norton.

Book with Corporate Authorship:

MLA United States Bureau of the Census. Statistical Abstract of the United States, 119th ed. Washington: GPO, 2001.

APA United States Bureau of the Census. (2001). Washington: *Statistical Abstract of the United States* (119th ed.). Washington: GPO.

Book with an Editor or Compiler:

MLA Baumback, Jonathan, ed. Writers as Teachers, Teachers as Writers. New York: Holt, 1970.

APA Baumback, J. (Ed.). (1970). *Writers as teachers, teachers as writers.* New York: Holt.

Item in an Anthology or Edited Collection:

MLA Minot, Susan. "Hiding." The Pushcart Prize, IX: Best of the Small Presses. Ed. Bill Henderson. New York: Pushcart, 1984, 31–42.

APA Minot, S. (1984). Hiding. In B. Henderson (Ed.). *The Pushcart prize, IX: Best of the small presses* (pp. 31–42). New York: Pushcart.

Introduction, Preface, or Afterword:

MLA Hughes, Ted. Foreword. The Journals of Sylvia Plath. Ed. Ted Hughes and Frances McCullogh. New York: Dial, 1982. 2–8.

APA Hughes, T. (1982). Foreword. In T. Hughes & F. McCullogh (Eds.). *The journals of Sylvia Plath* (p. 208) New York: Dial.

Translation:

MLA Tolstoy, Leo. Anna Karenina. Trans. Aylmer Maude. New York: Norton, 1970.

APA Tolstoy, L. (1970). *Anna Karenina* (A. Maude, Trans.). New York: Norton. (Original work published 1878).

Article in Journal with Continuous Pagination:

MLA Black, Davis S. "The Future of the Liberal Arts." The Georgia Review 44 (1995): 432–437.

APA Black, D. (1995). The future of the liberal arts. *The Georgia Review,* 44, 432–437.

Article in Journal That Pages Each Issue Separately:

MLA McCormick, Frank. "Donne, The Pope, and 'Holy Sonnets XIV.' " CEA Critic 2.4 (1983): 23–24.

APA McCormick, F. (1983). Donne, the pope, and "holy sonnets XIV." *CEA Critic,* 2 (4), 23–24.

Article in a Weekly or Biweekly Periodical:

MLA Fise, Harris. "The Politically Correct Disaster." Chronicle of Higher Education. 23 Feb. 1998: 5.

APA Fise, H. (1998, February 23). The politically correct disaster. *Chronicle of Higher Education,* 5.

Article in a Monthly Periodical:

MLA Hubbard, Thomas, R. "Vienna and Budapest: The Foreshadowing of WWI." Smithsonian Aug. 1994: 71–78.

APA Hubbard, T. R. (1994, August). Vienna and Budapest: The foreshadowing of WWI. *Smithsonian,* 71–78.

Article from a Newspaper:

MLA "New AIDS Vaccine Found." New York Times 14 Oct 1997: 1.

or

Grist, Tony. "Jazz Returns to Charlotte." Charlotte Observer, 21 Jan. 1990: 1+.

APA New AIDS vaccine found. (1997, October 14). *New York Times,* p. 1. Grist, T. (1990, January 21). Jazz returns to Charlotte. *Charlotte Observer,* p. 1.

Review:

MLA Creek, George. "Nightgames." Rev. of Burning Bright, by Marianne Bridges. Philadelphia Enquirer 7 Feb. 1990, sec. 1: 47.

APA Creek, G. (1990, February 7). Nightgames. [Review of the book *Burning bright*]. *Philadelphia Enquirer,* section 1, p. 47.

Editorial:

MLA "Perception vs. Reality." Editorial. The Asheville Citizen 16 Sept. 2000: 4.

APA Perception vs. reality. (2000, September 16). [Editorial]. *The Asheville Citizen,* p. 4.

Interview:

MLA Grisley, Robert K. Personal interview. 6 Jan. 1998.

or

Clinton, Bill. Interview with Katie Couric. Today. NBC. WNBC, New York. 3 Dec. 1997.

APA Do not list personal interviews on Reference page; identify fully in text.

Electronic Sources: Because electronic sources are relatively new and the technologies on which they depend continue to change rapidly, MLA and APA guidelines are continuing to change and evolve. Both groups tend to follow their same formats and punctuation as closely as possible. Many style guides and crib sheets for citing electronic resources are widely available online from various universities and commercial organizations. I strongly recommend consulting both the printed style manuals as well as the official MLA and APA websites (MLA at www.mla.org and APA at www.apa.org) for the latest news and updates concerning electronic information citation styles.

General Electronic Format:

MLA Author's Last Name, First Name. "Title of Document." Title of Complete Work (if applicable). Version or File number if applicable. Date of access <URL, or web address>.

APA Author's Last Name, Initial(s). (Date of work, if known). Title of Work. *Title of Complete Work in Italics.* Retrieved month, day, year, and path followed to site or URL.

Professional or Personal Web Document:

MLA Brennan, Laura. Best Practices in Community Disease Prevention. 1999. 11 Dec. 1999 <http://www.bestpracdis.org>.

APA Brennan, L. (1999). *Best practices in community disease prevention.* Retrieved December 11, 1999, from http://www.bestpracdis.org

Book or Scholarly Project Online:

MLA MacDonald, Ann Marie. Fall on Your Knees. 1996. Feminist Book Digitization Agenda. Ed. Kelly Gellar. U. of Oklahoma. 3 Mar., 2001 <http://www.ou.edu/fbda/macdonald/>

APA MacDonald, A. M. (1996). *Fall on your knees.* Ed. K. Gellar. Retrieved March 3, 2001, from the University of Oklahoma, Feminist Book Digitization Agenda Web site: http://www.ou.edu/fbda/ macdonald/

Article Based on a Print Source:

MLA Michigan, Franklin. "Waiting for the Night: Pop Culture and the Cult of Pleasure." Journal of Societal Trends 11 (July 2000): 19 pars. InfoTrac OneFile. 19 May, 2001 <http://www.infotof.com/st/>

APA Michigan, F. (2000, July). Waiting for the night: Pop culture and the cult of pleasure [Electronic Version]. *Journal of Societal Trends,* 11, 19 pars. Retrieved May 19, 2001 from InfoTrac OneFile database.

Interview:

MLA Kamp, Wilson. Interview with Andrea Thompson. "What Makes A Patriot?" Cable Network News. 27 Sept., 2001. 6 Nov. 2001 <www.cnn.com/interviews/011106.kamp.htm>

APA Do not list interviews on Reference page; identify fully in text.

Article from an Internet-Only Journal:

MLA Kennedy, Mickey. "Hot Stone Massage Used to Reduce Anxiety Disorder Symptoms." Homeopathic Times 2 (Feb. 2001): 10 Apr., 2001 <http://hempsoc.org/ht/vol2/hotstone>

APA Kennedy, M. (2001, February). Hot Stone Massage Used to Reduce Anxiety Disorder Symptoms. *Homeopathic Times,* 2. Retrieved April 10, 2001 from <http://hempsoc.org/ht/vol2/ hotstone>

E-Mail Message:

MLA Lagerfeld, Sam. "Lecture Notes." E-mail to the author. 26 Oct. 2000.

APA Do not list personal e-mail communications on Reference page; identify fully in text.

CHAPTER 35

Self-Criticism

Writing about abstract ideas may be the most difficult of all types of writing. The problem is often that writers know precisely what they mean but fail to recognize that their words do not express their meaning. The reader, however, knows only what the words actually say; we can't look into the writer's mind. The old excuse, I know what I meant, is never an excuse; writers are always responsible for verifying that their words express their intention. That verification occurs during both the revising and editing phases. It may involve the slow, thoughtful review of every word and sentence, not just once, but several times.

Accuracy and Precision

Several types of accuracy must be checked. Most important is the accuracy of summarized or quoted material. Not only is it a courtesy to the author you've read or the expert you've interviewed, it is also one of the most sacred rules of intellectual work: *Thou shalt not misquote.* Every word inside a quotation must be accurate, and ideas rephrased in your own words must be accurate to the *sense* of the original. Here is how one student writer expressed an idea he found in Charles W. Ferguson's book *Say It with Words.* I've placed Ferguson's original material to the left for you to compare.

Ferguson	**Student Version**
No generalization is wholly true, as Disraeli reminds us, including this one, but you will find it of great practical use to husband verbs.	In a chapter called "Mind Your Verbs," Ferguson shows us just how long attention has been paid to verbs: "Disraeli reminds us . . . you will find it of great practical use to husband verbs." And Disraeli was a prime minister of England in 1868!

The error here is serious. The student believes he has quoted accurately because every word inside the quotation appears in the original. But both Ferguson and Disraeli have been misrepresented. Either from careless reading or in a careless transferral of reading notes to manuscript, the student has botched the whole idea. Ferguson is paraphrasing Disraeli as saying that "no generalization is wholly true." Ferguson offers no indication that Disraeli ever said a word about verbs.

Unfortunately, this type of thing happens all too frequently to all of us when we work under pressure. We read too quickly; we write the paper late at night, glance over it hurriedly for spelling errors, and submit it. Critical thinking, however, demands a slow, attentive concern, not only to ideas others have presented but also to the way you represent those ideas. Here is how another student described a portion of Kate Millett's work on *Sexual Politics*.

Millett

. . . it was the Renaissance which furnished the first applied theories of education for women. Alberti's Della Famiglia is fairly representative of these. The purpose of such minimal training as it recommends is merely an aesthetic and convenient docility.

Student Version

Also Millett tells us that the education for women has risen as a sort of modern-day achievement of educating the lower levels of man to simply keep them content and satisfied. This is illustrated when Alberti said in Della Famiglia, "The purpose of such minimal training as it recommends is merely an aesthetic and convenient docility."

Like the previous student, this one attributes a portion of the author's ideas—this time, Kate Millett's—to someone she has referred to in her text. It was not Alberti who said, "The purpose of such minimal training . . ." Those are Millett's words. But the first part of the student's summary is also inaccurate because the student has not looked closely at his own words and considered what they mean: ". . . education of women has risen as a sort of modern-day achievement of *educating the lower levels of man. . . .*" Not only does Kate Millett say no such thing, it makes no sense. How can the education of women be aimed at educating the lower levels of man? What the student probably means is that Millett believes the education of women in the Renaissance was aimed at *satisfying* the lower levels of man. The failure to find the precise word makes a parody of the original material.

Another type of imprecision shows up in this student's paper:

The stock show champion was sired by a prize steer from Ross Perot's ranch.

Mr. Perot would no doubt have been surprised that a steer could sire anything since, by definition, a steer is a castrated bull.

Accuracy and precision include historical ideas:

> . . . it was Abraham Lincoln who was elected on the promise of freeing the slaves.

Lincoln, of course, promised nothing of the kind and probably would not have been elected if he had. Such a historical inaccuracy casts a dark shadow over the paper as a whole. If a writer can make this kind of error, how can we trust his or her other information to be sound?

A final illustration appears in this first-year student analysis of an essay on gun control:

> The First Amendment to the Constitution gives everyone the right to bear arms.

But it is the Second Amendment, not the First, that discusses the right to bear arms. Even the Second is not clear as to whether "everyone" has such a right. The precise wording of the amendment may refer only to the right to form a state militia. Did the student verify the number of the amendment or the actual wording? Obviously not.

Accuracy and precision in themselves seldom bring a writer praise; inaccuracy and imprecision will invariably bring condemnation.

Omissions

From the writer's point of view, the omission of a portion of an argument or even a single word may be terribly difficult to spot. I've often found myself reading a sentence four times before discovering that I've left out something, a phrase or word I could swear was there in print the first three times I read the sentence. Because our mind *knows* what the sentence is supposed to say, it tends to fill in any blanks. Unfortunately, the reader cannot.

Here's a student example I received last semester:

> Pitcher advised the divorcing parents to explain divorce to the young child in the following manner: This method will help ease the negative impact of the divorce on the child. Pitcher's method provides divorcing parents with a format that will help minimize the effect of divorce on the child.

The *method* around which the passage focuses is strangely absent. After some questioning, the student recognized a whole page of material was missing. The student's computer had apparently had one of those nervous breakdowns that are common. A page had vanished into the electronic mist. It was a problem that could—and does—happen to us all. But what should not have happened is that the student failed to reread her paper. She knew what she had written, but she failed to verify that all material had been printed.

Here's a different kind of omission:

> Art is also a form of therapy. Participating in creative with other people helps some individuals replace the loss of objects and to express their feelings openly.

As it is impossible to participate in "creative," a word must be missing. Creative *activities?* Creative *efforts?* Creative *arts?* We don't know. Neither do we know what the mention of a "loss of objects" means. It may be possible for participation in creative activities to help people express their feelings. But how does it replace a loss of objects? It turns out that the student had read a pamphlet on various mental problems that art therapists claimed to treat. Somewhere in that pamphlet an emotional condition was defined as arising out of a loss of "objects" that were of no particular worth, but that held symbolic value for the patient. The student failed to include that explanation. He knew in his mind what the phrase meant. After all, he had read the pamphlet. But he failed to consider that his audience had not. A definition or explanation for specialized concepts must occur on the page, not remain buried in the writer's mind. A single missing word can make nonsense of an otherwise valid argument.

Hidden Assumptions

We may so thoroughly believe something that we fail to realize others do not, that others might consider our beliefs only an *assumption.* If you believe that all human beings have souls, for example, you may argue that because Bob and Maria are human beings, they obviously have souls. The logic of your argument is valid, as long as we all agree on that first premise. Indeed, many reasonable arguments must begin with assumptions, because we can't possibly know everything. But if you present an argument based on an assumption without realizing that it is an assumption, you may find yourself being challenged.

After an essay in *Fortune* described the struggle between the Environmental Protection Agency and certain large industrialists in the Southwest, a student criticized the essay with the following argument.

> The author has attempted to make us believe that Schrieber, Danforth, Holman, and other factory owners are struggling over a principle involving individual rights. But how many times has that been the rallying cry for self-interest? The Southern states used a similar justification for breaking from the Union just because they didn't want to give up slaves. Actually, the real reason Schrieber and his kind are resisting efforts to clean up the air and water is simple. They are involved in big business. Money is more important than the environment. They have to answer to their stockholders, not to the trees.

The student seems to have presented a forceful argument. The final sentence seems especially strong. He tries to discredit both the author and the industrialists by arguing that their actions are based on self-interest. But what is the student's proof? Answer: *Those involved represent "big business."*

Something is missing. The proof rests on a hidden assumption that the student believes his readers share: All those connected with big business are greedy. Money, to such individuals, means more than the common good. Only if we agree with that *assumption* can we find the student's argument valid. If we question such generalities, however, we are in a position to challenge the argument as a whole. Are *all* big-business men greedy? Do *all* big-business men value money over the welfare of the nation? For a writer, the danger of the hidden assumption is that you may believe you've erected a convincing and logical argument when, in actuality, you've omitted its very foundation. As a result, the whole of it may come tumbling down.

The solution to all these problems—inaccuracy, imprecision, omissions—is to read your paper with the same critical attitude you use when you read someone else's work. You must apply the same criteria of logic, clarity, and concern for detail to your own essay that you expect to find in another's. The process of self-criticism is demanding, time-consuming, and often frustrating. But as Rimbaud once said, "Excellence costs less trouble than mediocrity." You can be sure that if you don't criticize your own work, your audience will. Better to be embarrassed in private than in public.

Practice

Check each of the following passages—all written by students—for inaccuracy, imprecision, or vagueness due to apparent omissions or for other problems that would cause confusion for a reader.

a. The two doctors are father and son who displayed two very interesting sides about vitamin C. The father told me that for colds, he tries to consult the patient to drink clear liquids. But his son goes much farther and tries to prevent the cold in the first place. Because a cold averages three persons per year, we know that prevention is more vital than cure. The son tries to get his patients to take massive doses of vitamin C before it gets them.

b. John Locke was not very bright if he believed in Natural Law. All scientific evidence shows that there are physical laws, but it is only a form of ego trip to believe that your personal moral values are God-given and form some kind of Natural Law or Absolute Law. John Locke was obviously enculturated into believing that the attitudes of his time were right and all others wrong. As common sense tells us that all men are not created equal, Locke was merely providing an argument that can only be described as wish fulfillment.

c. Burglars are of two varieties, the professional and the amateur. Most thieves are only interested in the merchandise they have come to steal, not inflicting bodily harm. . . . Most criminals work no harder than necessary to what they want . . . it is far easier for them to abandon a house with good locks on all doors and windows and look for one less protected," according to *Safety Strategy* by Jack de Cells. And evidence shows that what they want is televisions, tape recorders, and other electrical equipment. This has probably always been true such equipment is easier to sell than say clothes.

d. Katherine Anne Porter was trying to relate war and epidemic in her essay *Pale Horse, Pale Rider,* with epidemic as the rider and war as the horse. The horse carries his rider around, allowing him to cover more territory quicker and easier. Epidemic is not caused by war but war by an epidemic. World War I was a sign of the direction man was heading toward. War, although dating back into the ancient times, is a forerunner of death. War shows all the deathly sides of human nature. It causes people to want to die, to give up their lives, their will to live. There is a close knitting parallel between war and epidemic.

Manuscript Form

Preparing a manuscript to look professional is not difficult. The method shown in the following example is not the only way, of course. Many businesses, professions, and professors require that you follow a particular style sheet. The form described here is a simplified version of the one recommended by the Modern Language Association. In the *MLA Handbook for Writers of Research Papers,* you will find a more detailed and professional approach.

Rosa Rightly 1

Prof. Vern Dogood

Owen Hall 331

22 Mar 1988

How to Prepare Your Manuscript

The first page of your paper should look like this. Manuscripts should be typewritten on one side of the paper only. Always double-space and use margins of about one inch at top and bottom as well as on each side. If you are writing on a word processor, follow the same guidelines and be sure to print on a high-quality printer.

Number the first page one-half inch from the top of the page in the right-hand corner. Your name should appear in the upper left-hand corner, along with your instructor's: It's also wise to include the instructor's campus address or box number. If your paper becomes misplaced or lost, it can be

Rightly 2

forwarded. And most instructors will want you to give the date or the assignment number.

Double-space and center your title. Capitalize the first word, the last word, and all principal words. Then quadruple-space and begin your paper. Each paragraph should be indented five spaces.

The second and all succeeding pages of a professional-looking manuscript should look like this. Some instructors will not want you to number the first page, but all other pages should be numbered in the upper right-hand corner along with your last name. Attach all pages together with a paper clip. If you submit loose papers and pages become lost, you must assume responsibility.

No matter how good a typist you are, you must always proofread the final copy. Use dark ink and make corrections clearly. Few instructors will expect you to be a perfect typist, and few will objecat to a few, clear corrections.

Finally, don't conclude by signing your name or adding a "P.S." to explain why the paper is late. After you've typed the conclusion, simply stop.

Student Research Papers

The following student research papers provide two models. The first relies primarily on conventional library sources: dictionaries, scholarly books, and reference works. The second paper goes further and uses interlibrary loans, journals, and electronic research. Yet both are valid models of scholarship that pursue questions of value and seek out possible answers from a variety of sources. Both student writers integrate personal questions, insights and original insight into their essays, blending quotations and paraphrases with evaluation and assessment. The result in each case is an interesting paper, well researched, and intelligently written.

Kenneth Palmer was an adult commuter-student who had served in the navy before entering college as a first-year student. After reading Toni Morrison's *Beloved* for a humanities class, he became so intrigued with the names of slaves that he decided to focus his research on the subject. In "Call Me My Name," Kenneth opens with an imaginary lead. While he uses an informal style, he has included nine sources and numerous examples to substantiate his findings.

Kenneth Palmer

1

Professor Waterford

Humanities II

December 3, 1997

Call Me My Name

Dog Face, Beetle Nose, Frog. As a child I believed that repeating the rhyme "Sticks and stones will break my bones but names will never hurt me" would protect me from such school ground taunts. As I grew older, I knew better. Names can hurt. After researching the significant impact of names on African-American culture, I now realize names can at times evoke emotions and feelings from both ends of the spectrum: they can hurt as well as heal; they can bring sadness or joy; they can bolster self-esteem or create emotional pain far worse than physical injury.

Names are a curious phenomenon for numerous reasons. While methods, traditions, and customs vary, every human being as a member of a community is bestowed a name. Patrick Hanks and Flavia Hodges explain that names are cultural and are generally derived from native or religious beliefs (7). Leslie Alan Dunkling notes that names are also an identifying label which most people bear for reasons totally beyond their control, "like a suit of clothes or a dress which was chosen by somebody else, but which may fit very well nevertheless. If it does not fit, it can be changed for something that does" (Dunkling 48). A name brings individual identity to a person.

However, in *Black Names in America,* a book which cites the extensive research of Newbell Niles Puckett, editor Murray Heller points out that in the case of African-American slaves, a name (or lack of one) could "vilify, depersonalize and dehumanize" (Foreword V). Toni Morrison's novel, *Beloved,* reflects the material assembled by Puckett and also reveals how the inhumanities of slavery could well have affected and shaped the naming practice of African Americans. Morrison's skillful storytelling in her 1988 Pulitzer Prize-winning work illustrates remarkable authenticity in the careful choice of each character's name.

Palmer 2

An insight into African naming habits is necessary to understand how the African-American naming conventions differed from those of other civilizations. In Africa, as in other cultures, it was common practice to give a child a name that had some religious affiliation. To bestow a sacred name was a way to familiarize people with the qualities and history associated with the name (Puckett 48). *African American Voices of Triumph* cites *Tsukama* which means "a learner" and *Grabu* which means "have mercy on me" as names of two actual slaves taken from the Mende tribe of West Africa in 1839 and brought to America aboard the ship Amistad (56–57). Another African practice was to name a child according to the day of the week of his or her birth. In *Black Names,* J. L. Dillard provides two examples of typical male names used by African tribes: *Quashell* for males born on Sunday and *Quaco* for males born on Wednesday (8).

Loss of identity and naming conventions changed dramatically for Africans once they were captured by slave traders. While in transport, they were rarely called anything but *man slave* or *negro man.* However, the first man and woman brought aboard the ship were occasionally called *Adam* and *Eve* (Dunkling 147). The following, written by the slaver Thomas Watson in 1860, also provides evidence that slaves were at times temporarily named by the ship's crew:

> I suppose they . . . all had names in their own dialect, but the effort required to pronounce them was too much for us, so we picked out our favorites and dubbed them *Mainstay, Cat's Head, Bull's Eye, Rope-yarn* and various other sea phrases. (Puckett 6)

Once the Africans arrived at their port of destination, their original names, like their freedom, appeared lost forever. Reasons for the loss of their names vary. To American ears, the foreign sound of African names made them difficult to pronounce and remember. In addition, some tribal customs restricted the Africans from giving their names to strangers. Nevertheless, the main reason new names were supplied to slaves by their owners was simply because they were regarded as property. Owners felt they had the right to bestow a first name to their property (Dunkling 147).

Palmer 3

As a result, this became a method for the white slave holder to exercise control. By stripping Africans of their given names, the owner sought to reduce the slave to a non-person. This action made the slave owner appear more superior. In place of a name, it was prevalent to use *boy* or *nigger* which further reduced the social status of the slave. Once a slave received a name, he or she assumed some degree of dignity in the eye of the white owner, and this provided some relationship between them (Puckett 6). Meanwhile, when the slave assumed the surname of his master, he began to lose his own identity, and it became increasingly difficult to see himself as a separate human being. Julius Lester, in *To Be a Slave,* notes that in slave narratives, a slave was "never asked who he was. He was asked 'Who's nigger are you?' " (77). This further enslaved the black for it is a form of brainwashing. Without a feeling of self the slave found little reason to resist, and the slave owner found he did not have to control the slave with physical force.

Each time a slave was sold to a new owner, he was given the surname of the new master. This is revealed in an anonymous narrative taken from Bontemps-Hughs:

> A Negro has got no name. My father was a Ransome and he had a uncle named Hankin. If you belong to Mr. Jones and he sell you to Mr. Johnson, consequently you go by the name of your owner. Now where you get a name? We are wearing the name of our master. I was first a Hale; then my father was sold and then I was named Reed. (quoted in Lester 56)

In some ways I feel this loss of identity and loss of self was ultimately more cruel than any physical beating. Morrison illustrates the extreme loss of self when a slave named Paul D describes how the humiliation and abuse of slavery made him feel lower than a barnyard rooster—a rooster named Mister, who, in Paul D's eyes, was treated with more respect and dignity than he was (72).

So how did the white slave master choose a name for his slave? In *What's in a Name?* Leonard Ashley explains that given names of slaves were not substantially different from the names of whites during the same period (14). Names were simple and easy to shout (Dunkling 151). A sample from the collection of slave names taken by Puckett from 1619–1799 reveals that *Jack, Tom, John,* and *Will* were popular male slave names while *Mary, Jane, Sara,* and *Nan* were common among the female slaves (Ashley 14). In *Beloved,* Morrison is historically accurate when she chooses *Nan* as the name for the African slave woman who cares for Sethe as a child (62) and the biblical name of *Paul* for three of the Sweet Home men: Paul A, Paul D, and Paul F. All three slaves have the surname *Garner* which was given to them by the owner of Sweet Home (11).

Naming habits in some instances did differ from those of the whites (Dunkling 146). Owners with British heritage sometimes gave their slaves names of familiar places such as London, Cambridge, and York because they were easy to remember. Morrison uses a place name for Sethe's youngest daughter but not for the same reason. Amy Denver is the young white woman who befriends Seth as she tries to make her way to Ohio and freedom. Like Sethe, Amy is running from a life of servitude, but she puts her plans on hold and helps Sethe deliver her youngest daughter. Sethe is grateful and thinks the name is pretty. As a tribute to Amy, she names her baby Denver (85).

Some eighteenth-century slaves had names that could have been derived from actual jobs they were assigned. The name *Floor* appears four times in the lists of Puckett, and it has been suggested the name was given to a female slave whose job it was to keep the floors clean. However, another theory is that *Flora* was a common name among slaves and *Floor* might just be a form of it (Dunkling 150).

A first person account written in 1789 *The Interesting Narrative of the Life of Olaudah Equiano or Gustavus Vassas, the African,* is described in Marion Wilson Starling's study, *The Slave Narrative: It's Place in American History.* This memoir is the story of a Nigerian slave taken captive as a boy of eleven and sold several times before being bought by a British naval officer who consequently renames him Gustavus Vassa after a famous Swedish king (69). The narrative is one of the few written by a slave who can actually recall life in Africa and the brutal transition to slavery (*African American Voices* 28). Starling also notes the story of the son of an African prince taken from his tribe at age six-and-a-half. He is given the first name *Venture* because a ship's steward purchased him with his own money (78). At the age of thirty-one, Venture takes the last name of Smith in recognition of his respected third master (77).

Some slaves showed their defiance and resistance to slavery by not accepting the name they were given. John Blassingame's *The Slave Community: Plantation Life in the Ante-Bellum South* refers to a newspaper article that was reprinted in *The Journal of Negro History XXIV* in July 1939:

> A Georgia newspaper described two recaptured fugitive slaves in these terms: Run aways . . . Two new Negro young fellows; one of them . . . computed eighteen years of age, of the Fallah country, slim made, and calls himself *Golaga,* the name given here *Abel;* the other a black fellow . . . computed seventeen years of age of the Suroga country, calls himself *Abbrom,* the name given him here *Bennet.* (21)

A further example of slaves unwilling to give up their African names is evidenced by young Africans brought over on the *Wanderer* in 1858. This ship, one of the last legal slave ships, carried men and women from the Congo area who continued to practice their African language and customs after slavery ended in 1865 (*African American Voices* 72). An increased number of African names among free Negroes in 1830 provided additional confirmation [that] bolder slaves were in all likelihood more defiant and also sought freedom, while those who remained captives also remained without an individual identity (Dillard 22).

Other runaway slaves sought new identities to protect themselves from discovery. One example is the famous abolitionist and activist Harriet A. Jacobs who wrote *Linda: Incidents in the Life of a Slave Girl, Written by Herself* in 1861 under the pseudonym of *Linda Brent* (Starling 212). Another internationally known abolitionist, author and orator Frederick Douglass, changed his name from Frederick Bailey in an effort to remain free from the owner he escaped from in 1838 (*African American Voices* 60).

As a free people, some blacks chose to use formal first names, *Sam, Tom* and *Jim,* were replaced by *Samuel, Thomas,* and *James.* This reflects the former slaves need and desire for a feeling of greater dignity (Puckett 42).

Into the latter part of the eighteenth century, the Christian church represented freedom to former slaves not only in this world but in the one beyond. This explains their continued use of biblical names (48). But new variations of names began to emerge once slaves were freed. Since most were illiterate, they depended on someone who could read or write to record their name. *Liz* might be *Liza* or *Lizar* depending on who wrote it for them (41).

Freedom from slavery also brought freedom from conventional names for many former slaves. Sojourner Truth was born Isabel Baumfree in 1797. By 1843 she decided to devote her life to preaching, and when she converted to Christianity she changed her name (*African American Voices* 63). In his book *The Black 100: A Ranking of the Most Influential African-Americans: Past and Present,* Columbus Salley explains that *Sojourner* chose her first name because she planned to travel and show people their sins and chose the last name of *Truth* because she intended to "declare the truth unto the people" (61). In *Beloved,* Toni Morison's character *Stamp Paid* is born *Joshua* (184). After surviving the trials and ordeals of slavery (which included handing over his wife to his master's son), he changes his name as a message to himself and others. As former slaves they have met their obligation in life: "You paid it; now life owes you" (185).

Without a name of their own, freedom posed problems for some former slaves. Suddenly, many faced the decision of what to call themselves. This was not a problem for Morrison's character Baby Suggs. As a freed slave, she chooses not be known as *Jenny Whitlow,* the name on her bill of sale. For many years she had been called *Jenny* at Sweet Home, but in the wagon ride to freedom in Ohio, she finally finds the courage to tell Mr. Garner, her former owner, [that] this is not her name. *Baby* is the name her husband had called her, and *Suggs* was his surname. Once her son has bought her freedom, it feels natural to call herself *Baby Suggs* (143).

Before Freedom: 48 Oral Histories of Former North and South Carolina Slaves contains many interesting narratives which describe how other former slaves arrived at their choice of name. Three examples follow. According to Peter Clifton, "After freedom, when us was told we had to have names, Pappy say he loved his older marster Ben Clifton the best and him too that titlement, and I's been a Clifton ever since" (Hurmence 181–182). In another narrative, former slave Sarah Poindexter maintains she received the name *Poindexter* from the plantation she was born on in 1850. She explains that, like other slaves, she got the name honestly; and since she didn't have any other name, she planned to "keeps it to the end of the road" (Hurmence 177–179). George Briggs appears unusually proud of the name he had acquired. When asked his name he replies, "Give my name right flat, it's George Briggs. Give it round like this, George McDuffie Briggs" (Hurmence 167). I believe *George Briggs, Sarah Poindexter,* and *Peter Clifton* illustrate how having a name, even one derived from a former master, brings a sense of self-esteem and self-worth to an individual.

However, in *Early African-American Classics,* edited by Anthony Appiah, excerpts from Booker T. Washington's *Up from Slavery* reveal how some newly freed slaves felt it improper to assume the surname of their former owner. Instead, they took other surnames as a symbol for their first act of freedom. In addition, many produced middle initials which stood for no particular name at all. It was "simply a part of what the coloured man proudly calls his 'entitles' " (332). It is interesting to note that Booker T. Washington made up his name because he was embarrassed to tell the school teacher he didn't have one. He later found out his mother had given him the name *Booker Taliaferro.* As a result, the famous educator and scholar became known as *Booker Taliaferro Washington* (339). His positive comments about how he arrived at this name are shared in his story: "I think there are not many men in our country who have had the privilege of naming themselves in the way that I have" (339). He further suggests that having been born a slave made him a better person. He felt that if he had been born to a "more popular race" and had inherited a name, he probably would have depended on his ancestry and color to do what he had to do for himself. Because he had no ancestry, he resolved to make something of himself, and serve as an example for his children (340).

There appears to be solid historical reasons for the pride black Americans reveal in the names they chose for their children in modern times (Dunkling 159). The need for strong cultural ties is cited for the resurgence in the late 1960s for the use of preslavery African names as well as the names given to their ancestors by white slavers (Dillard 18). Unique spellings for common names such as *Teri* and *Toni* provide evidence that black Americans want distinction and are seeking to establish their own naming conventions (Ashley 13). They want to exercise their full freedom of expression because it was not so many years ago they were denied the choice to do so. Black Americans are not afraid to go outside the norm and are much more confident than white Americans when it comes to bestowing unusual first name. They don't feel pressured to go along with current fads: "These days black Americans give names freely; white Americans tend to remain slaves to their own naming conventions" (Dunkling 159).

Obviously slavery greatly influenced African-American names and made them unique to other cultures in many aspects. There is, however, one similarity shared by all societies: A name is a badge of identity which makes an individual feel like a real person. This is eloquently illustrated by Toni Morrison in *Beloved* when former slave Paul D is approached one evening by a strange, childlike, black woman who has mysteriously appeared at the 124 Bluestone Road home. As she struggles to confirm her own existence and drive Paul D away from Sethe, she asks him to "Call me my name" (117). She reminds us of a comment Dale Carnegie makes in *Remember Names:* "a person's name, is to that person, the sweetest sound in any language" (1).

Works Cited

African American Voices of Triumph: Perseverance. Vol 1. Virginia: Time Life, 1933.

Appiah, Anthony, ed. *Early African-American Classics.* New York: Bantam, 1990.

Ashley, Leonard R. N., *What's in a Name.* Maryland: Genealogical. 1989.

Blassingame, John W. *The Slave Community: Plantation Life in the Ante-Bellum South.* New York: Oxford UP, 1972.

Carnegie, Dale. *Remember Names.* New York: Dale Carnegie, 1977.

Dillard, J. L. *Black Names.* Ed. Josha A. Fishman. Hawthorn, New York: Mouton, 1976.

Palmer 9

Dunkling, Leslie Alan. *First Names First.* Michigan: Gale, 1977.

Hanks, Patrick, and Flavia Hodges. *A Dictionary of First Names.* New York: Oxford UP, 1990.

Hurmence, Belinda, ed. *Before Freedom: 48 Oral Histories of Former North and South Carolina Slaves.* New York: Penguin, 1990.

Lester, Julius. *To Be a Slave.* New York: Scholastic, 1968.

Morrison, Toni. *Beloved.* New York: Penguin, 1987.

Puckett, Newbell Niles. *Black Names in America: Origins & Usage.* Ed. Murray Heller, Boston, Massachusetts: G. K. Hall, 1975.

Salley, Columbus. *The Black 100: A Ranking of the Most Influential African-Americans: Past and Present.* New York: Carol, 1993.

Starling, Marion Wilson. *The Slave Narrative: It's Place in American History.* Boston, Massachusetts: G. K. Hall, 1981.

Tracy Wilson, an honors student, set out to write a conventional interpretation of a famous literary speech and its author. Finding almost no sources or materials in her college library, she turned to interlibrary loan and the Internet where, to her surprise, she found three conflicting versions of the same speech. Her research thereafter turned from a literary analysis to a textual, and scholarly, investigation. Tracy writes the essay informally, beginning with a personal experience and using the first person voice, but the research—and her final evaluation—are objective and well reasoned.

Tracy Wilson 1

Professor Benson

Karpen Hall 208

15 May 1997

Chief Seattle's 1854 Oration

In the summer of 1992, I bought a souvenir T-shirt from the Crossmen Drum and Bugle Corps which quoted an 1852 letter from Chief Seattle to President Polk. The Crossmen had used a supposedly accurate text by a Native American now featured on several sites on the World Wide Web whose words, in much of Europe, are called the "Fifth Gospel" (Kaiser 532). Like many others, the Crossmen accepted this letter as fact; however, since James K. Polk was dead in 1852, their use of this text is particularly troublesome.

In order to understand the implications of the widespread acceptance of Seattle's speech, we must first understand that three distinctly different versions of the address currently circulate through the world. The first and oldest was supposedly recorded by Dr. Henry A. Smith as Seattle spoke in 1854. This version was published in the *Seattle Sunday Star* in 1887. In Smith's text, Seattle laments the decline in the population of his people, states that he feels forsaken by his Great Spirit and hated by the Christian God, and agrees to move his people to a reservation if they are allowed unconditional access to holy ground ("Chief Seattle's 1854 Oration"—ver. 1). The second version, which is similar to Smith's, was translated from Smith's Victorian English into modern prose by William Arrowsmith. The Arrowsmith version contains the same images and argument, but modifies the grammar and structure. For example, the phrase "appears changeless and eternal" in the Smith version is changed to "looks eternal" in the Arrowsmith version ("Chief Seattle's 1854 Oration"—vers. 1 and 2).

The third and most famous version is the one believed to be a letter to President Franklin Pierce from Chief Seattle. This version was actually written in the 1970s by a film artist named Ted Perry, who used one of the supposed earlier texts of Seattle's speech as a basis for a film. His rendition is unlike the other two, however; it discusses treatment of the land while the other two discuss treatment of the people ("A Speech by Chief Seattle [Suquamish] in 1854"). Perry argues that his script for the film is original and he acknowledges that it is only loosely based on Seattle's speech. In the final version of the film, though, Perry is given no on-screen credit for having written the script. He claims he made it "clear" that the work was his, but the end product was attributed to Seattle and became the most widely quoted speech ever attributed to a Native American (Kaiser 514). Other better-known versions of the text also exist, but the Smith, Arrowsmith, and Perry versions are most often reprinted and considered to be "accurate."

In addition to the discrepancies among the texts, three problems immediately arise during any study of Seattle's speech. The first is that no official record of this speech or of a letter by Seattle exists in the National Archives, the Smithsonian Institute, or the Library of Congress (Clark 61). The only two speeches by Seattle which are documented in the National Archives were delivered at the signing of the Point Elliot Treaty; they are written in simple, concise prose and bear no resemblance to the more famous "poetic" speech (Clark 64; Kaiser 502–503).

The idea that the speech ever appeared in a letter of Chief Seattle's is probably not feasible. In the 1850s, letters from Native Americans to the president were directed through several channels. A letter by Seattle would have been read by a government agent, Col. M. T. Simmons, by Isaac Ingalls Stevens, who was governor of the Washington Territory in charge of Indian relations, and by several secretaries before reaching the president "Isaac Ingalls Stevens;" Clark 61). None of these offices has any record of a letter from Chief Seattle (Clark 61). Although one could argue that mishandling by racist government officials could account for missing documents, the fact that original documentation cannot be found anywhere is disturbing.

A second issue in dealing with this text is that no one can document its original language. According to Jerry L. Clark, Dr. Smith was fluent in "Duwamish" (62). Arrowsmith also claims that Seattle made his speech in Duwamish (Kaiser 505). However, neither gives a source for this information. In fact, Duwamish was not a language; the Duwamish and Suquamish people spoke a language called Lushotseed (505). According to Rudolf Kaiser, Seattle's speech was most likely spoken in Lushotseed; then translated into the Chinook jargon, a language most northwest coast Native Americans knew; and from that version, it may have been translated into English. We do not know which of these versions Smith may have been listening to while recording Seattle's speech (505). Without a native language text, scholars cannot create a literal translation or study the work in its original language, and the English version we have may have been spoken in one language, translated into Chinook jargon, and from the jargon, translated into English before it was recorded.

A third challenge in working with the speech is that those who have edited and recorded it have felt free to add their own modifications. For example, the three powerful end lines found in most printings of the address, "Let them be just and deal kindly with my people, for the dead are not powerless. Dead, did I say? There is no death, only a change of worlds," were added by either Clarence B. Bagley or John M. Rich, two men who wrote articles about Seattle's address in the early 1930s. ("Chief Seattle"—(ver. 1; Kaiser 506; Clark 65). Upon reading three of Bagley's books, none of which mention the 1854 oration, I find it more likely that Rich was the individual who added the lines. These three lines appear in most texts of the speech but are not included in Smith's supposedly original account (506).

The manner in which the possible text of Seattle's speech was recorded has its own series of problems. Scholars know Seattle was a real person, but it appears that Smith waited forty years before writing the first version of Seattle Speech. In the October 19, 1887 *Seattle Sunday Star* article, Smith describes Seattle and reconstructs his 1854 address based on journal notes ("Chief Seattle"—ver. 2). In this earliest version of the speech, Smith describes Seattle's voice as "deep-toned, sonorous, and eloquent" ("Chief Seattle"—ver. 2). After presenting his text, Smith states, "Other speakers followed, but I took no notes. . . . The above is but a fragment of his speech" (Kaiser 504–505). On his deathbed, Smith swore that the text was authentic and that he had reconstructed the entire address (Kaiser 504). However, even if Smith took detailed notes and had an excellent memory, the chances that his text are accurate are extremely slim. All versions of Seattle's supposed oration trace back to the text Smith himself admits is incomplete (Kaiser 508) and not recorded until forty years after the event.

To further complicate the speech's history, several accounts cast doubts upon Smith's claims. The local interpreter, B. F. Shaw, who survived to be interviewed in the twentieth century, did not remember any such oration by Chief Seattle (Clark 63). The source for this knowledge is a work by Ezra Meeker, who interviewed settlers from the Puget Sound area to produce an oral history (Clark 65). In his final version of his 1905 autobiography, *Frontier Remembrances of Puget Sound,* Meeker does not mention Seattle' speech (Clark 63). According to documents recording the negotiations of treaties with Native Americans, the widow of David S. Maynard, the doctor before whose office Seattle supposedly made his speech, had no recollection of anything like Smith's version of the speech (63).

Another question about the reliability of the text arises in one historians recording of the friendship between Maynard and Seattle. In *Pioneer Seattle and Its Founders,* Clarence B. Bagley calls Dr. Maynard "Seattle's warm friend"; later, Seattle is Maynard's "old time and steadfast friend"; (qtd. in Clark 9–10). But, in spite of allusions to their friendship, Bagley gives no reference to any speech by Seattle. Logically, if the friendship between Bagley and Seattle was important enough to warrant mention in the text, the author would see fit to also mention a moving speech given by Seattle on the steps of Maynard's office.

Similarly, historians' records contradict Smith's descriptions of Seattle. According to *History of Seattle,* edited by Frederick James Grant:

> In person Seattle was short and heavy, weighing as much as 180 pounds. He was round-shouldered, and by some it was fancied that he resembled in feature Senator Benton of Missouri. His face was refined and benevolent but not particularly strong. (62)

Clarence Bagley describes Seattle as "large in size, dignified in appearance, generous, kind, and unassuming, yet courageous and fearless in the face of danger." He continues the description with the fact that Seattle was bent with age and carried a staff (*History of Seattle* I 78). These perceptions of Seattle's physical appearance are completely unlike that given by Smith in his introduction to the first published version of Seattle's speech:

> Old Chief Seattle was the largest Indian I ever saw, and by far the noblest looking. He stood nearly six feet in his moccasins, was broad shouldered, deep chested and finely proportioned. His eyes were

> large, intelligent, expressive, and friendly when in repose, and faithfully mirrored the varying moods of the great soul that looked through them. He was usually solemn, silent and dignified, but on great occasions moved among assembled multitudes like a Titan among Lilliputians, and his lightest word was law. (Grant 433)

Another stumbling block before the question of whether or not Seattle would have made such a speech is the persistence of historians in referring to Seattle as friendly toward whites and certain that whites would act in his people's best interests. Grant's *History of Seattle* refers to his "well known friendliness" (62) and describes him as a "good friend of the whites" (71). Clarence Bagley refers to Seattle as "ever a loyal friend of the whites, which he showed to be sincere all through the Indian war of 1855–56" (*Pioneer* 9). Bagley also writes that Seattle manifested "his friendship for the whites on every occasion" and that no one ever regretted naming the city after him (Grant 27). Seattle "maintained a friendly attitude, having faith in the whites to do right by the Indians" (79). D. S. Maynard called Seattle "the greatest friend of the whites on this side of the continent" (qtd. in Carlson 7). Although these accounts are the perceptions of white men and could be biased, one must wonder whether or not they would have felt this way about a man who made a powerful speech questioning whether white civilizations would be considered "ever a friend" to the Indians.

Smith's deathbed claims, discrepancies in descriptions of Seattle's physical appearance, demeanor, and attitude toward whites, and a lack of references to his speech in so many historical resources, cause me to think that Smith either created the text himself or greatly embellished someone else's speech. To waste his last words on the authenticity of a speech which he says he heard at least forty years before is odd. His claim to authenticity might have been his way of dramatically imprinting himself into American history and thereby making himself immortal. Under the assumption that he was not senile, why else might he be so passionate about a long past event no one else seems to remember?

In fact, there are many similarities in the style of Seattle's speech and Smith's own introduction to it. These similarities might have occurred because Smith rewrote the speech in his own words based on his notes. However, one of the most memorable qualities of Seattle's speech is his use of natural imagery to describe his people. They "resemble the scattering trees of a storm-swept plain" while the white settlers are "like the grass that covers vast prairies." Similarly, Smith describes Seattle's voice as "like the ceaseless thunders of cataracts flowing from exhaustless fountains," a trait which is "as native to his manhood as the leaves and blossoms are to a flowering almond." Smith describes the crowd listening in silence "as instantaneous and perfect as that which follows a clap of thunder from a clear sky" ("Chief Seattle's 1854 Oration"—ver. 2). Perhaps Smith and Seattle simply had similar ideals about the relationship between man and nature, and these ideals seeped into the metaphors in their work. Or Smith might have written the speech himself, based loosely on an oration that may never have occurred, or which, if it did, he may or may not have taken notes on.

Even if Smith did hear a beautifully moving oration by Chief Seattle, he waited nearly forty years to rewrite and publish it. No matter how careful or well intended he thought he was, the text has to contain enough of his own thought to be considered his own text, not Seattle's. The story of Smith's recording of the text is one of the most readily available pieces of information about it, yet I have found no source who presents any form of disclaimer when publishing the speech. The only avenues which may now answer questions of authenticity are an examination of the diary of D. S. Maynard, if it survives, and a reading of everything Smith published in the *Seattle Sunday Star* to analyze tone and accuracy.

Societies around the world have absorbed Seattle's address as a statement of fact when it obviously can only be, at very best, partially true. Even more disturbing, portions of a film script written in the 1970s have been accepted as a letter written by a Native American chief in 1854. If the oration, supposedly given 150 years ago, is false, what else have we absorbed into our culture which is equally false? If editors have felt so free to change this text, then which other accepted texts have been tampered with?

The story of Seattle's speech illustrates the general willingness, even by editors and scholars, to accept information without question or protest. Other striking examples of this willingness to accept without question include assumptions of the authenticity of the Bible, the presidential statements of morality and practicality during the Cherokee Removal, and Hitler's successes in propaganda during World War II. Of course, the acceptance of Seattle's speech is not as dramatic, nor does it have such dire consequences. However, Seattle's 1854 oration can definitely been seen as an example of how easy it is for "false truths" to be accepted as reality.

Works Cited

Bagley, Clarence B. *In the Beginning: A Sketch of Some Early Events In Western Washington While It Was Still Part of "Old Oregon."* Seattle: Lowman and Hanford, 1906.

Carlson, Frank. "Chief Seattle." *The Bulletin of the University of Washington.* 3:2 (1903): 1–35.

Chief Seattle's 54 Oration [Smith ver. 1]. Indigenous People's Literature. 19 Feb. 1996 <http://indigenouspeople.org/nalit/seattle.htm>.

Chief Seattle's 1854 Oration (Arrowsmith ver. 2). Indigenous People's Literature. 19 Feb. 1996 <http://www.indigenouspeople.org/natlit/seattle.htm>.

Clark, Jerry L. "Thus Spoke Chief Seattle: The Story of an Undocumented Speech." *Prologue: Journal of the National Archives.* 17.1 (1985): 58–65.

Kaiser, Rudolf. "Chief Seattle's Speech(es): American Origins and European Reception." *Recovering the Word: Essays on Native American Literature.* Ed. Brian Swann and Arnold Krupat. Berkeley: U of California, 1987. 387–403.

McCarthy, James. *A Speech by Chief Seattle [Suquamish] in 1854 [Ted Perry Version].* 19 Feb. 1996 <http://www.formal.stanford.edu/jmc/progress/fake2.html>.

Index

Text Credits

Agee, James, Excerpt from *Let Us Now Praise Famous Men* by James Agee and Walker Evans. Copyright 1941 by James Agee and Walker Evans. Copyright © renewed 1969 by Mia Fritsch Agee and Walker Evans. Reprinted by permission of Houghton Mifflin Company. All rights reserved.

Ancevski, Dragi, "The Death of a Nation." Reprinted by permission of the author.

Anderson, Sherwood. "The Book of the Grotesque" from *Winesburg, Ohio* by Sherwood Anderson. Copyright © 1919 by B.W. Huebsch; Copyright 1947 by Eleanor Copenhaver Anderson. Used by permission of Viking Penguin, a division of Penguin Putnam Inc.

Angelou, Maya, "Sister Flowers" from *I Know Why the Caged Bird Sings* by Maya Angelou. Copyright © 1969 and renewed 1977 by Maya Angelou. Used by permission of Random House, Inc.

Anonymous, "Soup" from "Talk of the Town" in *The New Yorker,* January 23, 1989. Reprinted by permission. Copyright © The New Yorker Magazine, Inc. All rights reserved.

Arinze, Cardinal Francis, "Join Hands Across the Divide of Faith: Different Religions Must Begin to Cooperate to Overcome Society's Major Problems" May 1999 commencement address at Wake Forest University, Winston, North Carolina. Reprinted by permission of Cardinal Francis Arinze.

Berry, Wendell, "The Peace of Wild Things" from *The Selected Poems of Wendell Berry.* Copyright © by Wendell Berry. Reprinted by permission of Counterpoint Press, a member of Perseus Books, L.L.C..

Beattie, Ann, "Snow" from *Where You'll Find Me* by Ann Beattie. Reprinted by permission of International Creative Management, Inc. Copyright © 1986 by Ann Beattie.

CALVIN AND HOBBES © 1993 Watterson/Dist. By Universal Press Syndicate in Chapter 33.

Carlson, Peter, "Food for Thought" from "My Turn" in *Newsweek,* May 29, 1978. Reprinted by permission of the author.

Carter, Stephen L., "The Insufficiency of Honesty" from *Integrity* by Stephen L. Carter. Copyright © 1996 Perseus Books.

Christiansen, Rita Ann, "To Catch a Thief." Reprinted by permission of the author.

Clinger, Terrie, "An Unidentified Death." Reprinted by permission of the author.

Cox, Fred, "The Match." Reprinted by permission of the author.

Degnan, James P., Excerpt from "Masters of Babble." Reprinted by permission of the author.

Eighner, Lars, "Dumpster Diving" from *Travels with Lizabeth: Three Years on the Road and on the Streets.* Copyright © 1993 by Lars Eighner. Published by St. Martin's Press.

Erdrich, Louise, "Beneath My House" excerpt from "Foxglove" in the *Georgia Review,* Fall 1992, Vol. 46, No. 3, pp. 474–476. Reprinted by permission of the author.

Forstchen, William, "Academia Goes to War" in the *Asheville Tribune Weekly,* Nov. 20, 2001. Reprinted by permission of the author.

Gregory, Dick, "Shame" from *Nigger: An Autobiography* by Dick Gregory. Copyright © 1964 by Dick Gregory Enterprises. Used by permission of Dutton, a division of Penguin Putnam Inc.

Hall, Edward T., "The Arab World" from *The Hidden Dimension* by Edward T. Hall. Copyright © 1966, 1982 by Edward T. Hall. Used by permission of Doubleday, a division of Random House, Inc.

Harjo, Joy, "Remember" from *She Had Some Horses* by Joy Harjo. Copyright © 1983, 1997 by Thunder's Mouth Press. Appears by permission of the publisher, Thunder's Mouth Press.

Havens, James, "Stages on a Journey Westward by James Wright." Reprinted by permission of the author.

Hoagland, Edward, "Earth's Eye" from *Tigers & Ice: Reflections on Nature and Life* by Edward Hoagland. Copyright © 2000 Edward Hoagland. Reprinted by permission of The Lyons Press, a division of Globe-Pequot Press.

Key, Diane, "Truth in the Grotesque." Reprinted by permission of the author.

Lee, Chang-rae, "Coming Home" first appear in *The New Yorker,* Vol. 71, Issue 32, Oct. 16, 1995, pp. 164–168. Reprinted by permission of International Creative Management, Inc. Copyright © 1995 Chang-rae Lee.

Le Guin, Ursula K., "The Ones Who Walk Away from Omelas" Copyright © 1973, 1975 by Ursula K. Le Guin; reprinted by permission of the author and the author's agent, Virginia Kidd.

Levertov, Denise, "Love Poem" in *Life in Forest.* Copyright © 1978 by Denise Levertov. Reprinted by permission of New Directions Publishing.

MacKinnon, Catharine, "Sexual Harassment and Sexual Politics" an excerpt from *Feminism Unmodified Discourses on Life and Law* by Catharine MacKinnon. Reprinted by permission of the author

Mead, Margaret, and Rhoda Metraux, "Can the American Family Survive?" an excerpt from *Aspects of the Present.* Copyright © 1980 by Mary Catherine Bateson Kassarjian and Rhoda Metraux. Reprinted by permission of HarperCollins Publishers Inc.

Morris, Rebecca, "Student Power." Reprinted by permission of the author.
Reuse Chapter 15
AFE grant from previous edition. Student essay.

Mukherjee, Bharati, "American Dreamer," originally appeared in *Mother Jones,* January/February 1997. Copyright © 1997 Bharati Mukherjee. Reprinted by permission of the author.

Paglia, Camille, "It's a Jungle Out There" excerpt from *Sex, Art and American Culture* by Camille Paglia. Copyright © 1992 by Camille Paglia. Used by permission of Vintage Books, a division of Random House, Inc.

Palmer, Kenneth, "Call Me My Name." Reprinted by permission of the author.

Paterno, Holly, "Do You Speak American?" Reprinted by permission of the author.

Patterson, Orlando, "Hidden Dangers in the Ethnic Revival" in *The New York Times,* February 20, 1978. Copyright © 1978 by The New York Times Co.

PEANUTS (3–2–72) in Chapter 6. PEANUTS reprinted by permission of United Features Syndicate, Inc.

PEANUTS (11–2–74) in Chapter 24. PEANUTS reprinted by permission of United Feature Syndicate, Inc.

Pound, Ezra, "The River Merchant's Wife: A Letter" from *Personae* by Ezra Pound. Copyright © 1926 by Ezra Pound. Reprinted by permission of New Directions.

Rathbone, Charles, "Grandpa Was a Big Man." Reprinted by permission of the author.

Rodriguez, Richard, "Children of a Marriage" by Richard Rodriguez. Copyright © 1988 by Richard Rodriguez. Reprinted by permission of Georges Borchardt, Inc. for the author.

Rogers, Pattiann, "Trinity" from *Song of the World: New and Collected Poems, 1981–2001.* (Minneapolis: Milkweed Editions, 2001). Copyright © 2001 by Pattiann Rogers. Reprinted with permission from Milkweed Editions.

Rose, Mike, "Living South of L.A." Excerpt from *Lives on the Boundary: The Struggles and Achievements of America's Underprepared,* pp. 40–45. Reprinted by permission of The Free Press, an imprint of Simon & Schuster Adult Publishing Group, from *Lives on the Boundary: The Struggles and Achievements of America's Underprepared* by Mike Rose. Copyright © 1989 Mike Rose.

Rose, Wendy, "Three Thousand Dollar Death Song," reprinted from *Lost Copper* by Wendy Rose. Copyright © 1980 Malki Museum Press. Reprinted by permission of Malki Museum Press.

Ruggiero, Vincent Ryan, "Debating Moral Questions" from *The Art of Thinking: A Guide to Critical and Creative Thought,* Third Edition, pp. 29–30, by Vincent Ryan Ruggiero. Copyright © 1991 by HarperCollins Publisher Inc.

Seuss, Dr., Excerpt from *The Cat in the Hat* by Dr. Seuss, ® and copyright © by Dr. Seuss Enterprises, L.P. 1957, renewed 1986. Used by the permission of Random House Children's Books, a division of Random House, Inc.

Stafford, William, "Traveling Through the Dark" from *Stories That Could Be True* by William Stafford. Copyright © 1960 by William Stafford. Reprinted by permission of the William Stafford Estate.

Swir Anna, "I Wash the Shirt." in *Talking to My Body* by Anna Swir. Translated by Czelaw Milosz and Leonard Nathan. Copyright © 1996. Published by Copper Canyon Press: Port Townsend, WA.

Whitman, David, "Trouble for America's Model Minority" in *U.S. News & World Report,* Feb. 23, 1987, page 18–19. Copyright © 1987 U.S. News & Report. Reprinted by permission.

Whol, Anthony S., Excerpt from *The Victorian Family: Structure and Stresses* by Anthony S. Whol. Copyright © 1978 by Anthony s. Whol. Reprinted by permission of Palgrave.

Williams, William Carlos, "This Is Just to Say" from *Collected Poems: 1909–1939, Volume I.* Copyright © 1938 by New Directions Publishing Corp. Reprinted by permission of New Directions Publishing Corp.

Wilson, Tracy, "Chief Seattle's 1854 Oration." Reprinted by permission of the author.

Wright, James, five lines from "Stages on a Journey Westward" from *The Branch Will Not Break.* Copyright © 1963 by James Wright and reprinted by permission of Wesleyan University Press.

Younglove, Betty Anne, "The American Dream," from *U.S. News & World Report,* Dec. 8, 1986. Reprinted by permission of the author.